A COMPANION TO

JAMES JOYCE

EDITED BY
RICHARD BROWN

Blackwell
Publishing

BLACKWELL PUBLISHING
350 Main Street, Malden, MA 02148-5020, USA
9600 Garsington Road, Oxford OX4 2DQ, UK
550 Swanston Street, Carlton, Victoria 3053, Australia

First published 2008 by Blackwell Publishing Ltd

1   2008

Library of Congress Cataloging-in-Publication Data

A companion to James Joyce / edited by Richard Brown.
p.   cm.—(Blackwell companions to literature and culture; 52)
Includes bibliographical references and index.
ISBN-13: 978-1-4051-1044-0 (hardcover: alk. paper) 1. Joyce, James, 1882–1941—Criticism and interpretation. I. Brown, Richard, 1954–
PR6019.O9Z52715 2008
823'.912—dc22
2007015777

A catalogue record for this title is available from the British Library.

Set in 11/13 pt Garamond 3
by The Running Head Limited, www.therunninghead.com
Printed and bound in Singapore
by Fabulous Printers Pte Ltd

For further information on
Blackwell Publishing, visit our website at
www.blackwellpublishing.com

Contents

Illustrations

Acknowledgments

I'm happy to acknowledge the imaginative, prompt, courteous, and professional efforts made by each of the contributors to this volume and the depth and range of their enthusiasms and expertise which have made the project both conceivable in the first place and such an enjoyable and rewarding challenge in its coming to fruition. The intellectual resources of the international community of James Joyce studies never ceases to impress and many of the perspectives offered in this volume represent intellectual obligations and much-valued, friendly working relationships that have been established over several years of conference-going, editorial work on the *James Joyce Broadsheet*, and so on. I should offer special thanks to David Wright and the Department of English at the University of Auckland, New Zealand, for their hospitality and assistance in allowing me to open a genuinely antipodean vantage-point on the project during its early phase. I am grateful to my colleagues in the School of English at Leeds for the semester of study leave which allowed its completion. I'd also like to thank Emma Bennett and Karen Wilson at Blackwell for their advice, patience, and support at various stages in the making of the book, and David Williams, John Gaunt, and Jackie Butterley for hard work in the production of a complex text.

Material from some chapters has previously appeared in more or less different versions. Chapter 15 was delivered as the first A. N. Jeffares Memorial Lecture in the School of English at the University of Leeds in 2006. A version of Chapter 12 was originally read at the International Conference on the East-Asian Reception of James Joyce, held at Songsil University, Seoul, Korea, on November 4, 2006. Chapter 11, an earlier version of which appeared with the title "Joyce in the postcolonial tropics" in the *James Joyce Quarterly*, 39:1 (2003): 69–92, is included with the permission of that journal.

Harold Pinter kindly granted permission for the use of material in his possession and the quotation of copyright material in Chapter 19. Richard Prince, Miroslav Balka, James Coleman, William Anastasi, and Davide Cascio granted permission for the inclusion of images of their work in Chapter 20. David Wheatley agreed the publication of his poem in Chapter 21.

Editing a volume like this can make a range of demands. I'd like to thank my wife Jane and William, Charlotte, and Arthur for keeping me going with, and offering me occasional relief from the task.

Notes on Contributors

Richard Brown is Reader in Modern Literature in the University of Leeds, the author of *James Joyce and Sexuality* (1984) and *James Joyce: A Postculturalist Perspective* (reprinted 2005), and editor of *Joyce, "Penelope" and the Body* (2006). He co-founded in 1980 and co-edits the *James Joyce Broadsheet*, currently serves as Trustee of the International James Joyce Foundation, and has written widely on James Joyce and on such contemporary writers as Paul Muldoon, Ian McEwan, and Bob Dylan.

Maud Ellmann is Donald and Marilyn Keough Professor of Irish Studies at the University of Notre Dame. Her books include *The Poetics of Impersonality: T. S. Eliot and Ezra Pound* (1987), *The Hunger Artists: Starving, Writing, and Imprisonment* (1993), and *Elizabeth Bowen: The Shadow across the Page* (2004), which won the British Academy's Rose Mary Crawshay Prize.

Daniel Ferrer is Director of Research at the Institut des textes et manuscrits modernes (CNRS-ENS) in Paris. He is editor of the journal *Genesis*. The books he has written or co-edited include *Post-structuralist Joyce* (1984); *Virginia Woolf and the Madness of Language* (1990); *Ulysse à l'article: Joyce aux marges du roman* (1992); *Genetic Criticism: Texts and Avant-texte* (2004). With Vincent Deane and Geert Lernout he is currently editing the *Finnegans Wake* notebooks.

Finn Fordham is a Lecturer in Twentieth-Century English in the School of English Studies at the University of Nottingham. His publications include articles on Joyce, genetic criticism, modernism, and contemporary writing, and reviews for the *Guardian Review*. His *Lots of Fun at "Finnegans Wake"* was published in 2007.

Luke Gibbons is Keough Family Professor of Irish Studies, and Professor of English, and Film, Television, and Theater, at the University of Notre Dame. He is the author of *Gaelic Gothic: Race, Colonialism and Irish Culture* (2004), *Edmund Burke and Ireland: Aesthetics, Politics and the Colonial Sublime* (2003), *The Quiet Man* (2002), and *Transformations* *in Irish Culture* (1996), co-author of the pioneering book *Cinema in Ireland* (1988), and a contributing editor of the landmark *Field Day Anthology of Irish Writing* (1991). He is the co-editor (with Dudley Andrew) of "The Theatre of Irish Cinema," a special issue of *The Yale Journal of Criticism* (2002), and of *Re-Inventing Ireland: Culture, Politics and the Global Economy* (2002). He is currently working on *Joyce's Ghosts: Ireland, Modernity and the Memory of the Dead.*

Eishiro Ito is Associate Professor of English at Iwate Prefectural University, Japan. His field of research is modern Irish literature, particularly the works of James Joyce, W. B. Yeats, and Seamus Heaney. His recent research focuses on "Joyce and Orientalism," involving Jewish and East Asian studies.

R. Brandon Kershner is Alumni Professor of English at the University of Florida. He is author of *Dylan Thomas: The Poet and His Critics* (1977), *Joyce, Bakhtin, and Popular Literature* (1989), *The Twentieth-Century Novel: An Introduction* (1997); he also edited *Joyce and Popular Culture* (1996) and *Cultural Studies of Joyce* (2003).

Declan Kiberd is Professor of Anglo-Irish Literature at University College Dublin. Among his books are *Synge and the Irish Language* (1979), *Men and Feminism in Modern Literature* (1985), *Idir Dhá Chultúr* (1993), *Inventing Ireland* (1995), and *Irish Classics* (2000). He edited *Ulysses* for Penguin Twentieth-Century Classics (1992). A member of the Royal Irish Academy, he is a Director of the Abbey Theatre.

Christa-Maria Lerm Hayes is a Lecturer in Historical and Theoretical Studies in Visual Art at the University of Ulster, Belfast. She gained her PhD at Cologne University and was James Joyce Foundation Scholar in Zurich. She has published on contemporary Irish artists and interventionist arts practices. Her books include one on Joseph Beuys (2001, in German) and *Joyce in Art: Visual Art Inspired by James Joyce* (2004). The latter accompanied a large-scale art exhibition on the theme. She also curates for the Goethe Institut, Dublin.

Geert Lernout is Professor of English and Comparative Literature at the University of Antwerp where he is also director of the James Joyce Center. He is the author of *The French Joyce* (1990), and co-editor (with Wim van Mierlo) of *The European Reception of James Joyce in Europe* (2004), and has published widely on Joyce, Hölderlin, genetic criticism, textual editing, and the Bible.

Jane Lewty has served as Postdoctoral Fellow at University College London and Assistant Professor of British and Irish Literature at the University of Northern Iowa. She has published on Joyce, Pound, Woolf, and aspects of sound technology in modernist literature. A co-edited collection, *Broadcasting Modernism*, is forthcoming from the University Press of Florida. She is currently pursuing an MFA in Poetry at the Iowa Writers' Workshop.

John McCourt teaches at the Università di Roma. He is founder and co-director of the Trieste Joyce School. He is the author of *The Years of Bloom: Joyce in Trieste 1904–1920* (2000) and of *James Joyce: A Passionate Exile* (an illustrated biography). He guest-edited a special Trieste issue of the *James Joyce Quarterly* in 2001 and is currently editing *James Joyce in Context* for Cambridge University Press.

Vicki Mahaffey is Professor of Modern Literature at the University of York and the author of *Reauthorizing Joyce* (1988) and *States of Desire: Wilde, Yeats, Joyce and the Irish Experience* (1998). Her most recent book is *Modernist Literature: Challenging Fictions* (2007), which argues for the importance of the intellectual challenges presented by supposedly difficult modernist texts.

Katherine Mullin is Lecturer in the School of English at the University of Leeds. Her *James Joyce, Sexuality and Social Purity* was published in 2003. Her current project, *Working Girls*, explores the literary and cultural representations of typists, shop-girls, and barmaids between 1880 and 1920.

John Nash is Lecturer in English Studies at Durham University. He is the author of *James Joyce and the Act of Reception: Reading, Ireland, Modernism* (2006) and the editor of *Joyce's Audiences* (2002). He has contributed many essays and articles on Joyce, modern literature, and critical theory to books and journals.

Jean-Michel Rabaté has been Professor of English at the University of Pennsylvania since 1992 and is currently Professor of Comparative Literature at Princeton University. He is on the editorial board of the *Journal of Modern Literature*, and he is a Trustee of the James Joyce Foundation and a senior curator of the Slought Foundation, Philadelphia. He has authored or edited 30 books on modernism, psychoanalysis, theory, Joyce, Pound, and Beckett. Recent titles include *Given: 1) Art, 2) Crime* (2006) and *Lacan Literario* (2007). Forthcoming are *1913: The Cradle of Modernism* (2007) and *The Ethic of the Lie* (2008).

John Paul Riquelme is Professor of English at Boston University and author of *Teller and Tale in Joyce's Fiction* (1983) and *Harmony of Dissonances: T. S. Eliot, Romanticism, and Imagination* (1991). He has edited Fritz Senn's *Joyce's Dislocutions: Essays on Reading as Translation*, as well as *A Portrait of the Artist*, *Dracula*, *Tess of the d'Urbervilles*, and *Gothic and Modernism: Essaying Dark Literary Modernity*.

Krishna Sen is Professor of English at the University of Calcutta. She has published *Negotiating Modernity: Myth in the Theatre of Eliot, O'Neill and Sartre* (1999) and *Critical Essays on R. K. Narayan* (2003), and has edited the Penguin (India) edition of Ibsen's *A Doll's House*.

Mark Taylor-Batty is a Senior Lecturer in Theatre Studies in the School of English,

University of Leeds. His *Harold Pinter* was published in September 2001 and *About Pinter: The Playwright and the Work* in 2005. He is Associate Editor in Britain of the *Pinter Review*.

Luke Thurston is Lecturer in English at the University of Wales at Aberystwyth. He is the author of *James Joyce and the Problem of Psychoanalysis* (2004) and editor of *Re-inventing the Symptom: Essays on the Final Lacan* (2002).

Derval Tubridy is Lecturer in English and Visual Culture at Goldsmiths, University of London. She has published a monograph on *Thomas Kinsella: The Peppercanister Poems* (2001) and many articles on Samuel Beckett, James Joyce, the Dolmen Press, Literature and Philosophy, the *Livre d'Artiste,* and contemporary visual art. Her research has been supported by the Fulbright Commission and the British Academy.

Robert K. Weninger is Professor of German at King's College London and editor of *Comparative Critical Studies.* He has published several studies of Joyce and Arno Schmidt in German as well as *"Framing a Novelist": Arno Schmidt Criticism 1970–1994* (1995). His most recent monograph, *Streitbare Literaten*, was published in 2004.

Mark Wollaeger is Associate Professor of English at Vanderbilt University. He is author of *Modernism, Media, and Propaganda: British Narrative from 1900 to 1945* (2006) and *Joseph Conrad and the Fictions of Skepticism* (1990). He is editor of *James Joyce's "A Portrait of the Artist as a Young Man": A Casebook* (2003), and co-editor, with Victor Luftig and Robert Spoo, of *Joyce and the Subject of History* (1996).

David G. Wright is Senior Lecturer in English and Irish literature at the University of Auckland, New Zealand. He is the author of *Characters of Joyce* (1983), *Yeats's Myth of Self: The Autobiographical Prose* (1987), *Ironies of "Ulysses"* (1991), and *"Joyita": Solving the Mystery* (2002), and of articles about Joyce, Yeats, Harold Pinter, and Graham Greene.

Abbreviations and Editions Used

The following editions of Joyce's works have been used except where additional or alternative editions have been cited in the essay concerned. Abbreviations that are usual in Joyce criticism have been used for parenthetical references to these editions. These abbreviations are normally followed by page numbers, though in the case of *Ulysses* episode and line numbers are given throughout. For *Finnegans Wake* reference is to page and line number. In references to the Garland *Archive* of Joyce's manuscripts (*JJA*) the volume and page number are given.

D   Joyce, James (1992) *Dubliners* (first published 1914), ed. Terence Brown. London and New York: Penguin Books. In Chapter 22 the edition ed. John Wyse Jackson and Bernard McGinley, London: Sinclair Stevenson, 1995 cited as Joyce 1995 is used.

E   Joyce, James (1973) *Exiles.* London and New York: Penguin Books. (First published 1918.)

FW   Joyce, James (1939) *Finnegans Wake.* London: Faber and Faber.

GJ   Joyce, James (1968) *Giacomo Joyce.* London: Faber and Faber.

JJ   Ellmann, Richard (1982) *James Joyce*, revised edn. Oxford: Oxford University Press.

JJA   Joyce, James (1977–9) *The James Joyce Archive*, ed. Michael Groden et al., 63 vols. New York and London: Garland.

LI, LII, LIII   Joyce, James (1966) *Letters of James Joyce*, Vol. I ed. Stuart Gilbert. New York: Viking Press. Vols II and III ed. Richard Ellmann. New York: Viking Press.

OCPW   Joyce, James (2000) *Occasional, Critical and Political Writing*, ed. Kevin Barry. Oxford: Oxford University Press.

P   Joyce, James (2000) *A Portrait of the Artist as a Young Man*, ed. Jeri Johnson. Oxford: Oxford University Press. In Chapter 3 additional part and line references are given to Joyce, James (*A Portrait of the Artist as a Young Man*, 1993) ed. Hans Walter Gabler with Walter Hettche. New York and London: Garland Publishing. In Chapter 9, *A Portrait of the Artist as a Young Man: Text, Criticism and Notes*, ed. Chester G. Anderson, New York: Viking Press, 1968 cited as Joyce 1968 is used. (First published 1916.)

PE   Joyce, James (1992) *Poems and Exiles*, ed. J. C. C. Mays. London and New York: Penguin Books.

SH   Joyce, James (1956) *Stephen Hero*, ed. Theodore Spencer and rev. John J. Slocum and Herbert Cahoon. London: Jonathan Cape.

SL   Joyce, James (1975) *Selected Letters of James Joyce*, ed. Richard Ellmann. New York: Viking.

U   Joyce, James (1986) *Ulysses*, ed. Hans Walter Gabler. New York and London: Garland. (First published 1922.)

1

Introduction: Re-readings, Relocations, and Receptions

Richard Brown

The contribution of a volume on James Joyce to this series of Companions to Literature and Culture is not hard to justify in itself. Joyce's work has outstandingly developed the kind of academic interest that would especially repay such treatment, with an intellectually distinguished as well as highly diverse body of criticism having grown up around it, at times exponentially. Joyce's *Dubliners* (1914), *A Portrait of the Artist as a Young Man* (1916), *Ulysses* (1922), and, in its own way, *Finnegans Wake* (1939) have established quite unassailable places within the canons of twentieth-century modernistic literature, in Irish literature, more widely in the new, postcolonial, and global literatures in English, and in developments in the study of literary theory and culture, gender and sexuality, and so on. Joyce's distinctive cultural placement as an iconic founding figure of British, American, and Irish modernism, as well as his unique and emerging significance as a prototypical figure for the discussion of modern multinational and transnational European cultural identity, contribute to the sense of a writer whose importance to a variety of key interests and constituencies is hard to overestimate and continues to grow.

Joyce's work has been an inspiration to writers of prose fiction, poetry, drama, and film throughout the last century, with his status as a guru of the experimental or avant-garde frequently placing him at the forefront of significant cultural change. Innovations in literary and cultural theory (such as the revolutions in Continental philosophy associated with the post-1968 generation of Francophone intellectuals) as well as modern developments in academic empirical scholarship (such as historical and contextual study, reception study, and textual and genetic study) have frequently defined important stages of their progress in and through productive encounters with Joyce's work. Joyce's work remains authorial in a way that sometimes seems more comparable with the authorial status of a Shakespeare than with that of his modern contemporaries, whether you define that iconic position in relation to the newly independent Ireland, to the genre of twentieth-century prose fiction, or to our modernity itself.

Nevertheless aspects of Joyce's work once provoked scandal and can frequently remain awkward, typically no doubt because of misunderstandings that may arise from the scale and complexity of the work. Significant areas of the work remain less well known, despite such attempts to put them back on the agenda as we can see in approaches to his stage play *Exiles* (1918) (whose revival in the 1970s by Harold Pinter is discussed here and which was produced on the London stage in a substantial new production in 2006); his critical prose writing, political journalism, and reviews (that became more available when re-edited by Oxford University Press for World's Classics in 2001); his poetry (more fully collected in the Penguin Twentieth-Century Classics series in 1992); and the prose poem *Giacomo Joyce*, on which the first full volume of essays appeared last year (Armand and Wallace 2006). These works are all touched upon in this volume, though its emphasis is on the canonical and later work.

Adding an expansive new Companion on Joyce provides the opportunity to mark a moment in this re-approach to Joyce for our new century, presenting distinctively themed, critical readings of canonical texts and places of entry into the wide variety of current approaches within a single volume, and contributing informative pointers to current and possible future movements in the study of Joyce.

That there have already been two Companion volumes published on Joyce tells its own story and is another of the issues which face the editor of this one. The first, edited by Zack Bowen in 1984, contained 16 articles and two appendices written by a variety of academic and some non-academic enthusiasts and it retains much of value – not least in its broad intellectual frame. It offers a critical overview of each of the texts (including the less-well-known texts) with only a single final chapter offered on "The History of Joyce Criticism" (Bowen 1984). Alongside it the more contemporary Companion edited by Derek Attridge in 1990 and updated in 2004 thoroughly responds to the theory revolution of the 1970s and 80s with five chapters on texts, two on geographical and one on historical contexts, and four on the topics of feminism, sexuality, consumer culture, and colonialism/nationalism (Attridge 2004).

The format of this present volume allows for a larger number of more diverse essays and points towards an expansion of these categories, both of the possible contexts and of the themes that might inform our study of Joyce, whilst by no means exhausting the possibilities of such expansion. There is much of value in offering newly themed introductory readings, new contexts and locations for reading Joyce, and new kinds of material that mark the influence of Joyce on later imaginative literatures across the genres in a range of different cultures, as well as discussing how Joyce inspired the visual arts and the theatre, and the increasingly important Joyce of the cinema.

Of course there's an inevitable and necessary overlapping between categories here. Such overlapping means that some of the work of extending the range of texts receiving critical treatment can be seen in the thematic or contextual essays. For example, the essay by Mark Taylor-Batty, which treats *Exiles* most fully, appears in the "Approaches and Receptions" section and deals with the profound creative response to Joyce by Britain's Nobel laureate Harold Pinter – a work of reception that is perhaps distinctive to the medium of drama where a writer may both write and direct the work the others. His essay offers an example of a late twentieth-century English reception of Joyce that is not always recognized in Joycean studies. Derval Tubridy likewise extends the coverage of the volume when she engages the question of Joyce's poetry, and her chapter likewise invokes geography and contemporary literary reception – discussing Kinsella and the poetry of contemporary Ireland. John McCourt's essay on Trieste is the one that involves most discussion of *Giacomo Joyce*. Robert Weninger's essay on Joyce and German literature and that by Krishna Sen involve some treatment of the genre Joyce may be said to have invented (if not exploited), the short prose sketch or epiphany. There may not be a separate chapter here on Joyce and Paris but Jean-Michel Rabaté's essay on Joyce and French theory ensures that the developing avant-garde Parisian context for Joyce after the Second World War is not forgotten. Other essays confirm the renewed interest in Joyce's occasional writings as a lecturer and critic. It is the question of the biographical as well as that of the particular geographical context that emerges in John McCourt's essay on Joyce's Trieste in the "Contexts and Locations" section, as it does, perhaps more unexpectedly, in the opening biographical section of David Wright's. Chapters on Joyce's early publication in the modernist little magazines by Katherine Mullin as well as the spectral presence of "The Dead" in the cinema by Luke Gibbons and that of his later work in the new technology of radio by Jane Lewty further diversify this volume's coverage of both texts and their contexts. Unexpectedness and variety in the juxtapositions of these essays help both to expand and to redefine the ways in which Joyce might be understood.

Re-reading Texts

The shared perception that we return to the reading of Joyce's major texts and that we all agree that there is no single way of reading them paves the way I think for the section of exemplary textual readings by well-known critics that begins this volume. These essays by no means exhaust or even attempt to summarize mechanically the existing critical debate, but they do each combine a distinctive critical approach with the clarity and accessibility that is necessary for a reader new to the texts, and each offers a full bibliography which places their reading in the context of a debate, providing directions for further reading.

Since a primary goal of this volume is to refresh our approaches to Joyce's writing it seems especially appropriate that we begin with a chapter from Vicki Mahaffey, who writes on *Dubliners*, approaching the stories as descriptions of the habitual activities of the characters and also as texts which challenge the habitual assumptions that we might bring to them as readers, assumptions which Joyce's famously oblique narrative strategies might be shown to subvert. Mahaffey's underlying intention, as in her recent study *Modernist Literature: Challenging Fictions*, is to defend Joyce's apparent difficulty, even in these early works, and to show how the reader's confrontation with that difficulty can lead to substantial rewards (Mahaffey 2006). She achieves this through a reading of the stories in terms of their metaphors of economy and she explores the new kind of "covenant" between the author and the reader which Joyce's stories may be said to establish. Developing from a reading of the concept of "grace" in the story of that name, which she wittily exemplifies in the figure of the passing cyclist, she argues that elements in these stories invite a movement from the coercively contractual towards the kind of literary environment in which the reader's due care and attention can produce special insights. Such openness of the texts, as she argues in her account of "The Dead," can be compared to the cardinal Homeric virtue of hospitality – explored through its roots in the Greek words *xenos* and *mêtis* and in the Latin *hospes* – a virtue of his own writing which Joyce sees as problematic when absent from the society which his stories depict.

John Paul Riquelme explores *A Portrait of the Artist as a Young Man* as a text which stands closely beside an important predecessor: Oscar Wilde's *The Picture of Dorian Gray*. He considers the title's invitation to approach the book in terms of the visual arts and places his reading securely within the developing tradition of discussing the book's treatment of the maturing of Stephen's sexuality, taken here, in the spirit of recent queer theory, as fundamentally ambiguous in its orientation. Powerful dynamics of entrapment and constraint are seen to govern this and other aspects of Stephen's psychic and creative life and we are shown this especially in his encounter with the institution of the confession and its constraints which so intrusively govern his embodied sensibility. Riquelme notices the role of some minor characters, like Dante Riordan, Stephen's schoolfellow Heron, and his teacher Mr Tate, and he identifies imagery of snakes which appears in the discourses that terrorize Stephen's imagination of sin and guilt as well as appearing in one of the key points of reference for his aesthetic theory (as for that of many philosophic theorists of art of the previous century), the statue of *Laocoön* in the Vatican.

Maud Ellmann, returning to the vital theme of the body in *Ulysses*, confirms the enduring significance of that once-marginalized concern. In her essay she reiterates and develops the idea, first voiced by Beckett, that the language of *Ulysses* is not so much "about" the body as that it "enacts organic process": that the body and language are both circulatory systems. She builds from this to a reading of Stephen and Bloom in the early episodes in terms of the organs of the body and the cloacal, and of the Bloom in the middle episodes as he is engaged in the economics of wandering and return in the urban and domestic worlds which he inhabits. The final gendered "punch line" of *Ulysses* emerges here in the suggestion that it is through her body that Molly Bloom achieves the creativity that is so frustrated in Stephen Dedalus.

Finn Fordham offers a thoroughly new introduction to *Finnegans Wake* in terms of its approximations – or refusals to approximate – to the paradigm of the novel. Not only this but many other kinds of duality are said by Fordham to be characteristic both of the *Wake* and of the approaches to it that have been adopted over the years. In these approaches he sees a profound debate between those who do and those who do not want to understand it (at least in a conventional sense), between the philologists who accumulate knowledge and the theorists who argue that the very nature of *Finnegans Wake* is to call such knowledges into question. To approach *Finnegans Wake* is to enter a discussion concerning the fluid nature of language which Fordham ties to

Ezra Pound's favored sinologist Ernest Fenollosa, who is quoted in *Finnegans Wake*. He suggests that the discussion of nature and the natural, though it is not often invoked in the criticism of Joyce, can provide a paradigm for understanding this extraordinary text as it plies between opposed tendencies to "irrepressible category-smashing energy" and system-building. Fordham concludes by offering the reader examples of the Wakean transformation of two of the simplest elements of narrative: plot and character, describing what is usually held to be the central family plot or plots in the first sketches which Joyce wrote and what are usually held to be the central overlapping characters, character forms, or so-called "sigla" of the book.

Joycean Geographies: Biographical Contexts and Global Relocations

A second section on some of the places and contexts of Joyce's residence and reception offers a deliberate expansion of the usual range of places in which Joyce's work is understood, including nine essays whose keynote is their diversity. These are essays on familiar and unfamiliar geographical contexts for reading Joyce as well as ones which address theoretical problems of location more abstractly.

There is a recurrent debate in Joyce studies between the kind of cosmopolitanism that is implied by his several continental European places of residence and the kind of localism that is implied by his persistent return to the fictional subject-matter of Dublin. Each can be associated with a certain kind of politics. On the one hand the modernity and freedom of his cosmopolitanism is set against a backward-looking or procrustean aspect of the local, whilst on the other hand much recent work has tried to argue that it is his complex placement alongside the politics of an emerging national identity posed against repressive imperial domination that makes Joyce modern. No straight opposition between indigeneity and cosmopolitanism would do justice to the complex reformulation of the opposition between these terms either in Joyce's work or in the contemporary cultural arena. Questions of where to locate or to relocate James Joyce in a twenty-first-century, global culture are not so easily resolved as by a return to Dublin or even to the succession of Joyce's residences from Pola to Trieste, to Rome, Trieste, Zurich, Trieste, and Paris which are announced in the topographic by-lines that sign off *A Portrait* and *Ulysses*. As most readers will suspect, the "Gazeteer" of *Finnegans Wake* extends for hundreds of pages with its universalizing project of the overlapping of places through the alignments of their names.

There were different but no less significant cultural environments that informed the production and subsequent response to his work which recurrently radiated, for example, around literary London and which also depended vitally on Chicago and New York. Then there are the patterns of translation and/or literary reception which post-date the texts and make them come to figure in the many diverse narratives of Western European culture and of the cultural emancipation of one after another of the Western democracies and also the cultural modernization of Latin America, the former Eastern European countries, and the former imperial and postcolonial nations of the world. The reviews of three books in the February 2007 issue of the *James Joyce Broadsheet* bring some of the alternatives to the fore. Mark Sutton considers a book on *Finnegans Wake* by George Cinclair Gibson which places Joyce's last work in relation to Irish Gaelic myth and cultural history (Sutton 2007). Fritz Senn reviews the Joycean rediffusion throughout Europe alone, charted in Geert Lernout and Wim van Mierlo's 2004 volumes *The Reception of James Joyce in Europe*, which include some 29 articles on various Continental European countries, excluding Britain and Ireland though with an essay on Joyce and Irish-language writers (Senn 2007). This already encyclopedic project cries out for fuller extension around the other continents and language zones of the globe: a need to which this present volume can only gesture. Patrick O'Neill's *Polyglot Joyce* is among recent studies that have begun to pay attention to this global "multiplicity" of Joyces: the Joyces of the 65 languages used in the *Wake* but also the Joyce of the languages into which his works have been translated (O'Neill 2005). This, as Fritz Senn has himself long argued, may constitute one of the richest territories for exploring the phenomenon of *Joyce's Dislocutions*, where reading and interpretation may also themselves approximate to the activity of translation (Senn 1984).

Self-modernizing contemporary cosmopolitan Ireland is itself one among the places that has increasingly been led to reshape itself in the wake of the Joycean imagination. Yet if one wanted to locate Joyce as a force of cultural significance and of cultural emancipation for our time it would now appear too prudent even to limit that locationality to the well-developed academic centers of Britain, Europe, and North America, where most of the established academic authorities on Joyce are based. That would be to miss the larger picture of a writer whose liberatory cultural footprint, long planted on the bridges between Ireland, Britain, and Europe and between the larger Europe and North America, is now also poised to step out to the newer worlds of cultural communication that are opened up across the globe, between Europe with its rich inheritance of cultural diversity and Africa with its emerging national and pan-continental forms of cultural consciousness, or between Europe and America and Australasia and Asia that in their different ways have responded to Joyce.

English literary figures have written world histories from Walter Raleigh to H. G. Wells and the theorizing of a cosmopolitan ideal may be traced through Kant back to the Stoics (Nussbaum 1997), but our hotly debated contemporary impetus for global conceptions of culture and for a cultural conception of the global emerges hand-in-hand with rapid increases in the availability of cheap air travel, shared global problems such as climate change, and the everyday reality of instant global communications by means of the Internet. Global or cosmopolitan ideas may seem inevitably either homogenizing or idealistic. It may seem hard to imagine the cosmopolitan except in terms of the expert or even of an elite (Cucullu 2004). Perhaps the distinctive impact of Joyce's later writing is to imagine a world in which a remarkable variety of places retain their distinctiveness whilst also showing up the comical and surprising aspects of their similarities to each other, where their unexpected fungibilities may reside. At any rate the conception of modernism was always a partly national and a partly international one. For Raymond Williams as for Bradbury and McFarlane the urban spaces which distinguish its emergence as a cultural form and the places it frequently chooses to represent are the modern international or cosmopolitan cities of modernity: London, Paris, Vienna, New York, as well as Joyce's Dublin (Williams 1989; Bradbury and McFarlane 1970). The geographies of modernism, as a recent volume with that title attests, include a redefinition of nations, empires, locations and locationalities themselves (Brooker and Thacker 2005) and the postmodern cultural environment rapidly accelerates these trends. In late capitalism we see a rise of what Edward Soja has called the "prototopical" in which all places are the same place (Soja 1989) and may be driven all the more to pursue the specificities that Michel Foucault defined as "heterotopia" (Foucault 1986). Cultural productions can be defined as much in terms of the cultural environment, or what Pierre Bourdieu calls the "habitus," in which they are produced or consumed (Bourdieu 1993), even whilst these habitations themselves can come to seem transmuted through their simulacra (Baudrillard 1983), redefined through the hyperspatial disjunction of the body and its built environment (Jameson 1992), or morph into the intermediate or "non-places" of the airport or shopping mall (Augé 1995). That new nations continue to be born out of old empires and vice versa and that the places of culture are by no means always identical with those of geography or politics may be thought to play into the broad environment for our reading of the many-faceted multi-locatednesses of Joyce and his diasporic texts as much as such traditional terms as exile and displacement.

In the spirit of this situation the essays on Joycean places in this section are arranged into two broad sub-groups, the first dealing with European and the second with non-European locations, though no attempt at coverage of such locations is implied.

Geert Lernout, whose two-volume work on the reception of Joyce's work in Europe (edited with Wim van Mierlo) maps that field, here writes a more polemical essay. For Lernout the two traditions of reading Joyce are Irish and continental European and here he strongly defends the idea of Joyce as European writer, much of whose work can be understood to consciously subscribe to a broad continental European cultural tradition of "Daunty, Gouty and Shopkeeper" (*FW* 539 6) – a canon into which Joyce campaigned, for example, for an Ibsen to be admitted. That Joyce viewed "his own mission" along these lines is emphatically argued here as is the importance of his continental European defenders, most notably Valery Larbaud. His protagonists in *Dubliners*, in *Exiles*, in *Stephen Hero*, and in *A Portrait* and *Ulysses* and the sense of literary traditions and audiences which can be found in the critical writings and the letters and the multi-lingualism of *Finnegans Wake* are all invoked to add to this picture of a resolutely continental European Joyce.

John Nash writes a detailed historical essay on the specifics of Joyce's early reception in the context of an independent Ireland. Figures like Ernest Boyd and Daniel Corkery, who slighted or resisted the Joycean example in this national context, come into view, as does the critic Stephen Gwynn, who was among the first to see the distinctiveness of Joyce's Catholicism, and Shane Leslie, the Irish critic who called for *Ulysses* to be banned. We see here a counterview to the cosmopolitan perspectives of critics like Larbaud or Ezra Pound (who wrote of *Dubliners* in 1914 that "these stories could be retold of any town") and those of less-well-known Dublin-based critics who could concur that the setting of the works may be no more than "accident." According to Nash, on the historical coincidence between the appearance of *Ulysses* in 1992 hard on the heels of the Treaty of Independence, "not surprisingly, readers in Ireland found that the importance of the latter overshadowed the former." From Nash's essay the reader begins to get some bearings on the positions that were taken on Joyce early on in this complex and politically inflected terrain.

Joyce's first long-term alternative home to Dublin, the place where he cemented his relationship with Nora and where they began to bring up their children, was Trieste. John McCourt's essay on Joyce's Triestine home from home offers an elegant and well-informed account of the approaches that have been taken to Joyce's long residence there in the formative period of his writing. He charts Joyce's experiences there and argues strongly that it was "not accidental that it was in Trieste that Joyce began to form the theoretical skeleton of the ideas that Bloom would later come to embody . . . his refutation of 'the old pap of racial hatred' (*LII* 167) in its Irish configuration."

Robert Weninger's essay starts from a location which Joyce never inhabited in his person, though his first full work of translation was from the German of Gerhard Hauptman and his Zurich residence (which is not independently treated in this volume) made him a long-term inhabitant of a German-speaking city. "James Joyce and German Literature, or Reflections on the Vagaries and Vacancies of Reception Studies" crosses boundaries and links approaches, partly offering a study of sources for and receptions of Joyce in German literature but also addressing aspects of reception study (themselves a "Germanic" academic practice) which throw up particular connections that may call many of our assumptions about influence and relatedness into question. His essay selects intriguing and less-explored trajectories in the linking of Joyce and Gustav Freytag's *Soll und Haben* (*Debit and Credit*): a novel previously little known to Joyce critics though it sits on the shelves of Leopold Bloom's library in the "Ithaca" episode of *Ulysses*. This is balanced with an account of Joyce as a debatable influence on Heinrich Böll, surely significant at some level if elusive in point of fact, discussing the extent to which Böll might be said to have modernized himself in an encounter with Joyce and Ireland in the 1950s. Weninger goes on to reconsider the "connection, or ostensible non-connection," that marks the "interrelation" between Joyce and Rilke, both residents of Trieste, concentrating, for example, on the comparable use of the epiphanic in their works. His is an essay that makes connections with others in this group as well as anticipating the section on approaches and receptions that is to come.

Between continental Europe and its others, the essay by Richard Brown discusses Gibraltar: that other location which looms large at the climax of Dublin-bound *Ulysses*. This is another place where Joyce himself did not live but it is one that figures in his work and might encapsulate many of its concerns about place and context. The presence of this remembered other place of Molly Bloom's childhood that remains so vivid in her memory invites Joyce's readers to revisit the meticulously constructed and embodied locations in his work. Researching some approaches to this other place that have appeared in criticism thus far, the essay argues that this "other location" may offer a libidinal alternative to the book's main location, and one that anticipates contemporary cultural ideals. Joyce's image of Gibraltar serves as a cultural critique and as a paradigm for a cultural audience or community – linked by the richness and diversity of its respective inheritances – that Joyce's writings seem to envisage and even bring into being.

An engaged review of some of the distinctive contributions made by the postcolonial theory which has emerged in Joyce studies since the early 1990s can be found in Mark Wollaeger's essay on the analytical and tropical modes of Joycean postcolonial theory which is revised and updated here. Wollaeger's contention is that some tendencies in the postcolonial debate may paradoxically work to de-historicize Joyce, removing him from the lived cultural experiences and contexts and real histories in which he needs to be understood. One way beyond such a double-bind may be to break the binary modes and codes of such critical discourses to enable other histories to be told and familiar ones retold in new ways.

That there are other such histories can be demonstrated by the following three chapters in this book. It is, as Eishiro Ito writes, "fascinating to explore what James Joyce felt about Japan." Ito explores the few comments in Joyce's texts and letters and critical writings which relate to the key events of the period in Japanese history and to such well-known works in which Japanese culture is represented as Puccini's *Madame Butterfly*. Just as significant, though, is the reception of Joyce's work in Japan and the creative responses to it which Ito charts from the purchase of *A Portrait* by Ryunosuke Akutagawa as early as 1919. *Ulysses* was translated three times in the 1930s, beginning in 1931, with the result that many Japanese readers could enjoy it before those in Britain or America, and Joyce had at least three Japanese friends in Paris. Though Joyce's knowledge of the language was, Ito writes, "fragmental," over 80 Japanese words and phrases appear in *Finnegans Wake*. Ito explains that Chinese, Japanese, and other oriental references overlap in the *Wake*, perhaps deliberately, since he describes the transformation of Joyce's utopian phrase "United States of Asia" from a 1927 notebook entry to its final form, "United States of Ourania," which appeared in *Finnegans Wake*.

Further acknowledgment of the breaking and expanding of the mould of Joycean cultural awareness and contextualization can be seen in the essay by Krishna Sen on Joyce's encounter with India, which provides an extremely original perspective not only on some of the frequently ignored Hindu references in the encyclopedic *Finnegans Wake* but also on the ways in which contemporary Indian writers like Desai forge significant comparisons with Joyce. Compared to that in Eliot, Sen argues, India's presence is "spectral" in Joyce and vice versa. On the other hand she suggests that we could see Joyce as a critic more than as a purveyor or victim of Orientalist fantasy and that the Hindu and Buddhist "decorative iconography" of *Ulysses* may be transformed into a "greater synergy" between Western and Eastern religions and mythologies by the time of *Finnegans Wake*. The attempt to "hindustand" (*FW* 492 17) correspondences between Wakean figures and such deities as Agni and Shiva mentioned in the

Wake produces a richly inflected reading of some passages, phrases, and tropes from the *Wake* so that its familiar notions of dreaming and recirculation and even the aesthetics of the epiphany from Joyce's earlier writings can be seen in new lights. Sen finds an analogy between Stephen Dedalus, with his Aquinas-inspired ideas, and the spiritual-aesthetic experiences of Abhinavagupta of the eleventh-century *Abhinavabharati*, revealing aspects of the "transcultural nature of Joyce's thought" and reminding us that for Joyce in his "Drama and Life" essay of 1900 "beauty is the *swerga* of the aesthete." That canonical Indian writers in English from Vikram Seth to Salman Rushdie freely engage Joyce's texts in theirs and that such "counter-discursive" writers as G. V. Desani and Anita Desai acknowledge the Joycean example along with indigenous paradigms counteracts the impression of an occasional critical neglect. Joyce's interface with India and India's with Joyce are "subterranean," Sen argues, "but the results," as she shows in this densely packed account, "are no less rewarding."

New contexts for reading Joyce can take us far enough around the globe. Another rarely visited location for Joycean criticism is the subject of David Wright's essay on Joyce and New Zealand, which provides an intriguing example of the ways in which the expanded set of geographical and cultural horizons which are characteristic of our globalizing cultural consciousness can offer new information about contexts and new lights on the texts themselves. Much of Wright's essay is devoted to an account of Joyce's sister Margaret, who like many Irish Catholics emigrated to New Zealand, and the unearthing of her story leads Wright on to consider her possible appearance in "Eveline" and in *Ulysses*, the presence of New Zealand references in the texts including the haka in *Finnegans Wake* and then the cultural resistances to and influences of Joyce on subsequent New Zealand writers from Janet Frame to Maurice Duggan.

Such glimpses clearly suggest what a fascinating and dynamic cultural document a world encyclopedia of Joycean receptions and responses might turn out to be. As Joyce becomes a world author of the twenty-first century, the negotiation of cultural otherness refracted through such "fragmental" or "subterranean" connections as through the agglomerative carnival surreality of the later Joyce, can certainly present problems of "hindustanding" but also opens opportunities for the reader. We may be only beginning to glimpse the post-history of the diasporated Joycean text but then, as Ato Quayson has put it, postcoloniality is not so much a condition as a process and some aspects of this collection may reflect and indeed assist a little further in the process of decolonizing or postcolonizing Joyce.

Critical and Creative Approaches, Receptions, and Responses

Having sketched some unlikely as well as some more familiar contexts, we move to essayists, in this third and longest section, who write on themes that go beyond the geographical – though their essays may at least offer glimpses of such missing contexts as Paris and London and the links between modern Ireland and classical Greece. These essays bring us back to the works through the approaches taken to them by critics and scholars and by some creative artists over the years, charting critical methods that have defined or continue to define the intellectual agenda and selected aspects of the wide range of creative and cultural response that may be found in more contemporary work which can often be illuminated in terms of its relationship with Joyce.

That one of the most established of critical approaches to Joyce considers the debt which the title of Joyce's *Ulysses* announces to Homer makes the placement of Declan Kiberd's refreshing and distinguished essay on Homer and Joyce an especially welcome beginning to this section. Kiberd's prominence among Irish critics of Irish literature and of the creation of modern Ireland gives his argument about Joyce special interest. It is as an Irish Homer that he reopens *Ulysses*, but more particularly his theme is that it is the modernity of the *Odyssey* that Joyce's translation of it reveals. That all texts are rereadings of other texts is an underlying thread through all the essays in this volume and especially those in this section. Here the *Odyssey* is seen as Homer's anti-militaristic rereading of the *Iliad*: a work that anticipates the modern bourgeois world as much as it recalls the ancient one. This is the Homer which Horkheimer and Adorno open up when they explore the anti-mythological in his thinking. The epic is cinematic in its form, even its gods are seen as what Eric Dodds calls "monitions" and therefore closely alignable to Joyce's representation of mental interiority; its genius is in its location of the everyday in the epic simile's "as if." Kiberd's is an essay for our times when, as he says, Penguin Books sells more copies of James Joyce's *Ulysses* than of the *Odyssey*.

Kiberd reminds us that Joyce was not yet "James Joyce" when he wrote *Ulysses*, but it is the unabashed history of the appearance of this "James Joyce" of theory (the author as Michel Foucault's "inventor of discursivity") that Jean-Michel Rabaté offers here in what one might call a "companion" piece to his essay on Joyce's residences in Paris during the 1920s that appeared in the *Cambridge Companion* to Joyce. The group of intellectuals that formed around the periodical *Tel Quel* are claimed as the Parisian successors to the avant-gardism of the 1920s and 30s represented by the *transition* group and by Eugene and Maria Jolas, who were so supportive of Joyce. Readers who have been inspired by theory or had difficulty following its personalities and key debates will find much of value in this chapter, which focuses on the Paris of the 1960s and after and on the importance of Joyce to its cultural debates. Joyce is here placed in the development of the discourses represented by the *Tel Quel* group, and two great, if notoriously impenetrable, post-Joycean theoreticians, Jacques Lacan and Jacques Derrida, are here introduced with great clarity and command in terms of the substantial roles played, in their developing thought, by their encounters with James Joyce. Rabaté's essay gives a thorough and informative account of one of the most controversial and innovatory strands of cultural thinking in the humanities subject area since the 1970s – one which has often gone together with the study of Joyce.

Such theory may not always be easy or widely popular but it certainly engages with questions of popularity just as the belated academic acknowledgment of popular cultures has frequently depended upon an awareness of cultural theory. R. Brandon Kershner gives an informed overview of the ways in which discussions of popular culture in the academy have been especially useful in bringing new perspectives to Joyce's work and he combines this with a discussion of what we have come to know about Joyce and music, including the popular music that fills his work. Hampered at first by senses of the seriousness of literature that we may find in both F. R. and Q. D. Leavis (according to which popular literature was either overlooked or treated as a kind of addiction), Kershner explains the substantial recent changes in attitude and practice both in England and America, connecting the newer attention to popular culture with the rise of theory, of studies of sexuality, and of postmodernism. He details the contributions of a generation of Joyce scholars who have encouraged a celebration of the richness of this body of material in Joyce and also remind us of the extent to which such study continually presents questions about our disciplinary goals.

Preferring the selection of a few representative examples over the construction of an academic history, Daniel Ferrer's accessible and concise introduction to the excitement of studying Joyce's manuscripts begins by pointing out that all published texts begin as manuscripts and that, in Joyce's case, such texts as *Giacomo Joyce* and *Stephen Hero* have undertaken that transformation through the advocacy of academic editors whilst others (such as the volume of early *Finnegans Wake* sketches that was proposed for publication by Danis Rose under the title *Finn's Hotel*) have not. Joyceans, he suggests, may sometimes enjoy manuscript study not so much because it helps to clarify the substantial difficulties of the later Joyce, but because it promises to add a seemingly inexhaustible further supply of such difficulty. Approaching the text of *Ulysses*, so much the center of debate since Hans Walter Gabler's edition in the 1980s, Ferrer discusses instances where the study of Joyce's manuscripts can help correct an error in a published text and also those where a false editorial correction can be shown to have obscured highly complex intentions that need to be restored. The study of manuscripts reveals its own stories of foiled and changed intentions that can make the editor's quest for the definitive text an endless one. Such is the case with the passage about "Don Emile Patrizio Franz Rupert Pope Hennessy" from "Circe" that Ferrer shows to have developed through fortuitous routes to two quite different placements in different "final" versions of the text. Ferrer's examples grow still more complex and intriguing as he explores the composition of *Finnegans Wake* and the wealth of material that the manuscript archive can add to our knowledge of Joyce's creative experimentations even when these were not incorporated into published texts.

Four essays that follow give instances of the important place of Joyce's work in four different expressive media. Mark Taylor-Batty's essay provides a striking contribution to what is (even despite the mediating presence of Beckett and Tom Stoppard's play *Travesties*) a surprisingly rarely treated area – the importance of Joyce to later twentieth-century British drama – in a chapter which argues that the playwright Harold Pinter showed a good deal more enthusiasm for Joyce's one play *Exiles* than do many current academic supporters of Joyce's fiction. Taylor-Batty's research in the staging of Pinter's production of *Exiles* in London's Mermaid Theatre in 1971 unearths a correspondence with Beckett (in which Beckett recommends emphasizing the "apartness" of the characters on the stage) and plots the traces of Joyce's play in Pinter's subsequent writing, including the title of his play *Old Times*. Taylor-Batty also explores the theatrical potential of Joyce's "cat-and-mouse" work through Pinter's connection with it and the mutually informing perceptions about ambiguity, trust, and betrayal in human relationships and the "unpossessibility of the other" that is central to both writers. He also shows how both respond to an Ibsenite tradition. "Joyce harnesses Ibsen's structure, and undermines the traditional communicative function of stage dialogue to demonstrate how individuals might exile themselves from those who might best bring them comfort," Batty argues, whereas by contrast Pinter restores an Ibsenite sense of "duty to oneself."

In her recent 2004 exhibition and book on *Joyce in Art*, Christa-Maria Lerm Hayes has revealed more comprehensively than previous critics the extent to which visual artists can be seen as important heirs to Joyce. Taking them seriously as his "interpreters" and even "scholars" may, she argues, yield new perspectives for Joyce studies but also for the history of art. Invoking Derrida's concept of "performative interpretation" and "postproduction," she opts (after David Hopkins' *The Duchamp Effect*) for a discussion of what she calls the Joyce "effect," including, for example, his effect on the work of Richard Prince, a visual image of whose commitment to Joyce is offered as an illustration here. Lerm Hayes concludes that artists attracted to Joyce since the 1960s have found in him a precedent for their attention to forms and to "the fleeting nature of hierarchical power structures." Those "who have possibly most profitably responded to . . . Joyce, have done so obliquely and often irreverently or subversively," she claims, using as her examples works by Joseph Beuys, Patrick Ireland, Rebecca Horn, and James Coleman. Joyce reading groups may themselves represent a kind of cultural practice that aligns with that of "performative interpretation," she writes, and the "relational" work of the artist is also something that should be taken into account since artists like Tony Smith, Brian O'Doherty/Patrick Ireland and John Cage, Susan Weil, and Rauschenberg have been participants in such groups and they extend the dialogic trajectory that Lerm Hayes sees as the completion of Joyce's art.

For Derval Tubridy the dilemma of the Irish poet begins with that defined by Thomas Kinsella in 1928 between the relative attitudes taken by Yeats and Joyce to what Yeats called the "filthy modern tide," albeit siding with Joyce's modernity defined as an "ability to engage with the immediacy of Irish experience." Joyce's own poetry is, as Seamus Heaney and others have observed, hardly the most modern and experimental part of his oeuvre but the poetry of Joyce's prose is "central rather than supplemental," inspiring the range of contemporary Irish poets from Austin Clarke and Seamus Heaney to Paul Muldoon and Medbh McGuckian, according to this account, which includes glimpses of the less familiar Joycean presence in the Irish Gaelic poetry of Seán Ó Ríordáin. Fullest is Tubridy's account of Kinsella's 1997 collection of poems, *The Pen Shop*, which, she argues, rewrites Bloom's odyssey from the "Hades" episode of *Ulysses* in reverse, for the poet-speaker journeys through the center of Dublin in the opposite direction to the protagonist of *Ulysses*. But the contemporary writer has also partly outgrown Kinsella's dichotomy, being now able to "commute," to be both present and absent, local and international, at once.

Such cultural mobility might define the position of the Irish cultural critic who, like Luke Gibbons in his elegantly written chapter on John Huston's cinematic version of "The Dead," may find the cosmopolitan "haunted" by the specter of its local other as well as of the past which its modernity may purport to transcend. Contrary to the frequently voiced account, Gibbons claims, it was not Huston who introduced a nationalist "undertow" to Joyce's story. Rather Huston draws upon what are increasingly recognized in cultural history as the spectral and haunting aspects of the cinema as a modern technology and "medium," finding a "visual tonality" to capture nuances in Joyce's original that open up Dublin's modernity to an awareness of the voices it excludes. Story and film embody the same "spirit." He finds in the story and in Huston's film a "spectral modernity," one that comes "from the unrequited voices in the margins" such as "the 'servant girls', the lily flourishing and growing on the arms of Galway city."

Katherine Mullin's essay is on the also sometimes obscured cultural and sexual politics of the modernist little magazines in which Joyce's work first appeared: London's *The Egoist*, which serialized *A Portrait* and then *Ulysses; The Little Review* from Chicago, whose serialization of *Ulysses* got it into trouble with censorship; and *transition* in Paris, in which parts of *Finnegans Wake* were serialized in the 1920s and 30s. This is an engaged and engaging overview of this history in which a shared set of cultural problems concerning the role of literature in sex and gender politics across the international field hoves into view. In step with contemporary historicism, Mullin refuses the assumption that Joyce was completely aloof or alienated from the publications in which he wrote as if they were mere vehicles for his independent artistic vision, instead presenting a picture with a sharply formulated contextual edge in which the importance of Joyce to the agenda of the magazines as well as vice versa becomes more clearly apparent.

That Joyce's work is full of disembodied and distorted means of communication may be a familiar enough concept. In an essay as immersed in the history of radio technology as it is in the reading of the later Joyce, Jane Lewty takes this point and glosses it through the emergent communication technology of the radio which is referred to in *Finnegans Wake* but which also might provide an analogy for aspects of its communicative strategies. Patented by Marconi in 1900 the characteristic voicings and problems of the radio medium become a significant presence in *Finnegans Wake*. Lewty points out references to Irish, French, and BBC radio programmes, discusses the technical specifications of the radio set detailed in III.2, and makes a convincing case for the otological basis of much in *Finnegans Wake*. Joyce's visual impairments as well as his poet's fascination with the musical sound of words may make it all the more convincing to think of him as a writer of the ear. According to the argument in Sara Danius' book *The Senses of Modernism* (2002) we can observe a specialization of the senses in the forms of early twentieth-century modernity and its cultural technologies. That would appear to be confirmed in the specializations of our contributors too, if we contrast Lerm Hayes and Gibbons, who touch on Joyce and the visual, with, for example, Kershner's discussion of music and the world of sounds that Lewty foregrounds here.

It may not be entirely fortuitous that this collection ends with a chapter by Luke

Thurston on Joyce and psychoanalysis that imaginatively argues for the significant contemporaneity of his work with that emergent field of discourse in Freud and his subsequent direct influence upon the later twentieth century's interpretative sciences of the mind. Thurston develops some aspects of his recent book, exploring the connections between Joyce and Jung as well as supplementing aspects of Rabaté's earlier chapter on French theory with an extremely helpful account of Joyce's knotty relationship with Jacques Lacan which, as he explains it, hinges upon and closes our collection with the labyrinthine figure of the Borromean knot, in itself an irresolvable puzzle, though one that can in its way be resolved by a return to Joyce's texts.

It is nothing if not apparent that the reader of this volume might gain many different things from the variety of its contents and enjoy a wide range of exploratory journeys through geographical, historical, textual, linguistic, cultural, and psychological space. That Joyce's texts sustain repeated revisitations will be among the first of this reader's rewards but as the volume develops it should become apparent that the physical displacements around Europe that defined Joyce's writing life, the encyclopedic and multi-dimensional meaningfulness of his texts, especially his later works, and the extraordinary and repeated symbolic placement of his work at the center of many of the twentieth (and twenty-first) century's most innovatory developments in culture and thought make the Joycean journey an ever more diverse and far-reaching one whose many manifestations, contexts, and opportunities hardly seem likely to be exhausted or resolved any time soon.

BIBLIOGRAPHY

Armand, Louis and Clare Wallace (2006) *Giacomo Joyce: Envoys of the Other*. Prague: Litteraria Pragensia.

Ali, Zulfiqar (2007) "Review of Patrick O'Neill, *Polyglot Joyce* (Toronto: University of Toronto Press, 2005)," *James Joyce Broadsheet* 76 (February): 2.

Attridge, Derek (2004 [1990]) *The Cambridge Companion to James Joyce*. Cambridge: Cambridge University Press.

Augé, Marc (1995) *Non-Places: Introduction to an Anthropology of Supermodernity*. London: Verso.

Baudrillard, Jean (1983) *Simulations*. New York: Semiotexte.

Bohman, James and Matthias Lutz-Bachmann (eds.) (1997) *Perpetual Peace: Essays on Kant's Cosmopolitan Ideal*. Cambridge, MA: MIT Press.

Bourdieu, Pierre (1993) *The Field of Cultural Production*. London: Polity Press.

Bowen, Zack (1984) *A Companion to James Joyce*. Westport, CT: Greenwood Press.

Bradbury, Malcolm and James McFarlane (1976) *Modernism*. London: Penguin Books.

Brooker, Peter and Andrew Thacker (2005) *Geographies of Modernism: Literatures, Cultures, Spaces*. London: Routledge.

Cohen, Robin (2001) *Global Diasporas: An Introduction*. London: Routledge.

Cucullu, Lois (2004) *Expert Modernists, Matricide, and Modern Culture*. Basingstoke: Palgrave.

Danius, Sara (2002) *The Senses of Modernism: Technology, Perception and Aesthetics*. Ithaca, NY: Cornell University Press.

Eco, Umberto (1987) *Travels in Hyperreality*. London: Picador.

Foucault, Michel (1986) "Of other spaces," trans. Jay Miscowiec, *Diacritics* 16: 22–7.

Gibson, George Cinclair (2005) *Wake Rites: The Ancient Irish Rituals of "Finnegans Wake."* Gainesville: University Press of Florida.

Jameson, Frederic (1992) *Postmodernism, or the Cultural Logic of Late Capitalism*. London: Verso.

Lerm Hayes, Christa-Maria (2004) *Joyce in Art.* Dublin: Lilliput Press.

Lernout, Geert and Wim van Mierlo (2004) *The Reception of James Joyce in Europe.* London: Thoemmes Continuum.

Mahaffey, Vicki (2006) *Modernist Literature: Challenging Fictions.* Oxford: Blackwell.

Mink, Louis O. (1978) *A "Finnegans Wake" Gazetteer.* Bloomington: Indiana University Press.

Mishra, Vijay (1993) "Introduction," *Diasporas.* SPAN: Journal of the South Pacific Association for Commonwealth Literature and Language Studies: 34–5.

Nussbaum, Martha (1997) "Kant and cosmopolitanism." In James Bohman and Matthias Lutz-Bachmann (eds.) *Perpetual Peace: Essays on Kant's Cosmopolitan Ideal*: 25–37. Cambridge, MA. MIT Press.

O'Neill, Patrick (2005) *Polyglot Joyce.* Toronto: University of Toronto Press.

Quayson, Ato (2000) *Postcolonialism: Theory, Practice or Process?* Cambridge: Polity Press.

Raleigh, Sir Walter (1621) *The History of the World in Five Books.* London: William Iaggard.

Said, Edward (2001) *Reflections on Exile.* London: Granta.

Senn, Fritz (1984) *Joyce's Dislocutions: Essays on Reading as Translation,* ed. J. P. Riquelme. Baltimore, MD: Johns Hopkins University Press.

Senn, Fritz (2007) "Review of Geert Lernout and Wim van Mierlo, *The Reception of James Joyce in Europe.* London: Thoemmes Continuum," *James Joyce Broadsheet* 76 (February): 1.

Soja, Edward (1989) *Postmodern Geographies.* London: Verso.

Sutton, Mark (2007) "Review of Gibson George Cinclair, *Wake Rites: The Ancient Irish Rituals of 'Finnegans Wake.'* Gainesville: University Press of Florida," *James Joyce Broadsheet* 76 (February): 2.

Wells, H. G. (1927) *The History of the World.* London: T. Fisher Unwin.

Williams, Raymond (1989) *The Politics of Modernism: Against the New Conformists.* London: Verso.

PART I
Re-reading Texts

2

Dubliners: Surprised by Chance

Vicki Mahaffey

Readers who encounter Joyce's collection of short stories for the first time often come away with the impression that turn-of-the-century Dublin was an airless world, and that Joyce mercilessly arraigns its inhabitants for their helplessness. Using taut, spare prose, Joyce shines his interrogating beam of narrative attention on one telling detail after another. This process is not interrupted by the voice of that avuncular, editorializing third-person "omniscient" narrator we so often expect to hear when reading fiction. Instead, we are starkly confronted by selected "facts" about the lives of individual characters, and how we interpret those facts or respond to those characters is left to us. Readers tend to react to this narrative challenge in a predictable way: with boredom, avidity, depression, or moral judgment. Many readers patronize the characters as less self-aware and functional than the readers believe themselves to be. It is easy to feel protected from Joyce's scrutiny by the fiction, which is most often experienced as a one-way mirror rather than the "nicely polished looking-glass" that Joyce claimed it was (*LI* 64). When judging the characters, readers typically exempt themselves from those judgments, thereby neglecting the opportunity to look scrupulously for the "meanness" – in the less usual sense of the term, the thread of connection or commonality – between themselves and the characters they have deprecated.[1]

On subsequent readings, as familiarity with the stories grows, readers are apt to soften towards the characters. Effects they ignored at first become more prominent, such as the way Joyce's evocations of music offer a "virtual" soundtrack that complicates the meaning of his narrative slideshow of revealing details. When we familiarize ourselves with the music of "Silent, O Moyle" to read "Two Gallants," for example, its angelic-sounding Irish harp music in a minor key comes to accent the plaint of its lyrics, expressing a poignant yearning for long-awaited freedom. Such music, once heard, may awaken in the reader an uncomfortable sympathy for all of the characters: for the men reduced to petty machinations in an effort to gain a "sovereign" (a contemptibly small measure of sovereignty), as well as for the servant girl that one of the gallants sexually plays upon in order to get that sovereign. Other songs alluded to in

Dubliners – "I Dreamt I Dwelt in Marble Halls" ("Clay"), "I Sing Thee Songs of Araby" ("Araby"), "Arrayed for the Bridal" and "The Lass of Aughrim" ("The Dead") – similarly offer to put readers in closer emotional touch with the characters' half-buried, impossibly unrealistic dreams of escape or romance.

For all its sympathy with the plight of the characters, the narrative eye of *Dubliners* is not squeamish: it looks without blinking at the "little warm tricks," the "mean cosy turns," and "all the greedy gushes out through [the] small souls" (*FW* 627 17–19) of ordinary people, exposing the threadbare rationalizations and unacknowledged needs that render it unlikely that these particular people will discover the means to change. At the beginning and end of the collection, the uncompromising narrative scrutiny is momentarily relieved when two characters exhibit glimmerings of insight and self awareness: the young boy narrator of the early stories and Gabriel, the compromised protagonist of "The Dead." Those moments of new self-consciousness are tantalizing but undeveloped; "An Encounter," "Araby," and "The Dead" all conclude with this brief, undeveloped glimpse of a new way of seeing.

Dubliners, then, unlike its famous epic successor, *Ulysses*, is not comic fiction. Its characters, with only a few exceptions, are caught in habitual routines and ways of thinking, and it is difficult to imagine how these routines might be meaningfully interrupted or challenged. How did Joyce get from this anatomy of habit in *Dubliners*, conducted with "scrupulous meanness" in the primary sense of conscientious parsimony, to the narrative irrepressibility of the last half of *Ulysses*? If we understand comedy both as a narrative (as a trajectory that ends in a reaffirmation of community) and as a local effect (the sudden release of energy as two perspectives or possibilities unexpectedly collide) it becomes possible to see the boy's new appreciation of Mahony in "An Encounter" as proto-comic. When the boy realizes that he unconsciously patronizes Mahony, having always "despised him a little," and reacts with penitence, the convergence of his conflicting responses introduces a moment of irony into the text, so sudden and brief that it might be compared to the clash of meanings powering a pun. To adapt the words of Bloom in *Ulysses*, the boy briefly sees himself as others might see him (*U* 13 1058) – from the outside – which derails his perspective, allowing it to become softer and less haughty. At the same time, when the boy recognizes Mahony's ready responsiveness to his call, running "as if to bring [him] aid" (*D* 20), he appreciates an underlying connection between himself and Mahony that he had previously denied.

In these bursts of insight, we find the seeds of what will grow into the verbal and perspectival comedy of *Ulysses*. A writer can represent with fastidious accuracy the psychological and ideological mechanisms that subtly condition individuals to resist change, but how can a writer encourage a reader to look at him- or herself in the same light? How do people rendered smug or docile or desperate or profligate or abusive by habit gain access to a more dispassionate or objective view of themselves? As we can see from *Dubliners*, there is no known way to make this happen, at least not without shaming or breaking the spirit of the observer. Joyce can only create textual conditions in which self-recognition is possible, accenting that possibility by depicting characters who fail to achieve self-awareness. It is partly by chance, or perhaps by grace, that a character or a reader in a carefully controlled context may be inspired to apply what he sees in others to him- or herself. As Bloom remarks in *Ulysses*, "Some people . . . can see the mote in others' eyes but they can't see the beam in their own" (*U* 12 1237–8).

Although readers may feel that the effect of *Dubliners* is satiric, that is not its aim: it was designed, not to condemn its characters, but to expose the mechanisms of denial and dishonesty that prevent readers as well as characters from seeing themselves, and therefore others, clearly. When Joyce called *Dubliners* his "nicely polished looking-glass," he was deliberately aligning himself with Oscar Wilde's assertion in the preface to *The Picture of Dorian Gray* that it is "the spectator, not life, that art really mirrors." Joyce's strategy for crafting stories designed to spark self-recognition, the self-awareness that kindles a more sensitive acceptance of otherness, is to conduct something like an audit of his readers: an examination of their "accounts" of themselves. The word "audit" comes from the Latin *audire*, to hear, which accents the paradoxical nature of the problem Joyce was confronting: how does a storyteller – who is supposedly giving an account of life in Dublin – set up a narrative situation that makes audible the silent accounts of an unknown reader? Is it possible for fiction to facilitate a mutual accounting, in which the writer records an account in the hope of "hearing" how it tallies with the accounts of a reader? Or, to ask the question another way, how should we understand the overlap between the language of storytelling and that of accounting, both of which balance investment and return, or "earnings" and expenditures? "Tale" denotes a quantity or number as well as a story;[2] an account can be financial or narrative; to tell is also to count. Even "talent" has a similar double meaning: it designates an ancient weight and the value of that weight, which allows it to stand for wealth and riches, and also a special power or ability. To "tally" is to count and register, as well as to cause two things to correspond or agree (*OED*). The point of a "tale" is to expose a hidden deficit, so that it may be rectified. More ambitiously, a tale may call into question the unconscious accounting that creates and perpetuates expectations, expectations that limit the possibility and desirability of change.

It is important to consider the economies that operate in *Dubliners*, because reading is one such economy. The word "economy" derives from the Greek *oikos* (house) and *nemein* (control); it therefore designates quite literally a form of "home rule," which Bloom as a cuckold and an Irishman doubly lacks in *Ulysses*. The first meaning of "economy" is "management of a house," especially with regard to household expenses; economy connotes the careful management of resources (*OED*). As individuals, there is a need for economy in everything we do: the reckless waste of resources may mean not only bankruptcy, but dissipation of energy and even life (we can see this connection clearly emphasized in Flaubert's *Madame Bovary*, for example, where Emma's immense debt both precipitates and mirrors her suicide). Joyce points to economy as an important frame for understanding *Dubliners* on the first page of the collection, where the boy narrator identifies "*simony*" (the buying and selling of sacred things) as one of the words, along with *paralysis* and *gnomon*, that always "sounded strangely" in his ears (*D* 1). The sin of "simony" is a Christian cousin to the accusation of usury in

Jews that Joyce unmasks as hypocrisy in *Ulysses*; simony, like usury, depends upon a hungry materialism that sees everything as something that can be bought or traded. The simoniac is, by implication, greedy, eager to profit personally from supplicants' desires for love or forgiveness or knowledge. This kind of economy drives characters such as the priest in "The Sisters"; the boy narrator, whose mercenary predilections are highlighted by the name of a minor character, Mrs. Mercer, a pawnbroker's widow, in "Araby"; Mrs. Mooney in "The Boarding House"; Corley in "Two Gallants"; the canvassers in "Ivy Day in the Committee Room"; and, finally, Gabriel Conroy of "The Dead," who tries to compensate the servant girl in coin for her bitter, ungrammatical accusation that men are guilty of simony in their relations with women: "The men that is now is only all palaver and what they can get out of you" (*D* 178). Although simony is the most prevalent economy in *Dubliners*, Joyce briefly alludes to its complement and opposite, that of the wastrel, in "After the Race." This tale spotlights how much Jimmy Doyle is prepared to gamble for acceptance into the fast set; the extent of his losses is obscured by fatigue, alcohol, and filial irresponsibility, but his gambling nonetheless emerges as a kind of simony, in which a monetary cost has been paid in an effort to purchase the privilege of class.

Simony and profligacy are economies in that they are systems of spiritual or material (mis)management predicated upon an individual's confusion between tangible and intangible desires. They are not concerned with tallying profit and loss, nor do they constitute an intervention into the assumption that underlies careful accounting: the expectation that an investment of time, energy, or money should be repaid in equal or greater measure. Simony and profligacy represent possible orientations of an individual towards spiritual or material resources; they have relatively little to do with interpersonal exchanges. Social life – especially communication and commerce – is regulated according to two different economies that are often confused: an economy based on "contract" and one that follows the laws of a "covenant"; these two economies also describe two possible relations between an author and a reader, differing in the kind of expectations that both parties bring to the textual exchange. A contract economy offers stability and endorses an ideal of fairness, at least in principle. Like the contract itself, it depends upon reciprocal exchange, the expectation that an action will be repaid in kind, in roughly equal measure. It is designed to minimize exploitation motivated by self-interest and to limit reprisal for wrongdoing. In the language of Christianity, it is apparent in the mutually constitutive, reciprocal relations of sin and redemption; culturally and economically, it endorses the value of balancing debit and habit: owing and having. By extension, debit and habit correspond to two different modes of conduct: to be in debt is to be forced to live by one's wits (albeit stressfully), whereas to live by habit, or established routines, is to enjoy security while running the risk of stagnation. The contract economy is driven by an expectation of equal return, but it is also a means of creating communities;more specifically, it helps regulate a network of national, religious, and gender affiliations based on the ideal of fair exchange. What a contract economy cannot accommodate easily are the disruptions of chance: freedom, exception, or what Joyce, in *Dubliners*, evokes through an allusion to the fundamental Christian concept of "grace." (The Hebrew word for grace is *chesed*, or loving-kindness; the Greek word is *charis*, or gift.)

The covenant differs from a contract in that it is a one-way commitment: it is an oath or bond to adhere to right thought or action that commits only the person who makes it. A covenant can articulate a standard of behavior that the other party may be asked to uphold, but the other party is not bound to adhere to that code. A covenant, therefore, makes allowance for the free will of the other. If Christian theology is governed by three fundamental ideas – sin, redemption, and grace – the covenant economy is primarily indicated by the concept of grace. Grace designates a divine gift – it cannot be earned. Grace, or chance, works like mutation in Darwin's theory of evolution: it introduces the possibility of novelty or change into stable, self-perpetuating systems of behavior.

A contract economy grants a measure of social control to the members of a community, whereas a covenant economy recognizes and even celebrates the limits of control. A contract economy legislates fair treatment; a covenant economy leaves room for the vagaries of excess and deprivation: it draws attention to the intervention of chance, to the power of such intervention to destroy and to transform the stable and predictable economy of habit and debit. Christianity recognizes the original insufficiency of the human condition through its insistence upon sin as debt and its promise that this debt might be repaid or literally redeemed (to redeem is to buy back, to free by paying ransom). Sin – or debit – and its complement, redemption, lead to the point at which this spiritual accounting breaks down through the interruption of the unexpected and uncontrollable, whether disaster or miracle: this is the literally unaccountable moment of grace. For a reader, it is the moment of insight: unforeseen and previously unimaginable.

In "A Mother" and "Grace," we see the "ladylike" and the "manly," respectively, identified with two different economies, both of which are based on implied contracts, although the nature of the contract is different for men and women. For women, the expectation of return only works in the domestic arena of social etiquette. In "A Mother," Mrs. Kearney fails to understand that her expectations of fair treatment will only be honored with politeness, not with money. Her misunderstanding concerns a literal contract – her daughter's – that she believes to have been broken. Mrs. Kearney, however, mistakes the nature of the underlying social contract when she demands to be "repaid" (*D* 146) for her "homely" advice (*D* 136) by having her daughter paid the entire amount that was stipulated. Mrs. Kearney expects fairness in exchange for her "tact" (*D* 136); in return for her politeness, she demands recognition of "her rights." What she has not understood is that by speaking the language of the "ladylike," she has implicitly relinquished her claims to economic fairness or gender-blind justice, which is why her "conduct [can be] condemned on all hands" (*D* 147). Mr. Holohan, in particular, is hopping mad at the unladylike nature of her behavior, repeating, "That's a nice lady! . . . O, she's a nice lady!" (*D* 148). Mrs. Kearney's mistake was to expect "thanks" (*D* 136) for her contributions in the form of actual payment for her daughter. Specifically, in return for her help she expected respect for Kathleen's contract, despite the fact that she negotiated that contract not with a lawyer but with the decanter and the biscuit barrel. As Joseph Valente has shown, she confused friendly and polite behavior with business, not understanding that there are two separate economies for men and women – one social, the other monetary and legal – and that she tried to buy into one using the coin of the other (Valente 1995: 49–66).

In "Grace," Joyce explores not the ladylike, but the "manly," which he represents as another contract economy that operates in a different field: instead of trading in polite-ness, the businessman trades in money. In "Grace," Joyce turns to the world of the Church to provide the context for his anatomy of manliness, and he rather unexpect-edly suggests that for men the Catholic religion has no connection with what one feels: instead, it is about business, especially responsible accounting. We discover, through Father Purdon's sermon for the worldly, that Jesus asks only "one thing" of his fallible, indeed fallen, followers: "to be straight and manly with God" (*D* 174). A man's job is to "admit the truth," "to be frank and say like a man" whether "the books of his spirit-ual life" "tallied accurately with his conscience," and if they do not, to resolve to "rectify" them, to "set right" his accounts. The trademark of manliness, then, is accountability, although to a very low standard, whereas the trademark of ladylike behavior is *not* to hold men fiscally accountable for their promises. For both men and women, the rules of conduct (or habit) involve a notion of fair dealing based on an implied contract. If women extend friendly help, they will be "repaid" with politeness, and the debt will be canceled: the "currency" of exchange is consideration, not money. For men, Jesus will excuse their failings and peccadilloes if they balance their spiritual budget honestly against their con-sciences. This is a Jesuit economy that endorses the sufficiency of honest "confession" (without the necessity of atonement or change of behavior). What will not be tolerated is any imbalance between what is done (or spent) and what is declared, imposing only the lightest of responsibilities upon Catholic businessmen. Ladylike and manly behaviors are regulated by two separate economies, but they are both implicitly contractual.

If, in deals between men and women, biscuits are to be repaid with kindness, and if manliness is simply a manner of balancing the budget "frankly," so that simony is actu-ally the law of the church rather than a sin against it and what matters is how honestly one adheres to the laws of exchange, what are we to do with the concepts of accident, "grace," and "freedom"? If men are adjured to be "frank," should we perhaps attend more closely to the ironic possibilities that emerge when we consider the etymological root of "frank," which means "free"? (more precisely, free for those who belong to the enfranchised group.) In an economy based on the expectation of an exchange in kind, is freedom of response, or freedom of choice, or freedom from the bonds of belonging possible without the fear of reprisal? And what is the doctrine of "grace" but an asser-tion that salvation – literally health or wholeness of being – cannot be earned, is not regulated by the laws of exchange? The word "grace" is akin to the word "gratitude" (*grazia* in Italian, *graçias* in Spanish; *gratia* in Latin; *grâce* in French); it is a word that has no place in the marketplace, since it is an expression of an ontological indebted-ness that cannot be repaid in kind.

In order to appreciate the ironies of "Grace," the assurance that one can "retreat" into a church governed, like a brothel, by the "red light" of commerce (here "suspended before the high altar," *D* 172), where sins – or debts – will be forgiven to businessmen who promise not to doctor their accounts, we must contrast the meaning of "grace" with the ideal of a balanced budget, and interrogate the meaning of debt, or sin, in relation to habit, or the good conduct that is associated with prosperity and the desire to prosper (or accrue assets). I would argue that debt is akin to grace in the sense that both gesture towards the possibility of freedom offered by gratitude, a freedom that is compromised by an economy of balanced accounts and even exchange. Grace from debt cannot be expected: it is not governed by the rules of an exchange or bargain. Instead, grace *may* come from a *free* acknowledgment of inadequacy or indebtedness. Why can such an acknowledgment be liberating? Here is where the two economies overlap. An acknowledgment of indebtedness is potentially liberating because *debt* (from debit) is the opposite of *habit*. *Habit* comes from the Latin *habere*, to have, and it has come to designate apparel that is specific to a particular role as well as socially acceptable behavior. Habit is akin to custom, a word that is related to "costume,"[3] emphasizing the recognition that habitual or customary behavior is a form of role-playing. In such diurnal performances, the accent, in both habit and custom, falls on appearance (what is worn or enacted), and also on what is expected (by others and the self). What is expected is payment in kind for expenditure or effort: tit for tat, an eye for an eye, a balanced social budget that is free of indebtedness because "manliness" consists of honest accounting in which all debts have been repaid or confessed. What is wonderful and yet constricting about an economy of exchange is that it can so easily be regulated or controlled.

Chance, or grace, in contrast, is beyond human control. In Joyce's story, the "fall of man" is connected with an actual graceless tumble by a man full of spirits. An inebriated Mr. Kernan falls down the lavatory steps, biting his tongue in the process. His lack or want of grace triggers a compassionate and efficient response in "a young man in a cycling-suit" whose name we never learn. The young man washes the blood from Mr. Kernan and revives him with brandy. Mr. Kernan expresses his gratitude several times, hampered as he is by his wounded tongue: "I 'ery 'uch o'liged to you, sir," he says twice (*D* 151 and 152), and the narrator underscores the fact that "he expressed his gratitude" (*D* 152). The moment of "actual grace" in the story is Kernan's imperfect but genuine expression of gratitude to a nameless man who responds to him in a quick-witted and caring way that has nothing to do with that man's habit or his costume (cycling). It is, in essence, the readiness freely to depart from habit in response to a need that produces the kind of indebtedness that is associated with an equally free expression of gratitude. This moment stands in stark contrast to what passes as "grace" in the story itself: the plot hatched by Martin Cunningham (with the help of Mr. Power, M'Coy, and Mr. Fogarty) to make a "new man" of Mr. Kernan by taking him to a retreat at the Jesuit church on Gardiner Street. They all promise to "wash the pot," to confess or come clean, but their safe renewal of baptismal vows in the company of equally commercially-minded friends and acquaintances seems hollow and self-serving in contrast to the solicitude with which an unknown man voluntarily washes the blood from the face of a fallen man he does not know.

The man in the cycling-suit is the unsung hero of "Grace," the man who incites gratitude in Mr. Kernan, prompting him to speak despite his wounded tongue; the heroes are not the well-meaning friends why try to help him recover his respectability and manliness and resume the communal Catholic and pragmatic habits he has forsaken. Stephen Dedalus, in *Ulysses*, is also acutely aware of the importance of acknowledging and appreciating indebtedness as an antidote to habit, as we see not only when he structures an "avowal" of what he owes A.E. through a literal arrangement of vowels that begins with his name ("A. E. I. O. U." *U* 9 213), but also when he sends his telegram to Mulligan. Stephen's telegram is all about the ethical importance of acknowledging indebtedness through gratitude, a gratitude that acknowledges but cannot pay or cancel a "debt." *"The sentimentalist is he who would enjoy without incurring the immense debtorship for a thing done"* (*U* 9 550–1). A debt is an admission of inadequacy in which the inadequacy is seen not as a failure but as an opening, an opportunity for the other to respond freely with an offer of aid. If there is no acceptance of indebtedness, there can be no appreciation or love, no *charis*, no gift, no grace. And "appreciation" means increase – it is impossible to register appreciation in a spiritual economy designed merely to *balance* the budget.

In *Finnegans Wake*, Shem, like Mr. Kernan (and also, less explicitly, Mr. Power and Martin Cunningham), is described as someone who fell "into debit" as if off Eden Quay (*FW* 172 15–17). The fall – which marks the difference between the immortality of Eden and the mortality of humanity – signifies a condition of indebtedness or insufficiency that makes compassion and gratitude possible. Behind the shopworn ironies of marketable religion and male business communities lies an appreciation for the wild, compassionate, creative responsiveness of grace, free of the web of expectation and fairness that constitutes a dreary but stale habitus.

In "The Dead," Joyce examines the conflict between a contract economy and a covenant economy by focusing on hospitality. In this last story, hospitality serves as a rich metaphor not only for the social relation between host and guest, but also for a lover and the person he or she loves, and by extension for the relation between writer and reader. Although some people think of hospitality as a system of exchanges (associating it with an implied contract in which an invitation will be repaid in kind), hospitality is essentially an offering, a gift, a covenant that binds only the host to uphold a standard of careful conduct and respect for otherness; the guest is under no obligation to respond. This is also how Joyce writes: his writing is a kind of party, laced with intimations of death, to which readers are invited but in which they are not compelled to participate. The reader is a guest who is simultaneously a ghost at the word-fest of "The Dead" (the word "guest" is etymologically related to the word "ghost," *OED*). His party offers sensual pleasures of food, music, and dancing, and yet it also accommodates grimmer realizations about coldness, injustice, and mortality. He does not offer meaning directly, through a discursive presentation, but he has created conditions in which visitations of fresh understanding, like visitations of chance or grace, might happen.

In order to appreciate Joyce's "gift" of fiction to the reader, his covenant to realize the integrity of his vision that carries with it no responsibility to satisfy the reader's expectations,[4] it is necessary to look more carefully at the Irish hospitality Joyce ostensibly celebrated in "The Dead" in relation to its roots in Greek culture. In a letter to Stanislaus written on September 25, 1906, Joyce criticizes his representation of Dublin in *Dubliners* before the composition of "The Dead": "I have not reproduced its ingenuous insularity and its hospitality, the latter 'virtue' so long as I can see does not exist elsewhere in Europe." Joyce enclosed the word "virtue" in quotation marks, or what he called "perverted commas," which calls into question the description of Irish hospitality as a virtue; at the same time, he praises Ireland for an equally suspect characteristic: "ingenuous insularity." In his biography, after quoting Joyce's letter, Ellmann opines that Joyce "allowed a little of this warmth to enter 'The Dead,'" citing Gabriel's encomium to Irish hospitality in his speech as evidence (*JJ* 245): "I feel more strongly with every recurring year that our country has no tradition which does it so much honour and which it should guard so jealously as that of its hospitality" (*D* 203). Ellmann then comments, "This was Joyce's oblique way, in language that mocked his own, of beginning the task of making amends." We are all aware of the tinny insincerity of Gabriel's rhetoric during his speech, because he himself emphasizes it: when rehearsing his praise of the older generation's hospitality, humor, and humanity, he asks himself, "What did he care that his aunts were only two ignorant old women?" (*D* 192). Why, then, has the idea that "The Dead" celebrates Irish hospitality been so often affirmed?[5]

I would argue that Joyce, in the wake of Homer, understood genuine hospitality as something very different than what is presented in "The Dead"; to appreciate the meaning of what I am calling genuine hospitality – which the Irish typically do not exhibit in *Dubliners* – one has to return to its Greco-Roman roots, where hospitality is defined as a love of foreignness that is the basis of both eroticism and spirituality. Set against its Greek counterpart, the Irish hospitality of "The Dead" emerges as a compensatory self-deception that extends generosity primarily to the familiar (and therefore the familial[6]). In ancient Greece, hospitality embraces opposite extremes in that it is a familial courtesy extended above all to *strangers*, as we can see from the word itself. "Hospitality" comes from the Latin *hospes*, which denotes two things we have come to regard as opposite: both "guest" and "host," and also "friend" and "stranger." The same kind of relation pertains in Greek, where *xenos* denotes "friend" as well as "stranger." The paradoxical view of a stranger as a friend is essential to classical notions of hospitality; in the *Odyssey*, Zeus is described in Book 9 as "Zeus Xeinios," as one who attends to revered guests/strangers (Reece 1993: 5). As Sheila Murnaghan explains in her introduction to Stanley Lombardo's translation of the *Odyssey*, the rights and obligations surrounding hospitality constitute "some of the most highly valued and sacred principles of [Homer's] culture":

> The need to turn to strangers for shelter, food, and help with the next stage of a journey is a constant feature of life in the *Odyssey* . . . In extending hospitality, a host mitigates a stranger's foreignness, incorporating him for a time into his own household; he expresses a sense of universal human kinship based on a common subjection to fortune, which can drive anyone from home, and on common needs, above all the relentless demands of the belly (Murnaghan 2000: xxxii).

Hospitality is owed to all strangers, including beggars, and Odysseus frequently seems like a beggar when he asks for hospitality from strangers (from King Alcinous in Phaeacia, as well as from the suitors in his own hall).

We know that Joyce had been thinking about the *Odyssey* while writing *Dubliners*, because he once planned to include a story about Ulysses in Dublin in the collection. That makes it all the more striking that the Misses Morkan practice such a different form of hospitality than the one that shapes the events of the *Odyssey*. No strangers are to be found at the party in "The Dead"; on the contrary, "Everybody who knew them came to it, members of the family, old friends of the family, the members of Julia's choir, any of Kate's pupils that were grown up enough and even some of Mary Jane's pupils too" (*D* 175). The theme of social exclusiveness is underscored by Freddy Malins' mention of the negro chieftain singing in the Gaiety pantomime, to whom he attributes "one of the finest tenor voices he had ever heard." When the topic is not taken up with interest, Freddy asks sharply, "And why couldn't he have a voice too? . . . Is it because he's only a black?" (*D* 199). The exclusion of strangers is further stressed when Gabriel, before he begins his speech, thinks that "People, perhaps, were standing in the snow on the quay outside, gazing up at the lighted windows and listening to the waltz music" (*D* 203). Finally, the song, "The Lass of Aughrim," draws attention to the theme of exclusion by stressing the way that Lord Gregory leaves the lass and her dead baby out in the cold while he remains comfortably warm indoors. Gretta mourns over such exclusions, such indifference to the exposure of sickly others, when she remembers Michael Furey's ill-fated visit to her in her garden in Galway. "The Dead" constantly draws our attention to the crucial disparity between indoor warmth and exposure to the wetter elements outside, a difference that is inflected by inequality of class. The poorer people in Ireland, like Odysseus in the guise of a beggar in the *Odyssey*, are exposed to the inhospitable wildness of nature, including human nature, in ways that the gods find hard to forgive.

When we think of the *Odyssey* not only in relation to *Ulysses*, but also as a backdrop against which to measure the "scrupulous meanness" of *Dubliners*, it shows us, surprisingly, what virtue – richly present in Homeric epic – is missing from Joyce's Ireland: a vision of hospitality as divine and erotic wholeness, the quintessence of Homeric virtue. When we think of the Greek *xenia* or the Latin *hospes*, we are forced to abandon mutually exclusive oppositions between self and other, recognizing the strangeness of the self and the familiarity of the stranger. As classical scholars have long recognized, this is one of the main structural principles of the *Odyssey*, which is built not only around Alcinous' hospitality to Odysseus and the hospitality of Nestor and Menelaus to Telemachus, but also around egregious acts of *in*hospitality: Polyphemus' inhospitable reception of Odysseus and his crew (who have also violated the laws of hospitality themselves), and the suitors' ungracious abuse of Penelope's hospitality, on the one hand, along with their inhospitality to the returned Odysseus in the guise of a beggar, on the other.

Hospitality in ancient Greece represents a perfect equipoise between opposite extremes, in this case foreigner and native, that grows out of humility (thinking that

you yourself may some day be at the mercy of strangers), and also out of "divine" whole-ness, represented by the erotic and spiritual vitality of the Olympian gods. Once again, such wholeness is approximated in humans not only through hospitality, in which the distinction between stranger and friend is eradicated, but also through the special virtue that the always-thinking Odysseus and Penelope share, which is known in Greek as *mêtis*, or cunning. *Mêtis* denotes "intelligence, versatility, and a facility with words" (Murnaghan 2000: xviii), but it also connotes both duplicity and androgyny, a coin-cidence of contraries that connects it with hospitality. Both hospitality and *mêtis* are linked to disguise, since one of the main rules of Greek hospitality is that you cannot ask the identity of the guest until his needs for food, clothing, and sometimes rest have been met (which means that the guest is for a relatively long period "disguised"), and *mêtis* is also associated with disguise in that it is one of the Greek forms of the word "No-man," the name by which Odysseus identifies himself in reply to Polyphemus' enraged query (Murnaghan 2000: xviii). Finally, *mêtis* connotes androgyny, in that the term comes from the name of a goddess who personified cunning. Zeus impregnated Mêtis and then, fearful that she might bear a son who would overthrow him, swal-lowed her, and Athena, goddess of wisdom, was subsequently born from his head. By swallowing Mêtis, Zeus internalized female cunning, or duplicity (Murnaghan 2000: xxix); such an integration of male and female attributes is presented as conducive to survival. Athena loves Odysseus and Penelope precisely because they exhibit *mêtis*, like the goddess herself.

Clever, strategic duplicity in the Odyssean sense, or *mêtis*, is what Gabriel lacks, however, along with many of his fellow Dubliners. His resistance to the feelings of women, apparent in his exchanges with Lily, Molly Ivors, and Gretta, demonstrate this, as does the Pope's insensitivity to the effect of barring female singers from church choirs (Norris 1994). The lack of *mêtis* also helps to fuel the Irish suspicion of the British, their inhospitable scorn for invasive "strangers in the house."

The snow that buries thought and feeling at the end of "The Dead" both represents and denies, by turns, the doubleness of hospitality (and *mêtis*) that I have been uphold-ing as the virtues missing in *Dubliners*. To see how snow represents exposure and isolation, we have only to contrast it with the description of dawn at the beginning of Book V of the *Odyssey*: "Dawn reluctantly / Left Tithonus in her rose-shadowed bed, / Then shook the morning into flakes of fire."[7] Instead of evoking the fire of dawn, Joyce ends the anti-Odyssey of *Dubliners* with flakes of ice that signify the coldness of an inhospitable and hostile world. But the snow also connects opposite extremes, like hospitality and *mêtis*, linking the strange and the familiar, the living and the dead. The snow, then, like mortality, is a principle of connection as well as a force of isolation, and the emotional intensity of Joyce's lyrical ending depends on this doubleness of sig-nification. That doubleness is replicated on a purely verbal level by the word "snow," which sounds a negation softly introduced by a potential affirmation ("no" preceded by the suggestion of "yes"). In dialogue with the famous ending of *Ulysses* and its repeated affirmations of love and loss, the ending of "The Dead" resounds with "nos" antici-pated by a fainter "yes" of affirmation. Although most Romance languages lost the "s" in their words for snow, Irish (*sneacta*), German (*schnee*) and the Scandinavian languages all preserve the double echo of what in English couples affirmation with negation.

Why does Joyce present love and freedom as a mirage in Ireland at the turn of the twentieth century? Because he seems to have seen the Irish, like the Cyclopes and the suitors, as having disavowed the identity of stranger and friend by inviting only friends to their table, treating strangers with hostility or neglect. In Joyce's portrayal, his country-men have sided with Achilles by taking the view that victory is a product of macho force (*biê*) rather than a more feminine *mêtis*, as Odysseus contended (lxiii, Book 8, 120–1). The *Odyssey*, as Joyce seems to have known as early as 1907, was devoted to proving that Odysseus was right: Achilles dies in Troy, but Odysseus, mastermind of the fall of Troy through the ruse of the hollow horse, pregnant with soldiers, both survives and returns home, but only by embracing ambivalence, as well as by suffering and by deferring recognition. Odysseus might be said to have made a covenant with himself that freed him from a helpless dependence upon others. Instead of naively expecting help from strangers, he is able to design ways of enlisting their aid, thereby maximizing his chances of survival.

This digression by way of Greek notions of hospitality and *mêtis* illustrates the way one makes a covenant with oneself rather than fulfilling an implied contract to fulfill the reader's expectations. To make a covenant is to deliberately take the unknown and unknowable other into oneself, thereby generating a double consciousness that leaves the stranger, lover, guest, or reader free to respond in a variety of ways, unbound by authorial control. The author controls his or her world, not the reader's response; in turn, the author is not governed by the reader's expectations or desires. Unlike the individual driven by habit, for whom chance is an unwelcome disruption, the individual who has incorporated the unknown is receptive to change because he or she is open to the novelties offered by chance.

As Vladimir remarks in Samuel Beckett's *Waiting for Godot*, "habit is a great deadener" (Beckett 1986: 84). The habit-driven individual cannot easily experience freedom or enjoyment, as Joyce shows in "The Dead" through Gabriel's story about his grand-father's horse, Johnny:

> Johnny used to work in the old gentleman's mill, walking round and round in order to drive the mill. That was all very well; but now comes the tragic part about Johnny. One fine day the old gentleman thought he'd like to drive out with the quality to a military review in the park (*D* 208).

Gabriel goes on to describe how Johnny, when he sees King Billy's statue, begins to walk round and round the statue as if he were back at the mill, to the great indignation of his master, and Gabriel illustrates Johnny's embrace of his old habits by pacing "in a circle round the hall in his goloshes amid the laughter of the others" (*D* 209). Johnny's readiness to circle the statue, which is significantly a tribute to the Protestant William of Orange, his insistence on resuming his workday habits even on Sunday, illustrate the incompatibility of habit with freedom, change, or joy. Joyce uses Johnny to suggest that freedom from British rule would not in itself guarantee freedom for the Irish; on the contrary, radical freedom is a freedom from the expectations born of habit.

Hospitality to others – free from any expectation of return, although open to the chance of reciprocal desire – depends upon acceptance of the strangeness within the self. This is as true of the intimate form of hospitality – love – as it is of provisions of food and entertainment. Gabriel's expectation of reciprocal desire from Gretta stands in sharp contrast to Michael's mode of relating to her: he left his sickbed to bid her farewell, standing shivering in the rain. Michael takes a chance, exposing himself to discomfort and even death with very little hope of reward, unlike Gabriel, who safely (and warmly) foresees the repetition of intimacies he has experienced many times before (see, for example, his rehearsal of memories in *D* 214–15). Gabriel needs Gretta to respond to him, and when she seems "abstracted" he trembles with annoyance (*D* 218) and wishes he could control her: "He longed to be master of her strange mood" (*D* 218). As her story about Michael unfolds, the fires of Gabriel's lust turn to anger (*D* 220), and his anger in turn subsides into humiliation and shame (*D* 221). After Gretta's story is finished and she is asleep, Gabriel thinks, "He had never felt like that towards any woman but he knew that such a feeling must be love" (*D* 224). Gabriel has been surprised by chance: he planned an erotic escape with his wife, and instead he sees a ghost who in some ways emerges as more loving and hospitable, less demanding, than himself or his aunts. His epiphany, which aptly occurs on the Feast of the Epiphany, does not promise a definitive change in his thoughts or behavior. On the contrary, all it does is mark the intervention of a new thought, a new feeling, a new way of perceiving, which could possibly be the seed of some future change. Or not. We do not know what Gabriel's insight produced, only that he – hopeful, naive, hot with lust and anger – had a fleeting encounter with the end. Over the heads of the characters, Joyce directs his readers to think of Gabriel's vision of Michael as a brief conjunction of beginning and end, since Gabriel is the angel of the annunciation – the beginning of the Christian story – and Michael the angel of the Last Judgment, its final end. The story – and the volume – leave the reader with a double consciousness, a set of irreconcilable possibilities, and a taste of the novelty and freedom that cannot be experienced through habit.

In "The Sisters," at the very beginning of the collection, Joyce showed how habits of interpretation are formed: through the experience of a form of educational or doctrinal abuse in which learners are discouraged from interpreting meaning independently, by integrating knowledge and feeling (see Mahaffey 2007: 94). Instead, the young are taught to defer habitually, deferentially, to authority figures such as the priest; in the story, the boy has learned to substitute the priest's answers for his own. The boy learns to depend upon the priest's interpretations; he develops a set of expectations that are implicitly limiting, which is why, to his annoyance, after the priest's demise he discovers in himself "a sensation of freedom as if I had been freed from something by his death" (*D* 4). The boy has learned to quarrel with others, to scorn old Cotter, and to register the grammatical errors of the priest's devoted but uneducated sisters. He has entered a contract economy fueled by unconscious expectations that other people must match his own kind and level of achievement to be worthy of regard. However, as William Butler Yeats once wrote, "Out of the quarrel with others, we make rhetoric;

out of the quarrel with ourselves, poetry."[8] Unlike the boy at the beginning of the collection, Gabriel briefly quarrels with himself at the end of "The Dead." That self-interrogation, a product of freak chance, is an artistic covenant in embryo that also produces the finest poetry in the volume, its lyrical ending.

Near dawn, one of the narrative voices of *Finnegans Wake* asks, "Have we cherished expectations? Are we for liberty of perusiveness?" (*FW* 614 23–4). These are important questions, because to the extent that we cherish expectations, we are not actually endorsing liberty in reading. Instead, crippled by habit and motivated by unrealistic fantasies of liberation, we will be unable to recognize the potentially revelatory images of our own limitations in Joyce's "nicely polished looking-glass" (*LI* 64).[9]

NOTES

1   See Matthew Bevis (2007: chapter 4), who points out that according to Skeat's Etymological Dictionary (which Joyce has Stephen carry around with him in *Stephen Hero*), "mean" can be traced to a root meaning "common, general."

2   According to the *Oxford English Dictionary*, "tale" derives from the Old Teutonic word *tala*, "to mention things in their natural or due order; to enumerate, reckon." The meaning of "tale" as "enumeration" is now obsolete.

3   In a letter to Stanislaus (September 24, 1905), Joyce significantly asks whether it is possible for the priest in "The Sisters" to be buried in a habit (*SL* 75).

4   In fact, whenever possible Joyce violates the readers' expectations in an effort to bring them to consciousness.

5   Two critics who have challenged the critical commonplace that "The Dead" celebrates Irish hospitality are Vincent Pecora (1986) and Jean-Michel Rabaté (2001). Both arguments differ in significant ways from the one I am advancing here. Rabaté rightly refers to the hospitality exhibited in "The Dead" as "fake hospitality," but his main interest is to read

host and guest as father and son, respectively, and therefore to see them as simultaneously united and divided by a sexual secret alternately defined as incest and sodomy (Rabaté 2001: 176). Pecora's subtle and fascinating argument is that hospitality is the family name of Gabriel's individual generosity: although Gabriel prizes his generosity as a virtue, much as Ireland prizes its hospitality, both generosity and hospitality are culturally approved expressions of the deprivation that is endemic in society, even among the more privileged classes. When you are generous or hospitable, you allow yourself to believe that you are deliberately choosing that deprivation, which is then cloaked in the mythos of self-sacrifice and concern for others.

6   "Familiar" and "familial" derive from the same root.

7   Homer, *Odyssey*, trans. Stanley Lombardo, Book 5, ll. 1–3.

8   "Anna Hominis" (Yeats 1959: 331).

9   See Mahaffey (2004) for an account of the unrealistic fantasies that help characters to sustain their repetitive diurnal habits in *Dubliners*.

BIBLIOGRAPHY

Beckett, Samuel (1986) *The Complete Dramatic Works*. London: Faber and Faber.

Bevis, Matthew (2007) *The Art of Eloquence: Byron, Dickens, Tennyson, Joyce*. Oxford: Oxford University Press.

Mahaffey, Vicki (2004) "Joyce and gender." In Jean-Michel Rabaté (ed.), *Palgrave Advances in Joyce Studies*, pp. 190–205. London: Palgrave.

Mahaffey, Vicki (2007) *Literary Modernism: Challenging Fictions*. Oxford: Basil Blackwell.

Murnaghan, Sheila (2000) "Introduction" to Homer, *Odyssey*, trans. Stanley Lombardo. Indianapolis/Cambridge: Hackett.

Norris, Margot (1994) "Not the girl she was at all: women in 'The Dead.'" In Daniel Schwartz (ed.), *James Joyce's "The Dead": A Case Study of Contemporary Criticism*, pp. 190–205. New York: St. Martin's.

Norris, Margot (2003) *Suspicious Readings of Joyce's* Dubliners. Philadelphia: University of Pennsylvania Press.

Pecora, Vincent (1986) "'The Dead' and the generosity of the word," *PMLA* 101 (2): 233–45.

Rabaté, Jean-Michel (2001) *James Joyce and the Politics of Egoism*. Cambridge: Cambridge University Press.

Reece, Steve (1993) *The Stranger's Welcome: Oral Theory and the Aesthetics of the Homeric Hospitality Scene*. Ann Arbor: University of Michigan Press.

Valente, Joseph (1995) *James Joyce and the Problem of Justice: Negotiating Sexual and Colonial Difference*. Cambridge: Cambridge University Press.

Yeats, William Butler (1959) *Mythologies*. New York: Macmillan.

3

Desire, Freedom, and Confessional Culture in *A Portrait of the Artist as a Young Man*

John Paul Riquelme

Judging the Young Artist:
Autobiography, Nationhood, Sexuality

The question of how to judge Stephen Dedalus' progress toward artistic maturity has been central to interpretations of *A Portrait of the Artist as a Young Man*.[1] Facing considerable external and internal pressures concerning religious beliefs, disruptions in family life, and sexual desires, Dedalus wants to become an artist and to be free. Critics have disagreed widely about whether the details of the narrative indicate his current and future success or failure.[2] In that disagreement, the book's autobiographical element has played an important role. During the decades following the Second World War, when Joyce and modernism were shifting from being contemporary to being part of the canon of past literature, Joyce's life and the relation of his life to his works were of considerable interest to critics and readers. That was especially the case for *A Portrait* because, by contrast with Joyce's other published works, the book's title and many details of the central character's life invite an autobiographical reading. If the title were attached to a painting, one by Rembrandt, for example, who painted himself in many poses and costumes over the course of his life, the work would be a self-portrait of the artist when young. Much of the narrative is closely related to Joyce's actual experiences in Ireland, including the Jesuit schools that Stephen attends, first, Clongowes Wood College, a pre-eminent boarding school, and later, in Dublin, Belvedere College, and University College. Stephen's impending departure from Dublin at the end of the narrative parallels Joyce's own departures for the Continent in 1902 and, definitively, in 1904. The locales and dates printed after Stephen's journal, "Dublin 1904/Trieste 1914," pertain, on the one hand, to the decade-long period during which Joyce wrote *A Portrait*. They can also be read, on the other hand, as projecting the next stage of Stephen's life, which will include exile and writing, perhaps even the writing of a narrative based on his own youth. That latter implication is possible in part because Joyce does not make explicit the dates of the action. He must have known that many readers would think that "Dublin 1904" provided a reasonable year for Stephen's journal and his departure for unnamed locations, which could include Trieste. By not giving explanations, or even basic information, such as Stephen's age (mentioned in only one passage, when he confesses at 16), the narrator turns the task of formulating explanations and filling in missing details to us. "Trieste 1914" raises questions that are unanswerable within the narrative. Nor are there unambiguous indications concerning Stephen's likely success or failure in the future. Some critics, most notably Wayne Booth, have complained about Joyce's not providing clear signals for judging Stephen (Booth 1983). Identifying Stephen with Joyce enables a positive judgment, but it does so from outside the narrative. Because that identification is speculative, the narrative remains open to opposing interpretations.

Although there are good reasons to align Stephen Dedalus with James Joyce, the book is fiction, not autobiography, narrated in the third person, not the first (with the exception of the journal) about a character whose name differs markedly from the author's. For some critics, primarily during the postwar period, the unusual surname encourages a positive judgment, because the mythic reference invites us to read it not literally but symbolically.[3] The surname could suggest that Stephen is to be identified with Daedalus, the great craftsman, or artificer, of the ancient world.[4] But the mythic name can be read ironically, as calling attention to the large distance between Stephen's meager prospects and the name that he carries. If Daedalus is in some sense his father, the "Old father, old artificer" (P 213; 5 2791) whom he addresses in the book's famous closing line, then Stephen is the son, Icarus, who suffered an early demise because he was foolish. Symbolic readings proved unsatisfactory because they were often too far removed from the interlocking details of Joyce's sometimes intricately woven language, an aspect of his writing that has been widely praised and studied, particularly regarding his representations of characters' thoughts.[5] Joyce's ironic presentation of characters in debilitating situations involving individual and social paralysis in the 15 *Dubliners* (1914) short stories has sometimes been taken as setting the direction for his later, longer narratives, which are said to be largely concerned with modern alienation. Modernist literature was frequently interpreted in this way in the decades after the devastation of the Second World War. The rich texturing of Joyce's language and its networks of implications, however, suggest that alienation as an existential condition is not the defining element of his writing.

Alternative justifications for the celebration of Stephen Dedalus as Joyce or for the rejection of him as a failed artist or figure of alienated modernity have emerged regularly in recent decades in readings that assert the importance of historical contexts for understanding Joyce's narratives. These include political contexts that affect national and individual freedom and social contexts that influence the forms that gender and sexuality take. Attention to the historical framing of the action can help us place Stephen in meaningful relation to specific situations involving Ireland without reducing the work's relevance for non-Irish readers and situations. Once read primarily as a cosmopolitan, international writer who left Ireland early to live abroad, Joyce is now also recognized to be a distinctively Irish writer whose works invite readings in postcolonial terms. Critical responses to Joyce attuned to postcolonial theory have, however, frequently reflected a warranted skepticism about the fit between the theory and the Irish situation. Ireland was never a colony in the narrow sense, and Joyce was "semicolonial."[6] It is not that Joyce's Irish settings and cultural concerns previously went unrecognized, but for the most part they were treated as background in critical responses rather than as essential elements of foreground. Our understanding of Ireland's political history, with regard to empire and nationhood, and Joyce's relation to it has changed largely during the past quarter century in the wake of decolonization. Joyce's narrative is set in a late stage of empire, a stage in which some peoples under imperial rule were beginning to imagine independence in new ways. During such a period, imagining individual freedom is not separable from imagining political freedom in a postcolonial world that has yet to come into being. Joyce wrote *A Portrait*, a narrative about an aspiring writer who wishes to give a voice to his people, in the decade before the Easter Rising of 1916, the year in which *A Portrait* was published in book form. *A Portrait* and the Proclamation of the Irish Republic, the declaration of autonomy during the Easter Rising, are contemporaneous documents that contributed to creating a future Ireland.

Attention to the modern history of empire has increased our recognition of the book's political dimension, including especially its relation to Irish nationalism. The artist and art always emerge in contexts to which they necessarily respond. But the response is not narrowly determined by historical context. Other elements affect the life and the work. As Joyce presents Stephen as a child, adolescent, and young adult within a specific social context, his individuality emerges through intense physical and emotional experiences of sexuality that are affected by social pressures but not wholly defined by them. The effects of empire and individual sexuality converge in the tale of Stephen's development. Early in the narrative he lives in a boarding school in a homosocial atmosphere in which the naked male body and homosexual behavior, actual or imagined, affect the boys' lives.[7] Stephen's later frequenting of prostitutes as an adolescent is emphatically presented. The language of the villanelle he writes as a university student is highly erotic in a heterosexual way, but Stephen's thoughts suggest his identification with women. Critics have connected these representations of sexuality, both heterosexuality and homosexuality, to the late nineteenth-century writings in sexology that Joyce would have known, but they have read them as well in light of later understandings that emphasize feminist and queer perspectives.[8]

With regard to the latter, a crucial event in the rise of literary modernism, particularly for the Irish, during Joyce's adolescence and Stephen's was the imprisonment in England in 1895 of Oscar Wilde (1854–1900), the most successful Irish writer of the generation before Joyce's, for homosexual acts that carried criminal penalties.[9] Wilde's untimely death in exile followed his release from prison and hard labor. Although Wilde is not mentioned in *A Portrait*, readers of the book when it was published would have been aware of Wilde's writings, his trial, and his ruin as unspoken background for Stephen's story. No one interested in literature growing up in Ireland during the last decades of the nineteenth century could have been unaffected by Wilde's success in London and his subsequent conviction and imprisonment in England. Stephen would have read and thought about Wilde, who died during Stephen's university studies. Wilde's life raises issues of English–Irish cultural relations in combination with ones involving sexuality and art. A related mixture is apparent in Joyce's narrative. The phrase "a portrait of the artist" even occurs in the opening chapter of Wilde's *The Picture of Dorian Gray* (1891), an echo of whose title may be heard in Joyce's title.[10] Although Wilde's book presents homosocial and homoerotic relationships more insistently than does Joyce's, they play an important role in both narratives. A comparative (and, retrospectively considered, quite loud) silence about Wilde among writers and literary commentators lasted for fully three-quarters of the twentieth century. Renewed discussion of Wilde has helped make it clear that, when we discuss the cultural situation Joyce presents in *A Portrait*, the word *sexuality* means a pluralized *sexualities*, since the singular form expresses neither the diversity of heterosexuality, homosexuality, and bisexuality nor the multiple forms that gender identity has now been recognized to take.

The comparative silence about Wilde coincided in the later mid-twentieth century with an aversion to political discussion in literary interpretation. There was little appetite among the generation of critics touched directly by the devastation of the Second World War for thinking historically and politically about literature, in large measure because of the destructive politicizing of life, including art, that had preceded the war. Intellectual inquiries into literature's relation to politics, gender, and diverse alternative sexualities emerged in a significant way, primarily among critics born after the war, starting in the late 1960s. Our frames of reference for reading *A Portrait* now differ from those current a generation ago because of new discussions of empire and postcolonial nation-building, and new discussions of gender and sexualities. Our judgments about Stephen's potential, accomplishments, shortcomings, and values depend on close reading of Joyce's language. They also involve reading the language with attention to politics, especially national independence, and to gendered and sexualized feelings, thinking, and behavior. The values and goals at stake can be put in a direct way. Joyce's portrayal of the young Irish artist who is and is not the book's writer concerns desire and fulfillment, both individual and cultural, ranging from individual sexual desire to the desire to attain greater political freedom for the individual and the nation. Never a static condition, freedom is always freedom "from" and freedom "to," freedom from constraining influences of Church, state, and convention and freedom to bring something new into being, whether that be an unconventional life, a new kind of art, a new nation, or all three.

A Tale of Confessions and Constraints

Those constraining influences and their effects intermingle in the world in which Stephen Dedalus comes to maturity. Their presence and intertwined pressures are evident throughout *A Portrait* in the requirement and habits of confession that inform characters' thinking and behavior. Prominent moments in the narrative simultaneously involve confession and concern Stephen's sexual desires and gendered ways of thinking as he moves toward what may or may not be greater freedom for himself as an individual and eventually for the Irish. These moments occur in each of the five parts, from the threatened punishment, if the child does not apologize (in the first section of part one), to the young man's reconsidering his friendship with Cranly, who has acted as his confessor (at the end of the third section of part five). Between those moments, when Stephen is pressed to "admit" his sexual desires for a girl (in the third section of part two), he remembers the physically violent insistence, early in his schooling at Belvedere College, that he confess to holding heretical views. Stephen's experiences at the religious retreat in part three, which are physically and psychologically central to the narrative, result in the scene of Stephen's literal confession to a capuchin priest. Confession, desire, and freedom are also important, during the middle section of the climactic fourth part, when Stephen considers becoming a priest. Stephen's decision parallels his later response to Cranly. His reaction to Cranly brings a confessional relationship to an end, but the dynamics of confession and desire will continue to have a significant effect on Stephen, as does his Catholic upbringing even after he turns aside from the priesthood. Although his future artistic success is uncertain, at the end of the narrative by means of a transgendering imagination Stephen changes the dynamics of confession. Rather than being captive to the confessional, he takes important steps towards achieving greater freedom. His new attitudes and behavior are a significant achievement.

That the story of Stephen's life is a tale of confessions and constraints begins to emerge elliptically, without elaboration or explanation, in the brief opening segment. Because all five senses are evoked in these initial paragraphs, they have been read as introducing Stephen's early childhood as a matter of sense perceptions (Kenner 1956: 114). However important the senses are for a literal, context-free reading of this innovative beginning, the compressed presentation concerns not the senses primarily but an *embodied sensibility* that is being shaped, even before formal schooling begins, by pressures that are implicit in the juxtaposed details. Those details anticipate important aspects of the narrative that involve confession, desire, and freedom. The first-time reader who encounters the juxtaposed evocations of Irish political figures, reward, punishment, and the demand for an apology will not be aware immediately of their eventual mutual relevance. Our recognition of their defining, interwoven implications for Stephen's life develops only gradually and retrospectively. Like Stephen at this early stage of his development, we are not in a position to make sufficient sense of what we encounter. We and Stephen will understand more fully the politicized domestic situation structured by constraints on behavior, including restrictions on the objects of desire, that involve the Roman Catholic Church and the Irish conflict with England.

The act of confession, the disclosing of sins to a priest in order to obtain absolution, is not mentioned in the opening segment, but the threatening imperative to apologize contained in the vivid lines at the section's end are the first indication of the confessional culture in which Stephen is growing up.[11] It is not clear from the narration whether Stephen is speaking the italicized verse or hearing it chanted at him. In either case, the language and the event, like the rest of the section, make an impression on the child that is presumably indelible. The scene of threatened punishment is run together with the other elements, which, though apparently disparate, are linked by being included within the slightly longer paragraphs that begin when we learn about Dante's brushes. The repetitions, four times each, of "*Apologise*" and "*Pull out his eyes*" (*P* 6; 1 34–41), present emphatically the punishment and the prescribed means for avoiding it. The recurring violence and threats of violence that Stephen hears about, suffers, or observes close at hand begin here. The statement that "the eagles will come and pull out his eyes" is made by Dante, who is, as we learn later, a demandingly, unforgivingly devout Roman Catholic, one of the familial combatants in Stephen's disastrous first Christmas dinner with the adults.

When Stephen's mother expresses at the outset of the encounter the certainty that he "will apologise" (*P* 5; 1 31), she prefigures her later expectations for Stephen as a young adult, which he firmly rejects, concerning his compliance with the demands of the Roman Catholic faith. Beyond adolescence, Stephen's future does not involve doing penance for sins. Even the opening scene gives no indication that Stephen actually apologizes. Later, he either refuses to submit and admit or he submits and confesses only under great pressure and even then partially or with reservations, as when he chooses an out-of-the-way chapel for confession. The paragraph that introduces his mother's statement after "He hid under the table" (*P* 5; 1 30) also includes what is apparently Stephen's thought, which he may or may not have spoken, that he would eventually marry Eileen Vance. We learn later that Eileen is not a proper candidate for Stephen's affections because she is Protestant. Even though the narration does not indicate that a spoken childish wish to be married to a Protestant girl is the infraction that triggers the threatening demand for an apology, the sequence suggests it. It also prefigures distantly Stephen's indulgence in forbidden pleasures as an adolescent, for which he does penance.

The paragraph preceding that one also becomes relevant retrospectively. It presents Stephen as a model citizen of Dante's domestic universe, deserving of a reward whenever he brings a tissue paper. Dante's approval links him to the Irish politicians also mentioned in the paragraph, Michael Davitt and Charles Stewart Parnell, whom Dante for the moment admires because they are working, with the approval of many priests in Ireland, for Irish freedom by resisting English domination. Specifically, they were supporters of Home Rule, which would have involved limited autonomy for Ireland. This would not have been full separation from England, but it would have provided greater autonomy than had been possible since the 1801 Act of Union between Ireland and England. The Union dissolved Ireland's parliament but gave it representation within a parliament based in London whose large majority was English. During the Christmas dinner, in step with the Catholic Church in Ireland, Dante denounces Parnell for his sexual misbehavior, for being a sinner. The turn from approval to disapproval links Stephen, when he was told to apologize, with Parnell.

Several elements that become increasingly mixed and mutually defining in Stephen's life are touched on but not woven together yet in the opening: the demand to be contrite or else accept severe punishment, the limits on desire insisted on by the Catholic Church, and the history of British domination and Irish demands for greater freedom.

The particular combination affects individuals in the narrative who are at different stages of their lives. These include a small child who is growing up and a woman, probably permanently unmarried, who derives satisfaction from identifying male Irish leaders who are likely younger than she is with the items only she touches in private when she looks in the mirror to brush her hair. We learn from Stephen's thoughts after he goes to school that Dante, who acted as his teacher, was second only to a priest in her learning (*P* 8; 1 134–7). Stephen also remembers hearing that she had entered a convent but left before taking religious vows (*P* 29; 1 995–8). Like the priests, she turns against Parnell, because "Parnell was a bad man" (*P* 13; 1 339), unapologetic and deserving of punishment. When he is home at Christmas, Stephen remembers Dante's objections to his playing with Eileen because she was Protestant (*P* 29; 1 1000). The fact that Dante is, in effect, a female priest, a priest in skirts, anticipates the ambiguities about gender involving priests and confession later. The priestly woman blocks his access to his female object of desire. Later, priests who wear or mention womanly robes hear or invite his confessions about his sexual acts and his sexual preferences, and his soul becomes a female object of desire in a dynamic of confession that proceeds between boys and men in the midst of discussions about art and nationalism.

The elements become mutually defining in Stephen's experience. They coil around Stephen like the snaky demons that torment the souls in hell. It is an open question whether Stephen can free himself sufficiently by turning the restrictive coils to advantage somehow or by throwing them off. The possibility of political Home Rule for Ireland, as a step toward full independence, slipped away when the reaction to the Parnell adultery scandal undermined his political authority. The loss of that possibility is bound up with the kind of priestly rule and order within the Irish home that Dante insists on. The narrative to come intertwines Stephen's developing desires and gender-inflected self-understanding; the constraints, order, and rule that he decides he needs to move beyond; and his options for achieving "unfettered freedom" (*P* 207; 5 2544) and a voice for the Irish within or away from a politicized confessional culture under the rule of empire.

Giving Lip Service to Confession: Desire, Heresy, Literature, Politics

When Dante taught Stephen about geography (*P* 8; 1 131–4), she may have intentionally slighted the British Empire. Stephen is reminded of Dante's differently colored brushes when he looks in his geography book at the image of the earth in clouds that a classmate has decorated in the same colors. He also reads his name followed by the increasingly larger groups and places that he has written in his book in order to locate himself, starting with his class at Clongowes Wood College and moving out to "The Universe" (*P* 12; 1 300–8). The list conspicuously omits the British Empire, which, like Europe, could have a place between Ireland and "The World." A later scene-within-a-scene in part two involving writing presents Stephen's more direct rejection of English views and orthodoxies, as well as Irish Catholic ones, within a confessional frame that includes Stephen's adolescent sexual desire.

Stephen's rival and school friend Heron, a real but temporary ally in managing events at Belvedere, has seen Stephen's father, accompanied by a girl who is probably their own age, walking into the building where Stephen is to perform in a play. She is "E—— C——," the continuing object of Stephen's developing desire, for whom he attempted unsuccessfully to write a poem two years earlier, the Emma who inspires his erotic villanelle. After Heron admonishes Stephen twice to "Admit!" (*P* 65; 2 638) his interest in the girl, both times "striking him . . . with his cane across the calf of the leg" (*P* 65; 2 638–9), playfully but not altogether lightly, Stephen, "bowing submissively . . ., began to recite the *Confiteor*" (*P* 65; 2 643), the prayer said at the beginning of confession, whose first words, *Confiteor*, mean in Latin "I confess." Heron's chastizing (of Stephen) includes his criticism of Stephen both for a hypocritically chaste demeanor and for improper sexual desires. But those attitudes are arguably mixed in uncertain proportions with Heron's jealousy and anger that Stephen has a girlfriend, because Heron apparently does not and because Stephen is loosening the bonds of boyhood male solidarity.

Stephen asserts in part five in a conversation with Davin that he will "fly by those nets" (*P* 171; 5 1050) flung at him by his culture. The phrase suggests escaping the nets, but also flying by means of them, using them to his advantage. When Stephen speaks the words of the *Confiteor* as an "irreverence" (*P* 65; 2 645) to make Heron laugh "indulgently" (*P* 65; 2 644–5), he stages and transforms the confessional act to deflect Heron's aggressive insistence on confession into laughter. The reader has a reason to laugh, too, because an *indulgence* is a term for the remission of sin that is the intended result of a true act of confession. The generating of laughter displaces the threat Stephen faces, as it will again in part four when Stephen decides against becoming a priest. The scene of aggressive male action, about secretly having a female object of desire, that results in mock submission has the structure of a confessional act, from "admonition" (*P* 65; 2 651) through indulgence.

Before the scene is over, Stephen experiences "a sudden memory" (*P* 65; 2 647) of an earlier even longer, more physically and emotionally intense encounter (*P* 65–9; 2 647–795) in which Heron and two other boys, Boland and Nash, admonish him for being heretical and beat him with a cabbage stump and Heron's cane. The long-remembered narrative inset provides significant detail concerning Stephen's resistant response to his confessional culture. He has yet to arrive at the recognition that the *Confiteor* can provide a protective mask that he badly needs. When he dons that mask, Stephen gives only lip service to the prayer: "The confession came only from Stephen's lips . . ." (*P* 65; 2 646). He recites it while the remembered scene is presented at much greater length than the prayer would occupy. Like the threat of physical punishment in the book's opening and the violence of the unwarranted pandying, the recollected confessional scene leaves a lasting impression. Rather than deciding to conform and submit because of these accumulating experiences, Stephen is on the way to learning how to escape punishment without admitting.

The action in *A Portrait* regularly involves Stephen's acts of writing. At the time of the remembered scene, he is making determined efforts to produce the best weekly school essay on a regular basis while spending his free time reading "subversive writers" (*P* 66; 2 662–3). For one of his efforts, instead of praise from the lay English teacher, Mr. Tate, he draws the charge, made in front of the class, that his essay is heretical. By rephrasing slightly an assertion in the essay, Stephen effects "a submission" (*P* 66; 2 694) to the criticism that satisfies the teacher but not the other boys, some of whom pursue him later on a pretext that involves literature, heresy, and sexual impropriety but also implicitly the politics of national identity. There are enigmatic, sexually suggestive aspects to the action in the classroom though not involving a female object of desire. When Mr. Tate brings his charge against Stephen the teacher "dug with his hand between his crossed thighs" (*P* 66; 2 677–8). The action is odd, and not easy to visualize precisely. What exactly is he doing with his hand? The narrator stimulates us to wonder. The act might not in itself be so oddly suggestive, but the teacher's hand is further described as "delving" (*P* 66; 2 687), a word with a root that suggests digging. As Mr. Tate delves into the heretical essay, he is also digging with his hand between his thighs.

If this were an isolated oddly suggestive moment in the book, it might not be worth mentioning, but it is neither unique nor unimportant. Its importance has to do with Richard Brown's cogent insistence in *Joyce and Sexuality* that "Joyce's writing presses toward the revelation of this sexual heart of things which he especially strives to make evident in persons, phenomena and institutions that are normally supposed to be chaste" (Brown 1985: 127). Critics have suggested in compelling detail that the scenes at Clongowes evoke an intensely homosocial atmosphere, which includes the obscure but suggestive "smugging" (*P* 35; 1 1244).[12] The details invite us to understand the boys' social relations as infused by a homoerotic dynamic that is frequently just under the surface of the action or else breaking through to it. As Brown establishes, Joyce would have known the late nineteenth-century commentaries on what was called perverse sexuality when he included a significant number of homoerotic details in *A Portrait* that amount to "strong sexual undercurrents":

> Stephen's schoolfriends are implicated, like the Clongowes student Boyle, who 'was called Tusker Boyle but some fellows called him Lady Boyle because he was always at his nails paring them' [*P* 35; 1 1254–6]. Bertie Tallon has to play a female part in the Whitsuntide play at Belvedere and the incident is not allowed to pass without a teasing little exchange [*P* 62; 2 501–12] (Brown 1985: 103).

Joseph Valente cites Joyce's letters and an article he wrote on Wilde that make evident Joyce's recognition of the sexually charged atmosphere at boarding schools (Valente, 1998: 47, 70 n. 1). The word "queer," which occurs 18 times in *A Portrait*, means primarily *strange* or *peculiar*, but, as Valente has argued (Valente, 1998: 52–4) by focusing on Stephen's thought that "Suck was a queer word" (*P* 8; 1 150), at times the word *queer* evokes strongly the homoerotic implications that became attached to it within a few years of the publication of *A Portrait*. This is not the case for each occurrence of the

word, but it certainly is in that passage and in others.[13] One of those passages anticipates the suggestive implications of Mr. Tate's hand when the word *queer* occurs in
relation to the hands of another lay teacher who disciplines a student, Mr. Gleason,
who is slated to cane a boy for the "smugging" incident. The cane links the scene to
the encounters with Heron. When Stephen thinks about strokes from Mr. Gleason,
it is the hands that are presented as inciting a queer feeling. He feels a "queer quiet
pleasure inside him to think of the white fattish hands, clean and strong and gentle"
(*P* 38; 1 1356–7).

The schools are run by supposedly celibate priests for boys who are alternately too
young to understand about sexuality or old enough to have their passions disciplined,
controlled, and redirected. Although confession provides one way to deal with sexual
passions, as Stephen's thinking and actions in part four reveal, the re-channeling can
retain a strongly sexual quality. Confession involves a retrospective cleansing of passions already indulged, but, as Joyce evokes it, confession has its own sexualized aspects
and contexts, which can be variably and ambiguously gendered. The scene involving
Mr. Tate is not a literal scene of religious confession, but it is one with a suggestive
sexual inflection in which admission of error is expected.

Sexual indiscretion plays an important implicit role in the other portion of Stephen's
memory, involving Heron and literary preferences because Byron (George Gordon,
Lord Byron, 1788–1824), the English Romantic poet, was considered, as Boland
says, "a bad man" (*P* 68; 2 766), repeating Dante's words when she "ripped" the green
velvet back from her brush that symbolized Parnell" (*P* 13; 1 337). The boys who
punish Stephen stand in the place of Dante and in the place of censorious priests and
teachers as threatening figures who denounce Stephen's hero and Stephen's unorthodox thinking. Heron goes further than Boland by claiming that "Byron was a heretic
and immoral too" (*P* 68; 2 760). Forgetting momentarily the vows of silence that he
had made to himself (reaffirmed in part five), Stephen names Byron as the greatest
poet in impatient reaction to Boland's claim that Lord Tennyson (1802–92; Poet Laureate of England, 1850–92) was the best poet. The sharp contrast between the choices
is revealing. It is unclear what Heron knows about Byron's ostensible immorality. A
prolific, influential poet, Byron flagrantly violated the rules of propriety of his day and
of any other conceivable day, having numerous affairs with boys and women, including, apparently, an incestuous relationship with a half-sister. He was politically radical
and supported both social reform and revolutionary causes, including the Greek fight
for independence from Turkey, for which he gave money and his life. In Parliament he
spoke in defense of Roman Catholic rights.

By contrast with the iconoclastic Byron, Tennyson was an icon of English national
identity. His widely admired works included poems about Arthurian myths, which
were identified with English national origins. Heron tries to force Stephen to admit
"that Byron was no good" (*P* 69; 2 782), presumably as both a writer and a moral being.
Though beaten for his views, Stephen refuses to admit. Byron's literary greatness is
bound up for him with independence of thought and behavior, which are as much sexual
and political as artistic. Stephen's "no," repeated four times in the scene, anticipates the

refusal to serve that he expresses to Cranly near the narrative's end (*P* 201; 5 2297). We are invited to recognize in the preference for Tennyson over Byron what Stephen already understands, that English values have infiltrated thoroughly the views of the Irish, who are likely to accept as the greatest writer an icon of the nation that dominates them. Stephen refuses to participate in such deluded complicity involving moral censure and the adoption of English views. For Stephen, the subversive writers he reads are more likely to contribute to independence for himself and his nation than morally acceptable English imports assimilated into Irish tastes.

Confessional Turnings and the Snakes of Ireland

The one literal confession in the narrative occurs near the end of part three when Stephen decides he must confess because of the threat of damnation presented insistently during the religious retreat. Father Arnall's vision of hell derives largely from an English translation of *Hell Opened to Christians, to Caution Them from Entering into It*, by the Rev. F. Giovanni Pietro Pinamonti SJ.[14] The illustrated pamphlet is the source for much of Father Arnall's sermon on hell, and it is entirely believable that a priest in his position would have taken the pamphlet as his model. It might even have been circulated or distributed at retreats such as the one Stephen attends. The sermon and the woodcuts make it clear that Hell is a place of fetters and other constrictive punishments imposed by snakelike devils on the damned, who are "utterly bound and helpless" (*P* 101; 3 632–3). The woodcuts, one of which, "The Sting of Conscience," is reproduced here (Figure 3.1), provide an unforgettable visual correla-

Figure 3.1 "The Sting of Conscience." From *Hell Opened to Christians, to Caution Them from Entering into It*, by the Rev. F. Giovanni Pietro Pinamonti SJ (1688).

Figure 3.2 *Laocoön and His Sons* in the Vatican museum. Reproduced here from Gardner (1910–11).

tive for the threat to his freedom that Stephen feels for indulging his desires in sinful acts requiring confession. The preacher refers repeatedly to stings, "most cruel sting of the worm of conscience" (*P* 109; 3 973–4) and "the threefold sting of conscience, the viper which gnaws the very heart's core of the wretches in hell" (*P* 109; 3 994). In part five, after Stephen has chosen art over the priesthood, he tries to exorcize the serpents from his aesthetic universe by objecting to Gotthold Ephraim Lessing's famous treatise, *Laocoön, or The Limits of Painting and Poetry* (1766), whose title evokes the famous sculpture group (also reproduced as Figure 3.2) showing three human figures wrestling unsuccessfully with serpents that crushingly encircle them. Stephen's ideas about literature are at odds with images of reptilian constriction. By the time Stephen writes in his journal, he has shifted jokingly to other reptiles, crocodiles, whose name derives from a Greek root meaning both worm and circumcised man (*American Heritage Dictionary* 2000: 432). Stephen understands the threat of reptiles differently as he prepares to leave Ireland.

Richard Brown has pointed out the "transsexual implications" (Brown 1985: 103) in Stephen's interview with the director concerning the priesthood, but the earlier confession also involves cross-dressing and homosexuality obliquely. When Stephen confesses after the retreat, he does so discreetly, at a chapel away from home and school, to an old priest in "the brown habit of a capuchin" (*P* 119; 3 1419). During the confession, after Stephen admits to sins of impurity "with others" (*P* 121; 3 1448), the priest asks "With women, my child?" The question raises the possibility of an impurity that the priest has undoubtedly encountered before: Stephen could have committed acts with men or other boys as well or instead. That possibility is more evident when the director mentions the dress-like habits of the Capuchins. Stephen responds to the remark silently first by thinking of the "delicate and sinful perfume" (*P* 131; 4 293) brought to mind by the names of women's clothing, then by recognizing that the priest had "spoken lightly with design" (*P* 131; 4 305). The director is testing Stephen by inviting him to respond to an image of feminized priests, but to what end? He invites a response or even a confession from Stephen about womanly priests. How is Stephen to respond properly? He may be in a double bind of the sort that he experienced at Clongowes when Wells asked him if he kissed his mother before going to bed. Whatever preference Stephen expresses is likely to be in some way wrong, either in his own view or in the director's.

Earlier in part four, during his period of spiritual exercises, Stephen has recognized himself intensely as a soul gendered female in "dissolving moments of virginal self-surrender" in a spiritual "world of fervent love and virginal responses." "An inaudible voice seemed to caress the soul" as a spouse (*P* 128; 4 175). Recognizing that surrender is attractive for him because of renewed sexual longings, he imagines himself saved from sin "by a sudden act of the will or a sudden ejaculation" (*P* 128; 4 199–200) that gives him "a new thrill of power and satisfaction" (*P* 128; 4 202). For a priest who identifies with a feminine soul in spousal surrender, a womanly garment seems appropriate. The garb of the Capuchins includes not only a dress-like robe but a hood. The word *capuchin* derives from Italian words meaning "hood" or "cowl" (*American Heritage Dictionary* 2000: 278). When Stephen confesses to the Capuchin priest, he is submitting to God but through the vehicle of a celibate interlocutor in a dress-like robe whose cowl may well remind Stephen and the reader of Stephen's recurring memory of being on the tram with Emma. She wore her shawl as a cowl: "He heard what her eyes said to him from beneath their cowl" (*P* 58; 2 336). Stephen stands in reverie, desire, and surrender before the cowled figure. He crosses over from male penitent to feminized soul who, if Stephen became a priest, would occupy instead the confessor's place: "He had seen himself, a young and silentmannered priest, entering a confessional swiftly" (*P* 133; 4 397–8). That role also offers a thrill in the knowledge that he would hear sins "murmured into his ear in the confessional under the shame of a darkened chapel by the lips of women and of girls" (*P* 134; 4 439).

Stephen recognizes in the wake of these fluctuatingly gendered perspectives that the "chill and order of the life repelled him" (*P* 135; 4 496–7) and that his "destiny was to be elusive of social or religious orders" (*P* 136; 5 530–1). The decision not to accept a priestly vocation is accompanied by a smile and laughter of relief, which are remarkable because of their absence from earlier portions of the narrative: "He smiled to think that it was this disorder, the misrule and confusion of his father's house . . . which was to win the day in his soul" (*P* 137; 4 550). The narrator is giving us something to smile or laugh about as well, since Stephen's thoughts suggest a play on Home Rule as home misrule. The choice of misrule as a liberating truth about home has come by means of an intense oscillating of gendered perspectives, one that enables Stephen to experience the extremes of his embodied imagination's varying potentials.[15] The large swerves involving transgendering have contributed significantly to Stephen's aversion to the chill and order that would have permanently cast him in the role of priestly confessor, a primary functionary within a confessional culture. Instead, he will wear a different cowl and experience the crossing of genders as someone who attempts to invent new language rather than repeating the language of already prescribed rituals that contribute to restricting freedom. Refusing the priesthood means for Stephen wanting more than to be "schooled in the discharging of a formal rite" (*P* 186; 5 1676). As he writes his villanelle, Stephen thinks in an inflated way of imagination as a virgin womb. In a more material and embodied gesture, he makes "a cowl of the blanket" in imitation of Emma, who "had worn her shawl cowlwise about her head" (*P* 187; 5 1707). Rather than accepting restrictions concerning the objects of his sexual desire and his own variably gendered sensibility, Stephen oscillates, by means of a transgendering imagination, between roles. The crossing of sexual valences is part of his creative process, part of a loosening of the serpents' grip.

The Thrill and the End of Confession

In the late scene between Stephen and his friend Cranly, there is a strongly homosocial element that becomes briefly homoerotic after Stephen touches Cranly's arm once (*P* 200; 5 2241–2) and Cranly touches Stephen's five times (*P* 200, 201, 202, 203, 208; 5 2276, 5 2300, 5 2326, 5 2377, 5 2581). The last touch triggers a thrill in Stephen that is clearly homoerotic. After a pause Stephen responds to Cranly's question, about whether he wants to be alone, with another question: "– Of whom are you speaking?" (*P* 209; 5 2607). Cranly does not respond. Stephen's act has been read as a defining moment of bad faith and loss of freedom. In that reading, Stephen anxiously denies a homosexual attraction that the constricting conventions of his culture have tantalized him with throughout the narrative but also prevented him from accepting; further, the scene effects a reversal by showing Cranly rather than Emma to be the true object of Stephen's desire.[16] Arguably, however, a different kind of reversal is at work, a potentially liberating one that is enabled by Stephen's question. It is also difficult to see the flow of desire in the scene as directed toward Cranly rather than toward Stephen, considering that Cranly does nearly all of the touching. The implication there is significantly clearer than Mr. Tate's digging his hand between his thighs.

What Cranly says about being alone also has heterosexual implications that involve Stephen's attraction to Emma, an attraction that plays an important role in Stephen's transgendered imaginings. Cranly is recognizing and asking Stephen to recognize the possibility of becoming more involved with her in a conventional way rather than cutting himself off from marriage and a family in Ireland. If that is the case, then it is Cranly, not Stephen, who expresses but also denies his same-sex desire by encouraging a union that will keep Stephen from going away. Stephen senses Cranly's attraction to Emma and his friend's wish to be attached to her, which he alludes to in his journal (April 2). The situation is ambiguously homoerotic and heterosexual in its implications. Coming at the end of a narrative that is strongly accented in both directions, the scene mixes both. Like Heron, Cranly is jealous about the heterosexual object of desire but also jealous to keep his male friend within the orbit of male relations. In dealing with Heron, Stephen recognizes the confessional character of the encounter and reflects it back at his threatening confessor in order to share the recognition in a way that generates a laugh. In dealing with Cranly, Stephen enables a similar recognition but one that reverses Cranly's position from confessor to penitent by inviting him to respond to a confessional question. Having practiced both roles in actuality or in his intense imaginings, Stephen is not a captive of the confessional situation. Instead he can shift roles in a protean way that actually puts an end to the confessional relationship. When Stephen poses his question to Cranly, he effects a restaging of the moment in which the director encourages a confession from him about his desires, which Stephen withholds. With the director Stephen silently imagines a transgendering that leads him to extinguish the possibility that has been offered, which is for him to confess but also to take the role of priestly confessor. With Cranly, he goes a step further. After refusing to confess in response to the question, he poses a question of his own that displaces the confessor from his role. The interplay of sexual implications and roles is crucial for the scene. The "sexual heart of things," to use Brown's phrase, has a new beat, which Stephen is defining in a way that challenges the confessional character of his culture.

In effecting the reversal, Stephen has not wholly escaped the confessional cultural situation. That is not a closet from which he can emerge completely because it has been built so thoroughly and continuously into his life, though he can ventilate and re-design it. Rather than being a captive, Stephen is exercising choice within a situation that he cannot avoid but can affect. By bringing out the rules of the cultural game that has been playing him and his friends, he plays the game with modified rules. This is a step that Stephen has to take in order to shake, if not shake off, the rule of the home and the homeland by Dante and others like her. The motivations for shaking that rule, in favor of home misrule or some cognate unruly response to restraints, are not limited to rejecting religious beliefs. They include refusing to accede to deluded thinking that serves the rule of empire by damning, for being a "bad man," an effective political proponent of Irish freedom or a great iconoclastic English poet. Stephen feels a thrill when Cranly touches him a fifth time. And he was thrilled when he felt his soul being touched and tempted and when he imagined his role as confessor to women penitents. In these related situations, he imagines in himself or in his confessional partner the temporary actuality of a reversing, displacing experience, which can be a transgendering or a switch in confessional roles. The opportunities are thrilling, each the culmination of a long period of living in a confessional culture under empire in circumstances that are often between men. Stephen does not turn away from the cultural circumstances and pressures. He cannot. But he can turn them to partial advantage by redirecting their effects.

Gradually, Stephen has learned how to restage the scenes that Heron, Cranly, and the conventions of Irish society under the Catholic Church and the British Empire have arranged for him and all the Irish to play. He reaches a point at which he can respond with warmth, rather than his usual coldness, and feel his own desire by being thrilled while also understanding that the thrilling experience need not require him to accept the confessional cultural situation as it comes to him. He need not admit, nor pray for himself or others, nor stay. He will not be swept into an abiding commitment to the confessional role of either penitent or confessor. The confessional moment as culturally scripted is not the ultimately determining moment of his encounters with either the director or Cranly. It is instead part of a transforming process in which Stephen participates in an enabling, rather than a disabled, way, a process whose results for the individual and his culture are not predictable.

Beyond the Horizon of Confessional Constraints

We can predict that Stephen will not be confessing to Cranly or to a replacement for him and that he will not be anyone's priestly confessor. Stephen's refusals are marks of his resolve and also of wounds inflicted or warded off. Resolve is more in evidence than is injury in Stephen's journal, which can be read with various tones because the entries are comparatively brief and largely discontinuous. Unlike the book's elliptical opening segment, which evokes the pressures that will affect Stephen's embodied sensibility as it develops, the journal emerges as a provisionally concluding pause in the history of an already formed sensibility. The entries are by turns ironic, self-centered, humorously self-reflective, and inflated. Stephen reconsiders and admits things to himself in the journal under no threat of punishment and with no thought of doing penance. The threatening serpents have been displaced by jokes about crocodiles (March 30, April 3) that include Stephen as well as his friends. The implied laughter can remind us of Stephen's laughter as he decides against the priesthood.

Immediately prior to the final three entries, which express Stephen's goals in an inflated way, he reveals with humorous self-irony in a long entry that he continues to be attracted to Emma, who has just clearly rejected his advances (April 15). This is an important moment of recognition and self-confession for Stephen, an admission, by someone who regularly refuses to admit, that he is experiencing "a new feeling" (*P* 213; 5 2773), one that he immediately goes on to poke fun at. He also thinks about the Irish peasant as his antagonist but recognizes that he means the peasant no injury (April 14). The recognition is a moment of acceptance, though not submission, that turns Stephen's vehement, repeated "No" in a positive direction when he denies that he wants to force a submission: "Till he yield to me? No. I mean him no harm" (*P* 212; 5 2757). Stephen is trying to avoid the destructive consequences of forcing someone to yield, as he has regularly been pressured to do. The continuing attraction to Emma, carrying forward in a changed form a desire of considerable duration, and the acceptance of part of what Stephen feels he has to leave behind, suggest that Stephen is seeing himself and his oppositional counterparts in new ways. The oscillations in perspective that enable his new views may serve Stephen well as he sets out to create an independent life and independent art not narrowly defined by the constraints of a confessional culture.

Notes

1 The page number, given first, refers to the version edited by Jeri Johnson for Oxford World's Classics (Oxford and New York: Oxford University Press, 2000). The part and line numbers, given second, refer to the critical edition edited by Hans Walter Gabler with Walter Hettche (New York and London: Garland Publishing, 1993) and to the reprintings of the text established there by Vintage International (New York, 1993) and by W. W. Norton (New York, 2007). I wish to thank Marie-Anne Verougstraete for rendering the illustrations, and Gregory Castle and Jonathan Mulrooney for helpful responses to a late draft of the essay.

2 Hugh Kenner was the most influential of the Stephen-haters in postwar criticism. See Kenner 1956 and 1976. He was particularly skeptical about linking Stephen closely with Joyce, especially in the work of Richard Ellmann, who wrote the award-winning biography, *James Joyce* (1982 [1959]). Riquelme (1983) makes a positive case for Stephen by arguing that *A Portrait* is the book that Stephen eventually writes. Sosnoski presents an overview of the criticism through the mid-1970s. Among more recent critics, Mulrooney (2001) is negative about Stephen but not about the implications of the book for Ireland. Similarly, following Kenner, Valente (1998) blames Stephen but praises Joyce.

3 William York Tindall was a leading proponent of symbolic readings of Joyce in, for example, his *A Reader's Guide to James Joyce* (1959).

4 Joyce spelled the surname in the Greek way

in *Stephen Hero*, an unpublished novel drafted before *A Portrait*. He also used the pseudonym "Stephen Daedalus" when he published an early version of his story "The Sisters." Stephen Dedalus is a central figure in *Ulysses* (1922). Some critics run these three works together in order to interpret Joyce's artist character based on details from all the works, which they give equal weight. Although it is reasonable to identify the two identically named characters in the published works, arguments that depend on identifying Dedalus with his precursor in *Stephen Hero*, a book that Joyce never published, are methodologically questionable, as is the case with Nolan (1995).

5 See Burke (1964) for a critique of symbolic readings that stresses the elaborate networks in Joyce's language in *A Portrait*.

6 See Howes (2000) for a semicolonial reading of *A Portrait*. The title of the collection in which the essay appears includes the term "semicolonial." The introduction by Howes and Attridge focuses on Joyce and postcolonial studies. Gregory Castle (2000), a Joyce critic, includes several important essays on postcolonial thinking about Ireland.

7 Valente (1998) is particularly emphatic and detailed about the homosocial and homoerotic aspects of Stephen's experience at Clongowes Wood College.

8 Brown (1985) is a ground-breaking study concerning Joyce's reading in contemporary sexology. Valente's introduction to *Quare Joyce* (1998), "Joyce's (Sexual) Choices: A Historical

Overview," provides a lengthy list of influential critical writing about Joyce from a feminist perspective, but she shifts the terms of the discussion by drawing on the work of Eve Kosofsky Sedgwick, among others engaged in queer theory, concerning the mutual dependence of attitudes toward heterosexuality and homosexuality in the social world that Joyce represents. He draws primarily on Sedgwick (1985). Froula (1996) argues for Stephen's engagement with a "deeply buried" "vestigial female self" (47) as part of her defense of Joyce and Stephen from the charge of being anti-feminist.

9   In his introduction to *Quare Joyce*, Valente argues for "Joyce's debt to Wilde" (9), which is developed in other essays in the collection, including Valente (1998), and Mahaffey (1998).

10   First pointed out by Mahaffey (1998: 121, 134 n. 1), but also stressed by Valente (1998: 51).

11   Castle (1998) distinguishes between "sacramental" and "profane" confession in the narrative. The initial scene concerns what he would call profane confession. In my commentary, I am less concerned to distinguish the two kinds of confession than to bring out their common effects within a confessional culture that is heavily invested in both forms.

12   Mullin (2003) cites various critics who gloss smugging as homoerotic activity but suggests that it could be masturbation (92 n. 24).

13   In "Thrilled" (1998), Valente relies too heavily on Elaine Showalter's claim that *queer* had a homosexual meaning in the late nineteenth century. Attridge (2000: 63 n. 6) presents Valente's later thinking that, although *queer* has been documented to mean "male homosexual" only beginning in the 1920s, in the first decades of the twentieth century it was undergoing a se-

mantic shift that extends its suggestiveness in Joyce's narrative beyond the meaning *strange*. I find this modified position convincing.

14   That Joyce drew on this text (published originally in Italian in 1688) has been established by James R. Thrane (1960), who includes two of the eight woodcuts. All eight woodcuts are reproduced in the Norton Critical Edition of *A Portrait* (New York: W. W. Norton, 2007).

15   Castle (1998: 178) calls the oscillation "Stephen's ambivalent sexual identity." In his introduction to *Quare Joyce* (1998), Valente recognizes "the heightened lability of erotic valences in Joyce's writing" (5), but in "Thrilled" (1998) he consistently presents Stephen as unaware of a culturally induced bad faith in his gender identifications, a bad faith that involves him in anxiously denying his own engagement with homosexual desire. Our readings diverge, since Valente portrays Stephen as driven by the homophobic, misogynistic forces of his culture, and I see Stephen deflecting those forces in ways that loosen the bonds of confessional attitudes and behavior.

16   "Stephen's last unanswered question . . . virtually epitomizes homosexual panic as a neurotic obsession with the identity, status, and location of homo–hetero difference and virtually defines Stephen as its captive" (Valente 1998: 67). The double predication of "virtually" makes it unclear whether the question is, in fact, definite and epitomizing in the ways asserted, since logically these verbs do not allow for degrees. Concerning the reversal of positions, Valente asserts that "it is hard not to see Cranly as Stephen's *real* object of sexual rivalry rather than a rival for the favor of another" (Valente 1998:66).

BIBLIOGRAPHY

The American Heritage Dictionary of the English Language (2000), 4th edn. Boston: Houghton Mifflin.

Attridge, Derek (2000) "'Suck was a queer word': language, sex, and the remainder in *A Portrait of the Artist as a Young Man*." In his *Joyce Effects: On Language, Theory, and History*, pp. 59–77. Cambridge: Cambridge University Press.

Booth, Wayne C. (1983 [1961]) "The problem of distance in *A Portrait*." In his *The Rhetoric of Fiction*, pp. 323–6. Chicago: University of Chicago Press.

Brady, Philip and James F. Carens (eds.) (1998) *Critical Essays on James Joyce's "A Portrait of the Artist as a Young Man."* New York: G. K. Hall.

Brivic, Sheldon (2002) "Gender dissonance, hysteria, and history in James Joyce's *A Portrait of the*

Artist as a Young Man." James Joyce Quarterly 39: 457–76.

Brown, Richard (1985) *James Joyce and Sexuality.* Cambridge: Cambridge University Press.

Burke, Kenneth (1964) "Fact, inference, and proof in the analysis of literary symbolism." In Stanley Edgar Hyman (ed.) *Terms for Order*, pp. 145–72. Bloomington: Indiana University Press.

Castle, Gregory (1998) "Confessing oneself: *Homoeros* and colonial *Bildung* in *A Portrait of the Artist as a Young Man*." In Joseph Valente (ed.) *Quare Joyce*, pp. 157–82. Ann Arbor: University of Michigan Press.

Castle, Gregory (ed.) (2000) *Postcolonial Discourses: An Anthology.* Oxford: Blackwell.

Castle, Gregory (2006) "*Bildung* and the bonds of dominion: Wilde and Joyce." In his *Reading the Modernist Bildungsroman*, pp. 126–91. Gainesville: University Press of Florida.

Cheng, Vincent J. (1995) "Coda [to "Catching the conscience of a race"]: the case of Stephen D(a)edalus." In his *Joyce, Race, and Empire*, pp. 57–74. Cambridge: Cambridge University Press.

Church, Margaret (1981) "The adolescent point of view toward women in Joyce's *A Portrait of the Artist as a Young Man*." In Zack Bowen (ed.) *Irish Renaissance Annual* 1, pp. 158–65. Newark, NJ: University of Delaware Press.

Deane, Seamus (1985) "Joyce and Stephen: the provincial intellectual." In his *Celtic Revivals: Essays in Modern Irish Literature, 1880–1980*, pp. 75–91. London: Faber and Faber.

Eide, Marian (1998) "The Woman of the Ballyhoura Hills: James Joyce and the Politics of Creativity." *Twentieth-Century Literature* 44: 377–93.

Ellmann, Richard (1982 [1959]) *James Joyce*, new and revised edition, Oxford and New York: Oxford University Press.

Froula, Christine (1996) *Modernism's Body: Sex, Culture, and Joyce.* New York: Columbia University Press.

Gabler, Hans Walter (1998) "The genesis of *A Portrait of the Artist as a Young Man*." In Philip Brady and James F. Carens (eds.) *Critical Essays on James Joyce's "A Portrait of the Artist as a Young Man,"* pp. 83–112. New York: G. K. Hall.

Gardner, Percy (1910–11) "Greek Art." In *Encyclopaedia Britannica*, 11th edn. London and New York: Encyclopaedia Britannica.

Harkness, Marguerite (1990) "*A Portrait of the Artist as a Young Man": Voices of the Text.* Boston, MA: Twayne.

Henke, Suzette (1990) "Stephen Dedalus and women: a portrait of the artist as a young narcissist." In *James Joyce and the Politics of Desire*, pp. 50–84. New York and London: Routledge.

Howes, Marjorie (2000) "'Goodbye Ireland I'm going to Gort': geography, scale, and narrating the nation." In Derek Attridge and Marjorie Howes (eds.) *Semicolonial Joyce*, pp. 58–77. Cambridge: Cambridge University Press.

Jacobs, Joshua (2000) "Joyce's Epiphanic mode: material language and the representation of sexuality in *Stephen Hero* and *Portrait*," *Twentieth-Century Literature* 46: 20–33.

Joyce, James (2007) *A Portrait of the Artist as a Young Man: Authoritative Text, Contexts, Criticism*, ed. John Paul Riquelme. New York: W. W. Norton.

Kenner, Hugh (1956) "The *Portrait* in Perspective." In *Dublin's Joyce*, pp. 109–33. Bloomington: Indiana University Press.

Kenner, Hugh (1976) "The Cubist *Portrait*." In Thomas F. Staley and Bernard Benstock (eds.) *Approaches to Joyce's "Portrait": Ten Essays*, pp. 171–84. Pittsburgh, PA: University of Pittsburgh Press.

Kershner, R. B. (1989) *Joyce, Bakhtin, and Popular Literature: Chronicles of Disorder.* Chapel Hill and London: University of North Carolina Press.

Lawrence, Karen (1986) "Gender and narrative voice in *Jacob's Room* and *A Portrait of the Artist as a Young Man*." In Morris Beja (ed.) *James Joyce: The Centennial Symposium*, pp. 31–8. Urbana: University of Illinois Press.

Leonard, Garry (1998) "When a fly gets in your I: the city, modernism, and aesthetic theory in *A Portrait of the Artist as a Young Man*." In his *Advertising and Commodity Culture in Joyce*, pp. 175–207. Gainesville: University Press of Florida.

Lewis, Pericles (1999) "The conscience of the race: the nation as church of the modern age." In Michael Patrick Gillespie (ed.) *Joyce through the Ages: A Nonlinear View*, pp. 85–106. Gainesville: University Press of Florida.

Lowe-Evans, Mary (1990) "Sex and confession in the Joyce canon: some historical parallels." *Journal of Modern Literature* 16: 563–76.

Mahaffey, Vicki (1998) "Père-version and immère-sion: idealized corruption in *A Portrait of the Artist as a Young Man* and *The Picture of Dorian Gray*." In Joseph Valente (ed.) *Quare*

Joyce, pp. 121–38. Ann Arbor: University of Michigan Press.

Manganiello, Dominic (1980) *Joyce's Politics*. Boston and London: Routledge and Kegan Paul.

Manganiello, Dominic (1993) "Reading the book of himself: the confessional imagination of St. Augustine and Joyce." In James Noonan (ed.) *Biography and Autobiography: Essays on Irish and Canadian History and Literature*, pp. 149–62. Ottawa: Carleton University Press.

Mullin, Katherine (2003) "'True manliness': policing masculinity in *A Portrait of the Artist as a Young Man*." In *James Joyce, Sexuality and Social Purity*, pp. 83–115. Cambridge: Cambridge University Press.

Mulrooney, Jonathan (2001) "Stephen Dedalus and the politics of confession." *Studies in the Novel* 33: 160–79.

Nolan, Emer (1995) *James Joyce and Nationalism*. London and New York: Routledge.

Pinamonti, Rev. F. Giovanni Pietro SJ (1688) *Hell Opened to Christians, To Caution Them from Entering into It*. Dublin: G. P. Warren.

Riquelme, John Paul (1983) *Teller and Tale in Joyce's Fiction: Oscillating Perspectives*. Baltimore, MD and London: Johns Hopkins University Press.

Riquelme, John Paul (2004) "*Stephen Hero* and *A Portrait of the Artist as a Young Man*: transforming the nightmare of history." In Derek Attridge (ed.) *Cambridge Companion to James Joyce*, 2nd edn, pp. 103–21. Cambridge: Cambridge University Press.

Schwarze, Tracey Teets (1997) "Silencing Stephen: colonial pathologies in Victorian Dublin," *Twentieth-Century Literature* 43: 243–63.

Sedgwick, Eve Kosofsky (1985) *Between Men*. New York: Columbia University Press.

Sosnoski, James J. (1978) "Reading acts, reading warrants, and reading responses." *James Joyce Quarterly* 16: 43–63.

Spoo, Robert (1994) "Fabricated ghosts: a metahistorical reading of *A Portrait of the Artist as a Young Man*." In his *James Joyce and the Language of History*, pp. 38–65. New York: Oxford University Press.

Spurr, David (1999) "Colonial spaces in Joyce's Dublin," *James Joyce Quarterly* 37: 23–42.

Thrane, James R. (1960) "Joyce's sermon on Hell: its source and its backgrounds," *Modern Philology* 57: 172–98.

Tindall, William York (1959) *A Reader's Guide to James Joyce*. New York: Noonday Press.

Valente, Joseph (1998) "Thrilled by his touch: the aestheticizing of homosexual panic in *A Portrait of the Artist as a Young Man*." In Joseph Valente (ed.) *Quare Joyce*, pp. 47–75. Ann Arbor: University of Michigan Press.

Wollaeger, Mark A. (2003) *James Joyce's "A Portrait of the Artist as a Young Man": A Casebook*. Oxford: Oxford University Press.

4
Ulysses:
The Epic of the Human Body

Maud Ellmann

Samuel Beckett, in one of the first critical commentaries on *Finnegans Wake*, announced that Joyce's "writing is not about something. *It is that something itself.*" That something is the body: in the *Wake*, words do the things that bodies do, performing rather than describing bodily experience. "When the sense sleeps," Beckett writes, "the words go to sleep . . . when the sense is dancing, the words dance," and when the sense is drunk, the "very words are tilted and effervescent" (Beckett 1929: 14; added emphasis).

By uniting language with the body, word with flesh, *Finnegans Wake* brings to fruition an experiment that begins with *Dubliners*, and gathers pace with each of Joyce's subsequent works – namely to reincorporate the human body in the text. This experiment becomes explicit in *Ulysses*, which Joyce described as the "epic of the human body." It was his unblushing portrayal of the body that caused *Ulysses* to be banned throughout the prudish English-speaking world (Budgen 1972: 21). The ban was lifted in the United States in 1933 by Judge John M. Woolsey who, cautioning that *Ulysses* is "not an easy book to read or to understand," concluded that although its effect on readers is often "somewhat emetic, nowhere does it tend to be aphrodisiac" (*JJ* 436, 667). This verdict implies that it is better for our morals to be nauseated than aroused; yet in either case, the danger of the novel is located in its bodily effect upon the reader, not just in its frankness about bodies.

"About," as Beckett insists, is the wrong word. The present essay argues that *Ulysses* anticipates the *Wake* by transforming epic into body, and body into epic, through the use of a language that enacts organic processes, miming the activities of nerves and organs, such as peristalsis in "Lestrygonians," orgasm in "Nausicaa," seizures in "Circe." When Bloom eats his lunch, the language ruminates or chews its cud; when he masturbates, the language tumesces and detumesces; when he visits the brothel, the language is convulsed with locomotor ataxia, the spastic symptoms of tertiary syphilis. Phineas Fletcher had already attempted an epic of the human body in his *Purple Island* of 1633, but Joyce dismissed this precedent as "a coloured anatomical chart." "In my book," Joyce declared, "the body lives in and moves through space and is the home of a full human personality. The words I write are adapted to express first one of its functions and then another" (Budgen 1972: 21). Thus *Ulysses* strives to unite word and flesh in a secular version of the Incarnation, to make the English language breathe, digest, excrete, parturiate.

In the same period that Joyce was transforming the text into a body, Freud was interpreting the body as a text. According to Freud, the physical afflictions of hysteria stand for words debarred from consciousness, which are written on the body in the form of symptoms. In his well-known case-history of Dora, Freud interprets his patient's symptomatic cough as a sign of the forbidden things her mouth would like to do – speaking, eating, kissing, sucking (Freud 1905a: 29–32): an oral fantasy akin to the rapturous finale of *Ulysses*, when Bloom and Molly exchange kisses, seedcake, and yeses in their famous love scene on the hill of Howth. What Freud and Joyce have in common is the insight that such exchanges – of language, food, and sex – override commonsense distinctions between these categories, so that food can serve as a substitute for kisses, words as a substitute for food, and exchange itself as a substitute for sexuality. Food, words, and kisses function as circulating currencies in the economy of intersubjectivity; in Freud's terms, these currencies serve as symbolic equivalents of one another (Freud 1917).

To speak of "the body" in Freud or Joyce is therefore a misleading shorthand, since both writers conceive of language and the body as interpenetrating systems of exchange and circulation, which correspond to wider economic systems of the body politic. The city in *Ulysses* takes the form of a gigantic body circulating language, commodities, and money, together with the Dubliners whirled round in these economies. In the "Aeolus" episode, set in the offices of the *Freeman's Journal*, the newspaper is hailed as the "GREAT DAILY ORGAN" at the "HEART OF THE HIBERNIAN METROPOLIS," pumping misinformation into the collective bloodstream (*U* 7 84, 1–2). Meanwhile the transportation system circulates the characters, like corpuscles, on odysseys around the city's arteries. In *Finnegans Wake* Joyce describes Dublin as "this commodius vicus of recirculation," and this epithet pertains to the text itself, which recirculates the tales of myriad tribes, blending languages, literatures, and popular traditions (*FW* 3 2). Equally commodiously, *Ulysses* recirculates the Western literary canon, sponging off the works of its precursors much as Joyce himself sponged off handouts from his put-upon admirers. In this respect Joyce's literary borrowings vindicate his spendthrift habits by flaunting an economy of freeloading in place of the profit system based on bourgeois thrift (Osteen 1995; Tratner 2001).

To understand what Joyce means by "the epic of the human body," it is necessary to begin with his schemata for *Ulysses*, which assign bodily organs to most of the episodes.[1] Next, a close reading of Bloom's visit to the outhouse in "Calypso" reveals how Joyce implicates the body in language, language in money, and money in everything that circulates: sewage, semen, gossip, letters, telegrams, ads, popular songs, newspapers, commodities, disease, and the literary tradition – just to name a few. These circulating currencies resemble Freud's conception of the symbolic equivalents of the unconscious, whereby money, language, babies, excrement, and the imperiled penis are treated as interchangeable "gifts" (Freud 1917: 132). The next section of this essay investigates how these economies of word and flesh correspond to the Odyssean themes of exile and return that structure the action of *Ulysses*. The conclusion demonstrates how Molly Bloom's rhapsody in "Penelope" accomplishes what Stephen calls the "postcreation" by transforming the flesh into the word (*U* 14 294).

Inner Organs

Joyce wrote two schemata for *Ulysses* in which he assigned bodily organs to all but the first three episodes, which are devoted to Stephen's morning. Explaining this omission, Joyce declared that Stephen, as Telemachus, "does not yet bear a body."[2] Only when Bloom enters the stage in the fourth episode, "Calypso," does the body begin to assert its claims. Thus the organ designated for "Calypso" is "kidneys," in honour of Bloom's breakfast. Apart from listing organs, however, the schemata provide little inkling of the bodily vitality of Joyce's prose. Nor could the human body be reconstructed from the sum of its schematic parts. If the organs assigned to the episodes were put together, the mishmash would look weirder than Frankenstein's monster: a "heterogeneous mannequin" of kidneys, genitals, heart, lungs, esophagus, brain, blood, ear, muscles, bones, eye, nose, womb, nerves, skin, skeleton, unspecified "juices," flesh, and fat.[3] Furthermore, Joyce's schemata contradict each other: the Italian schema sent to Carlo Linati in 1920 designates "genitals" as the organ for "Lotus-Eaters," whereas the 1921 Gilbert/Gorman schema replaces "genitals" with "skin"; other discrepancies include "juices" (1920) versus "skeleton" (1921) in "Ithaca," and "fat" (1920) versus "flesh"(1921) in "Penelope."

One suspicion to be gleaned from the schemata is that Joyce, like Bloom, relishes the inner organs in preference to such superficies as legs and arms (with the proviso that Joyce's relish is purely intellectual; as far as his personal eating habits were concerned, Joyce reviled the offal consumed by Bloom with such enthusiasm, although a surfeit of Italian "paste" [pasta] made him long for Irish tripe and onions) (Maddox 1988: 105, 107). While the schematic body of *Ulysses* is equipped with several inner organs, it has no limbs, no head, no hair, no breasts, and not even a bottom: a surprising omission for a writer so obsessed with women's rumps and the "dirty things" they do (*SL* 186). As opposed to Deleuze and Guattari's conception of the body without organs, Joyce's schemata consist of organs without a body (Deleuze and Guattari 1983; Žižek 2003).

Bloom fantasizes about organs without a body in the "Hades" episode, during the funeral of Paddy Dignam, when he enjoys a private joke about the Catholic doctrine of the resurrection of the body, imagining how the dead would rummage around for their organs on the last day:

> Get up! Last day! Then every fellow mousing around for his liver and his lights and the rest of his traps. Find damn all of himself that morning (*U* 6 679–81).

This passage might be read as an ironic commentary on Joyce's own attempt in the schemata to resurrect the human body by "mousing around" for its scattered parts.

The fact that Bloom conceives of the body as a bunch of pumps may explain his predilection for inner organs, since he functions as a kind of pump (and pimp) in his capacity as advertising canvasser, flushing commodities through the intestinal passageways of commerce. Bloom's affinity with pumps, as well as his preoccupation with his large intestine, confirms the persistence of the "cloacal obsession" that H. G. Wells detected in Joyce's early writing: "how right Wells was," Joyce commented (*JJ* 414). But it is not so much the contents of cloacae that fascinate the author of *Ulysses* as the pumps and pipes through which these contents circulate. In "Lestygonians," Bloom imagines how a swallowed pin would navigate the cloacal networks of the body: "swallow a pin sometimes come out of the ribs years after tour round the body changing biliary duct spleen squirting liver gastric juice coils of intestines like pipes" (*U* 8 1047–50). Similarly, the Dublin waterworks are mapped in demented detail in "Ithaca," where the pedantic narrator traces the odyssey of water from Roundwood reservoir in County Wicklow through all the "subterranean aqueducts" that lead to Bloom's tap at 7 Eccles Street (*U* 17 165).

Joyce's fascination with such networks extends from the underworld of pipes to the overworld of tramlines, tracks, and cables, in which the modern city-dweller is enmeshed. Invading the privacy of the home, these networks insinuate the public in the private sphere, creating mysterious and uncontrollable relations of dependency. They remind Stephen of the umbilical cord that links humanity back to its first parents in the Garden of Eden, an association sparked off by the sight of two alleged midwives on Sandymount Strand:

> Number one swung lourdily her midwife's bag, the other's gamp poked in the beach. One of her sisterhood lugged me squealing into life. Creation from nothing. What has she in the bag? A misbirth with a trailing navelcord, hushed in ruddy wool. The cords of all link back, strandentwining cable of all flesh. Hello. Kinch here. Put me on to Edenville. Aleph, alpha: nought, nought, one (*U* 3 32–40).

Stephen, obsessed with the "sin darkness" of his own conception, links these insouciant Fates to the midwives who presided over his own birth (*U* 3 45). His fantasy that "number one" is carrying a misbirth in her bag reveals his fear of being an aborted artist, expelled by mother Ireland as a "misbirth with a trailing navelcord," rather than a living "wombfruit" (*U* 3 2, *U* 14 2). It is the "successive anastomosis of navelcords" that links every human infant back to Adam and Eve (*U* 14 300). But Stephen, who would prefer to create himself from nothing, feels strangled by this "strandentwining cable of all flesh." Nonetheless he allows himself to be distracted from his moody broodings by a pun: the term "cable" reminds him of a telephone wire, which prompts him to call up the Garden of Eden, giving the operator the telephone number for creation from nothing: nought, nought, one, preceded by the first letters of the Hebrew and Greek alphabets, aleph and alpha, which presumably stand for the first cause. This dazzling riff exemplifies Stephen's desire to slip by the nets of navelcords that bind him to his flesh and blood – his family, his country, and his body. At the same time, his umbilical reveries reveal Joyce's fascination with the cloacal networks that circulate the products of the body and the city.

In the nineteenth century, Ireland was used by England as a laboratory for new technologies of transportation and communication, which meant that these systems were considerably more advanced than the living conditions of the populace (Kiberd 1996: 23–4). In this respect Ireland itself consisted of organs without a body, its circulatory systems operating independently of both its heads – one in Rome and one in London – and of the concept of the nation as a unified integument. Joyce remarked that "modern man has an epidermis rather than a soul," but the epidermis of his native land was notable for its porosity rather than its power to contain or to exclude (Joyce 1977: 15). Ireland (as an early reviewer said of Stephen Dedalus) was too "thin-skinned" to enclose its emigrating thousands, or to insulate itself against incursions from its foreign masters (Deming 1970: 97). Thin-skinned Ireland may have inspired Joyce to thin the epidermis of his works by opening them up to other literatures and languages. At the same time he thins the skin of subjectivity, presenting the self as a nexus of exchange, rather than an autotelic monad. The "pale vampire," who stars in Stephen's only poem in *Ulysses*, represents the parasitical condition of the Joycean self, dependent on "recirculation" of the energies of others (*U* 3 397). Influences, whether literary, olfactory, or pestilential, pass in and out of the vampiric Stephen in the same way that the English literary tradition circulates through Joyce's writing, in a constant process of absorption and regurgitation.

Cloacal Obsessions

An appropriate place to launch an investigation of these circulatory systems is Bloom's visit to the outhouse in "Calypso."

> He went out through the backdoor into the garden: stood to listen [. . .]. The hens in the next garden: their droppings are very good top dressing. Best of all though are the cattle, especially when they are fed on those oilcakes. Mulch of dung. Best thing to clean ladies' kid gloves. Dirty cleans. [. . .]
>
> He kicked open the crazy door of the jakes. Better be careful not to get these trousers dirty for the funeral. [. . .]
>
> Asquat on the cuckstool he folded out his paper, turning its pages over on his bared knees. Something new and easy. No great hurry. [. . .]
>
> Quietly he read, restraining himself, the first column and, yielding but resisting, began the second. Midway, his last resistance yielding, he allowed his bowels to ease themselves quietly as he read, reading still patiently that slight constipation of yesterday quite gone. Hope it's not too big bring on piles again. No, just right. So. Ah! [. . .] He read on, seated calm above his own rising smell. [. . .] He glanced back through what he had read and, while feeling his water flow quietly, he envied kindly Mr Beaufoy who had written it and received payment of three pounds, thirteen and six (*U* 4 472–517).

In the nineteenth-century realist novel, despite its claims to verisimilitude, nobody ever goes to the toilet. Joyce, on the contrary, treats us to an unabridged account of this everyday heroic act. Affirming Bloom's insight that "dirty cleans," the squalor of the scene is counterbalanced by the immaculate precision of Joyce's prose. With a few clean strokes, Joyce crystallizes Bloom's humour and humanity, as well as his endearing foibles, such as his bourgeois fantasy of installing a summerhouse in the garden, and his scientific curiosity about the uses of excrement as fertilizer and detergent. Bloom's excrementitious musings recall another Irish avatar of the cloacal obsession, Jonathan Swift, especially Swift's mad scientist in the Academy of Lagado, engaged in "an Operation to reduce human Excrement back to its original Food," who welcomes Gulliver with "a close Embrace, (a Compliment I could well have excused)" (Swift 1986: 179). Readers of *Ulysses* might also feel they could excuse the compliment of being introduced to Bloom's excretions – but Joyce, like Swift, refuses to sanitize the human body. "Celia shits," Swift wrote, and so does Bloom.

The reason Bloom shits is that he eats – unlike Stephen, who does not eat, and only pees, at least within the pages of *Ulysses*. Remembering that Stephen "does not yet bear a body," one symptom of his incompleteness is his reluctance either to consume or to excrete solidities. Alcohol has rendered his imagination as diuretic as his bladder, and at this stage of his career it seems unlikely he will "bring forth the work" in solid form (*U* 14 1120). In Freudian terms, Stephen's preference for urination could be understood as a symptom of ambition: Freud speaks of "the intense 'burning' ambition of those who earlier suffered from enuresis" (Freud 1908: 175). Appropriately *A Portrait of the Artist* opens with a reference to Stephen's enuresis, which provides him with his first lesson in the art of dialectic: "When you wet the bed first it is warm then it gets cold" (*P* 5). In the "Proteus" episode of *Ulysses*, Stephen's fantasies about his future masterpieces culminate in an ambitious pee into the ocean, his "long lassoes" of urine soaring over the waves; and in "Ithaca" he engages in a peeing contest with Bloom, a former champion "who in his ultimate year at High School (1880) had been capable of attaining the point of greatest altitude against the whole concurrent strength of the institution, 210 scholars" (*U* 3 453, *U* 17 1194–6).

Since Stephen passes only water, it is curious that he distrusts "aquacities of thought and language" (*U* 17 240). Yet he remains unwilling or unable to pass solids; his urethral ambitions exceed his anal productivity. In *Finnegans Wake*, Stephen's successor Shem the Penman has learned how to alchemize his shit and piss into works of art, by writing on his body with his own excretions. Out of his workshop of filthy creation comes a Blakeian prophetic book, composed by the "corrosive sublimation" of "gallic acid on iron ore"; that is, Gaelic urine laced with gall and Gaul (*Ulysses* was first published in Paris, the Gauls being less prudish than the Gaels), branded in the excremental ore of Eire, and ironed with a dash of Irish irony (*FW* 185 27–186 8).

The jakes passage in "Calypso" illustrates what Hugh Kenner calls the "Uncle Charles principle," in reference to Joyce's description of another journey to the jakes in *A Portrait of the Artist*: "Every morning, therefore, uncle Charles repaired to his outhouse but not before he had creased and brushed scrupulously his back hair and brushed and put on his tall hat" (*P* 50; 2 12–14)). Kenner points out that there are invisible quotation marks around the word "repaired," because this is the creased and brushed terminology that Uncle Charles might have used to describe his own matutinal excursions (Kenner 1978: 15–38). The Uncle Charles principle therefore refers to free indirect discourse, in which the narrative voice is contaminated by the idiolect of the character.

When Bloom repairs to the outhouse in "Calypso," however, this contamination has grown too pervasive to allow for the insertion of inverted commas, or as Joyce called them, "perverted commas" (*LIII* 99). Perverted, because they insinuate a spurious hierarchy between the language of the narrator, supposedly omniscient and unbiased, and the limited perspective of the characters. Moreover, perverted commas impose boundaries between speakers, implying that their speech is private property. Joyce, by contrast, revels in his "commodius vicus of recirculation" in which language is always secondhand, the "last word in stolentelling" (a pun on stealing and Stollen, a German fruitcake, suggesting that Joyce's word-theft "[takes] the cake": *FW* 424 35). In the outhouse episode, the external narration alternates with Bloom's interior monologue, without signaling such transitions with perverted commas. This alternation between inside and outside mimics the peristalsis taking place in Bloom's intestines, as he digests the external world and expels his internal waste products. Bloom begins the chapter eating and ends it defecating, in the course of which his breakfast kidney undergoes an odyssey of metempsychoses, as it navigates its way through the rocks and whirlpools of his digestive tract.

Also striking is the correspondence between reading, excreting, and counting money established in the outhouse scene. It is clear that reading Philip Beaufoy's prize story in *Tit-bits* has a laxative effect on Bloom. Reading is commonly associated with eating rather than with defecating – think of the expression "devouring a book" – but Bloom reads "Matcham's Masterstroke" to ease his bowels and to wipe his arse, thus accomplishing what Freud might call "a displacement from the front of the body to the back" (Freud 1908: 172 n). Freud would also have appreciated the connection Bloom draws between anality and avarice by way of the familiar nursery rhyme: "The king was in his counting-house, / Counting out his money." In an essay that scandalized its early readers, "Character and Anal Erotism" (1908), Freud proposed that parsimony originates in anal retentiveness, and later argued that "interest in faeces is carried over first to interest in gifts, and then to interest in money" (Freud 1917: 132).

As if to illustrate Freud's principles, Bloom, sitting on his "throne," imagines himself as a miser, perhaps alluding to the stereotype of the tight-fisted Jew. Yet Joyce counters this stereotype by presenting Bloom elsewhere as a generous man whose spending is restrained by prudence rather than retentiveness. In the outhouse Bloom exercises the same prudence with his stool, "restraining himself," "yielding but resisting," and finally allowing "his bowels to ease themselves quietly as he read, reading still patiently, that slight constipation of yesterday quite gone. Hope it's not too big bring on piles again. No, just right." Similarly, Bloom donates five shillings to help Paddy Dignam's fatherless children – "not too big . . . just right" – whereas Stephen squanders money, murdering his goods with whores (*U* 14 276).

One of the funniest aspects of this passage is that everything Bloom thinks about his bowels also pertains to Beaufoy's prose: "Quietly he read, restraining himself, the first column and, yielding but resisting, began the second." Lawrence Rainey's argument that Bloom's choice of *Tit-bits* for his toilet paper "epitomizes the modernist contempt for popular culture" overlooks Bloom's evident enjoyment both in reading and in defecating, in the "litter" that goes in his eyes and out his arse – "litter" being Joyce's famous pun on literature, rubbish, and procreation in *Finnegans Wake* (Rainey 1998: 2). Bloom yields to *Matcham's Masterstroke* at the same unhurried pace that he yields to the exhortations of his bowels – "No great hurry. Keep it a bit." His bladder joins in at the end, his water flowing quietly as he counts up the money Philip Beaufoy must have earned out of his writing. Bloom – himself a would-be writer – "kindly envies" Beaufoy's success, marveling at the metempsychosis that transforms columns into guineas, words into cash. While Freud argues that faeces and money are treated as symbolic equivalents in the unconscious, Bloom here imagines words as the equivalents of cash and shit, aligning writing with excretion and expenditure.

These jokes on shitting and spending indicate that Joyce must have found Freud's theory of anal erotism hilarious – and so it is. Yet the fact that psychoanalysis is funny does not mean that it is false; Joyce saw jokes as the royal road to truth. "*In risu veritas*," he quipped; in laughter, as in wine, the truth will out (*JJ* 703). In *Finnegans Wake* Joyce speaks of being "yung and easily freudened," although elsewhere he tended to disclaim his debt to psychoanalysis (*FW* 115 22–3). "As for psychoanalysis it's neither more nor less than blackmail," he once declared – an enigmatic dismissal, to say the least (*JJ* 524). Yet in spite of his professed distrust of psychoanalysis, he sent his psychotic daughter Lucia into an abortive analysis with Jung, collected works by Freud, Jung, and Ernest Jones in his Trieste library, and made intensive use of Freud's case history of the Wolf Man in *Finnegans Wake*.

Probably the first instance of Freudian forgetting in the Anglophone canon occurs when Bloom forgets the name Penrose, the name of a voyeur who used to peep through the Blooms' windows, ogling their former married happiness: "a priestylooking chap [who] was always squinting in when he passed" (*U* 8 176–9). Bloom, as voyeur to his own memories of conjugal intimacy, finds himself in the much the same position as Penrose, whose name evokes such loaded terms as pens, rising penises, and roses, the last of which is Bloom's term for menstruation, as well as a pun on his own flowery name. Bloom also utters one of the first Freudian slips in literature, when he substitutes "the wife's admirers" for "the wife's advisors" – an error which is also a "portal of discovery," given Bloom's overt anxiety about his wife's adultery, as well as his covert admiration for his wife's admirers (*U* 12 767, *U* 9 232). Meanwhile the hallucinations of the "Circe" episode exemplify the techniques of Freudian dreamwork: the disguised fulfillment of forbidden wishes, the transformation of words into things, the resurgence of the day's residues, and the fusion of these residues with deeper memories and disavowed desires, bringing forth composite, overdetermined images – all these techniques contribute to Circe's phantasmagoria.

Throwaway Economics

Joyce and Freud's mutual concern with circulation could be understood as a response to the rise of a credit economy, which encouraged spending to keep money circulating, as opposed to Victorian economics which valued saving and frugality, epitomized in Mr. Deasy's tiresome refrain in "Nestor": "I paid my way, I paid my way" (*U* 2 251, 253). Michael Tratner has argued that modernity is characterized by the "normalization of debt," consumers being urged to borrow money in order to demonstrate their credit worthiness (Tratner 2001: 9). From this point of view Stephen's accumulating debts, rather than evidence of reckless improvidence, represent a means of gaining credit for the future – although it must be granted that Stephen never delivers on his promises, whether financial or artistic, during his life span in Joyce's fiction. Meanwhile Joyce portrays Dublin as a city founded upon debt, just as the Catholic Church is founded upon doubt; both are running on empty. Out of this dearth has arisen a parasitical economy consisting of the two activities portrayed in Joyce's story "Two Gallants": gambling and leeching. These activities become contagious, spreading into the economies of word and flesh, so that textual and sexual transactions trade in borrowed words and secondhand desires.

In economics as in other perils of the city, Bloom steers between antitheses, avoiding both the Scylla of the Victorian scrooge and the Charybdis of the modern shopaholic. With regard to sexual expenditure, however, Bloom foregoes prudence in the "Circe" episode, set in Bella Cohen's brothel, where Bloom spends his fantasies as lavishly as Stephen spends his money. Nonetheless the ultimate effect of Bloom's extravagance is to balance his libidinal economy. While Joyce said that Stephen "has a shape that can't be changed," Bloom's shape is as "solvent" as his assets, since solvency implies liquidity as well as backing. In "Circe," Bloom demonstrates his solvency by changing shape with every fantasy he entertains in nighttown, lionized and porcified by turns. As Lord Mayor of Bloomusalem, Bloom promises "Free money, free love and a free lay church in a free lay state" (*U* 15 1693); as sex-slave to Bella Cohen, he metempsychoses into a degraded sow. By performing his desires as hallucinations, Bloom prevents his hoarded fantasies from festering within. In this sense he exemplifies the mores of the new credit economy, in which expenditure, whether of money or sexuality, was regarded as beneficial to the body and the body politic (Tratner 2001).

Moreover, Bloom's role as ad-man in the marketplace of Dublin is to stimulate the circulation of goods and money. This means that Bloom disseminates commodities rather than producing them, just as he spends desires in the brothel rather than investing them for future gains. Thus the only sexual act that he forbids himself is the only act the Catholic Church does not forbid; that is, "complete carnal intercourse, with ejaculation of semen within the natural female organ" of his wife (*U* 17 2278–9). Bloom prefers to spill his seed, as he does in "Nausicaa," rather than to plant it in his wife; the death of their son Rudy has imposed a tacit prohibition on reproductive sex. Instead both spouses indulge in a kind of conspicuous consumption of desire: Bloom's hallucinatory extravagance in "Circe" finds its match in Molly's profligate imaginings in "Penelope," both spouses splurging for the thrill of waste. *Ulysses* ends with menstruation rather than conception, indicating that Molly is "fertilisable" but unfertilized, her blood squandered without recompense: "its pouring out of me like the sea" (Budgen 1972: 272; *U* 18 1123). Why does Molly Bloom menstruate? Not because she represents the fecundity of nature, as many critics have assumed, but because she does not: menstruation exemplifies the wastefulness of nature rather than its productivity. To menstruate is to lose the gamble of conception – in Stephen's idiom, another "godpossibled soul" has been "impossibilised" (*U* 14 225–6).

If gambling replaces productivity in Molly Bloom's menstrual economy, it also plays a central role in the homosocial pub culture of Joyce's Dublin. While women gamble by menstruating – if we take Bloom's word for it, almost every woman in Dublin is menstruating on June 16, 1904 – men bet on horses, staking their substance with no assurance of return. This throwaway economy depends on expenditure and miracle, rather than productive labour. "Throwaway" is the name of the horse that won the Grand National on Bloomsday at odds of 20 to 1, and the name implies both waste and luck; Dubliners throw away their money, but they also make throwaway remarks that sometimes hit their targets. The term "throwaway" inspires an extended play on words: in "Lotus-Eaters," Bloom offers his newspaper to Bantam Lyons with the throwaway remark, "I was just going to throw it away" (*U* 5 534). Lyons interprets this remark as a tip about the race, and rushes off to place a bet on Throwaway. Later Bloom is presented with a "throwaway" by a "sober Y.M.C.A. young man," which announces the arrival in Dublin of the Southern revivalist preacher John Alexander Dowie, bringing the good news that "Elijah is coming" (*U* 8 5–13). Bloom throws this throwaway into the Liffey, and from then on we receive bulletins of its odyssey downriver along with other floating signifiers, such as the torn remnants of Martha Clifford's letter to Henry Flower, as they wend their way towards the alphabet soup of the sea.

The term "throwaway" also applies to Joyce's narrative method, which exploits the adventitious and redundant on the principle that errors are the portals of discovery. Furthermore the superfluity of prose to plot indicates a throwaway economy of writing – Joyce wastes words. As *Ulysses* progresses, the tale and the telling drift apart, whole continents of language breaking off from the central narrative (Deane 1994: 184). This linguistic extravagance defies the bourgeois frugality built into the conventions of the realist novel, which supposedly budgets the supply of words to the demands of narrative. Joyce's language, on the contrary, bursts out of such constraints with wild, gratuitous performances, diverting rather than propelling the plot forward. These spendthrift habits grow increasingly conspicuous, the ratio of words to action widening with almost every chapter after "Lestrygonians." Most extravagant of all is "Oxen of the Sun," where Joyce tells the story of Mina Purefoy's childbirth in all the styles of the English literary tradition, although carefully excluding any women writers. Here male words compete with female flesh, the masculine imagination with the "uneared wombs" of female creativity (*U* 9 664). At the same time, Joyce's methods of pastiche and parody intimate that "creation from nothing" is impossible (*U* 3 35); the eared womb of the artist's brain can produce new works only by means of the "recirculation" of the past.

Returns

Joyce's neologism "recirculation" draws attention to the movement of return implicit in the concept of a cycle. Return is the structural principle of *Ulysses*; based on a return to Homer's *Odyssey*, which is itself an epic of return to origins, *Ulysses* stages the returns of the repressed, the past, the body, and the dead. These correspond to "returns" in the economic sense; that is, to the profits or losses that accrue from circulation, whether commercial, semantic, or libidinal. Thus the Odyssean theme of exile and return is implicated in the economics of expenditure and restitution. Bloom and Stephen, disbursed from their homes, circulate around the streets of Dublin, functioning as objects as well as subjects of exchange, as if they were the stakes in a gamble ventured by a hidden god. A parallel between their odysseys and those of money emerges in the "Ithaca" episode, where we are told that Leopold Bloom once marked a florin with three notches and launched it "for circulation on the waters of civic finance, for possible, circuitous or direct, return." "Had Bloom's coin returned?" the nameless questioner demands. The implacable reply is "Never" (*U* 17 981–8).

Does Bloom himself return to the home that he abandons to his wife and her suitors past and present? Like Odysseus, Bloom goes forth in exile and circles back to 7 Eccles Street, but it is unclear whether the Ithaca that he returns to is the same kingdom that he left in "Lotus-Eaters." In the meantime Molly has rearranged the furniture, and her lover Blazes Boylan has left his imprint on the bed, along with telltale flakes of Plumtree's potted meat. Does this mean that Bloom, like his florin, never returns to the place where both were "notched"? (Note that Odysseus is recognized in Ithaca by the "notch" or scar he received from a wild boar.) Does Bloom's exile represent a gamble, rather than a vicus of recirculation, insofar as there is no assurance of return? Dostoevsky, in his story *The Gambler* (1866), intimates that loss is more addictive than the possibility of gain, the fantasy of winning providing a pretext for the *jouissance* of limitless expenditure. In a similar way, the ambiguous *nostos* of *Ulysses* suggests that the promise of a homecoming may be merely an excuse for getting lost along the way.

Theodor Adorno claims that "it is part of morality not to be at home in one's home" (Adorno 1999: 39). Not to be at home is also crucial to Joyce's conception of morality; only the detachment of the exile enables him to write his chapters in the moral history of his country. "How could I like the idea of home?" Joyce protests in a letter to Nora Barnacle of 1904. "My mind rejects the whole present social order and Christianity – home, the recognised virtues, classes of life, and religious doctrines." In the same letter he dismisses his paternal home as "simply a middle-class affair ruined by spendthrift habits which I have inherited" (*SL* 25). What is more, an Irish artist writing in English can never be at home in language, as Stephen discovers in the *Portrait*, since every word he writes entails an exile from his indigenous tongue, compelling him to fret in the shadow of the language of imperialism (*P* 159; 5 558–9). To vary a quip of Oscar Wilde's, the English condemned Joyce to write in the language of Shakespeare.

Yet it was by forfeiting his home that Joyce regained it. When a friend asked him if he intended to return to Ireland, Joyce replied, "Have I ever left it?" (*JJ* 704). Jennifer Levine has pointed out that Joyce's "semicolonial" predicament sharpened his awareness that we are "never at home in language, not even in our mother tongue"; indeed, language exiles us from both our mothers and our tongues, estranging us from our own physicality (Levine 2004: 129). Yet it is only through our exile in words that we can come home to the flesh – and did we ever leave it? Language is the odyssey by which we leave the body in order to return where we started, and to know the place for the first time. "Where there is a reconciliation," Stephen says, "there must have been first a sundering" (*U* 9 333). Language sunders mind from body, yet also reconciles these opposing terms, since language is fashioned by the body, by the muscles of the mouth and hand. Mouths eat and kiss as well as talk, as Bloom and Molly demonstrate in their lovemaking on Howth Head; and as for hands, when a fan asked if he could kiss the hand that wrote *Ulysses*, Joyce retorted: "It's done a lot of other things too" (*JJ* 110).

If exile can represent a form of homecoming, return can also represent a form of exile. This principle applies to the style of *Ulysses*, which tugs in two directions, towards the realist tradition in the novel and away from it at once. In some ways this stylistic tug of war aligns with the contrast between Bloom and Stephen: Bloom the husband, who honours his filiations to home and family, versus Stephen the loner, who dreams of being father to himself, shaking off the claims of kin and country. In Bloomian mode, Joyce honours his filiations to the realist novel – this is evident in the humanity with which he treats his characters, the Dickensian exuberance of his homage to city life, and the density of his allusions to his literary predecessors. In sympathy with Stephen, however, Joyce also tries to fly by those nets, rejecting his homes in Ireland, the family, and the Anglophone tradition in the novel. Ultimately *Ulysses* remains faithful to the novel in much the same way that Bloom remains faithful to Molly – by indulging in a bit on the side. To pursue this analogy a little further, Bloom's masturbation corresponds to the self-reflexiveness of Joyce's language, which offers a relief, as opposed to a divorce, from the constraints of realism. "For this relief much thanks," Bloom quotes from *Hamlet*, hilariously out of context, after masturbating on the beach in "Nausicaa" (*U* 13 939–40). Besides the sexual connotation, this "relief" refers to the chapter's brief excursion into saccharine romanticism before the language detumesces into gritty realism.

In a curious way, Joyce's fidelity to realism gains strength through his philandering with baroque alternatives. Although his stylistic shenanigans remind us that fictional characters are not real people, but "alphybettyformed verbage," or constructs of the language, we still cherish the illusion of Bloom's reality (*FW* 183 13). In fact everything that Joyce does to de-realize Bloom – mythologizing him as Odysseus, Elijah, and the ghost in *Hamlet*, breaking up and reassembling the letters of his name, and finally abandoning his stream of consciousness, with its staccato rhythm and fireworks of wit, for the gradgrinding pedantry of "Ithaca" – all this verbal sabotage only makes the hero more real and more lovable.

Part of the fun of reading *Ulysses* is playing hide-and-seek with Bloom, as his name circulates through Joyce's prose, transmigrating into Henry Flower in the "Lotus-Eaters" episode, the Lord Mayor of Bloomusalem in "Circe," "L. Boom" in the printer's howler in the *Freeman's Journal* ("Eumaeus"), and flowers in the coda of "Penelope," where Molly affirms her paradoxical fidelity to Bloom by scattering blooms across the landscape of her memory. The transmigrations of Bloom's name recall the disguises of Odysseus, the consummate escape artist who slips out of the strandentwining nets of personal identity. But Bloom's vanishing tricks differ from those of Odysseus insofar as Bloom is constantly dissolving or "disselving" into language, only to bob up again in undiminished personality (*FW* 4 15, 608 5). Even in the heyday of poststructuralism, with its bracing scepticism about plot and character, readers of *Ulysses* never ceased to think of Bloom, as well as Molly, Stephen, and their fellow Dubliners, not only as real people but as old friends.

Perhaps we love Bloom because we lose him; Freud argues that that the finding of a love-object is always a refinding of an object previously lost (Freud 1905a: 222). When Bloom forgets his key to 7 Eccles Street, he foregoes the fixity of his identity in language, his name embarking on an independent odyssey. Even the letters of his name disband, like the ragged tail of sandwichmen advertising HELY'S in "Lestrygonians," where the letters wander off in several directions, with "apostrophe S" straggling behind (*U* 8 155). Stephen has also lost his key, having forfeited his access to the "omphalos," otherwise known as the Martello tower, to the convivial "usurper" Buck Mulligan (*U* 1 176; 1 744). Without their keys, Stephen and Bloom are exiled from their homes (Stephen has already left his first home, that "middle-class affair ruined by spendthrift habits"), and both are doubly exiled in the sense that they belong to deracinated peoples, Stephen being Irish and Bloom an Irish Jew. It is significant that both their homes are associated with the navel, the natal scar that marks the infant's exile from its first home in the mother's body. Buck Mulligan calls the Martello tower the "omphalos," referring to the navel of the world where the Delphic oracle issued prophecies, while the Blooms' home in 7 Eccles Street is associated with Calypso, the nymph who detained Odysseus in "a little navel of the sea" (Gifford 1988: 17). When Bloom and Stephen leave these navels, their exile represents a birth or miscarriage, yet neither hero fully breaks the navelcord that binds him to his home.

Joyce's image of the navelcord compares to the cotton thread with which Freud's grandson, in *Beyond the Pleasure Principle*, plays *fort/da* with a spool (Freud 1920: 13–16). In this famous vignette, little Ernst throws a cotton-reel into his curtained crib, crying "o-o-o-o," and then retrieves it with a sigh of "a-a-a-a." Freud interprets these two vocables as primitive attempts at the German words "*fort*" (gone) and "*da*" (here), and argues that the child substitutes the toy for his mother in order to control her exiles and returns. The spool therefore represents a reconciliation and a sundering, in Stephen Dedalus' terms, because it connects the child to the mother but also takes her place, substituting symbol for reality (*U* 9 334–5). In Joyce's writing, the recurrent image of the navel evinces a similar ambivalence: this primal scar marks our original connection to the mother and attests to our indebtedness to origins, but also marks the severance of this connection, sealing our exile from the womb. Throughout his work Joyce plays *fort/da* with Ireland, creating a symbolic substitute that he can throw away and reinstate at will, with the help of an elastic navelcord of prose. Meanwhile Bloom and Stephen play *fort/da* with their homes; Stephen throws away his family, Bloom his wife, in order to restore them in imaginary form.

The Flesh Made Word

Molly Bloom, meanwhile, curls up with her own imaginings. Whereas Joyce's heroes circulate around the streets of Dublin, Molly lingers in her little navel of the sea, and circulates her lovers through the strandentwining cables of her memory. Sex, for all its frequency in her imaginings, remains sex in the head. By presenting Molly as a creature entirely composed of her own thoughts, *Ulysses* overturns age-old stereotypes associating woman with the body, man with intellect. Not only does Joyce bring the bodies of his male characters into the limelight, with a candour that retains its capacity to shock, but he presents his heroine as pure mind, unmediated by the external narrator. Although Molly often thinks about the body, in all its glory and abjection, this is a body woven and unwoven in her words. For all the fleshliness of her imaginings, she epitomizes the incorporeal thinking substance that Descartes imputed only to the angels. I think, her monologue implies, and thought is what I am.

Joyce once said that "Ithaca" was the true ending of the book because "Penelope" had no beginning, middle, or end (*LI* 172). Ostensibly the contrast between "Ithaca" and "Penelope" epitomizes the age-old dichotomy between the Man of Reason and the Woman of Nature. But "Ithaca" presents reason as an obsessive-compulsive disorder, whereas "Penelope" reduces nature to the figment of a sleepy mind. Ever since the beginnings of Greek philosophical thought, femaleness has been conflated with everything that Reason has transcended, dominated, or simply left behind: the forces of nature, the instincts of the body, the death-dealing power of the earth-goddesses (Lloyd 1993). Joyce identified Molly Bloom with Gea-Tellus, a fusion of the Greek and Roman earth-goddesses, and declared that her soliloquy revolves around the female body, "its four cardinal points being breasts, arse, womb, and cunt" (*SL* 285). This famous pronouncement has obscured the fact that "Penelope" takes place entirely in Molly's head. Joyce thought "Penelope" "probably more obscene than any preceding episode," but Molly's obscenities have the paradoxical effect of purifying mind from body, since they substitute sexual fantasy for fleshly acts (*SL* 285). In this sense Joyce obeys Molly's entreaty to her maker: "O jamesy let me up out of this pooh" (*U* 18 1128–9). In her role as Penelope, Molly lifts herself out of the pooh, transcending the body by weaving and unweaving a virgin shroud of words.

Earlier Stephen speaks of Mother Dana "weaving and unweaving our bodies": an allusion to the Celtic mother-goddess, as well as to the Dublin literary journal *Dana*, edited by W. K. Magee, which rejected the first version of "A Portrait of the Artist" in 1904, inciting Joyce to re-weave his own self-portrait (*U* 9 376). In "Penelope" it is Molly who unweaves her portrait as a frowsty frump (this is how she is presented in "Calypso," a self-serving distortion on Bloom's part to justify his sexual inadequacy) in order to reweave an inviolable body out of words. One of Freud's more outrageous propositions was that weaving was women's sole contribution to civilization, invented to conceal their "genital deficiency" (Freud 1933: 132). But Joyce, by associating Molly with a weaving spider, its eight legs represented by her eight long sentences, pays tribute to the "weaver" who enabled him to write *Ulysses* without starving – Harriet Weaver, who financed the extravagances of his purse and pen (Joyce 1972: 499). The figure 8 also features in Molly's birthday on September 8, 1870, as well as in the mathematical symbol of infinity, the lemiscate or recumbent 8, which Joyce uses to designate the timelessness of the episode, as well as to evoke the female bottom.

"Bottom," according to Joyce, is a key word in "Penelope" (*SL* 285). Another key word is "because," and both these terms derive from Bottom's speech in *A Midsummer Night's Dream*: "It shall be called Bottom's Dream, because it hath no bottom." Thus one of the first bottoms we encounter in "Penelope" is the false bottom that the Blooms' former housemaid in Ontario Terrace padded out for Poldy's delectation (*U* 18 56). Like Shakespeare's Bottom, Molly conjures up a dream without a bottom, only a series of false bottoms, mirages of foundations such as the mother, the body, or the earth. Up until the eighteenth episode, Molly has been sidelined from the action of *Ulysses*, making her first appearance in "Calypso" as a disembodied grunt, and later as a disembodied arm, tossing a coin to the one-legged sailor in "Wandering Rocks." Such synecdochic sightings only call attention to her absence: to borrow her own words, she represents the "hole in the middle" of the action, the aperture through which the lady vanishes (*U* 18 151). Meanwhile Stephen insistently denigrates the feminine in favor of the masculine: in "Scylla and Charybdis" he claims that maternity depends upon the flesh, whereas paternity depends upon the word and signifies the triumph of "legal fiction" over fleshly fact (*U* 9 844). But Stephen can never be an artist until he learns that the word is the product of the flesh, whereas Molly demonstrates that flesh is also the product of the word. In "Oxen of the Sun" Stephen prophesies, "In woman's womb word is made flesh but in the spirit of the maker all flesh that passes becomes the word that shall not pass away. This is the postcreation" (*U* 14 292–4). But Stephen never fulfills his promise as an artist, and Joyce gives the last word to Molly. It is she who accomplishes the postcreation by transmuting her too too sullied, sallied, solid flesh into the angelic substance of the word.

Dirty cleans.

NOTES

1 The schemata are reproduced in Ellmann (1972: 186–8). Also available online at Michael Groden's Joyce website: http://publish.uwo.ca/~mgroden/notes/open01.html.

2 *"Telemaco non soffre ancora il corpo,"* note in Joyce's Linati scheme in Ellmann (1972: 186–8).

3 This is Malcolm Bowie's translation of Lacan's description of the body prior to the mirror-stage; see Bowie (1991: 27).

BIBLIOGRAPHY

Works cited

Adorno, Theodor (1999) *Minima Moralia.* London: Verso.

Beckett, Samuel (1929) "Dante . . . Bruno. Vico . . Joyce." In *Our Exagmination Round His Factification for Incamination of Work in Progress.* London: Faber and Faber.

Bowie, Malcolm (1991) *Lacan.* London: Fontana.

Budgen, Frank (1972) *James Joyce and the Making of "Ulysses."* London: Oxford University Press.

Deane, Seamus (1994) *A Short History of Irish Literature.* Notre Dame, IN: University of Notre Dame Press.

Deleuze, Gilles and Félix Guattari (1983) *Anti-Oedipus: Capitalism and Schizophrenia.* Minneapolis: University of Minnesota Press.

Deming, Robert H. (ed.) (1970) *James Joyce: The Critical Heritage*, 2 vols. London: Routledge and Kegan Paul.

Ellmann, Richard (1972) *Ulysses on the Liffey.* Oxford: Oxford University Press.

Freud, Sigmund (1905a) *Fragment of an Analysis of a Case of Hysteria.* In *The Complete Psychological Works of Sigmund Freud.* Vol. 7. Standard edn, general ed. James Strachey, 24 vols. London: Hogarth, 1953–74.

Freud, Sigmund (1905b) *Three Essays on the Theory of Sexuality.* Standard edn Vol. 7.

Freud, Sigmund (1908) *Character and Anal Erotism.* Standard edn Vol. 9.

Freud, Sigmund (1917) *On Transformations of Instinct as Exemplified in Anal Erotism.* Standard edn Vol. 17.

Freud, Sigmund (1920) *Beyond the Pleasure Principle.* Standard edn Vol. 18.

Freud, Sigmund (1933) *New Introductory Lectures on Psycho-Analysis XXXIII: Femininity.* Standard edn Vol. 22.

Gifford, Don (1988) with Robert J. Seidman. *"Ulysses" Annotated: Notes for James Joyce's "Ulysses."* 2nd edn. Berkeley: University of California Press.

Joyce, James (1972) *Joyce's "Ulysses" Notesheets in the British Museum*, ed. Philip F. Herring. Charlottesville: University of Virginia Press.

Joyce, James (1977) "L'influenza letteraria universale del rinascimento" (The Universal Literary Influence of the Renaissance), trans. Louis Berrone. In *James Joyce in Padua.* New York: Random House.

Kenner, Hugh (1978) *Joyce's Voices.* Berkeley: University of California Press.

Kiberd, Declan (1996) *Inventing Ireland: The Literature of the Modern Nation.* London: Vintage.

Levine, Jennifer (2004) "Ulysses." In Derek Attridge (ed.) *The Cambridge Companion to James Joyce*, pp. 122–48. Cambridge: Cambridge University Press.

Lloyd, David (1993) *Anomalous States: Irish Writing and the Post-Colonial Moment.* Dublin: Lilliput Press.

Maddox, Brenda (1988) *Nora: A Biography of Nora Joyce.* London: Hamish Hamilton.

Osteen, Mark (1995) *The Economy of Ulysses: Making Both Ends Meet.* Syracuse, NY: Syracuse University Press.

Rainey, Lawrence (1998) *Institutions of Modernism: Literary Elites and Popular Culture.* New Haven, CT: Yale University Press.

Swift, Jonathan (1986 [1732]) *Gulliver's Travels*, ed. Paul Turner. Oxford: Oxford University Press.

Tratner, Michael (2001) "The freedom to borrow in *Ulysses*." In his *Deficits and Desires: Economics and Sexuality in Twentieth-Century Literature*, pp. 19–45. Stanford, CT: Stanford University Press.

Žižek, Slavoj (2003) *Organs without Bodies.* London: Routledge.

Further Reading

Adams, Robert Martin (1966) *James Joyce: Common Sense and Beyond.* New York: Octagon Books.

Attridge, Derek and Marjorie Howes (eds.) (2000) *Semicolonial Joyce.* Cambridge: Cambridge University Press.

Attridge, Derek (ed.) (2004) *James Joyce's* Ulysses*: A Casebook.* New York: Oxford University Press.

Blamires, Harry (1996) *The New Bloomsday Book: A Guide through* Ulysses. London: Routledge.

Brown, Richard (1985) *James Joyce and Sexuality.* Cambridge: Cambridge University Press.

Brown, Richard (ed.) (2005) *Joyce, "Penelope," and the Body.* Amsterdam: Rodopi.

Cheng, Vincent (1995) *Joyce, Race, and Empire.* Cambridge: Cambridge University Press.

Connor, Steven (1996) *James Joyce.* Plymouth, UK: Northcote House.

Devlin, Kimberly J. and Marilyn Reizbaum (eds.) (1999) Ulysses*: En-Gendered Perspectives: Eighteen New Essays on the Episodes.* Columbia: University of South Carolina Press.

Froula, Christine (1996) *Modernism's Body: Sex, Culture, and Joyce.* New York: Columbia University Press.

Gibson, Andrew (2002) *Joyce's Revenge.* Oxford: Oxford University Press.

Gifford, Don (1988) Ulysses *Annotated: Notes for Joyce's* Ulysses. Berkeley: University of California Press.

Gilbert, Stuart (1958) *James Joyce's "Ulysses": A Study.* New York: Vintage.

Hart, Clive and David Hayman (eds.) (1974) *James Joyce's* Ulysses*: Critical Essays.* Berkeley: University of California Press.

Mahaffey, Vicki (1995) *Reauthorizing Joyce.* Gainesville: University Press of Florida.

Moretti, Franco (1996) *Modern Epic: The World-System from Goethe to García Márquez,* trans. Quintin Hoare. London and New York: Verso.

Mullin, Katherine (2003) *James Joyce, Sexuality and Social Purity.* Cambridge: Cambridge University Press.

Nolan, Emer (1996) *Joyce and Nationalism.* London: Routledge.

Norris, Margot (2004) *Ulysses.* Cork: Cork University Press.

Pearce, Richard (ed.) (1994) *Molly Blooms: A Polylogue on "Penelope" and Cultural Studies.* Madison: University of Wisconsin Press.

Rabaté, Jean-Michel (1991) *James Joyce, Authorized Reader.* Baltimore, MD: Johns Hopkins University Press.

Sherry, Vincent (1994) *James Joyce:* Ulysses. Cambridge: Cambridge University Press.

Spoo, Robert (1994) *James Joyce and the Language of History: Dedalus's Nightmare.* New York: Oxford University Press.

5

Finnegans Wake: Novel and Anti-novel

Finn Fordham

there are two signs to turn to, the yest and the ist, the wright side and the wronged side, feeling aslip and wauking up, so an, so farth.

(FW 597 10–12)

Finnegans Wake is neither a novel, nor an anti-novel: it is, rather, both. This means there is a plot and there is not a plot, protagonists emerge but all subjects are dissolved, it makes sense and is nonsense. There seem to be characters who have histories and qualities and who interact, but these characters are rendered impossible by being stretched and multiplied over time and space, far beyond the limitation of particular psychologically coherent mortal human beings, to become hybridized gods and animals, natural forces or even domestic objects. There seems to be a specific setting: a pub in the Dublin suburb of Chapelizod, called the Mullingar Inn. The pub actually exists and has a plaque proudly announcing that it provided the setting for the novel. But it also has a condensed cosmic location which puts "Allspace in a Notshall" (*FW* 455 29) and is nowhere arrived at: "touring the no placelike" (*FW* 609 2). It is a dream, a dream within a dream, and a dream *of* a dream; but being "a wake" it is also wakeful. Like many literary dreams, the dream is an alibi for the narrative to go anywhere it wants to and represents *aspects* of dreaming rather than an actual dream. Particular historical contexts seem powerfully recurrent – Anglo-Irish political relations from the mid-nineteenth century forward to the 1930s – and yet it contains elements of universal histories, taken from many sacred texts – the Old and New Testaments, the Egyptian Book of the Dead, the Koran – and is, equally, shot through with elements of the lives of Buddha and Mohammed. Such allusions seem to give it a "high" cultural status, and yet what Seamus Heaney recently described as the "explosion of vernaculars" in *Ulysses* becomes a big bang of vernaculars in *Finnegans Wake*. The widespread inclusion of cartoon characters like Popeye, Mutt and Jeff, and the Keystone Kops, alongside comical notes extracted from local newspapers, give popular culture a significant presence. In Rushdie's *Satanic Verses* the actress Mimi Mamoulian sees *Finnegans Wake* as a paradigm for cultural relativism:

> So comprehend please that I am an intelligent female. I have read *Finnegans Wake* and am conversant with postmodernist critiques of the West – i.e. that we have here a society capable only of pastiche: a "flattened" world (Rushdie 1998: 261).

Of course the paradox here is that *Finnegans Wake* authorizes this notion, proving with this very authority that, in such a world, while everything is "flattened" some are less equally flat than others.

The *Wake* blends the past (the "yest" of all our yesterdays) and present (the "ist" of our current existence). You can turn to the West – typified, at the time, as the world of the future, of particularity, rationality, progress, and technology – or to the East – typified, again at the time, as the world of the past, of universality, mysticism, tradition, and nature. You can read it like a grasshopper, jumping about and producing your own set of musically phrased series, or like an ant, moving in sequence diligently from beginning to middle to end, to finish (again) where you began. You can read its surface as a kind of pure nonsensical but expressive sound, caring little about skimming the scant appearance of sense, or you can submerge yourself deeply, pursuing the labyrinthine trails and clues that lead to other texts or discovering hidden but connected contexts. It is ordered and chaotic, a "chaosmos" (*FW* 118 21) as it describes itself in a coinage which is gaining currency, used by Umberto Eco and Gilles Deleuze among others, as if Joyce's new language has managed to introduce new terms for perceiving a new universe.

This perspective is deeply double and contradictory. "So," as it asks, "This Is Dyoublong?" (*FW* 13 4). How do you belong in a doubling city? Your double uncannily alienates you from yourself. This metropolitan amalgam produces paradox where no certainty about truth's belonging can ever fit in. This can be comically quirky as much as creepily unsettling. Either way, paradox is raised to a principle. Duality, binarism, dialectic, and two-ness are reflected in various paired characters: in the "twinsons" Shem and Shaun, in the parents HCE (father) and ALP (mother) doubled as the two servants Sackerson and Kate, the daughter Issy and her mirror-image, the conflicts between HCE and the people. (We will hear more about these later.) This principle may not be affirming the crude binarism of our thinking, so much as critically mocking it. There is moreover a challenge inside this radical contradiction: it must contradict itself, so that, at points, rather than being irremediably split it can also be unbrokenly singular and unified or, yet again, diversely multiple. Joyce sources this principle to Bruno's doctrine of the "coincidence of contraries" and "identity of opposites": the twins, as Joyce writes in a letter to his patroness, Harriet Shaw Weaver, are an embodiment of the Brunonian doctrine which Joyce described as "a kind of dualism – every power in nature must evolve an opposite in order to realise itself and opposition brings reunion" (*LI* 225).

Duality and Criticism

Reflecting this duality *Finnegans Wake* has divided critics. Its disregard for convention has alienated readers so that it appears to them as a philological curiosity, a waste of genius. But for others this negation is revolutionary. It is possible further to group the appreciative critical reaction into two large categories in an operation which is, like all binarisms, a way of managing or crudely mismanaging the enormously varied response to it. Dual approaches were identified in one of the first and most influential essays on *Finnegans Wake*, Samuel Beckett's 1929 "Dante . . . Bruno. Vico . . Joyce" from the collection *Our Exagmination . . .*:

> The conception of Philosophy and Philology as a pair of nigger minstrels [. . .] is sooth-ing, like the contemplation of a carefully folded ham-sandwich. [. . .] Giambattista Vico insisted on complete identification between the philosophical abstraction and the empir-ical illustration (Beckett 1929: 3).

In the history of the *Wake*'s reception there have been, on one hand, theoretical, ab-stracted responses to Joyce's writing as a series of experimental investigations into problems of form, language, history, identity, faith, fallenness, rationality, the un-conscious and the subconscious, memory, desire, universality, technology, the family, the human, and so on. On the other hand, there is the empirical, scholarly, genetic, source-hunting, annotative, closely text-based work, that might provide or assist exegesis. The "complete identification" of the two that Beckett sees in Vico is rare, but of course the two approaches can combine. Like the challenge of the work of thinking binary opposition into simultaneous combination, the critical challenge is to take up these approaches simultaneously. This chapter responds to this challenge by making a preliminary theoretical investigation into the *Wake*'s relation to Nature while also making, philologically, certain hidden structures of the *Wake* explicit.

Perhaps because Joyce wrote in Paris, and because of a powerful strain of Heidegge-rian philosophy there, many philosophical responses emerged in France. Writers, many now canonical in "theory," such as Jacques Lacan, Phillippe Sollers, Gilles Deleuze, Jacques Derrida, Hélène Cixous, and Julia Kristeva, found in *Finnegans Wake* a para-digm for certain kinds of thinking and writing which they were pursuing – especially in terms of language and the subconscious, the dissolution of the subject and of the human, the deferral of meaning and the overturning of "philosophies of presence." Their responses stem from an immediate grasp of the distorted linguistic surface of *Finnegans Wake*, rather than from any detailed scholarly investigation of its depths. Its symbolic form, achieved through its extraordinary crashing together of words and lan-guages, is sufficient provocation for philosophically exploring it. Just as "theory" has been influential in literary criticism generally, theoretical approaches have influenced the reception of the *Wake* and are still felt in work which makes general comments about the "language" of the book, which seeks to deny traditional novelistic elements like plot or character, and may adopt a studied indifference to exegetical techniques or source-hunting.

Arguably, the tide of such responses has receded. The freshest, most recent, work has appeared from the philological camp with the publication of the *"Finnegans Wake* notebooks at Buffalo." This is a culmination of the philological strain that appeared first in some of Joyce's own letters. The edition transcribes Joyce's notes and shows, where it can, their sources in other texts and the destinations of the notes as they were transferred into Joyce's drafts.

There has existed rivalry between these two camps which, in their mutual hostility, resemble the twins of the novel who resent each other. As the Mookse and the Gripes they exchange insults:

— Unuchorn!
— Ungulant!
— Uvuloid!
— Uskybeak!

(*FW* 157 3–6)

Roland McHugh, for instance, in his recent third edition of the *Annotations to Finnegans Wake* talks about theory as "vapid" and "fashionable" (McHugh 2005: vii), while the pursuit of exegesis and interpretation is seen as counter to Joyce's entire project: "Joyce worked seventeen years to push it away from 'meaning' adrift into language: nothing is to be gained by trying to push it back" (Kenner 1987: 304). One thing that unites all criticism of the *Wake* is a sense of incompleteness. *Exagmination . . .* came out ten years before *Finnegans Wake* was completed, so the writers were working only with fragments that were yet to receive heavy rounds of revision, and new episodes were still to be attached. Though criticism is now able to work with a book completed and published some 70 years ago, and which, textually, is far less of a muddle than *Ulysses*, we still share with that early criticism this problem or opportunity of incompleteness. In spite of the impossibility of encompassing the work, there is an enduring fear about its totalization and the reduction of its mystery through the philological approach. This fear often puts any knowledge about *Finnegans Wake* under suspicion.

Finnegans Wake lays the ground for this suspicion. Knowledge itself seems always already to have been ironized in various set pieces, such as the "quiz" chapter of I.6, or the "enquiry" of III.3, where four old fishermen are keen to divide up their catch: "spreading abroad on their octopuds their drifter nets, the chromous gleamy seiners' nets" (*FW* 477 11–12). Pursuits and displays of knowledge seem aggressive, anal, and ultimately overwhelmed, while the asking of unanswerable riddles, like "when is a man not a man?" (*FW* 170 5) is admirably cunning and subversive. Unwilling to categorize or identify, a romantic reading of *Finnegans Wake* would prefer to leave it in a wilderness "versts and versts from true civilisation" (*FW* 81 15). Such a reading would rather draw on and replicate in some parallel manner its obscurity and unreadability, as some notable responses have done, like that of John Cage's *Roaratorio*. Knowledge would detract from an anti-aesthetic in the work, described as the "KAKAO-POETIC [. . .] OF THE UNGUMPTIOUS" (*FW* 308 R2), and from its aim to disturb, disrupt, and challenge the reader to be thrilled by slopping masochistically about in its undifferentiated mass of "bogoakgravy" (*FW* 171 1). As Mme Raphaël, the person given the task of copying out Joyce's *Finnegans Wake* notebooks, said anxiously, "sometimes I feel as if I were floundering in a bog." To which Joyce replied, "Oh well, you have understood better than most people will after it is finished" (*JJ* 683). The failure to understand becomes a form of understanding and promotes a resistance to understanding.

Understanding it like this, as a wild natural object to be experienced rather than as a constructed text to be understood, turns the signs of its words and sentences into entities. The poet Basil Bunting vigorously expressed his feelings that such an art could imitate nature successfully enough to become like a natural thing:

> There are the Alps. What is there to say about them?
> They don't make sense. Fatal glaciers, crags cranks climb,
> jumbled boulder and weed, pasture and boulder, scree
>
> (Bunting 2000: 132)

Bunting was writing of Pound's *Cantos*, but his words can be applied to *Finnegans Wake* insofar as its mountainous difficulty makes it another modernist "moraine" whose long-term effects, like those of glaciers, will be felt far beyond our lifetime. Such "challenging" work courts difficulty in order to be separated from everyday linguistic signifying practice and to become a "thing itself" where "form *is* content, content *is* form" (Beckett 1929: 27). This critically early "deconstruction" of the text's referentiality sets up a tradition of experiencing, rather than reading, the text. This received corroboration in a response by critic Jean Cassou:

> Never has art approached nature so closely, or produced a work which resembled it so closely. One advances across its formidable noise as one would do across a world, across the world. . . . It is a concrete thing, organic, living with its own life . . . (Deming 1970: 471)

Knowledge will threaten such an "organic, living" world and our experience of it. It will subjugate it as territory and then set up fearsome defenses and passwords only known by an elite.

The "War on Language" as a Defense of "Active Nature"

This "organic, living" thing, this "bog," were the welcomed consequences perhaps of the "war on language" which Joyce said he had declared (*LI* 237). We might hazard reasons for this war: a romantic revenge against the acts of aggression done to the natural universe by language. Unable to evoke nature's particularity or its entirety, language fails reality and skews our perception of both. That language and nature might be incompatible appears in the famous (though flawed) work by sinologist Ernest Fenollosa:

> A true noun, an isolated thing, does not exist in nature. Things are only the terminal points, or rather the meeting points of actions, cross-sections cut through actions, snapshots. Neither can a pure verb, an abstract motion, be possible in nature. The eye sees noun and verb as one: things in motion, motion in things (Fenollosa 1973: 18).

This incompatibility becomes confrontational when our habit of producing and dealing with the isolated entities of words projects onto nature an idea of it too consisting of isolated things. This projection leads, according to a Romantic critique of human alienation from nature, to our large-scale division and exploitation of its spoils. Joyce was aware of Fenollosa's theories through their being championed by his friend Ezra Pound. Using his widespread technique of distorting allusions, Joyce reworked Fenollosa for one of the four old men analysing Yawn: "for if we look at it verbally perhaps there is no true noun in active nature where every bally being [. . .] is becoming in its owntown eyeballs" (*FW* 523 9–12). A language which wages war on language in order not to be made up of "true nouns," might manage to collapse this distinction and reflect nature or, at least, being "naturally" nonsensical, have no instrumental pretensions upon it. Straight true nouns may well seem to appear in *Finnegans Wake*, as on the first page with the words "Howth Castle" (*FW* 3 3), but these very quickly stop communicating an "isolated thing," since it is at once a building and the symbol of a person (as we shall see). And what kind of a "true noun" is that first composite word, "riverrun" (*FW* 3 1)? Neither a river nor a run, it is a nonce and nonsensical word, called into existence out of a nothingness which, at the moment it is called up, it evokes. What prevents "nouns" from being true in *Finnegans Wake* is both the potential multiplicity and nullity of their referentiality. *Finnegans Wake* hopes to reflect the way the universe of nature is meaningless but becomes infinitely meaningful.

"Active nature" is, moreover, a translation of Spinoza's term *natura naturans*, nature in the process of producing itself, sometimes rendered as "nature naturing." For Spinoza this processive nature is, paradoxically and counterintuitively, the eternally *un*changing being, God. God is not to be imagined as a distinct being producing the world, as Blake imagined a God-like Newton, wielding compasses to produce the world, but that which produces itself. A profane theology of nature emerges here that blends heresies with inversions of orthodoxies. What could be called his heretical Spinozistic pantheism can be gathered from remarks Joyce made in conversation:

> the parable of the lilies of the field touches on a deeper note, but one wonders why that parable was not taken further, and why the great subconscious life of Nature was ignored, a life which without effort reaches to such great perfection. . . . Nowadays the churches regard the worship of God through nature as a sin (Power 1999: 48).

Knowledge and the Resilience of Nature

The suspicion of knowledge as a means to grasp the work demonizes knowledge as necessarily abusive and panoptical power. This romantic reading fears for the book being tamed and disciplined. But this grows out of a fear of a totalization which, as mentioned above, can never come into being around the *Wake*. Knowledge of the *Wake* does not lead to total explanation, though it might qualify both philosophical and philological responses to it. The philological work of "textual genetics," as found in the edition of the notebooks, may provide facts (like the source of a quote in Fenollosa) but it cannot explain how the whole thing works or how to interpret such facts. The relations of textual unit to original context and to the context of its transferral are extremely varied and often difficult or impossible to determine. The facts that are garnered from the book, far from reducing the text, increase the ways in which the work can be approached.

With a sense that gaining knowledge of the text is defensible, I will now turn to two aspects that might be thought of as conventionally novelistic: plot and character. In providing knowledge about them, however, it will soon be seen how unconventional they are.

"Look at all the plotsch!" (*FW* 81 2)

The stories can be grouped into two areas: the early Irish sketches, and Earwicker's fall and family.

1. Irish sketches (1923)

Joyce set off on his new novel shortly after finishing *Ulysses* by making copious notes. In 1923 he drafted several sketches which make use of stereotypical icons of Irish culture who can be imagined as players in a comedic retelling of Irish history. The sketches often make use of philosophical discourse. They describe, roughly in order of their composition: 1) an old man, called "King Roderick," the last King of All Ireland, drinking the booze left by party guests, before slumping into a stupor; 2) a secret assignation between modernized versions of Tristan and Isolde, the former a rugby-playing college boy who quotes Byron and Hegel, the latter a flirty teenage "flapper"; 3) St. Kevin, a too-clean-to-be-true, fifth-century hermit who carefully isolates himself from the world on a small lake-island before making himself a baptismal tub; 4) a philosophical clash of visionary idealisms between an indigenous druid identified with the "immaterialist" Berkeley and a colonial missionary, St. Patrick, who brought Christianity to Ireland; 5) an encounter between a king and his subject who is supplied with the nickname "Earwicker" because he is catching earwigs out in his garden; 6) four old men, evoking the four "Annalists of Ulster," remembering their youth, and apparently promoting a theory of history which overlaps with "Vico and Hegel" (*LI* 406). Some other sketches have only recently, excitingly, come to light, bought by the National Library of Ireland in March 2006.

Joyce put several of these sketches aside, waiting for them to "fuse" in their own time. Nonetheless he would draw heavily on their themes and phrasing as he went on with his sketches, but he did not find "resting places" for many of the sketches themselves until the last stages of composition where some, it seems, were hurriedly adapted for the book that had grown without them.

2. Earwicker's fall

One reason for laying them aside seems to have been that the fifth of these sketches led to a series of other sketches that were closely linked to it. This sketch happened to be the one about a non-Irish character, the man given the name of "Earwicker," which Joyce picked up on a summer visit in 1923 to the English seaside resort of Bognor Regis. Joyce transfers this character with his Saxon-sounding name to Ireland, so he can symbolize both the invader and the settled outsider. Two related plots emerged from Earwicker: one concerned his fall and the other a defense of him in a letter written by his wife. Massively expanded, together these came to form the thinly threaded main plot that stretches over *Finnegans Wake* chiefly in Books I and III.

> a Woman of the World who only can Tell Naked Truths about a Dear Man and all his Conspira-
> tors how they all Tried to Fall him Putting it all around Lucalizod about Privates Earwicker and
> a Pair of Sloppy Sluts plainly Showing all the Unmentionability falsely Accusing about the Rain-
> coats (FW 107 3–7).

Anna Livia's letter, possibly a forgery or written down from Anna's dictation by one of their sons, Shem, is supposed to be delivered by the other son, Shaun. But, as we see in Book III, its delivery is repeatedly stalled. It is eventually discovered by a hen picking over a rubbish tip. It is described throughout one whole chapter (I.5), though its contents remain obscure. When it is finally presented (in Book IV) it is inarticulate and unconvincing, and will arrive too late even should it arrive at all: Earwicker is in fast decline. An alternative to the letter follows in the form of a monologue where she finally realizes his weaknesses: "All your graundplotting and the little it brought!" "I thought you were all glittering with the noblest of carriage. You're only a bumpkin. I thought you the great in all things, in guilt and in glory. You're but a puny" (*FW* 624 12–13, 627 21–4). But this realization is too late for her too, for she is in fast decline herself. Having momentarily risen above her husband she has to bow down to the inevitable arrival of death.

As with all versions of history, this story is made out of a tiny set of fragments selected from a whole, which is made of many other fragments. Others could have been chosen to produce a different narrative and therefore a different "message." It is certainly true, as it has often been observed, that the density and obscurity of the text militates against narrative. Nonetheless readers' drives to narrative should not be limited as much as they have been when it comes to the *Wake*. The construction of stories from within *Finnegans Wake* by readers themselves could be encouraged: it is an excellent example of a "*scrip-tible*" or "writable" text, using Roland Barthes's coinage. This liberating approach to texts can at the same time target narrative, as a tyranny of linearity that constrains readers from accessing a novel's "scriptability." But this view has in turn constrained readers' potential to write and rewrite stories of which there are many waiting to be told: with, through, and about *Finnegans Wake*.

Another constraining or constrained aspect of the so-called "traditional" novel is the existence of characters. The idea that characters are a restraint can be found in such statements as this by the writer Nathalie Sarraute in interview:

> Character, in my point of view, exists only as a deception, a facade; all that counts are the interior movements. In my later works even the facade of characters no longer exists: there are only consciousnesses where these tropisms are produced (Sarraute 1980).

As if in response to this type of view, there has been a backlash against the presence of characters in *Finnegans Wake*, something analyzed extensively by Adaline Glasheen in the late 1950s and onwards. But Sarraute's view is not much like the views Joyce expressed about his characters, nor do their novels resemble each other. So, again, with this brief defense of character in place, I will now attempt to draw an outline.

"All the charictures in the drame" (*FW* 302 32)

According to a reading of the quiz chapter of I.6, there are 12 characters or categories in *Finnegans Wake*: scarcely individuals, but rather "cumulative" or "composite" types. They have multiple incarnations that appear through different historical periods and different fictional universes to the point of blurring any defining edges they might manage to generate. They can be interpreted genealogically in a related series, or as fragments of a multiple or splitting personality, or as dream versions of a particular dreaming individual. Finnegan, Earwicker, and Haveth Childers Everywhere could be Mr. Porter's dream versions of himself as he sleeps; and Anna Livia an idealized dream version of his wife. Taken together they can be seen as the ironic subversion of attempts to present types as individuals. In the quiz they appear in the following order:

1:	E	HCE
2:	△	ALP
3:	□	The Title
4:	×	The Four
5:	S	Sackerson
6:	K	Kate
7:	O	The Twelve Customers
8:	⌒	The Twenty-eight Maggies
9:	⊕	The Vision
10:	⊥	Issy
11:	∧	Shaun
12:	⊏	Shem

The strange hieroglyphs are known as "sigla," which Joyce used in his notes to keep his "brains from falling about" (*LI* 216). Here are more details about each one:

1. HCE. See for example I.1 4–10, I.2–I.4, 126–39, 220, 355–8, 380–2, 532–54, and 564

"HCE" are the initials of the father, introduced as Humphrey Chimpden Earwicker. One clue in the quiz is that he is a "myther rector" (*FW* 126 10), an erector of myths, or an institutional cleric (a "rector") who puts mothers and myths to rights. He corresponds to large quantities of matter – a mountain, a city, a giant, and the producer of that matter too, so he is a founder of cities, a builder of roads, towers, and bridges. At the end of Book III Chapter 3 he boasts of these attributes, erecting myths of himself. But, like an insect (specifically, in his case, an "earwig") he is also insignificant and filthy, absorbed in the very matter he produces. In Book II Chapter 3 a confession of his fallenness is analogous to a fall of a huge pile of excrement: "Fall stuff" (*FW* 366 30). In various guises or incarnations, he has overindulged and become fat ("Falstaff"), has a hunchback and a stutter, stereotypically qualities of one who is guilty, embarrassed, or ashamed. At the start of the novel he is the bibulous builder of an Irish Babel, Tim Finnegan, while by the end he is the harassed innkeeper Mr. Porter. He is also associated with various British, Irish, or Anglo-Irish figures – like King Roderick O'Conor, the Duke of Wellington, Parnell, Oscar Wilde. His character absorbs other zealous heroes like Noah, the British Victorian journalist William T. Stead, Prime Minister Gladstone, imperial military commanders or even God himself. When he is Mr. Porter, there is an extended analogy between his bottom and Phoenix Park, both being very large examples of their kind. As well as a human, an insect, and a geological form, he has multiple "acronymic" identities that have in common, as initials, the letters H, C, and E. There are hundreds of these verbal incarnations: "He Can Explain," the "hubbub caused in Edenborough," "Howth Castle and Environs," "Here Comes Everybody," "Hang coersion everyhow!" and the hydrocarbon: H_2CE_3 (*FW* 95 12), smelly because it resembles H_2S. He is married to ALP.

2. ALP. See for example I.8 and 139, 220, 293, 615–28

ALP is Anna Livia Plurabelle, the mother. She is the River Liffey, the river which Dublin straddles. In the answer to Shem's riddle, she is a "dam night garrulous" (*FW* 139 18). Her qualities seem to balance those of her husband: "If Dann's dane, Ann's dirty, if he's plane she's purty, if he's fane, she's flirty" (*FW* 139 22–3). So where he is the bright day in which schemes, lines, and plans are drawn up, where work gets done and boasted of, but also where crimes come to light, she may be the murky night in which lines are blurred, work is undone, crimes are concealed, and sins are forgiven.

As a river she is associated with flowing volubility, the transience of speech and flux. She is also a force that makes civilization possible (by making fertile flood plains, and being a channel both for trade into interiors and out to lands beyond). ALP's grandiose incarnations are as Queens Victoria and Cleopatra, but in her association with the prankquean (pp. 21–3) she is an outlaw, quick, Irish, naughty, subversive; Joyce used the adjectives "Devious [and] shallow" to describe her (*LI* 302). Like Molly Bloom, she is shrewd but uneducated, happy to read romances (*FW* 28 26–7), indifferent to intellect. Complementing her husband, she defends and hopes to rescue him through her letter; she indulges him when he is miserable, cooking him omelettes which he ungratefully throws at her (*FW* 199 16–27), and even gets prostitutes round to cheer him up (*FW* 200 29–30). She is resourceful and gives out presents (*FW* 209 27 ff), though Joyce described these as the "ills flesh is heir to" (*LI* 302). Through all this she can be read then as an embodiment of patriarchy's traditional idealized female as a robust, generous, and forgiving figure, a feminized nature serving the ends of man, a "little oldfashioned mummy" (*FW* 194 32–3), whose time should by now be up. As with the initial letters of HCE, the letters A, L, and P are made to stand for many things, like "Auld Letty Plussiboots" (*FW* 415 3), "Annshee lispes privily" (*FW* 571 26) or "ambling limfy peepingpartner" (*FW* 580 25–6). We hear from her directly in the lengthy closing monologue that rounds up the novel – for many, its most beautiful extended passage.

As Mr. and Mrs. Porter, HCE and ALP make love, but unsatisfactorily, and, as they do so, the text teases them by making satirical use of the language of cricket commentary.

3. The Title, or Square

The third question in the quiz concerns the title of the novel, something Joyce, a compulsive riddler like Shem, kept secret from everyone except his wife Nora. He teased his generous patron Harriet Shaw Weaver about it, as an only partially successful ruse, to keep up her flagging interest in the novel. The square symbol for the novel (or for the title that stands for it) can stand for a house, a pub, an asylum, a hospital – any institutional edifice. Like this square the novel has four "sides," though they're far from equal, "I am making an engine with only one wheel . . . The wheel is a perfect square!" (*LI* 251). The title itself, *Finnegans Wake*, finally guessed in August 1938, is "nothing Grand nothing Splendid" (*FW* 140 03–4), an indication of a kind of lowliness that is consistent with the song that the title steals from: "Finnegan's Wake." This was an Irish-American comic song from the 1860s about a builder who is thought to have died but whose corpse, lying at his own wake, nonetheless stirs when whiskey is spilled and splashes on his face (*JJ* 708). Joyce transformed the title of the song by removing the apostrophe. The title then becomes a sentence in which Finnegans (the plural noun) do (verb in the present tense) wake up.

4. The Four. See for example 13–14, II.4, III.3, and III.4

The fourth question in the quiz asks us to consider four old men, at this point embodied as the four main cities of Ireland: Dublin, Cork, Galway, and Belfast. Sharing the names Matthew, Mark, Luke, and John with the biographers of Christ, they are associated with ancient mediums of Christian revelation, and represent quests for historical truth. Yet they are also associated with being lost in the past and getting blotto. Their siglum points to Christ's crucifixion and to the four points of the compass, each being assigned one of these points: Matthew is North and Ulster (and it is not too hard, in III.3, to hear his Belfast accent), Mark is South and Munster, Luke is East and Leinster (making him probably a Dubliner), and John is Connacht, a province which includes Galway.

They feature as judges at a trial, detectives in a criminal investigation, four ancient historians, psychoanalysts, psychical researchers. Joyce figured them first as four old men tut-tutting over youthful illicit sexuality, as they spy on a tryst at night between the teenagers Tristan and Isolde, while also recalling their own youthful sexual exploits (II.4). They are associated with great age, as old as the geographical forms of the four cardinal corners or "waves" of Ireland. Their most extensive appearance is in III.3 where they hold a "starchamber quiry" over the character Yawn (a version of "Shaun").

Watchful and nosy, Matthew is their leader, the most aggressive of the interrogators, reflecting perhaps the economic power in the North, its wealth stemming from the shipbuilding in Belfast's docks. But in III.3 they are all eventually dumbfounded by their witness whose extraordinary facility of ventriloquial transformation reduces them until all they are capable of is a drunken acquiescent hiccuping:

— Hoke!
— Hoke!
— Hoke!
— Hoke!

(*FW* 552 31–4)

5. S. See for example 141, 221, 429, 530, 556

"Sackerson" would appear to be HCE's servant or his servile flip side. His is a small role: he is "unconcerned in the mystery" (*FW* 221 10). He serves drinks in the pub, cleans up after the customers and clears the rubbish out through the town. His job of cleaning extends to the moral zone where, as a night watchman, he seems to police sexual activities and is therefore given the name of "seequeerscenes" (*FW* 556 24). As the "blond cop" (*FW* 186 17) "constable Sistersen" (*FW* 186 19) he is ordered to defend Shem from attack, but is as likely to be spying on him. There is something melancholic and misanthropic about him: he is heard at one point producing the following garbled message:

— *Day shirker four vanfloats he verdants market.*
High liquor made lust torpid dough hunt her orchid.

(*FW* 530 23–4)

This nonsense transcribes sounds that he produces but the actual misunderstood words behind them are the following from Ibsen's *Tim min Ven Revolutions-Taleren*:

I sorger for vandflom til verdensmarken.
Jeg laegger med lyst torpedo under Arken

This, in turn, translates as:

> You deluge the world to the topmost mark.
> With pleasure I will torpedo your ark.

A policeman and a sneak, his S marks him out as the snake into which Satan was transformed, as if his snooping is what will bring about the end of paradise or a revolutionary apocalypse.

6. Kate. See for example 79, 141–2, 221, 531, 556

Kate is, socially, the lower-class flipside of ALP and, as a servant-maid, the female equivalent of Sackerson. She is associated with a busy-bee energy of cleaning and an impatience at dirt being left anywhere: "And whowasit youwasit propped the pot in the yard and whatinthe nameofsen lukeareyou rubbinthe sideofthe flureofthe lobbywith. *Shite*! Will you have a plateful? Tak" (*FW* 142 5–7). She also prepares food with the energy of a cancan dancer: "I started so hobmop ladlelike, [. . .] to kick the time off the cluckclock lucklock quamquam camcam potapot panapan kickakickkack" (*FW* 531 23–5). Somewhere beside this energy there is a suggestion of sexual dalliance between her and HCE, but this is hard to pin down. Her job of cleaning and the way she picks through all the rubbish (*FW* 79 27 ff) means she is associated with the hen who finds the letter when picking over the rubbish tip. She is superstitious: reading tea leaves, swearing with Catholic idioms ("glory to God!," "in the name of St Luke!") and sighting ghosts (*FW* 556). As the key keeper, she opens doors and winds the clock and in this is the principle of trying to keep things going: "the show must go on" (*FW* 221).

7. The Twelve. See for example 142, 221, 373–80, 496–9, 557

The Twelve Customers are "the people": twelve men of a jury, twelve apostles, twelve barons, the Irish parliament (or "Dail"), the twelve tribes of Israel, customers in a pub, representatives of guilds and citizens of the state and society. Their siglum and the number 12 – like the hours on a clock face or the signs of a zodiac – represent a certain kind of unifying circularity, a group of multiple members representing a yet greater multiplicity. They are "Murphys" (*FW* 142 29), that is, typical Irishmen. They are any crowd and the Finnegans of the title who are supposed, inevitably, to wake. During the book, however, they are often far from awake, but "ruled, roped, duped and driven" (*FW* 142 23), and as such are Gods of sleep, hence "Morphios" (*FW* 142 29). They shift between devotion and animosity towards HCE, the singular mythic hero. As the audience of the ballad (*FW* 43–5) and as turfed-out customers (*FW* 373 ff), we can see forms of social conflict between a leader and his people, or a tradesman and his customers.

8. The Twenty-eight Maggies. See for example 92–3, 142–3, II.1, especially 220 and 235–40, III.2 (430), III.3 (470, 499), 558

The Twenty-eight are the flipside of "the people," and are Joyce's portrait of femininity en masse, or rather his ironized picture of certain pictures of this. Unlike the Twelve, they are lithe and attractive, associated with flowers and dancing (*FW* 281), the colors of the rainbow (*FW* 226–7), and the letters of the alphabet (*FW* 147). They represent a pretty-pretty formalist aesthetic but often get tinged with an eroticism that is suspect because they are either too young or too old. Humbert Humbert recalls their incarnation as rainbow girls in Nabokov's *Lolita* (Fordham 1999: 100). Joyce seems first to have introduced them as schoolgirls from Saint Bridget's "national night-school" (*FW* 430) who listen to Jaun's long sermon in Book III Chapter 2. They often embody contradiction: "they were never happier, huhu, than when they were miserable, haha" as if going through some moody adolescent crisis (*FW* 558 25). They are attracted always to Shaun, to whom they sing songs of praise or mournful psalms (*FW* 235 and 470), rather than Shem, whom they despise and laugh at for smelling of drains (*FW* 92 and 93). In one of their hymns (*FW* 471) they sing twenty-nine words for peace in different languages, of which Joyce said: "This word was actually sighed around the world in that way in 1918" (*LI* 264). So they represent, again, another kind of multiplicity, but more harmonious and ceremonious, and less aggressive, than the Twelve. One of them is specified as Issy, HCE and ALP's daughter, Shem and Shaun's sister.

9. The Vision

The ninth question has a siglum attached to it which appears scarcely anywhere else in the book, a circle with a cross in it. This mandalic wheel-like form might also be what you see through a telescope or a gun-sight. Imagined in this way it corresponds to a concentrated vision of the work itself, the content or intention of the whole thing. It is the double of the square above. The question in the quiz wonders what someone would see after a day in the city ("the sooty") and were given a peek at this extraordinary thing. The confusion would be such that all they could manage would be a projection of what they seem to themselves: "*what*" asks the question "would that fargazer seem to seemself to seem seeming of?" (*FW* 143 26–7). The answer given is "A collideor-scape!" (*FW* 143 28). This wonderful word is a collision itself, of the words "collide" and "kaleidoscope" and the suffix "-scape," found in such words as landscape and seascape. In the process it combines two opposite alternatives in one: centripetal collision or centrifugal escaping. If the work is kaleidoscopic then it is colorful – more colorful than the perceived darkness of the *Wake* usually allows us to see.

The last three questions concern the three children: Issy, Shaun, and Shem.

10. Issy. See for example pp. 27, 143–8, 157–9, II.1 (220, 226, 248), II.2 (the footnotes), III.2 (457–61), III.3 (527–8), III.4 (556)

Issy is HCE's daughter. One of the old men wonders if she is "the clou historique" (*FW* 528 14), a clue to the riddle of the whole story, the character around which everything in the novel rotates. As we have seen, Isolde featured in an early sketch. The sketch was laid aside but the character remained, turned into Earwicker's daughter and the object of her brother Jaun's attention (III.2). To his long sermon she responds suggestively, "your name of Shane will come forth between my shamefaced whesen with other lipth I nakest open my thight," and requests him to "Coach me how to tumble, Jaime, and listen, with supreme regards, Juan, in haste, warn me which to ah ah ah ah . . ." (*FW* 461 25–7, 30–2). In the next section that Joyce drafted she appears addressing her mirror image, reassuring, scolding, teasing, gossiping, and fantasizing. Through this address, she seems to have split in two and one of the four analysts thinks she might be a hysteric (*FW* 528 13). In III.4 she is Isobel the daughter of the Porters, "the darling of my heart [. . .] she is so pretty, truth to tell, wildwood's eyes and primarose hair, . . . like some losthappy leaf" (*FW* 556 14–19). Often she is alone, reduced to addressing her mirror, dolly, imaginary pet, or lover – or trying to get the attention of her brothers, who are too busy arguing. Similar but more extreme than Alice in Wonderland, she dissolves and drowns in tears. The three children do all play together in II.1 ("Nightgames") and the boys compete for her, but she is made to stop playing and dissolves in tears again. She occupies the footnotes in Book II Chapter 2 (260–308). Doubled by her mirror image it becomes possible to layer her over the "pair of dainty maidservants" before whom H. C. Earwicker exposed himself (*FW* 34 19). Through that layering comes a suggestion of incestuous feelings, already explicit in Jaun's lecture to Issy in III.2 and built up in III.4 where she is "dadad's lottiest daughterpearl" (since, in Genesis, Lot and his daughters committed incest). A "clou" for the four judges, she is "clou" for critics too. Incestuous desire around Issy becomes the motive for the way the deformed language of the *Wake* is always trying to shove something out of sight. The prevalence of "insects" for instance is explained as a sublimation of a repressed but powerful presence of "incest".

11 and 12. Shaun and Shem

These final questions ask about Shaun and Shem, the twin sons of HCE and ALP. As we have seen, they developed around ALP's letter: Shem the Penman is supposed to be its writer and Shaun its deliverer. Into this structural pairing, Joyce could throw in any number of conflicting polarities and symbols: Christian and Jew, priestly preacher and poet – philosopher, angel and devil, soldier and pacifist, arithmetic and geometry, nationalist and anarchist, pure and impure, eye and ear, speech and writing, white and black, high and low, meat and fish, the frank and the fake, being and seeming, worker and layabout, space and time, justice and mercy, ant and grasshopper, stone and tree, death and life, Catholic archbishop and pagan high priest, noble Brutus and mean and hungry Cassius. Joyce used the "C" of Cain for Shem's siglum and the A of Abel for Shaun's, but in his rewrite of the myth he seems to mistrust the righteousness of the victim Abel and sympathizes with the outlawed exile Cain. This mistrustful inversion of authorized history gets extended to the fact that, being twins, it is often difficult to ascribe these qualities with any certainty. As Jacob faked being Esau, they can counterfeit each other and at times they swap positions. Rivals for the most part, occasionally they come together, as at the end of II.2 and in II.3, where it seems they plan (*FW* 308) or celebrate (*FW* 354) the demise of their tyrannical father.

11. Shaun. I.7, III.1–3. 556

Joyce took the name of Shaun from the character Shaun the Post in Dion Boucicault's 1865 Irish melodrama "Arrah-na-Pogue." Boucicault's character embodies a certain kind of Irish heroism, an eloquent and gallant Irish Catholic peasant who sings the 1798 "The Wearing of the Green," a song subsequently banned by the British during the Fenian uprising of 1867.

Another common name for Shaun is Kevin or Frank, as we see in the first and the penultimate chapters. He is a goody-goody: "Kevin's just a doat with his cherub cheek" (*FW* 27 5), and as "Frank Kevin" he is to be the "commandeering chief of the choirboys' brigade" (*FW* 555 16–17). He embodies purity and becomes known as "Stainusless" (*FW* 237 11). This transforms the name Stanislaus of Joyce's brother, just as Joyce used his own first name as Shem.

Shaun is the most verbose "character" in a book of garrulous speakers: he holds the stage in I.7, III.1 and III.2. He predominates in III.3 also but has become a medium for all the other characters. Voluble and a hypocritical moralist, he continually assassinates his brother's character and warns his sister, for whom he holds a scarcely repressed attraction, away from him. He thus resembles Laertes as he warns Ophelia about Hamlet. Into Shaun's turn of phrase and attitude, Joyce also wove in the words of one-time friend Wyndham Lewis, who wrote an aggressive critique of Joyce in his *Time and Western Man* (1927). An indication of Joyce's satirizing Lewis (and Shaun) is found in the title's "translation" into Wakese as "*Spice and Westend Women*" (*FW* 292 6). The relationship between Lewis and Joyce underpins Joyce's hilarious rewrite of Aesop's Ant and the Grasshopper (*FW* 414–19). In the original the musical and spendthrift Grasshopper has to accept that he has wasted his resources, unlike the Ant who has selfishly invested for the winter of his old age. In Joyce's idealistic rewrite the "gracehoper" gets the last laugh over the "ondt" (Danish for "evil"), as if the temporality of a musical art will outlast capitalism's spacious empire.

12. Shem. I.7

Unlike the long answer to question 11, the answer to the brief question 12 consists of just two words: "*Semus sumus*" (*FW* 168 14), meaning "we are the same." This statement of equality feels reconciliatory after all the conflict described in question 11. The brevity reflects the way that, unlike Shaun's immense verbosity, Shem is often perfunctory in his speech. He defends himself as Mercius to Shaun's Justius (in I.7) and voices the Gracehoper's verse in III.1. But after Shaun's diatribe all he comes out with is: "Quoiquoiquoiquoiquoiquoiquoiq!" (*FW* 195 6). Shem quacks because he is both quackers and a wise fool imitating a duck, as if to say with a naive dismissiveness: "nonsense to all this nonsense." Like the text, Shem initiates riddles rather than clarificatory glosses. Hence him being the questioner in I.6 and his asking in I.7 "the first riddle of the universe: . . . when is a man not a man?" (*FW* 170 4–5). Our knowledge of Shem is, however, mediated mostly through a remorselessly critical Shaun, much of whose language Joyce found in early negative reviews of *Ulysses* (Landuyt 2002). Shem is a disagreeable writer, a forger and narcissist who writes the history of the world in his own excrement on his own skin (I.7), a wastrel musician (*FW* 414), a shaman-style dancer (*FW* 462). Shaun's invectives are poisonous but clearly fueled by jealousy. We cannot really trust any of what he says about Shem: Shaun is envious presumably in part because of Shem's intelligence, which punctures many of his beliefs. An example of this occurs in II.2 when Shaun (as Frank) is unable to do the geometry problem of constructing an equilateral triangle. He asks Shem (as Dolph), who shows him how. In the process Dolph comments that the triangle resembles their mother's privates (*FW* 296 31). This is too much knowledge for Frank Kevin, who wallops him so that Dolph sees stars: "its the weight you strike me to the quick . . . I'm seeing rayingbogeys ring round me" (*FW* 304 5–9). In this narrative, certain kinds of knowledge are shown to be the radically destabilizing seeds of the conflict between the twins: that any "philosophical" abstraction (as can be found in the ideal world of pure geometry) can be identified with the "empirical illustration" (as can be found in the "practical biology lessons"). The identification is shocking as it makes explicit, in libidinous terms, concealed libidinous elements that, having been repressed, re-emerge in a misformed manner as a pursuit of knowledge as power. Time and time, in *Finnegans Wake*, the quest for knowledge and origins runs in parallel with a pursuit of sexual knowledge, origins, or power.

Answers to the quiz may end here, but questions about the *Wake* will of course continue. The introduction I offer here falls into two parts while bringing together two approaches to the *Wake* – philosophical, in which some relations to "nature" were discussed, and philological, where some of its structures were described. The latter grew out of a defense of knowledge about certain "traditional" novelistic components such as plot and character as legitimate for understanding *Finnegans Wake*. However, the challenge of the *Wake*, as indicated at the start, is that any such knowledge achieved, and any defense of achieving it, have to be considered beside a simultaneous negation of them, through that principle of contradictory duality and the identity of opposites, that may be called "Brunonian." In the history of the criticism of *Finnegans Wake* as in the narratives of *Finnegans Wake*, there is a dramatic conflict between rival Romantic conceptions of knowledge: between the Romanticism of enlightenment, in which a heroic knowledge can be a powerful subversion of all that one once held to be true, and an anti-enlightenment Romanticism in which knowledge is demonized for being that which forces splits between subjects and objects, between humanity and the natural universe. Through these splits, so the argument goes, we feel alienated or we try to compensate by becoming masters of the material universe. *Finnegans Wake* does not resolve this conflict, but presents and may then produce in us an endlessly unfolding narrative of movements that reflect such a conflict. This in turn reflects the way we are caught up in this unresolvable conflict in our perceptions of the universe itself, where we may turn out to feel ourselves as both subjects and objects, merged components of an "everintermutuomergent" world (*FW* 55 12) whilst also separated from it. The continually surprising language of *Finnegans Wake* manages to turn this conflict away from being an angst-ridden and tragic existential perception into a slapstick comic version of this predicament of human knowledge, nature, and power.

But since this dualism means that only half-truths are ever available with respect to the *Wake*, then all that has been covered here must be acknowledged as a set of half-truths too.

BIBLIOGRAPHY

Attridge, D. (ed.) (2004) *The Cambridge Companion to James Joyce*. Cambridge: Cambridge University Press.

Attridge, D. and D. Ferrer (eds.) (1984) *Post-Structuralist Joyce*. Cambridge: Cambridge University Press.

Beckett, Samuel et al. (1929) *Our Exagmination Round His Factification for Incamination of Work in Progress*. London: Faber and Faber.

Bishop, J. (1986) *Joyce's Book of the Dark: Finnegans Wake*. Madison: University of Wisconsin Press.

Brivic, S. (1995) *Joyce's Waking Women*. Madison: University of Wisconsin Press.

Bunting, Basil (2000) *Complete Poems*. Newcastle upon Tyne: Bloodaxe.

Deane, Vincent, Daniel Ferrer, Geert Lernout (eds.) (2001) *The Finnegans Wake Notebooks at Buffalo*. Turnhout: Brepols.

Deming, Robert H. (ed.) (1970) *James Joyce: The Critical Heritage*. London: Routledge.

Fenollosa, Ernest (1973) "From the Chinese written character as a medium for poetry." In Donald Allen (ed.) *Poetics of the New American Poetry*, pp. 13–35. New York: Grove Press.

Fordham, F. W. (1999) "Censorship in the wake of the *Wake*." In Katarzyna Bazarnik and Finn

Fordham (eds.) *Wokol Jamesa Joyce'a*, pp. 97–108. Krakow: Universitas.

Glasheen, Adaline (1977) *The Third Census of Finnegans Wake*. Berkeley: University of California Press.

Groden, M. et al. (eds.) (1979) *The James Joyce Archive*. New York and London: Garland Publishing, Vol. 2.

Hayman, D. (ongoing) *The James Joyce Scholars' Collection*. Available at <http://digicoll.library.wisc.edu/JoyceColl>

Hofheinz, Tom C. (1995) *Joyce and the Invention of Irish History: Finnegans Wake in Context*. Cambridge: Cambridge University Press.

Kenner, Hugh (1987) *Dublin's Joyce*. New York: Columbia University Press.

Landuyt, Inge (2002) "Joyce reading himself and others." In John Nash (ed.) *Joyce's Audiences*, pp. 141–51. Amsterdam: Rodopi.

Lernout, Geert (1990) *The French Joyce*. Ann Arbor: University of Michigan Press.

McHugh, Roland (2005) *The Annotations to "Finnegans Wake,"* 3rd edn. London: Johns Hopkins University Press.

McHugh, Roland (1976) *The Sigla of "Finnegans Wake."* Austin: University of Texas.

McHugh, Roland (1981) *The "Finnegans Wake" Experience*. Dublin: Irish Academic Press.

Power, Arthur (1999) *Conversations with James Joyce*. Dublin: Lilliput Press.

Rabaté, Jean-Michel (1991) *Joyce upon the Void: The Genesis of Doubt*. Basingstoke: Macmillan.

Read, Forrest (ed.) (1967) *Pound/Joyce*. New York: New Directions.

Rose, Danis (1995) *The Textual Diaries of James Joyce*. Dublin: Lilliput Press.

Rushdie, Salman (1998) *The Satanic Verses*. London: Vintage.

Sarraute, Nathalie (1980) Interview with Ruth Ann Halicks in *The Artful Dodge* 2. Available online at <http://www.wooster.edu/artfuldodge/interviews/sarraute.htm> (no page number given).

Svevo, Italo (1972) *James Joyce*, trans. Stanislaus Joyce. New York: City Lights Books.

Theall, Donald F. (1997) *James Joyce's Techno-Poetics*. Toronto: University of Toronto Press.

PART II
Contexts and Locations

6

European Joyce

Geert Lernout

From the very beginning of his writing career the work of James Joyce has been read in two different ways and this has resulted in a divergence of reception that he himself was in no small part responsible for. For some readers he was essentially an Irish writer, somebody who had managed to portray life in the capital of the Emerald Isle in particularly interesting ways and whose works could only be understood when situated in the literary context of the Irish Revival. Joyce's main accomplishment would then be that he had put the "seventh city of Christendom" on the literary map, that he had given voice to a city, a land, and a people that had not yet been depicted by a major writer. This is Joyce as the Irish Dante, Goethe, and Shakespeare, the great national poets who in *Finnegans Wake* have been turned into a single and sufficiently mercantile and European "primed favourite continental poet Daunty, Gouty and Shopkeeper, A.G." (*FW* 539 5–6). It is clear from this reference and from the resonance of these names that this self-portrait of the writer is not entirely unflattering.

But this view of Joyce's achievement is not without its problems, first of all the fact that he has quite a few competitors for the title of national poet, even among his contemporaries, two of them with Nobel Prizes during Joyce's lifetime. And we know that later in life Joyce (correctly) considered William Butler Yeats as the greater poet. A more important problem with the view of Joyce as a writer of Ireland is that in the most successful part of his life he seems to have openly rejected the label. Not only did he hold on to his British passport after the establishment of the Irish Free State in 1922, he also refused to join the Irish Academy that had been founded by the two other national poets, Shaw and Yeats, and of course he spent almost his entire writing career in continental Europe. During his lifetime Joyce never became the national poet, neither of the country under English rule nor of the Free State, because this is an acclamation that can only be made by the citizens of that state or their representatives. Joyce only began to be considered a valuable asset to his native country 40 years after his death. And a final problem: if he acknowledged that he had given voice to something, then it was not to a country, a people or a land, but to "the seventh *city* of Christendom." Joyce never showed much interest in or sympathy for the rest of Ireland, with the possible exception of Cork and Galway, two cities with family connections. If Joyce saw himself as an Irish writer it was, as the *Finnegans Wake* quotation makes clear, in the first place as an Irish writer *in a European context.*

Despite all of these arguments and under the influence of a postcolonial interpretation of the history of Ireland, the Irish Joyce has been quite prominent in criticism. This is not the place to argue in full with these readings, what I will do instead is present the case for a different view of Joyce's achievements as a writer. Of course the alternative is not that Joyce was primarily an English or a British writer. He did see his work as part of the general field of literature in English, but Joyce felt that his work belonged to a wider and decidedly European context.

Of course it is also not my intention to deny the fact that Joyce *can be read as* an Irish writer: critics such as Enda Duffy (1994), Vincent Cheng (1995), Christine van Boheemen-Saaf (1999), and Andrew Gibson (2002) have demonstrated that it is possible to read Joyce's works in the light of an anti-revisionist Irish variant of postcolonial theory, just as it was once possible to read it in the light of deconstruction, psychoanalysis, feminism, or even post-Thomist Catholic philosophy. But this view of Joyce's writing has very little to do with the way Joyce himself thought of his writing or with the way that his writing was read by his contemporaries, and these are the focus of this essay. The Irish Joyce is the result of an overtly political reading of a writer's work that may well have implications for academic or real-life politics in the twenty-first century, but that has only tenuous connections to the writer or to his work. James Joyce saw himself explicitly as a European writer; he wrote his major works while living on the European continent, in the context of a general European culture, and this was recognized by representative critics from within that culture.

Joyce's View of His Own Mission

Joyce always saw literature in a much wider context than a purely Irish one and this attitude is already central to one of the earliest of his writings. In the essay he read for the Literary and Historical Society at University College he began the historical part of his argument with the Greek drama that is the most valuable "this side of the Caucasus" (*OCPW* 23). Then he moves on to the victory of literature over drama in England with "the Shakespearean clique" that later came to be replaced in its turn by what he calls the New School, writers who were bound (by the inner logic of the "dramatic drama") to supplant the preceding and obsolescent forms. The stage for this discussion is explicitly international and for Joyce the old school consists of the French Corneille, the Italian Trapassi, and the Spanish Calderón (it is probably a little joke on the young critic's part that the three have "Peter" as their given names). A casual remark may involve two European artists – "Even the least part of Wagner – his music – is beyond Bellini" (*OCPW* 24) – and Joyce's frame of reference throughout is not Irish but openly European. Joyce gives Shakespeare an important role in his history of drama, but most of the members of the New School mentioned are Europeans. Both in his essay on Ibsen for the *Fortnightly Review* and in "The Day of the Rabblement," Joyce defends this New School against a hostile audience. It is in the latter text that Joyce most explicitly expresses his European allegiances: he explicitly accuses the directors of the Irish Literary Theatre of breaking their promise to produce European masterpieces in Dublin: the result is that their theater "must now be considered the property of the rabblement of the most belated race in Europe." Instead of producing Ibsen, Tolstoy, or Hauptmann, the Irish Literary Theatre "by its surrender to the trolls has cut itself adrift from the line of advancement." Irish art has no history in drama and this lack of a tradition forces it to find influences elsewhere: all of the examples of the New School are Russian, French, Norwegian, Spanish, German, Italian, Belgian. When Joyce discusses the writers of the Irish Literary Theatre, it is clear that none of them measures up to Joyce's exacting European standards: although George Moore may once have had a "place of honour among the English novelists," at present he is "struggling in the backwash of that tide which has advanced from Flaubert through Jakobson to D'Annunzio" (*OCPW* 50–1).

In 1907 Joyce explained the relationship of Ireland to the rest of the world in a lecture at the Trieste *Università popolare*: the role of his native country in the history of Europe is stressed and the idea of a true-blood Irishness rejected, and Joyce even claims that all those of his countrymen who have some degree of self-respect should leave the country. The speaker disdains the futile appeals to past greatness and closes with the thought that he will not see the day when Erin will be once again the Hellas of the north.

When we read Joyce's letters or the testimonies of his brother Stanislaus, we can only conclude that Richard Ellmann's portrait of a Joyce who was extremely critical of Ireland from the very beginning of his career as a writer is not unfair. In fact, this is not essentially different from the similar image in Herbert Gorman's biography that was corrected by Joyce himself. Gorman speaks of Joyce's first stay in Paris as a *hegira* and in his description of the young Joyce in Dublin he consistently stresses the writer's estrangement from his native culture. As early as 1902, before leaving for Paris, Joyce's sense of alienation in Ireland is compared to the words of Dumas *père* in the 1850s:

> Oh, gentlemen! you who are engaged in matters of French dramatic art, ponder this seriously. France, with its powers of assimilation, ought not to restrict itself to National Art. She ought to seize upon European Art, cosmopolitan, universal art – bounded in the North by Shakespeare, in the East by Aeschylus, in the South by Calderon and in the West by Corneille. It was thus that Augustus, Charlemagne and Napoleon conceived their Empires (Gorman 1941: 74).

Joyce's decision to leave Ireland in 1904 is described in no less lofty words:

> The desire, like a hot iron, had been prodding him for a long time. His disaffection with Dubliners and Dublin, an aggravation of the spirit troubling him since the autumn of 1902 when his brief wild-goose flight to Paris had given him – despite his poverty –

a tantalizing taste of a broader civilization, was now an incurable malady of the mind intensified by nearly all that he saw and heard (Gorman 1941: 123).

It is all too clear to Gorman that Joyce could not possibly stay in Dublin and become a writer. Young Joyce's disdain for Ireland was matched by his allegiance to "the great world that lay beyond the frontiers of Ireland": not England, "but Continental Europe, the Europe of Ibsen and Maeterlinck and d'Annunzio and Giacosa and Hauptmann where a man could write without being smothered by religious and social obligations and oppressions" (Gorman 1941: 124–5).

It is clear from the contemporary sources and from this authorized biography that Joyce saw himself as part of a European cultural context. It is all too clear from his writings on the subject and from what his friends tell us, that he felt that he had to leave Ireland in order to become and remain a writer, despite the fact that from the beginning he almost exclusively wrote about Dublin. This impression is confirmed when we take a closer look at his work.

Artistic Europe in Joyce's Work

In the stories of *Dubliners* the oppressive atmosphere of the Dublin setting cannot disguise the fact that the protagonists are all attracted by a wider world: one of the reasons why the narrator of "The Sisters" is fascinated by Father Flynn is that the latter has studied in Rome and tells stories about a world beyond Dublin; the boy in the first story of the book dreams of exotic lands ("Persia, I thought") as do the heroes of "Araby" and "Eveline." Most of these stories oppose the meanness of present-day Dublin with an alternative that can only be found outside of Ireland: for Little Chandler the exotic is London and Paris. Even the Dublin pub where Chandler meets his old friend is foreign enough to boast waiters who speak French and German. Ignatius Gallaher does not disappoint, he addresses the waiter as "garçon" and "François." The difference between life in Dublin and the world outside is clearest in "The Dead," where Joyce finally goes beyond the polemics that had already been explored by George Moore in the stories of *The Untilled Field*. Gabriel Conroy is quite like the intellectual heroes of Moore's Irish fiction, culturally sophisticated, with holidays on the Continent and, of course, clothes to match:

> — And what are goloshes, Gabriel?
> — Goloshes, Julia! exclaimed her sister. Goodness me, don't you know what goloshes are? You wear them over your . . . over your boots, Gretta, isn't it?
> — Yes, said Mrs Conroy. Guttapercha things. We both have a pair now. Gabriel says everyone wears them on the continent.
> — O, on the continent, murmured Aunt Julia, nodding her head slowly (*D* 181).

Like Gabriel Conroy, the hero of *Exiles* is a European Irishman who has distinctly Continental habits: even back in Dublin Richard Rowan subscribes to Italian newspapers.

Most of the self-portraits of Joyce in his mature work are writers who have returned to Dublin but find it difficult or impossible to remain true to their vocation. Richard Rowan himself blames his exile on the "cold blighted love" of his mother (*E* 24), but part of his decision to go and stay away has to do with the hardness of heart that Beatrice seems to believe he has inherited from his mother. His son Archie speaks Italian and the father is keenly aware of the lack of local interest in his work (only 37 copies of his book are said to have been sold in Dublin). In that context the position at the university offered to Richard cannot be anything other than a temptation. On the other hand, his friend and supposed ally Robert Hand says that Richard's Virginia cigars "Europeanize" him and he even claims that the new Ireland can only come into existence if she first becomes European.

In his notes to *Exiles*, Joyce rather pedantically makes it clear that his play must be read strictly in a European context. Not only does he refer to the inadequacy of Shakespeare and Spinoza's description of jealousy (preferring the scholastic definition), the change of perspective from the lover to the husband is supported by reference to "the lost pages of *Madame Bovary*" (*E* 150), to two contemporary Italian plays, and to an unnamed number of works by the French writer Paul de Kock. Again the stage for this play is not strictly Irish: in the notes Joyce writes, "Europe is weary even of the Scandinavian women (Hedda Gabler, Rebecca Rosmer, Asta Allmers) whom the poetic genius of Ibsen created when the Slav heroines of Dostoievsky and Turgenev were growing stale. On what women will the light of the poet's mind now shine? Perhaps at last on the Celt" (*E* 158). The characters and the playwright may be Irish, but the intended audience and the art itself are European.

In *A Portrait of the Artist as a Young Man* and in *Ulysses*, Europe and exile are even more prominently present and although we hardly ever leave Dublin, a Continental exile seems to be always an option, in the former case as the possibility of an escape from the restrictions of Stephen's youth, in the latter as a horizon, despite the Dublin *couleur locale* that gives *Ulysses* so much of its charm. In those chapters of *Stephen Hero* that have survived the theme is expressed most succinctly: in Chapter XVI Stephen's isolation in the college could not be more pronounced and the lines are drawn all too clearly. For him, "Isolation is the first principle of artistic economy" (*SH* 37), and it is on his own that he develops his ideas on art: "ancient art in this context meaning art between the Balkans and the Morea and modern art meaning art anywhere between the Caucasus and the Atlantic except in the sacrosanct region." Modern art seems to be everywhere in Europe, except in an Ireland where Stephen's fellow students regard "art as a continental vice" (*SH* 38). Despite all of this, Stephen knows he is not alone:

> Indeed he felt the morning in his blood: he was aware of some movement already proceeding out in Europe. Of this last phrase he was fond for it seemed to him to unroll the measurable world before the feet of the islanders (*SH* 39).

At the head of the new European movement in literature is Ibsen, who is the modern equivalent of Dante, Shakespeare, and Goethe as "the first poet of the Europeans"

(*SH* 46). The battle lines are clearly drawn: according to his fellow students Stephen's essay for the Literary Society is but "a reproduction of the decadent literary opinions in the exhausted European capitals" (*SH* 107), a symptom of the modernist decadence that has afflicted all of Europe, except for the Emerald Isle. For young Stephen, as for the Pope, Ireland is but "the afterthought of Europe," and in the discussion with Madden about learning Irish he argues there is nothing to be gained from a Gaelic and Catholic peasant Ireland that will turn its back on what it calls the "materialism" of the rest of the civilized world. That world is decidedly modern: an urban and secular culture that is not English but part of a wider pan-European and even "Aryan civilization." When Madden accuses him of despising the Irish peasants because they lack sophistication, Stephen replies that he admires the Irish peasant's cunning (*SH* 59). Despite the fact that the novel was never finished, it is clear from what survives of *Stephen Hero* that Stephen Daedalus, much like the young James Joyce as he appears in his essays and letters, saw his artistic mission as a revolt against the values of the culture he grew up in. His art was not only going to be part of a European modernity, he intended to put Ireland on the literary map and his aesthetic plans are just a part of what he intends to do with his life:

> He, at least, though living at the farthest remove from the centre of European culture, marooned on an island in the ocean, though inheriting a will broken by doubt and a soul the steadfastness of whose hate became as weak as water in siren arms, would live his own life according to what he recognised as the voice of a new humanity, active, unafraid and unashamed (*SH* 199).

In *A Portrait of the Artist as a Young Man* Stephen devotes much less time and space to the discussions about life and art with his family and friends, but the general outline of his relationship with Ireland and with Europe remains the same.

Stephen Dedalus is not quite at home in Ireland and from the beginning of the book he is acutely aware of his precarious position in the culture he has grown up in. His awareness of his own mission is consistently mirrored in the growing distance between his artistic ambitions on the one hand and the values of those around him, family, friends, and teachers, on the other. Continental Europe offers the possibility of a different kind of life and it is especially in his diary at the end of the novel that young Stephen most clearly expresses his disgust with the Celtic Ireland that some of his fellow students dream of, as when he writes about the deep thoughts that were brought back from the west of Ireland by one of his friends or when he mentions the spell of arms and voices, as the arms of roads or of tall ships that "are held out to say: We are alone. Come. And the voices say with them: We are your kinsmen. And the air is thick with their company as they call to me, their kinsman, making ready to go, shaking the wings of their exultant and terrible youth" (*P* 213). Stephen sees himself as a relative of the foreign voices that will carry him away from Dublin and Ireland.

Although we find out in the first chapter of *Ulysses* that the young poet's escape was all too brief, in returning from Paris Stephen has definitely acquired a European aura that is recognized by family and friends. Buck Mulligan has taken over the role of

Stephen's sparring partner and from the beginning of the book the differences between them are pronounced. Like the other Dublin tempters in Joyce's work, Mulligan proposes a project of Europeanizing (here Hellenizing) Ireland, but it is clear that Stephen believes Mulligan has more in common with his Oxford friend Haines. Buck complains of Stephen's "Paris fad" of drinking his tea black, he refers to Stephen's headgear as a "Latin quarter hat." Later on in the book professor MacHugh claims that Stephen's loose tie looks like that of a Paris communard and Myles Crawford hopes that the young writer will follow in the footsteps of none other than Ignatius Gallaher in order to fulfil the ambition to "paralyse Europe as Ignatius Gallaher used to say" (*U* 7 628).

In the discussions with Mulligan and Haines in the first chapter Stephen is exposed to the different options available to the young Irishmen of his generation but he refuses them all. He will not serve the British Crown, neither will he show allegiance to the Roman Church or the Irish cause. The native option is ironically dismissed when the milkmaid, the real-life representative of the Irish folk, turns out to think that Haines' Irish is French. Ironically it is the Britisher Haines that seems to be the only person in the room capable of speaking the language of the oppressed. For the three Irishmen present Irish as a language is at best something only for "them that knows," and more important is the cost of the milk, which the possibly illiterate woman calculates quickly and quite effortlessly.

There is a clear distinction in Joyce's writing between those who leave Dublin and those who stay behind: even the returned exiles dress and speak differently, eat and drink differently. They wear Latin quarter hats, smoke bandit cigars, drink their coffee black and put lemon in their tea. In the case of Stephen these habits are mirrored by his multi-lingual erudition, which is nowhere more evident than in the *monologue intérieur* of the "Proteus" chapter. And it is here too that we are given information about Stephen's brief Continental adventure. The young artist still rejects his native land, probably for the same reasons as in *Stephen Hero* and *A Portrait*, but the possibility of an escape (and thus of a genuine artistic career) seems to be no longer available. When he talks with the Dublin journalists and intellectuals in "Aeolus" or "Scylla and Charybdis," he is keenly aware that he is seen as a promising figure but that unlike his friend Mulligan he does not yet belong to the inner circle of young writers around George Moore, the sole representative in Dublin of the new European literature.

Leopold Bloom represents not just a new character in Joyce's fiction, but one that, as John McCourt has demonstrated, represents a type of person that belonged more to Trieste than to Dublin. Not only is Bloom *l'homme moyen sensuel*, as an uncircumcised and non-kosher Jew he is an outsider in any company he finds himself in. Despite the fact that he was born in Ireland and feels Irish, nobody else in the book seems to be willing to accept him as one of their own. When we first meet him, the sunlight in the street makes him dream of an exotic East and one of the first things we learn of him is that his wife is Spanish and that he is fond of olives, lemons, and oranges. Yet in this and the other Bloom chapters there is very little on his mind that distinguishes Bloom from all the other inhabitants of Dublin. His alterity seems to be wholly in the mind of the beholder, just like Bloom thinks of Nannetti: "Strange he never saw his real country. Ireland my country" (*U* 7 87–8). It does not even seem to occur to him that according to the same logic he himself would not be Irish. In "Aeolus" it is professor McHugh who makes the point that the Irish, with the Jews and Greeks, are a spiritual race that can only stand in opposition to the materialism of the Roman and the British empires: "We are liege subjects of the catholic chivalry of Europe that foundered at Trafalgar and of the empire of the spirit, not an *imperium*, that went under with the fleet at Aegospotami" (*U* 7 565–8). Later on, in "Scylla and Charybdis," the talk of the Dublin intelligentsia concerns itself almost as much with European writers as it does with the minutiae of Shakespeare research. Despite the fact that all of them seem to be aware that a new generation of Irish writers is ready to make their mark, "Our national epic has yet to be written, Dr Sigerson says. Moore is the man for it" (*U* 9 309–10).

From what we learn of Bloom's way of thinking, in his interior monologue, in his discussions with others, and even in his hallucinations in "Circe," it is clear that he is a socialist and secularist, who will publicly argue against religious and nationalist bigotry, if need be. In a way Bloom, more than Stephen, represents Joyce's own political and ideological position. As a relative outsider to both the church and the nation, he can comment on both, but from a distance that is unavailable to Stephen. The latter's position towards Ireland and to its place in Europe does not seem to have changed at all since the end of *A Portrait of the Artist as a Young Man*. Neither Stephen nor any other narrative instance in the book demonstrates any kind of sympathy with the nationalist or anti-Semitic sentiments expressed by minor characters such as Haines, Deasy, the Citizen, or Skin-the-Goat.

When Stephen does address the issue of his own allegiance to Ireland, he hides behind mockery, as when he tells Bloom that the latter is mistaken in thinking that he must be important because he belongs to "the *faubourg Saint Patrice* called Ireland for short" (*U* 16 1160–1), whereas perhaps the exact opposite is the case: "But I suspect, Stephen interrupted, that Ireland must be important because it belongs to me" (*U* 16 1164–5). When Bloom fails to understand what he means, Stephen replies, "We can't change the country. Let us change the subject" (*U* 16 1171). The young artist has reached the point where Bloom's socialist and anti-nationalist utopia of universal brotherhood ("Free money, free rent, free love and a free lay church in a free lay state," *U* 15 1693) is no longer attractive. It is this sense of disenchantment with politics in Stephen that may have given Richard Ellmann and other critics the impression that after the First World War Joyce himself had become noncommittal in political issues. But reading through his correspondence it is impossible to document any change of heart on the crucial issues of religion, aesthetics, or politics.

This is also evident in *Finnegans Wake*: again Joyce writes about Dublin and once more his hero is not Irish. Both HCE and Shem are foreigners: they dress and eat differently. The latter is even accused of being a farsoonerite: "he would far sooner muddle through the hash of lentils in Europe than meddle with Irrland's split little pea" (*FW* 171 5–6). The Shaun-like narrator claims that the artist figure Shem is everything except genuinely Irish:

an Irish emigrant the wrong way out, sitting on your crookedsixpenny stile, an unfrill-frocked quackfriar, you (will you for the laugh of Scheekspair just help mine with the epithet?) semi-semitic serendipitist, you (thanks, I think that describes you) Europasianised Afferyank! (*FW* 190 36–191 4)

It is in the figures of Shem and Shaun (Cain and Abel) that Joyce has most clearly pictured the artist figure that we already know from the autobiographical fiction as the counterpart of the mentality of his native land represented by his twin brother Shaun. Shem is like the other autobiographical figures in Joyce's fiction: he is "self exiled in upon his ego" (*FW* 184 6–7) and at the end of Book I Chapter 7 he is directly accused by his brother:

a nogger among the blankards of this dastard century, you have become of twosome twiminds forenenst gods, hidden and discovered, nay, condemned fool, anarch, egoarch, hiresiarch, you have reared your disunited kingdom on the vacuum of your own most intensely doubtful soul (*FW* 188 13–17).

The View from Europe

Like his writer-characters Joyce could only become a writer by a deliberate form of self-exile on the European continent and, when he continued to write about Ireland, it was with the same critical distance as most modernist writers of his generation show their own particular national or social origins. Joyce seems to have started his career as a writer in roughly the same way that he had described in his autobiographical fiction, and we have seen that the idea of what he was doing remained constant in his work until the end of his writing career. But this self-understanding was also very much part of the way he presented his work to the reading public and this is clear from *A Portrait of the Artist as a Young Man* onwards when after the final words of the novel about the hero leaving his fatherland we read the triumphant words

Dublin, 1904.
Trieste, 1914. (*P* 213)

These names and dates mark the successful attempt by the artist as a young man to escape Ireland and to become, after an apprenticeship of ten years, the writer who has become capable of finding a new way to describe the process that has made him a writer in the first place. When we read of Joyce's efforts to publish his early works, when we follow the negotiations about *Dubliners* with his Irish publishers, it is obvious that Joyce the writer has exactly the same ideas about his artistic ambitions as Stephen Dedalus. Like the other cosmopolitan writer George Moore in his Irish works *The Untilled Field*, *The Lake*, and *Hail and Farewell*, Joyce seems to have come to the conclusion that it was impossible to be a writer in Ireland. When we look at his reactions to the period of the Troubles and the civil war and to the first two decades of the Free State, we can only conclude that on this important topic he never really changed his mind.

This is also quite clear when we read of Joyce's life in Trieste, Rome, Zurich, and Paris. Although he continued to be interested in Dublin and the minutiae of life there, he was all too aware that he would never have been able to become a writer if he had not left. So he stayed away. In the 1920s he even developed ideas about Ireland that old Dublin friends such as C. P. Curran found outrageous: when in the summer of 1922 his wife and children had been caught in the crossfire between the IRA and Free State troops in Galway, Joyce insisted on considering the incident an attack against his own person.

More positively, the rejection of Ireland (in this case an objective and subjective genitive) is impossible to understand without the realization that as a writer he felt he belonged to a larger context than that of Ireland. We have already seen that the frame of reference of the young man was a modern movement on a scale that was not only much larger than Ireland but most assuredly also wider than that of English literature. While still in Dublin he was apparently keeping up with the new literatures from Russia, Germany, France, Italy, Norway, and Belgium; in most cases he even read these works in the original language. In Pola, Trieste, and Zurich he kept up this interest in European literature and he continued to read German, Italian, and French contemporary writers. It was only relatively late in his career, in Paris, that he seems to have adopted (or pretended to adopt) the Olympian stance that he did not read contemporary authors, an attitude mirrored in Nora Joyce's excuse after the war when André Gide asked about the other writers she had met: "Sure, if you've been married to the greatest writer in the world, you don't remember all the little fellows" (*JJ* 743). In reality Joyce's relations with other writers in the European cities where he spent most of his life do show that he saw not only his own work but also theirs as part of a context that included the best works by the best writers in all European languages. When he first read Italo Svevo's novels he told the Italian writer that there were passages in *Senilità* that even Anatole France could not improve upon (*JJ* 272).

Joyce saw his work as part of a European context, not as the literature of Ireland or even of what is now sometimes called "literature in English." This is clear when we look at the care he took in choosing translators in the different European countries (O'Neill 2005) and in helping his work along in all these different national and cultural contexts by advising and sometimes even choosing his own critics, an attitude documented in the case studies collected in *The Reception of James Joyce in Europe*.

One of the moments when Joyce seems to have been most conscious of the manner in which his work should be presented to the reading public was in the 1920s, when he had just decided to spend his middle years in Paris and not in London, where he was originally headed. Ellmann puts it like this: "He came to Paris to stay a week and remained for twenty years" (*JJ* 482). Although there may have been other and more practical reasons for his failure to move on to London, it was certainly important to Joyce that he found an unexpected acceptance in a Parisian literary culture that had been carefully prepared for his arrival by Ezra Pound. In his interesting study *Our Joyce: From Outcast to Icon* Joseph Kelly has claimed that beginning in 1914 the American writers Ezra Pound and T. S. Eliot managed to turn the basically Irish writer who wrote for an Irish audience into the international writer of modern classic works. It is clear that

Pound and Eliot saw Joyce's work as belonging to the same wider European context that they themselves considered the real playing field of modernist literature, not English or Irish literature. This was true not just for the way in which Joyce's work should be read but also for how it could be read. In a letter to John Quinn, Pound pointed out that "an Irish catholic with local knowledge has very little advantage over the outsider with good grounding in literature when it comes to understanding *The Portrait*" (Deming 1970: 113). Against Kelly it should first be admitted that the context that was described in the first part of this essay shows that Joyce by 1914 did not need lessons in European modernism from the two American poets. In its attempt to defend Joyce against American cosmopolitanism, Kelly's book fails to see Joyce's work in the context that the author himself chose for his work – and that is a decidedly European one.

In this context Valery Larbaud's efforts for Joyce's reputation are crucial. After the war Larbaud had become one of the influential voices of the most modern trends in French literature. His endorsement of *Ulysses* was just as important to Joyce's reputation in France as it was on the rest of the European continent, in the United Kingdom, in the United States, and in Ireland. In France it established Joyce, seven years before the translation of *Ulysses*, as a classic in the modernist and European vein. In his discussion of the French reception Sam Slote has pointed out that virtually "all reviews of Joyce's work in France in the 1920s and 30s (and many elsewhere) refer to Larbaud's essay" (Lernout and Van Mierlo 2004: 363). On most of the Continent and especially in those countries where France was considered as the arbiter of literature and culture, the publication of the lecture in *Nouvelle revue française* (*NRF*) was usually the first thing that readers heard of Joyce and it was Larbaud's portrait of the artist as a European modernist that most often established the earliest reception of Joyce's works in many different countries. Famously, Larbaud stressed that Joyce was Irish in a European and decidedly non-English vein: "He is what we call a pure 'Milesian': Irish and Catholic of old stock, from the Ireland that benefits from some affinities with Spain, France, and Italy, but for whom England is a strange land which cannot be made closer even by the commonality of language" and he made the claim that with Joyce's *Ulysses* "Ireland made a sensational re-entry into European literature." As Slote points out, this description of Joyce's position almost certainly would have been impossible without the author's own input (Lernout and Van Mierlo 2004: Deming 1970: 363).

The claim for Joyce as a European writer was not without its international impact: the Irish-American literary critic Ernest Boyd, who had published a book on the Irish renaissance, replied in the May 28, 1922, issue of the *New York Herald Tribune*. First Boyd did not believe that there was any such thing as a European literature and in any case Joyce could only be understood within the compass of "the facts of Ireland's literary and intellectual evolution" (Deming 1970: 302). Boyd argued that Joyce's work even refutes the idea that the book could be European: "To claim for this book a European significance simultaneously denied to J. M. Synge and James Stephens is to confess complete ignorance of its genesis, and to invest its content with a mysterious import which the actuality of references would seem to deny" (Deming 1970: 305).

Boyd's essay (and the controversy that followed) was welcome enough for Joyce,

who urged his friend Larbaud to answer the attack with another essay that was published in the *Nouvelle revue française* in 1925. By that time Boyd had written another
article in the New York *The World* in which he merely repeated his profound disagreement with Larbaud's *démarche* which he now described as an attempt to turn Joyce into
a "coterie author" (Deming 1970: 321). Without going into detail, this debate was not
between a sophisticated French writer and a benighted Irish isolationist: in 1917 Joyce
had thanked Boyd for his review of *A Portrait* in *New Ireland* and Boyd explained in his
essay how difficult it had been to publish a number of positive reviews of that book in
the pages of Irish nationalist magazines that were extremely critical of Joyce and of the
other writers of the revival. Boyd had been educated in Switzerland and Germany and
in a way he did for French literature what Larbaud had done for English writers. He
collected and edited the stories of Balzac and Maupassant, translated Anatole France,
and wrote introductions for Zola's *Nana* and Casanova's *Mémoires*.

The terms of the discussion between Larbaud and Boyd clearly demonstrate that
the issue of Joyce as an Irish or as a European writer was present at the very beginning of Joyce's international literary career. His status as a European writer seems to
have been equally important to the early English or American critics who do not tire
of comparing him with other European writers. Critics hostile to *A Portrait* and *Ulysses*
claim that he is an Irish Zola, whereas Margaret Anderson compares *A Portrait* favor-
ably to Romain Rolland's *Jean-Christophe* and to the Danish writer Martin Anderson
Nexo's *Pelle the Conqueror* (Deming 1970: 118) and Hart Crane finds only Baudelaire
to compare with the author of *Ulysses* (Deming 1970: 124). Although Joyce was an
enthusiastic self-promoter from the start, he could not have foreseen that the mostly
sexual "scandal of *Ulysses*" would have an intellectual counterpart with the Larbaud
– Boyd discussion, and it was especially the translation of the *NRF* piece in Eliot's
Criterion that made an impression on critics in Ireland and England. In *Nation & Ath-
enaeum* John Middleton Murry specifically argued against the notion of *Ulysses* as part
of "high European literature" (Deming 1970: 195), which he rather idiosyncratically
defines as "the artistic acknowledgement of and submission to the social tradition of
Europe." Murry sees Joyce as an anarchist whose extreme individualism makes him
"the man with the bomb who would blow what remains of Europe into the sky," but
his excessive anarchism has made him "socially harmless" (Deming 1970: 196). Murry
merely confirms that Joyce belongs to the European literary avant-garde.

That this association was important to Joyce is clear when we look at the ways in
which Joyce engineered the reception of his work into the major European countries:
Italy, France, Germany. First of all he seems to have made sure that the translations
of his work appeared in the right chronology: *A Portrait of the Artist as a Young Man*
before *Ulysses*. When we look at the way in which his work was read in those European
countries that Joyce himself took an interest in, it is clear that despite local differences
almost all of the early readers of his work seem to have agreed on the fact that this
Irish writer wrote European literature. That even without interference from Joyce local
critics could see his work in European terms is demonstrated by the earliest Italian
review of *A Portrait* in the Florentine journal *Il Marzocco*. Without Joyce's "help" Diego

Angeli read the novel in precisely such terms that seem to have been so welcome to Joyce that he translated the review himself for inclusion in *The Egoist*. Angeli claimed that as an Irishman Joyce "has found in himself the strength to proclaim himself a citizen of a wider world," and as a writer, "inheriting the most traditionalist of all European literatures, he has found a way to break free from the tradition of the old English novel and to adopt a new style consonant with a new conception" (Deming 1970: 114). The end of the review even captures some of the tone of the final paragraph of "The Day of the Rabblement": "We must welcome [James Joyce] with joy. He is one of those rude craftsmen who open paths whereupon many will yet follow. It is the first streaks of the dawn of a new art visible on the horizon. Let us hail it therefore as the herald of a new day" (Deming 1970: 116). At least one Italian critic did not need Joyce himself to come to this conclusion.

Because neither English nor French were widely read or taught in Germany, the real reception of Joyce's work only began in 1927 with the publication of *Ulysses* in translation. In his early article in the October 1925 issue of *Die literarische Welt*, Ernst Robert Curtius (a specialist in French and European literature) began by saying that many considered *Ulysses* "the *Divine Comedy* of our age" (Füger 2000: 106) and he ended with the statement:

> No matter what one's final conclusions about Joyce's work are, it is impossible to deny that as a monumental project it is much superior to the unadventurous and pretentious modernism of much contemporary literature. Its unmistakable greatness can only appear where decades of absorption in the grand traditions of the European spirit are coupled with real originality and tireless artistic labour (Füger 2000: 108).

It is not clear how much Curtius had benefited from Joyce's direct help (already in 1924 Joyce had given Curtius' name as a possible German translator of *Ulysses*), but as a specialist in French literature who in 1919 had published a book on the innovators of French literature, Curtius certainly knew of Larbaud. In the introduction to his essay he mentions that Larbaud's photo was displayed at Sylvia Beach's bookshop in Paris, which he called "the headquarters of the Joyce community" (106) and in his book *Französischer Geist im neuen Europa* (1925a) he had written about Joyce's influence on Larbaud.

For the period immediately after the publication of the German *Ulysses*, Breon Mitchell has documented the enormous stylistic influence of *Ulysses* on the work-in-progress of three prominent German modernist writers, Alfred Döblin's *Berlin Alexanderplatz* (1929), Hans Henny Jahnn's *Perrudja* (1929), and Hermann Broch's *Die Schlafwandler* (1931–2). This success among peers was almost certainly responsible for the surprisingly central role of Joyce in the expressionism debate among German and Soviet Marxists that has been discussed in detail by Robert Weninger in *The Reception of James Joyce in Europe*. Whether one rejected Joyce as a bourgeois decadent, like Karl Radek and Georg Lukács, or whether one defended his stylistic innovations, as Ernst Bloch and Bertolt Brecht did, both parties in this debate accepted the Irish writer's central role in European literature.

We may not agree with Larbaud's analysis of the central importance of Joyce's *Ulysses* in the European literature of his day, but we cannot deny two facts. One is that this view coincided with Joyce's self-understanding and the other that all over Europe critics and writers read Joyce's work initially from Larbaud's perspective. In most cases the acceptance or dismissal of Joyce's contribution to European literature had more to do with whether one accepted or dismissed the general drift of "modern" (not necessarily modernist) European literature between the two wars.

Master of Languages

There is one aspect of Joyce's work that is too easily overlooked nowadays, both in the increasingly monolingual English-speaking world and in an increasingly bilingual Europe where more and more people speak English as a second language. Joyce was an actively multi-lingual writer whose frame of reference was not just the literature of Ireland and England, but also that of France, Italy, Belgium, Germany, Austria, Switzerland, Denmark, and Norway. At least on one level, and no matter what other reasons Joyce may have had for his artistic choices, *Finnegans Wake* represents an attempt to capture Ireland as a part of Europe in its multi-cultural but also multi-lingual reality. Ironically it is this aspect of his final work that today makes the book so difficult to read. People like Joyce and Beckett who could read Latin, French, Italian, and German are a dying breed in Ireland, in the United Kingdom, and in the countries on the European continent where only English has survived as a second language. Whereas the interest in English has created a larger market for Joyce's earlier works, future readers of *Finnegans Wake* all over Europe will need more and more annotations and translations.

The evidence in his criticism and his theoretical essays, in his literary works and his correspondence, and finally in testimonies of friends and family, demonstrates that Joyce saw himself as part of a European modernist literature. In most European countries his work was read in that context and his novels were rejected or accepted accordingly. The early reception of Joyce's work in the Irish Free State shows that his major works were rejected precisely for this reason: Joyce was thought to belong to the group of modern writers in Europe. It was only in the 1980s, when Ireland began to transform itself into a modern European state, that Joyce's work was finally accepted on his own terms. Some writers seem to be too important to belong exclusively to their native country: some of them are forced into exile, like Dante; others leave of their own accord, like Joyce and Beckett. Just as Samuel Beckett is not French, James Joyce is not Irish. Neither of them wanted to be merely Irish and this might be a good time to acknowledge that both of them do belong to that select group of national poets of a Europe that now includes Ireland and the United Kingdom: Dante, Goethe, Shakespeare, Joyce, Beckett.

Bibliography

Angeli, Diego (1917) "Un romanzo di gesuiti," *Il Marzoccoi*, 12 August, 2–3.

Bloch, Ernst (1935) "Großbürgertum, Sachlichkeit und Montage." In his *Erbschaft dieser Zeit*, pp. 166–87. Zürich: Oprecht and Helbling.

Boyd, Ernest (1923) *Ireland's Literary Renaissance*. London: Grant Richards.

Broch, Hermann (1931–2) *Die Schlafwandler*. Zürich: Rhein Verlag.

Broch, Hermann (1936) *James Joyce und die Gegenwart*. Vienna: Herbert Reichner.

Cheng, Vincent (1995) *Joyce, Race, and Empire*. Cambridge: Cambridge University Press.

Curtius, Ernst Robert (1925a) *Französischer Geist im neuen Europa*. Berlin: Deutsche Verlags-Anstalt.

Curtius, Ernst Robert (1925b) "Das verbotene Buch; James Joyces *Ulysses*," *Die literarische Welt* 1 (22): 5.

Deming, Robert H. (1970) *James Joyce: The Critical Heritage*, 2 vols. London: Routledge.

Döblin, Alfred (1928) "*Ulysses* von James Joyce," *Das deutsche Buch* 8: 84–5.

Döblin, Alfred (1929) *Berlin Alexanderplatz: Geschichte vom Franz Biberkopf*. Berlin: S. Fischer.

Duffy, Enda (1994) *The Subaltern Ulysses*. Minneapolis: University of Minnesota Press.

Füger, Wilhelm (ed.) (2000) *Kritisches Erbe: Dokumente zur Rezeption von James Joyce im deutschen Sprachbereich zu Lebzeiten des Autors. Ein Lesebuch* (Critical Heritage: Documents on the Reception of James Joyce in the German-Speaking Countries during his Lifetime). Amsterdam: Rodopi.

Gibson, Andrew (2002) *Joyce's Revenge: History, Politics and Aesthetics in "Ulysses."* Oxford: Oxford University Press.

Gorman, Herbert (1941) *James Joyce: The Definitive Biography*. London: John Lane/The Bodley Head.

Jahnn, Hans Henny (1929) *Perrudja*. Berlin: Kiepenheuer.

Jahnn, Hans Henny (1930) "James Joyce: *Ulysses*," *Der Kreis* 6: 735.

Kelly, Joseph (1998) *Our Joyce: From Icon to Outcast*. Austin: University of Texas Press.

Larbaud, Valery (1922a) "James Joyce," *Nouvelle revue française* 103: 385–409.

Larbaud, Valery (1922b) "The *Ulysses* of James Joyce," *Criterion* 1 (1): 94–103.

Larbaud, Valery (1925) "A propos de James Joyce et de *Ulysses*; Réponse M. Ernest Boyd," *Nouvelle revue française* 108: 5–17.

Lernout, Geert (1990) *The French Joyce*. Ann Arbor: University of Michigan Press.

Lernout, Geert and Wim van Mierlo (2004) *The Reception of James Joyce in Europe*, 2 vols. London: Thoemmes Continuum.

Lukács, Georg (1935) "'Größe und Verfall' des Expressionismus," *Internationale Literatur (Deutsche Blätter)* 1: 153–73.

Lukács, Georg (1936) "Der Niedergang des bürgerlichen Realismus," *Das Wort* 1 (6): 53–67.

Mitchell, Breon (1976) *James Joyce and the German Novel: 1922–1933*. Athens: Ohio University Press.

Moore, George (1903) *The Untilled Field*. London: T. Fischer Unwin.

Moore, George (1905) *The Lake*. London: Heinemann.

Moore, George (1911–14) *Hail and Farewell*. London: Heinemann.

O'Neill, Patrick (2005) *Polyglot Joyce: Fictions of Translations*. Toronto: University of Toronto Press.

Slote, Sam (2004) "Après mot, le déluge." In Geert Lernout and Wim van Mierlo (eds.) *The Reception of James Joyce in Europe*, pp. 362–81. London: Thoemmes Continuum.

Van Boheemen-Saaf, Christine (1999) *Joyce, Derrida, Lacan and the Trauma of History: Reading, Narrative, Postcolonialism*. Cambridge: Cambridge University Press.

Weninger, Robert (2004) "James Joyce in German-speaking countries: the early reception, 1919–1945." In Geert Lernout and Wim van Mierlo (eds.) *The Reception of James Joyce in Europe*, pp. 14–50. London: Thoemmes Continuum.

7

"In the Heart of the Hibernian Metropolis"? Joyce's Reception in Ireland, 1900–1940

John Nash

The reception of James Joyce in Ireland has been – like Joyce's attitudes to his native country – a sometimes contradictory and muddled affair. Perhaps we should expect no less from any major site of reading but the particular historical circumstances of twentieth-century Irish life have surely exacerbated the already substantial difficulties of reading Joyce. The question of how Joyce was read by his compatriots is therefore a fascinating and necessary one, offering its own peculiar cultural narratives. One of the implications of what follows is that Joyce's work offers us several different receptions: not only does his work provoke divergent responses but so too can his historical significance be variously understood. The reputation of a major writer can offer a glimpse into the contestations of history that have structured our understanding of the past and of ourselves. Moreover, "reception" – with its implied response "after the event"– can be misleading: it is forged not only by readers but also by the contexts that help shape reading and it is even engaged by Joyce's texts themselves (which are closely concerned with questions of reading, reception, and the formation of literary value). Whereas I will show something of these complications of reception, this essay for the most part focuses on specific readings of Joyce's significance in an Irish context.

The author's well-known semi-autobiographical character, Stephen Dedalus, asserted that Ireland was important insofar as it belonged to him. It might be said from the point of view of his Irish reception, that Joyce was important insofar as he belonged to Ireland. This problematic of "belonging" is central both to Joyce's work and to the ways in which he has been read (and not read) in Ireland. It will be the focal point of the following examination of Joyce's reception in Ireland from his first published work through to the early 1940s. The following section examines the role of Joyce in three contemporary surveys of Irish literature, showing some of the differing traditions into which he was inserted. The next two sections consider specific responses to Joyce's works from within Ireland, prior to the publication of *Ulysses* in 1922 and afterwards.

Placing Joyce in Histories of Irish Literature

It is impossible to consider Joyce's reception in Ireland in the years in which he was writing without facing the massive, and massively difficult, task of placing him in relation to both the Irish Literary Revival and to the cultural project of Irish Ireland. As we will see, Joyce has variously been ignored and claimed as a Revivalist, and dismissed and asserted as a writer of Irish Ireland and the Catholic people. As these paradoxical interpretations suggest, Joyce's reception must be understood as an aspect of – and contribution to – the shifting political, cultural, and religious traditions that crossed Ireland, and furthermore these divisions that Joyce knew too well have to be seen in the wider context of Ireland's relations with Britain and its moves towards political independence. His reception then does not consist simply in a line of literary critics and writers who responded to his work; it is instead a contributory part of its contexts, a part of the living history of Ireland which can still be seen today in the government-sponsored appropriation of Joyce's image and the many Joyce-related tourist activities that adorn Dublin's streets.

Joyce's very absence from some critical accounts is itself noteworthy, for "reception" is not only a narrative of critical opinions but also a set of assumptions that govern what is *not* said. This is perhaps particularly true in the case of Joyce, for he famously struggled to be published in the early years of his career. Indeed something of the divergence of Joyce from established revivalism can be seen in the history of the Maunsel publishing press, which had been influential in the promotion of that movement over the previous decade and a half. Maunsel famously rejected *Dubliners* (between 1909 and 1912) – around the time of the release of the well-reviewed *Collected Works* of the dramatist J. M. Synge (posthumously published in 1910) – for fear of offending its readers and patrons.

Given the well-known history of Joyce's non-publication, his reception, then, also consists precisely in his *not* being read (a fact of which he was well aware). Some indication of this ignorance – a difficulty that continues to beset Joyce's reputation – might be gathered from some critical histories of Irish literature of the period. These volumes are significant not only for what they say about how individual writers were read at the time but also because, in relating one writer to another, they represent different attempts to forge traditions (and even canons) of Irish literature in the period of independence; that is, following the 1921–2 Treaty and the publication of *Ulysses*. In this way, reception needs to be thought of as an active shaping of cultural value. In his important 1916 promotion of revivalist writing, *Ireland's Literary Renaissance* (published by Maunsel), Ernest A. Boyd neglected to mention Joyce but, as we will see, corrected this in the 1923 expanded edition. Through the 1920s and 30s, when Joyce was among the most celebrated living writers in Europe, the tradition of "Irish Ireland" could implicitly dismiss Joyce as part of an Anglo-Irish literary culture whose "insolence" was "Ascendancy minded" primarily because, it seems, he lived abroad (Corkery 1931: 26). As we will see, however, in the 1920s there were also some who would propose Joyce as the exemplary figure that Irish Ireland sought (Brown 1988: 78).

Although Boyd and Corkery both slighted Joyce, they did so from differing cultural viewpoints, of which they may be taken as representative. Their initial non-engagement with Joyce is itself emblematic of the way that Joyce fell between two camps. Born and privately educated in Dublin, Ernest A. Boyd worked for a few years on the staff of the *Irish Times* before joining the British Consular Service and then settling in New York in 1920. This absence qualified him to join Corkery's list of "wild geese." He would have been a natural champion of those writers dismissed by Corkery as "Ascendancy minded." Unlike Boyd, Corkery was from Cork and educated by the Presentation Brothers; he became a forceful proponent in the Irish Ireland brand of nationalism promoted by D. P. Moran's *The Leader* in the early years of the century. After the War of Independence (1918–21), Corkery was closely associated with Eamon de Valera and Catholic orthodoxy. He became Professor of English at University College Cork in 1931. So Boyd and Corkery were politically divergent but both were engaged in the attempted formation of a critical tradition in the nascent Irish state: Boyd's second edition coming out in 1923 just after independence; Corkery's book appearing at the start of the following decade after de Valera had assumed power.

Corkery divides Irish writers into two camps: the Ascendancy writer, by which he means the revivalists and most obviously Yeats ("the all too sophisticated alien-minded poetry of the 'Celtic Revival', dead tired as it is"); and "the writer for the Irish people" – the example he gives in his famous study is in fact an Anglo-Irishman, J. M. Synge, who "although an Ascendancy man, went into the huts of the people and lived with them" (Corkery 1931: 27). Corkery suggested that émigré writers still took Ireland as their topic but did so under the influence of their new domicile: the content might be Irish life but the "treatment": would be "imposed" by "alien considerations" (Corkery 1931: 5). Joyce merits only two mentions by name in Corkery's introductory polemic: the first to list him as one of those emigrant "wild geese" of Irish letters (along with Ernest Boyd and nearly 30 others), and the second in connection with "the religious consciousness" that Corkery says is "so vast, so deep, so dramatic' in the Irish people. This bizarre later allusion to Joyce comes just after Corkery's suggestion that owing to the rigidity of moral standards in the country, "only about Irish life can a really great sex novel be written these days." Sex and religion clearly brought Joyce to mind, for Corkery immediately goes on to explain Joyce's having "gone astray" from the Church despite its nearly "holding him fast" (Corkery 1931: 20). Corkery's implicit suggestion that Joyce's writing had a prurient and unsavoury interest in sexual matters is indicative of a widespread "labeling" of Joyce – and *Ulysses* in particular – among the respectable Catholic middle classes in the 1920s. As we will see, this would be one of the dominant themes of his Irish reception; but, at the same time, Joyce's name and work would also be used by opposing positions. Despite Corkery's implicit dismissal of Joyce, his analysis of Irish writing was influential for a later, famous rejuvenation of Joyce's "national belonging" by Thomas Kinsella in the 1960s. Like Corkery, Kinsella locates a fundamental break in Irish literary tradition with the loss of the Irish language; unlike Corkery, he finds that Joyce is the "voice to speak for Irish reality" since that loss (Kinsella 1970: 65). It is evident, then, that even the non-reading of a writer can effect his later reception.

Boyd's *Ireland's Literary Renaissance* exemplifies one of the major themes that would become familiar in later critical analyses: Joyce emerges as very much an Irish writer, but one that was yet indebted to a European literary heritage to the extent that he seemed at a crossroads between traditions. Boyd's account is an overview of the Revival and associated writing; Stephen Gwynn's, on the other hand, delineates a longer national tradition that goes back to the early nineteenth century and links this English-language tradition to centuries of literature in Irish. As we will see, whereas Boyd is evasive of religious and political analysis, Gwynn stresses Joyce's cultural positioning and his relation to recent historical events. Within the emerging field of Irish literary criticism, then, we find a number of different versions of an Irish national literature and, as a result, varying accounts of the significance of Joyce.

In *Ireland's Literary Renaissance*, Boyd traces the growth and variety of what he and others called the "Celtic Renaissance," or what we would now call the Irish Literary Revival. Stating that most criticism has been "written from an essentially English point of view" (Boyd 1923: 10), Boyd begins from the reasonable premise that Irish writing ought to be considered on its own terms rather than in comparison to, or as a subset of, English literature. Yet even in this, Boyd implies a definition of what is properly Irish literature that would be at odds with Corkery's admonition that the Revivalists were somehow not authentically Irish but "servants of the English people" (Corkery 1931: 19).

Boyd's attitude to Joyce is simultaneously both respectful and somewhat slighting. In the first edition of his book, Boyd found no place for Joyce. In the expanded 1923 edition, however, Joyce is given ten pages (out of 427 pages of text). If, nowadays, that seems a slim section, then Joyce is at least given more pages than any other prose writer. Even so, he cannot rival the three whole chapters (66 pages) dedicated to Yeats. Boyd's ambivalence can be further traced in the fact that although Joyce – along with George Moore – is seen as pre-eminent among novelists and short-story writers of the period, Boyd's organization clearly implies the dominance of poetry and drama over prose, which occupies only one (the last) of his 15 chapters. Part of the difficulty of placing Joyce then, was his generic distinction from many other Revival period writers and the historical lack of a strong national tradition in the novel. Furthermore, Boyd makes clear from the first section heading of this final chapter that prose has been "The Weak Point Of The Revival" (Boyd 1923: 374). Joyce's importance for this survey of the Revival is, then, distinctly qualified. His is a "daring and extraordinary genius" but still a "tributary" to "the stream" of Irish literature. Indeed, one of the strengths of Boyd's work is its contextual depth and range: the chapters on Yeats begin with a reminder that he was not "the beginning and the end" of the Revival but also consider alongside the now canonical writers important precursors like Standish O'Grady and Douglas Hyde as well as significant but lesser figures such as T. W. Rolleston and Katherine Tynan.

As with other Irish critics, such as Shane Leslie, Boyd takes issue with the influential French critic Valery Larbaud, who had asserted that through Joyce Ireland re-entered European literature. To some Irish readers, this was to slight the country's intellectual history. The effect of the championing of Joyce as a European writer — as did Larbaud, Pound, and Eliot — was to sever Joyce from his Irish context (and Pound in particular seems to have deliberately aimed at this; he did after all write an essay called "The Non-Existence of Ireland" [Pound 1965b]). Yet Joyce's reception in Ireland has consistently brought these flights of "universal" fancy crashing back to the earth of Dublin. Indeed, Boyd already recognizes the extent to which Joyce's standing at large was being shaped from elsewhere, declaring that he suffered a "prematurely cosmopolitan reputation, the unkind fate which has always overtaken writers isolated from the conditions of which they are a part" (Boyd 1923: 404). Boyd's ambivalence continues, however, in that he both pulls Joyce out of Europe and reinserts him there. While "no Irish writer is more Irish than Joyce" it remains unclear exactly how this is the case. We are told that *Ulysses* features an analysis and "Meticulous detailed documentation of Dublin" (Boyd 1923: 411) and that Stephen and Bloom are "two types of Dubliner such as were studied" in his short stories. But the authors that Boyd cites for comparison are all, apart from Moore, European (and even Moore, of course, was heavily influenced by French naturalism): Flaubert, Romains, Zola, and the Expressionists. Boyd makes a familiar distinction between form and content in *Ulysses* which would be repeated in later Joyce criticism, arguing that "the 'European' interest of the work must of necessity be largely technical, for the matter is as local as the form is universal" (Boyd 1923: 411). This idea of a "universal" appeal that is derived from European naturalism is a point inherited by Boyd from Ezra Pound's promotion of Joyce. The precise place occupied by Joyce in relation to Irish society and writing is not argued by Boyd, whose references to Joyce bearing the "imprint" of "his race and traditions" are left vague. It would take others, notably John Eglinton and W. B. Yeats, to flesh out that imprint. For Boyd, perhaps he too could not escape the "English" perspective that he abjured, sensing that there was "no sign" of Joyce's influence in Ireland but that his "daring technique" found followers across the Irish Sea (Boyd 1923: 7). Joyce, then, remains an enigmatic figure in Boyd's survey, both the fulfillment of the promise of George Moore and not quite securely placed. Surely Boyd's evasion of Joyce's relationship with the Church lay behind his inability to define his role in relation to the Revival: the distinctiveness of Joyce's Catholic heritage providing him with a formal means and intellectual context that would have enabled that relationship to be more fully analyzed.

Others, however, found Joyce's Catholic background and subject matter to be central to his importance. In a newspaper article first published in 1923, Stephen Gwynn saw Joyce as "the first notable force to appear in it [Irish literature] from the Catholic population" (Gwynn 1923: 299). The Oxford-educated son of a Church of Ireland vicar, Gwynn was also one of the Revival's most important critics, writing many reviews and reports on the Irish Literary Theatre as well as his own fiction, and championing its cause in his capacities as critic and Nationalist MP for Galway from

1906 to 1918. His survey, *Irish Literature and Drama in the English Language* (1936) was drawn up with the benefit of commentary on Joyce from the 1920s by Eglinton and others. It included a significant entry on Joyce in the context of ideas of a national tradition that owes much to "native Irish literature" in Irish (Gwynn 1936: 13) and which cannot be considered apart form the political history of the country. This analysis, then, bears some resemblance to Corkery's but it does not carry the same national charge as the Irish Ireland movement. The significance of the recognition of Joyce as a writer from Catholic Ireland will be considered later; for now, what is striking about Gwynn's volume is the relative emphasis on Joyce as the final writer of note in his volume, even if the praise is tempered: Joyce "holds high rank indisputably" and *Ulysses* has "affected or infected the whole of Europe" (Gwynn 1936: 200–1). In a volume in which Yeats is not named in a chapter title, Joyce comes to the fore as more representative of the path the nation has trodden. As with Boyd, it appears that it was the furor caused by *Ulysses* that forced Irish critics to take notice of Joyce, even if they preferred his earlier work (as clearly Gwynn did).

It is possible to see from the narratives of national literary history composed by Boyd, Corkery, and Gwynn that Joyce's contemporaries were unsure of his place in Irish writing. In part this is because the making and remaking of a notion of "Irish writing" was itself a preoccupation of the previous decades, and in part it is due to the more obvious difficulties of placing a writer whose work appears to reject so many possible traditions. The surveys by Boyd and Gwynn are important in that they cast Joyce into competing narratives of Irish writing, pitting him amidst the Revival and not as an opponent of it, as later became the dominant interpretation in Joyce studies when – rather simplistically – Joyce was read over against Yeats. These strands of interpretation will be significant for our later consideration of some specific, differing readings of Joyce, by Yeats and defenders of the Catholic Church, in the 1920s. First, however, it is necessary to see how those interpretive strands developed through the reviews that Joyce met with prior to Independence and *Ulysses*.

Reading Joyce before 1922

It is important to understand the ways in which Joyce's fortunes were from the first measured with the Revival in mind. As an aspiring writer, Joyce had attempted to set himself apart from the older generation of Revivalists such as Yeats whom he considered to be compromised by various political conciliations with, first, a particularly Anglo-Irish nationalism and, later, with the Gaelic League. Perhaps it was Joyce's own attitude that initiated the critical tradition that dominated twentieth-century Irish literary studies of reading the fortunes of Yeats and Joyce as emblematic of broader social history. Yet Joyce's difference from that older generation was less oppositional than it might appear, despite his own best efforts at defining himself individually. Even when his individuality was attested, it was done so by reference to his peers. Thomas Kettle's praise of *Chamber Music* in the *Freeman's Journal* in 1907 – one of the first public reviews of Joyce in Ireland – made clear that Joyce's poems were devoid of "the folklore, folk dialect, or even national feeling" then so common (Kettle 1907: 37). Joyce later distanced himself from these Elizabethan-style lyric verses and certainly they inspired an oddly un-Joycean response in some readers: the reviewer for the *Irish Daily Independent*, for example, was apparently under the impression that poetry was an exclusively rural pastime. He suggested that they were "poems that lying in the shade amid the scent of new-mown hay one would read and dream on, forgetful of the workaday world" (Anon. *c.* 1907: 42; *LII* 332–3 n. 3). Joyce's choice of this extract to publicize his poems (in a leaflet of press notices) exemplifies his attitude to reviews of his work in general: he *did* care about his reception and was able to use it to suggest the many ways in which his work could be read, even if the response was hostile. (As we will see with *Ulysses*, Joyce even promoted his work by citing critics' opposing interpretations.)

Despite being the author of some short stories and an ongoing autobiographical novel, Joyce was known to many in his youth as a poet (Yeats apparently continued to think of him as a poet for many years). Joyce's stories for the *Irish Homestead* (published in 1902) – whose subtitle, "a journal of agriculture and co-operation," indicated its mixture of a conservative, rural bias and liberal, self-help attitude – had been loosely commissioned by one of that older Revivalist generation, the theosophist, writer, and painter George Russell (known by his pseudonym AE, under which he appears in *Ulysses*). The stories, later incorporated into *Dubliners* with some modifications, met with a difficult reception. Russell had appealed to Joyce "not to shock the readers" (*LII* 43) but the paper's editor, H. F. Norman, received "numerous letters of complaint from his readers both in the city and in the country," as Joyce himself acknowledged (Witemeyer 1995: 524). It has been argued that it was precisely Joyce's realism that was incongruous with the expectations of an Irish readership – especially the rural readers of the *Homestead* – and that consequently it is this, rather than their symbolism, that made his stories radical (Kelly 1998: 31, 62). However, this argument simplifies the complexity of Joyce's generic formulations in these early stories. It was not their realism per se so much as their disparagement of traditional pieties that made Joyce's stories unpalatable to Norman and some among the *Homestead*'s circulation. The point remains, however, that from the first Joyce's writing found an uncertain reception amid ordinary Irish readers.

Irish critics were slow to appreciate Joyce's significance, even if some of his fellow writers were already attuned to him. Reviewers of *Dubliners* and *A Portrait* had to contend with generic originality that they found difficult to place. One reader of *Dubliners* in 1914 found that the stories offered "pen portraits of great power" but that the types of character depicted detracted from the whole even though they could recognizably be seen in Dublin (Anon. 1914: 68). Later readers would have the benefit (or perhaps the difficulty) of following the comments of Ezra Pound in the English-based *Egoist*. Pound declared that Joyce was so utterly different from the "'Celtic' imagination (or 'phantasy' as I think they now call it)" that it was "surprising that Mr. Joyce is Irish" (Pound 1965a: 28). His work might be set in Dublin but that seems merely to have been an unfortunate accident: "these stories could be retold of any town" (Pound 1965a: 29). Pound's frequent pieces on Joyce consistently took this line and were no doubt somewhat influential among Irish reviewers too. The *Freeman's Journal* reviewer of *A Portrait* in 1917 agreed with Pound's approach: "it is an accident that Mr Joyce's book should have Dublin as its background" (Anon. 1917a: 98).

Pound might also be said to have been responsible for another dominant strain in Joyce criticism when declaring at once simply and enigmatically, "He is a realist" (Pound 1965a: 28). As it turned out he would be too "realist" for most of his Irish readers. That *Freeman's Journal* review of *A Portrait* echoed the important Victorian English man of letters Matthew Arnold by saying that "to see life steadily one must see it whole" but balked at the "wholeness" of life that Joyce saw. Joyce, the review claimed, "drags his readers after him into the slime of foul sewers" (Anon. 1917a: 98) – an image that would be repeated in later criticism. It was suggested that English critics saw this as typically Irish in a way that spoke more to their "complacency" (Anon. 1917a: 99) than to their perspicacity (the unnamed target is probably H. G. Wells' review two months previous to this).

The public reception of Joyce was thus from the start bedeviled by charges of immorality: the pious "rabblement" whom Joyce had attacked in his youth returned to revenge him. The apparent immorality of Joyce's writing – a charge that was of course fueled by his depiction of the Church in *A Portrait* – was often associated with what critics called realism, which begs the question: if it was both realistic and immoral why complain at the book and not at life? The anonymous reviewer in *Irish Book Lover* is a good example of this tendency, noting that "Mr. Joyce is unsparing in his realism" but the "brilliant descriptive style" is altogether too racy. "No clean-minded person," the writer says, "could possibly allow it to remain within reach of his wife, his sons or daughters. Above all, is it art? We doubt it" (Anon. 1917b: 102). (Perhaps unconsciously, Joyce echoes this line at *FW* 94 9–10.)

Alongside Joyce's public reception in newspapers and books, there was also a private reception, one that formed in letters and opinion without being written for wider consumption but which nonetheless fed back into public reputation. In a notable example of this private reception, Yeats had already, in 1915, supported Joyce to the English novelist Edmund Gosse, then secretary of the Royal Literary Fund. Yeats argued that *Dubliners* showed "the promise of a . . . great novelist of a new kind" and that Joyce was "the most remarkable new talent in Ireland today." Joyce indeed benefited from these comments: he secured funding. A private reference could enable public esteem. Some years later, Yeats – unknown to Joyce – defended him from the political sniping of Gosse behind the private doors of the Saville Club in London at the end of 1922 (Foster 2003: 708). Others such as Pound wrote many private letters in support of Joyce to influential editors, critics, and collectors. It is usually impossible to gauge the effect of a non-public reception but it is all the same a crucial aspect of a writer's reputation, especially in a context where the writer is not widely read. Owing to his perceived obscurity and immorality, and of course the censorship of him in other countries, Joyce's reputation in Ireland was certainly formed in part through private opinion.

Reading Joyce in the 1920s

The historical coincidence of *Ulysses*, published in February 1922, and the Treaty of Independence, signed at the end of 1921, has given later critics much to speculate over. At the time, not surprisingly, readers in Ireland found that the importance of the latter overshadowed the former. With opinion over the treaty constituting what the historian F. S. L. Lyons has called "the great divide" (Lyons 1985: 439), the country swiftly fell into a bitter civil war. The Free State of the 1920s and 30s has often been characterized by historians as a period of conservative, rural populism (Brown 1985: 168) allied with "draconian" security measures (Lyons 1985: 488) which combined to form a social repressiveness in which the Catholic Church came to exert a heavy influence on both the ordinary citizen and the legislature (Keogh 1994). Indeed, Joyce's reputation came to the public fore in the protracted debates over the censorship bill in the late 1920s.

There is a further complexity to Joyce's reception in this period that needs to be recognized: Joyce maintained a strong interest in his own reception – especially in Ireland – and was sent newspaper clippings of reviews by agencies as well as by friends and relatives at home. But this interest did not stop there: Joyce further responded by referring to a number of critics in his writing. *Ulysses* had made allusion to Joyce's apparent rejection by figures such as George Russell and John Eglinton. This process gained momentum with the publication of *Ulysses*. In 1922–3 Joyce followed newspaper reports of the political turmoil in Ireland at the same time as taking a keen interest in the reviews of *Ulysses*; it was in this context that he began to write *Finnegans Wake*. Not long into the composition of that book, Joyce wrote to Weaver declaring his intention to answer the critics of *Ulysses* in his new work. A number of critics have discussed Joyce's allusions in "Work in Progress" to critical responses to *Ulysses*: Joyce directly mimicked Shane Leslie (see *FW* 33 19–21 and Leslie 1922a: 225) and many more reviewers (see for example Landuyt 2002). It is important, then, to understand not only that literary reception contributes to a broader political and cultural context but also that it can feed back into literary composition. Joyce's writing is an excellent example of this more complex notion of reception. Moreover, not only does it create a loop between texts and readers but it also, in Joyce's case, highlights the essential social contexts in which that reading should be understood (see Nash 2006a). The following comments seek to show both that reception needs to be understood in this dialogic sense and something of the complexity of the context within which Joyce's work circulated and from which his reputations emerged.

The complex and inconsistent character of critical debate in the immediate post-treaty period, with the civil war (1922–4) and unsettled politics, reflects the social turmoil of these years. That Joyce could be named in the case for each side in the censorship debates says as much about the period as it does about Joyce's writing. The point may be illustrated with reference to the reviews of *Ulysses* by two prominent critical figures: Shane Leslie and John Eglinton. In the 1920s the question of

Joyce's relationship not only with the nation but especially with Catholicism dominated his reception in Ireland. In some readings, Joyce appears as a renegade Catholic,
an example of the need for Church and state censorship; in others, Joyce's background
is enough to qualify him as a Catholic writer and voice of the newly emergent independent Ireland that is throwing off the habits of colonial rule. The significance of
Joyce's Catholic upbringing for his Irish reception may be shown by the fact that one
reviewer, Shane Leslie, wrote two subtly different reviews (both in the autumn of
1922) – one for an English audience in the prestigious *Quarterly Review* and the other
for Irish readers of the *Dublin Review* (which he edited). In the *Dublin Review* the offen-
siveness of *Ulysses* is specifically against Catholicism, but in the *Quarterly* it is generally
against "all ideas of good taste and morality." The two reviews carry many directly
contrasting phrases as if they have undergone a cultural translation. For example, to
(presumably English) readers of the *Quarterly*, *Ulysses* was an "Odyssey of the sewer"
but in the *Dublin Review* it was a "Cuchulain of the sewer." This comparison sets the
tone: in the *Quarterly*, Leslie's reference points belong to European "high culture"; in
the *Dublin Review*, they are distinctly Irish and predominantly Catholic. To readers of
the English journal, Joyce appears as a literary "genius" led astray; to readers of the
Irish journal, he is a badly lapsed Catholic. He underlines the need for readers to be
familiar with both Catholic "lore and citation" and the conditions of Dublin in 1904.
In Leslie's reviews, Joyce has let down his "fellow country-men" to the extent even
that *Ulysses* should be removed from "Catholic houses" and "its reading and communication be made a reserved case" (Deming 1970: 201). This bifocal response speaks to
Leslie's own background and cultural confusion, and the fact that Joyce echoed some
of Leslie's words in *Finnegans Wake* only adds to the sense of an irresolvable, bifurcated
reading of Joyce's texts (see Nash 2006b).

The following edition of the *Dublin Review* carried a response to Leslie's piece.
Among numerous objections to *Ulysses* raised by C. C. Martindale was one that
must have struck a chord with Leslie for he too made the same point in his article for
English readers in the *Quarterly*. Martindale gives as an example of Joyce's "crooked"
perception his "offensive habit of introducing real people by name" (Martindale
1922: 205). One such "real person" introduced by Joyce into *Ulysses* was the critic
John Eglinton (the pseudonym of W. K. Magee), who for the past two decades had
been a notable presence in the new Revivalist-era literary establishment. The fact that
Joyce had offered his earliest draft of *A Portrait* to Eglinton for publication in *Dana*,
in the National Library in 1904, only for Eglinton to reply that he could not print
what he did not understand, makes the character "John Eglinton" a suitable antagonist for Stephen Dedalus in the Library episode. Eglinton's review of *Ulysses* appeared
in his "Dublin Letter" for *The Dial* in October 1922 (a partially erroneous handwritten
"copy" was sent to Joyce) and it certainly picked up the echo of that moment in 1904.
Eglinton notes somewhat self-consciously that the book portrayed "that company of
real imaginary personalities whom we know better than our nearest acquaintances,
perhaps better than ourselves" (Eglinton 1922: 436) The formulation "real imaginary" might be awkward but it gets at the crux of Joyce's formal development of a

mode in which the fictional and the historical entwine. Recollecting discussions at the
National Library, Eglinton later twinged at reading "things actually said" (Eglinton
1935: 148).

Perhaps precisely because of his estrangement from Joyce, Eglinton was in some
ways a perceptive reader of him: that he could never quite overcome his personal and
cultural distaste for Joyce oddly enabled an assessment that might not otherwise have
had the clarity (and bias) of distance. His review of *Ulysses* in *The Dial* had doubted
whether this "massive work is of good augury for Irish literature." It was, Eglinton
judged, both a "masterpiece," the most important recent Irish work of literature,
and "a violent interruption of what is known as the Irish Literary Renasence" (Eglinton 1922: 437). In fact, Leslie's review in the *Quarterly* had made a not dissimilar
claim for *Ulysses* as a "Clerkenwell explosion in the . . . classical prison of English literature" (Leslie 1922a: 234). Indeed Eglinton's "letter" implies an analogy between
the "monstrous explosion" that recently blew up the Archives office and Joyce's
own "violent interruption." These comments – with their overtones of direct political action – suggest that Joyce's work was itself a politically violent and potentially
decisive moment in Irish social as well as literary history. Eglinton's view was based
on a perception of Joyce as a Catholic writer (as opposed to "the Protestant-minded
Shaw" [Eglinton 1922: 435]), a label that he attaches to the writer from the start with
the backhanded comment that his readers are mostly among recent graduates of the
National University (formed in 1908 to provide a non-denominational education in
which Catholics would readily participate). So far from seeing that Joyce's work might
cause offence to pious Catholics was Eglinton that he declared bluntly that Dublin
lacked a communal spirit that could be offended by his "crude realism" (Eglinton
1922: 435). In later years Eglinton deepened this characterization of Joyce. In 1929,
with literary opinion across Europe asserting Joyce's importance, Eglinton argued that
his significance lay in a more local, political sense: with Joyce, he argued, "the mind of
Catholic Ireland triumphs over the Anglicism of the English language" and "perhaps
for the first time in an Irish writer, there is no faintest trace of Protestantism: that is, of
the English spirit." Foreign critics were at a loss given their ignorance of "Joyce's race
and upbringing" (Eglinton 1929: 459).

In their "letters" from Dublin to a British and American potential readership,
Eglinton and Joseph Hone – not unlike Stephen Gwynn (above) – presented Joyce as
the first decolonized Irish writer, a by-product of what Hone called "Catholic democ-
racy in Ireland" (Hone 1923: 298). Hone's analysis of Joyce at the beginning of 1923
is acute and historically loaded: despite his distaste for Joyce's "struggle for freedom,"
he sees the importance of a Catholic writer who writes with "perfect freedom" (Hone
1923: 297, 299). Clearly, this combination was a seeming paradox to many of Joyce's
reviewers and to the literary establishment, a "paradox" that sparked the use of Joyce's
name in the forthcoming censorship debates. The association made by Eglinton and
Hone between Joyce and the new independent and Catholic-dominated state was necessarily more complex because Joyce's emigration and skepticism (both national and
religious) meant that no easy cultural correlation could be drawn. Indeed, Eglinton

appears to recognize this when he says that "it would be advantageous for the critical comprehension of Joyce . . . that a country should be found for him" (Eglinton
1929: 459). Despite his hostility to Joyce, Eglinton was perhaps the first serious critic
to write about Joyce's work in this way, at a time when Pound's version of Joyce as
utterly disconnected from Ireland was setting the dominant model for future generations of critics. Indeed Eglinton's reading of Joyce may be most significant for what it
implies rather than for what it directly states: that is, that Joyce's writing represented
a momentous challenge to the Anglo-Irish domination of Ireland's cultural and political life. As such, Eglinton offers an uncanny earlier version of what later critics, such
as Seamus Deane, writing from a very different perspective, see as Joyce's critique of
colonial rule.

Eglinton's version of Joyce thus differed hugely from Shane Leslie's: the former read
Joyce as inevitably a Catholic writer, the latter saw him as an affront to the Church.
This sense of *Ulysses* as a book that could be taken in contrary ways was exacerbated
by its difficulty. Critics could even disagree as to whether or not it was wellreceived,
and Joyce reveled in these divergent responses. The flyer of press notices that Joyce
gathered for publicity for *Ulysses* emphasized its controversial reception, even citing
contrary opinions. Joyce arranged for Eglinton's phrase that the novel had been
"received with enthusiasm by those who provisionally determine literary fame in
Ireland" (Eglinton 1922: 435) to be juxtaposed with Leslie's "from Dublin as yet we
have heard only jocular contempt" (Leslie 1922a: 225).

Leslie's call for *Ulysses* to be banned did not materialize: numerous copies were purchased through arrangement with bookshops who subscribed via Sylvia Beach. Roughly
25 copies of the first edition were sold through four bookshops in central Dublin in
early 1922 alone. We know from Beach's list of subscribers that significant Revivalist figures such as Yeats and Lennox Robinson subscribed, as did a number of other
individuals, some of whom would be disappointed not to receive one of the thousand-
copy limited edition (see Nash 2006a: 100–3). However, *Ulysses* remained a scarce
commodity in Ireland for decades, with Joyce's reputation as a dangerously irreligious
writer well established.

Until the past decade or so, it was common to characterize Joyce's politics as
Dominic Manganiello did: "Joyce preferred to be outward-looking" and "aimed to
Europeanise Ireland" as against the "narrow nationalism" of the "dogmatic and domestic" Eamon de Valera (Manganiello 1980: 189). This retraces the grounds of a debate
that began in Ireland in the 1920s (even prior to the completion of *Ulysses*) and continued through that decade. While Pound had asserted that Joyce was in the line of
Flaubert and others, in Dublin some were already claiming Joyce as the "native" writer
that Irish Ireland had lacked. Joyce's friend, Con Curran (who later became registrar
to the Supreme Court), argued in the mid-1920s that Joyce and Yeats were two poles
of a cultural distinction that structured Irish writing, clearly favoring the former's
"virile, sometimes astringent quality" (Curran 1926: 484). In fact, as Terence Brown
has shown, the confining nature of this debate over Joyce's politics was already being
exposed in the 1920s. Thomas MacGreevy (the poet and one of the 12 *Exagmination*

critics supervised by Joyce) asserted Joyce's European lineage as part of a specifically Catholic tradition. In doing so, he suggested that an Anglo-Saxon perspective (and an Anglo-Irish one) was cut off from the bulk of an Irish and European common inheritance (Brown 1988: 79–80). This appropriation of Joyce as a Catholic writer – and an anti-imperial one at that – became one of the key rereadings of Joyce in the 1920s as Joyce's reputation became the scene for opposing sides in the censorship debates.

The supposed oppositional duality of Yeats and Joyce that has been a sort of short-hand account of twentieth-century Irish literary and cultural history was an invention of their reception (notably given voice by Thomas Kinsella in the 1960s). In fact, Yeats' response to Joyce – and Joyce's to him – was a more complex affair. In the summer of 1922 Joyce had written a sharp letter to Lady Gregory complaining at the lack of public recognition he received in Ireland, and the following summer Yeats did publicly praise *Ulysses*. In summer 1923 he invited Joyce to Dublin, promising a new generation of "many" admiring readers (*LIII* 77), and later that year he praised Joyce's originality at a student debate in Trinity College, likening him to Tolstoy and Balzac. The report in the *Irish Times* noted how Yeats valued Joyce as having the "intensity of a great novelist," only to qualify this immediately by admitting that "The novel was not his . . . *forte*" (Yeats 1923: 4). Once again, Joyce read this report and drew on Yeats' comments when drawing up advertising material for *Ulysses*. In the early 1920s, then, encouragement for Joyce came from a perhaps less obvious source, at a time when some previous supporters, notably Pound and Stanislaus Joyce, and many of the first readers of "Work in Progress," were either lukewarm or openly hostile to his later work.

Yeats again invited Joyce to Dublin, this time to his revived *Aonach Tailteann* (a sort of cultural festival), but Joyce predictably declined to attend and instead followed reports in the newspapers. When it came to the literary prizes, presented at the Royal Irish Academy, Yeats made it clear that Joyce's non-residence had excluded him but praised *Ulysses* as the best prose by any Irishman since Synge. By inviting Joyce and publicly praising *Ulysses*, Yeats set about provoking the Catholic authorities and the new government into a public debate over censorship through which he hoped to reshape the cultural standing of the Free State. At the same time, he must have realized the extent to which the government was publicly tied to the Church and that such a debate would backfire into precisely the form of repressive censorship bill he feared. Not surprisingly, organs such as the *Catholic Bulletin* were only too happy to engage Yeats in the controversy he sought (Foster 2003: 267–8). This must have had resonance for Joyce: after all, *Ulysses* had not been placed on the Index or banned in the Free State. Yeats hoped that by organizing a cultural festival which honored writers of diverse opinions he could promote a conception of Irishness which was not only "not Catholic" but even directly opposed to Church institutions. While provocative to the Catholic establishment, this was also an attempt to promote a public discourse that would be appropriate to his vision of the new state, and Yeats found in Joyce's antagonism to Church piety the perfect exemplar for this project. Yeats' public praise for Joyce was thus always mixed with an emphasis on his "obscenity": at the Trinity debate he had called *Ulysses* "as foul as Rabelais" and at the *Aonach Tailteann* he repeated the claim (Yeats 1923: 4; Foster 2003: 168). Joyce went on to echo some of Yeats' remarks in *Finnegans Wake* (see Nash 2006a: 150–1).

Joyce's relationship with Catholicism was thus a notable feature of a key cultural debate of the 1920s, with both sides in the censorship debates enlisting Joyce as an example for their arguments. For Leslie and later writers in the *Catholic World*, *Ulysses* typified the need for strong Church leadership in the new state; for others such as Yeats and Russell (in his liberal organ the *Irish Statesman*, revived in 1923) tolerance of Joyce's work was a benchmark for the liberalism of the new state (see Brooker 2004: 193–4). For yet others, such as Eglinton, Joyce's success obliquely represented the bewildering rise to power of a Catholic middleclass from which he was alienated by upbringing and temperament. The extent to which Joyce would have recognized himself in any of these portraits is another story.

Succeeding generations would mould Joyce according to their own needs: the counter-Revivalists like Seán O'Faoláin and Frank O'Connor would, in their different ways, cite Joyce as the primary source of Irish realism (again, opposing him to Yeats) while at the same time asserting their own more "authentic" realism. Both former students of Corkery's, these short-story writers attempted to speak for "the people." In the year after Joyce's death, and not long after the death of Yeats, Cyril Connolly's influential English literary journal, *Horizon*, published a special number on Ireland in which Joyce hardly merits a mention. O'Faoláin wrote on Yeats and "the younger generation"; O'Connor looked to "the future of Irish literature." Joyce is almost entirely overlooked between them, gaining merely a parenthetical aside from O'Connor to "prove" that "the literature of Catholic Ireland is dominated by its material," unlike that of Yeats or Synge (O'Connor 1942: 59). Joyce thus stands alongside Pádraic Colum and Edward Martyn as a Revivalist Catholic, one who could not transcend the conditions he drew upon. The curious slighting of Joyce by these writers intent on making their own path partially echoes that of their former mentor, Corkery, while their later recognition of him would set the scene for Kinsella and then Deane's traditions of a national literature of which Joyce is "the true father" (Kinsella 1970: 65).

It can be seen, then, that Joyce's reputation in Ireland was bound up with the nation's own national, cultural, and religious struggles and debates. The forging of his reception is thus both the creation and the fabrication of Joyce, whose name comes to stand as shorthand for a range of complex and sometimes contrary ideas. While he has been seen as both a Revivalist and not, a Catholic writer and national figure as well as a European and liberal one, it might be tempting to conclude that Joyce's reception only ever confirms the values of the reader. Yet such a reading would "flatten" Joyce into his reception. In fact, what contemporaries increasingly came to see as Joyce's literary and socio-cultural significance – as the major writer of prose and of realism in the Revival period, as the major writer of the period from a Catholic background, as one whose anti-imperial sentiments and a political skepticism make him a modern, national figure – continues to shape our reading of him today.

BIBLIOGRAPHY

Many – but not all – of the early reviews of Joyce's work have been collected in Deming. Where appropriate, they have been cited from Deming (in which case they have been listed by author, date, and page reference to Deming); others have been cited from their original source where Deming either omits them altogether or has made significant cuts.

Anon. (1914) *Irish Book Lover* (November), vi (4): 60–1. In Deming 1970: 68–9.

Anon. (1917a) *Freeman's Journal* (April 7): n.p. In Deming 1970: 98–9.

Anon. (1917b) *Irish Book Lover* (April–May 1917) viii (9–10): 113. In Deming 1970: 102–3.

Boyd, Ernest A. (1923) *Ireland's Literary Renaissance*. Dublin: Grant Richards.

Brooker, Joseph (2004) *Joyce's Critics*. Madison: University of Wisconsin Press.

Brown, Terence (1985) *Ireland: A Social and Cultural History, 1922–1985*. London: Fontana.

Brown, Terence (1988) "Yeats, Joyce and the Irish critical debate." In *Ireland's Literature: Selected Essays*. Dublin: Lilliput.

Corkery, Daniel (1931) *Synge and Anglo-Irish Literature* Cork: Cork University Press, 1931.

Curran, C. P. (1926) "On the north side," *Irish Statesman* (July 10): 484.

Deming, Robert H. (1970) *James Joyce: The Critical Heritage*, 2 vols. London: Routledge and Kegan Paul.

Eglinton, John (1922) "Dublin Letter," *The Dial* (October) lxxiii: 434–7.

Eglinton, John (1929) "Irish Letter." *The Dial* (May) lxxxvi: 417–20. In Deming (1970): 459.

Eglinton, John (1935) *Irish Literary Portraits*. London: Macmillan.

Foster, R. F. (2003) *W. B. Yeats: A Life. Vol. II: The Arch-Poet 1915–1939*. Oxford: OUP.

Gwynn, Stephen (1936) *Irish Literature and Drama in the English Language: A Short History*. London: Thomas Nelson and Sons.

Hone, Joseph (1923) "A letter from Ireland," *London Mercury*, v (January): 306–8. In Deming 1970: 297–9.

Kelly, Joseph (1998) *Our Joyce: From Outcast to Icon*. Austin: University of Texas Press.

Keogh, Dermot (1994) *Twentieth-Century Ireland: Nation and State*. Dublin: Gill and Macmillan.

Kettle, Thomas (1907) *Freeman's Journal* (June 1): n.p. In Deming 1970: 37.

Kinsella, Thomas (1970) "The Irish writer." In W. B. Yeats and Thomas Kinsella, *Davis, Mangan, Ferguson? Tradition and the Irish Writer*, pp. 57–70. Dublin: The Dolmen Press.

Landuyt, Ingeborg (2002) "Joyce reading himself and others." In John Nash (ed.) *Joyce's Audiences*, pp. 141–51. Amsterdam: Rodopi.

Leslie, Shane (1922a) *"Ulysses," Quarterly Review* 238 (October): 219–34.

Leslie, Shane (1922b) [Domini Canis] "Ulysses," *Dublin Review* clxxi (July, August, September): 112–19.

Lyons, F. S. L. (1985) *Ireland since the Famine*. London: Fontana.

Manganiello, Dominic (1980) *Joyce's Politics*. London: Routledge.

Martindale, C. C. sj (1922) "Ulysses," *Dublin Review* clxxi: 273–6. In Deming 1970: 204–6.

Nash, John (2006a) *James Joyce and the Act of Reception*. Cambridge: Cambridge University Press.

Nash, John (2006b) "'English audiences and Irish readers': the cultural politics of Shane Leslie's reviews of *Ulysses*." In Andrew Gibson and Len Platt (eds.) *Joyce, Ireland, Britain*, pp. 139–52. Gainesville: University Press of Florida.

O'Connor, Frank (1942) "The Future of Irish Literature," *Horizon* V (25): 55–62.

O'Faoláin, Seán (1942) "Yeats and the younger generation," *Horizon* V, 25: 43–54.

Pound, Ezra (1965a [1914]) "'Dubliners' and Mr. James Joyce," *The Egoist* I: 14. In Forrest Read (ed.) *Pound/Joyce*, pp. 27–30. New York: New Directions.

Pound, Ezra (1965b [1915]) "The non-existence of Ireland," *New Age* VXI: 17. In Forrest Read (ed.) *Pound/Joyce*, pp. 32–3. New York: New Directions.

Witemeyer, Hugh (1995) "'He gave the name': Herbert Gorman's rectifications of *James Joyce: His First Forty Years*," *James Joyce Quarterly* 32: 523–32.

Yeats, W. B. (1923) "The modern novel: an Irish author discussed," *Irish Times* (9 November): 4.

8

His *città immediata*:
Joyce's Triestine Home from Home

John McCourt

I myself did not fully comprehend the importance in Joyce's life of his sojourn in Trieste.

(Frank 1979: 82–3)

Oh how I shall enjoy the journey back! Every station will be bringing me nearer to my soul's peace. O how I shall feel when I see the castle of Miramar among the trees and the long yellow quays of Trieste! Why is it I am destined to look so many times in my life with my eyes of longing on Trieste?

(*SL* 193)

For the best part of forty years, the principal font of information about Joyce's life was undoubtedly Richard Ellmann's comprehensive and stylish 1959 biography, *James Joyce*, which remained not only the indispensable map of a complicated life but also a largely unchallenged one. In more recent times, various aspects of Joyce's biography have become the focus of new scrutiny and cracks and omissions in Ellmann's extraordinary mosaic have begun to emerge. It still seems unlikely in the foreseeable future that any single work will challenge Ellmann's immense opus, though several more recent studies have provided shorter, less ambitious alternatives. Morris Beja's *James Joyce: A Literary Life* (1997) was the first and the best of these various short biographies that include works by Edna O'Brien, Ian Pindar, and Andrew Gibson. Elsewhere, studies limited to just one period or one aspect of Joyce's life have expanded on and sometimes corrected Ellmann's work: works that fall into this category include Bruce Bradley's *James Joyce's Schooldays* (1982), Brenda Maddox's *Nora* (1988), Peter Costello's *James Joyce: The Years of Growth, 1882–1915* (1992), John Wyse Jackson and Peter Costello's *John Stanislaus Joyce: The Voluminous Life and Genius of James Joyce's Father* (1998), Peter Hartshorn's *James Joyce in Trieste*, and Renzo S. Crivelli's *James Joyce's Triestine Itineraries* (both 1997), and John McCourt's *The Years of Bloom, Joyce in Trieste 1904–1920* (2000). Collectively these works have profitably rewritten and re-evaluated the first two-thirds of Joyce's life, while at the same time exploring new contexts and influences on his writing. The work done in Trieste especially over the past decade has brought about a considerable re-evaluation of his years in the city and of the impact that it had upon him. Nino Frank, quoted above, was not the only one to not entirely realize the import of the Trieste period. Thankfully, the wrongheadedness of Stanislaus Joyce's comment that Trieste had offered his brother James little or nothing in the way of literary inspiration, that the "cosmopolitan atmosphere of the Trieste of the early twentieth century did not inspire him at all. Trieste did not give Jim anything"[1] has gradually been exposed for what it is – more a reflection of his own vexed relationship with the Adriatic city that was his home for 50 years (from 1905 until his death in 1955) than a just appraisal of what Joyce might have been able to draw from the place. Crucially, Stannie's remarks can be read as a summary of Ellmann's own sense of Joyce's Trieste experience and hence it has led mainstream Joyce criticism to downplay the importance of his years in the city. Foremost in Ellmann's biography is the focus on Joyce's struggle for survival in what he paints as a bleak and dispirited city, a struggle which had been alluded to by the writer himself in *Finnegans Wake* in the oft-quoted line "And trieste, ah trieste ate I my liver!" (*FW* 301 16).[2] Indeed, Joyce more than occasionally gave vent (with the melodramatic overstatement which was his wont) to the frustrations he had to live through during his time in Trieste. In 1924 he wrote to Harriet Shaw Weaver of "the long drudgery and disappointment in Trieste (I scarcely ate anything, taught until late every night and bought one suit of clothes in nine years [. . .]) and then the labour of *Ulysses* must have undermined my strength. I was poisoned in more ways than one" (*LI* 215–16). Joyce did, of course, try his hand at a number of alternative careers in Trieste – he lived by teaching private language lessons and at the Berlitz School, later at the Scuola Commerciale di Perfezionamento of the Società fra gli Impiegati Civili (an evening school for trainee clerks) and at the Scuola Superiore di Commercio "Revoltella." He also earned his keep by working as a translator (mainly of commercial correspondence), a cinema entrepreneur (when, armed with Triestine expertise and capital, he opened Ireland's first permanent cinema, on Mary Street in Dublin) in 1909, and a journalist (he wrote nine front-page articles for *Il Piccolo della Sera* and – unsuccessfully– sought to work as a correspondent for *La Stampa* in Torino and *Il Mattino* in Naples) before taking up the part-time occupation of sales representative for the Dublin Woollen Company in Trieste. Joyce's somewhat dispersive nature infuriated Stanislaus, as can be seen in this excerpt from his diary, written when Joyce had decided to pursue a career as a tenor:

> Now that his writing is 'definitely off', I take little interest in the budding *tenorino*, that has failed as a poet in Paris, as a journalist in Dublin, as a lover and novelist in Trieste, as a bank clerk in Rome, and again in Trieste as a Sinnfeiner, teacher, and University Professor (*Triestine Book of Days*, October 12, 1908).

Joyce showed promise in all of these trades but was not sufficiently interested to fully succeed in any of them. His was thus, as Ellmann has amply shown, a frustrating fight to stay afloat, a sometimes heroic struggle for literary affirmation over 11 tough and sometimes dark years spent in the Adriatic city. Ellmann's version is rich with in-depth discussions of Joyce's innumerable difficulties in Trieste, at the Berlitz, with his landlords, with Nora, and with his brother Stanislaus. Furthermore, for Ellmann, the Ireland that Joyce was contemplating from afar for his fiction remained the almost exclusive intellectual focus and influence in these years. Yet this position is unnecessarily limiting and cuts Joyce off from the currents of modern Italian and European literary, cultural, and political ideas that were very much present in Trieste and to which he had been drawn from Ireland in the first place. Colin MacCabe's comment adds authority to this view:

> Ellmann's biography, magnificent achievement that it is, is sadly wanting in its descriptions of Joyce's political beliefs. Joyce's comments are constantly reduced to the ramblings of a great artist: "Trieste resembled Dublin, too, in its Irredentist movement; the similarity here was so striking that Joyce found he could interest his Italian friends in Irish political parallels, *though no doubt he would have compelled them to listen in any case.*" [*JJ* 196; MacCabe's emphasis]. The trivialization of this last phrase distracts attention from the real political similarities between Ireland and Italy at the turn of the century (MacCabe 1978: 141).

It also fails to take into account that Joyce might have been just as interested in his audience's complex political predicament(s) as he set out to create fiction with such a markedly European dimension. In a less specific but equally cogent manner, Bernard Benstock's words are also salutary:

> The Grand Critical Cliché is that Joyce took his native city with him wherever he wandered, whereas it is far more accurate to view Joyce as a voyager who travelled light, fully expecting to find whatever he needed wherever he was. Constantly setting his stage as Dublin, he set up his prompter's box in whatever city he resided in and boxed in his stage with "foreign" echoes from the wings – continental correctives (Benstock 1994: 32).

While Ireland would always be Joyce's principal subject matter, he would also gradually allow himself to be influenced by the various adopted cities of his extended exile even if it is true that he initially seems to have been indifferent as to where his exile would be staged (although he was not backward about letting people know of cities he clearly did not feel up to the task – hence the "naval Siberia" that was Pola, the "filthy hole" [*LII* 114] that was Ancona, and the "the stupidest old whore of a town" [*LII* 198] that was, in an echo of Martin Luther, Rome). Trieste was different. The cosmopolitan Adriatic port was, in Philippe Soupault's words, "the unrecognized city par excellence" (Soupault 1979: 110), more than just another city among the many. It became his second home, despite everything, on and off for some 20 years, or as he put it in *Finnegans Wake*, his "città immediata by alley and detour with farecard awailable these getrennty years" (*FW* 228 23–4). Not for nothing would he leave the city only to always come back (even after the First World War when Paris already beckoned), not for nothing would he talk to his friend Alessandro Francini Bruni of Trieste as "*la mia seconda patria*" (my second country), and would he look on himself after leaving Trieste definitively in 1920 as being twice exiled and a "*Tergestime Exul*" (*SL* 268) (an exile from Trieste or Tergeste to give it its Latin name). Later he would choose to downplay the fierce struggle he had lived there while trying to balance his precarious writing career with the demands of his family, and would have Herbert Gorman, his first biographer, write of him taking his place in "the variegated life of Trieste with the pleasure of a dolphin diving in familiar waters. Every aspect of the city seemed to please him . . ." (Gorman 1941: 142). He also was careful to have Gorman quote him saying of life in "Old Auster and Hungrig" (*FW* 464 27–8): "I cannot begin to give you the flavour of the old Austrian Empire. It was a ramshackle affair but it was charming, gay, and I experienced more kindnesses in Trieste than ever before or since in my life. Times past cannot return but I wish they were back" (Gorman 1941: 143). It was precisely the empire's ramshackle, rickety nature that appealed to Joyce, who usually did little to hide his "hostility towards all political state formations" (Nolan 2000: 78).

In recent years, several critics have begun to explore and describe what it was about Trieste that made it such a special location for Joyce. Peter Hartshorn has written that "Joyce understood that Trieste was valuable as the place from which he could clearly view Dublin, the focus of his life's work. Svevo in his Milan speech on Joyce, observed, 'A piece of Ireland was ripening under our sun'" (Hartshorn 1997: 137). Hartshorn concludes by quoting Joyce's friend Philippe Soupault, who wrote that the "Trieste period . . . is without doubt the most important of all his life." While in Trieste Joyce published *Chamber Music*, composed the great body of *Dubliners*, wrote *A Portrait* in its entirety, penned his only prose work not to be set in Dublin, *Giacomo Joyce*, and wrote several chapters of *Ulysses*. It was, as Soupault points out, during the time in Trieste "that he became aware of the grandeur and importance of his life's work; it was at this period that he detached himself definitively from our world in order to conceive the Joycean universe" (Soupault 1979: 110). With good cause, then, Renzo Crivelli has written of the role of Trieste as that of a "placentary city" (Crivelli 1996: 10) that helped nurture the budding novelist. More than a mere reflection of Dublin or just some neutral, detached place in which Joyce felt he had physical and psychological space to write, Trieste played a crucial role in forming Joyce as a writer and furnished him with vital material for his fiction. Svevo sensed this and later claimed

> that we Triestines have a right to regard him [Joyce] with deep affection as if he belonged in a certain sense to us. And as if he were to a certain extent Italian. In Joyce's culture there is a marked Italian bias. [. . .] it is a great title of honor for my city that in Ulysses some of the streets of Dublin stretch on and on into the windings of our old Trieste. [. . .] Trieste was for him a little Ireland which he was able to contemplate with more detachment than he could his own country (Svevo 1972: no pages given).

To the Irish critic Boyd, who asserted that *Ulysses* was merely the product of prewar thought in Ireland, Valery Larbaud tellingly replied, "Yes, in so far as it came to maturity in Trieste."

Part of the attraction of Trieste lay in the fact that it was such an intellectually challenging city, a lively melting pot of peoples and their culture, politics, literature, religion, fashion, music, and ideas, in Soupault's words "the most beautiful, the most European crossroads in all Europe (Soupault 1979: 110). The linguistic and religious mix of "tarry easty" (*FW* 228 23–4) – *la terra dell'est*, this eastern land worth tarrying in – left an indelible mark on Joyce. On a daily basis, he was meeting scores of people, drawn from all over Europe, many of whom routinely spoke several languages. Not untypical was Stannie's Russian pupil, "a restless and particularly vulgar gentleman who speaks several languages, Russian, a smattering of Moscovite, Croatian, Serbian because it is so like Croatian, French because they speak French at home, German because he studied in the University of Graz, Italian because he was reared in Trieste, and a little English" (*Book of Days*, August 15, 1915). It is hard to see the polyglot author of *Finnegans Wake* not being at home in this city that Stannie called "a funny place for languages" (*Book of Days*, October 18, 1908) and which was little short of a linguistic babel. The clamour of foreign tongues took hold of Joyce, who felt increasingly estranged from English and, frustrated at not being able to publish *Dubliners*, actually thought of translating some of the stories, and even of abandoning his mother tongue (as he would partially do, years later, in the *Wake*):

> He spoke of unlearning English and learning some other language – Italian or French – because his stories would never be accepted by an English publisher. He said there was no use in his writing them if they would never be published (*Book of Days*, April 6, 1907).

Scipio Slataper, contemporary of Joyce and author of *Il mio Carso*, the book which attempts to define *Triestinità*, describes well how the city was caught between Mittel-Europa, Imperial Austro-Hungary, which promised economic growth, and Mediterranean Italy ("Illbelpaese" *FW* 129 27), which appealed more to the Irredentist sentiment dear to the majority in the city:

> It is the torment of two temperaments, the commercial [Austrian] and the Italian, which collide and nullify each other, and Trieste cannot suppress either of the two: this is the double spirit, otherwise it would kill itself. Whatever is necessary for commerce is a violation of the Italian aspirations, just as any real commercial gain damages the spirit (Slataper 1912, quoted in Robinson 2001: 325).

Stanislaus Joyce describes the problem, from the point of view of Triestine *Irredentismo* in his diary:

> How, for example, do Italians hope to maintain the *italianità* of Trieste, when in the city you have, on all hands, childless families, and in the surroundings a threatening and hostile Slav population with families of from six to twelve? These Slav families are poor and have many boys, who begin early to strike out for themselves, while Italian families are from one to three – probably one boy and two girls. Now girls don't count, when they marry they change everything, religion, nationality, language, prejudices, even appearances. The Italians here complain just of this, that the children of the half-Italian blood in the suburbs speak Slav and do not understand *italiano* (*Book of Days*, August 14, 1907).

Herbert Gorman, writing under Joyce's shadow, put it more succinctly, writing of how the Triestines were caught between "the emotions of the heart and the sovereignty of the pocket book," a phrase which echoes Joyce's own cutting comment about their nationalist impulses in *Giacomo Joyce*: "Ay. They love their country when they are quite sure which country it is" (*GJ* 9). The semicolonial complexities of Trieste, so different from those Joyce had abandoned in Ireland, add fuel to the literary fire from which he would forge modern literature's most convincing affirmation of cultural hybridity – Leopold Bloom. It is not accidental that it was in Trieste that Joyce began to form the theoretical skeleton of the ideas that Bloom would later come to embody, most important his refutation of "the old pap of racial hatred" (*LII* 167) in its Irish configuration. It was in his sometimes contradictory "Ireland, Island of Saints and Sages" lecture that Joyce asserted that no race could boast of being pure because none was and nowhere was this belief better exemplified than in Trieste with its intermingled ethnic groups drawn from all over Europe that managed to maintain vital elements of the languages and cultures they had abandoned, even generations after settling there. As Claudio Magris and Angelo Ara put it,

> All the groups which lived in Trieste looked elsewhere to a far-off country, identifiable only through an imaginary projection. The Italians looked, like the Irredentists, to Italy, or at least saw Italy as a reference point, feeling that they lived in a world apart, or at least the most passionate standard-bearers did; the Germans and the Austro-Germans looked beyond the Alps, while the Slovenes waited for the awakening of their land, or later, that of the Slavs in the Empire (Ara and Magris, 1982, 17).

With so many of the population of Trieste maintaining such strong ties with their countries of origin, Trieste was living proof of Bloom's seemingly impossible formulation that a nation was not simply "the same people living in the same place" but also, and essentially, a variegated diaspora of "the same people living in different places" (*U* 12 422–9).

Small surprise then that this city came to play a vital role in shaping Joyce's creative development, to the extent that despite, or perhaps because of, the hard struggle he had to make a living there as a language teacher, he later came to believe – as his friend Alessandro Francini Bruni (his fellow teacher in the Berlitz School, first in Pola and later in Trieste) stated – that "his personality had been formed in Trieste."[3]

Joyce had first arrived in Trieste in 1904, aged, like Stephen Dedalus, 22; when he left some 16 years later he was, like the central character of *Ulysses*, that "cultured all-roundman" Leopold Bloom, 38. In those years Joyce lived many of the experiences that would enable him to put flesh on his Middle European Dubliner, Bloom. The cultural environment of Trieste was lively and varied: in addition to the dominant *Il Piccolo* and its evening version *Il Piccolo della Sera*, Trieste boasted a surprisingly bulky range of daily and weekly newspapers and periodicals, all of which were politically affiliated; there was also much literary activity, indeed one need only mention a couple of contemporary Triestine writers, such as Italo Svevo, Silvio Benco (a Triestine D'Annunzio), the poet Umberto Saba, and consider the prominent presence of groups of both *Vociani* and *Futuristi* in the city. Marinetti referred to Trieste as one of the three capitals of Futurism, along with Paris and Milan, but the city is also deserving of more prolonged investigation as an important location in the development of European modernism *tout court*. Theater was also an enduring passion for the Triestines. Each night the city's impressive theaters offered an eclectic range of plays (from Shakespeare to Shaw, from Ibsen to Pinero to Italian contemporaries such as Praga and Giacosa, whose *La Crisi* and *Tristi Amori*, respectively, influenced Joyce in the writing of *Exiles*). Lyric opera was also popular and the Italian tradition, represented by figures such as Donizetti, Verdi, Puccini, and the local artist Antonio Smareglia, whom Joyce knew, were regularly patriotically pitched against Wagner. Lectures and readings were organized on a bewildering range of subjects by a countless number of associations and study circles. If all that was not enough, one could take in a film at one of the city's dozen or so permanent cinemas. Joyce and Nora often did so and so taken was Joyce by this new medium that he convinced a group of Triestine businessmen to finance his founding of the Cinema Volta on Mary Street in Dublin as Dublin's first permanent cinema in 1909. Joyce knew he was onto a good thing but was not sufficiently interested to manage it for more than a short period and the whole enterprise folded within six months.

Joyce also found an unusual mix of religions in Trieste and had little trouble earning the title he later coined in *Finnegans Wake* of "Jimmy the chapelgoer" (*FW* 587 35–6). Communities of Armenian Mechitarists, Swiss and Valdesian Protestants, Lutherans, Anglicans, and Methodists existed side by side with the larger and more prominent religious groups. Joyce regularly attended the splendid neo-byzantine Serb Orthodox Church of San Spiridione and the impressive gem that was the Greek temple, the Church of the Most Holy Trinity and San Nicolò – the *"ciesa dei greghi"* as the Triestines called it – and rewrote his short-story "The Sisters" following a visit to Mass there. In these churches he lived the experience of being an outsider peering in at rituals he did not fully grasp, an experience, this, that would be useful to him later when he placed Leopold Bloom in a parallel situation at Mass in Westland Row in Dublin.

Joyce went to Easter services in various Catholic churches but more often than not in the Church of Sant' Antonio Taumaturgo, located at the end of Trieste's Canal Grande, surely one of the shortest grand canals in the world. Joyce had a laugh at its expense in a letter to Svevo, when he wrote: "Anna Liffey would be the longest river in the world, if it was not for the canal that comes from far to wed the great God, Antonio Taumaturgo, and then changes its mind and goes back as it came" (*LIII* 133). He also found in Trieste a large Jewish population and regularly visited the synagogue, where he found a surprising number of his students, as his brother Stanislaus remembered in his *Triestine Book of Days*:

> He asked had the Jews any theology in the sense that Catholics have one, and was the priesthood with them a caste or a profession. Also he wanted to know whether they had a school of theology in which it was necessary to study, and lamented that none of his

pupils ever seemed to know anything about the religions to which they were supposed to belong (*Book of Days*, September 8, 1908).

Joyce's friendship with Ettore Schmitz (Italo Svevo) allowed Joyce the chance not only to bombard the Triestine novelist with questions about the Jews but also to get to know well the man who became his principal model for Leopold Bloom. But Schmitz is also important because of his understanding of Joyce's predicament as a writer. More than anyone else, he sensed the importance of Trieste in Joyce's developing creative consciousness and his testimony to this effect is a crucial one because for a very long time he seems to have been the only one to have realized the depth and breadth of this impact, perhaps because he was one of the very few to have witnessed at close range the mechanics of Joyce's writing process in the years leading up to the First World War and to have contributed personally much valuable information in response to Joyce's persistent questions (especially about the Jews and the Hebrew language).

Joyce's fondness for Trieste was genuine and complex. Although he often despaired of the drudgery of endless rounds of English language lessons, and although he was to leave the city several times (spending six months in 1906 and 1907 in Rome in the vain hope of an easier life, undertaking three visits to Dublin and an extended stay in Zurich for the period of the First World War) he always returned voluntarily, recognizing Trieste as both a refuge and an adopted home. As he put it to Nora in September 1909 in a letter written to her from Dublin,

> *La nostra bella Trieste*! I have often said that angrily but tonight I feel it true. I long to see the lights twinkling along the riva as the train passes Miramar. After all, Nora, it is the city which has sheltered us. I came back to it jaded and moneyless after my folly in Rome and now again after this absence (*LII* 249).

Like many other recently arrived immigrants he found little difficulty in adapting to the rhythms of the busy port city and to its many pleasures: "una buona mangiata, un caffè nero, un Brasil, il Piccolo della Sera, e Nora, Nora mia, Norina, Noretta, Norella, Noruccia ecc ecc" (*SL* 191). He quickly learnt its ways and mastered its dialect, *Triestino*, "one of the richest, one of the most 'composite' (languages) in the world that Joyce listened to with passionate attention" (Soupault 1979: 110). *Triestino* was a sort of *lingua franca*, a linguistic glue which held together many peoples – Italian, Austrian, Slav – not to mention "the Greeks and the Jews and the Arabs and the devil knows who else from all the ends of Europe" (*U* 18 1587–9), all of whom worked in harmony to make the city thrive and prosper.

Joyce never confused *Triestino* with standard Italian, which the Triestines referred to as *regnicolo*, as can be seen in his one hundred-odd letters written in a mixture of both to his brother Stanislaus (who joined him in Trieste in 1905 and lived and worked there until his death on June 16, 1955), to his children, Giorgio and Lucia, and to his friends Ettore Schmitz and Alessandro Francini Bruni.[4] Proof of his mastery of Italian is to be found in the translation of J. M. Synge's *Riders to the Sea* which he made with his Triestine friend, the multi-lingual lawyer and man of letters Nicolò Vidacovich. This is a remarkably controlled achievement, which manages often to reproduce the flow of Synge's lines and, by careful use of rhythm, mirrors and sometimes even intensifies the original tragedy.

But Joyce had to study hard to achieve such fluency and mastery of Italian. He read widely and rapidly, regularly turned his English lessons into discussions in which he practiced his own Italian and even Triestine, and took sporadic lessons in Italian language and literature with his Tuscan friend Francini Bruni. The lessons began in the early period in Pola and continued for a time after they had both transferred to Trieste. Evidence of this is to be found in a large notebook Joyce kept with the title "Italiano"[5] inscribed in his own hand on the cover and which contains an eclectic variety of handwritten passages in Italian and a further 20 pages of useful Italian idioms, commonplace phrases, and key vocabulary which he had painstakingly noted down. Usually the key phrase was underlined as in the following examples: "Parenzo è il capoluogo dell'Istria" (Parenzo is the provincial capital of Istria), "La via S. Caterina è una traversa del Corso," "Stando all'ultimo censimento la città di Trieste . . ." (according to the last census the city of Trieste . . .), "La neve fioccava fitta fitta" (the snow fell steadily, steadily). The passages were taken from Luigi Barzini's *La Metà del Mondo*, Raffaello Fornaciari's *Letteratura Italiana*, Gabriele D'Annunzio's *Il Trionfo della Morte* (a great favorite of Joyce's; according to Stanislaus, Joyce felt that "D'Annnunzio has done for the novel what Ibsen did for the drama" (*Triestine Book of Days*, November 30, 1907), Libero Merlino's *I Principi dell'Anarchia*, Torquato Tasso's *Aminta*, Giacomo Leopardi's *Pensieri*, A. C. Firmani's *Tacito e le sue opere*, Paolo Giacometti's *La Morte Civile*, Brunetto Latini's *Il Libro delle Bestie*, and Francesco Bricolo's *I Drammi dell'Irlanda* (this was actually written by Lucien Thomin and translated by Bricolo).

But a casual reader of Joyce who might expect to find Joyce's most significant works peppered with easily identifiable, studied Italian or with Triestine phrases or references might well at first be a little disappointed. The city of Trieste is mentioned directly just once in *Ulysses* in the scene in the Eumaeus episode in which the sailor recounts seeing a stabbing in a Triestine brothel:

> Possibly perceiving an expression of dubiosity on their faces the globetrotter went on, adhering to his adventures.
>
> — And I seen a man killed in Trieste by an Italian chap. Knife in the back. Knife like that.
>
> Whilst speaking he produced a dangerouslooking claspknife quite in keeping with his character and held it in the striking position.
>
> — In a knockingshop it was count of a tryon between two smugglers. Fellow hid behind a door, come up behind him. Like that. *Prepare to meet your God*, says he. Chuk! It went into his back up to the butt (*U* 16 576–82).

Looking for the obvious in Joyce's writings often leads the reader astray and causes key clues surreptitiously lurking in unsuspected corners of his prose to be missed. The attentive reader will gradually come to realize the need to delve deeper in order to find

Trieste's influence, which, in reality, adds a shadowy layer to all of Joyce's works. Space here allows for but a few examples. The stories of *Dubliners*, for instance, which Joyce completed in Trieste during his early years there, bear a few names borrowed from people Joyce met in Trieste, such as that of his first singing teacher there, Francesco Riccardo Sinico (1869–1949), whose name the Irish writer would give to Captain and Emily Sinico in "A Painful Case." The extraordinary eight matching syllables contained in the name of Joyce's employer at the Berlitz School, Almidano Artifoni, would be recycled for Stephen Dedalus' Italian teacher in *A Portrait of the Artist as a Young Man* and in *Ulysses*. Another Triestine name which would reappear in *Ulysses* in a daring act of Joycean cultural relocation was that of Moses Dlugacz, Joyce's student from 1912 to 1915. Dlugacz, a cashier with the Cunard Line in Trieste, was an ardent Zionist who was born on January 12, 1884, in Galicia, was ordained Rabbi when he was 15, and was well known for his efforts to promote the teaching of Hebrew. During the First World War Dlugacz worked in Trieste as a provisions merchant in a small shop on via Torrebianca, which supplied cheese and meat to the Austrian army fighting along the Isonzo river near Trieste, a fact, this, which induced Joyce to rather roguishly have him appear in *Ulysses* as the "ferreteyed porkbutcher" of Upper Dorset Street, the only shopkeeper in the book who is not listed in Dublin's *Thom's Directory*, a singular example of "an acculturated Irishman, an assimilated Irish Jew who finds a highly pragmatic way to recycle Orientalist propaganda" (Caraher 2007: 139), but who simply would not have been possible for Joyce without the intermediary experience of Trieste. Significantly, Dlugacz keeps advertisements in his shop for the model farm at Kinnereth, and Molly mentions him as that "queerlooking man in the porkbutchers" who "is a great rogue" (*U* 18 911–12), thus managing to embody both a nostalgia for a lost homeland and a multi-cultural assimilated presence in Dublin, much like that of the real Dlugacz in Trieste.

But Joyce found more than just bit players in Trieste. In a very real way the city furnished him with many vital elements for the central characters of *Ulysses* – Leopold and Molly Bloom. While *Ulysses* is primarily a book about Joyce's Dublin, the Dublin it presents is no longer the provincial city of *Dubliners* that stifled the young writer and forced him to depart, rather melodramatically, for exile and Europe; rather it is a cosmopolitan metropolis which resounds with echoes from all over the Continent. While the central characters of *Ulysses* are all genuinely and vitally Dubliners, Stephen Dedalus brings with him a Greek coloring, Leopold Bloom has vital Middle European, Austro-Hungarian, Jewish backgrounds and his wife Molly is decidedly Mediterranean, having been born in Gibraltar, the daughter of Major Brian Tweedy and Lunita Laredo, his Spanish-Jewish wife. Joyce could never have found this combination of backgrounds and identities in Dublin but there seems little doubt that he found it in Trieste, a city noted for its multi-cultural and multi-ethnic fabric. He drew on "the cummulium of scents in an italian warehouse" (*FW* 498 31) – Trieste – which was his "città immediata" (*FW* 228 22–3), the major source of many of the "foreign" and especially Jewish elements which enrich the book. To complement the little he knew about the Jewish situation in Ireland,[6] he visited Trieste's synagogues (a new one was inaugurated in 1912 as the biggest in Europe) and its Jewish shops and businesses, and, from his many Jewish friends and students – a mixture of rich businessmen, Irredentists, Zionists, and their offspring ("the society of jewses," *FW* 423 36) – put flesh on the character of Leopold Bloom, whose very name may be the result of a cross enacted by Joyce with the names of two people he knew in Trieste – Leopoldo Popper and Luis Blum.[7]

Perhaps the key text for any understanding of Joyce's Triestine absorption is *Giacomo Joyce*, his brief and fragmentary Triestine novelette – or compendium of what he described to Pound as his "prose sketches"[8] – written sometime between 1911 and 1914 and located overwhelmingly in the Adriatic city. *Giacomo Joyce* is largely written in English with several interwoven foreign elements – Italian, Triestino, and German. It comprises just 16 handwritten pages written on both sides of 8 large sheets with uneven gaps between the paragraphs or entries or fragments of text. Among other things it presents a portrait of Joyce at around 30 finding himself fascinated by a young Triestine girl, and an image of a newly continentalized Joyce coming to terms with the clash of complex Middle European and Italian identities and cultures that made Trieste such a singular place.

The hybrid Italian-Irish title, *Giacomo Joyce*, evokes a different vision of the writer from the one to which we are accustomed, suggesting a man who has undergone a process of transculturation and is now very much at home in his adopted city, who is comfortably acclimatized to life in Trieste and steeped in Italian culture, literature, and language – an Italianized Irishman pleased to stray into the shadows of many an illustrious Italian Giacomo before him, such as Leopardi, Puccini, and Casanova (as well as the nineteenth-century Irish poet Joyce translated as Giacomo Clarenzio Mangan in his lecture prepared for, but never delivered at, the Università Popolare in Trieste). (Mangan, Joyce noted, also enjoyed "an affair of the heart between him and a pupil of his, to whom he gave lessons in German" [*OCPW* 56], and thus provided a convenient model for the situation sketched in *Giacomo Joyce*.)[9]

As various offical documents relating to Joyce in Trieste show, he was habitually referred to as Giacomo (or sometimes Giac.) and he seems to have enjoyed adopting the name and indulging in the various Triestine nuances it evoked. He signed a letter written in the Triestine dialect to Italo Svevo "Giacometo"[10] and another, dated September 8, 1920, to Francini Bruni, "Jacomo Del Oio, sudito botanico" (*SL* 268–9). In this case the "Jacomo" is Giacomo spelt in Triestine dialect: the *sudito botanico* a corruption of *suddito britannico* "British subject," which Joyce of course was; while the "del Oio" carries a second conscious hint of Joyce's financial woes in its echo of a Triestine idiom *scampar coi bori de l'oio* "to flee from the paying of debts". He re-evokes these money troubles in another letter written on February 20, 1924, which mentions "S. Giacomo in Monte di pietà" (*LI* 211–12), referring to the working-class district of Trieste which bore his name and was just up the street from his house in via Bramante (he changed the name slightly from *San Giacomo in monte* – "Saint James on the hill" – to the more apt *San Giacomo in Monte di pietà* – "Saint James in the pawnbrokers" – a place he was forced to visit as a customer all too often during his Triestine years). Finally, in a letter written in the unhappy 1930s to Lucia, he ironically referred to himself as "Giacomo Giocondo" – "James Joyful" (*LIII* 352–3).

Giacomo Joyce is dominated by a mysterious young Triestine lady whose depiction by Joyce genuinely represents a turning point for him as a creative writer and which would later come to nourish the more complicated female characters of Molly Bloom and Anna Livia Plurabelle. Equally powerfully inscribed in the pages of Joyce's text is the city of Trieste, which is not simply a location for this chronicle of a failed, impossible love story, but a key protagonist in the development of the narrative. As Carla Marengo Vaglio has shown (1998: 91–106), Joyce attempts "to illustrate Trieste from within, giving a sort of moral portrait of it (the streets, the harbour, the market, the hospital, the theatre, the house of Baron Ralli, the Israelitic cemetery, the cloudy Carso mountains, trams, the 'huddled browntiled roofs, testudoform' (*GJ* 8)." He does this with a series of effects, the most important of which is the visual, and which borrows much from both art and cinema, evoking both painterly and cinematographic techniques:

> The sellers offer on their altars the first fruits: greenflecked lemons, jewelled cherries, shameful peaches with torn leaves. The carriage passes through the lane of canvas stalls, its wheel-spokes spinning in the glare. Make way! Her father and his son sit in the carriage (*GJ* 8).

> *The lady goes apace, apace, apace* . . . . . Pure air on the upland road. Trieste is waking rawly: raw sunlight over its huddled browntiled roofs, testudoform; a multitude of prostrate bugs await a national deliverance (*GJ* 8).

What seems initially to be detached physical description soon reveals itself to function on other levels. The final brief passage discloses a political underside in its masterly evocation of the city's Irredentist movement which was such a powerful force in Joyce's time in the image of the "prostrate bugs" waiting to be emancipated from the Austro-Hungarian Empire.

Joyce's brief poetic sketchbook is also his homage to "docile Trieste" (*GJ* 10), that singular semicolonial city that challenged so many of his artistic and political beliefs through its composite and often contradictory nature, and played a such a key role in allowing him turn his provincial Hibernian metropolis of Dublin into a great European city of modernism.

NOTES

1 Quoted in Crise (1995: 20 and 22).
2 This phrase is a direct translation of the Italian idiom "mi sono mangiato il fegato" but there is also, of course, an echo of Paul Verlaine. Joyce's Triestine friend, the poet, Dario de Tuoni, later recalled (2002: 128) that Joyce often recited

Verlaine: "Or pausing where the shades grew darker, he would exclaim in a mysterious and saddened tone: *O triste, triste était mon âme / A cause, à cause d'une femme.*"

3 Francini Bruni made these remarks in a partially unpublished interview with Richard Ellmann

in July 1954. Ellmann's notes are to be found in the Richard Ellmann Collection at the McFarlin Library of University of Tulsa.

4 For a detailed discussion of Joyce's use of Italian see Zanotti (1999: 16–63).

5 The original document is kept in the Cornell Joyce Collection and a facsimile version is available in Groden et al. (1979: 1–105).

6 See Ó'Gráda (2006).

7 See McCourt (2000: 217–38).

8 On April 9, 1917, Joyce wrote to Pound from Zürich: "As regards stories I have none. I have some prose sketches, as I told you, but they are locked up in my desk in Trieste" (Read 1967: 105).

9 For alternative readings of this influence see McCourt (2004: 145) and Mahaffey (2006: 53).

10 Reproduced from Stelio Crise's "Joyce e Trieste" in Crise (1995: 44–5).

BIBLIOGRAPHY

Ara, Angelo and Claudio Magris (1982) *Trieste: Un identità di frontiera*. Turin: Einaudi.

Beja, Morris (1997) *James Joyce: A Literary Life*. London: Fourth Estate.

Benco, Silvio (1979) "James Joyce in Trieste." In Willard Potts (ed.) *Portraits of the Artist in Exile: Recollections of James Joyce by Europeans*, pp. 49–58. Dublin: Wolfhound Press.

Benstock, Bernard (1994) "Paname-Turricum and Tarry Easty: James Joyce's città immediata." In Claude Jacquet and Jean-Michel Rabaté (eds.) *James Joyce 3: Joyce et l'Italie*, pp. 29–37, special issue of *La Revue des lettres modernes*. Paris: Lettres Modernes.

Bosinelli, Bollettieri and Maria Rosa (1970) "The importance of Trieste in Joyce's work, with reference to his knowledge of psycho-analysis," *James Joyce Quarterly* 7 (3, Spring): 177–9.

Bradley, Bruce (1982) *James Joyce's Schooldays*. Dublin: Gill and Macmillan.

Caraher, Brian (2007) "A 'ruin of space, shattered glass and toppling masonry': reading nightmares of orientalist history in Joyce's *Ulysses*." In Sebastian Knowles, Geert Lernout, and John McCourt (eds.) *Joyce in Trieste: An Album of Risky Readings*, pp. 131–49. Gainesville: University Press of Florida.

Costello, Peter (1992) *James Joyce: The Years of Growth, 1982–1915*. Dublin: Kylie Cathie.

Crise, Stelio (1995) *Scritti*, ed. Elvio Guagnini. Trieste: Edizioni Parnaso.

Crivelli, Renzo S. (1996) *James Joyce: Itinerari Triestini/Triestine Itineraries*, trans. John McCourt. Trieste: MGS Press Editrice.

Davison, Neil, R. (1996) *James Joyce, Ulysses, and the Construction of Jewish Identity*. Cambridge: Cambridge University Press.

De Tuoni, Dario (2002) *Ricordo di Joyce a Trieste/ A Recollection of Joyce in Trieste*, eds. Renzo S. Crivelli and John McCourt. Trieste: MGS Press.

Doria, Mario with Claudio Noliani (1991) *Grande Dizionario del Dialetto Triestino Storico, Etimologico, Fraseologico*. Trieste: Finanziaria Editoriale Triestina.

Francini Bruni, Alessandro (1922) *Joyce intimo spogliato in piazza*. Trieste: La Editoriale Libraria.

Francini Bruni, Alessandro (1979) "Joyce stripped naked in the piazza." In Willard Potts (ed.) *Portraits of the Artist in Exile: Recollections of James Joyce by Europeans*, pp. 7–38. Dublin: Wolfhound Press.

Frank, Nino (1979) "The shadow that had lost its man." In Willard Potts (ed.) *Portraits of the Artist in Exile: Recollections of James Joyce by Europeans*, pp. 73–105. Dublin: Wolfhound Press.

Gorman, Herbert (1941) *James Joyce: A Definitive Biography*. London: The Bodley Head.

Groden, Michael et al. (eds.) (1979) *The James Joyce Archive*, Vol. 2. New York and London: Garland.

Hartshorn, Peter (1997) *James Joyce and Trieste*. Westport, CT: Greenwood Press.

Joyce, Stanislaus (n.p.) *Triestine Book of Days*. A entire photocopy of this document is kept in the Richard Ellmann Collection at the McFarlin Library of University of Tulsa.

MacCabe, Colin (1978) *James Joyce and the Revolution of the Word*. London: Macmillan.

Maddox, Brenda (1988) *Nora*. London: Hamilton.

McCourt, John (2000) *The Years of Bloom: James Joyce in Trieste 1904–1920*. Dublin: Lilliput Press.

McCourt, John (ed.) (2001) *James Joyce Quarterly* 38 (3 and 4, Spring and Summer).

McCourt, John (2004) "Joyce's Mangan: a romantic model?" *Joyce Studies in Italy* 8: 135–52.

Mahaffey, Vicki (2006) "Giacomo Joyce." In Louis Armand and Clare Wallace (eds.) *Giacomo Joyce: Envoys of the Other*, pp. 26–70. Prague: Litteraria Pragensia.

Nolan, Emer (2000) "State of the art: Joyce and postcolonialism." In Derek Attridge and Marjorie Howes (eds.) *Semicolonial Joyce*, pp. 78–95. Cambridge: Cambridge University Press.

Ó'Gráda, Cormac (2006) *Jewish Ireland in the Age of Joyce: A Socioeconomic History*. Princeton, NJ and Oxford: Princeton University Press.

Potts, Willard (ed.) (1979) *Portraits of the Artist in Exile: Recollections of James Joyce by Europeans*. Dublin: Wolfhound Press.

Read, Forrest (1967) *Pound/Joyce: The Letters of Ezra Pound to James Joyce*. London: Faber and Faber.

Robinson, Richard (2001) "A stranger in the House of Hapsburg: Joyce's ramshackle empire," *James Joyce Quarterly* 38: 321–39.

Schloss, Carol (2003) *Lucia Joyce: To Dance in the Wake*. New York: Farrar, Straus, and Giroux.

Slataper, Scipio (1912) *Il mio Carso*. Florence: Libreria della Voce.

Soupault, Philippe (1979) "James Joyce." In Willard Potts (ed.) *Portraits of the Artist in Exile: Recollections of James Joyce by Europeans*, pp. 108–18. Dublin: Wolfhound Press.

Svevo, Italo (1972) *James Joyce*, trans. Stanislaus Joyce. New York: City Lights Books.

Vaglio, Carla Marengo (1998) "Giacomo Joyce or the Vita Nuova." Franca Ruggieri (ed.) *Joyce Studies in Italy* 5 Rome: Bulzoni Editore.

Zanotti, Serenella (1994) "Per un ritratto dell'artista 'italianato' note sull'italiano di James Joyce con edizione di un testo" *Studi Linguistici Italiani* 25 (1): 16–63.

9

James Joyce and German Literature, or Reflections on the Vagaries and Vacancies of Reception Studies

Robert K. Weninger

Approaches to Reception and Influence

Once upon a time and a very good time it was, the greatness of an author was measured by the influence he or she had exerted on later generations of writers. It was the time when the cult of originality ruled supreme and to be influenced was considered tantamount to being a writer of lesser genius, leading even in recent scholarship to such titles as *The Burden of the Past* (Bate 1971) or *The Anxiety of Influence* (Bloom 1973). It was the age of nationalism, when great writers were regarded as showcases of the nation's grandeur and their literary masterpieces were taken as proof of its cultural supremacy. Their influence and hence "conquests" were seen as a mirror of the country's intellectual and ideological superiority over other nations and cultures (or, inversely, compensating, as in Germany's case in the second half of the nineteenth century, for its economic delay and as yet unfulfilled imperial aspirations). Goethe in France, Shakespeare in Germany,[1] Rousseau in England, these are just a sampling of the topics that demonstrated, or were supposed to demonstrate, the eminence and predominance (not just) of one's literary heritage.

Reception studies have come a long way since these heady days of nationalistic favoritism and narrow-mindedness. And in all fairness, comparative literary criticism – in particular following the nationalistic fervor and racial fanaticism of the First and Second World Wars – more often than not struck a humane, anti-nationalist and conciliatory note rather than advocating nationalist or racist zeal. Indeed, the still young history of the discipline suggests that most of its early proponents, people like Hugo Meltzl de Lomnitz at the University of Cluj in Romania, subscribed to a cosmopolitan and polyglot agenda that consciously positioned itself institutionally as a counterbalance to the distinctly national bias of the modern philologies at most European universities of the time.[2]

During the heyday of literary theory – the two decades roughly between the mid-1960s and mid-1980s – literary influence and fortune studies went through a number of methodological permutations to become what we today call reception theory, with its various strands of reader-response theory, reception aesthetics and reception history. By the same token, traditional influence and analogy studies have experienced a similar methodological permutation to become subsumed under the more general heading of transtextuality or intertextuality. But regardless of whether we are dealing with fortune or reception, influence or intertextuality, reception studies (in a broad generic sense encompassing all the above aspects) still tend to gravitate towards the great writer, our substantial progress in methodological awareness notwithstanding. "Great writers," those who constitute our canon (at any given moment, one should add warily, since aesthetic canons fluctuate considerably over time), have invariably been the focus of reception studies, partly because they provide the most fertile ground for research, but partly also because literary scholars (and in particular the aspiring doctoral candidate: I myself graduated with an influence/reception study of this kind) need some justification for their endeavors, and what better ticket into the ivory tower – or onto the book market – than the study of the most seminal and widely accepted authors?

James Joyce is just such a "great author." And "James Joyce and German Literature," the subject of this essay, must inevitably result in some form of reception study. But just what form should it take? Within the limited space of one article, it would be impossible to survey *in toto* Joyce's influence on German literature; that is, the multiple receptions of Joyce by some four or five generations of authors writing in German. Even within this one linguistic tradition (which is divided into German, Austrian, and Swiss German-language writers), Joyce's accumulated *Wirkungsgeschichte* amounts to a vast and intractable terrain that has been covered piecemeal by numerous scholars in countless essays, books, and published and unpublished MA theses and PhD dissertations. A second option would be to discuss Joyce's reception selectively *pars pro toto*, his impact on an individual German writer, Alfred Döblin, for instance, or Thomas Mann, or Arno Schmidt. It would pose no difficulty to name forty or more German-language authors who have been influenced more or less tangibly by Joyce's *Ulysses* and/or *Finnegans Wake* – and these are only the cases where a direct influence can be documented (see Weninger 2004). Inversely, and since reception history by definition must have at least two vectors, one pointing forward from Joyce, the other, also pointing forward, but to Joyce, one could ask how Joyce was influenced by German writers, Johann Wolfgang von Goethe (1749–1832) for example, whose *Wilhelm Meister* figures prominently at the beginning of "Scylla and Charybdis," the library chapter of *Ulysses*, where we read, "And we have, have we not, those priceless pages of *Wilhelm Meister*. A great poet on a great brother poet" (*U* 9 2–3). Or the revered Gerhart Hauptmann (1862–1946), two of whose plays the early Joyce translated into English; at the close of his 1901 essay "The Day of the Rabblement," Joyce, not yet 20, proclaims rather self-conceitedly, but nonetheless prophetically,

Elsewhere there are men who are worthy to carry on the tradition of the old master who is dying in Christiania [i.e. Henrik Ibsen]. He has already found his successor in the writer of *Michael Kramer* [i.e. Gerhart Hauptmann], and the third minister will not be wanting when his hour comes [i.e. James Joyce]. Even now that hour may be standing by the door (*OCPW* 52).

Or Friedrich Nietzsche (1844–1900), the "neatschknee" of *Finnegans Wake* (FW 346 2), whose Dionysian concept of drama features as early as 1900 in Joyce's formative essay "Drama and Life" (*OCPW* 22–9), written at the young age of 18, and whose *Übermensch* appears as late as 1939 in *Finnegans Wake* as "*Overman*" (FW 302 left).

In short, there are many trajectories this essay could take. But rather than rehearse what has already been said and done – and what not has already been said and done in the interminably vast tracts of Joyce scholarship, rivaled only by the even more limitless scholarship on the works of William Shakespeare? – I hope to illuminate a few of the remaining white patches that define the geo-literary map of the Joyce–German cosmos; and in so doing I hope also to shed light on some of the vagaries and vacancies of reception studies. As the major reception studies series *The Reception of British and Irish Authors in Europe* – with volumes among others on Virginia Woolf (2002), Ossian (2004), Laurence Sterne (2004), Walter Pater (2004), James Joyce (2004), and Byron (2005) – illustrates, the "old" concept of influence remains as indispensable an analytical tool of reception studies as ever, its overlap and recent rivalry with the term intertextuality notwithstanding. In terms of influence, reception studies always possess two vectors: influence *on* an author *by* others and influence *by* an author *on* others. The old-style French school of comparative literature traditionally premised any such influence study on a so-called *rapport de fait*, a demonstrable factual link between two authors and their works. Such factual links are typically made manifest by an explicit mention of a name or title of an earlier author either in a literary work by a later author or in her or his letters, diaries, or interviews; a *rapport de fait* can also take the form of a translation or adaptation of an earlier author's work by a later author.[3] As tangible as they may be, limiting oneself to the study of *rapports de fait* can be problematic, however; on occasion they hold out more promise of results than an actual comparative reading will yield, and they tend to occlude or marginalize the less palpable kind of intertextual link, for example an analogy or affinity between literary contemporaries, which in their own right can constitute a third vector of influence studies, even if an actual influence has not taken place.

The reception history of Joyce in German literature is full of such occlusions in part because influence often occurs negatively rather than positively, an author feeling pressured to demonstrate precisely that he was not influenced by his predecessor – influence again being taken as an unwelcome sign or token of epigonality (viz. Harold Bloom's *Anxiety of Influence*, where wilfully swerving away from one's precursor plays such a crucial part in the psychological formation and artistic development of "strong, authentic authors" [Bloom 1973: 30]) – in part because an influence like that of Joyce is often disseminated indirectly via intermediaries. Thus Breon Mitchell correctly pointed out in his important study *James Joyce and the German Novel 1922–1933* that "by the

mid-thirties . . . it would not be surprising to see a German writer mix inner monologue and third-person narrative in his novel without ever having read a word of Joyce
– provided he had read *Berlin Alexanderplatz* or *Perrudja*," the former by Alfred Döblin,
the latter by Hans Henny Jahnn, both of whom substantially revised their novels-in-
progress under the immediate spell of the freshly published German translation of
Ulysses in 1927 (Mitchell 1976: 177). What I would like to spotlight in the following,
therefore, are examples of each of these three vectors, examples that, on the one hand,
have not yet been sufficiently explored by Joyce scholars but which, on the other hand,
provide fresh insight into the complex nature and sometimes fluid dynamics of reception studies.

Gustav Freytag as Influence

The first of these lesser-explored German trajectories is the mid-nineteenth century
novel *Soll und Haben* by the novelist, playwright, and essayist Gustav Freytag (1816–
95). Freytag's novel is the only foreign-language publication in Leopold Bloom's small
but select personal library of "inverted volumes improperly arranged" (*U* 17 1358),
as if his eclectic collection of some 23 "scintillating titles" (*U* 17 1359) – ranging
from *Thom's Dublin Directory* through *The Beauties of Killarney* (author anonymous),
William O'Brien's *When We Were Boys*, and Robert Ball's *The Story of the Heavens* and
The Philosophy of the Talmud, to Hozier's *History of the Russo-Turkish War* – could ever
be properly arranged. The sparse "catalogue" entry for Freytag's novel reads: "*Soll und
Haben* by Gustav Freytag (black boards, Gothic characters, cigarette coupon bookmark at p. 24)" (*U* 17 1383–4). Neither the book nor its author are ever mentioned
again in *Ulysses*, or anywhere else in Joyce's work for that matter. The appearance of
Freytag's novel in *Ulysses* poses a veritable enigma for interpreters, as Erwin Steinberg
and Christian Hallstein have only very recently pointed out, not just because it is a
book in German but also because it exhibits a strong anti-Semitic bias, which explains
why the novel later found itself ostracized, at least in Germany, as part of the prehis-
tory of German Nazism (Steinberg and Hallstein 2003). But what is a book like this
doing here, they ask, occupying valuable space on Leopold Bloom's two bookshelves?
Does Bloom know German? Can he read Freytag in the original? Well, as a matter of
fact, we cannot be quite sure: after all, earlier that day in the "Hades" chapter, Bloom
had mused about his pregnant wife Molly and prematurely deceased son Rudy: "Got
big then," he recollects. "Had to refuse the Greystones concert. My son inside her. I
could have helped him on in life. I could. Make him independent. Learn German too"
(*U* 6 82–4). If it is unclear here whether Bloom was intending to teach himself or his
son German, we do know that Rudolph Virag, Bloom's father, was born a Hungarian
Jew and lived, among other places, in Vienna. And of course, during the second half of
the nineteenth century, many Hungarians, as Austro-Hungarians, would have spoken
German more or less fluently. Indeed, among the "fractions of phrases" Bloom remembers his father using are some German words, namely "das Herz . . . Gott . . . dein"

(*U* 17 1885–6).[4] However, even if he did know German, which is the more likely scenario, the lines suggest that Bloom never progressed far enough into the novel to learn of its anti-Semitic tendency, for is this not the conclusion we are to draw from the bookmark placed between pages 24 and 25? Now, I do not know which edition of Freytag's *Soll und Haben* Joyce is describing here; the narrator's bibliographical referencing skills are clearly not up to scratch. But there is something peculiar at play here, one of the many vagaries of reception that I refer to in my title and that Steinberg and Hallstein refer to as a textual "silence." I have before me the one-volume 1858 edition of the popular and well-circulated translation of Freytag's novel into English, published under the title *Debit and Credit* and prefaced by a Chevalier Bunsen. This preface was intended for an English audience and is not contained in any German version that I know. Page 24 of this edition marks the end of Bunsen's preface and Freytag's "Dedications," with Chapter One beginning on page 25. Hence, if Bloom had possessed this English edition instead of a German one, he would not even have read the first page of the novel. So what? You might think with Bloom: "Coincidence" (*U* 11 713), and leave it at that. But there is more to this than meets the eye. Let us assume for a moment that Joyce knew the English translation (or even that Bloom might have owned this English version rather than the German one), what else might be noteworthy? For one thing, there is Bunsen's astonishing remark (for those like T. S. Eliot who immediately recognized the importance of Joyce's ingenious idea to construct myth as a "continuous parallel between contemporaneity and antiquity" and as "a way of controlling, of ordering, of giving a shape and a significance to the immense panorama of futility and anarchy which is contemporary history" [Eliot 1975, 177]) that "Every romance is intended, or ought to be, a new Iliad or Odyssey" (Bunsen in Freytag 1858: viii). Moreover, if we wonder where and why Bloom ever obtained a copy of this book in a language that he may not understand, the answer could lie in Bunsen's opening comment:

> To form a just conception of the hold the work has taken of the hearts of men in the educated middle rank, it needs but to be told that hundreds of fathers belonging to the higher industrious classes have presented this novel to their sons at the outset of their career [. . .] (Bunsen in Freytag 1858: vii).

Are we to assume, then, that Rudolph Bloom, né Virag, Leopold Bloom's father, who was probably conversant in German, presented Freytag's novel to his son and that Leopold Bloom planned on presenting it in turn to his son Rudy as a kind of male family heirloom? But as if that were not enough, toward the end of his preface Chevalier Bunsen draws a parallel between the Poles in their relationship with the Prussians in the German–Polish borderlands, where much of the novel plays, and the Catholic Irish in their relationship with Irish Protestants. The relevant passages read (and we need to substitute Poles for Catholic Irish and Germans for Protestants):

> The two national elements may be thus generally characterized: The Prusso-German element is Protestant; the Polish element is Catholic. Possessing equal rights, the former

is continually pressing onward with irresistible force, as in Ireland, in virtue of the principles of industry and frugality by which it is animated. . . .Forming, as they once did,
with the exception of a few German settlements, the entire population of the province,
the Poles have become, in the course of the last century, and especially since the removal
of restrictions on the sale of land, less numerous year by year. In Posen proper they constitute, numerically, perhaps the half of the population; but in point of prosperity and
mental culture their influence is scarcely as one fourth of the whole. On the other hand,
in some districts, as, for instance, in Gnesen, the Polish influence predominates in the
towns, and reigns undisputed in the country. The middle class is exclusively German or
Jewish; where these elements are lacking, there is none (xviii–xix).

As regards Freytag's portrayal of Jews, Bunsen notes somewhat euphemistically:

> It is a pretty general feeling in Germany that Freytag has not dealt altogether impar-
> tially with this class, by failing to introduce in contrast to the abandoned men whom he
> selects for exhibition a single honest, upright Jew, a character not wanting among that
> remarkable people (xviii).

Ironically, in *Ulysses* Joyce reverses this numerical imbalance: *his* novel parades precisely the "single honest upright Jew" who in Freytag's novel is so conspicuously
lacking. However, from the textual evidence alone there is no way that we can deduce
conclusively whether these intertextual connections represent mere "reminiscences
of coincidences, truth stranger than fiction" (*U* 17 323), or whether they have been
planted by design. All we can say is, knowing how scrupulously Joyce attended
to every detail of his novel, that there must be some reason, some particular logic
why Bloom is made to own a German edition of Freytag's mid-nineteenth-century
anti-Semitic novel even if the precise intention on Joyce's part remains occluded, as
Steinberg and Hallstein rightly conclude. *Ulysses* remains "silent," they maintain,
"about the meaning of that uniqueness or the reason the Blooms would have such a
volume on their bookshelf" (Steinberg and Hallstein 2003: 547).

Ultimately, the focus of Steinberg and Hallstein's article is the stratagems critics
employ when they attempt to recover authorial intentions from insufficient textual
evidence – something we do more often than we think and without realizing it.
They use the example of Gustav Freytag's novel to illustrate how critics often stake
out authorial intention where in actual fact what is created is only the critic's "personal fiction" of what a text means.[5] Influences, too, are like this, "personal fictions"
that arise from our linking of literary personages (Goethe and Joyce, Joyce and Arno
Schmidt) or works of world literature (*Wilhelm Meister* and *Ulysses*, *Finnegans Wake* and
Zettels Traum). Such linkings enable us to construct stories of genealogy and inter-
dependence, give and take, debit and credit. I do not want to depreciate the value of
these stories: we need them to make, and to make sense of, literary history. But what
really goes on in authors' minds will of course remain forever shrouded, as my next
example will show.

The Potential Connection with Heinrich Böll

A similar void or vacancy surrounds the relationship between Joyce's works and the postwar German writer, political essayist, and translator Heinrich Böll. Critics agree that the Nobel Prize-winner of 1972 underwent a period of transition during the early 1950s. With novels like *Und sagte kein einziges Wort* (1953) and *Haus ohne Hüter* (1954) he successfully abandoned his *Trümmerliteratur* signature style which was permeated by the experience of war, death, and physical and spiritual deprivation. New motifs and more contemporary settings emerged as Böll increasingly lashed out both in his fiction and in his essays against the moral hypocrisy and inhuman materialism of the Phoenix-like economic resurgence of *Wirtschaftswunder* Germany. At the same time, a gradual but tangible shift away from the largely unsophisticated realism of Böll's literary beginnings was taking shape, leading him to the much more elaborate forms and sophisticated configurations of such books as *Billard um halbzehn*, his landmark novel of 1959, which exhibits extensive symbolical cross-referencing, or *Gruppenbild mit Dame* (1971), with its unprecedented complexity of character portrayal.

This shift or new departure may well be attributable at least in part to Böll's getting to know the work of James Joyce around 1954 when he began traveling to Ireland (see Weninger 1998). Indeed, the earliest mentionings of Joyce in Böll's work occur in his popular travelogue *Das irische Tagebuch*, which was published in 1957. It is worth noting, however, that none of these comments is formulated in a way that would presuppose more than a superficial knowledge of Joyce's writings. And later, too, we find only the occasional allusion to or mention of the Irish writer in Böll's literary work. Nor does Joyce or his œuvre figure prominently in Böll's countless essays and interviews on writers and writing. Even in the short article "Über den Roman" (On the Novel) of 1960, which deals specifically with the modern novel and would provide a natural opportunity to acknowledge his indebtedness to Joyce, Böll refers neither to *A Portrait of the Artist as a Young Man* nor to *Ulysses*, not to mention *Finnegans Wake*. This fact in itself is rather astonishing, considering Böll's genuine interest in Irish literature (he goes on in the 1960s and 70s to translate, together with his wife, the works of numerous Irish writers into German, among them Brendan Behan, John Millington Synge, and George Bernard Shaw). Tellingly maybe, the narrator of Böll's novel *Gruppenbild mit Dame* deems Leni Gruyten, the book's central character, only a "potential" reader of Joyce. "To be sure," he speculates, "– if frivolous books of this sort had ever come within her reach as potential reading matter –, she would have become a Proust-reader rather than a reader of Joyce."[6] It is quite possible that Böll, like his fictional narrator, considered Joyce's work far too frivolous to merit scrutiny. For all we know, Böll may actually never have skipped through more than a couple of pages of his work (which, as we know, often suffices to get a rough but nevertheless first-hand impression of Joyce's techniques). So despite the occasional mention, despite that isolated *rapport de fait*, Joyce leads at best an eclipsed life in Böll's literary household.

However, as elusive as the link between the Irish and the Germans writer might be, it seems ironical that, at least since the appearance of *Billard um halbzehn* in 1959, critics have not ceased to tie Böll's turning to experimental techniques to the influence of James Joyce. But any attempt to pinpoint the formal correspondences – most frequently cited among them are Böll's increased use of interior monologue and montage techniques after the mid-1950s – seems doomed if only because these echoes or parallelisms can be attributed as easily, if not more convincingly, to influences other than that of Joyce. The mediators were more likely Alfred Döblin or William Faulkner, writers with whose works Böll was demonstrably familiar. Whatever the case, Böll himself cautions us to beware of the pitfalls of influence studies; in an interview of 1971 he remarks acutely from a writer's point of view:

> One does not consciously copy a style, at least practically, but rather one seeks one's own expression within the tensions of the author one currently considers exemplary. The process is fascinating, but I don't believe it reveals anything about the quality of an author to know who has influenced him. Sometimes I am inspired by some stupid movie I have seen and in some corner of it there's an idea that I find attractive but that is kitsch. It can become more important as an entry point than reading the complete works of, say, Camus, who I think is very interesting and who was immensely important for me.[7]

This comment is useful in that it reminds us to heed Claudio Guillén's cautionary words when he observed that "an influence need not assume the recognizable form of a parallelism, just as every parallelism does not proceed from an influence" (Guillén 1971: 35).

Because Joyce's formal innovations in *Ulysses* or *Finnegans Wake*, his two most celebrated works, are so uniquely distinctive, any similarity or parallelism is quickly noted and equally quickly attributed to his influence even when other contenders present themselves. What this focus on *Ulysses* or *Finnegans Wake* frequently makes us overlook, however, is that there are other avenues through which Joyce's works might have impacted on a writer like Heinrich Böll. (Not to mention the fact that, at least until the mid-1950s, Böll would have possessed neither the time nor the energy to devote himself to any sustained reading of Joyce's rather obscure and intractable masterpieces; following his return from the front lines of the Second World War, the former *Wehrmacht* soldier was preoccupied with a very different kind of battle, namely one for his and his family's very survival in war-torn Germany.) In the 1950s, when Böll seems to have first encountered Joyce's writings, he was primarily preoccupied with short prose forms rather than with the bulkier genre of the novel; hence it is not unlikely that Böll encountered the Joyce of *Dubliners* before discovering the Joyce of *Ulysses*. We can infer as much from a remark made during an interview given in the mid-1970s: "Since I still believe," he tells his interlocutors Nicolas Born and Jürgen Manthey, "that I am by nature a short-story writer [*ein Kurzgeschichtenschreiber*], I have taken most interest in those colleagues of mine who are writers of short stories" (Böll 1977: 50). If we take this comment seriously and focus our attention less on formal similarities and parallelisms between, say, *Billard um halbzehn* and *Ulysses* and more on theme, tone, narrative pitch, and mood, we might notice that a number of Böll's shorter prose texts, and in particular those written in the mid-1950s when he started traveling to Ireland, exhibit tangible convergences with Joyce's own short stories in *Dubliners*.

As I have argued elsewhere, Böll's *Das irische Tagebuch* as well as his remarkable short story "Im Tal der donnernden Hufe" (In the Valley of Thundering Hoofs), both of which were published in 1957, carry such eminently Joycean overtones. While the contentual parallels are less palpable than the affinities in tone and mood, the similarities — conjoined with the fact that we can assume Böll's familiarity with Joyce's *Dubliners* — can justify reading these stories against the interpretative backdrop of such Joycean meta-concepts as "paralysis" and "gnomon," bringing to the fore their more sinister hues. Not surprisingly, both authors' short narratives have been mistaken for simple, uncomplicated, and unmediated depictions of everyday life. In the case of Joyce's *Dubliners*, critics have long since become aware of the existential abyss that lurks beneath their seemingly straightforward naturalistic surface and have corrected their readings accordingly, establishing in the process what Bernard Benstock has called "gnomonic criticism" (Benstock 1976: 428). In Böll's case, it seems high time to take a fresh look at, and to re-evaluate, the purportedly "uncritical" and socially less involved tales of the middle period of his career, including *Das irische Tagebuch*, and to attend "gnomonically" to the existential silences and veiled psychological meanings that lie behind and beneath the seemingly uncomplicated surfaces of these narratives.

Ostensible Non-connection with Rilke

What Böll's remarks also point to is that no serious writer likes to be considered derivative. The naming game of influence remains as intimidating, injurious, and damaging to authors as ever — even in our current condition of postmodernity in which what was once embarrassing and stigmatizing influence is oftentimes too easily elevated to, or conflated with, consciously cunning citationism. Nevertheless, and fortunately, since the advent of intertextuality around the 1960s, attitudes have changed significantly and this kind of rigid exclusionary practice and stigmatization of influence has by and large become obsolete in literary theory and criticism, although maybe less so in terms of *Literaturkritik*, i.e. book reviewers' attitudes towards originality and epigonality. While intertextual relationships where no *rapports de fait* are found to exist may indeed be less tangible, they are frequently no less illuminating and worthwhile pursuing, especially when they obtain between works conceived or written at about the same time, documenting some form of common Zeitgeist, or spirit of the age. An often cited example is Joyce writing his revolutionary *Ulysses* in Zurich during the heyday of the equally revolutionary and anti-institutional art movement Dadaism all the while Lenin lived around the corner preparing his Bolshevist version of a modern political revolution. The fact that no literary historian dared to venture where tangible *rapports de fait* were felt to be lacking allowed the playwright Tom Stoppard to capitalize all the more liberally on this historical coincidence. In his 1975 play *Travesties*, a wonderfully farcical drama, Stoppard has James Joyce, Tristan Tzara, and Lenin, these three very different revolutionaries, all of them exiles on foreign soil and operating within a foreign culture and language, meet and interact, ironically without ever really taking notice of one another.

Another such relationship, one from which quite substantial correlational insight can be extracted, as we shall see, is the connection, or ostensible non-connection, between Joyce and the Prague-born German-language writer Rainer Maria Rilke (1875–1926).[8] However, in order to investigate this – as yet – unexplored vacancy of reception in more detail we need to backtrack for a moment to Joyce's biography. On December 1, 1902, a 20-year-old James Joyce leaves Dublin for Paris. It is his first trip abroad. Like many a young student separated from home for the first time, he initially cannot bear to stay longer than three weeks, heading home to spend Christmas with his parents on December 22. Ellmann records: "The prospect of going home, even if he was seasick on the way, was delightful" (*JJ* 115). Joyce returns to the French capital on January 17, 1903, where he remains until April 11, when his mother's failing health forces him once again to return home. "By the third week in February," Ellmann reports, "hunger had become Joyce's principal theme in his letters home. Scarcity was succeeded by famine, famine, after a brief splurge, by scarcity and famine again, diminuendos of stomach twinges followed by crescendos of starvation" (*JJ* 122). Living in the Hotel Corneille, 5 rue Corneille, the aspiring young artist meets with little success; his articles, with which he was hoping to improve his dire financial situation, are either not accepted or their publication is delayed. Already in December he had given up on his planned medical studies, so he now immerses himself in literature and philosophy in the Bibliothèque Nationale and the Bibliothèque Sainte-Geneviève instead – he is "up to his eyes in Aristotle's psychology," Joyce writes to his brother Stanislaus on February 8. With his regular nourishment being more intellectual than alimentary – "My next meal will be at 11 a.m. tomorrow (Monday): my last meal was 7 pm last (Saturday) night. So I have another fast of 40 hours" (*LII* 28, 34, 35), he admits to his father around March 8 – his health soon begins to deteriorate. "Damnably cold here," he complains the next day to Stannie, maybe summarizing not only the weather but also the social and intellectual climate he encountered in Paris.

At about the same time and a couple of streets further down, in the rue Toullier, another aspiring young writer had taken up residence in the Latin Quarter. He too had come from afar, from Denmark, originally of noble stock, but now, not unlike Joyce, impoverished and hungry. This young artist has no acquaintances worth mentioning; he traverses the city, observing, reflecting, taking notes:

> How ridiculous. I sit here in my little room, I [. . .] who am twenty-eight years old and completely unknown. I sit here and am nothing. And yet this nothing begins to think and thinks, five flights up, on a gray Paris afternoon, these thoughts: Is it possible, it thinks, that we have not yet seen, known, or said anything real and important? Is it possible that we have had thousands of years to look, meditate, and record, and that we have let these thousands of years slip away like a recess at school . . . (Rilke 1990: 22).

"I have taken action against fear," he notes elsewhere. "I sat up all night and wrote" (Rilke 1990: 16–17). His writing is his only elixir, and it is through it that he is learning to read the reality of the city around him:

> I think I should begin to do some work, now that I am learning to see. I am twenty-eight years old, and I have done practically nothing. To sum it up: I have written a study of Carpaccio, which is bad; a play entitled "Marriage," which tries to demonstrate a false thesis by equivocal means; and some poems (Rilke 1990: 19).

Are we not immediately reminded of James Joyce, who at this point in time has written a mere handful of essays on such subjects as Ibsen, Mangan, and "Drama and Life"; a drama entitled *A Brilliant Career* (written and destroyed in 1901, maybe because it too attempted "to demonstrate a false thesis by equivocal means"?); and a smattering of largely mediocre verse? In Paris in early 1903 he seems also to have been writing a comedy. But this, too, like *A Brilliant Career*, has not survived. And how frustrated must Joyce have been to receive the following lines from William Butler Yeats:

> I think the poem that you have sent me has a charming rhythm in the second stanza, but I think it is not one of the best of your lyrics as a whole. I think that the thought is a little thin. Perhaps I will make you angry when I say that it is the poetry of a young man who is practising his instrument, taking pleasure in the mere handling of the stops (*JJ* 114).

Joyce's counterpart in the above example, the 28-year-old Danish artist, is, as some may already suspect, not a real author. Rather, he is the fictional character Malte Laurids Brigge, created by Rilke at the very moment when Joyce was composing *A Portrait of the Artist as a Young Man*, namely the years 1903 to 1910.[9] We know from Rilke's biography that Malte Laurids Brigge's experiences in Paris are modeled on the author's own experiences in the French capital. Rilke was about to turn 27 when he arrived there on August 28, 1902, only three months before Joyce. Nor did Rilke stay long, like his Irish counterpart. Rilke found Paris too unwelcoming and oppressive. He wrote to his close friend and occasional companion Lou Andreas-Salomé (better known to many in the Anglo-Saxon world for her close ties with the philosopher Friedrich Nietzsche) on July 18, 1903:

> I must tell you, dear Lou, that Paris was an experience for me not unlike the Military School that I attended; at the time I was seized by a great anxious amazement; now again I was overpowered, as if in total confusion, by a dread of everything that is called life.[10]

While Rilke was already an established writer in the German-speaking world at this point in time – he had published a number of respectable volumes of poetry, in particular in 1902 *Das Buch der Bilder* – he had little international renown; his most famous volumes of poems were still to come, the *Neue Gedichte* of 1907 (Volume 1) and 1908 (Volume 2, *Neue Gedichte anderer Teil*), his *Sonette an Orpheus*, published in 1923, and his supreme achievement, the *Duineser Elegien*, also published in 1923. And, of course, Rilke was not yet the author of *The Notebooks of Malte Laurids Brigge*, the 1910 novel that was to become one of the earliest showpieces of German modernism and one of its defining moments. All the while Joyce was still an *inconnue*. Understandably, the two men – both of whom would come to rank among the greatest writers in their respective literary traditions – never met, and why should they have?

And yet, even beyond the mere biographical coincidence of their living in more or less the same location at more or less the same moment in time, there are links between these two literary heavyweights that seem to take us beyond the realm of mere literary parallelism. The following quote sets the stage, I believe, for one of the most remarkable accidental – that is, non-causal – intertextual linkages in early twentieth-century modernism: "Ah, but poems amount to so little," Malte speculates,

> when you write them too early in your life. You ought to wait and gather sense and sweetness for a whole lifetime, and a long one if possible, and then, at the very end, you might perhaps be able to write ten good lines. For poems are not, as people think, simply emotions (one has emotions early enough) – they are experiences. For the sake of a single poem, you must see many cities, many people and Things, you must understand animals, must feel how birds fly, and know the gesture which small flowers make when they open in the morning. You must be able to think back to streets in unknown neighborhoods, to unexpected encounters, and to partings you had long seen coming; [. . .] But you must also have been beside the dying, must have sat beside the dead in the room with the open window . . . (Rilke 1990: 19–20).

While Rilke wrote more than ten good lines in his lifetime, it is amazing to note in hindsight just how clairvoyantly he is predicting in 1910 his own future and the culmination point of his career in the early 1920s. Yet, in some ways, Malte is also describing James Joyce's literary trajectory (setting aside for the moment the generical argument about poetry). But more importantly, Malte is formulating a literary programme that comes close to one of Joyce's central aesthetic concerns during those early years of the twentieth century. Rilke's translator here has highlighted the issue for the English-language reader by giving the word "thing" (German *Ding*) in upper case as "Thing." Between Rilke's first sojourn in Paris in 1902–3, with his formative encounter with the sculptor Rodin, and the completion and publication of *The Notebooks of Malte Laurids Brigge* in 1910 lie the years when Rilke composed his "New Poems." In these, Rilke creates and gives form, in poetic language rather than critical discourse, to a uniquely modern theory of the apperception of a "Thing" (*Ding*). These poems subsequently became known in German as Rilke's *Dinggedichte* ("Thing" poems) and they represent one of German literature's pre-eminent contributions to the history of twentieth-century poetry. Rilke's poetological program was less to describe things in poetry than to make them, "to create things" (*Dinge zu machen*), he writes to Lou Andreas-Salomé, "not solid written things – [but] realities that spring from my craft."[11] Through poetry, things both become reality and create reality. As one critic noted, Rilke's *Dinggedichte* aim to craft, as do Rodin's sculptures that served as Rilke's model, "static situations and visions of situations, in which a slice of our emotional life presents itself, without clamor and without a sigh, like a thing."[12]

This is the context also for Malte Laurids Brigge's persistent attempt to formulate an aesthetics that would carry *his* poetry beyond its current impasse. In one of the earliest sections of Malte's notebooks, Rilke has him reflect, "I am learning to see. I don't know why it is, but everything enters me more deeply and doesn't stop where it once used to. I have an interior that I never knew of" (Rilke 1990: 5). Shortly thereafter he notes,

> Have I said it before? I am learning to see. Yes, I am beginning. It's still going badly. But I intend to make the most of my time. For example, it never occurred to me before how many faces there are. There are multitudes of people, but there are many more faces, because each person has several of them . . . (Rilke 1990: 6).

This new sensation of seeing things for the first time, and of seeing them more clearly and intensely than ever before, is encapsulated most vividly in the following passage, a passage, however, that belongs not to the final version of the novel but to an earlier draft:

> These clarities [*Klarheiten*] are so peculiar; one never expects them. They hit you when you are getting into a bus, or when you are sitting in a restaurant with the menu in your hand, while the waitress is standing close by – : suddenly you are unable to see what is printed on the menu, you can no longer imagine eating: because a clarity has hit you, just now, while you were looking at the menu, reading the names of dishes, sauces or vegetables, just at that moment it hit you [. . .] today this kind of clarity came to me on the Boulevard des Capucines when I was crossing the wet road weaving through the heavy traffic trying to get to the Rue Richelieu, there, right in the middle, it lit up within me and for a second was so bright that I could see not just a very distant memory but also some rather peculiar relationships which connected an early and seemingly irrelevant event to my life (Rilke 1997: 218–19; my translation).

Composed during a visit to Rome during the winter of 1903–4, this posthumously published early draft of the novel's first pages pre-dates Proust's *Du Côté de chez Swann*, the first volume of *A la Recherche du temps perdu*, by some ten years and was composed roughly at the same time (namely February 1904, as far as we know) that James Joyce was beginning to write *Stephen Hero*, the first chapter of which was drafted in January and February 1904.

In other words, at the very moment when Joyce is collecting epiphanies and formulating a theory of the epiphany in his Paris notebooks in early 1903, Rilke has his protagonist Malte Laurids Brigge draft a similar aesthetics in his Paris notebook. And just when Joyce is incorporating his theory of the epiphany into Chapter 25 of *Stephen Hero* around the second half of 1905, Rilke has just drafted the first pages of a novel, to be entitled *The Notebooks of Malte Laurids Brigge*, that contain a comparable theory of the "sudden spiritual manifestation" of objects or situations.

Stephen's (and hence of course Joyce's) definition of epiphany runs as follows:

> he meant a sudden spiritual manifestation, whether in the vulgarity of speech or of gesture or in a memorable phase of the mind itself. [. . .] First we recognize that the object is *one* integral thing, then we recognize that it is an organized composite structure, a *thing*

in fact: finally, when the relation of the parts is exquisite, when the parts are adjusted to the special point, we recognize that it is *that* thing which it is. Its soul, its whatness, leaps to us from the vestment of its appearance. The soul of the commonest object, the structure of which is so adjusted, seems to us radiant. The object achieves its epiphany (*SH* 216 and 218).

The narrator continues:

He believed that it was for the man of letters to record these epiphanies with extreme care, seeing that they themselves are the most delicate and evanescent of moments. He told Cranly that the clock of the Ballast Office was capable of an epiphany (*SH* 216).

Not only is *Malte Laurids Brigge* replete with such epiphanies, many of which might have been lifted directly out of Joyce's own collection of such epiphanic "visions," but most of Rilke's *Dinggedichte* might rightly be characterized as poetic equivalents of such Ballast Office manifestations of "whatness." But, as Morris Beja notes in the most thorough study of Joyce's and other modernists' use of epiphanies to date, Joyce conceives them as "produced much less frequently by concrete objects than by events, people, snatches of talk, gestures, dreams, phases of the mind" (Beja 1971: 80).[13] Throughout much of his novel Rilke, too, seems to focus epiphanically less on objects than on people, memories (in particular of Malte's childhood), death and illness, ghosts and masks, or the sites and sights of Paris, its houses, streets, shops, hospitals, and institutions; at times we even encounter epiphanies of reading, for instance Malte's comments on Baudelaire's poem "Une Charogne" (72) or his meditations on the "reading" of such medieval tapestries as *La Dame à la licorne* (127–31). Sections xi and xiii of *Malte Laurids Brigge* provide particularly instructive examples of how Rilke weaves such epiphanic tableaux or short poems in prose that revolve around objects, persons, and everyday events into the tapestry of his novel:

xi: Today we had a beautiful autumn morning. I walked through the Tuileries. Everything that lay toward the East, before the sun, dazzled; was hung with mist as if with a gray curtain of light. Gray in the gray, the statues sunned themselves in the not yet unveiled garden. Single flowers in the long parterres stood up to say: Red, with a frightened voice. Then a very tall, thin man came around the corner from the Champs-Elysées. He was carrying a crutch, but it was no longer thrust into his shoulder-pit: he was holding it out in front of him, lightly, and from time to time he hit the ground with it, firmly and loudly, as if it were a herald's staff. He couldn't repress a joyful smile, and smiled, past everything, at the sun, the trees. His step was as bashful as a child's, but extraordinarily light, filled with memories of an earlier walking (Rilke 1990: 17–18).

xiii: In the street below there is the following group: a small wheelbarrow, pushed by a woman; lengthwise across the front of it, a barrel-organ. Behind that, a small crib in which a baby is standing on firm legs, chuckling with delight under its bonnet, not wanting to be sat down. From time to time the woman turns the organ handle. Then the baby immediately stands up again, stamping in its crib, and a little girl in a green Sunday dress dances and beats a tambourine lifted up toward the windows (Rilke 1990: 18–19).

Similarly, in his *Dinggedichte* Rilke focuses as often on people and events as on objects. "Pont du Carrousel" for example, an early (and still rather immature) prototype composed in 1902 when Joyce was in Paris for the first time, revolves around the poet "seeing" a blind man, envisioning his essence:

Pont du Carrousel

That blind man standing by the parapet,
Gray as some nameless empire's boundary stone,
He is perhaps that thing-in-itself-alone
To which Eternity's image Time is set,
The silent centre of the starry ways;
For all around him strives and struts and strays.

Right, with inflexible deliberation;
Flag over many wavering faiths unfurled;
The dusky entrance to the underworld
Among a superficial generation.

(Rilke 1939: 18)[14]

For comparison's sake, here are two of Joyce's epiphanies, one as it occurs in *A Portrait of the Artist as a Young Man*, the second as it appears in the author's notebooks:

The quick light shower had drawn off, tarrying in clusters of diamonds among the shrubs of the quadrangle where an exhalation was breathed forth by the blackened earth. Their trim boots prattled as they stood on the steps of the colonnade, talking quietly and gaily, glancing at the clouds, holding their umbrellas at cunning angles against the few last raindrops, closing them again, holding their skirts demurely.

And if he had judged her harshly? If her life were a simple rosary of hours, her life simple and strange as a bird's life, gay in the morning, restless all day, tired at sundown? Her heart simple and wilful as a bird's heart? (Joyce 1968: 216).

The children who have stayed latest are getting on their things to go home for the party is over. This is the last tram. The lank brown horses know it and shake their bells to the clear night, in admonition. The conductor talks to the driver; both nod often in the green light of the lamp. There is nobody near[.] We seem to listen, I on the upper step and she on the lower. She comes up to my step many times and goes down again, between our phrases, and once or twice remains beside me, forgetting to go down, and then goes down. . . . . Let be; let be. . . . . And now she does not urge her vanities, – her fine dress and sash and long black stockings, – for now (wisdom of children) we seem to know that this end will please us better than any end we have laboured for (Joyce 1968: 268).

Clearly, one must be cautious not to expect too direct a correlation between the actual contents of Stephen's/Joyce's epiphanies and Malte's/Rilke's visions; the resemblance lies more in the atmospherics and the resonance of a given situation and the relevance, if not revelation, ascribed to a particular motif within its narrative context. Both Rilke and Joyce are providing a distinctive tonal perspective on a seemingly immaterial scene or object, lifting them out of their insignificance and bestowing on them a symbolical latitude that they otherwise lack. But while both Joyce and Rilke look at these epiphanies or visions as revelatory in nature, and while both are concerned with a "seeing" that is simultaneously an unveiling of the nature or essence of an event or a thing, they seem to present divergent models of how such a sudden spiritual experience comes about. In terms of sequencing, Joyce begins with the object or event which induces in the beholder a sudden manifestation of its "whatness." Rilke's Malte, by contrast, seems to be struck by the sudden spiritual manifestations as a consequence or extension of a pre-existing inner disposition: "Because you were a revealer, a timelessly tragic poet," Malte says, refering as much to Ibsen (as critics assume)[15] as to his own creator,

> you had to transform this capillary action all at once into the most convincing gestures, into the most available forms. So you began that unprecedented act of violence in your work, which, more and more impatiently, desperately, sought equivalents in the visible world for what you had seen inside. There was a rabbit there, an attic, a room where someone was pacing back and forth; there was a clatter of glass in a nearby bedroom, a fire outside the windows; there was the sun. [. . .] But this wasn't enough: finally towers had to come in and whole mountain-ranges; and the avalanches that bury landscapes spilled onto a stage overwhelmed with what is tangible, for the sake of what cannot be grasped (Rilke 1990: 83).

In his study of the epiphany, Morris Beja at one point notes, "this book [. . .] attempts to show that, even if Joyce had never lived and Stephen had never roamed the streets of Dublin, what they both called »epiphany« would still have been a profoundly important presence in the contemporary novel" (Beja 1971: 14). Indeed, what could better corroborate this thesis than Rilke's poetry and his novel *The Notebooks of Malte Laurids Brigge*, created at the very moment when Joyce was conceiving and drafting his concept? The fact remains, however, that it was Joyce and not Rilke who provided literary scholars with this most convenient and suggestive of words to discursively link and classify the fascinating array of versions and adaptations of "a sudden spiritual manifestation" in twentieth-century literature, although in some ways not Joyce's *Stephen Hero* or *A Portrait of the Artist as a Young Man*, but rather Rilke's poetry might be said to constitute the ultimate epitome of the epiphany.

However we look at it, (re)reading Joyce against the background of Rilke and (re)reading Rilke against the backdrop of Joyce helps us not just to better understand the affinities between their works, but also to better define the major aesthetical and philosophical trends that characterized European modernism. It seems hardly coincidental that both of their life's stories and both of their life's work approximate more than any other modernist's œuvre what Georg Lukács has called the "transcendental homelessness" (*transzendentale Obdachlosigkeit* [Lukács 1977: 32]) of modernity and the modern novel.

Conclusion

In conclusion, I hope to have shown that, despite the fact that we know of no direct factual link either between Rilke's and Joyce's lives or their œuvres, a comparative reading of their work can shed considerable light on the period and its intellectual heartbeat. Such less defined contact zones between writers surely must have as much a role to play in the future of reception studies as those more "pronounced" relationships – with direct links attestable through *rapports de fait* as is the case with Gustav Freytag and Heinrich Böll – that continue to form the staple of influence studies and comparative literary "normal science." And yet, and as we saw, even "causal" and seemingly unproblematical relationships like those between Gustav Freytag's *Debit and Credit* and Joyce's *Ulysses* or those between Joyce's works and Heinrich Böll's often produce rather unexpected interpretative difficulties. An "influence" is rarely as straightforward an analytical tool as one would hope.

So despite their traditional antagonism, most influence studies tend to revert to intertextual arguments about formal analogies, parallelisms, echoes, or traces as soon as they attempt to move beyond positivistic collation of facts and data to actual interpretative practice. Likewise, an intertextual interpretation will rarely convince without the substructure of influence – as for example evidenced in the recent work of Gérard Genette (1982), who subsumes under the term intertextuality much that would have qualified as influence in earlier comparative studies. The days are over when a Roland Barthes could pronounce with such unassailable conviction the incompatibility of influence and intertextuality:

> The intertextual in which every text is held, it itself being the text-between of another text, is not to be confused with some origin of the text: to try to find the "sources", the "influences" of a work, is to fall in with the myth of filiation; the citations which go to make up a text are anonymous, untraceable, and yet *already read*: they are quotations without inverted commas (Barthes 1977: 160).

That is to say, the intertextual vistas opened up for interpreters by the study of less palpable and non-causal connections like those between Rilke and Joyce serve as useful counterparts to the interpretations produced by a more traditional approach premised on causal relationships. They are complements, not combatants. Indeed, much as the "Author" and authorial intention were proclaimed dead or defunct by theorists like Barthes or Michel Foucault in the mid-1960s and much as the "Author" – who was never really dead of course, just eclipsed by theory – staged a successful comeback in the 1990s, influence too was maybe too prematurely pronounced extinct (cf. Burke 1992 and Jannidis 1999). If we take a critical look back at the trajectories of both literary theory and literary critical practice over the past half-century we might note that, in many ways, the very practice of intertextuality itself now seems little more than an extension of the older paradigm of influence, complementing and refining rather than supplanting or usurping it.

NOTES

1 I use Shakespeare in Germany advisedly because, especially toward the end of the nineteenth century, Germans tended to regard Shakespeare as "their own" (*unser Shakespeare*). This was not least due to the many (excellent) translations of Shakespeare's works into German, among others by such seminal writers as Christoph Martin Wieland (1762) and August Wilhelm Schlegel and Ludwig Tieck (1797–1801 and 1825–33), and the innumerable stagings of his plays throughout the century, not to mention the profound influence that Shakespeare's plays had on German writers. The prime example is, of course, Johann Wolfgang von Goethe's *Wilhelm Meisters Lehrjahre* of 1795, cited in the "Scylla and Charybdis" chapter of *Ulysses*, the very chapter in which Stephen alludes to Shakespeare's domineering role in German turn-of-the-century intellectual life with the caustic remark "He [Shakespeare] was made in Germany . . . as the champion French polisher of Italian scandals" (*U* 9 766).

2 Cf. most recently Saussy (2006) and Damrosch (2006).

3 Cf. Jean-Marie Carré, one of the leading scholars of the French School: "La littérature comparée est une branche de l'histoire littéraire: elle est l'étude des relations spirituelles internationales, des *rapports de fait* qui ont existés . . . entre les œuvres, les inspirations, voire les vies d'écrivains appartenant à plusieurs littératures" (cited in Guyard 1951: 5).

4 Steinberg and Hallstein argue that all the German words Bloom uses are also Yiddish expressions; while this may be so, I am not convinced that Joyce would have been so sure about this. It seems more likely that for him, as for any reader of *Ulysses* who knows German, these words would ring German. However, I fully agree with their conclusion: "Taking this into account," they write, "there is no persuasive evidence in *Ulysses* to show that either Rudolph or Leopold Bloom knew (or did not know) German sufficiently well to read a novel such as *Soll und Haben*" (Steinberg and Hallstein: 546).

5 For more on this topic cf. also my (1995) survey of Arno Schmidt criticism, *Framing a Novelist: Arno Schmidt Criticism 1970–1994*.

6 "Ganz sicher ist – wären solche frivolen Bücher auch nur als potentielle Lektüre in ihre Nähe geraten –, sie wäre eher ein Proust- als eine Joyceleserin geworden" (Böll 1974: 64; my translation).

7 "Man schreibt ja nicht bewußt den Stil nach, praktisch wohl, sondern sucht seinen eigenen Ausdruck innerhalb der Spannungen des Autors, den man im Augenblick für vorbildlich hält. Der Vorgang ist interessant; aber ich glaube nicht, daß es irgend etwas über die Qualität eines Autors sagt, von wem er beeinflußt ist. Manchmal z.B. werde ich angeregt von einem blödsinnigen Film, den ich sehe, wo in irgendeiner Ecke eine Idee ist, die ich interessant finde und die vielleicht kitschig dargestellt ist. Das kann viel wichtiger sein, als Einstieg wichtiger werden, als die Gesamtlektüre von etwa Camus, der für mich interessant, sehr wichtig war" (Böll 1971: 7–8; my translation).

8 Born in Prague at a time when that city was one of the intellectual hubs of the Austro-Hungarian Empire, Rilke is "German" here of course exclusively in terms of language.

9 Rilke's text is cited from the translation by Stephen Mitchell (Rilke 1990).

10 "Ich möchte Dir sagen, liebe Lou, daß Paris eine ähnliche Erfahrung für mich war wie die Militärschule; wie damals ein großes banges Erstaunen mich ergriff, so griff mich jetzt wieder das Entsetzen an vor alledem was, wie in einer unsäglichen Verwirrung, Leben heißt" (Engelhardt 1974: 23; my translation).

11 "nicht plastische, geschriebene Dinge – Wirklichkeiten, die aus dem Handwerk hervorgehen"; quoted after Holthusen (1971: 86).

12 "statische, bildhaft beruhigte Situationen und Stimmungsbilder, in denen sich ein Stück gefühlter Welt, ohne Seufzer und Aufschrei, wie eine Sache präsentiert"; quoted after Holthusen (1971: 86).

13 It is worth pointing out that the relationship between Joyce, the epiphany, and Rilke that I highlight here is neither referenced nor discussed in Beja's excellent survey of the epiphany in the modern novel.

14 Pont du Carrousel:

Der blinde Mann, der auf der Brücke steht,
grau wie ein Markstein namenloser Reiche,
er ist vielleicht das Ding, das immer gleiche,
um das von fern die Sternenstunde geht,
und der Gestirne stiller Mittelpunkt.
Denn alles um ihn irrt und rinnt und prunkt.

Er ist der unbewegliche Gerechte,
in viele wirre Wege hingestellt;
der dunkle Eingang in die Unterwelt
bei einem oberflächlichen Geschlechte.
(Rilke 1948: 119)

15 Cp. Manfred Engel's commentary (Rilke 1997: 260).

BIBLIOGRAPHY

Barthes, Roland (1977) *Image – Music – Text*, sel. and trans. Stephen Heath. New York: Hill and Wang.

Bate, Walter Jackson (1971) *The Burden of the Past and the English Poet*. London: Chatto and Windus.

Beja, Morris (1971) *Epiphany in the Modern Novel*. London: Peter Owen.

Benstock, Bernard (1976) "The Kenner conundrum: or who does what with which to whom," *James Joyce Quarterly* 13: 428–35.

Bloom, Harold (1973) *Anxiety of Influence*. New York: Oxford University Press.

Böll, Heinrich (1971) *Im Gespräch: Heinrich Böll mit Heinz Ludwig Arnold*. Munich: Richard Boorberg Verlag.

Böll, Heinrich (1974) *Gruppenbild mit Dame*. Cologne: Kiepenheuer und Witsch.

Böll, Heinrich (1977) "'Ich habe nichts über den Krieg aufgeschrieben.' Ein Gespräch mit Heinrich Böll und Hermann Lenz." In Nicolas Born and Jürgen Manthey (eds.) *Literaturmagazin 7*, pp. 30–74. Reinbek: Rowohlt.

Burke, Sean (1992) *The Death and Return of the Author: Criticism and Subjectivity in Barthes, Foucault and Derrida*. Edinburgh: Edinburgh University Press.

Damrosch, David (2006) "Rebirth of a discipline: the global origins of comparative studies," *Comparative Critical Studies* 3: 99–112.

Eliot, T. S. (1975 [1923]) "*Ulysses*, order, and myth." In Frank Kermode (ed.) *Selected Prose of T. S. Eliot*, pp. 175–8. New York: Harcourt Brace Jovanovich.

Engelhardt, Hartmut (ed.) (1974) *Materialien zu Rainer Maria Rilkes "Die Aufzeichnungen des Malte Laurids Brigge."* Frankfurt: Suhrkamp.

Freytag, Gustav, with a Preface by Chevalier Bunsen (1858) *Debit and Credit*. New York: Harper.

Genette, Gérard (1982) *Palimpsestes: La littérature au second degré*. Paris: Éditions du Seuil.

Guillén, Claudio (1971) *Literature as System: Essays toward the Theory of Literary History*. Princeton, NJ: Princeton University Press.

Guyard, Marius-François (1951) *La Littérature comparée*. Paris: Presses Universitaires de France.

Holthusen, Hans Egon (1971) *Rilke*. Reinbek: Rowohlt.

Jannidis, Fotis (ed.) (1999) *Rückkehr des Autors. Zur Erneuerung eines umstrittenen Begriffs*. Tübingen: Niemeyer.

Joyce, James (1968) *A Portrait of the Artist as a Young Man: Text, Criticism, and Notes*, ed. Chester G. Anderson. New York: Viking Press.

Lukács, Georg (1977) *Die Theorie des Romans. Ein geschichtsphilosophischer Versuch über die Formen der großen Epik*. Darmstadt and Neuwied: Luchterhand.

Mitchell, Breon (1976) *James Joyce and the German Novel 1922–1933*. Athens, OH: Ohio University Press.

Rilke, Rainer Maria (1939) *Poems*, trans. J. B. Leishman. London: Hogarth Press.

Rilke, Rainer Maria (1948) *Ausgewählte Werke, Vol. 1: Gedichte*. Frankfurt: Insel.

Rilke, Rainer Maria (1990) *The Notebooks of Malte Laurids Brigge*, trans. Stephen Mitchell. New York: Random House (Vintage).

Rilke, Rainer Maria (1997) *Die Aufzeichnungen des Malte Laurids Brigge. Kommentierte Ausgabe*, ed. and commentary by Manfred Engel. Stuttgart: Reclam.

Saussy, Haun (2006) "Exquisite cadavers stitched from fresh nightmares: of memes, hives, and selfish genes." In Haun Saussy (ed.) *Comparative Literature in an Age of Globalization*, pp. 3–42. Baltimore, MD: The Johns Hopkins University Press.

Steinberg, Erwin and Christian Hallstein (2003) "Probing silences in Joyce's *Ulysses* and the question of authorial intention." *James Joyce Quarterly* 40: 543–54.

Weninger, Robert (1995) *Framing a Novelist: Arno Schmidt Criticism 1970–1994*. Columbia, SC: Camden House.

Weninger, Robert (1998) "Böll and Joyce, Joyce on Böll: a gnomonic reading of Heinrich Böll's *Irish Journal*." In Joachim Fischer, Gisela Holfter, and Eoin Bourke (eds.) *Deutsch-Irische Verbindungen. Geschichte–Literatur–Übersetzung*, pp. 133–43. Trier: Wissenschaftlicher Verlag.

Weninger, Robert (2004) "James Joyce in German-speaking countries: the early reception 1919–1945" and "The institutionalization of 'Joyce'. James Joyce in (West) Germany, Austria and Switzerland 1945 to the present." In Geert Lernout and Wim van Mierlo (eds.) *The Reception of James Joyce in Europe*, pp. 14–69. London: Continuum.

10
Molly's Gibraltar: The Other Location in Joyce's *Ulysses*

Richard Brown

A new reader of *Ulysses* turning to the final pages of the book and having heard the usual things about it – its having been set on a single day in 1904, its being packed with the minutiae of the minds of its central characters, and its being set in Joyce's home city of Dublin – may well be surprised to find that the atmospheric location which is most strongly present in that conclusion is not Dublin at all. Neither is it any of the three locations in which Joyce lived during the composition of the book which are named in the closing signature "Trieste-Zurich-Paris 1914–1921" (*U* 18 1611–1). It is, rather, the Gibraltar of the 1870s and 80s, of Molly Bloom's birth, upbringing, and memory. And whereas the detailed particularities of Joyce's Dublin urban space and the interiority of his character's minds have often seemed to offer the defining paradigms of modernism's geography (Williams 1975: 291–3; Bradbury 1976: 96–104), Molly's Gibraltar is a place and non-place that adds another environment, providing a sense of gendered, racial, and libidinal otherness that is relatively neglected but essential to the book and also to our developing understanding of the imagined spaces of modernity. The question "Where?" is the final question of the penultimate "Ithaca" episode (*U* 17 2331) and if, as has recently been suggested (Ziarek 1994: 264), one possible way of reading the episode that follows is as an answer to that question, then one version of that answer could be construed in terms of this "Gibraltar."

Though Gibraltar was not somewhere Joyce himself visited, though its presence in *Ulysses* is often only half-acknowledged by criticism, and though Gibraltar itself (unlike many of the other places associated with Joyce in this volume and elsewhere) has yet to develop a tradition of cultural or academic reception of Joyce's work,[1] there would seem an increasing desire in Joyce criticism to explore the context of this fertile and suggestive concluding location of *Ulysses* as a significant other place and site of meaning in the book. This seems appropriate since Joyce's Gibraltar is among the most positively described locations in the book and its treatment must surely count as one of the most significant, most atmospheric, not to mention sexiest, treatments of Gibraltar that exist in modern English, adding significantly to the ways in which it has been presented whether in imaginative or non-fictional literature. Though surprising and distinctive, Joyce's Gibraltar is inevitably heir to a diverse literary tradition that includes the Greek, Roman, and medieval European epics and English writers like Defoe, George Borrow, and Tennyson and Browning. Joyce's treatment may also be placed alongside that of a close contemporary like Ezra Pound, who, unlike Joyce, did visit Gibraltar on more than one occasion and wrote about it in Canto XXII (Carpenter 1988: 88–9), but is less satirical than that of the latter in perspective and tone and might rather anticipate that of a more recent novelist, Marguerite Duras, in whose novel *Le Marin de Gibraltar* a sailor from Gibraltar is the mysterious object of the heroine's projected or possibly fantasized desire (Duras 1952).

In British military history Gibraltar, as Andrew Gibson has argued, has often been represented as a proud if somewhat rigid symbol of intransigence (Gibson 2002), a place locked in an isolating military history that might thereby dislocate it from the cultural and from a sense of the future. Certainly Gibraltar appears as a byword for "fixture" in a rare other appearance at the conclusion of the remaining fragments of Joyce's *Stephen Hero* (*SH* 239). But it appears in *Ulysses* as a place of layered mythic inheritance, of ambivalence and of gendered desire – as a garrison town that is neither quite city nor country, as a peninsula that is neither quite mainland nor island – poised in the liminal space between Europe and North Africa, a bit less like some aspects of the Dublin of 1904 and more akin, perhaps, to the global promises of the twenty-first century and beyond. Such a Gibraltar is some distance from the images of other places which we have in the book. Its military associations may sometimes have made Gibraltar seem a place of "no," but Molly's memory turns it into the place of what Jacques Derrida among others have explored as literature's most famously celebratory and communicative "yes" (Derrida 1992).

In rough quantitative terms around a fifth to a quarter of the concluding episode alone contains material set in Gibraltar (enough to make it the book's second or, as we might say, most significant "other" place). In 1904 Gibraltar was celebrating its own 200th anniversary, the anniversary of its British government, since the occupation in 1704, a fact which Joyce apparently knew and to which drew he attention in his allusion to the moment which Molly almost scoffingly recalls as one when "4 drunken English sailors took all the rock from them" (*U* 18 756). To some this history of English occupation marks the primary interest of Gibraltar in terms of its status as "another colonial city," as the annotation to its first mention in the "Calypso" episode in the 1990s World's Classics edition of *Ulysses* (Johnson 1993: 794) notes. Susan Bazargan, for example, contributes to the critical debate on "Penelope" in this vein, arguing that, on the basis of her coming from Gibraltar, Molly can be analyzed as an example of colonized subjectivity, drawing on the divided or dialogized condition of the colonial subject as defined by Homi Bhabha and the working of gender hierarchies in the structure of colonial authority as discussed by Ashis Nandy (Bazargan 1994). Joyce announces the Gibraltar connection as being significant at the very start of his introduction of the Blooms but it is not until the "Cyclops" episode that the perspective of the colonized in the context of colonial history is announced as being relevant to it and then only in the exaggerated political language of the nationalist barroom where it is described as a place "now grabbed by the foe of mankind" (*U* 12 1249). Joycean allusiveness more typically works to dislodge the potentially destructive force of such binaries. In "Calypso" it is the comic fact of the Blooms' "old style" brass bedstead which has come from Gibraltar (Molly has even allowed Bloom to suppose that it comes from the Governor's residence *U* 18 1212–13) that sets off the train of Bloom's thoughts on the role of the place in Molly's past (*U* 4 60–2) and this may, amongst other things, invite an association with another part of his British inheritance on which Joyce freely borrows, that of Shakespeare and the bequest to Anne Hathaway of the "secondbest bed" that is the subject of discussion in the "Scylla and Charybdis" episode's theorizings about Shakespeare.

In a book where the life of the modern city and the conditions of colonialism have so frequently produced points of entry for critical debate, the complex cultural associations that play into Joyce's Gibraltar make it hard to define it only as a city or as a colony in the classic senses. Anyway the latter term would conceal a host of complex particularities that it is neither easy nor even especially helpful to reduce to the simple binary opposition of colonizer and colonized. Following Bazargan's lead, for instance, we might say that, from the much-discussed Spivakian point of view, Molly, as an Irish woman, may fit the condition of being silenced by a double colonization (Spivak 1988). But Molly's mixed origins – her father the occupying Irish soldier "Major" Tweedy and her mother the shadowy "jewess looking" (*U* 18 1184) Lunita Laredo – make her more complex in her ethnicity and social placement than might be supposed. She is a good deal more confident and empowered in this condition and in her gendered individuality than picturing her as a doubly colonized victim would suggest. In Gibraltar she is enough the colonizer to enjoy garrison privileges and the "cantankerous," "rock scorpion" Mrs. Rubio as a housekeeper or maid, and in Dublin her "Spanish type" looks give her some extra cultural capital which she exploits in her singing career. There is a clear case that Gibraltar was chosen by Joyce to give him a credible opportunity to pose a heroine of somewhat mixed ethnic background alongside his partly Jewish hero Leopold Bloom, and Molly is placed there in a position of some social status and power so that her Gibraltarian aspect is not so much a condition of disempowerment as one of displacement and desire.

Enda Duffy has ingeniously suggested that the "subaltern" point about Molly's imaginative displacement to Gibraltar might be that "it transgressed the unspoken rule that the natives of that colony will keep to their own territory" (Duffy 1994: 183–4). It may indeed be that Gibraltar gives Molly somewhere other to go than Dublin, at least in her imagination, which empowers her in relation to her immediate environment. And it may be the more complex varieties of social "otherness" that are sometimes represented in contemporary theoretical discussions of the condition of postcoloniality or in the processes of postcolonizing that most helpfully open up the vision of Gibraltar as constructed in Molly's memory in the book (Quayson 2000). Molly, for instance, remembers Mrs. Rubio's sense of indigenous nativist resentment about the event of the occupation, but she does not share it. Any reader turning to the end of *Ulysses* will be more likely to be struck by the good-humoured image which she has of the place as a sensuous and sensual environment of warm weather, natural growth, children's games, commercial transactions, romantic and erotic possibilities achieved, diverse and peacefully coexisting cultural and ethnic mixtures and so on:

> I was thinking of so many things he didnt know . . . the Spanish girls laughing in their shawls and their tall combs and the auctions in the morning the Greeks and the jews and the Arabs . . . yes and those handsome Moors all in white and turbans like kings asking you to sit down in their little bit of a shop . . . and the sea the sea crimson sometimes like fire and the glorious sunsets and the figtrees in the Alameda gardens yes . . . and the pink and blue and yellow houses . . . Gibraltar as a girl where I was a Flower of the mountain . . . and how he kissed me under the Moorish wall and I thought well as well him as another . . . (*U* 18 1582–1604)

There is certainly a sense of magical transformation rather than of political oppression here. The longer passage of her memory begins at a moment of intimacy with Bloom's kiss on Howth Head and what has happened there, and this is underpinned with the idea that the whole imaginative landscape is somehow "other" to Bloom's experience. Her ecstatic response to his kiss seems coincident with or maybe even depends upon the "many things he didn't know" in which otherness and the libidinal may be vitally connected. Her Gibraltar memory is an indication of both her alterity and her interiority. Furthermore, in the line "where I *was* a Flower of the mountain" (*U* 18 1602; my emphasis), readers might spot the ecstatic development of Molly's earlier thought "he said I was a flower of the mountain" (*U* 18 1576). Here she apparently drops the implied acknowledgment that Bloom's gallant compliment is a metaphor. Instead Molly sees herself as apparently quite literally having been transformed back into the flower she once was. The impression of ecstatic transport is further underscored by the rogue capitalization of "Flower," which may well strike observant readers as appropriate enough since we know of Bloom's libidinal alter-ego name Henry Flower from earlier in the day and it is conceivable that, as well as his "official" name Bloom, it is also the Bloomian world of covert domestic romance that she is in the process of adopting in saying "yes" to his proposal here. The flower metaphor becomes "the one true thing he said" as she morphs momentarily into the myth.

There is much in the detail of Gibraltar as it appears through the episode that invites critical discussion but several contextual factors play into and support the sense of pleasure that frames its presentation at this moment. The place is invoked through layers of Molly's association with the moment when Leopold "proposed" to her on Howth Head in what we may assume, through the book's meticulously constructed internal time-scheme, to have been sometime in the summer of 1888, not long after her arrival in Dublin, when she was about 18 years old. Molly associates the pleasurable memory of that event with a previous occasion, some few years earlier, when she was about 14 or 15, when she was out with her first serious boyfriend Mulvey in various places on the rock and as they enjoyed some share of exploratory sexual intimacy including the orgasm she gives him with her hand on his "last day."

From one psychoanalytic point of view Susan Stanford Friedman has argued that, if we seek to substantiate in detail Richard Ellmann's much-accepted view that Joyce chose the date of June 16, 1904, for *Ulysses* to commemorate the day when he and Nora Barnacle first went out together, it is in the memories of the Bloom's courtship and especially in Molly's recall of her sexual intimacies with Mulvey in Gibraltar that this courtship is actually presented in the book (Friedman 1993: 54). We do not see Stephen Dedalus as being much like the young Joyce of 1904 in this respect. However, some displacement of the intimacies of the young Joyces, perhaps even of some of the intimate details of their courtship recalled in Joyce's love letters of 1909 (*SL* 182), may play into the placement of Molly's memories of her girlhood in Gibraltar, which takes on its eroticized and romanticized atmosphere partly because of this, as in Molly's mind Gibraltar is reconstructed in the manner of a hot date on Howth Head on a sunny day.

Meanwhile, readers of Joyce's *A Portrait* may be excused for consciously or unconsciously importing the structure of feeling implied in the narrative paradigm of that earlier book. The Stephen of *A Portrait* is poised at the end of that text to leave the constraining Dublin of his adolescence and expectations for some other supposedly better and freer location. He is no closer to sharing his escape with a partner than is the Stephen of *Ulysses* and the place to which he is voyaging is shadowy and symbolic by contrast with the places he leaves. We see little more than a vision of the "white arms of roads" which give him the "promise" of welcome, as do "the black arms of tall ships" (*P* 213). We might extrapolate from the authorial by-line "Dublin 1904/Trieste 1914" that Joyce envisaged it was for somewhere like Trieste and for something not unlike his own Triestine experiences of young family life and freedom that Stephen was departing: a place of happiness a bit like the idealized Trieste of Ewan MacGregor's 1990 film version of Brenda Maddox's biography *Nora* (MacGregor, 1990). But it is not stated in the text that this is so. Some mysteriously distant other location perhaps along the lines of the romanticized Buenos Aires of the story "Eveline" may be imagined. Given the location of the story of the mythic Daedalus in classical Crete we may be forgiven for having an image of some mythic or idealized Mediterranean destination (perhaps Stephen's roads even conjure to some geographically minded readers an echo of adjacent "Rhodes"), but this is not stated either. It seems obvious enough, though, that the promises set up in this narrative paradigm may inflect the way we may want to read the end of *Ulysses* as forward-looking and utopian as much as it is retrospective, reminding us that it may be Molly Bloom in *Ulysses* who is to be thought to have been its boldest traveler, possibly indeed its best example of an Odyssean "exile" whose dreams are of her home and show some traces of a longing to return.

The political question of the "colonial" in the history of the rock, then, is strongly inflected by these complex emotional displacements on the part of the character and the author. Resentment is hardly the governing feeling since Molly is immersed in the libidinal aspects of a complex inheritance of cultural diversity. She feels herself aligned to the military garrison through her father's placement as a part of the garrison community engaged there. She tends to see military uniforms as an attractive aspect of masculine self-display rather than as a political symbol or threat, more sensitive to them as a mark of masculinity rather than as one of national obligation. Despite the strong moral and political views in the nationalist community about such conduct, she has been happy to enjoy an affair with the English Lieutenant Gardner since her marriage to Bloom and even to pass on to him Mulvey's Claddagh ring (*U* 18 867). Elsewhere in the episode she is shown as an enthusiast for Kipling, the late Victorian poet of empire, and such politically incorrect attitudes seem to have placed her as an apologist for the cosmopolitan amongst her more nationalist neighbors in Dublin and her enthusiasm for the Gibraltar of her youth may be seen as a part of this stance. Paul O'Hanrahan has made the point that the location of Gibraltar figures precisely in Molly's imagination as an alternative to negative aspects of her image of her Dublin environment (O'Hanrahan 2006). And this too may align to the general associations of gendered otherness that define her as an independent individual, as desirable because somewhat different from other women in Dublin at the time as well as subtly similar to and different from Bloom.

The Exegetical Tradition

Part of the interest of discussing Molly's Gibraltar emerges from the fact that significant earlier critics such as Stuart Gilbert and Frank Budgen, whose ideas often took the hint from Joyce himself, did not give much more than hints on the question of how to read this presence in the book (Gilbert 1952; Budgen 1972). The question of the setting of Molly's memories is not one on which Joyce commented in his 1921 explanatory letter about the final episode, nor is the place one on which he wrote in his nonfictional or critical writings or in his fiction outside of *Ulysses*, besides a couple of references to the Pillars of Hercules in *Finnegans Wake* (*FW* 16 4 and 128 36). As we have seen, the biographical approach does not get us anything like as far as it usually does with Joyce. But there are many critical insights that have accumulated from which a fuller picture of the role of this setting might appear, and Gilbert and Budgen themselves provide two useful directions.

Gilbert was the first to explore the allusive epic or mythic links: sketching the complex connections that tie Joyce's use of a modern Gibraltar into the classical Homeric subtext of his novel. Gilbert, the classicist, seems to digest relatively easily these typically complicated and unsettling components according to which:

1 Joyce's Molly Bloom is to be identified with *both* the Homeric Penelope *and* the Homeric Calypso, the person from whom Bloom – Odysseus departs in the morning and to whom he returns at night. This double identification is confirmed in Joyce's Linati schema (see Ellmann 1972).
2 Calypso is the daughter of Atlas and the Atlas Mountains are the mountains on the African side of the Straits of Gibraltar.

3 Calypso lives on the distant Western island Ogygia, which, according to Joyce's favored Homericist Victor Bérard, might be identified with the bay of Gibraltar (see Seidel 1975).

4 "Calpe," the Greek name for the bay of Gibraltar, sounds a bit like Calypso and means "cup" or "bowl," reinforcing this identification from a classical Greek or even the "Phoenician" geographical perspective that emerges from Bérard.

5 Because of 1 above, there might even be some connection between Gibraltar and Penelope's rocky island home of Ithaca.

Gilbert is keen to place these associations in a further symbolic connection with the Greek and Roman earth- goddesses Gaea and Tellus. So the Gibraltarian connection is by no means all he has on his mind and broader elements of gynomorphic geographic symbolism come into play. The point about Gibraltar as such here, succinctly made by Michael Seidel, whose *Epic Geography* developed the study of Joyce's use of Bérard more than most other Joyce critics, might be that the placement of Molly Bloom's childhood memories in Gibraltar adds a dimension to the mythic parallel or analogy that begins to return the setting of the novel away from the Dublin locality and back towards the environment of its Mediterranean epic original (Seidel 2002: 144). The fact that Gibraltar is a viably Homeric location in the Joycean text turns realism back to the mythic and cultural memories of Europe. Indeed it potentially redraws the boundaries of the real and symbolic in the text in many suggestive ways. Some of these may include such connections with epic geographies but they also include the deliberate association of the two pseudo-Odyssean sailors of the book, Mulvey and the sailor from "Eumaeus," D. B. Murphy, if laconically, with this location (*U* 17 611–23).

Calypso's island is one of the most luxuriously described environments in the *Odyssey*, as it is also, for instance, in the seventeenth-century French reworking of the story by François de Fénélon, *Telemachus*, which was one of the better-known literary works of its period (translated by Tobias Smollett, amongst others), as Joyce would have known. Here the story is retold as that of the wanderings of Telemachus and right from the start the son as nearly falls victim to the charms of the nymph, as had his father. The luxuriousness of such visions of Ogygia may also be echoed in Joyce's Gibraltar. In Joseph Lennon's recent study of *Irish Orientalism*, the representation of Ireland itself as Ogygia by Roderic O'Flaherty and other writers from the seventeenth century adds further to the pattern of associations to which Joyce may have been exposed and meanwhile thoroughly problematizes the oppositions between self and other upon which they depend (Lennon 2004: 58–114).

Richard Ellmann, without a specifically biographical connection to highlight in this case, in *Ulysses on the Liffey* adds a further dimension to the range of allusions that are important to Gibraltar in making a connection with the post-Homeric representation of Ulysses' last voyage that we find in Canto XXVI of Dante's *Inferno*. Here the story of the hero's fatal last voyage beyond the Pillars of Hercules and Dante's mysterious references to *"una montagna, bruna / per la distanza"* ("a mountain, brown from the distance") add greatly to associations of mysterious otherness surrounding the place.

That Dante's *Ulysses* was a favorite for Triestine resident and Italian-speaking Joyce is hardly in doubt and that it was also an important point of cultural reference for his modernist contemporaries can be seen in that it also has a role in the allusive sub-text of T. S. Eliot's *The Waste Land* (Eliot 1971: 128). The Gibraltar of Pound's *Cantos* is multi-ethnic and commercial, like Joyce's, but the atmosphere and tone are much less celebratory. Amongst many other possible associations it may be no coincidence that Wagner's heroine Brünnhilde is made captive on a rock by her father Wotan, from whence she is released by the hero Siegfried, though (perhaps because Bloom is said to find Wagner "a bit too heavy"; *U* 16 1736) this has come up less often in criticism and, as will become apparent, Molly's other location may well be as strongly constructed from popular-cultural as from such high-cultural musical sources.

In reading Joyce the danger, as Samuel Beckett said, is often "in the neatness of identifications" and the tendency of allusive criticism is to conflate otherness into the same (Beckett 1929). Alongside myth we should always try to place a sense of history. Consequently, to my mind, one of the most significant historical contributions on the question of Joyce's Gibraltar came in the 1960s in the work of Robert Martin Adams. For Adams the whole point was that Gibraltar was "outside the realm of his [Joyce's] own personal experience." However, the reality of the modern place is still vividly glimpsed in the text and that partly explains the mechanics of the representation. Joyce researched contemporary guidebooks and built details of street and shop names from that research into his text using the *Gibraltar Directory* much as he did with *Thom's Dublin Directory* for the Dublin scenes, and, according to Adams at any rate, "from no other motive, it would seem, than to enrich his social background" (Adams 1967: 231–3). Many of the Gibraltar place, personal, and business names are glossed in Gifford and Seidman's notes from such sources. For all the brilliance of his discoveries, though, and the Copernican shift that they imply, Adams' critical conclusions seem cautious, literal, even bathetic. Yet they open up a window on a *Ulysses* the depth and detailed particularity of whose locations are constructed by such researched use of published documents rather than, for example, recalled from personal experience, and they can consequently point to social realities as much as to personal memory and myth. Adams' approach encourages a sense of the comparability of Joyce's Dublin, which he did know, with his Gibraltar, which he did not, both being equally visible as symbolic and strategic locations within the text. If we go back to that explanatory letter of 1921 we do see that Joyce had asked Frank Budgen in 1921 for another source, a book on the *Sieges of Gibraltar* (*SL* 284–5) and this might further suggest this alternative direction of exploring the interest of the modern history as well as mythic significance of the place.

Further conspicuous advances in our knowledge of Joyce's "Penelope" in the 1970s and 80s were based on opportunities for the detailed understanding of Joyce's research in and use of source materials on Gibraltar that were provided by genetic and notebook study associated with the publication of the Garland facsimile archive. Books by Philip Herring (especially his study and transcription of the *"Ulysses" Notesheets in the British Museum*) and the detailed study of "Penelope" by James van Dyck Card explored the extent of Joyce's use of certain key texts including books such as *A History of the Late Siege of Gibraltar* by John Drinkwater, *A History of Gibraltar and its Sieges* by Frederic Stephens, and, above all, Henry Field's *Gibraltar*, published in 1889.

In what is the fullest of the attempts to place Joyce's treatment within a wide discursive history of writings about Gibraltar so far, Gibson shows that the sieges and what we may call "siege discourse" have been a powerful, if not the most powerful, paradigm in histories of Gibraltar throughout the nineteenth century, and in England Gibraltar gained almost "sacred status" through such military-historical narratives. However, it is not the history of the sieges of Gibraltar that dominates the "Penelope" episode for all that this might have made a convenient Homeric analogy for Joyce or an opportunity to explore the morals of Molly's sexual fidelity at a basic level. According to Gibson, Joyce's treatment of Gibraltar in the episode is unique among the books he might have read for its discursive elements of "budding sexuality (18 769–72, 777–8, 787–825, 850–3); lewdness (18 440); sensuousness, color, and warmth (19 605–11, 973, 1598–1603); literature (18 652–7), music (18 644), games (18 1583–4); splendid scenery (18 399–400, 790–2), exotic flora and fauna (18 665, 784–7, 871, 973–5)." (Gibson 2002: 262–3). We might call this Molly's "female" narrative of personal childhood happiness, the senses and romance as opposed to an official "masculine" military discursive history of siege and defense. There might, of course, be an analogy to be drawn with Joyce's evasion of a traditionally moralistic treatment of Penelopean sexual fidelity here too. Taking issue with Bazargan's critique of Molly as the symptomatic victim of a stereotypically colonized mentality, Gibson argues that this place provides "an image of the possibility of ordinary sanity and happiness that Joyce finally presented to Ireland in the year of its independence" (Gibson 2002: 272).

A related but distinguishable sense of the Gibraltar material in "Penelope" can be found in a recent essay by Paul O'Hanrahan, where these aspects of the place are contrasted with frustrating aspects of her experience of her Dublin environment rather than with the assumptions of colonial discourse. O'Hanrahan contrasts her associations of the cold weather and a sense of constraint in Dublin with her enjoyment of the wide vistas, warmth, and sun of her Gibraltar memories. He points out the occasionally sordid or squalid sexual scenes in Dublin (the image of the copulating dogs and the men outside the urinal) and contrasts these with the "preference for *al fresco* sex, preferably at a height," in Gibraltar (O'Hanrahan 2006: 193–4). Here Gibraltar may provide her with a high point of pleasurable experience against which both her marriage and her affair can be assessed.

Drawing on both of these approaches, then, it would make sense to see Joyce's deployment of his complex image of Gibraltar as a double critique both of the narrownesses and limitations of colonial discourse and of the entrapments of the contemporary city, and, of course, it has other critical dimensions too, which its thorough embedding in such wide-ranging cultural associations may leave too varied to be ever fully resolved.

The Multi-ethnic Field

Among Joyce's source books the 1889 book *Gibraltar* by the American traveler Henry Field has become the best known, especially as the source for the enthusiastic and emotional mood, which is an important component of the "gynomorphic" or feminine style of the discourse. Joyce's use of Field is also significant in its underlining of aspects of the peacefully coexisting ethnic alterities that are so important for Joyce's picture of the place.

Field quotes "a lady correspondent" who writes, "I never tire of the brilliant sunsets, the gorgeous clouds, with the snow-capped mountains of Granada for a background" (Field 1889: 14–15). Joyce follows Field in apparently overestimating the visible proximity of the Sierras here and they have many other details in common. Further miscellaneous correspondences include his frontispiece photograph of the Alameda Gardens (a special favorite place for Molly, which she mentions three times in the episode and once in "Cyclops") and references to the Levanter (Field 1889: 46), to the "cavalry at San Roque" (Field 1889: 70), and the bull ring at La Linea (Field 1889: 112) all of which form moments in her memories. Molly feels sympathy for "the sentry in front of the governors house," "poor devil half roasted" (*U* 18 1585, 6), and she notes that she "could see over to Morocco almost . . . and the Atlas mountain with snow on it" (*U* 18 859–60). Field notes that a "little house furnishes a shelter for officer on duty, who from its flat roof, with his field-glasses, sweeps the whole horizon, north and south, from the Sierra Nevada in Spain, to the long chain of the Atlas Mountains in Africa" (Field 1889: 14).

As several critics have noted, the celebration of Gibraltar's multi-ethnic integration links Joyce and Field. Field says,

> there is a singular mixture of characters and countries, of races and religions. Here Spaniards and Moors who fought for Gibraltar a thousand years ago, are at peace and good friends, at least so far as to be willing to cheat each other as readily as if they were men of the same religion. Here are the long-bearded Jews in their gabardines; and the Turks with their baggy trousers, taking up more space than is allowed to Christian legs; with a mongrel race from the Eastern part of the Mediterranean, known as Levantines, and another like unto them, the Maltese; and a choice variety of natives of Gibraltar, called "Rock Scorpions," with Africans blacker than the Moors, who have perhaps crossed the desert, and hail from Timbuctoo (Field 1889: 334).

Field is not alone in this kind of account. The account of Gibraltar in George Borrow's *The Bible in Spain* (many editions from the 1840s to end of the century) has a similar account of the demographic mix:

> here walked a group of officers, there a knot of soldiers stood talking and laughing. The greater part of the citizens appeared to be Spaniards but there was a large sprinkling of Jews in the dress of those of Barbary, and here and there a turbaned Moor (Borrow: 710).

The demographic basis of such impressions might be clarified by placing alongside them the account of the numbers of soldiers and civilians and the races or at least religions of the population which were given in the contemporary *Gibraltar Directory*: "The population at the end of 1878 was 25,700, including the military; the civil population divided as follows: Protestants, 1,203; Roman Catholics, 15,296; Hebrews, 1,465; Mohammedans, 44" (*Gibraltar Directory 1883*: 20).

Molly follows Borrow and Field in her enthusiastic glosses on this mix. In this respect Joyce's presentation of Gibraltar may function not just as an emotional contrast for Molly from the day-to-day constraints of Dublin domestic life, but as a kind of political contrast, pointing up, especially in relation to the kind of racial exclusions of which Bloom finds himself a victim in the "Cyclops" episode, the dangerous potential of some contemporary nationalist discourses to resort to an idea of homogenous indigeneity to define their community. Critiques of the assumption of homogenized indigeneity take many forms in *Ulysses* but one of them may be in this utopian multiethnic picture of Gibraltar with which the book concludes.

Molly's Gibraltar is also a good deal more "Spanishy" (Bloom's term for her from "Sirens," *U* 11 731) than the usual narrative account and this can be seen in the place names, in characters like Mrs. Rubio, and in Molly's own half-Spanish background. The *Directory* would have given him these distinctive names and atmospheric details of its "stairs" and "ramps" and donkey carts. In this passage Joyce favors the Spanish name "Calle las Siete Revueltas" for Mill Lane, just as he does Calle Real for Waterport Street (*U* 18 763):

> those names in Gibraltar Delapaz Delagracia they had the devils queer names there father Vilaplana of Santa Maria that gave me the rosary Rosales y OReilly in the Calle las Siete Revueltas and Pisimbo and Mrs Opisso in Governor street O what a name Id go and drown myself in the first river if I had a name like her O my and all the bits of streets Paradise ramp and Bedlam ramp and Rodgers ramp and Crutchetts ramp and the devils gap steps (*U* 18 1463–9).

Bloom thinks in "Calypso" that she has "Forgotten any little Spanish she knew" (*U* 4 59–60) but she thinks, "I haven't forgotten it all" (*U* 18 1472). Mrs. Rubio has given her a novel by "Valera" (Juan Valera Y Alcala Galiano) to read and a fair smattering of Spanish words and phrases from "horquilla" (*U* 18 751), to "como esta" (*U* 18 1471–2), to "dos huevos estrillados senor" (*U* 18 1486–7), or the half-remembered Spanish word *sereno*, in Molly's usage "serene" (*U* 18 1597), turn up in her thoughts and throughout the book. Sometimes Spanish and Gibraltarian themes and associations easily merge and overlap without strict border lines. This happens to absurd effect in "Eumaeus," where Bloom meanderingly explains to Stephen that "my wife is, so to speak, Spanish, half that is" (*U* 16 879). He adds that this implies she is hot-blooded and then, with wonderfully circular Eumaean logic, that Parnell's mistress Kitty O'Shea, "the English whore," was also hot-blooded and therefore "if I don't greatly mistake she was Spanish too" (*U* 16 1413). (O'Shea was not actually Spanish, of course.) Bloom then shows off Molly's photo to emphasize the point about her appearance (*U* 16 1425–55), perhaps revealing an unconscious link (which is later made explicit by Molly; *U* 18 564) between his attraction to Molly's exotic Spanish looks and a pornographic picture of a couple having sex in Spanish dress which he keeps in his drawer (*U* 17 1810).

Her construction of the Spanish flavor of her childhood memories seems also to go hand in hand with the pair of popular musical songs, "Waiting" and "In Old Madrid," which she sang in Gibraltar and which formed part of her repertoire when she first came to Dublin. The second of these is half-quoted at the close of the book in the line "2 glancing eyes a lattice hid" (*U* 18 1596). This song and the breathy "Waiting" are mentioned and half-quoted several times: in "Sirens" (*U* 11 730–4, 1004); in "Nausicaa" (where Gerty MacDowell is also apparently immersed in the erotics of anticipation; *U* 13 209 and 669); and in "Eumaeus" (where Bloom shows Stephen the picture of Molly singing the song; *U* 18 1432); and throughout "Penelope" (*U* 18 617, 678–9, 736–7, 1335–41, 1595), where the songs frequently overlap. David Pierce reproduced an illustrated postcard in *James Joyce's Ireland* (Pierce 1992: 61) that admirably captures the atmosphere of "In Old Madrid." It is an unashamedly populist and stereotypically "Spanishy" picture of Gibraltar as well as of the role of the sense of difference or the mildly exotic in sexual attraction that we get from the use of such sources. Even Molly refers to it as "in old Madrid stuff silly women believe" (*U* 18 736), though words from the song figure in her thoughts about her relationships with Bloom, Stephen, Boylan, and the Stanhopes as if such stereotypes are often part and parcel of the mechanics of desire.

The Sephardic community in Gibraltar and the tradition of religious toleration are regularly invoked by writers from Defoe onwards and by critics of Joyce. Molly recalls having been playful and comfortable in taking Mulvey to the "jews burial-place" (*U* 18 834) on a date. Her family connection to a "jewess looking" mother (*U* 18 1184) may be one reason, but then she mentions the Catholic Cathedral of Santa Maria more than once, has a rosary, and has certainly adopted Catholicism at some point, so it is not made especially clear to which ethnic or cultural grouping she most feels she belongs. Molly's recall of "the old longbearded jews in their jellibees" (*U* 18 687) and of the language on the gravestones seems part of her enjoyment of the diversity of the place. She is also made to recall the Genoan community at Catalan Bay and to make associations between it and other places in Italy where Bloom has apparently promised to take her on a honeymoon (*U* 18 974, 985).

The awareness of Gibraltar's proximity to Africa and the Africanness and related Orientalism of Joyce's presentation of it in "Penelope" and in "Calypso" also deserve attention. Mrs. Rubio worships a black-skinned image of the virgin in the cathedral (*U* 18 759). Molly can "see over to Morocco almost the bay of Tangier" (*U* 18 860), she imagines various semi-mythic connections with the other side of the straits such as "the way down the monkeys go under the sea to Africa" (*U* 18 793–4) and "the sand-frog shower from Africa" (*U* 18 871), and she recalls "listening to that old Arab with the one eye and his heass of an instrument singing his heah heah aheah" (*U* 18 700–1). She thinks "Id have to get a nice pair of red slippers like those Turks with the fez used to sell" (*U* 18 1494–5), one of a thread of references to the Turkish in her reality, of which Bloom's dream of Molly "in Turkish costume" in "Circe" or Stephen's half-remembered dream of Haroun al Raschid (*U* 3 365–9) may form a fantastical anticipation and counterpart. And at the climax of the episode she recalls "those handsome Moors all in white and turbans like kings asking you to sit down in their little bit of a shop" (*U* 18 1593–4).

A new fascination with black bodies was shown by modernist artists from Picasso's *Demoiselles d'Avignon* of 1907 (several of whose faces are famously copied from African masks), in Joseph Conrad, in the presence of the writer Rabindranath Tagore (to whom Joyce fleetingly compared himself in a letter [*LI* 165] and Djuna Barnes recalled him mentioning in a review [Herring, 1995:215]), in Jean Rhys (herself half-Caribbean), and in several other high-modernist writers, especially Nancy Cunard, known to Joyce from his arrival in Paris, who was to scandalize the society of the 1930s through her relationship with black jazz musician Henry Crowder and edited her celebration of the Harlem renaissance under the title *Negro*.

Molly's reference to "handsome Moors" does not suggest quite so well developed a curiosity about ethnic alterity as Cunard's but does add to an impression of the conflation of the landscapes of the two sides of the straits that is first set up in "Calypso" when Bloom thinks of Molly's Gibraltar and the train of associations sets him wandering around the city with old Tweedy as sentry then "through awned streets. Turbaned faces going by. Dark caves of carpet shops" (*U* 4 86–98). This description has clearly become one of an Islamic Moroccan townscape, presumably Tangiers, rather than anything in Gibraltar itself, but the conflation is appropriate in a way since volumes like the *Gibraltar Directory* which Joyce used included brief descriptions of Ceuta and Tangiers as possible destinations for travelers (as well as nearby places on the Spanish side like Tarifa and Ronda which are mentioned by Molly), and they emphasize the local color of streets and carpet shops and, for example, the reedy Moorish wind instruments which are sometimes compared to the sound of the bagpipes. Bloom meanwhile himself construes this scene through his immediate popular cultural source, the pantomime *Turko the Terrible*, and aspects of his and Molly's experience accrue oriental glosses from his visit to the "Hammam" in "Lotus-Eaters" (*U* 5 502) through to her appearance "in Turkish costume" accompanied by a humanoid camel in "Circe" (*U* 15 298–330), as in his mind "Spain, Gibraltar, Mediterranean, the Levant" (*U* 4 211) merge rapidly into each other and into fantasy. Stephen too recalls that even his mother enjoyed *Turko the Terrible* in happier days (*U* 257–9) and has his oriental half-remembered dream of Haroun al Raschid (*U* 3 365–9).

"The B Marche Paris"

Joyce deploys senses of gendered alterity alongside ones of ethnic alterity to create a Molly Bloom who constructs the details of her remembered Gibraltar through mildly exotic images of popular culture, and she is herself in part constructed as an object of desire, wittingly or unwittingly, through stereotypes that may derive both from her and from Bloom's and also Stephen's absorption of the orientalist stereotypes in the popular cultures in which they live. Perhaps, though, her actual memories of Gibraltar do allow her a place in remembered reality which is significantly other to the more fantastical constructions of their imaginations. Her sense of the red slippers sold by the Turk and the "bit of a shop" run by the "handsome moors" may, for that matter, also be connected to a thread of references to shops and shopping in the episode which include, as we have seen, such markers of social reality as the local Gibraltar shop names of Benady Brothers and Abrines that appear in the text.

Via her memories of her most important childhood friend Hester Stanhope, who has left Gibraltar to go to live in Paris, we may also make a connection to another kind of reality beyond the text's layers of constructedness in "the B Marche Paris" to which she twice refers (*U* 18 613, 858) since Hester has bought her the present of a frock from there. This store is Le Bon Marché, Paris's oldest department store, amply mythologized in Emile Zola's *Au Bonheur des Dames* (The Ladies' Paradise) as early as 1883, which is located on the rue de Sèvres and not of course to be confused with the newer and now better-known department stores of the Boulevard Haussmann, as Gifford and Seidman's notes seem to do (Gifford and Seidman 1988: 617). Since when he was writing the episode Joyce himself was living in what might have seemed to be another partly utopian location, the Paris of the 1920s, and indeed for some of that time in the Boulevard Raspail apartment which was just around the corner from Le Bon Marché, this train of associations brings us right back from the imagined Gibraltar of the 1870s and 1880s to the social and biographical context in which he was writing. The libidinal, cosmopolitan, much-mythologized literary Montparnasse of the later 1920s of Hemingway (who moved in across the street from Valery Larbaud's apartment where Joyce completed "Penelope," Larbaud, Gertrude Stein, Nancy Cunard, Djuna Barnes, and Jean Rhys, as well as the closer circle of Sylvia Beach, Robert McAlmon, Winnifred Ellerman (Bryher), and Samuel Beckett, of which he was to become the central focus, was becoming Joyce's reality, and one which no doubt differed in many ways from the Dublin of 1904, let alone the Gibraltar of the 1870s and 80s. The avant-garde daughters of shipping magnates more than lowly mariners were his accomplices. Yet, as I have attempted to show, the ways in which he wrote about those 1870s and 80s may deliberately anticipate aspects of the kind of "future" which he was himself experiencing at the time.

A final cluster of associations that might help us define the presentation of Gibraltar in *Ulysses* emerges from Molly's remembered friendship with both Hester Stanhope and her husband, who represent an important cosmopolitan attachment for her that is briefly connected to Paris but also deeply associated with writing (inasmuch as we see Hester through her affectionate postcard to Molly, *U* 18 612–25), and reading (since Hester has been the main source for her adolescent curriculum of fiction-reading that includes the books by Wilkie Collins, Mrs. Braddon, Bulwer-Lytton, Mrs. Henry Wood, Margaret Hungerford, and Defoe that she has read in Gibraltar as part of that friendship and which seem to remain among the more substantial literary experiences which she recalls). It is well known that two previous Stanhopes associated with

Gibraltar are combined in the naming of Joyce's characters: a former governor of the garrison and Lady Hester Stanhope, the eighteenth-century traveler and diarist who stopped in Gibraltar on her way to the Middle East. Bloom's retention of the Gibraltar Garrison library copy of the *History of the Russo-Turkish War* on his bookshelf in "Ithaca" (that we assume he has acquired through his father-in-law) may even further underline that association with Gibraltar as a place of reading in *Ulysses*.

It is, however, thoroughly characteristic of the discourse of "Penelope" that the friendship with the Stanhopes is so entirely believably imagined through the eyes of a fictional Molly Bloom that we need to remind ourselves of these allusive correspondences from time to time. The sense of authentic personally-experienced details which are not so evidently mediated by official print discourses or even easily accessible popular-cultural sources is delivered up in the description of this friendship and the other glimpsed half-recalled characters like Mulvey and Captain Groves, and in countless other details that make up the episode such as references to the childrens' games "all birds fly and I say stoop" and "washing up dishes" (*U* 18 1584), or the memory of running joyfully down Willis' Road, or the incident of bursting the biscuit bag, which communicate a simple sense of experienced everyday fun.

Joyce, in his references to the "indispensable countersign" to Bloom's "passport" (*SL* 278), seems to have thought of the "Penelope" episode and of his principal female character in terms of the difference of perspective that she brings to bear on the events of the day as an independent corroboration (or otherwise) of the book's claim to reality. An important aspect of this independent perspective comes from the geographical otherness of her memories of her childhood and their wealth of "so many things he didn't know" (*U* 18 1582). But Gibraltar is not just other to Bloom and Stephen, or, for that matter, to Joyce himself. It is deftly construed in the text as marked by alterities of gender and ethnicity that provide a powerful alternative to or double critique of the conventional discourses of intransigence associated with British military historiography and of the assumptions of racial homogeneity in some contemporary nationalist discourses.

As such it provides more than a nostalgic or romanticized personal memory, being the significant other location of the text's modernity in which its personal and political desires and aspirations can be articulated and confirmed.

NOTE

1   I should acknowledge here that an earlier version of this chapter was delivered as an invited lecture at the Jewish Museum in London on the occasion of a celebration of the 300th anniversary of the Jewish community in Gibraltar.

BIBLIOGRAPHY

Adams, Robert Martin (1967) *Surface and Symbol.* Oxford: Oxford University Press.

Bazargan, Susan (1994) "Mapping Gibraltar: colonialism, time and narrative in 'Penelope.'" In Richard Pearce (ed.) *Molly Blooms: A Polylogue on "Penelope" and Cultural Studies,* pp. 119–38. Madison: University of Wisconsin Press.

Beckett, Samuel (1929) *Our Exagmination Round His Factification for the Incamination of Work in Progress.* London: Faber and Faber.

Borrow, George (1907) *The Bible in Spain.* London: John Murray.

Bradbury, Malcolm (1976) "The cities of modernism." In Malcolm Bradbury and James McFarlane. *Modernism,* pp. 95–104. London: Penguin.

Brooker, Peter and Andrew Thacker (eds.) (2005) *The Geographies of Modernism.* London: Routledge.

Brown, Richard (ed.) (2006) *Joyce, "Penelope" and the Body.* Amsterdam: Rodopi.

Budgen, Frank (1972 [1937]) *James Joyce and the Making of "Ulysses" and other Writings.* London: Oxford University Press.

Card, James van Dyck (1984) *An Anatomy of "Penelope."* Rutherford: Farleigh Dickenson University Press.

Carpenter, Humphrey (1988) *A Serious Character: The Life of Ezra Pound.* London: Faber and Faber.

Cunard, Nancy (ed.) (2002 [1934]) *Negro.* New York: Continuum.

Derrida, Jacques (1992) "Ulysses gramophone: hear say yes in Joyce." In Derek Attridge (ed.) *Acts of Literature,* pp. 253–309. London: Routledge.

Devlin, Kimberley J. and Marilyn Reizbaum (1999) *Ulysses: En-gendered Perspectives.* Columbia: University of South Carolina Press.

Drinkwater, John (1905) *A History of the Siege of Gibraltar (1779–1783).* London: John Murray.

Duffy, Enda (1994) *The Subaltern "Ulysses."* Minneapolis: University of Minnesota Press.

Duras, Marguerite (1952) *Le Marin de Gibraltar.* Paris: Gallimard.

Eliot, T. S. (1971) in Valerie Eliot (ed.) *The Waste Land: A Facsimile and Transcript of the Original Drafts Including the Annotations of Ezra Pound.* London: Faber and Faber.

Ellmann, Richard (1972) *"Ulysses" on the Liffey.* London: Faber and Faber.

Fénélon, François de (1994 [1685]) *Télémachus,* ed. and trans. Patrick Riley. Cambridge: Cambridge University Press.

Field, Henry (1889) *Gibraltar.* London: Chapman and Hall.

Friedman, Susan Stanford (1993) "Self-censorship and the making of Joyce's modernism." In her *Joyce: the Return of the Repressed.* Ithaca, NY: Cornell University Press.

Gibraltar Directory, The (1883) Gibraltar: Tito Benady.

Gibson, Andrew (2002) *Joyce's Revenge: History, Politics and Aesthetics in "Ulysses."* Oxford: Oxford University Press.

Gifford, Don and Robert J Seidman, (1988) *"Ulysses" Annotated: Notes for James Joyce's "Ulysses."* 2nd edn. Berkeley: University of California Press.

Gilbert, Stuart (1952) *James Joyce's "Ulysses": A Study.* London: Faber and Faber.

Herring, Phillip (1972) *Joyce's "Ulysses" Notesheets in the British Museum.* Charlottesville: University Press of Virginia.

Herring, Phillip (1995) *Djuna: The Life and Work of Djuna Barnes.* London: Viking.

Johnson, Jeri (ed.) (1993) *James Joyce's* Ulysses: the 1922 Edition. Oxford University Press.

Lennon, Joseph (2004) *Irish Orientalism.* Syracuse, NY: Syracuse University Press. .

MacGregor, Ewan (dir.) (1999) *Nora.* Dublin: Volta Films.

O'Hanrahan, Paul (2006) "The geography of the body." In Richard Brown (ed.) *Joyce, "Penelope" and the Body,* pp. 189–95. Amsterdam: Rodopi.

Pearce, Richard (ed.) (1994) *Molly Blooms: A Polylogue on "Penelope" and Cultural Studies.* Madison: University of Wisconsin Press.

Pierce, David (1992) *James Joyce's Ireland.* New Haven, CT: Yale University Press.

Quayson, Ato (2000) *Postcolonialism: Theory, Practice or Process.* Cambridge: Polity Press.

Seidel, Michael (1975) *Epic Geography: James Joyce's "Ulysses."* Princeton, NJ: Princeton University Press.

Seidel, Michael (2002) *James Joyce: A Short Introduction.* Oxford: Blackwell Publishing.

Spivak, Gayatri Chakravorty (1988) "Can the subaltern speak?" First given as lecture in 1983 and subsequently reprinted in Patrick Williams and Laura Chrisman (eds.) *Colonial Discourse and Postcolonial Theory*, pp. 66–111. Hemel Hempstead: Harvester Wheatsheaf. Subsequently revised in *Critique of Postcolonial Reason.* Cambridge, MA: Harvard University Press, 1999.

Stephens, Frederick (1870) *A History of Gibraltar and Its Sieges.* London: Provost.

Williams, Raymond (1975) *The Country and the City.* London: Paladin.

Ziarek, Ewa (1994) "The female body, technology and memory in 'Penelope.'" In Richard Pearce (ed.) *Molly Blooms: A Polylogue on "Penelope" and Cultural Studies*, pp. 264–87. Madison: University of Wisconsin Press.

11

Joyce and Postcolonial Theory: Analytic and Tropical Modes

Mark Wollaeger

Having suggested in 1983 that nothing of value has ever emerged from interpreting Joyce on the basis of Ireland, Franco Moretti must feel a bit like Forster's Leonard Bast in the moment of his death: in the last few years alone at least nine books have fallen down on his head (Moretti 1988: 190). They started raining down steadily in 1992 with Patrick McGee's treatment of Joyce in *Telling the Other: The Question of Value in Modern and Postcolonial Writing*, followed in succession by, among others, David Lloyd's *Anomalous States: Irish Writing and the Post-Colonial Moment* (1993), Enda Duffy's *The Subaltern* Ulysses (1994), Emer Nolan's *James Joyce and Nationalism* (1995), and Vincent Cheng's *Joyce, Race, and Empire* (1995). The last decade having seen many more books along similar lines, the deluge is not likely to stop anytime soon (though concepts of transnationality and globality seem poised to siphon off a good deal of the energy). But if Moretti has been answered, some versions of postcolonial criticism have effectively negated the historical gains achieved by the reterritorializing of Joyce. The difficulty is not simply the perennial methodological problem of mediating between history and theory. Much of the attenuation of history in postcolonial readings of Joyce derives from Joyce's overdetermined availability as a postcolonial subversive par excellence.

I am not concerned here to enter into debates about whether Joyce *should* be considered a postcolonial writer, nor whether Ireland can properly be located under the increasingly capacious umbrella of the postcolonial.[1] It seems to be indisputable that, as Vincent Cheng has put it, "Joyce wrote insistently from the perspective of a colonial subject of an oppressive empire" (Cheng 1995: i). Rather, I argue that specific qualities of Joyce's work and several pre-existing trends in Joyce criticism made it possible, in the early years of postcolonial work on Joyce, for critics to re-dress a familiar modernist or poststructuralist Joyce in the vestments of postcoloniality without seriously engaging Irish history or substantially revising longstanding perspectives on Joyce as a high-modernist innovator. Although no one wants Joyce the God of Modernism to become Joyce the Patron Saint of the Colonized, the seemingly easy fit between Joyce and the postcolonial sometimes ended up being as much a liability as an opportunity.

So, in hopes of promoting the opportunities opened up by the confluence of Joyce and postcolonial studies, this chapter undertakes a simultaneous critique of postcolonial theory and its early appropriation in Joyce studies. It would be wrong to lay blame entirely on Joyce's critics: problems in postcolonial treatments of Joyce also throw into relief shortcomings in postcolonial theory itself. To this end the chapter takes up representative critical and theoretical texts from what I will call the first and second waves of postcolonial Joyce studies in order to suggest how criticism in the future might de-routinize its protocols in order to revivify the dead and dying metaphors that often govern postcolonial discourse. Early signs of a third wave are already apparent, and they promise, I will suggest, to render obsolete some of the criticisms advanced in this chapter. But as Irish orator John Philpot Curran might have remarked, had he lived to a very advanced age, the price of theory is eternal vigilance.

Analytic and Tropical Modes and the Language of Postcolonialism

As prelude to this project, I need to introduce a distinction between analytic and tropical modes of criticism. By "analytic" I mean to characterize the deployment of a metalanguage that aspires to engage with the language of its object of study without becoming implicated in that language. Stringently disciplining its own language, the analytic mode does not necessarily entail turning a blind eye to poststructuralist insights into the hidden ubiquity of figuration in even the most scientific of discourses. Rather, it aims to establish a provisional set of stable truths in order to throw into relief particular features of literary texts and their contexts. With "tropical" I mean to allude to tropes in order to characterize criticism that self-consciously deploys metaphor as part of its practice. (I prefer the word "tropical" to "tropological" owing to the trace of geography in tropical, as well as the implication of "logos" or "logical" dropping out of "tropological," a word with the true scholastic stink about it.) The tropical mode does not necessarily entail the kind of self-reflexive commentary that seems more interested in its own twists and turns than in its object of study. The best tropical criticism exploits its own capacity for figuration to bring into sharper focus what is peculiar to its object of study. The distinction between the analytic and the tropical does not line up neatly with historical versus deconstructive, though much historical work is analytic and all deconstructive is tropical. Paul Gilroy's *The Black Atlantic* (1993), for instance, aims to be both historical and tropical, and deconstruction aspires to be simultaneously analytic and tropical. As part of a continuum, the analytic and the tropical are not mutually exclusive; each always inhabits the other. And while I may betray a preference over the course of this inquiry, I do not want to establish a hierarchical relationship between them. In theory, each can accomplish the kind of renewal and de-routinization I value in criticism. A few more words about Gilroy will help clarify the basis of my critique of postcolonial studies of Joyce.

In *The Black Atlantic*, Gilroy attempts to think through race in cultural studies by organizing his book around a historically grounded trope, "the image of the ship," and this strategy helps to produce an inclusive analytic perspective without losing sight of the material history of the middle passage. As both trope and historical fact, the complex image of the ship – "a living, micro-cultural, micro-political system in motion" (Gilroy 1993: 4) – allows Gilroy to theorize "intercultural positionality" in resonantly concrete terms, and so keeps him continuously engaged with the trans-atlantic circulation of idea, bodies, and artifacts that motivates his theoretical and historical project. It is precisely this sustained engagement with material history that tends to get lost in theoretically informed postcolonial criticism of Joyce.

It has become commonplace in recent years to observe that the reader of much postcolonial theory and criticism may feel like Stephen in *Portrait*, who finds himself "glancing from one casual word to another on his right or left in stolid wonder that they had been so silently emptied of instantaneous sense" (*P* 150). "Subversion," "exposure," "dislocation," "hybridity": some tropes are dead, others are dying. "Dislo-cation" no longer has the same purchase it must have had once; "nomadic" has stepped in as an improvement, with its suggestion of the historical movement of actual bodies, yet under the influence of a Deleuzian sublimation nomadic is rapidly going the way of dislocation. Many of us keep reading through what Stephen understood as "heaps of dead language" (*P* 150), however, because the issues addressed are interesting enough to make the effort of translation worthwhile. The point is not to voice the kind of complaint that became common in mass circulation publications such as the *New York Times Book Review* when poststructuralism first hit the scene; namely, that criti-cal jargon is just too difficult to understand. Rather, what makes for problems is that, unlike in Gilroy, the governing critical tropes in postcolonial criticism can seem exces-sively abstracted from the cultural and historical materials under discussion, and as a result the lives of historical subjects and the imagined lives of literature can disappear from view, turning the critical discourse into an entirely self-referential affair. Reasons for this unproductive abstraction can be traced back to some key issues in postcolonial studies.

Theoretical language always emerges from a particular historical situation, but it may not always transcend that situation. Critical tropes uprooted from their points of origin and endlessly transplanted may lose not only their vitality but their power to differentiate among diverse cultural phenomena. To what extent can models of post-coloniality derived from post-Second World War African or Anglo-Indian literature be mapped onto early century decolonization in Ireland? How do differences between settler and non-settler colonies register in the theoretical language derived from study of one or the other? Do issues of racial difference and geographic proximity inflect key terms? Consider Anglo-Irish versus Anglo-African and Anglo-Indian relations. With Africa and India, racial difference and geographic distance evidently made it possible for the English to imagine remaking the colonized in their own image. For when viewed from afar or safely distanced in ethnography, the cultural relativism fos-tered by early century cross-cultural contact became palatable. Accordingly, Marlow's intense anxiety in *Heart of Darkness* arises because the "remote kinship" he senses with

Africans in the Congo is no longer sufficiently remote (Conrad 1969: 540). In India, English educational policies, in Macaulay's words, aimed to create "a class of persons, Indian in blood and colour, but English in taste, in opinions, in morals, and in intellect" (quoted in Ashcroft 1995: 430), an ideal which looked good from afar but which broke down, as Forster so memorably showed in *A Passage to India*, on closer inspection. With Ireland, however, racial similarity and geographic proximity produced a need to push the Irish away by transforming them into racial others, and the reception of Darwinism, as L. P. Curtis first showed, gave the English a way of locating Celtic peoples alongside Africans and not far from apes on the hierarchically ordered racial tree of humanity (Curtis 1968). Such Africanizing of the Irish is of course an important context for much Irish literature, and Cheng's *Joyce, Race, and Empire* reads racial stereotyping in Joyce in the light of Curtis' research and through the lens of postcolonial theory. But when Cheng invokes Homi Bhabha's "colonial mimicry," which is derived primarily from Indian experience and depends on a logic of assimilation underlying perceptions of cultural difference and sameness, he does not address the problem of transferability (e.g. Cheng 1995: 120, 285–6). Of course Bhabha does not either, but the point is that valuable work such as Cheng's could counter the ungrounding of Bhabha's tropes by reflecting on what happens when they are imported into Ireland.

The general problem of the reach of critical categories has been underscored in postcolonial studies by debates over the language of postcolonial theory. The dominant discourse of postcolonial theory derives largely from poststructuralism and has been criticized most trenchantly by Arif Dirlik, who reads postcolonial theory as a discourse of self-legitimation for self-identified Third World intellectuals who are expressing not so much their "agony over identity" as their "newfound power" in the First World academy, all at the expense of analyzing the role of global capital in producing the very historical conditions postcolonial studies takes as its point of departure (Dirlik 1994: 339). Chief offenders for Dirlik are Gayatri Spivak and Homi Bhabha, for whom the term "hybridity" serves to disguise their own privileged locatedness in elite Western universities. Benita Parry, focusing on the tendency for the historical subjects of colonialism to be effaced by the abstraction of postcolonial discourse, has offered a complementary critique (Parry 1987). To her credit, Spivak has self-consciously struggled with this very issue, most notably in her often-cited article "Can the Subaltern Speak?" (Spivak 1988), and though the conceptual complexity and telegraphic compression of her writing play into the critiques offered by Parry and Dirlik, it would be difficult to dispute her genuine engagement with the problem of mediating between the historical particularity of the peoples she discusses and the desire to generalize the significance of their lives within an encompassing theoretical perspective. Indeed, this issue becomes one of the main burdens of Spivak's *Critique of Post-Colonial Reason* (1999). To anticipate some of my later remarks, Joyce criticism, in contrast to Spivak's multi-layered response, has often been too quick to answer in the affirmative to Spivak's question by saying, in effect, "if you want to hear the voice of the subaltern, just listen to Joyce." And Dirlik's critique of postcolonial discourse as a mode self-legitimation has not lost its potency now that postcolonial criticism is no longer practiced mainly by Third World intellectuals. On the contrary, the fact that post-colonial criticism has become such a marketable commodity and is practiced so widely makes it all the more likely that its ostensible political commitment to the victims of imperialism will be overshadowed by its promise of professional advancement.

Deconstruction, Bakhtin, and Postcolonial Appropriations

Dirlik's and Parry's skepticism of the way critical discourse can fold back on itself and lose touch with its historical ground suggests why Joyce studies tends to exacerbate the ungrounding of critical discourse that troubles postcolonial theory. There are at least two ways in which pre-existing developments in Joyce criticism have contrib-uted to a de-historicized appropriation of a body of theory that is already in danger of severing its own historical roots. One is the poststructuralist emphasis on Joyce's deconstruction of binary oppositions; the other is the assimilation of Mikhail Bakhtin's theory of the novel into Joyce studies (Bakhtin 1981).

In the postcolonial appropriation of deconstruction, the architectural metaphor-ics of "deconstructing" are replaced by the politicized valences of "subverting" and "exposing," and the targeted binaries are no longer speech/writing or inside/outside but self/other or colonizer/colonized. The space in between gets called "hybridity," a trope that wears thin when criticism does not acknowledge, as Robert Young does, that hybridity comes in many forms and operates differently in diverse historical situ-ations. Possibly the trope that translates most effectively between critical domains is center/periphery, for there rhetorical reversibility can be correlated with the historical interplay of specific metropolitan and colonial discourses as well as with the shuttling of bodies between empire and colony. But the transposition is valuable only if the correlation between rhetoric and historical action is rigorously worked out. Undoubt-edly Joyce was fascinated by the tendency of opposites to coalesce or polarities to reverse – hence "jewgreek" meets "greekjew" in *Ulysses*. But to engage in a mechani-cal politicizing of the dismantling of oppositions in Joyce as evidence of a generalized anticolonial subversiveness risks obscuring the ways in which Joyce was ambivalently invested in the very forms of power he seems to subvert. Paternity may be a "legal fiction" but it is a fiction Joyce does much to empower. Exaggerations and schema-tizations, moreover, may obscure the subtler ways in which Joyce's texts may have participated in Irish political history, for instance through the invention of forms of cosmopolitan identity that became materially important during the agonizing process of Ireland's decolonization. As Alan Liu has observed in a critique of cultural criticism, "an ideological subject 'contained' in history-as-representational-structure" differs from "a principle of action contained in politics-as-regulated-activity" (Liu 1989: 64). A direct correlation between the deconstruction of binary oppositions and the subver-sion of political authority should not simply be assumed.

One might expect Bakhtin's poetics of utterance to militate against facile invo-cations of deconstructive writing as political subversion, but in fact the reception of

Bakhtin has operated otherwise. Early on, the dominant tendency in Anglo-American criticism was to assimilate Bakhtin into a residual New Critical template that valued complexity, managed multiplicity, and a delicate counterpoise of contradictory voices bound within the individual work. Given the multiple voices in Joyce's texts, such a model held an obvious appeal, and with dialogism construed as a principle of order immanent in a closed textual system rather than as an assertion of the intrinsically social and ideological character of language, formalist criticism did not need to stretch to accommodate Bakhtin (e.g., Wollaeger 1990). But Bakhtin was welcomed not simply because he could be read as an avatar of New Criticism. Dorothy Hale has shown that Bakhtin was readily absorbed by deconstruction and poststructuralist humanism alike, owing to their common adherence to a set of beliefs about the novel that has underwritten both formalist and cultural-studies approaches to the novel from Henry James to the present day. Hale has called this masterplot of narratology "social formalism"; namely, "belief in the novel's special power to arouse sympathy" along with a correlative tendency "to attribute social efficacy to the form as well as the content of novels" (Hale 1998: 9–10). "The deconstructive interpretation of Bakhtin," she argues, "finds in his work an ethical imperative to honor the impersonal diversity that is language; the humanists find in Bakhtin a new reason to honor the plurality of subjects that are instantiated through language" (Hale 1998: 118). Clearly the fit with Joyce is nearly perfect: in the wake of Richard Ellmann's influential biography of Joyce, Leopold Bloom has often been interpreted as an expression of Joyce's liberal humanism, and Hélène Cixous, who wrote her dissertation on Joyce at the Sorbonne, is only one of many poststructuralists, Jacques Derrida and Jacques Lacan among them, who have read Joyce's writing as the epitome of *écriture*.

Postcolonial theory's appropriation of Bakhtin made it easy to understand Joyce's polyphonic-deconstructive-humanism as postcoloniality waiting to be named as such. In the course of an essay critiquing *The Empire Writes Back*, an influential 1989 anthology of postcolonial studies, Vijay Mishra and Bob Hodge suggest that its contextual strategies are underwritten by the dialogism of Bakhtin and that a Bakhtinian model of the novel threatens to have the decidedly problematic effect of making the novel-as-form intrinsically postcolonial. That is, to the extent that Bakhtin's polyphonic reading of the novel necessarily dialogizes or carnivalizes official history, "the novel form makes the post-colonial redundant"; it follows that all counter-historical critiques logically ought to take novelistic discourse as their primary source material (Mishra and Hodge 1994: 280). If this argument has the virtue of explaining why the novel remains, despite some excellent recent work on poetry (e.g. Ramazani 2001), the privileged genre of postcolonial studies, it also casts light on Joyce's overdetermined availability as an icon of postcolonial subversion: Bakhtin can make the postcolonial appropriation of Joyce seem inevitable, if banal. "The political implications of the linguistic experimentation of both Joyce and Rushdie appear obvious," Keith Booker writes, "especially when viewed through the eyes of Bakhtin" (Booker 1991: 203). That depends, of course, on what kind of vision one attributes to Bakhtin, and in this early foray into postcolonial treatments of Joyce, Bakhtin functions to make an aesthetic claim look like a historical one. When Colin MacCabe described Joyce as "the very prototype of the postcolonial artist" in 1988, he wished to draw attention not only to the potential political valence of Joyce's "broken English," but also to Joyce's role as producer of Irish colonial experience for consumption by the imperial metropolis, a historical locatedness nowhere addressed in Booker's comparison of Rushdie and Joyce (MacCabe 1988: 12). The material grounding of "linguistic decolonization," in such a reading, is ultimately attenuated beyond recovery.

I do not mean to suggest that the fit between Joyce and postcolonial theory depends entirely on a common interest in the dismantling of binary oppositions or that the linking of the two amounts to little more than a species of linguistic mirroring. On the contrary, the fit between Bakhtin and Joyce, and between Joyce and deconstruction, should throw into relief their shared interest in otherness, a concern that is obviously fundamental to postcolonial studies. It should also provide points of reference for a historical understanding of Joyce's genuine interest in otherness. But the formalistic nature of Bakhtin's reception and the persistence of deconstructive reading strategies that not only coincide with but to some degree derive from Joyce's own textual practice have contributed to the tendency simply to reuse existing theoretical templates under the rubric of postcoloniality, a tendency further exacerbated by professional pressure to produce a steady flow of fashionable criticism. How is it, then, that some postcolonial critics manage to escape the cul-de-sac of routinized critical gestures while others, encumbered with dead metaphors, ultimately lose touch with the historical conditions that give postcolonial studies its *raison d'être*? An attempt to answer this question returns us to my distinction between analytic and tropical criticism.

Familiar and Unfamiliar Tropes: The Same Anew

The most effective tropical criticism, I have suggested, promotes rereading from a new conceptual orientation through the deployment of tropes that remain engaged with historical forces beyond the text. Two of the most interesting arguments in the first wave of postcolonial treatments of Joyce, Enda Duffy's *The Subaltern* Ulysses (1994) and David Lloyd's chapter on Joyce in *Anomalous States* (1993), both employ the tropical mode effectively, yet their critical tropes have related weaknesses.

Duffy's master trope, introduced in his first sentence, quickly became notorious: "Might an IRA bomb and Joyce's *Ulysses* have anything in common?" (Duffy 1994: 1). Duffy goes on to pursue a sophisticated analysis of violence, modernism, and postcolonialism in which the differences between modernism and postcolonialism as aesthetic categories are dissolved, reconstituted, and then redeployed along the axis of political violence. Arguing that Joyce's formal innovations carry a conjectural, proleptic force that conjures new possibilities for postcolonial subjectivity, Duffy sometimes disavows the bomb trope but always returns to it in one form or another. Lloyd's tamer but equally productive trope is "adulteration," a canny reformulation of "hybridization" that is meant to get at a paradoxical process of simultaneous multiplication and homogenization played out in Irish nationalism's attempt to create a unified Irish identity from within the unifying flood of English commodities saturating Ireland.

The relative strengths and weaknesses of these two tropes depend on a trade-off between defamiliarization and aptness. Duffy achieves a defamiliarization of *Ulysses* as a text of cosmopolitan modernism while reclaiming it for an Irish audience, and yet the bomb trope is problematic on several grounds. First, it seems tonally out of key with *Ulysses*. Duffy wants the bomb to help us hear in the "perverse polysemy" of the novel, "the ambivalent, almost fearful searching of the novelist for codes within which to encapsulate the horror – and the potential – of the revolutionary moment" (Duffy 1994: 11), but this account of Joyce's stylistic disruptions and generic discontinuities catches tonalities that are more Conradian than Joycean. Whether or not Joyce was aiming to capture the horror of revolution, I do not think he was ever very fearful about finding the right codes. Further, though the bomb may open new possibilities for critical reflection, it may ultimately be more constricting than liberating. Given the political vicissitudes of Northern Ireland, with the IRA at one moment seeming on the verge of laying down their arms and the next reneging, I wonder how many Irish readers would want Duffy's *Ulysses* delivered to their doorsteps. Of course, Duffy might say that this is just the point: we need to restore the more threatening version of the novel in order to resist the academic domestication of modernism that Lionel Trilling lamented long ago in his essay "On teaching modern literature" (1965). Still, if the IRA bomb trope effectively evokes Joyce's shattering of novelistic form in *Ulysses*, it also risks a presentism that allows the critic's historical moment to override the author's by indulging (though Duffy himself is Irish) a recognizably American form of sentimental Irish Republicanism.

Lloyd's trope is more in tune with Joyce on multiple levels: "adulteration" not only picks up the obvious connections among Joyce's personal obsession with adultery, its thematization in his texts, the story of Parnell, and the "popular myth of origins for Irish nationalist sentiment" in the adulterous relationship between the King of Leinster and the High King's wife; it also posits Joyce's hybridized style as the exact aesthetic correlative for adultery in the social sphere: each substitutes "multiplication of possibility" for the "order of probability" instituted by the legal fiction of paternity (Lloyd 1993: 106, 109). Lloyd is also sensitive the problem of transferability, and for that reason proposes adulteration as a more appropriate trope than hybridization. Lloyd appropriates Bakhtin critically as well by elevating the chronotrope – the historically variable ways in which the time – space conjunction is construed – over heteroglossia. The limitation of Lloyd's adulteration is that it cedes so much ground to Joyce's own master trope that it loses some of the defamiliarizing power of Duffy's bomb. One need not fully credit Derrida's oddly exhilarated despair over the claustrophobia induced by the entrapping power of Joyce's textual labyrinths to worry that too often Joyce continues to manage his reception from beyond the grave by leading critics to historical intertexts that suit his own ends (Derrida 1992: 281).

Where do things stand now, when the surfeit of postcolonial theorizations has begun to elicit the sort of exasperation epitomized in the title of a 1998 book, *Beyond Postcolonial Theory* (San Juan, Jr.), not to mention the more aggressively dismissive (and misconceived) 2005 title *Against the Postcolonial* (Serrano). The first wave of post-colonial Joyce criticism coincided with a surge of interest in race and modernism in 1994 that soon spilled over into Joyce studies (e.g. North; Doyle). Criticism also began to focus more intently on specifically Irish history, sometimes merely to rebuke the supposed excesses of theory, but more fruitfully to illuminate Joyce's complex positioning between British imperialism and Irish nationalism (e.g. Fairhall 1993; Tymoczko 1994; Nolan 1995; Gibbons 2000). But with the high theory of the 1980s migrating into postcolonial studies, Joyce criticism has also seen an increasing number of highly theorized postcolonial approaches, and these typically rely on a predominantly analytic mode.

The Analytic and the Psychoanalytic: Bhabha and the Ghosts of History

The defining feature of the second wave of postcolonial Joyce criticism is its reliance on psychoanalytic theory, chiefly as mediated by Bhabha; representative in this context are Christine van Boheemen-Saaf's *Joyce, Derrida, Lacan, and the Trauma of History* (1999) and the collection of essays edited by Ellen Carol Jones, *Joyce: Feminism/Post/Colonialism* (1998). Consideration of these books will lead to my concluding reflections on how tropical and analytic modes bear on the future of postcolonial criticism of Joyce.

In *Joyce, Derrida, Lacan, and the Trauma of History* Van Boheemen-Saaf's ambitious goal is to articulate a mode of reading attentive to affect in order to prevent a repetition of history's pain. Primarily analytic in approach, the book also lays great emphasis on a governing trope. Invoking Spivak's "Can the Subaltern Speak?," Van Boheemen-Saaf wants to elevate hearing over enunciation: "I suggest that it is our responsibility to endeavor to learn to hear the text speak" (van Boheemen-Saaf 1999: 78). It is this ethical claim on readers that distinguishes Joyce's postcoloniality from a purely formal deconstruction of discourse, and van Boheemen-Saaf argues that her postcolonial Joyce is "new" and perhaps "disconcerting" because she locates "his struggle with difference not as a theme in his work, nor as an attempt to redress injustice *in* representation," but as the coded expression of a traumatic story that has been forgotten *owing* to representation (Van Boheemen-Saaf 1999: 17: emphasis original). Van Boheemen-Saaf argues that Joyce's work, properly read, reveals the "trauma" of Irish history, with trauma understood in the psychoanalytic sense of experience that cannot be understood or articulated but only relived or repeated as symptom. The elusiveness of meaning in Joyce is itself a symptom of the traumatic absence produced by Irish history, and the trauma of Irish history is largely a linguistic matter, for the loss of the Irish language made articulation possible only through the language of the colonial oppressor. Joyce's work is also traumatic in another sense: it constitutes a traumatic event in literary history that subsequent literature and criticism are still repeating, in part through contradictory responses to Joyce's texts (Van Boheemen-Saaf 1999: 6–7). The critic's role is to help readers and culture more generally to work through the trauma of literary history caused by Joyce by giving us access to the trauma of Irish history encoded in Joyce's texts and the trauma of literary history enacted in their reception. Joyce's work, in this reading, becomes a ghost story and the critic as psychoanalyst helps us to hear, and cope with, the voices of the dead.

Much of this is very appealing, but with the "postcolonialism" of Van Boheemen-Saaf's subtitle justified mainly by the historical fact of English colonial rule and the virtual disappearance of the Irish language, the reduction of Irish history to the loss of the Irish language within a Lacanian model of subjectivity – i.e. a purely textual one – dissipates any concrete sense of the effects of Irish history on living subjects. Certainly it makes sense to think about Joyce's "broken English" within the framework of "minority discourse" as theorized by Deleuze and Guattari – a discourse that turns the dominant language toward new and subversive ends – but without any attention to specific instances of discursive appropriation (for instance of the sort Joyce practices in the "Cyclops" episode in relation to particular rhetorical practices), the assertion that Joyce's experimental writing indexes a historically remote linguistic trauma remains a provocation to work not yet done. Although *Joyce, Derrida, Lacan, and the Trauma of History* aims to "to refine" Bhabha's claim in *The Location of Culture* (1994) that postcolonial writing is fundamentally deconstructive, its ability to articulate the affective dimension of the historical trauma encoded in Joyce's textual practice is limited by its very reliance on Bhabha. How can one distinguish, using Bhabha's assimilation of Lacan, between the alienation experienced by an Irish subject entering into English and the alienation produced, according to Lacan, by the very accession into the symbolic order of language?

Bhabha also plays a big role in Jones' volume *Joyce: Feminism/Post/Colonialism* (1998), which includes an impressively wide range of approaches. From Peter Hitchcock's meditation on the relationship between literary and political representation in the washerwoman episode in *Finnegans Wake* to David Spurr's elegant Derridean riff on forgery and colonization, Bhabha looms large. Jones' introductory essay argues, under Bhabha's influence, that Joyce creates a liminal space of culture difference – the space of hybridity and colonial ambivalence – from which the repressed other can speak. If fewer essays in the volume take up precisely this line of thinking than Jones' introduction would indicate, several in fact do. Most interesting for my purposes is Gregory Castle's essay "Colonial Discourse and the Subject of Empire in Joyce's 'Nausicaa.'"

Castle intervenes in the debate over Gerty McDowell's agency in the "Nausicaa" episode of *Ulysses* by means of a pivotal invocation of Bhabha. The Gerty debates turns on whether she is in effect wholly constituted by consumer culture, as Thomas Richards argues in *The Commodity Culture of Victorian England* (1990), or deliberately self-fashioning, as others have contended. After a masterful survey of the critical terrain, Castle begins his intervention with an approving citation of Bhabha's concept of colonial mimicry, linking it to Spivak's critique of positivist formulations of the subaltern, and, in a move that closely resembles Van Boheemen-Saaf's linkage of Bhabha and Derrida, closes his theoretical introduction by citing Henry Louis Gates' observation that "what Jacques Derrida calls writing, Spivak, in a brilliant reversal, has renamed colonial discourse"; this entails "the corollary that all discourse is colonial discourse" (Castle 1998: 122, 123). This assertion effectively erases any distinction between post-colonial and poststructuralist discourse as well as between different kinds of colonial discourse. If all discourse is colonial discourse, and all discourse answers to Derrida's account of writing, then "Nausicaa," like everything else, must be self-subverting and therefore postcolonial. Ultimately, Castle values Gerty as an instance of Bhabha's colonial ambivalence because "the subject position of the female subaltern" is "the site of a liberatory ambivalence within colonial discourse" (Castle 1998: 144). But with no real grounds for differentiating among kinds of discourse, the attribution of agency to Gerty risks making Joyce the empty vehicle for the critic's desire for political engagement. Could Gerty's ambivalent location within colonial discourse not just as well be debilitating? It would be more effective (and accurate) to embrace one's own agency by saying, in effect, "here's how Joyce *can* be read and here's why it is important to do so." Hitchcock's essay on the washerwomen maintains a steady interest in human agents and labor outside the text by thinking about ways in which Joyce both illuminates and occludes the labor of actual washerwomen. To endow Gerty's "subaltern" voice with liberatory power simply because she is a woman, in contrast, erases the complex materiality of actual women's lives by essentializing the feminine as a form of subversion in itself.

Should the sentimental erasure of historicity be ascribed to Bhabha himself or to a "citational Bhabha"; that is, to a postcolonial icon worn thin by too much handling? Although Bhabha certainly cannot be held responsible for all those whose carry papier-mâché replicas of his helmet into battle, some of his early work reads like a blueprint for the dehistoricized work of his followers. Consider an extraordinary sequence in a 1990 essay, "Interrogating Identity: Frantz Fanon and the Postcolonial Prerogative," in which the ghost of history, Banquoesque, sits down at Bhabha's table and demands a response.

Having broached Fanon's question, "What does a black man want?," Bhabha begins to problematize the notion of a culturally specific sovereign subject that Fanon's question purportedly presupposes before invoking what he calls "a celebrated gathering of poststructuralist thinkers" – Lacan, Foucault, and Lyotard – who in effect provide celebrity endorsements for the concept of the decentered subject that Bhabha takes (in an unspoken paradox) as the essence of the subaltern subject (Bhabha 1994: 56). Break to a new section: the ghost of history has materialized to accuse Bhabha of "a form of linguistic or theoretical formalism" that makes it "impossible to give meaning to cultural specificity" (Bhabha 1994: 57). Instead of responding directly to the charge, Bhabha asks what "cultural specificity" might mean and by way of an answer indulges in an unpersuasive reading of a poem by Adil Jussawalla that culminates in Bhabha's unacknowledged substitution of the phrase "cultural difference" for "cultural specificity." This substitution absorbs the idea of specificity into the more abstract concept of difference, in effect turning cultural specificity into Derrida's *différance*. The ghost makes its presence felt again when Bhabha feels compelled to explain why his reduction of cultural specificity to a purely linguistic phenomenon does not amount to "a schematic, poststructuralist joke" (Bhabha 1994: 59). *Ceci n'est pas une blague*, we are informed, owing to "Derrida's passing remark that the history of the decentered subject . . . is concurrent with the emergence of the problematic of cultural difference within ethnology" (Bhabha 1994: 59). Rather than argue that the notion of the decentered subject emerged in response to increased cross-cultural contact (as in Clifford), Bhabha simply concludes from their temporal coincidence that it is difficult, perhaps impossible, to "draw the line between languages . . . cultures . . . disciplines . . . people" (Bhabha 1994: 59). Which is to say that what we really talk about when we talk about cultural specificity is epistemological uncertainty (cf. Resch 1997).

The evanescence of history in Bhabha suggests why Fanon, as Keith Booker has observed, makes very few appearances in postcolonial treatments of Joyce (Booker 2000: 10–14). Bhabha's mediation of Fanon has had the effect of inventing a Fanon in which ambivalence is privileged over analysis of class conflict (Gibson 1999). Why go back to Fanon, who never loses sight of actual social struggle, when you can get what you need from Bhabha, a theory of resistance which emerges from the aporias of writing and obviates the need to undertake historical research? While it is important to acknowledge that Bhabha's early essays are not as strong as his later work and that even his early essays on Fanon have had the salutary effect of inaugurating a productive rereading of Fanon in postcolonial studies, Bhabha's governing tropes, in the hands of others, have become even more dead, if such a thing is possible, than they were before. If, as Ian Baucom has nicely remarked, "we inevitably discover that everything is 'hybrid' we might as well close up shop, or reconcile ourselves to the fact that we really are Bouvard and Pécuchet" (Baucom 1997: para. 18).

From Analytic Cleansing to Tropical Rebirth: Voicing Joyce

Which returns us to the distinction between the analytic and the tropical: does one offer a better way out of the dictionary of received ideas? Not really. At its best the analytic mode can cleanse our critical vision. Joseph Valente's "Between Resistance and Complicity: Metro-colonial Tactics in Joyce's *Dubliners*," for instance, pursues a critique of Michel de Certeau, theorizes what he calls British "metro-colonialism" as a substitute for the terms "colonial," "anti-colonial," or "postcolonial"; and provides an entirely fresh reading of "A Little Cloud" (Valente 1998) that illuminates the rest of *Dubliners* as well. But the tropical mode can often contribute forcefully to a critical renewal simply because the transformative power of metaphor offers an effective way to breath life into language that has suffered so many deaths. For all its limitations, Duffy's bomb did much to shake up received notions of Joyce. What's a critic to do?

If easy answers abounded, we would all look forward to reading widely in contemporary criticism more than most of us do. But I believe that heightening one's awareness of what each mode can do can serve as a provocation to more thorough historical scholarship guided by flexible theoretical models. Theory will always be crucial to opening up new ways to make literature matter to our own moment, but the routinized redeployment of theory untempered by new archives, new forms of contextualization, and a keen sense of rhetorical complexity – a kind of tone-deaf textual processing – tends to give theory a bad name by blunting its vision and wadding its ears.

How then might one re-explore some questions raised by Van Boheemen-Saaf's attempt to enrich the way we "hear" Joyce? When Stephen imagines a drowned body bobbing to the surface in the opening pages of *Ulysses* – "Here I am" (*U* 1 675) – the voice of the past comes explicitly to the surface, just as it does again a few episodes later when Bloom imagines a voice from the past emanating from a gramophone as he wanders among the dead. What does it take to make the corpse of the past speak and what is the nature of the voice we listen to? Answering such questions would require a resuscitation of the trope of voice as part of the broader effort to reinvigorate the dead lexicon of postcolonial criticism.

One clear sign that postcolonial treatments of Joyce have outgrown their birth pangs is Majorie Howes' fine overview, "Joyce, Colonialism, Nationalism" (2004), in which she picks out the best possibilities the field has offered (thereby providing a sweet antidote to the astringency of the present chapter) and weaves together a strong case for what postcolonial perspectives can contribute to Joyce studies. Along the way, she pauses for a moment over Stephen's conversation with the Dean of Studies at university, a de rigueur passage for postcolonial studies. Reflecting on their momentary impasse over the provenance of the word "tundish," Stephen thinks: "How different are the words *home*, *Christ*, *ale*, *master*, on his lips and on mine! . . . His language, so familiar and so foreign, will always be for me an acquired speech. I have not made or accepted its words. My voice holds them at bay" (*P* 159). Adopting precisely the kind of historical perspective elided in earlier treatments, Howes observes the pertinence of Ireland as a settler community, noting that "Stephen recognizes his identity as Irish, conceives of that Irish identity in opposition to Englishness, and recognizes his Irishness as a divided condition, so that English is both 'familiar' and 'foreign'" (Howes 2004: 257, 261). One might add that, far from being traumatized, Stephen ultimately recognizes that he knows the English language better than the Dean does, triumphantly recording in his diary that "tundish" is not a quaint Gaelicism in comparison with the Dean's "funnel," but "English and good old blunt English too." Stephen thus strikes the first blow in what became Joyce's quest to reappropriate the English language from the colonizers, as many have felt he finally did in *Finnegans Wake*.

Grasping the question of Stephen's voice historically, Howes deftly links such moments to Ireland's dual status "as both an agent and a victim of British imperialism" (Howes 2004: 254). At the same time, by analyzing the inscription of colonialism and nationalism in Joyce's texts not just at the level of "the formal qualities of each text as a whole" but also at the level of the word, Howes also sustains a sense of voice as trope – as a figure within the text that links Stephen to multiple forms of authority. Joyce often used the trope of the voice to suggest that individual consciousness is a cacophony of public voices inhabiting the seemingly private theater of the mind, and in *Portrait* Stephen struggles to find a voice he can consider his own within "the din of all these hollowsounding voices," the babble, that is, of competing authorities that echo in his mind. By showing how "ivory," circulating from context to context and establishing new associative links, becomes "a node in a web that is at once linguistic, political, and historical" (Howes 2004: 257), Howes in effect (in my extrapolation of her thinking) links the recirculation of key words within *Portrait*'s complex narrative mode – discussed by Hugh Kenner under the rubric of "Joyce's voices" (Kenner 1978) and by Vicki Mahaffey as a continual process of linguistic reframing (Mahaffey 2003) – to the problem of voice as Stephen experiences it: how can he establish his voice as artist? The question of vocation and voices in *Portrait* thus leads directly to the climax of *Ulysses* in the "Circe" episode, in which Stephen, shortly before being decked by a British soldier, taps his forehead and remarks, "in here it is I must kill the priest and the king" (*U* 15 4436–7). The problem of inner versus outer voices in *Portrait*, claustrophobically played out in Stephen's inability to hear the polyvocality of the text over the "din" of his inner demons, takes on dramatic, embodied life in "Circe" in the form of the inescapable, crude voice of arbitrary authority: "I'll wring the neck of any fucking bastard says a word against my bleeding fucking king" (*U* 15 4644–5). Here are words – what the law might call fighting words – of which Stephen cannot easily say, "My voice holds them at bay" (*P* 159).

What are the powers of voice, then, within the colonial matrix Joyce maps in his texts? This is the kind of question that postcolonial criticism has increasingly come to address in ways that move beyond earlier attempts to insert Joyce into a master discourse provided by postcolonial theory. And as new ways to historicize texts emerge, new analytic lenses may provide new ways to revivify critical tropes. In the future, for instance, postcolonial approaches to voice may draw on the rapidly expanding field of media studies, and I will close with a few conjectures about the ways in which a media-inflected perspective on voice could restore material histories conducive to a continuing revivification of voice. Metaphors, after all, have a way of dying on us when we are not listening.

Growing attention to the place of acoustic experience in modernity has shown how new sound technologies were changing the status of human voice at the turn of the century (e.g. Kittler 1990; Kreilkamp 1997). This would appear to be a concern of Derrida's brilliantly comic "*Ulysses* Gramophone: Hear Say Yes in Joyce," in which, while musing over telephones, telegrams, and gramophones, he suggests that "the motif of postal difference, of remote control and telecommunication, is already powerfully at work in *Ulysses*" (Derrida 1992: 268). But in fact Derrida is not concerned with situating *Ulysses* in relation to the shift from a postal to an information-machine epoch. German media theorist Friedrich Kittler has discussed how the mechanical reproduction of the voice by the gramophone effectively detached the voice from the body and from consciousness, fragmenting the human in a way that threw definitions of the human into doubt (Kittler 1999: 21–114). For Derrida the gramophone is useful largely as a metaphor for articulating the peculiar properties of the word

"yes," which he traces throughout *Ulysses*: "yes" is the affirmation that precedes linguistic utterance, the assertion that makes it possible to say something as elemental
as "I am here," and it is also always a response to an other; thus "yes" epitomizes the
"gramophone effect": it must "archive its voice in order to allow it once again to be
heard" (Derrida 1992: 276). "Gramophone" is consequently more interesting for
Derrida as evocation of the transhistorical distinction between writing and hearing/
speech (gramo-phone) than it is as a historical index of the turn-of-the-century effort
to understand a new sound technology in terms of the more familiar technology of
writing.[2] Wishing to privilege the historical over the tropical (though whether he
actually does so is open to dispute), Kittler veers in the opposite direction by positing
a techno-determinism in which culture and even the human are effects of technology.

Given that technology itself should be understood as an extension of human desires
that in turn shapes and ramifies those desires, a more dialectical approach is called for.
As Garrett Stewart has suggested, the arc in Hugh Kenner's work from *Joyce's Voices*
(1978), in which voices are always grounded in implied characters, to the technolo-
gized voices in *The Mechanic Muse* (1987), reveals the need for a new theory of voice.
Ideally, that approach would combine the tropical acuity of Derrida's gramophone
with the materiality of Kittler's. If the gramophone, typewriter, and telephone rob
Joyce's voices of their "phenomenality as overheard speech," our consequent "acknowledgment of the voiceless mechanics of textuality" (Stewart 1990: 254) also requires
us as readers to recognize our own embodied role as "the vehicle," in the words of *Portrait*, "of a vague speech" (*P* 85). Joyce speaks to us by speaking through us, and the
voice travels only through the circuit of the body.

To write in this way of the embodied voice may seem a form of excessive literal-
ism, but only by restoring a sense of the literal voice can we appreciate the relationship
between metaphors of voice and the historical situations from which they arise.
When Stephen reflects about the Dean, "How different are the words *home*, *Christ*,
ale, *master*, on his lips and on mine!," the passage underscores differences of pronunciation: "Stephen, or Joyce, has cunningly chosen words that demonstrate very well
the main phonic differences between the speech-systems of the English and Irish capitals" (Burgess 1973: 28). American scholars were less likely than the Englishman
Anthony Burgess to recognize that Stephen feels the weight of the Dean's authority
in his metropolitan accent because non-British speakers embody Joyce's voices differently. We can extend this literal and material difference – the variability of embodied
voicing – into a metaphoric one by thinking of it as the space of a particular version of
coloniality in *Portrait*, one barely glimpsed through the inward gaze of Stephen's consciousness, but traceable beyond the text in the discrepant appropriations of English
that followed the British Empire across the globe. Within the greater polyvocality of
Ulysses, in which voices tend to assert their autonomy – taking on bodies, for instance,
in "Circe" – the voices readers silently supply map a complex range of postcolonial
differences in a world in which new communication networks, travel, diaspora, and
migration place pronunciation and linguistic difference center stage as markers of
national and transnational identities. The staging of vocal difference through juxta-

position in *Ulysses* is superseded in *Finnegans Wake* by evocations of simultaneous difference, or difference as simultaneity. The eye registers multiple verbal possibilities as if seeing down through semitransparent strata, yet the readerly act of supplying a voice necessarily ousts multiple possibilities by regrounding the text in the body, which can supply only one voice at one time and in one place. The dizzying multiplication of Joyce's voices-in-waiting thus offers the experience of locatedness in the moment of reading as a momentary stay against confusion. Voicing the text we hold it at bay, if only for a moment, grounding it in a particular point on the spatial and temporal grids of empire before releasing it again into circulation.

The historical embeddedness of voice points toward a relatively untapped area of future research in postcolonial treatments of Joyce: his global reception. Some very useful books have already mapped Joyce's reception in the United States and France (e.g. Segall 1993; Lernout 1990), and Joseph Brooker has recently expanded the inquiry to include England and Ireland while also addressing the ways in which Joyce has been invoked in debates about nationality and internationalism, and about humanism and posthumanist theory (Brooker 2004). Rebecca L. Walkowitz has mined a similar vein, arguing that in eschewing the "heroic pieties" of Irish nationalism on one hand, and a vaguely humanistic "planetary belonging" on the other, Joyce "proposes instead that anticolonialism and antiracism require a model a model of cosmopolitanism that values triviality, promiscuous attention, and . . . 'canceled decorum'" (Walkowitz 2006: 86). Yet systematic, close attention to the revoicing of Joyce around the world is barely under way. In "Comparative Colonialisms: Joyce, Anand, and the Question of Engagement," Jessica Berman provides one model by exploring "the complex intertextual web linking Joyce's *Portrait* to Anand's early writings, most notably his novel, *Coolie*" (Berman 2006: 465). Far from a straightforward influence study, the essay sees the texts as mutually illuminating of occluded political dimensions in both Joyce and Anand; in so doing, Berman aims "to realign modernism along global lines" (Berman 2006: 466). Given the complex voicing of Joyce around the world, the rapidly developing field of transnational perspectives on modernism would benefit greatly from a comprehensive study of Joyce's global reception modeled on Brooker's. After all, as a character in Salman Rushdie's *The Satanic Verses* remarks (revoicing the language through an evocative colonial stutter): "The trouble with the Engenglish is that their hiss hiss history happened overseas, so they dodo don't know what it means" (Rushdie 1992: 343). The English here can stand in for Anglo-American and European critics of Joyce. As Rushdie's character implies about English imperialists, if we do not rethink our horizons, we too may end up dodos, hissed.

NOTES

1 For a critique of the relevance of postcoloniality to Ireland, see Kennedy (1992–3); for an opposing view from within Joyce studies, see Mays (1998).

2 Derrida's focus is not entirely unhistorical, however, as he points out that Joyce's success in keeping the professors busy for a hundred years was predicated on his anticipation of the

ways in which the evolving academy would exploit new communications and data storage or retrieval technologies in order to create

"a crazy accumulation of interest in terms of knowledge blocked in Joyce's name" (Derrida 1992: 280).

BIBLIOGRAPHY

Ashcroft, Bill, Gareth Griffiths, and Helen Tiffin (eds.) (1995) *The Postcolonial Studies Reader*. London and New York: Routledge.

Attridge, Derek and Marjorie Howes (eds.) (2000) *Semicolonial Joyce*. Cambridge: Cambridge University Press.

Bakhtin, M. M. (1981) *The Dialogic Imagination*, ed. Michael Holquist, trans. Caryl Emerson and Michael Holquist. Austin: University of Texas Press.

Baucom, Ian (1997) "Charting the Black Atlantic," *Postmodern Culture* 8 (1) (no page numbers).

Berman, Jessica (2006) "Comparative colonialisms: Joyce, Anand, and the question of engagement," *Modernism/Modernity* 13: 465–85.

Bhabha, Homi (1994) *The Location of Culture*. London and New York: Routledge.

Booker, M. Keith (1991) "*Finnegans Wake* and *The Satanic Verses*: two modern myths of the fall," *Critique* 32: 190–207.

Booker, M. Keith (2000) "*Ulysses," Capitalism, and Colonialism: Reading Joyce after the Cold War*. Westport, CT: Greenwood Press.

Brooker, Joseph (2004) *Joyce's Critics: Transitions in Reading and Culture*. Madison: University of Wisconsin Press.

Burgess, Anthony (1973) *Joyceprick*. New York and London: Harcourt Brace Jovanovich.

Castle, Gregory (1998) "Colonial discourse and the subject of empire in Joyce's 'Nausicaa.'" In Ellen Carol Jones (ed.) *Joyce: Feminism/Post/Colonialism*, pp. 115–44. Amsterdam: Rodopi.

Cheng, Vincent J. (1995) *Joyce, Race, and Empire*. New York: Cambridge University Press.

Cheng, Vincent J. (1996–7) "Of canons, colonies, and critics: the ethics and politics of postcolonial Joyce studies," *Cultural Critique* 35: 81–104.

Clifford, James (1992) "Travelling cultures." In Lawrence Grossberg, Cary Nelson, and Paula A. Treicher (eds.) *Cultural Studies*, pp. 96–116. New York: Routledge.

Conrad, Joseph (1969) *Heart of Darkness*. In Morton

Dauwen Zabel (ed.) *The Portable Conrad*. New York: Penguin.

Curtis, L. P. (1968) *Anglo-Saxons and Celts: A Study of Anti-Irish Prejudice in Victorian England*. Bridgeport, CT: University of Bridgeport Press.

Curtis, L. P. (1971) *Apes and Angels: The Irishman in Victorian Caricature*. Washington, DC: Smithsonian Institution Press.

Deleuze, Gilles and Félix Guattari (1986) *Kafka: Toward a Minor Literature*, trans. Dana Polan. Minneapolis: University of Minnesota Press.

Derrida, Jacques (1992) "*Ulysses* gramophone: hear say yes in Joyce." In Derek Attridge (ed.) *Acts of Literature*, pp. 253–309. New York and London: Routledge.

Dirlik, Arif (1994) "The postcolonial aura: third world criticism in the age of global capitalism," *Critical Inquiry* 20: 328–56.

Doyle, Laura (1994) *Bordering on the Body: The Racial Matrix of Modern Fiction and Culture*. New York: Oxford University Press.

Duffy, Enda (1994) *The Subaltern "Ulysses."* Minneapolis: University of Minnesota Press.

Fairhall, James (1993) *James Joyce and the Question of History*. Cambridge and New York: Cambridge University Press.

Gibbons, Luke (2000) "'Have you no homes to go to?': James Joyce and the politics of paralysis." In Derek Attridge and Marjorie Howes (eds.) *Semicolonial Joyce*. Cambridge: Cambridge University Press.

Gibson, Nigel (1999) "Thoughts about doing Fanonism in the 1990s," *College Literature* 26 (2): 96–117.

Gilroy, Paul (1993) *The Black Atlantic*. Cambridge, MA: Harvard University Press.

Hale, Dorothy J. (1998) *Social Formalism: The Novel in Theory from Henry James to the Present*. Stanford: Stanford University Press.

Hitchcock, Peter (2000) "Joyce's subalternatives." In Derek Attridge and Marjorie Howes (eds.)

Semicolonial Joyce, pp. 23–42. Cambridge: Cambridge University Press.

Howes, Marjorie (2004) "Joyce, colonialism, and nationalism." In Derek Attridge (ed.) *The Cambridge Companion to James Joyce*, pp. 254–71. Cambridge: Cambridge University Press.

Jones, Ellen Carol (ed.) (1998) *Joyce: Feminism/Post/Colonialism*. Amsterdam: Rodopi.

Kennedy, Liam (1992–3) "Modern Ireland: post-colonial society or post-colonial pretensions?" *Irish Review* 13: 107–21.

Kenner, Hugh (1978) *Joyce's Voices*. Berkeley: University of California Press.

Kenner, Hugh (1987) *The Mechanic Muse*. New York: Oxford University Press.

Kittler, Friedrich (1990) *Discourse Networks, 1800/1900*, trans. Michael Metteer, with Chris Cullins. Stanford: Stanford University Press.

Kittler, Friedrich (1999) *Gramophone, Film, Typewriter*, trans. Geoffrey Winthrop-Young and Michael Wutz. Stanford: Stanford University Press.

Kreilkamp, Ivan (1997) "A voice without a body: the phonographic logic of *Heart of Darkness*," *Victorian Studies* 40 (2): 211–44.

Lernout, Geert (1990) *The French Joyce*. Ann Arbor: University of Michigan Press.

Liu, Alan (1989) "Wordsworth and subversion, 1793–1804: trying cultural criticism," *Yale Journal of Criticism* 2 (3): 55–100.

Lloyd, David (1993) *Anomalous States: Irish Writing and the Post-Colonial Moment*. Durham, NC: Duke University Press.

MacCabe, Colin (1988) "Broken English." In Colin MacCabe (ed.) *Futures for English*, pp. 3–14. Oxford: Manchester University Press.

Mahaffey, Vicki (2003) "Framing, being framed, and the Janus faces of authority." In Mark A. Wollaeger (ed.) *James Joyce's A Portrait of the Artist as a Young Man: A Casebook*, pp. 207–43. New York: Oxford University Press.

Mays, Michael (1998) "*Finnegans Wake*, colonial nonsense, and postcolonial history," *College Literature* 25 (3): 20–43.

Miller, James (2000) "Is bad writing necessary? George Orwell, Theodor Adorno, and the politics of language," *Lingua Franca* 9 (9): 33–44.

Mishra, Vijay and Bob Hodge (1994) "What is post(-)colonialism?" In Patricia Williams and Laura Chrisman (eds.) *Colonial Discourse and Post-Colonial Theory*, pp. 276–90. New York: Columbia University Press.

Moretti, Franco (1988) *Signs Taken for Wonders*, rev. edn. trans. Susan Fischer, David Forgacs, and David Miller. London and New York: Verso.

Nolan, Emer (1995) *James Joyce and Nationalism*. London and New York: Routledge.

North, Michael (1994) *The Dialect of Modernism: Race, Language, and Twentieth-Century Literature*. New York: Oxford University Press.

Parry, Benita (1987) "Problems in current theories of colonial discourse," *Oxford Literary Review* 9 (1): 27–58.

Ramazani, Jahan (2001) *The Hybrid Muse: Postcolonial Poetry in English*. Chicago: University of Chicago Press.

Resch, Robert Paul (1997) "The sublime object of liminality: a critique of Homi Bhabha," *Journal for the Psychoanalysis of Culture & Society* 2 (2): 109–20.

Richards, Thomas (1990) *The Commodity Culture of Victorian England*. Stanford: Stanford University Press.

Rushdie, Salman (1992) *The Satanic Verses*. Dover: The Consortium.

San Juan, Epifanio, Jr. (1998) *Beyond Postcolonial Theory*. New York: St. Martin's Press.

Segall, Jeffrey (1993) *Joyce in America: Cultural Politics and the Trials of Ulysses*. Berkeley: University of California Press.

Serrano, Richard (2005) *Against the Postcolonial: "Francophone" Writers at the Ends of the French Empire*. Lanham, MD: Lexington.

Spivak, Gayatri Chakravorty (1988) "Can the subaltern speak?" In Cary Nelson and Lawrence Grossberg (eds.) *Marxism and the Interpretation of Culture*, pp. 271–313. Urbana: University of Illinois Press.

Spivak, Gayatri Chakravorty (1999) *A Critique of Postcolonial Reason: Toward a History of the Vanishing Present*. Cambridge, MA: Harvard University Press.

Spurr, David (2000) "Fatal signatures: forgery and colonization in *Finnegans Wake*." In Derek Attridge and Marjorie Howes (eds.) *Semicolonial Joyce*, pp. 245–60. Cambridge: Cambridge University Press.

Stewart, Garrett (1990) *Reading Voices: Literature and the Phonotext*. Berkeley: University of California Press.

Trilling, Lionel (1965 [1961]) "On the teaching of modern literature." In his *Beyond Culture*, pp. 3–30. New York: Viking.

Tymoczko, Maria (1994) *The Irish Ulysses*. Berkeley: University of California Press.

Valente, Joseph (1998) "Between resistance and complicity: metro-colonial tactics in Joyce's *Dubliners*," *Narrative* 6 (3): 325–40.

Van Boheemen-Saaf, Christine (1999) *Joyce, Derrida, Lacan, and the Trauma of History: Reading, Narrative and Postcolonialism*. New York and Cambridge: Cambridge University Press.

Walkowitz, Rebecca L. (2006) *Cosmopolitan Style: Modernism beyond the Nation*. New York: Columbia University Press.

Wollaeger, Mark (1990) *Joseph Conrad and the Fictions of Skepticism*. Stanford: Stanford University Press.

Young, Robert (1995) *Colonial Desire: Hybridity in Theory, Culture, and Race*. London and New York: Routledge.

12

"United States of Asia": James Joyce and Japan

Eishiro Ito

Introduction

When Stephen Dedalus hears Rector Father Conmee praising Saint Francis Xavier's missions in the East, including Japan and China, in *A Portrait of the Artist as a Young Man*, non-Christian Asian readers might feel menaced by "a great soldier of God" and their hearts, like Stephen's heart, would "wither up like flowers of the desert that feel the simoom coming from afar" (*P* 91).

It is fascinating to explore what James Joyce felt about Japan. In a letter to his brother Stanislaus on November 6, 1906, Joyce showed his interest in Japan's military power at that time: "Japan, the first naval power in the world, I presume, in point of efficiency, spends three million pounds per annum on her fleet" (*LII* 188). His comment refers to the recent history of Japanese victories in the First Sino-Japanese War (1894–5) and the Russo-Japanese War (1904–5). The entry "Japan" in the fifteenth volume of the eleventh edition of the *Encyclopaedia Britannica*, which Joyce often consulted, expanded to a 119-page article with ten sections and references to additional reading. It begins: "JAPAN, an empire of eastern Asia, and one of the great powers of the world" (*11th Britannica* 15: 156). In his 1907 Italian lecture "Ireland, Island of Saints and Sages" Joyce described the Japanese as "Nipponese dwarfs" (*OCPW* 119). The *Britannica* entry "JAPAN" includes the following description: "It is true that the Japanese are shorter in stature than either the Chinese or the Koreans," and continues, "the average height of the Japanese male is only 5 ft. 3½ in., and that of the female 4 ft. 10½ in., whereas in the case of the Koreans and the northern Chinese the corresponding figures for males are 5 ft. 5¾ in. and 5 ft. 7 in. respectively" (*11th Britannica* 15: 164).

Many of Joyce's contemporary writers, like Ernest Francisco Fenollosa, W. B. Yeats and Ezra Pound, were very interested in Japanese culture. Joyce liked Puccini's opera *Madame Butterfly* very much and repeatedly called Nora "little Butterfly" in a letter to her dated November 1, 1909 (*LII* 258), a comparison that may have arisen from her legally unstable marital status which was also experienced by several prominent Western men at the time, including Lafcadio Hearn (1850–1904), British scholar Basil Hall Chamberlain (1850–1935), and diplomat Sir Ernest Mason Satow (1843–1929) (Makino 1992: 125–9). Joyce knew about Japan through two other operas mainly set in Japan: W. S. Gilbert and Arthur Sullivan's *The Mikado* (1885), and Sydney Jones' *The Geisha*, (1896). *Ulysses* and *Finnegans Wake* contain allusions to *The Mikado* and *The Geisha* and allusions to *Madame Butterfly* and to that opera's main setting, Nagasaki, have been found in several parts of *Finnegans Wake*. Since the 1990s these "Japanese operas" have often been criticized as being based on what Edward W. Said calls "Orientalism," or as examples of colonialism in their vision of a passive and tragic Asia.

However, in the early twentieth century Japan was not a colony of any country. In this essay, I will introduce the general attitude regarding Japan in world affairs in Joyce's time and then explore Joyce's reception of Japan in his works and the Japanese reception of Joyce from a postcolonial perspective.

The Rise of the Empire of Japan in *Ulysses*

Japan almost completely isolated itself from the world during the Edo Period from 1639 to 1854. Exceptions were made with Korea, China, and the Netherlands only for trading purposes. It was the nation's policy to exclude Christianity and the influence of Western countries because the Tokugawa Shogunate believed that it was the best way not to be invaded by powerful Western countries. The government noticed Christianity could be a great threat to their social hierarchy, based on neo-Confucianism, and they also desired to enjoy a monopoly of trading with some chartered purveyors.

When the United States of America awakened Japan from peaceful times with overpowering military strength in 1853, Japan had to be forced to conclude unequal treaties (extraterritoriality and loss of customs autonomy) with the Great Powers: the Treaty of Amity and Commerce between America and Japan in 1858 was followed by the same treaty with the United Kingdom, France, the Netherlands, and Russia in the same year. From then on, Japan's earnest wish was to abrogate the unfair treaty. To do so, Japan had to become one of the Great Powers under the slogan of *Fukoku-Kyohei* (building up a rich country with a strong army). It was not until 1911 that Japan achieved the abrogation of the unfair treaty, with the result of the First Sino-Japanese War and the Russo-Japanese War. Sun Yat-sen (1866–1925), father of modern China, admired Japan's achievements in his memorable speech on pan-Asianism (or Greater Asianism; *Da Yaxiyazhuyi*) in Kobe, Japan on November 28, 1924. Despite Sun's appeal for pan-Asianism against Western colonialism, however, some Japanese politicians and the military authorities conceived a horrific, wrong idea. The Japanese army became desperately immersed in founding colonies in East and Southeast Asia and ruling them, frequently perpetrating impermissible and inhumane acts on other Asian races, and later Japan vainly justified itself with the hypocritical name of the *Dai-Toa Kyoei-ken* (Greater East Asia Co-prosperity Sphere) between 1940 and 1945.[1] Few people in Japan dared to impugn colonialism in public for fear of the special political police at that time.

The Russo-Japanese War (1904–5) was a conflict between Imperial Russia and the Empire of Japan that arose from their rival colonialist ambitions in Manchuria and Korea. The Japanese government regarded Korea as a lifeline because the peninsula was geopolitically close to Japan. The major battlefields of the war were Port Arthur and the Liaodong Peninsula on the Yellow Sea, the railway line from Port Arthur to Harbin in Manchuria, and the sea area around the Korean Peninsula including the waters off Incheon (February 8–9, 1904), off Ulsan (August 14, 1904), and off Busan (May 27, 1905). At sea, as well as on land, the war was brutal. The total casualties of Russia were at least 134,817 killed in action or taken prisoner and 170,000 missing in action, and of Japan 87,983 killed in action and 290,000 missing in action.[2] Although Russia had an army three times as large as that of Japan, successive defeats had shaken Russia's confidence in her invulnerability since the Napoleonic wars; Russia had had to separate its forces into several areas including the Black Sea and a revolution occurred in 1905, which threatened the stability of the government.[3] Russia decided to negotiate peace with the offer of mediation by US President Theodore Roosevelt, winner of a Nobel Peace Prize for this effort, who arranged the Treaty of Portsmouth, New Hampshire on September 5, 1905. Russia ceded the southern half of Sakhalin Island to Japan and evacuated its army from Manchuria. It also recognized Korea as being under Japanese influence. However, this victory formed a remote cause of later tragedies, including the Japanese annexation of Korea in 1910.

What did Irish people think of the Russo-Japanese War in June 1904? Joe Hynes says, "It's the Russians wish to tyrannise" (*U* 12 140). In some quarters, the Russo-Japanese War was regarded as evidence of Russian desire for world dominion (Gifford 1988: 320). In fact, both the *Freemans Journal* and the *Evening Telegraph* devoted unusually large space to the events of the Russo-Japanese War, (1904–5), in which a victorious Japan forced Russia to abandon its expansionist policy in the Far East, becoming the first Asian power in modern times to defeat a European power. Irish people, still building their nationalism under British control, must have been greatly encouraged by Japanese military prowess.

The following passage from *Ulysses* is a good example of the general Irish reaction to the war: "Simon Dedalus takes him off to a tee with his eyes screwed up. Do you know what I'm going to tell you? What's that, Mr O'Rourke? Do you know what? The Russians, they'd only be an eight o'clock breakfast for the Japanese" (*U* 4 114–17). As Gifford notes, O'Rourke's prediction of the outcome was not entirely inaccurate: Japanese successes in the opening months of the war would have made O'Rourke's prediction look sound on June 16, 1904 (Gifford 1988: 72). Richard M. Kain observes that the war occupies so small a place in the narrative of *Ulysses* that one could not expect a reader to recall that it had been even mentioned (Kain 1947: 175). However, Joyce cunningly put several references into *Ulysses*, as these newspapers reported the halfway mark on the previous day.

A review of Inazo Nitobe's *Bushido: The Soul of Japan* (1899) appeared in *Dana: An*

Irish Magazine of Independent Thought (no. 11, March 1905), 11 years before the Easter Rising of April 1916. It begins: "WAR compels attention." D.N.D., the reviewer, considered the reason why a minor Asian country like Japan could beat a major European country like Russia. He regarded Bushido as the military code of Japanese ethics: "It is true courage to live when it is right to live, and to die only when it is right to die" (*Dana* 1970: 327). The Irish became interested in Japan and its culture at that time, seeking for a way to be independent from the British Empire.

In "Oxen of the Sun" there is a description of the Japanese fleet's effective high-angle fire against the vulnerable thinly armored decks of the Russian ships at the first sea battle off Incheon on February 8–9, 1904: "Jappies? High angle fire, inyah! Sunk by war specials. Be worse for him, says he, nor any Rooshian" (*U* 14 1560–1). The *Evening Telegraph*, June 16, 1904 (p. 2, col. 4), reported "a renewal of activity on the part of Russia's naval commanders," though that renewal was to lead to further Russian losses during the summer of 1904.

The war is remembered by Bloom again with some other headlines of *The Evening Telegraph* in "Eumaeus": "Great battle, Tokio" (*U* 16 1240) As Gifford notes, it refers to "THE WAR. / BIG BATTLE AT TELISSA. / RUSSIAN DEFEAT. / Japs Take 300 Prisoners and 14 Guns. / Press Association War Special. / [datelined] Tokio, Thursday" (*Evening Telegraph*, June 16, 1904, p. 2, col. 9).[4] Telissa is on the Liaodong Peninsula just west of North Korea (Gifford 1988: 552). The narrator of "Eumaeus" mentions this: "The Germans and the Japs were going to have their little lookin, he affirmed" (*U* 16 1001–2). As Gifford notes there are two interrelated factors: "Japan was demonstrating that it had a powerful if limited navy in the Russo-Japanese War . . . The corollary was that both the Germans and the Japanese were interested in a colonial expansion that threatened to bring them into conflict with the expansionist policies of the British Empire" (Gifford 1988: 548).

There are also some direct descriptions of Japan in *Ulysses*, which show the popularity of the Japanesque at that time: Mrs. Cunningham appears in merry-widow hat and kimono gown and "glides sidling and bowing, twirling japanesily" (*U* 15 3856–8).[5] It seems that Joyce had positive feelings about Japan and Japanese culture when he composed *Ulysses*.

The Early Reception of Joyce in Japan

James Joyce was first referred to in Japan in Yonejiro Noguchi's article about *A Portrait of the Artist as a Young Man* in 1918 (*Gakuto* literary magazine, March 1918 issue). The next year Ryunosuke Akutagawa, one of the most famous novelists of the time, bought two books by James Joyce, including *A Portrait*. He was much impressed with Joyce's technique, especially with the boy narrator of the first chapter. Later he tried to translate some fragments of the novel under the title "Dedalus."

The first Japanese article about *Ulysses*, by Mirai Sugita, was published in the literary magazine *Eigo-Seinen*, December 15, 1922 issue. In 1925 Daigaku Horiuchi wrote an article titled "Shosetsu no Shin-Keishiki toshiteno 'Naiteki-Dokuhaku'" (Interior Monologue as a New Novel Form), mentioning that the narrative style of *Ulysses* was influenced by Edouard Dujardin's *Les Lauriers sont coupés* (*Shincho* literary magazine, August 1925 issue).

The first influential academic introduction was made in "Joyce's *Ulysses*" by Prof. Kochi Doi (Tohoku Imperial University) in the *Kaizo* magazine, February 1929 issue, in which Doi introduced and analyzed the structure of the novel and its relationship with *A Portrait*. Doi was said to have known *Ulysses* in 1922 when he stayed in Boston, but it was in 1923 in Edinburgh that he acquired a copy and read it. Since then, many Japanese scholars, including Junzaburo Nishiwaki, Yukio Haruyama, and Kazutoshi Fukunaga, have begun to write on *Ulysses*, sometimes comparing it with Marcel Proust and Virginia Woolf.

The impact *Ulysses* has had on Japan is extremely wide for many Japanese people who like European literature. Japanese readers could enjoy the first Japanese translation of *Ulysses* in 1931, even earlier than most American and British readers had the novel. The first legal American edition (Random House, January 1934) was made available after Judge John M. Woolsey's famous decision, and British readers were able to buy the first legal British edition (Bodley Head) in September 1937. The 1931 Japanese translation was probably the third, after the German translation (1927) and the French translation (1929).

The first complete Japanese translation of *Ulysses*, by Sei Ito, Sadamu Nagamatsu, and Hisanori Tsuji, was published by Daiichi-shobo, Tokyo, in 1931–4.[6] The second translation (by Sohei Morita, Hirosaburo Nahara, Naotaro Tatsuguchi, Takehito Ono, Ichiro Ando, and Eitaro Murayama) was published by Iwanami-shoten, Tokyo, in 1932–5. The earliest Japanese translation of *A Portrait*, by Matsuji Ono and Tomio Yokohori, was published by Sogen-sha, Tokyo and Osaka in October 1932. The first complete Japanese *Dubliners*, by Sadamu Nagamatsu was published by Kinsei-do, Tokyo, in September 1933. After the war, the third *Ulysses*, by Sei Ito and Sadamu Nagamatsu, was published by Shincho-sha, Tokyo, in 1955.[7]

As opposed to its fate in the UK and America, *Ulysses* was at first not legally labeled as obscene in Japan because either the translators or the publishers purposely deleted or omitted some obscene sentences and paragraphs from the earlier editions of the Japanese translations in order to avoid censorship. However, despite their endeavors, the sale of the second half of the first translation was banned "under charges relating to descriptions of the imaginary middle-aged woman's sexual desire" on May 30, 1934, soon after publication on May 25.

The translation of Herbert Gorman's *James Joyce: His First Forty Years*, by Sadamu Nagamatsu, was published by Kosei-kaku, Tokyo, in June 1932. The first study book on James Joyce, titled *Joyceana: Joyce Chushin no Bungaku-undo* (Joyceana: The Literary Movement Spearheaded by Joyce), by Yukio Haruyama, was published by Daiichi-shobo, Tokyo, in December 1933. After that, Joycean publications seldom appeared until the 1950s because of the Second World War – Japanese people could not read English books and translations openly.

Since the first translation of *Ulysses* was published in 1931, numerous ambitious writers tried to follow Joycean methods, especially the stream of consciousness. One of the earliest *Ulysses* influences can be seen in the lesbian novel "Manji" (1928), of Junichiro Tanizaki (1886–1965), in which Tanizaki has a woman narrator use a Joycean interior monologue.[8] It also influenced Riichi Yokomitsu (1898–1947), whose short fictional piece "Kikai" (literally "Machine") appeared in the *Kaizo* literary magazine, September 1930 issue. "Kikai," as Yokomitsu claims, is narrated by the "fourth person" (as opposed to the "third person") in that it is narrated by four "I-narrators" like the four gears of the machine. It is often said to have been influenced by Joyce and Marcel Proust. Yokomitsu's narrative technique was very refined and sophisticated for the time in Japan.

Yokomitsu's friend Yasunari Kawabata (1899–1972; Nobel Prize laureate) bought the original texts of *A Portrait of the Artist as a Young Man* and *Ulysses* to compare with each Japanese translation, and once imitated Joyce's techniques in his notebooks, as he confessed later. Kawabata is said to have read a part of the Japanese translation of *Ulysses* serialized in the literary coterie magazine *Shi to Genjitsu* (Poetry and Reality) in September 1930. Kawabata, who once majored in English literature in Tokyo Imperial University (later he transferred to the Japanese Department), was especially impressed by Joyce's interior monologue and used it in at least two of his early novels, *Hari to Garasu to Kiri* ("Needle, Glass and Fog," 1930) and *Suisho Genso* ("Water Crystal Dream," 1931).

Kawabata wrote an article titled "James Joyce's *A Portrait of the Artist as a Young Man*" in January 1933, and in "Joyce no Kotoba kara" (From Joyce's Words) he discussed *Ulysses*, "Work in Progress," and even Joyce's "Anna Livia Record" (September 1932). He commented in the review of *A Portrait* (January 1933) that "James Joyce's *Ulysses* was the greatest destruction and construction in the record of literature: it was the creation of a new universe for literature." It is not so easy, however, to find Joyce's influence in Kawabata's works or in Yokomitsu's, because both tried hard to establish self-contained "modern Japanese novels." Kawabata later denied that foreign literature, including that of Joyce, greatly influenced his works ("Sakka ni Kiku" or "Interview with a Writer"). However, it is an undoubted fact that both made efforts to learn Joyce's technique of interior monologue.

As Min Taeun notes in "'An Encounter': Blooms Day and Goobo's Day," Park Taewon, generally regarded as the first Korean Joycean novelist, went to Japan to study at Hosei University between 1930 and 1931 and was exposed to the Western psychological novels which were challenging young Japanese authors in that specific year (Min 2004: 106). Significantly, five of the six translators of the Iwanami edition of *Ulysses*, excepting Ichiro Ando, were either professors or graduates of Hosei University, as Kyoichi Kawaguchi (2005: 168) points out. It was Toyoichiro Nogami, president of Hosei University, who introduced the Hosei group to Shigeo Iwanami, president of the publisher Iwanami-shoten. Iwanami initially asked Nogami to translate *Ulysses*, but Nogami transferred the honor to the group led by Sohei Morita on account of pressure of work. They began to translate *Ulysses* in 1929; the first volume (of five) was published in February 1932.

Sei Ito's group, on the other hand, set about translation in June 1930 and it soon appeared serially in their coterie magazine *Shi to Genjitsu*. The first half (episodes 1–13) was published in December 1931. However, during translation, what were later called the "Hosei University Troubles" occurred in 1933 with the origin of the antagonism between Nogami and Morita: both were pupils of Soseki Natsume (1867–1916), famous novelist and lecturer in English literature at Tokyo Imperial University. The troubles ended with the result that Nogami was placed on the temporarily retired list and that Morita left the university with many other professors.

Park Taewon must have had many chances to read Joyce in Japanese during his stay in Tokyo. The early 1930s was a miraculous time in the history of Japanese Joycean studies. If Park came to Japan in the late 1930s or later, he would not have so easily found Japanese Joycean books at bookshops and in libraries. The Second Sino-Japanese War and the Pacific War against the allied forces led by the USA and the UK badly affected studies of English literature in Japan. The atmosphere of Japanese society strictly restricted people using and learning the language and culture of *Kichiku Bei-Ei* ("Brutal America and Britain"). Japan had been among the most advanced countries in Joycean studies before the Second World War, but Joycean scholars and their students had to lie dormant and had very few chances to publish their articles and translations during the war.

The Fall of the Empire of Japan in *Finnegans Wake*

Finnegans Wake includes numerous Asian elements as well as other non-European elements.[9] Joyce used many Japanese or Japanese-compounded words in his works, particularly in *Finnegans Wake*. Approximately 80 Japanese(-compounded) words are used throughout the final text. Doubtless he could not speak Japanese very well and his knowledge about Japanese was fragmental. Probably he had some friends who spoke Japanese fluently, and sometimes, judging from the entries, just listened to their conversation: most of the Japanese words in the *Wake* are basic Japanese words used in daily speech. Joyce might have learned some Japanese words by listening or from the *Encyclopaedia Britannica* article.[10] That was certainly the most convenient source for him. It also includes the lists of Japanese rivers and cities Joyce referred to in the Anna Livia chapter. The River Sendai (*FW* 196 19: "Sendai"), and likewise two other rivers, the Kiso (*FW* 203 35: "kisokushk") and the Ishikari (*FW* 207 24: "Ishekarry") are included in the list of the Japanese rivers (*11th Britannica* 15: 156).

In Paris, after writing *Ulysses*, Joyce met at least three Japanese who knew each other and could teach him some Japanese words and culture. The only Japanese figure described as being on friendly terms with Joyce by Richard Ellmann in his biography is Yasushi Tanaka (1886–1941), a painter born in Iwatsuki, Saitama, who was frequently invited with his wife by Joyce to restaurants and bistros in Paris around 1920. Tanaka painted Nora and Lucia Joyce around 1921. However, Joyce seems to have been far closer to Mrs. Tanaka (Louise Gebhart Cann, an American), who wrote an article on *Ulysses* for the *Pacific Review* published by the University of Washington.[11] On July 15, 1926, Joyce met Takaoki Katta (1886–1976), born in Matsue, Shimane, an English professor at Yamagata Higher School (now Yamagata University), and Katta was delighted with what Joyce called "the japlatin" (*LI* 242).[12] Three months later, on October 27, 1926, at Joyce's apartment, Joyce met Ken Sato (1886–1960). Born in Sasaya, Fukushima, Sato was a playwright, novelist, and translator of Saikaku Ihara's works. Joyce gave him a signed *A Portrait of the Artist as a Young Man* and a signed *Ulysses*.[13] Sato published the French translation of selected works of Saikaku Ihara, *Saikakou Ebara: Contes d'amour des samourais* in 1927 and the English translation, *Quaint Stories of Samurais by Saikaku Ibara*, thanks to Sylvia Beach's linguistic assistance, in 1928. They are the same selection mainly from *Nanshoku Okagami* (Gay Tales of the Samurai, orig. 1687). However, it is unclear if Sato gave Joyce a copy of either of the translations. Enough research, however, has not yet been done regarding the degree to which the three Japanese – Tanaka, Katta, and Sato – taught Japanese words and culture to Joyce.

The Buffalo Notebook VI.B.1.178 contains "Yellow River / China's sorrow" (MS 47474–164: *JJA* 48 95: July 1925). It appears in the final text: "Lying beside the reeds I saw it. Hoangho, my sorrow, I've lost it!" (*FW* 213 6–7). This passage is full of meaning for Chinese history. In 1938, during the Second Sino-Japanese War, the nationalist troops under the orders of Chiang Kai-Shek broke the dike holding back the Yellow River in order to stop the advancing Japanese troops. This resulted in the flooding of an area covering 54,000 km² and the death of between 500,000 and 900,000 people.[14]

As if Joyce had predicted the Japanese hypocritical slogan "Dai-Toa Kyoei-ken" (Greater East Asia Co-Prosperity Sphere), he wrote "United States of Asia" in his notebook for *Finnegans Wake* (VI.B.3.073/MS 47474–97, BMA: *JJA* 47 495) in September 1927. When this phrase appeared in the final text, however, it was modified: "he shall produce nichthemerically from his unheavenly body a no uncertain quantity of obscene matter not protected by copriright in the United Stars of Ourania" (*FW* 185 28–31). This obviously refers to the fact that Joyce's copyright of *Ulysses*, with its uncertain quantity of obscene matter, was not protected in the United States of America and Eurasia, and that Joyce also knew that his copyright was not protected in Japan, either.[15] Why did Joyce not keep the word "Asia"? Presumably because it may have reflected the Asian state of tension which later caused the Second Sino-Japanese War (1937–45). Joyce would probably have been disappointed at the Asian states, particularly at the Empire of Japan: Sun Yat-sen's speech on pan-Asianism in November 1924 might have echoed in the phrase "United States of Asia" as Joyce's utopia. It is highly likely that when some Chinese revolutionaries or the Paris branch of the Chinese Communist Party discussed Sun's idea in a bistro in Paris, Joyce happened to be there and fragmentally heard their conversation at that time.

The Buffalo Notebooks are full of fragmental words. They contain the following three words related to Asia; two of them were written in early 1924:

VI.B.6.117: Asiatic (MS 47471b-67, *JJA* 47 379, Jan.–Feb. 1924, *FW* 191 4)
VI.B.6.129: Europasianised Afferyank (MS 47471b-67, *JJA* 47 379: Jan.–Feb. 1924, *FW* 191 4
VI.B.33.032: Asialand (VI.C.6.164 (c), Feb.–Apr. 1931)

Joyce inserted the Japanese-compounded words into *Finnegans Wake* little by little, especially in 1926, 1927, 1929, 1937, and 1938. Although the earliest insertion (*FW* 475 2: "Jeeshee," etc.) could date back to 1924 when Joyce had an interest in Japanese, the majority were put into the text in later manuscripts; more than half of them were presumably interpolated between 1936 and 1938. This is probably because the Second Sino-Japanese War attracted Joyce's attention to East Asia. He paralleled the Asian conflicts with the European conflicts of imperialism. *Finnegans Wake* indirectly reflects numerous conflicts and wars including wars up to 1939. However, his attempt has not been sufficiently understood by readers because the "Work in Progress" was "completed" and published as *Finnegans Wake* in 1939 in the middle of the world conflicts that later expanded to become the Second World War.

In addition, Joyce sometimes confused several Japanese words with Chinese ones, or he tended to combine some Japanese words with Chinese on purpose. The sounds he tried to represent with the alphabet are not often correct, or very frequently sound like pidgin Japanese. C. George Sandulescu argues, concerning Joyce's language list in *The Language of the Devil*, that the order of the languages is very significant: "Next on the list, two languages – Chinese and Japanese – are placed together for reasons of geographical vicinity, similarity of exotic flavor, and like appearance of the script" (*sic*) (66). This is the list of Japan/China contrasts in *FW*:[16]

Japan/China contrasts in FW		*Insertion date**	*MS no. (JJA)*
FW 81 33–4	Nippoluono/Wei-Ling-Taou	May 1938	47476a-189v (*JJA* 49 400)
FW 343 15	yup/scoopchina's	1937	47480-26 (*JJA* 55 49)
FW 435 27	chine/jupan	1936	47486b-386 (*JJA* 61 407)
FW 485 36	chinchin/nipponnippers	1936	47486b-456 (*JJA* 61 443)
FW 486 11	a chink/a jape	April–May 1937	47487-56 (*JJA* 62 109)
FW 583 18	china's/japets	? 1925	47482a-42 (*JJA* 60 81)
FW 611 4–5	chinchinjoss/tappany	Mid-1938	47488-169v (*JJA* 63 169)

*Each date indicates the time when the insertions of both elements were completed.

As this chart shows, most of the insertion dates of Japan/China were between 1936 and 1938 when the tension between the two countries became severe and erupted into the Second Sino-Japanese War in 1937. Joyce added some Japan/China elements later to express the strife between Shem and Shaun, Mutt (Muta) and Jute (Juva), Butt and Taff, and Berkeley and St. Patrick.

The sunrise in the East is described in the beginning of Book IV, the last chapter of *Finnegans Wake*, when the publican Earwicker falls asleep while HCE is about to wake up. The rising sun is also the symbol for Japan, as her national flag shows. The opening of the Asian chapter, which begins with the reciting of the Sanskrit word meaning "the twilight of dawn" three times — "Sandhyas! Sandhyas! Sandhyas!" (*FW* 593 1) — reminds us of the last line of T. S. Eliot's *The Waste Land*: "Shantih shantih shantih" (Skt. "peace"), which is often used as the closing line in the chanting of the mantras. It seems that Joyce purposely used the Sanskrit word here, being conscious of *The Waste Land*. The sound of the word "waste" can echo the sounds of both "east" and "west."

Louis O. Mink indicates in *"Finnegans Wake" Gazetteer*, that Joyce regularly pairs Japan with China, but there seems little reason to connect this with other important pairings in the *Wake*, despite the fact that, by Joyce's own account, the dialogue between Archdruid Berkeley and St. Patrick (*FW* 611–13) represents them as speaking pidgin English and "Nippon English" respectively (Mink 1978: 364). As Jacques Mercanton tells us in "The Hours of James Joyce," he was asked by Joyce, "Isn't it contradictory to make two men speak Chinese and Japanese in a pub in Phoenix Park, Dublin?" (Mercanton: 213). It makes sense at least for Asian readers. Joyce paralleled the relationship between Japan and China with that between Celts and Christianity or Irish Bishop Berkeley and the English evangelist to Ireland. The Japanese bonze St. Patrick practically propagates Christianity to the Chinese philosopher Archdruid, who takes, according to *Ulysses*, the "veil of space with coloured emblems hatched on its field" (*U* 3 417–18).

Joyce mentioned this conversation in a letter to Frank Budgen on August 20, 1939: "Much more intended in the colloquy between Berkeley the arch druid and his pidgin speech and Patrick the arch priest and his Nippon English. It is also the defence and indictment of the book itself, B's theory of colours and Patrick's practical solution of the problem" (*LI* 406). The Japanese "Patriki San Saki" (*FW* 317 2) reappears to discuss color/colorism/colonialism with the Chinese Archdruid George Berkeley (*FW* 611–13), reflecting the two Sino-Japanese Wars.[17] Using two Japanese words related to colors, "shiroskuro" (white and black, *FW* 612 18) and "Iro" (color, *FW* 612 20), "Same Patholic" (*FW* 611 10), an aggressor "quoniam [Lat. "since"], speeching, yeh not speeching noh man" in the Noh theatrical performance (*FW* 611 10–11), finds the practical answer for the argument on colors of "pidgin fella Balkelly" (*FW* 611 5). Patrick seems to affirm colorism or colonialism and desire to "displace tauttung" (Ch. daodong: orthodox tradition of the Way: morality/virtue) before Berkeley (*FW* 612 8). The Yellow River (Huanghe) is described again "in a hunghoranghoangoly tsinglontseng" [Ch. "(the) Blue Dragon Meeting(?)" (Qinglong + ceng)] "while his comprehen-durient [comprehensive enduring Orient]" (*FW* 611 29–31).[18] The Chinese did not resist Japanese imperialism in the beginning and watched Japanese forces "peacefully" conquer Chinese territory piece by piece until the Battle of Lugouqiao (the Marco Polo Bridge Incident) on July 7, 1937, when the Second Sino-Japanese War finally broke out. During the Battle of Shanghai (August 13, 1937–November 9, 1937), on October 23, the Japanese troops broke through Chinese lines, forcing them to make an orderly retrograde operation further south in the hilltops of the Blue Dragon Ridge with casualties of some 30,000: "The Battle of Shanghai was a military defeat but a morale-boosting victory for the Chinese" which let America and Britain know that China was ready to fight against Japan.[19]

Their conversation seems to suggest the Chinese resistance against the Japanese army in the 1930s. The Japanese St. Patrick dominates over the Chinese Archdruid in this argument probably because it reflects that many Europeans, including Joyce, believed that Japan still held a dominant position in Manchuria and China at that time. "Rumnant Patholic" (*FW* 611 24) did "kirikirikiring" (*FW* 612 11: Jap. *kirikirimai*: "to put the screw on") "Bilkilly-Belkelly" (*FW* 611 27). In the process of the dialogue, the Japanese and the Chinese are antipodal. However, as St. Patrick, once a kidnapped British slave boy to Ireland, revisited there to convert the country to Christianity and as a result Druidism merged into Irish Christianity, Joyce seems to suggest that the two Asian countries can be united reversing the dominance in turn. From a postcolonial perspective, it is notable that in one spectrum of the prisms of the rainbow ("ruin-boon" *FW* 612 20) here, the Japanese imperialist turns into the Russian General, the Chinese Berkeley into Buckley, an Irish soldier in the Crimean War, who shoots the General in defecation (*JJ* 398).[20]

Conclusion

In the 1907 Italian lecture "Ireland, Island of Saints and Sages," Joyce wrote.

> I find it a bit naïve to heap insults on the Englishman for his misdeeds in Ireland. A con-queror cannot be amateurish, and what England did in Ireland over the centuries is no different from what the Belgians are doing today in the Congo Free State, and what the Nipponese dwarfs will be doing tomorrow in some other lands (*OCPW* 119).

As we have seen, through "the cracked lookingglass of a servant" (*U* 1 146), Joyce directly or indirectly reflected the three wars related to Japan – the First Sino-Japanese War, the Russo-Japanese War and the Second Sino-Japanese War – in *Ulysses* and *Finnegans Wake*. The *casus belli* of those wars was desire for colonies in Manchuria and Korea. It seems that Joyce regarded Korea as an equivalent to his native Ireland, which, in Joyce's lifetime, was already divided into two regions by the British Empire. So Joyce's angle on the Japanese Empire is rather ironic, although in the beginning Joyce and other Irish people thought it good that a minor Asian country like Japan had defeated one of the Great Powers. However, as Japan began to devote itself to imperialism, Joyce was deceived in his expectation of the "United States of Asia," although it did not come to the surface. Joyce died on January 13, 1941 in Zurich, so he could not know what was to happen on December 8, 1941: the Japanese surprise attack on Pearl Harbor, the start of the Pacific War, or the Second World War in Asia, which ended with the Japanese unconditional surrender and the end of Japanese impe-rialism on August 15, 1945. What would Joyce have thought and said if he had still been alive at that time? Joyce did not stand for imperialism or colonialism.

Joyce would also have found it rather naive to heap insults on Japan for her misdeeds in Korea and China. It will depend on us Asians as to whether Joyce's idea of the "United States of Asia" or Sun Yat-sen's Pan-Asianism will come true in the twenty-first century.

NOTES

1 Manchuria, the puppet state ruled by the Empire of Japan between 1932–45, was also governed under the two similar disguised slogans of Chigaku Tanaka: *hakko ichiu* ("eight corners of the world under one roof") and *gozoku kyowa* (harmony among five races: Koreans, Manchurians, Mongolians, Chinese, and Japanese). The state aimed at achieving *Odo Rakudo*, that is, paradise ruled by the way of the emperor. It was the Japanese army, however, who disharmonized *Gozoku Kyowa* and tried to control the other races.

2 Cf. "Russo-Japanese War" from Wikipedia: <http://en.wikipedia.org/wiki/Russo-Japanese_War> accessed October 4, 2006.

3 The Japanese victory greatly owed to the Anglo-Japanese Alliance made in 1902 (the end of Britain's splendid isolation) because the UK did not wish Russia to advance southwards. Since the UK did not approve the Russian Baltic Fleet to go through the Suez Canal, the fleet had to pass the Cape of Good Hope, taking far longer. The Japanese had the advantage of much shorter supply lines than the Russians. In addition, the Japanese Navy had six modern battleships and most of them were based on the British style at the start of the war in 1904.

4 The war-related headlines of the *Evening Telegraph* dated June 16, 1904 (p. 2, col. 9) are: THE WAR. / BIG BATTLE AT TELISSA. / RUSSIAN DEFEAT / Japs Take 300 Prisoners and 14 Guns. / SERIOUS RUSSIAN LOSSES. / Dispatch from Gen. Kuropatkin / VLADIVOSTOCK SQUADRON. / The Korean Straits Fight- / RUSSIAN WARSHIPS. / Reported Capture. / Jap Transports Captured- / Feared Heavy Loss of Life. (Cf. also *Freeman's Journal*, June 16, 1904.)

5 See also *U* 6 57: "geisha," *U* 17 1531–2, *U* 17 1570–2, etc.

6 Translating *Ulysses*, Sei Ito was deeply influenced by James Joyce and his literary technique. Later Ito had gone to court to defend his translation of D. H. Lawrence's *Lady Chatterley's Lover* (abridged trans. 1935; completed trans. 1950), classified "obscene" by the public prosecutor in 1950. The Japanese branch of the Association of Poets, Playwrights, Editors, Essayists and Novelists (PEN) and the Bungei Club (the Japanese association of literature) supported Ito. It took six years for the court to convict him and the publisher of publishing "pornography" or an "obscene book." After the trial Ito published his autobiographical novel *Wakai Shijin no Shozo* ("A Portrait of the Poet as a Young Man") in 1956.

7 The fourth translation of *Ulysses*, by Saiichi Maruya, Reiji Nagakawa, and Yuichi Takamatsu, was published by Kawade-shobo, Tokyo, in 1964. The fifth (the revised edition with detailed notes by Hideo Yuki), by Saiichi Maruya, Reiji Nagakawa, and Yuichi Takamatsu, was published in 1996–7; its paperback edition was released in late 2003. Two more new translations are now (autumn 2006) in progress (partially published).

8 The interior monologue itself had been already lectured on in the English Department of Tokyo Imperial University since *c.* 1900 when some English professors lectured on William James. It became popular among some ambitious novelists through Joyce's works.

9 Cf. Tindall, (1969: 307) "Matters of the East, both Near and Far, crowd this chapter. Egypt, India, China, Japan are here, along with their creeds and languages: Moslemism, Hinduism, and Buddhism, Sanskrit, pidgin English and Nippon English. Here to serve no occult purpose, these oriental matters are here to assist the sun, which, after all, rises in the East. Complex no doubt, Joyce was almost never deep." I agree with Tindall's opinion in that this rising-sun chapter is full of eastern elements. However, Joyce seems to have made some profound implications (with no occult but some faithful documentary purposes) related to the (especially Far) East in this chapter. Sheldon Brivic has allowed me to read his unpublished outstanding article on the Asian elements of *Finnegans Wake* and assured me of the importance of Asia in *FW*.

10 Joyce's notes on Japanese (esp. Tokyo) from *The Finnegans Wake Notebooks at Buffalo* include: VI.B.10.118: *obi* = stomacher (*FW* 384 3: early 1927); VI.B.29.005: (Stockholm v.s. Tokyo): *Sumida R, Niponbashy* (Nihonbashi), *Shim-*

bashi; VI.B.29.006: *Yedo* (old name of Tokyo): *shogun* (*FW* 535 20: *JJA* 59 126: February 1930): *Secourda* (Sakurada): *Shiba*: *Ukayehno* (Ueno); VI.B.29.007: *Asacusa*: *Fu-chiji* (prefectural governor): *Shicho* (mayor); VI.B.29.008: Press: *tokio* (Tokyo): *kioto* (Kyoto) (*FW* 550 28; MS 47484b-453; *JJA* 59 196; March 1930); VI.B.29.196: *bonze* (*FW* 536 9; MS 47484b-432; *JJA* 59 172; March 1930).

11 See *JJ* 491, etc. Cf. also *LI* 150 and *LIII* 31. See Ito (2004: 37).

12 Cf. Yasuo Kumagai, (2002) (VI.B.12: 113). See Ito (2004: 37–8).

13 On September 8, 2002, Yasuo Kumagai and Ito went to Ken Sato's house in Fukushima City and met his son, Yoichi Sato, who kindly showed us articles Sato had, including the two signed books (Ito 2004: 38).

14 Cf. Yellow River: Wikipedia: <http://en.wiki pedia.org/wiki/Yellow_River>; accessed October 9, 2006.

15 According to Paul Léon, 22 letters with enclosures were sent between Joyce/Léon/Sylvia Beach and the Japanese translators/publishers of *Ulysses* in 1932–4. See Joyce 1992: 6, 28, 224–5. According to Joyce's letter to T. S. Eliot, two Japanese pirated editions of *Ulysses* had appeared and 13,000 copies been sold to date (June 20, 1932; *LI* 320). One of the Japanese translators sent Joyce a 200-yen cheque, but Joyce returned it, saying, "2,000 yen would be suitable." It does not seem that the Japanese publishers paid the amount Joyce suggested. John Gadby advised Joyce and Léon to accept the "small sum offered" and they sent Joyce's receipt dated April 24, 1934 to the publishers. Roughly calculating, 200 yen in 1932 would be equivalent to 129,000 yen in 2004 (about 868.6o at the exchange rate of September 26, 2006). Probably 200 yen was too low to obtain Joyce's permission, but 2,000 was too high for the Japanese translators to pay.

16 This chart is reproduced from Ito (2004).

17 "Patriki" is a Japanese way of pronouncing "Patrick," and "San Saki" is Joyce's unique Japanese translation of "saint": "san" (Mr., Miss, Mrs., etc.) + "saki" (in front of > ahead/above > high/holy). See Ito (2004: 43).

18 The word "hunghoranghoangoly" can be deconstructed into three East Asian words plus the English suffix "-ly": Hung + horang + Huanghe (the Yellow River) + -ly. In AD 576 in Korea, Chin-Hung, the 24th king of the Silla Dynasty, established the Hwa-Rang (lit. "flower of youth"), which later developed as the Korean martial art "hwa-rang-do." However, there seems no special connection between Huanghe and the Hwa-Rang. Another possibility is that "-hoan-" might suggest *Huang-hai* (the Yellow Sea). It is considered at any rate that the word "hunghoranghoangoly" suggests some resistance against the Japanese Army either in Korea or in China in the early twentieth century. Also, "Tseng" of "tsinglontseng" is a common family name in China.

19 Cf. World Affair Board: "how could we forget the history! – In memory of Sino-Japanese war (1937–1945) 1." It is also believed in China that blue dragons are the sign of the coming spring and that they are the symbol of the East. It is to be remembered that Shanghai, now one of the most comprehensive industrial and commercial cities of the world, was originally a fishing town developed under Western imperialism after the Opium War in 1842 and once occupied by the Japanese army during the Second World War. Shanghai is referred to in *Finnegans Wake* at least twice (*FW* 398 28 and 485 24) and the phrase "synthetic shammyrag" might imply Joyce's sympathy with Shanghai as a colonial city which became ruined in a series of battles with Japan as Dublin (the "synthetic shamrock" city) was during the Easter Rising and the Irish Civil War.

20 Cf. Tindall (1969: 319): "If Berkeley is Buckley is in the sense of united *bouchal*, Patrick must be the Russian General, who, reversing the story, shoots Buckley. The "Thud" (*FW* 612 36) of fallen Buckley is parallel to the "Shoot" (*FW* 610 33) that fells the General" (319).

Special thanks to Sheldon Brivic, who checked this article and gave me valuable suggestions.

BIBLIOGRAPHY

Dana: An Irish Magazine of Independent Thought, vol. 1 (May 1904–April 1905). (1970) New York: Lemma Publishing Corporation.

Dublin Evening Telegraph, June 16, 2004. (1996) Edinburgh: Split Pea Press.

Encyclopaedia Britannica (1910–11) 11th edn., 29 vols. Cambridge: Cambridge University Press.

Freeman's Journal, June 16, 2004 (special edition).

Giedion-Welcker, Carola (1979) "Meeting with Joyce." In Willard Potts (ed.) *Portraits of the Artist in Exile*, pp. 256–80. San Diego, CA: Harvest/HBJ.

Gifford, Don, with Robert J. Seidman (1988) *"Ulysses" Annotated*, rev. edn. Berkeley: University of California Press.

Hodgert, Matthew, J. C. and Ruth Bauerle (1997) *Joyce's Grand Operoar: Opera in "Finnegans Wake."* Urbana and Chicago: University of Illinois Press.

Ito, Eishiro (2004) "The Japanese elements of *Finnegans Wake*: 'Jishin, Kaminari, Kaji, Oyaji,'" *Joycean Japan* 15 (June): 36–50.

Joyce, James (1992) *The James Joyce–Paul Léon Papers in the National Library of Ireland: A Catalogue*, compiled Catherine Fahy. Dublin: National Library of Ireland.

Joyce, James (2001–3) *James Joyce: The "Finnegans Wake" Notebooks at Buffalo*, VI.B.1, 3, 6, 10, 25, 29, and 33, eds. Vincent Deane, Daniel Ferrer, and Geert Lernout. Turnhout: Brepols.

Kain, Richard M. (1947) *Fabulous Voyager: James Joyce's "Ulysses."* Chicago: University of Chicago Press.

Kumagai, Yasuo (2002) "'Takaoki Katta' (VI.B.12: 113)," *Genetic Joyce Studies* 2 (Spring) <http://www.antwerpjamesjoycecenter.com/GJS/kataplus/katta/katta.htm>; accessed October 2, 2006.

McHugh, Roland (1976) *The Sigla of "Finnegans Wake*," London: Edward Arnold.

McHugh, Roland (2006) *Annotations to "Finnegans Wake."* 3rd edn. Baltimore, MD: Johns Hopkins University Press.

Mercanton, Jacques (1979) "The hours of James Joyce." In Willard Potts (ed.) *Portraits of the Artist in Exile*, pp. 206–52. San Diego: Harvest/HBJ.

Min, Taeun (2004) "'An encounter': Blooms Day and Goobo's Day," *James Joyce Journal* 10 (2) (Winter): 105–16.

Mink, Louis O. (1978) *"Finnegans Wake" Gazetteer*. Bloomington: Indiana University Press.

Rose, Danis (1995) *The Textual Diaries of James Joyce.* Dublin: Lilliput Press.

Said, Edward W. (1979) *Orientalism*. New York: Vintage Books.

Sandelescu, C. George (1987) *The Language of the Devil.* Gerards Cross: Colin Smythe.

Tindall, William York (1969) *A Reader's Guide to "Finnegans Wake."* New York: Syracuse University Press.

Wikipedia, the free encyclopedia: <http://en.wikipedia.org/wiki/Main_Page>; accessed September 1–November 26, 2006.

World Affair Board, "How could we forget the history! – In memory of Sino-Japanese war (1937–1945) 1.": <http://www.worldaffairsboard.com/showthread.php?t=5443>; accessed November 26, 2006.

Works cited (Japanese)

Fukuda, Rikutaro (1980) *Hikaku-Bungaku no Shoso* (Aspects of Comparative Literature). Tokyo: Taishukan-shoten.

Inoue, Teiji (2000) *Tanaka Yasushi Mangekyo* (The Kaleidoscope of Yasushi Tanaka). Tokyo: Gallery Hongo.

Kawaguchi, Kyoichi (2005) *Showa-shonen no "Ulysses"* ("Ulysses" in the Early Showa Era [early 1930s]). Tokyo: Misuzu-shobo.

Makino, Yoko (1992) *Lafcadio Hearn: Ibunka-taiken no Hate ni* (Lafcadio Hearn: At the End of His Intercultural Experience). Chuo-kosho 1056. Tokyo: Chuo-Koron-sha.

Suzuki, Yukio ed. (1982) *Joyce kara Joyce he* (From Joyce to Joyce). Tokyo: Tokyo-do.

13

Where Agni Araflammed and Shiva Slew: Joyce's Interface with India

Krishna Sen

Must we wring the neck of a certain system in order to stuff it into a contemporary pigeon-hole, or modify the dimensions of that pigeon-hole for the satisfaction of the analogymongers? Literary criticism is not book-keeping.

(Beckett 1972 [1929]: 3–4)

Joyce and India

Joyce remains a spectral presence in the literatures of India as India does in Joyce. The interface implicit in "that european end meets Ind" (*FW* 598 15–16) is complex and often problematic – it is not as easy to speak in quantifiable terms of filiations and affiliations as it is with Eliot. Eliot's impact is palpable and well documented – M. S. Ramaiah lists over 600 dissertations and publications till 1988, while the volumes edited by P. Lal and R. S. Sharma demonstrate Eliot's points of contact with Indian culture. Tagore admired "Journey of the Magi" enough to translate it into Bengali as "Tirthayatri" ("The Pilgrims") and accorded Eliot pride of place in his seminal essay "Adhunik Kavya" ("Modern Poetry"), while Bishnu Dey's "Mr. Eliot among the Arjuns" (Tambimuttu and March 1965: 96–102) names several creative writers of the post-Tagore era who responded creatively to Eliot.

Much of this has to do with Eliot's accessibility to the Indian mind. His study of Sanskrit and Patanjali's metaphysics during his second stint at Harvard from 1911to 1912 (Eliot 1934: 43–4) is often cited, and his hieratic utterances, spiritual themes, and frequent references to Hindu and Buddhist theology engender a sense of familiarity. There are skeptical voices, such as Mohamed Elias' "Orientalism in *The Waste Land*" (Sharma 1994: 34–40), but titles such as V. Rai's "*The Waste Land* and the *Ramcharitmanas*" (Sharma 1994: 31–3) are more common. Joyce's parodic tone and scatological bent require a different kind of orientation – it is difficult to imagine an essay on *Ulysses* or *Finnegans Wake* along the lines of N. Eakambaram's "If an Advaitin were to read *Murder in the Cathedral*" (Sharma 1994: 84–96).

As essays such as "Home Rule Comes of Age" demonstrate, Joyce was well aware of India, and of the similarities between the political conditions in India and Ireland as colonies of England (*OCPW* 142–4). Yet he does not access Indian religious and philosophical systems as readily as he uses Greek and Egyptian mythology. Because of the relative scarcity of the references, the Indian elements in his work have not been researched as exhaustively either. In her informative study of Joyce's contacts with Eastern thought in general, Suzette Henke refers to his extensive use of E. A. Wallis Budge's multivolume *The Egyptian Book of the Dead*, and states that he "had read Frazer's *The Golden Bough* along with the Kabbalah, the Koran, and various studies of Eastern mysticism" (Henke 1986: 313–14, 316). For Indian religions, however, Henke falls back on J. S. Atherton's speculation in his *Books at the Wake* that Joyce's "knowledge of Hindu myth came from three sources – Helena Petrovna Blavatsky's *Isis Unveiled*, her *Mahatma Letters*, and a German text by Heinrich Zimmer entitled *Maya der Indische Mythos*" (Henke 1986: 316 n. 10). The philosophical and factual haziness of Madame Blavatsky and the carefully cultivated Orientalist mystique of Zimmer are only too apparent in Stephen's and Bloom's figurations of India in *Ulysses*. Stephen's cavalier equation in the "Scylla and Charybdis" section of Madame Blavatsky's esoteric Theosophical God with the Buddha in terms of a Hindu/Buddhist/Meso-American pastiche (jumbling continents, histories, and mythologies, just as Blavatsky does in *Isis Unveiled: A Master Key to the Mysteries of Ancient and Modern Science and Philosophy*), is a case in point:

> Yogibogeybox in Dawson Chambers. *Isis Unveiled.* Their Pali book we tried to pawn. Crosslegged under an umbrel umbershoot he thrones an Aztec logos, functioning on astral levels, their oversoul, mahamahatma. The faithful hermetists await the light, ripe for chelaship, ringroundabout him. [. . .] Lotus ladies tend them i'the eyes, their pineal glands aglow. Filled with his god he thrones, Buddh under plantain. Gulfer of souls, engulfer (*U* 9 279–85).

Stephen's lubricious "lotus ladies" or *apsaras* (divine damsels in Hindu mythology) parallel Bloom's voluptuous illusions of a "hothouse" East in "Lotus Eaters" – "The far east. Lovely spot it must be: the garden of the world, big lazy leaves to float about on [. . .] Those Cinghalese lobbing about in the sun in *dolce far niente*, [. . .] Sleep six months out of twelve. [. . .] Lethargy" (*U* 5 29–34). Bloom's soporific Buddha tropes his decadent East – "Buddha their god lying on his side in the museum. Taking it easy with hand under his cheek. Josssticks burning. Not like Ecce Home. Crown of thorns and cross" (*U* 5 328–30). In Buddhist iconography the reclining Buddha is emblematic of *mahaparinirvana* or final release from the cycles of karmic rebirth.

Granted, these sentiments reflect consciousnesses dramatized (Stephen the clever young man, the laboriously cosmopolitan Bloom), and need not be attributed to Joyce. In fact, Joyce was sharply satirical about the commercial exploitation of Orientalist fantasy in the popular British press, as is evident from his review of Aquila

Kempster's *The Adventures of Prince Aga Mirza* in Dublin's *Daily Express* (September 17, 1903; *OCPW* 82–3). Besides, Stephen and Bloom are equally irreverent about the Christian mysteries, and about what the arrogant young Stephen of *Stephen Hero* disdainfully dubs "the half-witted God of the Roman Catholics" (*SH* 215). In *Ulysses*, Stephen parodies "Hiesos Kristos, magician of the beautiful," and dispatches Christ "to the plane of buddhi" along with Blavatsky's Theosophical God, even as he mock-heroically intones Sri Krishna's words about the omnipresence of the divine from the ninth book of the *Bhagavad Gita* – "I am the fire upon the altar. I am the sacrificial butter" (*U* 9 63–4). Bloom, for his part, compares the Holy Communion to cannibalism (*U* 5 352). Yet his glib application in "Lestrygonians" of the doctrine of *karma* to the "holocaust" involving "all those women and children excursion beanfeast burned and drowned in New York" (*U* 8 1146–7) is stereotypical of Western notions about reincarnation – *karma* has to do not with the mode of death, but with the liberation of the *atman*.

As compared to *Ulysses*, where Hindu and Buddhist iconography functions as decorative exotica, *Finnegans Wake* demonstrates greater synergy between "Western and Osthern Approaches" (*FW* 604 26), and a more rigorous endeavor to "hindustand" (*FW* 492 17). The Viconian *ricorsi* and the Oedipal subtext of the *Wake* are reprised, among other motifs, through the Hindu myths of Agni, Shiva, and Manu. The *Rigveda* hails Agni (fire; the Hindu god of fire), along with water, as the "ritual elements" without which no life is possible. The cyclical structure of the *Rigveda* begins and ends (*Rigveda* I: 1 and X:191) with hymns to Agni, also known as Pramantha (etymologically akin to the Greek "Prometheus," who is variously described as the "Fire-Giver" or "Fire-Bringer"). *Rigveda* I:1 celebrates Agni as the recipient of the "Agnihotra," the ritual oblation of clarified butter (*ghee*) into the holy fire that initiates any Hindu *puja* or act of worship, which is mandatory if the devotee's offerings are to please the gods – it is the "Agnihotra" that is referred to in the "Agni araflammed" (Lat. *ara*, altar) of *Finnegans Wake* (*FW* 80 24).

Several incidents in the myths of Agni parallel situations in *Finnegans Wake*. The *Vishnu Purana* hails Agni as the eldest child of Prajapati Brahma (the Vedic "Lord of Progeny" or Supreme Creator), and hence a type of Everyman, of whom HCE is the prototype in the *Wake*. Yet Agni also represents the Earwicker offspring. In the *Shatapatha Brahmana*, Brahma describes Agni as the devourer of his progenitor (paralleling the "eatupus complex" [*FW* 128 36] of HCE's Oedipal son Shaun):

> Then Prajapati thought, "I have given birth to this Agni, this eater of food, from my own self. But there is no food here but me . . . .." Then Agni turned toward Prajapati with a wide-open mouth . . . [However] by making an offering [of clarified butter], Prajapati gave birth to himself and saved himself from Agni, from Death, who was about to eat him (O'Flaherty 1988: 10–11).

In folklore, Agni is said to consume his progenitor because the wood that is used to kindle or give birth to fire is itself destroyed. However, the paradox is that Agni is also a giver of life, for though he consumes the human body in the Hindu funerary rite of cremation, he simultaneously releases the Self or *atman* for rebirth or reincarnation (*Rigveda* X:16). In the tropology of *Finnegans Wake*, Agni is thus HCE; then, as "*Ad Regias Agni Dapes*," he is invoked at the arraignment or "exagmination" of HCE (*FW* 497 5) as the fire that burns and cleanses the world of sin; concurrently, he symbolizes Shaun; and he is also an emblem of *ricorso* (death and rebirth). This Hindu myth provides an analogue that universalizes the argument of the *Wake*.

Shiva is less well served in Earwicker's "dream monologue" (*FW* 474 4). He is part of the Hindu Trinity of Brahma, Vishnu, and Shiva, symbolizing the cyclic process of the creation, preservation, and destruction (followed by re-creation) of the universe. The *tandavanritya*, the cataclysmic dance of cosmic destruction signaling the possibility of rejuvenation that Shiva enacts in his incarnation as Nataraja, could well have been emblematic of "the Phoenican wakes" (*FW* 608 32). Shiva appears in the *Vedas* only as Rudra or the "Implacable Destroyer" – it is in the much later *Puranas*, comprising Vedic commentary and a variety of ancient and local lore, that he emerges as the phallic god of fertility. It is this non-Vedic and telluric Shiva, the lord of the phallus or *lingam*, who is foregrounded in the *Wake*.

The reference to the Puranic (as opposed to the purely Vedic) Shiva occurs early in *Finnegans Wake* in the description of the iconic tower (standing for all towers and all skyscrapers, and clearly a phallic symbol) that "Bygmester" Finnegan/HCE built – "a waalworth of a skyerscape of most eyeful hoyth entowerly, eriginating from next to nothing and celescalating the himals and all" (*FW* 4 35–5 1). The "himals" are the lofty Himalayas, the traditional site of Shiva's *tapasya* or meditation, but "eriginating" suggests both "erogenous" and "vertiginous." The phallic Shiva is perhaps meant to prefigure Earwicker's primal sin in the Wakean Garden of Eden, Dublin's Phoenix Park, with its phallic obelisk (also called "Phornix Park" [*FW* 80 6], suggesting fornication), where HCE and his daughter Issy (Iseult to her father's "Tristan") exposed themselves to each other. It is, however, not this kind of voyeuristic sexuality that is suggested in either the *Linga Purana* or the *Brahmanda Purana*, the two major sites of chthonic Shaivite doctrine and liturgy, where the *lingam* (usually imaged as a column of fire spanning the cosmos) represents the mystic origin of all nature and the source of all life and fertility. In fact the *Brahmavaibarta Purana* recounts how, in a towering fit of rage, Shiva reduced Kamadeva (Eros, the god of sexual love) to a heap of ashes through the radiance of his third eye for attempting to distract him from his meditation. Anna Livia Plurabelle, HCE's "consort," is no chaste Parvati (Shiva's consort) either. Though the references to Shiva seem to identify the *ricorso* with sexual *jouissance* – "Phall if you but will, rise you must" (*FW* 4 15–16) – the "secular phoenish" sadly reduces Shiva the cosmic Dancer and Destroyer (or Slayer) to the cartoon character of "Simba the Slayer of his Oga" (*FW* 203 32).

Finnegans Wake uses to greater effect another Hindu trope of cyclical existence – the *mahamanvantara* or millennial cycle of years. In Hindu mythology each millennium represented the reign of a "Manu," all of whom are types of the original man named Manu, who may be compared to the Biblical Adam or the Adam Kadmon of the Kabbalah. The *Matsya Purana* (and not the *Markandeya Purana*, as the exclamation "Play him, Markandeyn!" [*FW* 525 28] seems to suggest) states that Vishnu in the guise of a fish rescued the archetypal Manu from certain death in the Primal Flood. This near-death/rebirth motif is invoked in Shaun/Yawn's reverie in the fifteenth section of the *Wake* when he ponders his "soul's groupography" (*FW* 476 33) – "Hep! I can see him in the fishnoo! . . . Manu ware!" (*FW* 525 27, 32). In diving into the depths of his psyche to search out his own identity, Yawn discovers his father, and realizes that he reprises HCE as the later Manus replicated the archetypal Manu. In this complicated dreamwork HCE emerges as both the rescuer and the rescued, Vishnu as well as Manu. Yawn's delineating HCE as *"Our Human Conger Eel!"* (*FW* 525 26), and his assertion that they would "land him yet, slitheryscales on liffeybank, times and times" (*FW* 526 1), indicate that HCE has been "metandmorefussed" (*FW* 513 31) into a Vishnu figure, or what Hinduism would describe as an *avatar* of Vishnu. Vishnu the Preserver is also often figured as the Eternal Sleeper who, like HCE in his "svapnasvap" (*FW* 597 4; Sanskrit for "dream-sleep"), dreams the entire creation.

The dreamer in *Finnegans Wake* (now simultaneously HCE and Yawn) wakes shortly after this episode to "a future of maybe mahamayability" (*FW* 597 28), "of the yere of the age of the madamanvantora" (*FW* 598 32–3). The clever juxtaposition of "madam" and "man" in the Joycean millennium ensures that ALP and all her incarnations will partake of it, as will HCE and all his incarnations. Both the *Brahmanda Purana* and the *Devi Bhagavata Purana* identify Mahamaya as the consort and one half of Brahma. In her incarnation as Durga she is the averter of evil. But the awakened dreamer in *Finnegans Wake* can hope only for "maybe mahamayability." This uncertainty about redemption creates a sense of despair – "Take thanks, thankstum, thamas" (*FW* 598 15). "Thamas" is *tamas* (meaning both "inertia" and "darkness"), which is named in the *Brahmanda Purana* as one of the three *gunas* or qualities of matter, the other two being *rajas* (energy) and *sattva* (rightness, truth). Barring a brief invocation to the sun, "reneweller of the sky, thou who agnitest" (*FW* 594 2), it is *tamas* that marks the final section of the *Wake*. The aged Anna Livia's concluding thoughts in the coda of *Finnegans Wake* as she prepares to return to the "obluvial waters of our noarchic memory" (*FW* 80 25) – "My leaves have drifted from me. All. But one clings still" (*FW* 628 7) – is shot through with *tamas*, just as *rajas* had vitalized Molly Bloom's coda, "and yes I said yes I will Yes" in *Ulysses* (*U* 18 1608–9).

Yet there is the suggestion of rebirth, too, in "vidnis Shavarsanjivana" (*FW* 597 19): the Sanjivani Mantra was the occult charm for immortality. The last section of *Finnegans Wake* begins with the threefold invocation "Sandhyas, Sandhyas, Sandhyas" (*FW* 593 1). *Sandhya* is "evening," which signifies the evening of life and yet also prefigures the dawn, and the chant is clearly intended to echo the liturgy of the Mass, "Sanctus, Sanctus, Sanctus," signifying the Resurrection. So the dying Anna becomes, as it were, a child again, exclaiming, "Far calls. Coming, far!" (*FW* 628 13). "Far" is Danish for father, and in the old woman's confused imagination this father figure is her dead husband HCE, who comes like Neptune or some great mythical fish to carry her away into the river of oblivion – "Carry me along, taddy . . . Us then. Finn, again!" (*FW* 628 8–14). "Finn" is both the finny "Fishnoo" and Finn MacCool, the legendary

Irish warrior whose master Finegas trapped the "salmon of knowledge" that Finn also tasted. The *sattva* or truth gleaned from Anna's experience of *tamas* is the intuition of resurrection. Her final unfinished sentence – "A way a lone a last a loved a long the" (*FW* 628 15–16) – loops the text round and back to its opening word, "riverrun," by way of "a commodius vicus of recirculation" (*FW* 3 1, 2).

The circular structure and cyclical world-view of *Finnegans Wake* stands at odds with the linearity of Western notions of time – "Teems of times and happy returns. The seim anew. [. . .] Northmen's thing made southfolk's place [. . .] Latin me that, my trinity scholard, out of eure sanscreed into oure eryan" (*FW* 215 22–7). Yet one cannot infer from this that Joyce accepted Eastern systems as having greater validity – "sanscreed" is both "Sanskrit" and "sans [without] creed." Moreover, Hindu mythology does not constitute the only "Osthern" paradigm of *ricorso* – circularity is as inherent in the Kabbalistic concept of metempsychosis and in certain ancient Egyptian belief systems as in the Hindu doctrine of karmic reincarnation, all of which Joyce used eclectically in *Ulysses* and *Finnegans Wake*. The overarching structural principle of the Viconian *ricors* in the *Wake* probably offered an acceptable (albeit exceptional) European model of circular time that could be universalized through analogy with other similar models.

If one were prepared to go further and bypass Beckett's "analogymongers" with their tyrannical demand for exact equivalents, it would be rewarding to compare certain Indian aesthetic systems with Joyce's poetic theory, especially his concept of epiphany. An "epiphany," that "most delicate and evanescent of moments," is defined in *Stephen Hero*, the earlier version of *A Portrait of the Artist as Young Man*, as "a sudden spiritual manifestation, whether in the vulgarity of speech or of gesture or in a memorable phase of the mind itself." According to Stephen, even "the clock of the Ballast Office was capable of an epiphany":

> Imagine my glimpses at that clock as the gropings of a spiritual eye which seeks to adjust its vision to an exact focus. The moment the focus is reached the object is epiphanized. It is just in this epiphany that I find the third, the supreme quality of beauty (*SH* 216–17).

The more extended discussion of the aesthetic theory in *A Portrait* itemizes the three qualities of beauty that Stephen extrapolated from St. Thomas Aquinas' *Summa contra Gentile* as follows: "Aquinas says: *Ad pulcritudinem tria requiruntur, integritas, consonantia, claritas*. I translate it so: *Three things are required for beauty, wholeness, harmony, and radiance*" (*P* 178; italics in original). The experience of the "epiphany" is therefore coeval with *claritas* or "radiance."

To experience an epiphany the auditor or viewer has to pass through a twofold process. The first stage is *integritas* or "wholeness," in which "the esthetic image is first luminously apprehended as selfbounded and selfcontained." In the second stage, "the synthesis of immediate perception is followed by the analysis of apprehension" as the mind senses the *consonantia* or harmonious "rhythm of its structure [. . .] the result of its parts and their sum" (*P* 178). The third stage or *claritas* is the epiphanic flash that renders palpable an aesthetic beauty that has no referent outside itself, being its own truth – "beauty is the splendour of truth. I don't think that it has a meaning" (*P* 174).

The aesthetic emotion is contemplative – Stephen describes it as "the luminous silent stasis of esthetic pleasure" (P 179).

There are interesting parallels between this schema and certain aspects of Sanskrit aesthetics. Ancient Indian philosophical and aesthetic systems were hospitable to the cognitive model Stephen outlines. Bharata, in his *Natyashastra* (second century BCE), hailed *kavya* or poetry as the fifth Veda. Bhartrhari's *sphota* theory (fifth century CE) held that the linguistic sign itself could communicate a sudden insight, as with the word "Om" (*Vakyapadiya* I:1). *Sphota*, however, pertains to the nature of language and not to the psychology of the recipient. For that one must turn to the theory of *rasa*, which is also a modality of perception.

However, it is not Bharata's conception of *rasa* as an objective phenomenon dependent upon the judicious construction of the art object that is applicable here so much as Abhinavagupta's more complex enunciation of *rasa* as subjective experience in his *Abhinavabharati* (eleventh century CE).[1] For Abhinavagupta, the experience of *rasa* went beyond mere literary understanding and became a psychologically transforming experience – *sattva udreka prakasamaya* or "the revelation of an effulgent truth [*sattva*]" (Bhat 1984: 54). This experience could only be achieved by the *sahrdaya* (the sensitive person). Abhinavagupta posits a five-stage schema outlining the psychology of the aesthetic experience. To summarize G. K. Bhat's tabulation (Bhat 1984: 54–5), these five stages are:

1. Grasping the meaning or import of what is presented (*sabda-jnana*).
2. Going beyond the specific meaning to an intuitive realization that takes a vivid and almost tangible form before one's mental eye (*sadharanikarana*).
3. This mental state is neither too detached nor too involved. In this "personal-impersonal" condition, the *sahrdaya* partakes of the original emotion of the artist (*hrdaya-samvada*).
4. A complete merging into the art-experience follows (*tanmayibhavana*).
5. A state of pure awareness (*samvid*) is now attained, in which the activity of the mind is stilled (*visranti*) and the relish or *rasa* of the experience is fully apprehended.

Stages 1, 2, 4, and 5 are akin to Stephen's aesthetic theory as outlined in *A Portrait*.

For Abhinavagupta one of the ends of the art experience was the perception of beauty, which he distinguished from other kinds of cognition. The difference between the *rasa* experience and practical knowledge parallels Stephen's provocative equation in *A Portrait* of pornography with didactic literature as "improper arts" that seek to inculcate different kinds of practical knowledge – "The feelings excited by improper art are kinetic, desire or loathing. Desire urges us to possess, to go to something: loathing urges us to abandon, to go from something. [. . .] The arts which excite them, pornographical or didactic, are therefore improper arts" (P 172). Bhat glosses Abhinavagupta on this matter as follows – "*Rasa*-experiences differ from empirical experiences because the latter are hampered by practical considerations of gain or avoidance, and so lack the ability to perceive beauty" (Bhat 1984: 57). Abhinavagupta also distinguished the aesthetic experience from the religious experience – the *yogi's* detachment from the material world hinders his perception of the balanced arrangement of details (Stephen's *consonantia*) that goes into the production of aesthetic beauty.

The second end of the *rasa* experience, according to Abhinavagupta, was *ananda* or joy, which is again different from normal pleasures as well as from religious ecstasy. Kapil Kapoor says of Abhinavagupta's concept of *ananda*, "So *kavyananda* [the joy derived from the aesthetic experience] is different from both *visayananda* [material pleasures] and *brahmananda* [spiritual bliss]" (Kapoor 1998: 116). The material source of this joy is the worldly experience that goes into the making of the art object; Stephen, too, spoke of the artist as "a priest of the eternal imagination, transmuting the daily bread of experience into the radiant body of everliving life" (*P* 186). When there is total empathy with the art object, the Self is transformed into *ananda* and becomes fully receptive to the *rasa* of the experience. This *ananda* or the radiant joy of the mind is close to Stephen's *claritas*.

There is a clear resemblance between Stephen's aesthetic theory and the ideas on art in Joyce's Paris and Pola Notebooks. Yet in "Drama and Life" (1900) Joyce is not as dismissive of the grossness of the real world as is his young hero:

> A yet more insidious claim is the claim for beauty. [. . .] Beauty is the *swerga* [glossed by Joyce as "The Heaven of the Gods in Hindu literature"] of the aesthete; but truth has a more ascertainable and a more real dominion. Art is true to itself when it deals with truth (*OCPW* 27).

The narrator says in "The Oxen of the Sun" episode in *Ulysses*, "For who is there who anything of some significance has apprehended but is conscious that that exterior splendour may be the surface of a downwardtending lutulent reality" (*U* 14 17–19). That in his practice Joyce sought to go beyond Stephen's quest for the pure ideal in order to combine verisimilitude with idealism is evident from his dual allegiance to Defoe and Blake in the two-part lecture he delivered in March 1812 at the Università Popolare Triestina, entitled "Verismo et idealismo nella letteratura inglese (Daniele De Foe – William Blake)" (*OCPW* 163–81, 269–85). What Joyce sought to realize in his work was a composite unity of the material and the ideal, Defoe's realism coupled with Blake's metaphysics. Both *Ulysses* and *Finnegans Wake* can therefore be character-ized as allotropic narratives that simultaneously occupy two contradictory worlds, the intensely particular and the intensely mystical.

Once again Abhinavagupta offers an interesting parallel. According to Kapil Kapoor, the *Abhinavabharati* recognizes two kind of cognition – "cognition of external objects" and "cognition of the bhavas [loosely translated as the emotional states that constitute the Self] internal to the cognizing self." Kapoor explains that while the first kind of cognition requires the normal cognitive apparatus of the mind, the second kind of cog-nition must be made cognizable by consciousness itself – the first kind is like seeing a horse in real life, and the second kind is like seeing a horse in a dream (Kapoor 1998: 115). Both these modalities of cognition as delineated by Abhinavagupta occur in powerful ways in *Ulysses* and *Finnegans Wake*.

A comparison between Joyce's poetics and the aesthetics of Abhinavagupta, however anachronistic, illuminates the transcultural nature of Joyce's thought. Western poetics, at least till the twentieth century, tended to revolve around dichotomized binaries – Aristotle and Plato, or neoclassicism and Romanticism (which Joyce identified with Defoe and Blake respectively). The attempt to unite opposites, in this case Defoe as well as Blake, within a single literary paradigm argues for the kind of dialectical thinking typical of Eastern world-views, though not as a general rule of the West. As Joyce wrote in his review of Ibsen's *When We Dead Awaken*, what drew him most to the play was Professor Rubek's conversion, in which "there is involved an all-embracing philosophy, a deep sympathy with the cross-purposes and contradictions of life, as they may be reconciliable with a hopeful awakening – when the manifold travails of our poor humanity may have a glorious issue" (*OCPW* 48).

India and Joyce

Vikram Seth's *A Suitable Boy* has a hilarious episode set in the 1950s of an English Literature syllabus committee in an Indian university where Joyce becomes the site of a bitter confrontation between the Ancients and the Moderns. The pompously conservative Head of the Department, Professor Mishra, is not only convinced that the "unreadable *Ulysses*" and the "worse than unreadable *Finnegans Wake*" would tempt students to indulge in "sloppy and ungrammatical writing," but is apprehensive lest the venal "ending of *Ulysses*" corrupt the "young and impressionable women whom in our course it is our responsibility to introduce to the higher things of life." Mishra's opponent, the young and generally peaceable lecturer, Dr. Pran Kapoor, who has risked a much-needed promotion to champion *Ulysses*, is seized with a "sudden murderous impulse . . . And all this over Joyce, he said to himself" (Seth 1993: 52–3).

That scenario has changed since the 1970s, with "Araby" now staple fare on undergraduate courses on the short story, while no MA syllabus in English literature is complete without either *A Portrait* or *Ulysses*. Rushdie satirizes Joyce's newly acquired status as an intellectual cachet for India's Anglophone urban elite in *The Satanic Verses*. Mimi Mamoulian attempts to impress Saladin Chamcha with her sophistication by flaunting her acquaintance with *Finnegans Wake* – "So comprehend, please, that I am an intelligent female. I have read *Finnegans Wake* and am conversant with postmodernist critiques of the West, e.g. that we have a society capable only of pastiche: a "flattened" world" (Rushdie 1989a: 261). Yet Mimi's proleptic equation of *Finnegans Wake* with postmodernism signals the typical Indian response to Joyce as being an abstruse writer. The element in Joyce's work that could have brought him close to the Indian reader, his anticolonial stance – as manifested in several essays on the Irish Question, in "Two Gallants" in *The Dubliners*, in many episodes of *Ulysses*, and in the sequences from *Finnegans Wake* analyzed by Vincent J. Cheng (Cheng 1992: 260–8) – is rarely recognized in the vernacular press.

Even in Calcutta (now Kolkata), well known for its penchant for all things artistic, it is difficult to find extensive coverage of Joyce in the hundreds of Bengali "little magazines" that devote so much space to Neruda, Kundera, or Borges.[2] European modernism was discussed in Pramatha Chaudhury's *Sabujpatra* (*The Green Journal*, founded in 1914) – but its contents were not widely appreciated. A search through the archives of *Desh* (*The Nation*), a prestigious literary journal with a well-deserved reputation for acknowledging the avant-garde, discloses only three pieces on Joyce. Two of these are translations of stories from *Dubliners* – Tarun Sarkar's 1946 rendering of "Araby" entitled "Andhakar" ("Darkness"), and Krishna Dhar's 1948 version of "Counterparts," titled "Pratikriya" ("Reaction"). Sarkar's brief biographical sketch identifies Joyce as a great British writer of Irish origin, the author of *Dubliners*, *A Portrait*, *Ulysses*, and *Finnegans Wake*, and a rebel against conventional notions of form and content in the novel. The third contribution, captioned "Dubliner Odysseus," is an extremely perceptive reading of *Ulysses* by the noted Bengali *littérateur* Manabendra Bandopadhyay.

"Dubliner Odysseus" ("The Odysseus of Dublin," Bandopadhyay 1962: 831–8) begins with a detailed analysis of Dujardin's *Les lauriers sont coupées* and its influence on Joyce. It goes on to illustrate the connection between language and the flow of mental processes or stream of consciousness by translating some of Bloom's ruminations into Bengali. It then examines the cinematic technique of *Ulysses* and the way this technique anticipated the grammar of Eisenstein's cinema. Finally, it links these observations to the element of "plotlessness" and the handling of time in the novel. Joyce himself is here the Odysseus figure, apparently straying from the set path of novel-writing, yet ultimately always aware of his unique destination.

That unique fictional destination impacted Indian fiction in different ways. It must be remembered that, in the first half of the twentieth century, the major vernacular literatures foregrounded psychological analysis and the motif of the alienated individual, not simply because of Western modernism, but as a response to India's specific historical situation, and the ideological crisis of an educated and introspective middle class called upon to adapt to a challenging social milieu undergoing rapid transition. In Bengal the exploration of the psyche begins with the novels of Tagore and his contemporaries. Naturally, there was interest in the technique of the interior monologue, but the motivating impulse could have come from Joyce or Proust or Gide, all of whom were known to these writers. In the sphere of the Indian novel in English, G. V. Desani's *All About H. Hatterr* (1972) uses counterdiscursive strategies as in *Ulysses*, although Desani also acknowledged Sterne. In the 1960s, Raja Rao's *The Serpent and the Rope* (1960) and Anita Desai's *Cry, The Peacock* (1963) make effective use of interior monologue. From the 1970s onwards, Salman Rushdie, I. Allan Sealy, and Amit Chaudhuri have used alternative narrative models which they have indeed related back to Joyce, but they also acknowledge other European paradigms, as well as indigenous modes such as the *purana* and the classical *raga* that use the same strategies of circularity, digression, and allusiveness that mark the stream-of-consciousness technique.

In the vernacular literatures, a notable use of interior monologue is seen in the Oriya novelist Gopinath Mohanty, whose *Lagna Bilagna*, and especially *Paraja*, have won immense critical acclaim for their successful deployment of this experimental form. Bengali fiction, too, produced notable examples. In a footnote to "Dubliner Odysseus" (Bandopadhyay 1962: 833 n. 1) the author cites Buddhadeb Bose's *Lal Megh* ("The Red Cloud," 1931) as the first stream-of-consciousness (*chetanaprabaham-ulak*) novel in Bengali, followed in Bose's oeuvre by the musings of Somen in *Nirjan Swakkhar* ("The Lonely Sign"), the railway journey in *Anya Konokhane* ("Some Other Place"), and especially the celebrated coda to *Tithidore* (roughly translatable as "The Phases of the Moon," 1948). In the last lines of *Tithidore* the aging Rajenbabu broods over the anxieties and alienation of middle-class existence:

> Darkness, darkness. [. . .] silence . . . the whole house silent . . . the universe silent [. . .] a life . . . heart . . . pulsating heart . . . eyeless, open-eyed, the open window dark . . . darkness outside, stars in a black sky . . . afar . . . on the shore . . . the other shore . . . being . . . not-being . . . becoming . . . for all eternity . . . the silent stars diffusing the sky look on . . . (Bose 2000: 328; my translation).

The drama of consciousness recurs in Gopal Halder's *Ekada* ("Once"), *Ek Deen* ("Some Day"), and *Anya Deen* ("Some Other Day"), a trilogy concerning the anguished memories and dreams of three captured freedom fighters sentenced to death by the British Raj, each part occurring within a single day, as in *Ulysses*. There is also the eponymous hero of Jibanananda Das' *Malyaban* (1948), memorably emerging from a nightmare about his own insecurities at the end of the novel – "Talking animatedly in the half-darkness, the sun, thunder in the root, tempestuous gales, the mothers, the whores, Utpala's [Malyaban's wife's] guffaw, the sound of the sea, of blood, of death, hearkening to the dissonant flow of the endless winter night Malyaban awoke" (Das 1986: 165; my translation).

The long footnote to "Dubliner Odysseus" also names Dhurjatiprasad Mukhopadhyay's trilogy – *Antahshila* ("The Hidden Spring," 1935), *Abarta* ("The Vortex," 1937), and *Mohana* ("The Estuary," 1943) – as an example of psychological fiction. In one of the earliest reviews of *Antahshila* (*Chitrali*, January 1935), Indira Devi Chaudhurani observed, "Though the form of this novel is not original, it is relatively new in Bengali literature. It brings to mind <u>Virginia Woolf's *Mrs. Dalloway*</u>" (Mukhopadhyay 2002: 440; my translation; underlining as in the original). In *Antahshila*, Khagendranath, a young intellectual affiliated with the avant-garde *Sabujpatra* group who reads Ortega y Gasset, Anatole France, and C. K. Scott Moncrieff's translation of Proust, discourses with ease on European art from Tintoretto to the Impressionists, and considers himself a universal man, the product of all cultures and all histories. He muses on the form of the novel in the course of a long meditation on art:

> The novel has a main strand surrounded by many broken wavering threads. Their worth lies in their being peripheral. [. . .] Many a minor <u>phrase</u> wanders around the main theme. In earlier times, the relationship between the central and the subordinate was like that between the Brahmin and the *sudra* [untouchable], or the king and his vassal, absolute and preordained – this is known as <u>unity of action</u>. But life in our times is

multifarious and richly textured, so unity is no longer valued! [. . .] All that one looks
for is a pleasurable whole as in Joyce's *Ulysses*. [. . .] Sometimes I wonder, will I find the
ultimate reality through art? [. . .] As playful gusts whirl together the small and the big,
the useful and the useless, just so the focal and the ancillary come together. [. . .] That is
when scattered flowers become a garland (Mukhopadhyay 2002: 175, 177; my translation; underlining as in the original).

In his Foreword to *Antahshila*, the author declared that Beauty could not be realized
through the "realist" and "naturalist" modes, or even through "romantic realism," and
that he sought to evoke beauty not in terms of stream of consciousness but through
the concrete, in the manner of Cyril Connolly (Mukhopadhyay 2002: 66; underlining
as in the original). In view of his having invoked *Ulysses*, could this idea of a beauty
approached through the "concrete" also be akin to Stephen's theory of the epiphany
from the Ballast Office clock from *Stephen Hero*?

The Bengali novel by and large took a different turn after the 1940s. Grappling
with the double trauma of the Bengal Famine (1942) and Partition (1947), and compelled to engage with the pressures of modernization, literature turned away from the
palimpsest of consciousness to gritty realism or nostalgic evocations of the vanishing idyll of rural Bengal. A rare instance of a late psychological novel is Kamalkumar
Majumdar's *Golap Sundari*, translated into English by Asok Mitra as *Rose Beauty*.[3] The
novel opens with the coalescence of object and sensation in the mind of Bilas:

> Bilas was elsewhere, for, right before him against the low sky, bubbles, the colour of
> the young Sun, occasionally turning blue all too suddenly, floated around. One, then
> another, and then so many and still so many, even as the stars swim into view in rows out
> of the oncoming dusk, the well-rounded luminous bubbles bobbed up and down, their
> shapes issuing like pure notes in the upper register from a shepherd's pipe across green
> fields afar on an autumn afternoon; [. . .] these bubbles have a way of receding from view
> even while they are there before you. . . This must have troubled him. For, he had set him-
> self in the past to writing poetry, struggling all by himself day after day, without end in
> the mists of his own selfconsciousness (Mitra 1995: 13).

In his "Translator's note," Mitra refers to Majumdar's intimate knowledge of Proust
and surmises that this may have been one of the inspirations behind the use of montage
in *Golap Sundari* (Mitra 1995: 9). But without speaking in terms of direct inspiration, is not the tone of Bilas' reverie reminiscent of Stephen in *A Portrait*, with only
the green fields of autumn situating the scene in Bengal and not in Ireland? Artists
working on the same theme at the same time in widely separated locations manifest
the kind of similarity that proclaims the universality of the Zeitgeist.

Compared to the vernacular literatures, several Indian English novelists turned to
Joyce not for his rendering of human psychology, but for his subversive use of the colonizer's language, English. Joyce was unequivocal in his belief that "the Irish language,
although of the Indo-European family, differs from English almost as much as the language spoken in Rome differs from that spoken in Teheran." Interestingly, he locates
the Irish language squarely in the domain of the Other – "This language is eastern in

origin, and has been identified by many philologists with the ancient language of the Phoenicians" (*OCPW* 110). This is clearly a counterdiscursive stance. According to Francis Mulhern, who cites as his evidence Stephen's conversation with the Dean of Studies about the hegemony of English in *A Portrait* (*P* 158–9), this is "the writing of one for whom 'English' could not be self-identical, a literary practice whose 'roots' lay in the history of colonialism" (Mulhern 1990: 260). Citing the same passage from *A Portrait*, Said draws out its political undertone – "Joyce's work is a recapitulation of those political and racial separations, exclusions, prohibitions instituted ethnocentrically by the ascendant European culture throughout the nineteenth century" (Said 1991: 48). The point has also been noted by Derrida in his essay on Joyce – "What matters is the contamination of the master by the language he claims to subjugate, on which he has declared war" (Derrida 1984: 156). Fredric Jameson finds in Joyce a "multiethnic [. . .] creole" (Jameson 1991: 302), and the colonial interface is analyzed in the essays in Attridge and Howes' *Semicolonial Joyce*. James Snead relates Joyce's radical language to his radical form, "indirectly challenging the European nationalisms and even imperialisms that had allowed for only token levels of hybridization" (Snead 1990: 236). Rushdie, naming Joyce, says, "perhaps, above all, what is going on is politics" (Rushdie 1982: 8).

It is only the occasional minor talent that attempts to replicate Joyce. This is the case with Sanjib Datta's little-remembered Wakean novel, *The Judas Tree*. Its "infralapsarian" (Datta 1984: 138) angst, mannered cynicism (life is a "bum ballocky back of a zero blanked to every honest calculation" [Datta 1984: 1]) and deliberately oracular inconclusive conclusion ("body. There is the body and heart of the body . . . heart I speak in, heart I spit out" [Datta 1984: 444]), are no more than clever approximations through a welter of words. Major Indian English writers rearticulate rather than repeat Joyce.

In his Introduction to Desani's *All About H. Hatterr*, Anthony Burgess compared both its structure and language to *Ulysses*. Desani invokes both *A Portrait* and *Ulysses* in his tongue-in-cheek description of his Indian English novel written in Indian English, which throws potential British publishers into a "trilemma":

> So to Betty Bloomsbohemia: the Virtuosa with knobs-on. [. . .] I did the best I could. *A.* A man's choice, Missbetty, is conditioned by his past: his experience. [. . .] That's all why this book isn't English as she is wrote and spoke. *B.* [. . .] I didn't know myself, poor devil! What I had gone and done. *Qua* artist, I was drawing on my unconscious obviously (Desani 1972: 16–17, 20).

Hatterr, Desani's alter ego, apprentices himself to seven oriental sages in succession in his desperate search for antique wisdom. Sadly, this is frustrated by his equally desperate attempts as a Eurasian ("Biologically, I am fifty-fifty of the species" [Desani 1972: 31]) to play the colonial sahib, the "real blightah, suh" (Desani 1972: 248), in a fruity mixture of "babu English" and bazaar slang – "Every little helps [. . .] old feller! Whiskey ja soodavesi, met het *leetle* spuit*wasser*! La, what a cup final!" (Desani 1972: 163; italics in the original). Hatterr's Hindi invocation to "mata meri" ("Mother"

Mary, the Blessed Virgin; Desani 1972: 248) is the colonized subject's revenge by appropriation.

Rushdie's intertextual use of Joyce has been well documented – Keith M. Booker and Ronald Bush have exhaustively catalogued Joycean reminiscences in *The Satanic Verses* (Booker 1991: 190–208; Bush 1998: 129–50). Yet over and above the specific reminiscences, it is Joyce's polyphonic and circular structures, urban settings, and allusive hybrid language that resonate through Rushdie's multi-voiced narratives, Bombay cityscapes, and mongrelized Hindi–Urdu–Marathi–Babu English chutnification of the colonizer's language. That the many connections with Joyce are not accidental is proved by Rushdie's echoing Stephen's resolve to use "silence, exile and cunning" to preserve his freedom as an artist during the Iranian *fatwa* following publication of *The Satanic Verses* – "The Muslim world is full of censors these days, and many of its greatest writers have been forced into silence, exile or submission. (The Joycean option of cunning seems unavailable at present)" (Rushdie 1989b: 26). Less well known than Rushdie's oeuvre but equally indebted to the tradition flowing from Swift through Joyce to Desani and Rushdie is I. Allan Sealy's gargantuan, polyvocal, and irreverently hybrid *The Trotter-Nama*, with its mocking insight into "don't know what-all nonsense" such as "geography is everywhere but history happens only in England!" (Sealy 1999: 403–4).

A different tradition emanating from Joyce is the fiction that searches out the epiphany in the trivial and the mundane. Mulk Raj Anand wrote in his "Afterword on the Genesis of *Untouchable*" that "I was struck by the compassion of Joyce's vast epic narrative *Ulysses*, about the symbolic lives of Mr. and Mrs. Bloom [. . .] during one day in Dublin in the year 1905" (Anand 1940). *Untouchable*, too, is set within a single day and its characters are both individual and symbolic. It is, however, Amit Chaudhuri among Indian English novelists who is closest to this aspect of Joyce – that is, the construction of "epiphanies, which, though produced in the conditions of ordinariness and chaos, redeem that ordinariness into a heightened awareness" (Chaudhuri 2003: 125). In "Joyce remembered," Chaudhuri acknowledges learning from Joyce that "the uncovering of the miraculous in the post-industrial, post-colonial, metropolitan commonplace might be a legitimate literary ambition [. . .] of the bourgeois [. . .] novelist." Moreover, Joyce "became a facilitator of my recuperation of my Indian, specifically, my Bengali, sensibility," because "Irishness, to me, like Bengaliness, was a colonial, urban invention of, at once, great magnitude and particularity and specificity and location, a quite astonishing response to Empire, industrialization, and, among many other things, the English language" (Chaudhuri 2004: 8). So in the final lines of *A Strange and Sublime Address*, the glimpse of a cuckoo in a dusty garden in crowded Calcutta becomes the passport to wonder for a band of schoolboys – "'It's eating the orange flower,' whispered Abhi. But it must have sensed their presence, because it interrupted its strange meal and flew off – not flew off, really, but melted, disappeared from the material world. As they watched, a delicate shyness seemed to envelop it, and drew a veil over their eyes" (Chaudhuri 2001: 109).

Joyce's interface with India and India's with Joyce are subterranean as compared with other, more overt influences, but the results are no less rewarding. Said's observation on

Ulysses is useful here – "The image for writing changes from *original inscription* to parallel script, from tumbled-out confidence to deliberate fathering-forth" (Said 1991: 135; emphasis in the original). Though Stephen's vision of the artist in the "Scylla and Charybdis" section of *Ulysses* is of a self-authorizing figure who has no need for origins or literary "fathers," the act of reading Joyce against the background of India illuminates mutual connections in the reciprocity of artistic inspiration – "the one substrance of a streamsbecoming. Totalled in toldteld and teldtold" (*FW* 597 7–9).

NOTES

1   For the development of this idea, I would like to acknowledge my discussion with Professor Kapil Kapoor of the School of Languages, Jawaharlal Nehru University, New Delhi.

2   Some of India's major languages – each with a rich recorded literary tradition (Tamil literature, for example, goes back to 100 BCE) – are at least as different from one another as English is from Russian. Indians read the literature of other parts of the country in translation – either in English or in their own vernacular. Because of firsthand knowledge, all the detailed examples from the vernacular that follow are from Bengali literature.

3   I would like to thank Dr. Chinmoy Guha, Reader, Department of English, University of Calcutta, for drawing my attention to Asok Mitra's English translation of *Golap Sundari*, and also for his kind assistance while searching through the archives of *Desh*.

BIBLIOGRAPHY

Anand, Mulk Raj (1940 [1935]) *Untouchable*. London: Penguin.

Attridge, Derek and Marjorie Elizabeth Howes (eds.) (2000) *Semicolonial Joyce*. Cambridge: Cambridge University Press.

Bandopadhyay, Manabendra (1962) "Dubliner Odysseus" [The Odysseus of Dublin], *Desh* 29 (22): 831–8.

Beckett, Samuel (1972 [1929]) "Dante . . . Bruno. Vico . . Joyce," in Samuel Beckett et al., *Our Exagmination Round His Factification for Incamination of Work in Progress*. London: Faber and Faber.

Beckett, Samuel et al. (1972 [1929]) *Our Exagmination Round His Factification for Incamination of Work in Progress*. London: Faber and Faber.

Bhat, G. K. (1984) *Rasa Theory and Allied Problems*. Baroda: MS University.

Booker, Keith M. (1991) "*Finnegans Wake* and *The Satanic Verses*: two modern myths of the fall," *Critique* 32 (3, Spring): 190–208.

Bose, Buddhadeb (2000 [1948]) *Tithidore*. Calcutta: New Age Publishers.

Bush, Ronald (1998) "Rereading the exodus: Frankenstein, Ulysses, The Satanic Verses*, and other postcolonial texts." In Karen Lawrence (ed.) *Transcultural Joyce*, pp. 129–50. Cambridge: Cambridge University Press.

Chaudhuri, Amit (2001 [1991]) *A Strange and Sublime Address* in *Freedom Song: Three Novels*. New York: Knopf.

Chaudhuri, Amit (2003) *D. H. Lawrence and "Difference": Postcoloniality and the Poetry of the Present*. Oxford: Clarendon Press.

Chaudhuri, Amit (2004) "Joyce remembered," *The Telegraph*, Calcutta, Sunday, April 18: 8.

Cheng, Vincent J. (1992) "The general and the sepoy: imperialism and power in the museyroom." In Patrick J. McCarthy (ed.) *Critical Essays on James Joyce's Finnegans Wake*, pp. 260–8. London: Macmillan.

Das, Jibanananda (1986 [1948]) *Malyaban*. In his *Collected Works*, ed. Debesh Roy, Vol. 2. Calcutta: Pratikshan.

Datta, Sanjib (1984) *The Judas Tree, A Novel*. Calcutta: Datta.

Derrida, Jacques (1984) "Two words for Joyce." In

Derek Attridge and Daniel Ferrer (eds.) *Post-Structuralist Joyce*, pp. 145–59. Cambridge: Cambridge University Press.

Desani, G. V. (1972 [1948]) *All about H. Hatterr.* London: Penguin.

Dhar, Krishna (1948) "Pratikriya" [Reaction – a Bengali translation of Joyce's 'Counterparts' from *The Dubliners*], *Desh* 15 (25): 521–4.

Eliot, T. S. (1934) *After Strange Gods: A Primer of Modern Heresy.* London: Faber and Faber.

Henke, Suzette (1986) "James Joyce, the East and Middle East: literary resonances of Judaism, Egyptology and Indian myth," *Journal of Modern Literature* 13 (2): 307–20.

Jameson, Fredric (1991) *Postmodernism, or the Cultural Logic of Late Capitalism.* Durham, NC: Duke University Press.

Kapoor, Kapil (1998) *Literary Theory: Indian Conceptual Framework.* New Delhi: Affiliated East–West Press.

Lal, P. (ed.) (1965) *T. S. Eliot: Homage from India.* Calcutta: Writers' Workshop.

Mitra, Asok (1995) *Rose Beauty* [an English translation of Kamalkumar Majumdar's *Golap Sundari*]. Calcutta: Papyrus.

Mukhopadhyay, Dhurjatiprasad (2002) *Complete Works*, Vol. I, rev. edn. Calcutta: Dey's Publishing.

Mulhern, Francis (1990) "English reading." In Homi Bhabha (ed.) *Nation and Narration*, pp. 250–64. London: Routledge.

O'Flaherty, Wendy Doniger (ed. and trans.) (1988) *Textual Sources for the Study of Hinduism.* Chicago: Chicago University Press.

Ramaiah, M. S. (1988) *Indian Responses to T. S. Eliot.* Calcutta: Writers' Workshop.

Rushdie, Salman (1982) "The empire writes back with a vengeance," *The Times*, July 3: 8.

Rushdie, Salman (1989a) *The Satanic Verses.* New York: Viking.

Rushdie, Salman (1989b) "The book burning," *New York Review of Books*, March 2: 26.

Said, Edward W. (1991) *The World, the Text, and the Critic.* London: Vintage.

Sarkar, Tarun (1946) "Andhakar" [Darkness – a Bengali translation of Joyce's "Araby"], *Desh* 14 (3): 100–2.

Sealy, I. Allan (1999) *The Trotter-Nama, A Chronicle.* New Delhi: IndiaInk.

Seth, Vikram (1993) *A Suitable Boy.* New Delhi: Viking.

Sharma, R. S. (ed.) (1994) *Indian Response to T. S. Eliot.* New Delhi: Atlantic.

Snead, James (1990) "European pedigrees/African contagions: nationality, narrative, and communality in Tutuola, Achebe, and Reed." In Homi Bhabha (ed.) *Nation and Narration*, pp. 231–49. London: Routledge.

Tambimuttu T. and R. March (eds.) (1965) *T. S. Eliot: A Symposium.* London: Cass.

14

Joyce and New Zealand: Biography, Censorship, and Influence

David G. Wright

Family Ties

A most immediate and substantial link between James Joyce and New Zealand is a little-known biographical one. His sister Margaret, having come to New Zealand as a nun in 1910, stayed and taught in the country for the rest of her life, a period of over 54 years. She thus joined that large group of Irish immigrants helping to run New Zealand's Catholic education system.

Margaret was born in Dublin on January 18, 1884, two years after James, and was baptized at St. Joseph's Chapel of Ease in Roundtown. She was invariably known to her family as Poppie. According to Noel Purdon, who interviewed Margaret in 1962, she claimed that her nickname derived from the color: "It was because of my red cloak that I used to wear for my sodality, and someone said, 'She looks just like a poppy.' . . . It was a nice name . . . and Jim always pronounced it to me as if he were bursting a bubble right in front of my face. Jim was a tease" (Purdon 1993: 4). After her mother died in 1903, Margaret stayed at home for six years, looking after her younger siblings. But she had intended for some time to become a nun, and in August 1909 she joined the Sisters of Mercy at Callan, County Kilkenny, where she began studying at St. Brigid's Missionary School. She spent nearly three months training in Kilkenny, and her departure for New Zealand occurred during Joyce's visit from Trieste to Dublin in November 1909. On November 10 Joyce wrote to his brother Stanislaus in Trieste from the family home that "Poppie will be here tomorrow on her way to New Zealand" (*LII* 261). Margaret was encouraged to believe that Joyce made this visit to Dublin in order to say farewell to her. No doubt he was glad to be present, but his visit had other main motives, including the Volta cinema project. According to Father Godfrey Ainsworth, Joyce told Margaret at this time that if she should ever wish to return to Europe she should let him know, though it remains unclear whether he promised explicitly to pay her fare (Ainsworth: 7).

Among the orders she might have joined, the Sisters of Mercy may have appealed to Margaret because they were a teaching order and in a position to send her overseas. She appears to have welcomed the decision to deploy her in New Zealand because it served to take her as far as possible from her family. Not that she felt hostile to them, but she probably had come to resent the demands they made on her. Besides, in joining the order she was supposed to renounce all worldly ties, and to sail for New Zealand was to relinquish her family connections decisively. According to Ainsworth, Margaret told him: "I thought to myself, 'Well now, I haven't much to sacrifice' and the only thing I had to sacrifice was my love for my own people [. . .] and that was my sacrifice" (Ainsworth: 7). According to James Feehan, Margaret informed him that Joyce had suggested the idea of New Zealand to her in the first place. Feehan claims that Joyce had urged her to "do something really heroic and witness at the uttermost parts of the earth" (Feehan 2000: 132). This claim cannot be confirmed. After she left Ireland, in any event, Margaret never returned, and she never saw any of her relatives again.

As a nun, she took the name Sister Mary Gertrude. She was sent first to Greymouth, on the west coast of the South Island. There, she was received as a novice on July 13, 1910, then pronounced her final vows on July 13, 1912. She also spent some time in a smaller town nearby called Runanga. The Greymouth area was an austere district, mostly sustained by the local coal mining industry, and with quite a harsh climate by New Zealand standards: persistent rain, numerous thunderstorms, and even occasional tornadoes. Apart from the rain, it must have appeared very different from Dublin.

In 1949, nearly 40 years after her arrival in New Zealand and at the age of 65, she was transferred to Loreto Preparatory College for Boys in Christchurch, on the east coast of the South Island. Christchurch was then a city of just over 150,000 inhabitants, Victorian in its architectural appearance and to some extent in its social tone, and with strong musical and cultural traditions. Its climate is gentler than that of Greymouth, more like that of Dublin, and altogether it would have been a comfortable place to retire. In fact, Margaret was probably moved because of a perceived need for an extra music teacher in Christchurch, and she duly continued teaching music to the pupils of Loreto College for the next 15 years, until three weeks before her death. She was diagnosed with stomach cancer in 1963, earning much praise for her courageous response to her illness. She died in Calvary Hospital, Christchurch, on Sunday March 1, 1964, at the age of 80. On March 3 a Requiem Mass was celebrated at St. Joseph's Church in the suburb of Papanui. Thus she had been baptized at one St. Joseph's Church, and had her funeral at another, on the opposite side of the world. She was buried in the nearby Waimairi Cemetery, where her gravestone lies among a group of identical ones commemorating other Sisters of Mercy. Six of her young music pupils, wearing their blue school uniforms, carried her coffin, having reportedly begged to be allowed to do so. On her death certificate, her father's occupation is listed as "revenue inspector."

Margaret's former colleagues and pupils speak highly of her, though all stress that she could be a stern disciplinarian. Mary Buchanan, for example, studied with her for seven or eight years in the Greymouth era, and reports that "she was an excellent teacher but also very very strict. [. . .] God help you if you hadn't done your practice. [Yet] my initial education from her was invaluable. So much so that I became very proficient at sight reading music [. . .] and at the age of 84 I am still an active musician and organist at two Catholic churches in Christchurch" (email to author, February 9, 2005). Gary Lennon is the deputy rector of St. Bede's College, a well-regarded boys' high school in Christchurch, and he studied with Margaret at Loreto College between 1949 and 1952. While he refers to her in an email as "Sister Gertie," and calls her "diminutive but forceful," he also stresses that she engendered great loyalty and respect from her pupils, and that more than fifty years after studying with her, he still goes to visit her grave (email to author, 31 January 2005).

Margaret's communications with James Joyce during the later parts of his life are rather mysterious. They did stay in contact. On July 19, 1933, Joyce wrote to his de facto secretary Paul Léon complaining that Margaret had not received a photograph – evidently one which he had asked Léon to send to her. She had presumably written directly to Joyce to report the photograph's non-arrival (Fahy 1992: 10). On October 18, 1933, Joyce wrote to Stanislaus, reporting that "I had a letter from Poppie. She was operated, the usual thing, I expect, but is now better" (*LIII* 288). We have no other details of this operation, and Joyce's letter shows that Margaret had disclosed few details to him. But the reference does prove that Margaret wrote to him in the 1930s, at least occasionally. Presumably she knew his current address in Paris, which changed often; that suggests reasonably frequent communication. On September 4, 1936, Joyce wrote to Léon asking him to send his daughter Lucia's book to Margaret (Fahy 1992: 23).

Unfortunately, Margaret's later letters to Joyce seem to have disappeared. They are not among the catalogued Paul Léon papers in Dublin and no sign of them seemingly appears at Buffalo, Cornell, or other likely locations. They may be in a library somewhere uncatalogued, or they may be in a private collection, or they may have been lost or destroyed, possibly by Joyce himself. We really have no idea how often she might have written to him. More often than he wrote to her, seems a reasonable guess. But unless any letters surface, nothing precise can be asserted about this correspondence.

In her 1962 interview with Purdon, Margaret claimed that "I had nothing from [James] but a telegram after the earthquake when he wanted me to come back [to Europe]" (Purdon 1993: 5). There was a major earthquake in New Zealand in 1929, usually called the Murchison earthquake and centered not far from Greymouth, where Margaret then lived. It mostly avoided major population centers and inflicted relatively slight casualties (fewer than twenty deaths in all), but it caused considerable property damage and was mentioned in European newspapers, so Joyce apparently wrote to Margaret expressing concern. He felt apprehensive about earthquakes as he did about thunderstorms, having written to Stanislaus on September 18, 1905, "Have you heard of the earthquake in Calabria? [. . .] Some phenomena of nature terrify me" (*LII* 108).

Margaret seems to imply in the interview that with this exception, Joyce did not write to her during her years in New Zealand. However, there are good reasons to query this declaration. Ainsworth asserts that Joyce did write to her on several occasions, and Sister Margaret Ann, once Margaret's superior at Loreto College, believes that he may even have written as often as every six weeks. We might suspect his letters were less frequent than that, though it seems that Margaret remained, after Stanislaus, the sibling to whom Joyce felt closest. Margaret clearly retained her esteem for Joyce even though his rejection of Catholicism pained her and she felt embarrassed by his reputation as the author of morally suspect books. And Joyce seems to have respected Margaret's dedication to her calling, despite his own reservations about the Church.

However, it is clear that his letters to Margaret were all destroyed on her instructions around the time of her death. Ainsworth claims to have had the letters in his own hands shortly before that time, though he refrained from making copies, and has provided few clues to the contents of the correspondence. He does confirm that he saw the telegram James sent in 1929 after the earthquake, asking if Margaret was safe and if she wanted to return to Europe. Apart from that topic, they presumably discussed family matters, and no doubt exchanged some information about the places where they lived.

Margaret's obituary in the *Tablet* in March 1964 includes an intriguing claim: that in 1925 Joyce attended a rugby game in Paris between the visiting New Zealand national side, the All Blacks, and a French team (if this happened, it would have been on January 11, 1925). Incidentally, the 1924–5 All Black side became known as "the Invincibles," since they never lost a match on their tour of Europe. That nomenclature might well have appealed to Joyce, though presumably they acquired this name only towards the end of the tour. The story goes that Joyce was taken with the Maori dance and chant, the haka, a version of which was performed by the team at the beginning of each All Black game, as it still is today. The obituary claims that Joyce then wrote to Margaret asking her to send him the Maori words of the haka with an English translation, and that the words were later incorporated into *Finnegans Wake*.

A slightly modified version of a Maori haka does indeed appear in the *Wake* and is discussed below (*FW* 335), but it seems impossible to establish from surviving evidence that Joyce requested this material from Margaret or that she supplied it. However, there is no doubt that Joyce's source for his *Finnegans Wake* haka material was the particular haka specially written for the 1924–5 All Blacks to perform on their tour of Europe. It was written by two team supporters during their voyage to Europe, and it is quite distinct from the "Ka Mate" haka which the All Blacks have otherwise regularly used for about a hundred years. Roland HcHugh in his *Finnegans Wake* annotations, drawing on information supplied by Bruce Biggs to *A Wake Newslitter* in 1962, cites a different original haka and supplies a translation of it (McHugh 1991: 335). That original does share a few phrases with Joyce's version. But the 1924–5 All Black haka is virtually identical with the one Joyce includes. And Joyce must have seen the official English translation of the All Black haka, too, because he echoes it closely on the same page of the *Wake*. For example, part of the original haka appears in the official translation as follows – the leader speaks some of the lines, and the team speaks the others:

Let us prepare ourselves for the fray. . . . We are ready. . . . The New Zealand storm is about to break. . . . The sound of the breaking. . . . The New Zealand storm waxes fiercer. . . . The height of the storm (Masters 1928: 160).

In Joyce's text, between portions of slightly modified Maori words, appear these phrases:

Let us propel us for the frey of the fray! Us, us, beraddy! [. . .] The Wullingthund sturm is breaking. The sound of maormaoring. The Wellingthund sturm waxes fuercilier. The whackawhacks of the sturm (*FW* 335 15–19).

So we can be certain which haka Joyce used as his source, though none of this proves either that he went to the game and heard the haka there, or that he asked Margaret for the words. The haka words and translation appeared in many newspapers, and a newspaper was probably where Joyce saw the printed text.

Ainsworth claims that Margaret had read none of Joyce's mature works until he showed her a copy of *A Portrait of the Artist as a Young Man* in 1961. Sister Margaret Ann mentions that, on some earlier occasion, she herself had been reading the *Portrait* as part of an English literature course: on noticing the title, Margaret Joyce had expressed shock and asserted that she would never read such a book herself. But Ainsworth observes that when he showed Margaret the novel she leafed through it, evidently taking it for a literal transcript of Joyce's own life, and remarking that her own recollection of some incidents differed from his. Rather touchingly, she claimed that she herself had been the girl who was with John Joyce (or Simon Dedalus) in the audience for the Whitsuntide play at Belvedere, and who is described by the other boys as "ripping." In the novel, the girl in question is apparently not Stephen's sister but his sometime girlfriend E— C—.

It seems unlikely that Margaret ever looked at *Ulysses* or the *Wake*. Purdon claims he remarked to her during his interview in 1962 that Joyce's works show how much he adored his family. He then quotes Margaret's reply:

I will *never* read his later writings and I will never, *never* know. But it is kind of you to say he remembered us well. Not simply me, I know that, but all of us. Something from the past at least stays for us. Father was always mortgaging everything. He used to say to me, 'Poverty, my dear, is not shameful; but it is uncomfortable.' Well, it's no longer uncomfortable and I forget even the bad times at St Peter's Terrace. Jim was a lovely boy to me, whatever (Purdon 1993: 5).

During the interview, however, Margaret did claim to recall some of Joyce's childhood writing, done while the family was still living together. In particular, she remembered a line he had written at the age of nine, though whether this line had once formed part of "Et Tu, Healy" or of some other long-lost poem remains unclear. In any case, it is a line allegedly by James Joyce which has apparently been printed only once before, so it should be included here for the record. According to Margaret, the line reads, "Do not hamper the man at the wheel" (Purdon 1993: 5).

Antipodean Content

Whether Joyce learnt anything significant about New Zealand from Margaret or not, the country features obliquely in his work from time to time. In an essay he wrote at the age of 16 on the subject of "Subjugation," he cites New Zealand as a location where land was appropriated from indigenous people by European settlers in the nineteenth century (*OCPW* 7). In this essay he expresses an assumption about the superiority of the settlers which seems offensive to a modern reader, though it should be noticed that he also draws attention to the loss undergone by the indigenous people, a loss which historically has been addressed in New Zealand only recently. It also appears that Joyce already took New Zealand as an instance of otherness, as the antithesis of Ireland or Europe, a status it would retain in some of his later writings.

In *Dubliners* there is a motif of Antipodean escape, though it is marked by ambivalence about whether such an escape from Dublin is wise. While Australia and South America are the destinations specifically mentioned, Joyce must have had New Zealand in mind in one context at least. The story "Eveline," from the earliest stages of its development, incorporates unmistakable allusions to Margaret Joyce. Like Eveline, she had formally promised her mother "to keep the home together as long as she could" (*D* 33). Like Eveline, moreover, Margaret "had hard work to keep the house together and to see that the [. . .] young children who had been left to her charge went to school regularly and got their meals regularly" (*D* 31). In childhood, Margaret had played Eve in Joyce family theatricals – Eveline's name designates her as a "little Eve" – and her nickname Poppie is echoed in Eveline's nickname Poppens. By the time Joyce finished revising the story's text in 1910, adding at that stage a pointed reference to Blessed Margaret Mary Alacoque, Margaret had become a nun, taken the name Sister Mary Gertrude, and sailed to New Zealand. Besides echoing both her baptismal name and her religious name, Margaret Mary Alacoque is especially associated with the Sacred Heart – as is St. Gertrude. Cumulatively, these references confirm Margaret as an important antecedent for Eveline, and suggest that the decisions Margaret made about her future – becoming a nun and accepting a posting to New Zealand – formed part of Joyce's speculations about the possibilities open to a person in Eveline's situation, at least as he prepared the story for publication. Feehan claims that Margaret had had the notion not only of becoming a nun, but also of going to New Zealand, as early as 1903 (Feehan 2000: 129). If this claim is true, Margaret's experiences seem all the more likely to have been in Joyce's mind even as he first drafted the story in 1904. Eveline is granted a suitor, as Margaret was not, but decides against leaving Ireland with him. While we learn nothing of her subsequent life, becoming a nun would seem to be one of the few possibilities remaining open to her.

In *Ulysses*, Joyce includes a brief scene set in the Dedalus household, which we can assume to be approximately based on the Joyce household as it was in June 1904 (*U* 10 258–97). The father and sons of the family are absent, temporarily in the case of the father (whom we observe frequenting the pubs of Dublin) and permanently in the case of at least one son (Stephen Dedalus declares during the novel that he will never return to his father's house). The sadly improvident family home is being managed by the Dedalus daughters Maggy, Katey, Boody, and Dilly. The first three of these also appear in *A Portrait of the Artist as a Young Man*, though Maggy's name is there spelt "Maggie" (*P* 146). Maggy may well be based on Margaret. On June 16, 1904, Maggy, like Margaret on that date, is clearly the one managing the household. She dispenses food and keeps tabs on the family's movements. It is Maggy who admonishes Boody when Boody alludes to "our father who art not in heaven" (*U* 10 291–3). The scene in *Ulysses* thus seems a compassionate portrayal of the dispiriting home which Margaret was running by 1904, and whose stresses would later help project her to her future as a nun in New Zealand.

New Zealand also features on several occasions in *Finnegans Wake*, though the references do not seem pointed or consistent enough to establish any real thematic emphasis. The phrase "Rosbif of Old Zealand!" (*FW* 171 1–2) echoes Fielding's "Oh! The roast beef of old England," and establishes a polarity between New Zealand and the British Isles which may also underlie subsequent allusions. Another passage, "The Pills, the Nasal Wash (Yardly's), the Army Man Cut, as british as bondstrict and as straight-cut as when that brokenarched traveller from Nuzuland" (*FW* 156 28–30), recalls Macaulay's *Review of Ranke's History of the Popes*: "She [the Roman Catholic Church] may still exist in undiminished vigour when some traveller from New Zealand shall, in the midst of a vast solitude, take his stand on a broken arch of London Bridge to sketch the ruins of St Paul's" (McHugh 156). And in the "Anna Livia" section, the name "Waiwhou" (*FW* 202 12) echoes the Waihou River in New Zealand, though it may have been chosen simply for its sound qualities.

The most intriguing invocation of New Zealand in the *Wake* remains the Maori haka:

> Au! Au! Aue! Ha! Heish!
> As stage to set by ritual rote for the grimm grimm tale of the four of hyacinths, the deafeeled carp and the bugler's dozen of leagues-in-amour or how Holispolis went to Parkland with mabby and sammy and sonny and sissy and mop's varlet de shambles and all to find the right place for it by peep o'skirt or pipe a skirl when the hundt called a halt on the chivvychace of the ground sloper at that ligtning lovemaker's thender apeal till, between wandering weather and stable wind, vastelend hosteilend, neuziel and oltrigger some, Bullyclubber burgherly shut the rush in general.
> Let us propel us for the frey of the fray! Us, us, beraddy!
> Ko Niutirenis hauru leish! A lala! Ko Niutirenis haururu laleish! Ala lala! The Wullingthund sturm is breaking. The sound of maormaoring. The Wellingthund sturm waxes fuercilier. The whackawhacks of the sturm. Katu te ihis ihis! Katu te wana wana! The strength of the rawshorn generand is known throughout the world. Let us say if we may what a weeny wukeleen can do.
> Au! Au! Aue! Ha! Heish! A lala!

> (*FW* 335 4–23)

Roland McHugh glosses the Antipodean content in this passage by noting that "neuziel" alludes to New Zealand, and "maormaoring" to the Maori race or language. Wellington, the capital city of New Zealand, is invoked twice, though of course the Duke of Wellington is also present.

Joyce's text juxtaposes conflicts in different places and at different times. Underlying the passage is the long-running *Wake* jest about Buckley shooting the Russian general. Meanwhile, the Maori haka serves to transpose the Napoleonic Wars to the other side of the world (and possibly to the later nineteenth century, if Joyce had the New Zealand Wars, once called the Maori Wars, in mind). If Joyce did indeed learn that the haka had been performed at a rugby game in Paris, he might have been amused that this cultural manifestation of the new world had been translated into the heart of the old world, thus reversing the direction taken by the name "Wellington" as it moved from a battle on French soil to denote a place in a distant colony. The repeated references to a Wellington "sturm," moreover, appear to link human conflicts with meteorological ones. This *Wake* passage, in its reference to a Maori perspective and its use of antithesis, faintly echoes Joyce's invocation of New Zealand in that essay he had written more than forty years earlier.

Joyce and Censorship

In New Zealand during the twentieth century, censorship of publications operated much as it did in Britain or the United States, but may have been even more stringent. *Ulysses* was banned from the time of its publication in book form until the 1930s. (A similar fate met D. H. Lawrence's *Lady Chatterley's Lover* and Vladimir Nabokov's *Lolita*.) In her biography of the poet and short-story writer R. A. K. Mason (1905–71), Rachel Barrowman reports that Mason received a copy of *Ulysses* which had been smuggled into New Zealand from Britain by the egregious expatriate author Geoffrey de Montalk (Barrowman 2003: 91). In 1931 Mason agreed to give a talk on Joyce to the Auckland Literary Society, but this talk in turn was "promptly banned" after "the professor of English [at Auckland University College] borrowed and read a copy of *Ulysses*" (Barrowman 2003: 137).

In 1932 Mason felt concern that his poetry collection, *No New Thing*, might cause offence when it was published in Britain. But the New Zealand poet A. R. D. Fairburn, then living in Britain, reassured him that there would be no problem in a country where "it is unnecessary to begin a discussion on James Joyce by determining whether or no he is pornographic. Intelligent people raise their eyebrows & gape blankly if you come out with irrelevancies of that sort" (quoted in Barrowman 2003: 158). This judgment suggests that Fairburn considered New Zealand more timid than Britain over issues of censorship, and it also seems indicative that he should choose Joyce as his particular example.

Rachel Barrowman adds that Mason did eventually discuss Joyce in a lecture he delivered in the city of Hamilton in May 1932. The lecture's topic was "Modernism in Literature." Mason asserted in this lecture that "qualities arousing wrath of old women in petticoats against James Joyce are the same qualities of greatness as brought querulous protests from moralists against Shakespeare" (quoted in Barrowman 2003: 165). He claimed that art endures because it deals with "the strongest, deepest, most abiding instincts of humanity." Also,

> the great characteristic of the modern age was the realisation of change, and the greatest poet of change, he argued – the greatest of those who "turn all their power to finding out more and more about the stream," among them Lawrence, Yeats and Housman – was Joyce (Barrowman 2003: 165).

Mason argued further that the most important influence on the development of modern literature was psychology, which had introduced to it an almost mythical dimension, as in Joyce's work.

Censorship of *Ulysses* did not end altogether after the ban on the novel was lifted. When Joseph Strick's film version first screened in New Zealand in the late 1960s, it was subjected to a curious form of censorship. At the time cinemas were oddly regarded as public places, and bad language was therefore strictly forbidden. Thus the chief censor initially decided he should ban the film outright, because of Molly Bloom's use of four-letter words. Yet he understood that *Ulysses* was a classic novel, already studied in the universities, and he felt reluctant to withhold the movie version from the public altogether. So he decided that it could be legally shown – but only to all-male or all-female audiences. This was not standard practice in New Zealand, no other film appears to have been treated in the same way, and the censor was subjected to widespread and even international ridicule for making the ruling. Most cinemas obediently screened Strick's *Ulysses* to men on one day and women on the next, but at least one university daringly bent the rules by screening it to an audience of men and women, with a rope down the center of the cinema to keep the sexes safely separate. As these variously constituted audiences sat through Strick's quiet and totally uninflammatory film, they must surely have wondered what the problem was. In any case, times have changed. The Sean Walsh movie version of *Ulysses* now circulates around New Zealand unhindered, despite its numerous bedroom (and bathroom) scenes, while Fionnula Flanagan's sexually explicit *James Joyce's Women* screened complete on a local television station in the early 1990s. There are no signs that New Zealand society has been harmed by exposure to such material.

Spheres of Influence

Claims are often made that Joyce "influenced" one writer or another, and several New Zealand authors seem to be cases in point. Yet we need to distinguish shared literary methodology and common cultural climate, on the one hand, from specific and measurable literary influence on the other.

Two of New Zealand's most widely known authors, Katherine Mansfield (1888–1923) and Janet Frame (1924–2004), both read at least some of Joyce's work. Both display qualities in their writing which in combination can seem "Joycean": autobiographical impulses, attempts at direct transcriptions of psychological states and the consciousness of central characters, epiphanic moments, and experimental use of language. Literary influence, however, is difficult to demonstrate in either case. Like Virginia Woolf, who also displayed all of these traits, both Mansfield and Frame were quite capable of discovering and refining such methods without direct reference to Joyce or anyone else.

Mansfield's collections of stories do resemble Joyce's *Dubliners* in their attention to the position of women, the place of victims in general, and social difficulties arising in colonial societies. But Mansfield, a remarkable literary innovator, developed her distinctive tone at around the same time as Joyce developed his. There seems to be no specific evidence, at least within her creative writing, that she ever read *Dubliners*. She did read the *Portrait*, and she had seen at least part of the text of *Ulysses* as early as mid-1918 (*JJ* 443). Evidently she read the full text of the novel in 1922. Her response to *Ulysses* seems to resemble Woolf's response: she found it obscure and vulgar, but also felt compelled to admire the psychological subtlety evident in Joyce's portrayal of Bloom and Molly. Nevertheless, there is no sign that *Ulysses* influenced her own writing, and she died only a year after it appeared in book form.

Frame began writing in the 1950s, and by that time Joyce had been sufficiently assimilated into the culture that it was difficult to say whether a "Joycean" trait discernible in another writer's work actually derived from him directly or not. There is little obvious reason to trace any specific aspect of Frame's writing back to her reading of Joyce. W. B. Yeats, in fact, appears to have been a more lingering influence on her work.

Two other New Zealand authors, less well known internationally than either Mansfield or Frame, display more demonstrable and declared debts to Joyce: R. A. K. Mason and, especially, Maurice Duggan (1922–74). Both of them, as it happens, were themselves partly of Irish family background.

Mason is known primarily as a poet, and he appears to have read Joyce's *Pomes Penyeach* in 1930, but his poetry does not resemble Joyce's at all. His short stories are less widely known but they do seem to contain Joycean moments. Rachel Barrowman notes that Mason's short story "Springtime and the Sick-Bed" was published in late 1930. In it,

> a man decides to abandon his invalid wife, bedridden and pain-racked by chronic asthma, after years of giving up his life (as he now realises) to her care. In the cold clear air of an early spring morning, as he splits kindling in the backyard, he comes to the sudden realisation "that all his life of self-sacrifice was only a sham and hypocrisy. . . . He had often wrung his hands for death to give her rest: now he saw that it was his own rest that he wished for." The story is a Joycean moment of epiphany, its form an interior monologue (Barrowman 2003: 138).

Barrowman adds that

it was in his short stories, which he himself described (to one publisher) as "fairly 'advanced' psychological studies," rather than in his poetry, that Mason's interest in Joycean modernism at that time – in "that fantastic twilit jungle where amid the mops and mows of nightmare apes and owls Mr Joyce and the Lancashire lout prance hand-in-hand to the sweet pipings of Professor Freud," as he jotted in his notebook – was most evident (Barrowman 2003: 165).

But Mason did not experiment with stream-of-consciousness narrative. James Bertram, reviewing Mason's "Springtime and the Sick-Bed," remarked that "this seems to me a small masterpiece . . . perhaps a little Joycian [*sic*] (the early Joyce of *Dubliners*)." But he thought Mason "a strong enough individualist to absorb any such influence" (quoted in Barrowman 2003: 165).

The New Zealand writer most clearly and deeply influenced by Joyce appears to be Maurice Duggan, who was also an intriguing character in his own right. Though Duggan had been born in New Zealand, he shared with Joyce a strong background of Irish Catholicism, partly repudiated but partly inescapable. Like Joyce he suffered problems defining his relationship with family, Church, and country, struggled with health issues and had difficulties with alcohol; like Joyce, he also died in his fifties. He wrote several groups of short stories dramatizing his relationship with a society which he found problematic, and these included a series of linked stories focusing on a character called Lenihan. (Joyce's character Lenehan features in *Dubliners*, and he also appears in more episodes of *Ulysses* than any other minor character.) It is worth lingering over Maurice Duggan's case, since it shows the impact Joyce could have on New Zealand literature in a writer who consciously chose to assimilate him.

Maurice Duggan bought a 1928 Shakespeare & Co. edition of *Ulysses* secondhand on November 9, 1943, about the time he himself began writing stories. According to Ian Richards' fine biography of Duggan,

> Maurice read it over and over until it almost fell to pieces. He could scarcely contain his excitement at Joyce's rich phraseology and endless virtuosity, at the Irish writer's ability to transform everyday life into something beautiful and significant through language. Maurice felt that his personality developed after reading *Ulysses*. From Joyce he also learned that writers were people who had problems with their parents, who had abandoned all religious faith, and who took gloomy consolation in their art. Many years afterwards he commented: "Between the beginning of *A Portrait of the Artist as a Young Man* and the end of *Finnegans Wake* lies everyman's domain and all literature, our hopes, fears and velvet curtains" [letter to John Reece Cole, November 7, 1962]. Maurice could even quote passages of Joyce from memory in a facsimile of an Irish brogue (Richards 1997: 56).

So there can be little doubt of Duggan's willingness to attend to Joyce's example.

It seems, moreover, that he believed Joyce's linguistic resourcefulness and richness might serve as a counterweight to the drab naturalism which he sometimes felt, fairly or otherwise, to characterize more typical New Zealand writing. He wanted more attention paid to language, less to plot and character. As Richards notes, "for Duggan [. . .] language was always pre-eminent, to which [belief] each new story presented a fresh challenge. Writing was not about recording reality, but about managing a reality of one's own. It was about style" (Richards 1997: 159). In the pursuit of enlivening qualities like those he detected in Joyce's writing, Duggan also adopted a painstaking and Joycean attention to detail. He once boasted that in a whole day's writing he had produced a total of 50 words. And of his story "Voyage," Duggan declared to his friend and mentor, the New Zealand writer Frank Sargeson, that "I am rather proud of the sentence 'Brown leaves drifting enticed her out . . .' which took me three days, three days to get" (quoted Richards 1997: 144). These remarks closely recall Joyce's famous observation to another friend called Frank (Budgen) that he had already gathered the words he needed for a particular sentence, but was now making great efforts to arrange them into the best possible sequence. For at least one of Duggan's stories, titled "A Small Story," he wanted speeches to be designated by dashes, presumably a mode of presentation he had learned from Joyce. The story did not appear this way, however: as in the first edition of *Dubliners*, somebody insisted on normalizing the dashes to inverted commas before the text was published.

As a sample of Duggan's writing which seems to echo Joyce in most of its sentences, here is a paragraph from the story "Voyage" (1956). It includes the sentence which, Duggan told Sargeson, he had taken three days to write:

> Sunk at its moorings a houseboat lay in water that covered all but one corner of the tilted gable and the top of a doorway, a dark rectangular cave. In the liquid shadow a striped pillow floated by a head of flaxen hair spread on the tide. The damp hair weaved and shifted on the broken current. One waited some Ophelia, some Osyth reading her ancient book, embowered in that blistered paint, shrined in those waterlogged boards, to float from the dark with each shift of the tide. Brown leaves drifting enticed her out under the bare witchfingers of the hanging willows that plucked at her weeded hair. But only a rope end washed from the sunken doorway (Duggan 1981: 120).

Here, the sentence "One waited some Ophelia . . ." seems much too direct, explicit and "authorial" for Joyce, too little anchored in the perceptions of a character in the fiction. With that exception, however, these sentences could easily have come from a Joycean context such as Stephen Dedalus' meditations in the opening episodes of *Ulysses*. In their spare punctuation, use of apposition, aquatic imagery, adjectival richness, introspective intensity, and precision of observation they appear markedly Joycean.

In 1944 Duggan wrote a story called "Faith of Our Fathers," expressing hostility to the Catholic Church. Of this story, Richards remarks that

> its aura of failure and frustration, in conception at least, would not be out of place among the stories of Joyce's *Dubliners*, which Duggan had read a few months before [his copy is dated 8 July 1944]. . . . His ability to embed words of subtle commentary in his opening paragraphs indicates that he had absorbed techniques also from his careful reading of Joyce (Richards 1997: 71).

"Faith of Our Fathers" includes the claim "If you are brought up in a religion until you are twenty you still have it when you are ninety, probably." And the story states that "real, considered blasphemy must taste like bravery." This emphasis shows "a determination, like [that of Joyce], to replace his faith with literature" (Richards 1997: 72).

Duggan seems also to have endorsed Joyce's views about the impersonality of the artist. Accordingly, in his work

> there is no intruding narrator even to imply things, so that "A Small Story" takes on an apparent objectivity. This is reinforced by the story's style. Because the authorial voice is so noticeably reduced to a mere tonal presence, because the two scenes are presented without flashbacks or gaps in time, because characters' thoughts are mostly unreported, and because most of the action advances through dialogue, it is not surprising that "A Small Story" should seem almost dramatic. Duggan may have adapted this technique in part from James Joyce's "Ivy Day in the Committee Room" (Richards 1997: 154).

On other occasions, Joyce's influence on Duggan arguably became less benign. Two reviews by New Zealand critics suggested as much. Ray Copland remarked that Duggan "had looked longer and more lovingly at his sentences than he did at the places and the people he describes," and Bill Pearson commented that "in Mr Duggan's stories things don't change or develop. Something is revealed, perhaps, or someone is disillusioned, but things stay the same. His vision is static, held still by adjectives and a painter's interest in colour and patterns of colour" (quoted in Richards 1997: 217). Much the same could be said of Joyce's work, and these comments may show that different expectations were held about New Zealand literature (though Pearson did stress that his comments were meant to be simply descriptive, not pejorative). The first sentence of Duggan's story "Sunbrown" could have been taken directly from *Ulysses*: "In solitary position, posed among grassgreen and treegreen, leaning, he lay" (Duggan 1981: 52). In its own context, though, it seemed to some readers to be overwritten. This story was initially rejected for publication as "too much borrowed from Joyce and badly put together" (Richards 1997: 77). And Duggan's story "Mezzanine Reading" includes the manuscript of a story by a fictional character, which "is crammed to the brink of incomprehensibility with Joycean neologisms, and begins, 'Quiet of dewmooned afternight of deathsmells. This secret circle of drab-dead bodies, bonereaching. . . . Ignoceremened from clatterheaving slothveyance by gruntacheod drabby they passed in mourning procession'" (Richards 1997: 83).

In Duggan's later writing career he also appears to have assimilated the influences of Nabokov and Beckett. His story "Riley's Handbook" (1970), for example, is strikingly reminiscent of a text like Beckett's *Molloy*. But the influence of Joyce also remained active till the end. One of Duggan's last works, "The Magsman Miscellany," seemed to his friends as Joycean as anything he had written earlier. As Richards remarks, in this story "Duggan comes as close as perhaps is conceivable to painting a complete self-portrait in words, while still remaining within the recognizable boundaries of fiction. This was the final use, and arguably the most brilliantly unconventional, that he was able to discover for language and for style" (Richards 1997: 405).

In the Academy

Joyce's works have featured in New Zealand university courses for many years. Some of those who teach and research his writings today first studied *Ulysses* in Ray Copland's graduate course at the University of Canterbury in the early 1970s. These days Joyce appears among the authors taught in English departments throughout the country, most typically through the inclusion of *A Portrait of the Artist as a Young Man* in undergraduate courses on modern fiction. His other texts feature less often among material taught to undergraduates, but do appear at graduate level. At the University of Otago Chris Ackerley offers a course on ambiguity in *Ulysses*, which also includes *Dubliners* and the *Portrait* as set texts. *Ulysses* appears on the booklist for Brian Boyd's course on narrative at the University of Auckland. Also at Auckland, David Wright regularly teaches a course on modern Irish authors which includes *Dubliners* and *Ulysses* (together with the work of Yeats, Synge, and Beckett, among others) and occasionally a course solely on Joyce which samples *Finnegans Wake* and looks in detail at the other prose works, including Joyce's play *Exiles*. These courses are all popular, and a number of the students who take them go on to carry out their own research projects on Joyce.

Several New Zealand academics have also published research on Joyce, or are working on him currently. David Wright has published *Characters of Joyce* and *Ironies of "Ulysses,"* as well as many articles, including "Joyce's Debt to Pinter," which assesses the influence of *Exiles* on Harold Pinter's *Old Times*, and "The Secret Life of Leopold Bloom and Emily Sinico," which investigates one aspect of the relationship between *Dubliners* and *Ulysses*. He is currently completing a book for the University Press of Florida which analyzes the relationship between these two texts in more detail. He has given papers at three recent international Joyce conferences, all of which have been subsequently published. Ray Copland published a pioneering article on the "Ithaca" episode of *Ulysses*. *James Joyce Quarterly* has published articles by Chris Ackerley (on opera in "Sirens") and Brian Boyd (on the priest in "Telemachus"). Chris Ackerley is planning a book drawing on his doctoral thesis about ambiguity in *Ulysses* and his graduate course on the same topic. His various publications on Beckett have often alluded to Joyce as well. In Brian Boyd's forthcoming book *Heads and Tales: On the Origin of Stories* he attempts an evolutionary (Darwinian) account of fiction, using examples from Homer to Art Spiegelman, and will devote a chapter to *Ulysses* to show that such an approach can deal non-reductively with high-modernist texts. His work on Nabokov has also involved many comparisons with Joyce and the tracing of Joycean allusions. Richard Corballis of Massey University has recently published an essay on Joyce and Wilde. Chris Ackerley and Richard Corballis also attend international Joyce conferences from time to time, and Richard Corballis has given papers on Joyce at various other conferences as well. Thus the state of Joyce studies in New Zealand universities, given the small size of the country, appears to be healthy and vigorous enough.

Some Conclusions

Joyce never paid prolonged or concentrated attention to New Zealand. All the same, several links and patterns do emerge from the data and quietly insist on being noticed. Family, racial, and religious associations underlie Joyce's continuing contact with his sister in New Zealand, and the influence he exerted on New Zealand writers. Not all New Zealand's writers especially admired Joyce. But it may be that Joyce's emergence in the early part of the twentieth century as a detached commentator on Irish identity, and as a revolutionary influence on English literature, elicited sympathetic responses in a society on the other side of the world which was busily redefining itself and its own literature at much the same time. New Zealand remained a very British society in many respects, at least until the time of the Second World War, but also had a pressing and increasing need to develop an identity of its own. An Irish author who wrote in English yet challenged British writers at their own game, and who always insisted on remaining true to his own vision, could seem an apt guide and role model in such endeavors.

Maurice Duggan is the New Zealand writer who responded most directly and enthusiastically to Joyce's example and there have been subtler and less measurable effects on a range of others as well. The very fact that in New Zealand *Ulysses* was subject to stringent official censorship, and that this censorship even extended to a movie version of the novel shown as late as the 1960s, obliquely marked Joyce as a persistently valuable liberating influence, one to set against the forces of repression.

Joyce may also have been ahead of his time in foreshadowing the broad international response to his own work, and more generally the increasing globalization of the modern world, a pattern which would ultimately extend to encompass even New Zealand. As Richard Ellmann always stressed, Joyce summoned into being the audience he needed. That New Zealand appears to respond to his works with a level of enthusiasm belying its size may speak to particular and quite diverse aspects of the country. But it also reflects the curious manner in which, from whatever angle or distance we think to approach him, Joyce always seems to be already there waiting for us at some point along the way.

BIBLIOGRAPHY

Published sources

Ackerley, Chris (2000–1) "'*Tutto è sciolto*': An operatic crux in the 'Sirens' episode of James Joyce's *Ulysses*," *James Joyce Quarterly* 38: 197–205.

Akenson, Donald Harman (1990) *Half the World from Home: Perspectives on the Irish in New Zealand 1860–1950*. Wellington: Victoria University Press.

Barrowman, Rachel (2003) *Mason: The Life of R. A. K. Mason*. Wellington: Victoria University Press.

Boyd, B. D. (1978) "A plain-clothes priest," *James Joyce Quarterly* 15: 176–9.

Copland, R. A. and G. W. Turner (1969) "The nature of James Joyce's parody in 'Ithaca,'" *Modern Language Review* 64: 759–63.

Corballis, Richard (2002) "Wild essence of Wilde: Joyce's debt to Oscar in *Ulysses*." In Uwe Böker,

Richard Corballis, and Julie A. Hibbard (eds.) *The Importance of Reinventing Oscar: Versions of Oscar Wilde during the Last 100 Years*, pp. 159–68. Amsterdam: Rodopi.

Costello, Peter (1992) *James Joyce: The Years of Growth 1882–1915*. London: Kyle Cathie.

Duggan, Maurice (1981) *Collected Stories*, ed. C. K. Stead. Auckland: Auckland University Press.

Fahy, Catherine (comp.) (1992) *The James Joyce–Paul Léon Papers in the National Library of Ireland: A Catalogue*. Dublin: National Library of Ireland.

Feehan, James A. (2000) *An Hourglass on the Run: The Story of a Preacher*. Dublin: Mercier Press.

McHugh, Roland (1991) *Annotations to "Finnegans Wake,"* rev. edn. Baltimore, MD: Johns Hopkins University Press.

Mason, R. A. K. (2003) *Four Short Stories 1931–35*. Auckland: Holloway Press.

Masters, Read (1928) *With the All Blacks in Great Britain, France, Canada and Australia 1924–25*. Christchurch: Christchurch Press.

Purdon, Noel (1993) "Bloomsday with Poppie," *Independent Monthly*, June: 4–5.

Richards, Ian (1997) *To Bed at Noon: The Life and Art of Maurice Duggan*. Auckland: Auckland University Press.

Watson, Chris and Roy Shuker (1998) *In the Public Good? Censorship in New Zealand*. Palmerston North: Dunmore Press.

Wright, David G. (1983) *Characters of Joyce*. Dublin: Gill and Macmillan.

Wright, David G. (1988) "Joyce's debt to Pinter," *Journal of Modern Literature* 14: 517–26.

Wright, David G. (1991) *Ironies of "Ulysses."* Dublin: Gill and Macmillan.

Wright, David G. (1999–2000) "The secret life of Leopold Bloom and Emily Sinico," *James Joyce Quarterly* 37: 99–112.

Unpublished sources

Ainsworth, Father Godfrey. "James Joyce and Sister Gertrude Joyce." Unpublished paper. Supplied by the Sisters of Mercy, Christchurch.

Larsen, Daniel. "Poppie." Unpublished essay on Margaret Joyce.

Telephone interviews with Sister Margaret Ann and Sister Hilary Swanson, Christchurch (about Margaret Joyce).

Email correspondence from Mary Buchanan and Gary Lennon, Christchurch (about Margaret Joyce); email correspondence from Roger Horrocks (about censorship of Joseph Strick's movie version of *Ulysses*).

Conversations with Peter Simpson (about Joyce and New Zealand literature) and Margaret Edgcumbe (about Joyce's use of the haka).

PART III
Approaches and Receptions

15

Joyce's Homer, Homer's Joyce

Declan Kiberd

"Odysseus is not a hero," a Jesuit priest told James Joyce at Clongowes Wood College, but the young boy disagreed (O'Connor 1967: 104). All his life, he would admire the canny wanderer who survived challenges by a mixture of will-power and craftiness. He told Pádraic Colum that the Greek epics were "outside European culture" (O'Connor 1967: 77), a fact which left Homer free to experiment with new ideas of narrative and character. Much the same was true of Joyce's own predicament: he was not yet "James Joyce" when he wrote *Ulysses*, but a relatively unknown artist from a peripheral country and so at liberty to attempt strange, unprecedented things without provoking choruses of disapproval. Over one hundred generations of humankind separated him from Homer, yet somehow the *Odyssey*, with its tales of travel and encounters with unfamiliar peoples, seemed the quintessentially modern story. Small wonder that Penguin Classics have sold far more copies of it than of the *Iliad*.

Through the centuries, the *Odyssey* had exercised a magical appeal over many authors, who wished only to retell it in poetry or in verse. But the chances of producing something worthy to stand beside the original were almost nil. "You are only a second-rate poet," scoffed one journalist to Patrick Kavanagh on reading his sonnet called "Epic," only to receive the amused rejoinder: "Since Homer, we all are" (O'Brien 1974: 64). But Kavanagh had his wisdom too:

> I inclined
> To lose my faith in Ballyrush and Gortin,
> Till Homer's ghost came whispering to my mind.
> He said: "I made the Iliad from such a local row.
> Gods make their own importance."

> (Kavanagh 1972: 136)

Although as a child Joyce loved the Lamb version of the *Odyssey*, he was himself rather scathing about "feeble and second-rate" versions by many other artists: "there is little point in imitation on this scale unless it is a means of saying something new" (Jenkyns

1992: 53). He also realized that Homer had performed the repetition trick first, using the *Odyssey* to reduce its predecessor and rival the *Iliad* to the status of a mere footnote. Homer's own travel tale provided perhaps the first major model of how a prior text could be trumped. Early in the narrative, he has Telemachus suggest that many people enjoy the latest version of a story far more deeply than they relish any of its predecessors.

A modern reviser of ancient texts must be like a good lover: faithful without seeming so. If it would be a sin for him or her to neglect a past work, the other great offence would be to repeat it exactly. Joyce felt himself animated by Homer's own unfinished energies. "The spirit of Homer was always beside me to sustain and encourage me," he said, "I believe that this was the first time that he did such a thing, since he could hardly have been concerned with all those feeble imitations that every second generation feels duty-bound to produce" (Potts 1979: 158). If the arts lie dreaming of what is to come, then Homer's ghost may have been waiting for just such a translator, capable of taking a deeper x-ray of his narrative than any prior version could offer. For Homer would have known, as all writers must, that only the future has critical methods subtle enough to bring out all the vital elements of the original work. Being multi-plotted, epic must always contain within it all possible future narratives.

If Odysseus was destined to travel across space and time, so also was the *Odyssey*. It represents, in the words of Carol Dougherty, "not so much the story of a journey as the journey of a story" (Dougherty 2001: 75). With its layered structure of flashbacks, reveries, inscribed tales, and multiple narrators, it has an oddly modern feel to it. Odysseus is himself a recognizably modern kind of protagonist. His authority to tell a story comes less from the Muses than from the pressure of a felt experience. Like his later analogue, Leopold Bloom, he has learned his lessons in "the university of life" (*U* 17 555–6). When Calypso promises immortality if he will only stay with her, he says no, in what must be the first ever tale in which a human refuses such an offer; and his canny creator knew that there would be other, future Odysseys, even as Joyce humbly sensed that there would be later versions of his *Ulysses*, such as Derek Walcott's *Omeros*.

Odysseus was hardly a conventional military hero – more a kind of modern conscientious objector. He knew that the official reason for the war – defense of the ancestral culture – was trumped up, since the real underlying motive was the search for raw materials and new markets. Accordingly, he tried to dodge the recruiting sergeant, but to no avail. Much as he rejected military heroics, he also refused the role of sexual conqueror. Circe, the Sirens, Calypso: these women take the sexual initiative in wooing their men, much as Bloom is given seedcake by Molly at their first lovemaking on Howth Head. Far from being a sexual predator, Odysseus seems rather like an absolute bourgeois, who knows how to be passive and vigilant, how to *wait* – a forecast not just of the modern intellectual, Hamlet, but of the secret charm of café society. He is supposed to be intent on returning to Ithaca, a journey which might have taken a couple of weeks but instead consumes many, many years, and, as he tarries, he anticipates something of the pleasures of the modern *flâneur*, something of the spectatorial delights of a Leopold Bloom. Bloom also knows the pleasures of delay, even as he sets out from Molly's boudoir: "in the act of going, he stayed to straighten the bedspread" (*U* 4 308–9).

"Who will deliver us from the Greeks and Romans?" asked many a Romantic author, to which Joyce answered "I will." The root meaning of "translate" is "conquer," because the translator half-hopes to displace the original text, or at least to release the energies latent in it but as yet not fully expressed. It is as if one molecule, brought into contact with another, releases a new "third" energy after their collision. To remember any past work, one must agree to forget many of its elements, and so the involuntary memory, often triggered by associative mechanisms, will have not just an element of surprise but also the force of a revelation. In Joyce's case, what is revealed is the modernity of Homer's greatest tale. Joyce understood that the modern mind was attracted to primitive art not simply as a reaction against the dessication of the new order, but as an expression of the fact that his generation had yet to master the new technology. They were, in effect, still the primitives of the electronic civilization. T. S. Eliot said that Joyce used Homer's story as a way "of controlling, of ordering, of giving a shape and a significance to the immense panorama of futility and anarchy which is contemporary history" (Eliot 1923: 681). But Homer was himself using his tale in the attempt to impose a semblance of order on a chaotic world which had, in fact, been shattered by his hero's travels and by what he had found on them. *The Odyssey* was "trying to construct a reading of the worlds and peoples of its own mythic past in order to make sense of a tumultuous and volatile present" (Dougherty 2001: 9) and so Homer decoded various alien cultures in order to recode them for his own, much as Joyce would turn Homer's "then" into his own "now."

Theodor Adorno and Max Horkheimer described the project of the *Odyssey* as an attempt to destroy mythical thinking and replace it with the rational order of a trading world. In the tale, Odysseus is treated often as a traveling salesman or barterer, and even taunted in Book Eight for being a profiteering merchant rather than an aristocratic athlete. His refusal to be seduced by the song of the Sirens is really a rejection of the mythical by a prudent rationalist (Adorno and Horkheimer 1979: 32). The bourgeois wins by doing nothing, by simply waiting, by deferring gratification: Odysseus refuses to eat the lotus-plant or the sacred cows and opts instead to be both sacrifice and priest, in an astonishing anticipation of the role of Jesus in the New Testament. In like manner Bloom offers Stephen Dedalus the inadvertent eucharist of coffee and a bun at the climactic meeting of *Ulysses*.

The bourgeois ego thus owes its existence to the sacrifice of the present to the future, even as the *Odyssey* deferred some of its gratifications until *Ulysses*. In the old story, Odysseus saves his life at one point by losing his very name, just as Jesus will offer a "new" code by which whoever loses his life will save it, and in Joyce's book Bloom will eventually become simply "the man." In all of these narratives, a passive but caring person achieves a sort of divine status, at once victim and god, by virtue of a sort of anonymous celebrity. Odysseus' name was a compound of *outis*, Greek for "nobody" and *zeus*, meaning a "god," and his tale was a parable of how to use your ordinariness and anonymity to win a final victory. (This was the application of the same technique of the "everyday" by which Homer was trumping the war-driven *Iliad.*) Among the lotus-eating sybarites, Odysseus triumphs by just working hard; and, when faced with the one-eyed monster, he bribes him with a drink in yet another audacious anticipation of the words of Jesus consecrating the bread and wine: "Take, Cyclops, and drink. Wine goes well with human flesh" (Adorno and Horkheimer 1979: 67). Bloom will offer his secular equivalents, coffee and bun, to Stephen, as a revised version. If sacrifice was once designed by humans to deceive gods, now it is designed by godlike humans as a sacrifice offered ultimately to themselves.

Joyce seized on this anti-mythological thinking behind the *Odyssey*, in order to free his own generation from old, useless myths. He knew that the First World War was not a battle for love and honor among nations but a pretext for the steel barons to seek new outlets and markets. As Shakespeare's Hamlet would do, Odysseus feigned madness, in the attempt to avoid bloody battle. His visit to the underworld was important mainly for his triumphant return from Hades, by which the protagonist annulled the idea of death and the storehouse of myths which encoded it. That liberation, too, would be repeated in the life of Jesus (who "descended into Hell, but the third day rose again from the dead"), and of Leopold Bloom in entering and exiting Glasnevin Cemetery.

The notion of an underworld is as crucial to Joyce as his dramatization of the subconscious. If the Celtic hero Cuchulain might walk again through the streets of Dublin, as Yeats suggested, then so also might Odysseus. Yeats simply put on plays rendering ancient Ireland in his contemporary theater, but Joyce felt that a truer way in which to evoke past people might be to imagine them in our space, not us in theirs. Louis Aragon beautifully captured the underlying concept in his *Paris Peasant*: "our cities are peopled with unrecognised sphinxes" (Aragon 1994: 27). So, just as the rebels of the 1916 Rising used the underground passages of Dublin for communication and escape, so did Joyce expose the life beneath the city's surface, not only in the story of how Tom Rochford rescued a man from an underground gas chamber ("He's a hero," *U* 10 492), but also how the underground passages in the tale of Cuchulain might insinuate themselves back into the city's story. The man, like Tom Rochford or Cuchulain, who comes back safe and hale from his foray underground is the true and only hero of the spirit.

If the *Odyssey* was arguably the first major assault on mythological thinking, then *Ulysses*, by lacerating the earlier, now-sacred text, is guilty of nothing more than an application of Homer's underlying logic. The modern translator is never merely an aggressor, for he or she also helps to create the aura of the *original*. But by setting a new text into vibration with the ancient one, they also serve to decanonize the original. Homer, in this scheme, becomes a botched, incompletely imagined, ur-version of Joyce, much as Simon Dedalus is presented in *Ulysses* as an unsatisfactory father of Stephen. Every major work of art contains and reinforces our sense of the strangeness of its original, even as it shows how elements of the modern may be found latent in the prehistorical. The converse is also true. Elements of the prehistorical may sometimes be found in the modern, which is forever in danger of lapsing back into mythological mentalities, as in the anti-Semitic outbursts against Bloom in the "Cyclops" chapter. (Autocratic nationalists have often hated and despised travelers and seafarers, who are notoriously hybrid and innovative in their sense of cultural identity.)

Joyce sensed that the surviving elements of premodern thought in his world might yet become the basis for a common culture in the future and that they need not signal repression or denial. That, after all, was the understanding upon which Yeats and his collaborators were basing the Irish literary revival, and there is good reason to see Joyce as someone who felt himself a part (however angular a part) of that movement. If the story of Odysseus anticipates many features of the lives of the civic bourgeoisie, that may say more about the vulnerability of that modern class than it does about the permanence of the ancient world, for *Ulysses* is, among other things, an elegy for the public-spirited bourgeois world that was fast disappearing as Joyce wrote his book. A central theme right through the *Odyssey* is its insistence that the solitary traveler really is alone, isolated by his own sophistication from the superstitious activities among primitive peoples, whose codes he views with the incredulity of a scandalized anthropologist. The song of the Sirens is, by definition, based on the pull of the past, and the worship of that past, though seductive, can only strike the busy Odysseus as an attempt to wish away the challenges of the present. Bloom voices a similar reservation when he rephrases the old patriotic song "Who Fears to Speak of Ninety-Eight?" as "Who fears to speak of nineteen-four?" (*U* 11 1072–3). Calypso, Circe, the Sirens themselves are all nothing but "a stylisation of what can no longer be celebrated" (Adorno and Horkheimer 1979: 43). Small wonder, then, that Joyce would key his own lament for a dying civic bourgeois culture to such a story of lost worlds. Ithaca began to generate elegies to lost cultures at just that moment when it began to appropriate and abolish them, much as the modern discipline of sociology began to emerge only when society was no longer felt to fit like a glove. The logic of the *Odyssey* is the same as that in so many tales which involve a shipwreck – that "the solution to Old World problems would be found only in the ideal, Golden Age setting of the New World across the seas" (Dougherty 2001: 85), on the other side of a shipwreck. The catastrophe must precede the clarification, to paraphrase a character in *Ulysses*, before the tables of the law can be set down in the language of the outlaw.

That new land may in fact simply be one's old land returned to and seen now in a fresh light. It is dangerous to leave one's country, as Joyce showed in his play *Exiles*, but more dangerous still to go back to it. Odysseus returns to Ithaca a chastened man, but with a sense that he may now know enough to see his place as if for the first time. The Exodus narrative of the Old Testament was different, since it told the story of a type of return, long delayed, to a land which the people of Israel had never possessed (Hartog 2001: 20) and in which a messiah would appear. The Greeks were different, not feeling the need for a messiah and sensing that all their gods were near at hand.

The gods of the Greeks were social beings, possessed of a past and a present reality. They were made in man's image, not pictured as mythical monsters or fabulous birds, but as people with human organs. This humanization was itself a bold and modernizing act. It suggested that if man could create gods in his image, then he might himself be godly (Finley 2002: 139). The returned Odysseus at the close has the knowledge, even omniscience, of a god, although in his disguise he looks like a traveling beggar. By a similar logic, both Jesus and Bloom never seem more godlike than when they appear most bereft. To become a nomad is to have no place in which to lay your head – it is to give up all identity. Odysseus' great fear of dying at sea and drowning in the water, without clean burial, is of being a "nameless one." The equivalent modern fear might be of massification, of being lost in the crowd, or even at a more personal level of drowning in one's own unconscious zones (since the sea is often a dream image of the unconscious). All through *Ulysses*, Stephen and Bloom seem to fear that they are drowning in the spray of phenomena, and the body washed up out of the sea in the opening episodes might well be read as Joyce's satiric dismissal of Homer and the uses to which he will put the dead sailor in the rest of the narrative.

One of the reasons why Telemachus sets out in pursuit of his father is to establish a viable identity for himself. Years without a father have left a vacuum and so his journey is a search for authority rather than a revolt against it, a search for a meaning (even more than an answer) to his question. Like father, like son. Telemachus never quite catches up with his target, finding in pursuit a kind of happiness. His trajectory parallels his father's rather than intersecting with it, much as Stephen will trace parallel lines through most of *Ulysses* with Leopold Bloom. In the event, he learns little about his father, but he does discover how to share in his journey – his own journey to a self-formed identity, his father's to an exemplary role (Brann 2002: 149).

Telemachus sets out to discover what men are saying about his father and, if necessary, to build an appropriate tomb. On his travels he enters that condition of non-identity, already well known by his father, for a nomad by definition can never be anybody in particular. "My mother says I am Odysseus's son, but I myself cannot tell, for no one really knows his father himself" (Brann 2002: 148). The very separation of both protagonists epitomizes the psychic problem. For Joyce, this was the fear of many men – that they were not the true biological fathers of their designated children, but for Homer (as for Shakespeare) that became also a pressing problem for sons, no longer sure of their own fathers. (Such a doubt may, in part, account for Hamlet's hesitation about enacting the revenge called for by his dead "father.") Telemachus bravely and wisely concludes that he must take his given father on trust. All of these uncertainties help to explain the lure of Calypso or of the Sirens with their promise of immortality: but they are false muses, whose poetry of the past would only empty men like Odysseus or Telemachus of their selfhood.

The true muses are the gods, who guide the traveler often to faraway places (as if the *Odyssey* also functions as a sort of prospectus for settlers and tourists), often under cover of the darkness of the night. This gives Homer's story its astonishingly cinematic quality, for it is a narrative filled with "jump cuts." There is no gradual transition from one scene to the next. Every setting is arbitrarily *just there* as a "given" at the start of each episode, in a book whose tales have the weird but lucid discontinuity of a dream. *Ulysses* proceeds in similar fashion: there is no explanation, for example, as to how

Leopold Bloom ends up on Sandymount Strand at 8 p.m. And neither Odysseus nor Bloom appears at the outset of either tale. Odysseus only comes into his story in Book Five, by which time he has evoked a crescendo of expectation, since in all the earlier scenes a huge point is made of the disastrous effect of his absence on family, friends, and the body politic. Bloom, for his part, appears only in the fourth episode of *Ulysses*, and his emergence is quite sudden, arbitrary, unannounced, and unexpected.

Ulysses may have been the first artistic work to centralize the very process of *thinking*, but in doing as much it was simply taking to a logical conclusion a discovery of Homer: that thought itself is godly. For him it was not just a god but the god, not something to be bounded by human form. Athene is at once an external god and a projection of human thought processes – which is to say, interior monologue. In the primitive world, people did not recognize thought as coming from their own minds and so emotions such as anger, nervousness, and desire were identified with organs of the body like the lungs, stomach, or heart. (One way of reading the organ-for-every-episode scheme in *Ulysses* would be to interpret the book as putting that world back together again, but in the form of a completed human body.)

Like all storytellers and human psychologists, Homer was intrigued by those vital moments in life when characters act impulsively, as if under the sway of forces greater than themselves. E. R. Dodds in *The Greeks and the Irrational* called these moments "monitions" which "allow us to ascribe all sorts of mental events to the intervention of some god" (Dodds 1951: 11). Literature is filled with instances of people who act with decisive or tragic effect, as if their will were not their own:

> Whenever someone has a particularly brilliant or a particularly foolish idea; when he suddenly recognises another person's identity or sees in a flash the meaning of an omen; when he remembers what he might well have forgotten or forgets what he should have remembered, he or someone else will see in it, if we are to take the words literally, a psychic intervention by one of these anonymous supernatural beings (Dodds 1951: 11).

This sounds remarkably like some of the interior monologues of Joyce's masterpiece: "Often he is conscious of no observation or reasoning which has led up to them. But in that case, how can he call them 'his'?" (Dodds 1951: 11). All of which is to suggest that there are severe limits to what modern people call "individuality." Some force has inserted such thoughts, outside the thinker's formal control, much as a clap of thunder seems to arise from a source outside the usual pattern of the weather. (Joyce was terrified of thunderclaps, perhaps because he thought of them as monitions from angry gods. When someone pointed out to a quaking Joyce that his children were not at all frightened, he replied that that was because they had no religion.)

What makes Homer so subtle and, in a sense, so modern is his recognition in the *Odyssey* that often the thinker alone can visualize the prompting god, who remains invisible to everyone else. The clear implication of this is that some sort of projection of people's inner states has led humans to create gods, by whom the creators then feel themselves possessed. This would explain some of the obsessive-compulsive behaviour of Stephen Dedalus and Leopold Bloom in the "Circe" sequence of *Ulysses*, as it also accounts for the ways in which a proud person can offload responsibility for some types of behaviour:

> When he acts in a manner contrary to the system of dispositions which he is said to "know", his action is not properly his own, but has been dictated to him [. . .] Acts resulting from these impulses tend to be excluded from the self and ascribed to an alien origin [. . .] especially acts such as to cause acute shame to their author (Dodds 1951: 17).

No deed done by persons is ever fully their own, for men and women never quite find the conditions in which they must act to be those which they would ideally have chosen. As the Player King warns in *Hamlet* (Act 3, Scene 2): "Our thoughts are ours / Their ends none of our own." Joyce, by a weird kind of analogy with the monitions, may have installed Homer as one of his gods, only to feel possessed by him, so that *Ulysses* is not just Joyce's own work but also that of the spirit which guided his hand as he wrote. The attempt to seize a life as peculiar to the self is the wisdom sought by Homer, by the authors of the New Testament Gospels, and by Shakespeare, as well as being the basis of the story in the *Odyssey*, the life of Jesus, and *Hamlet*, but that attempt can never be wholly successful, being conditioned by many forces from the past which suggest that experience is always somehow more real than the rather frail, tenuous selves on which it is imposed. Just when he or she is about to innovate and do something radically new and unprecedented, a ghost from the past appears and seeks to return the script to somewhat more familiar lines.

For the epic poet (unless he is Walt Whitman) does not speak of himself; rather the Muse, goddess of inspiration, speaks through him, being invoked at the outset, whether by Homer, Virgil, or Milton. Homer used his own invocation in order to protest against rival versions of his stories, much as Joyce himself would prove jealously dismissive of the claims of other modern masters. In *Ulysses* the inspiratrice speaks only at the end, but the entire book is a telling example of how the hidden gods intervene, by analogy with the Muse, through monitions and forces which are latent in the everyday self. And, at the close, the book seems to have developed a separate, independent consciousness, which still sings through Joyce, but has moved well beyond him. That consciousness was, perhaps, born in the "Oxen of the Sun" episode and is summed up by the soliloquy of Molly Bloom in such a style as to make it seem to float free of the intentions of its creator.

The wisdom to be gleaned from the *Odyssey* is clear enough: that there is nothing better in life than when a man and woman live in harmony and that such happiness, though felt intensely as a truth by the couple themselves, can never be fully described. It can merely be evoked, either by comparison or by contrast. Homer set out to heroicize the domestic, even as Joyce wished to domesticate the heroic. Although these are not exactly identical processes, the results have much in common. The major, characteristic device of Homer is the "normalization" technique of recalling a touching, homely image in the midst of a terrifying battle: "as when the farmer ploughs his field" (Brann 2002: 138–9). The whole of *Ulysses* might be taken as just such an extended hymn to the dignity of everyday living, when cast against the backdrop of the First World War, in which young men went naively to battle seeking extreme sensations of exaltation or debasement after the long peace.

It is as if Joyce has turned Homer inside out and made the "as if" similes the key to the entire narrative, rather than having them function just as passing moments of beautiful relaxation within it. In a more localized and concrete sense, the "as if" similes of Homer might be taken to lie behind not only the interior monologues but also the daydreams and reveries of Bloom throughout the book. It has been said that the epic similes of Homer are designed not simply to escape battle, but "to project the excruciating enormities of battle onto an integral world of peaceful and homely work" (Brann 2002: 139). This is also very like the effect which Joyce achieves, when scenes from or responses to the First World War break in upon (however anachronistically) the meditations of his characters: "I hear the ruin of all space, shattered glass and toppling masonry, and time one livid final flame. What's left us then?" (*U* 2 9–10). The war features repeatedly in the text ("killing any finelooking young men," as Molly laments; *U* 18 396), but as something ancillary rather than primary – as a final measure of the unsurpassable sweetness of the middle range of human experience. It is as if Joyce had all the time anticipated Tom Stoppard's little joke: "What did you do in the Great War, Mr. Joyce? I wrote *Ulysses* – what did you do?"

All that might seem like a charter for a complacent banality, but at the time it was very much a minority viewpoint among intellectuals. Even the liberal humanist Freud was convinced that decades of peace had left the youth of Europe supine and spineless. And so he welcomed the era of the mass-grave and the testing of the moral fibre of nations. "Life has become interesting again – it has recovered its full content," he opined, bemoaning the fact that during the prolonged peace it had seemed to become "as shallow as an American flirtation" (Kiberd 1992: 16). In those prewar years, cults had grown up around boy-scouting, mountain-climbing, Arctic expeditions – anything that allowed men to assert a jeopardized virility and to escape from taunts of emptiness and effeminacy at home. The link between all this and empire-building was obvious enough, and Joyce was keenly aware of the use to which the classical texts of Greece and Rome were put in the classrooms of Britain and Ireland. A cult of manly strength, cut loose from clear ethical moorings, had led to the jingoism finally unleashed in the First World War. As early as 1905, Joyce had written to his brother Stanislaus,

> Do you not think the search for heroics damn vulgar — [? . . .]
> I am sure, however, that the whole structure of heroism is, and always was, a damned lie and that there cannot be any substitute for individual passion as the motive power of everything — (*LII* 81).

That attack on heroics is really a critique of the idea of imperial mastery over subject peoples; yet Joyce's own project, while employing the Nestor episode to deride the false use of the classroom classics in 1904, offers a renewed version of the older educational project.

Ulysses is brave enough to celebrate the feminine while attacking the merely genteel, and its writer would probably have agreed with Henry Stanley that "England is becoming effeminate and soft from long inactivity, long enfeeblement of purpose, brought about by indolence and ease, distrust of her own powers and shaken nerves" (cited in Lasch 1991: 299). Joyce, after all, was the man who boasted that he could find nobody in Ireland with a faith to match his own (*LI* 63), and this at a time when Sorel was contending that epic still had a future, being "an anticipation of the kind of work that ought to be carried on in a highly productive state of society" (Lasch 1991: 314). Such a society would make for strong, self-reliant individuals, such as the republican John Wyse Nolan in *Ulysses*, who, because he knows how to stand up to the British, will never fall into the error of hating them, and who in his own relaxed self-acceptance is easily open to the Jewishness of Bloom.

Bloom's charm, like his heroism, is inadvertent and never conscious of itself as such. He no more knows his own effect on others than he realizes that in his wanderings through Dublin he might be re-enacting the voyage of Odysseus. "The healthy know not of their own health," wrote Thomas Carlyle, "but only the sick" (Lasch 1991: 236). The real problem posed for Freud and Stanley by the long peace was not the absence of a fibre-testing war but rather the fact that virtue, if it grows overly aware of itself, becomes sickly. It was in that precise context that William James could contrast "the health, brightness and freshness" of "the bloody old heathens of The Odyssey" and "the essentially definite character of all their joys," with "the over-cultivated and vaguely sick complainers of today" (Lasch 1991: 287). Odysseus, like Mr. Bloom, accepted the universe and held to the here-and-now. Hamlet, like Stephen Dedalus, wished that it might all dissolve.

The quotidian world of work, to which people rise each morning, is affirmed in the *Odyssey*: Penelope at her weaving, the farmer at his ploughing, these are among its defining images. Hamlet has no distraction from his worries but the assumption (real or imagined) of madness, but for Odysseus this is a mere trick done to outwit the press gang. An epic character like Odysseus is no more subject to change than a Leopold Bloom: theirs is not the world of the bildungsroman, for at the end "their experiences leave them more like themselves than ever" (Moretti 2000: 114). *Ulysses* teases the reader by opening as might the conventional novel of growth, but from the fourth episode it turns its focus onto Mr. Bloom, already 38 years old and too mature to develop as might the youthful hero of a nineteenth-century novel. Joyce, in fact, may not know how to produce a bildungsroman except in this aborted form. He can set up a meeting between his Telemachus and Odysseus near the end, but he cannot tell how the younger man will turn into a convincing version of the senior one.

Shakespeare had something of the same problem in showing how exactly the naive Hamlet of Act 1 becomes the mature sage of Act 5; and so he removed Hamlet, as Telemachus is removed by Homer, from some of the central episodes of his narrative. Both men had hoped (like Stephen at the close of *A Portrait of the Artist as a Young Man*) to excite the sympathies of the *demos* with their program – only to fail utterly. The problem of writing such a bildungsroman has been well captured by Eva Brann: "we need an identity in order to learn but learning is supposed to confer an identity" (Brann 2002: 51). Growing into an adult state allows a person to absorb energies which, once selfhood is found, can be applied to an interpretation of the world, but if, lacking identity, Stephen in *Ulysses* is not fully free at all times to learn, he may at least hope to study at close range just how an older man, possessed of selfhood, can take on the world. Bloom can no more narrate this wisdom in words than Odysseus can for Telemachus; it is merely a case of both men in each story "arriving" at the same moment at a place that could be called home.

Odysseus fears that Penelope will have aged; Bloom worries that his wife is not faithful. The Greek wanderer speaks to his wife as if she is still young, to be courted over again, but in Joyce's version it is Molly who sets herself the task of a renewed wooing.

The famous interpolated story of Eurycleia discovering the identity of Odysseus by seeing his old scar and recalling how he got that wound offers a long retrospective reverie in mid-action. Told on the verge of the long-postponed finale, this is Homer's technical trick, by which he can deliver delayed gratification in yet another form, and it is offered as a momentary pause in mid-narrative, a memory which consumes but a moment of consciousness-time even though it takes far longer to hear or read it through. Joyce in *Ulysses* opened many similar portals into the remembered past at various points in his unfolding of the action on June 16, 1904. In somewhat similar mode, just as Homer's characters break in upon one story in order to tell another, so also do Joyce's males, competing for narrative time in funeral carriage or in pub. Both the *Odyssey* and *Ulysses* repeatedly cannibalize earlier sections of their own tale, and each is written in a way which shows itself deeply alert to its own reception as a literary performance. Some of the internal audiences for tales within the works suggest parallels with the external audience (just as the listeners to Stephen in the National Library episode may be that part of Joyce's readership on which he hopes to wreak a merry revenge).

Interpreters of the *Odyssey* often try to recover its immediate effect on its first audience, and so also readers of *Ulysses* hope for the sort of "innocent" analysis possible only to its initial audience in 1922. The problems posed for both sets of interpreters are, in fact, identical: each work is now over-familiar to scholarly commentators, who fail to open themselves at a given moment to the exfoliations which might (but did not) ensue. Congealed readings need to be challenged in order to allow to each moment in the unfolding text the openness which it once had. There are missed meetings, or missed accounts of vital meetings, all through both stories, and each one has plenty of time for the sort of nondescript individual who might well have been passed over in a more conventionally heroic tale. The drunken Elpenor was no great fighter, nor were his wits of the foremost, but in his death by falling from a roof he becomes the prototype for Paddy Dignam, a decent man whom Dubliners have taken the liberty of burying.

Many other ordinary people are given their moment of prominence by the aristocratic Homer: a nurse, a swineherd, a bard. When Odysseus returns to Ithaca at the end, he moves among his servants like a god in disguise, testing their fidelity, much as

Jesus rejoins his disciples after the crucifixion or as Bloom returns to his familiar pos-
sessions at Eccles Street. Eumaeus grieves for the missing master who is in fact already
present and cries out for that which is lost, even as it has already been found. *Ulysses*,
in its lament for a lost world, may find even in the energy expended on elegy a basis
for the recovery of its inner codes, because a tradition will always live on, even in the
lament for its passing. Stephen says, with some self-disgust, "dead breaths I living
breathe" (*U* 3 479), but that breathing is done over a "green grave," as the very dead
Homer helps to reactivate a culture.

Like Homer, Joyce belongs to everyone and to no one – but to the lover of literature most of all, who might turn to his text, as the Greeks turned to the *Odyssey*, for
their ideas of virtue and decency. The epics of other nations (and even those of the
Greeks and of the children of Israel) fed that mood of manic nationalism that drove
Europeans over the edge of madness in 1914 – but these past epics were subverted and
reconfigured by Joyce. Nor was the surgery required of him all that radical. For both
the *Odyssey* and the New Testament stood out from other epics in their willingness to
treat ordinary life and ordinary people as subjects of innate dignity. In a sense, both of
these prior works had already questioned ancient epic notions of aristocratic milita-
rism, long before Joyce mocked those notions even more fully.

BIBLIOGRAPHY

Primary reading

Adorno, Theodor and Max Horkheimer (1979) *Dialectic of Enlightenment*, trans. John Gumming. London: Verso.

Ahl, Frederick and Hanna M. Roisman (1996) *The Odyssey Re-Formed*. Ithaca, NY: Cornell University Press.

Brann, Eva (2002) *Homeric Moments: Aids to Delight in Reading The Odyssey and The Iliad*. Philadelphia, PA: Paul Dry Books.

Dodds, E. R. (1951) *The Greeks and the Irrational*. Berkeley: University of California Press.

Dougherty, Carol (2001) *The Raft of Odyseus: The Ethnographic Imagination of Homer's Odyssey*. London: Oxford University Press.

Finley, M. I. (2002) *The World of Odysseus*. New York: New York Review Books.

Griffin, Jasper (1980) *Homer*. London: Oxford University Press.

Hartog, François (2001) *Memories of Odysseus: Frontier Tales from Ancient Greece*, trans. Janet Lloyd. Edinburgh: Edinburgh University Press.

Homer (1993) *The Odyssey*, trans. and ed. Albert Cook. New York: Norton Critical Edition.

Jenkyns, Richard (1992) *Classic Epic: Homer and Virgil*. London: Bristol Press.

Kiberd, Declan (1992) "Introduction" to James Joyce, *Ulysses: The Student's Annotated Edition*. London: Penguin Classics.

Louden, Bruce (1999) *The Odyssey; Structure, Narration and Meaning*. Baltimore, MD: Johns Hopkins University Press.

Secondary reading

Aragon, Louis (1994) *Paris Peasant*, trans. Simon Watson Taylor. Boston, MA: Exact Change.

Eliot, T. S. (1923) "Ulysses, order and myth," *Dial* 75: 480–3; reproduced in Richard Ellmann and Charles Feidelson (eds.) (1965) *The Modern Tradition*. New York: Oxford University Press.

Gilbert, Stuart (1968 [1930]) *James Joyce's "Ulysses."* London: Peregrine Books.

Grana, Cesar (1964) *Bohemian versus Bourgeois: French Society and the French Man of Letters in the Nineteenth Century*. New York: Basic Books.

Kavanagh, Patrick (1972) *Collected Poems*. London: Martin, Brian, and O'Keefe.

Lasch, Christopher (1991) *The True and Only Heaven: Progress and Its Critics*. New York: Basic Books.

Moretti, Franco (2000) *The Way of the World; The* Bildungsroman *in European Culture*, trans. Albert Sbragia. London: Verso.

O'Brien, Darcy (1974) *Patrick Kavanagh*. Lewisburg, PA: Bucknell University Press.

O'Connor, Ulick (ed.) (1967) *The Joyce We Knew*. Cork: Mercier Press.

Potts, Willard (ed.) (1979) *James Joyce: Portraits of an Artist in Exile*. Dublin: Wolfhound Press.

Stoppard, Tom (1975) *Travesties*. London: Faber and Faber.

16

The Joyce of French Theory

Jean-Michel Rabaté

The treatment of Joyce by French theorists has often been called glib, offhand, mysti-fying, or not very accurate. Such, for instance, is the picture that emerges from Geert Lernout's groundbreaking and systematic overview, in *The French Joyce*, whose stric-tures have given a bad name to most of the "Joyce of French Theory" (Lernout 1990). It is not my intention to reopen the critical debate that followed this publication more than 15 years after the initial discussion, especially as I figure among the French Joy-ceans as an example of a critic who has been led astray by theory and then found a way back to a more rational or "scientific" approach by way of textual studies and genetic criticism (if not in quite so linear a path as this seems).[1] Now that reception studies of Joyce have become more systematic and comprehensive (Lernout and Van Mierlo 2004), it is time to take a more distanced look back at a period dominated by theory, and one when, for some at least, theory was inevitably French. I will focus on two moments that repeat the same stakes, add up the same tally of losses and gains: the *transition* moment in the late 1920s and 30s and, more especially, the *Tel Quel* moment in the late 1960s and 70s. My aim will be to assess what these theoretical avant-gardes have brought to us today, beyond their historical value as testimonies to the interpene-tration of experimentalism and theory.

The first obvious common feature of these two reviews is that they were both based in Paris. It is useful to go back to the moment of Joyce's decision to come to Paris. We know that Joyce hesitated for a few years after his arrival in Paris in July 1920, and that he thought for a while that he would only stay until *Ulysses* was completed before moving to London (Rabaté 2004). His final decision to stay in Paris was partly con-nected with the impression that he found there not only a safe haven but also a place where young people, including artists, critics, and writers, would look to him respect-fully. This impression was due mostly to the initial enthusiasm of Valery Larbaud, soon relayed by the utter devotion of Eugene and Maria Jolas in the late 1920s. Joyce's friendship with Eugene Jolas was almost predetermined by parallel trajectories in philosophy, politics, and aesthetics. It corresponds to a last happy avant-garde, clearly an exception as the 1920s led to the 1930s. It was with Joyce in mind that Jolas and his friends had announced the death of the novel: "The Novel is dead/Long Live the Novel" – a proclamation to be found at the end of *transition* 18 in a manifesto-like tract asserting "The novel of the future will take no cognizance of the laws imposed by professors of literature and critics" (*transition*, 18, 1929: n.p.). Already then, Joyce was taken as a pioneer who has put an end to the novel with *Ulysses* so as to engage with a different mode of verbal experimentation. Perhaps indeed Joyce had believed then that he could bypass the old "literary genres" and grapple with a new aesthetics and the dream of creating a "new language."

This utopia could only have been brought by a sense of crisis; a crisis that is analyzed in Jolas's editorial in *transition* 15. In "Super-Occident," Jolas takes stock of the crisis in values, economic, and spiritual, following the Crash of 1929. He surveys the various movements around him and finds that he cannot identify with any of their programs: Surrealism is groping toward the Spirit, the Bauhaus praises pure functionality, proletarian art apes bourgeois philistinism, fascism has perverted the Nietzschean utopia. A new individual is needed so as to blend the particular and the universal, the conscious and the subconscious: "But before this development is possible, a continuous subversive action will have to take place" (*transition*, 15, 1929: 13), a position which postulates a revolution: "Never has a revolution been more imperative" (15). However, this revolution will be limited to the domain of the word: "We need the word of movement, the word expressive of the great new forces around us. . . . The new vocabulary and the new syntax must help destroy the ideology of a rotting civilization" (15). Here is the foundation of a Parisian avant-gardism that will last until *Tel Quel* in the 1980s. For Jolas takes Joyce as the main example of a new word that can destroy a rotting civilization: his "Work in Progress" provides the realization of the "new Mythos."

The "mythos" of a new word implies a scientific basis in linguistics, and this is why the contributors to *transition* found it in Ogden's and Richards' linguistic theories. In *Our Exagmination*, John Rodker sends his reader to *The Meaning of Meaning* in order to illustrate how the mind invents "hybrid formless onomatopoeic" to express certain feelings (Beckett et al. 1972 [1929]: 142–3). *The Meaning of Meaning* is a very influential book that starts by refuting Saussure's theory of the sign as being uniquely "philological," too far from "things" and therefore not "verifiable" scientifically, and too determined by the categories of one language, French (Ogden and Richards 1968: 5–6). Having given their own definition of meaning as a triangular arrow linking Symbol, Thought, and Referent, the authors devote their second chapter to the classical conception of "the power of words" (Ogden and Richards 1968: 11). They discuss Mauthner's nominalism (a strong influence on Beckett and Joyce) and Hugo's mystical conception of the *Verbe* as God, and finally provide an example of how language works even when it means almost nothing. When a writer like Lewis Carroll writes "*The gostak distims the doshes*" (quoted in Ogden and Richards 1968: 46) one can still make good sense of it, at least thanks to the prevalence of grammar (one could say "*the doshes are distimmed by the gostak*"). This would be what takes place with Joyce's "synthetic" language. Like Ogden, Joyce believes that meaning percolates through our activities into the world of symbols we inhabit. Language is more a "mode of action" or a "gesture" than an expression of thought. If Joyce's own linguistic theories owe more to Jousse and Saussure taken together than to Ogden and Richards, it is clear that Ogden's and Richard's psychological pragmatism finds its way into the *Wake*, at least when reformulated as a theory of generalized mime: "lead us seek, lote us see, light us find, let us missnot Maidadate, Mimosa Multimimetica, the maymeaminning of maimoomeining!" (*FW* 267 1–3).

Like the practitioners of *Tel Quel*, Jolas and Gilbert wanted to develop a rigorous theory of semiotics thanks to Ogden's and Richards' definitions. For instance, Stuart Gilbert's "Functions of Words" (*transition*, 18: 203–5) discusses the loaded term "revolution." He uses this word to distinguish a symbolic from an emotive function of language: "The revolution of the word" aims at promoting the secondary, non-utilitarian function of language, so as to address the *aura*, the "light vapour which floats above the expression of the thought" (204). A true revolutionary is one who will compose a personal "syntax," not merely in the linguistic sense, but in the etymological sense of "setting things together." As soon as expression is privileged over communication (as the Manifesto insists it should be) then this new "syntax" can explore the "dream world" and create a new vision, therefore a new reality.

All the critics of *transition* describe the poetics at work in Joyce's musical prose and babel of languages – aspects that were rarely studied by the scholars of the following generation. The collection *Our Exagmination . . .* (announced in issue 16/17) gives pride of place to Beckett's wonderful essay, partly dictated by Joyce, which is meant as a general introduction to the collection as well as to the *Wake* and is constructed to be as introductory as possible. One of the earliest pieces, Elliot Paul's "Mr. Joyce's Treatment of Plot" (*transition*, 9) was published in 1927, 12 years before the final publication of the *Wake* itself. Besides remarking on the circular structure of the work, Paul introduces the new treatment of characters in the *Wake*. The curious collapsing of "plot" with "characters" is to be read positively. Paul knows that, except for a few archetypal motifs such as the "Fall," the *Wake* does not intend to create a "story," as it is a matrix of stories in which Time and Space are elastic: "the characters are composed of hundreds of legendary and historical figures, as the incidents are derived from countless events" (*Our Exagmination*: 134). Clumsy and vague as some pages are, they nevertheless convey the pleasure of discovery, they unabashedly enjoy a new type of writing defined as a new "polyphony" (136). Paul stresses that, however baffling, the *Wake* respects the syntactical structures of English. The avant-gardism of the "apostles" never pushes them into a position of "radical break" with the past, which was the case with the French reception of Joyce by *Tel Quel* in the 1970s.

Our Exagmination attempts very seriously to construct the new reader needed by Joyce's last work. John Rodker's essay is typical of this effort when it presents Joyce's achievement as a "complete symbiosis of reader and writer" (143). Joyce's text will echo this with a rhetorical question: "His producers are they not his consumers? Your exagmination round his factification for incamination of a warping process" (*FW* 497 1–3). The joint effect of the *transition* critics was less to explicate a text's fundamental unreadability than to make readers participate in its deciphering. Both initiated exegetes and lay readers should work together in an original understanding of the production of the text's meaning, first of all because the meaning is not given but made. This insight will be a central tenet in the version of Joyce propounded by *Tel Quel* in the late 1960s.

Since Joyce had by then become the keystone figure for the international avant-garde in Paris, it is not surprising that he was to loom large for *Tel Quel* in the 1960s and 70s. His experiments with language have acted as a testing ground for all the avant-gardes and their attendant critical discourses. The deployment of the fabled "interior monologue" was just the first step in a mounting escalation of claims and sweeping gestures. Joyce's uncanny adaptability excited admiration and none of the critical schools forgot him. He often stood as a privileged testing ground for the validity of their methods. Joyce soon became synonymous not only with avant-gardist experiments but with high theory and this identification was achieved by the *Tel Quel* group in so far as it condensed French theory at its peak.

For two decades, the review *Tel Quel* managed to be more than a literary periodical: between 1960 and 1982 it promoted a sophisticated international avant-garde. The review summed up a whole state of mind, standing for what is now seen with nostalgia as the age of theory. Its deployment of typically avant-garde shock tactics, political denunciations, and ideological reversals never prevented it from constantly amassing cultural capital. Avoiding sociological reductionism (Kauppi 1994) and hagiography, glossing over staggering palinodes (Forest 1995; Ffrench and Lack 1998; Ffrench 1998), a historical perspective yields an understanding of the link established by *Tel Quel* between the cultural politics of the avant-garde, the wish to take literary production into consideration, and the promotion of a new "science" of signs, writing, and textuality. Theory could not thrive without these three elements and they were promoted together by the members of *Tel Quel*.

Philippe Sollers dominated the periodical, being the only founding member who always figured on the editorial board. The review's rise to fame, contradictions, and collapse should be seen as historical and cultural symptoms, compromise formations that condense an entire Zeitgeist. Philippe Joyaux (his real name, symptomatically not that far away from that of Joyce) consciously strove after literary models: early Dantean and Joycean identification was followed by mimetic re-enactments of Céline, and then Dante, Joyce, and Céline blended in the writing of *Paradis*, Sollers' own work-in-progress. Radical literary experimentations like those of Joyce were for him a site of subversion of middle-class complacency and resistance to totalitarianism: Joyce's later work would be the best antidote against Fascism. Sollers arranged to his advantage the editorial power games that gave a stamp to the review just as evolution of the magazine gathered speed and reflected adequately the acceleration of French history in the watershed years before and after May 1968.

Tel Quel was launched by Le Seuil, a Paris press known for its left-wing Catholic sympathies and its wish to promote the new "human sciences." The two personalities who presided over the birth of the magazine were Jean-Hedern Hallier and Sollers.

Hallier was soon to fight with his partners and to discredit himself in dubious political ventures. The new school that they first endorsed then criticized was the *nouveau roman*, whose practitioners would often salute Joyce as a radical predecessor – Joyce was important for Robbe-Grillet, Sarraute, and Beckett. By the mid-1960s Joyce was not a central author in the *Tel Quelian* canon. In 1963, Umberto Eco had published in *Tel Quel* a chapter of *Opera Aperta* on Joyce and the Middle Ages, but this was an exception. By the mid-1960s the review appeared as serious, committed, aiming at disseminating the theory and practice of a literary structuralism which looked very much like a revised version of Russian formalism. The Parisian avant-garde had found new bearings when it perceived its affinities with the avant-gardes that had been active in Moscow, Leningrad, and Prague in the 1920s. When Tzvetan Todorov presented the texts of the Russian poets and critics in his *Théorie de la littérature* in 1965, the names of Khlebnikov, Brik, Chlovski, Jakobson, and Eikhenbaum were news in French circles. Todorov relayed by *Tel Quel* put an end to the obscurity surrounding these authors. When Julia Kristeva arrived upon the scene a year later, she brought a similar Slavic expertise to the group as she completed the formalist picture by adding new references to the semioticians of the Tartu school and to Mikhail Bakhtin, then unknown in France. Not only was the history of the avant-garde sanctioned by reference to a previous movement which had established political credentials, a concrete proof was also given that one could be a "formalist" (that is, interest oneself in exploring the literariness and literality of poetic and novelistic languages) and a revolutionary at the same time. This led to a first filtering of reception through a Joyce mediated by Bakhtinian concepts of parody, multi-voicedness, heteroglossia and historical links with a Rabelaisian popular culture.

The first issue of the journal with a cluster of essays on Joyce was published in 1967; there Jean-Pierre Faye introduces Philippe Lavergne's very competent translation of the Shem chapter. This is preceded by the philological notes of the translator and also by a very useful analysis of the *Wake*'s language by Jean Paris. Paris takes three words, "Venissoon," "Cweamy," and "Notshall" and he lists all their echoes and "overtones" in various languages and contexts. Paris makes use of at least thirty languages and says that only a computer could list all the implied meanings (Paris 1967: 61–3). However, between Todorov's *Theory of Literature* and Julia Kristeva's *Semeiotike* (republishing in 1969 essays previously published in *Tel Quel*), a whole revolution had taken place in the field of literary semiotics. Sollers had been interested by the asides on Joyce made by Derrida in his Introduction to Husserl's *Origin of Geometry* (Houdebine 1982: 36) and he asked him to contribute regularly. Derrida's impact was immediately felt and his name was called upon more and more frequently in the pages of the review. Derrida then referred to Joyce when, in 1968, he published a brilliant essay on "Plato's Pharmacy" whose seventeenth endnote ominously described the "whole of this essay, being itself nothing else, as one will soon have understood, than a reading of *Finnegans Wake*" (Lernout 1990: 60). This meant that all his deconstructive strategies could be understood as footnoting *Finnegans Wake*. Derrida introduced another dimension through a questioning of the main presuppositions that underpinned structuralism, while remaining close to many references shared by the structuralists, like the Saussurean idea that there are only differences in language. Like Georges Bataille's review *Critique*, but more visibly, *Tel Quel* provided the young philosopher with a tribune, a sounding board, a constant invitation to engage with literary issues. Derrida identified in Sollers' novel *Nombres* the utopia of a purely textual novel soon to become the hallmark of *Tel Quel*: resolutely "experimental" texts half way between poetry and prose. Like *Finnegans Wake*, they did not represent anything but just exhibited the functioning of language. By showing the codes, cogs, and wheels of literary language, the production of a new poetic and political truth would hopefully shatter the dominant repressive ideology.

Thus Joyce had a central place in the double helix, literary and ideological, which caught theory in its vortex. The volume put together by *Tel Quel* in the fall of 1968, *Théorie d'ensemble*, shows the insertion of Joyce into the lists of key names of innovators – in two texts by Sollers, we move from a first list ("Dante, Sade, Lautréamont, Mallarmé, Artaud, Bataille") to a second list which includes him: "Lautréamont, Mallarmé, Roussell, Kafka, Joyce, Artaud, Bataille" (*Tel Quel* 1968: 71, 404). "General Theory" aimed at creating the impression of a group similar to the Surrealists, of a collective approach with a scientific slant, for it refers obliquely to the series of mathematical treatises on set theory (*théorie des ensembles*) written jointly by the anonymous group of Parisian mathematicians who called themselves Groupe Bourbaki. The volume highlights the key role of Foucault, Barthes, and Derrida, whose names are separated from all the other contributors. Foucault opens the volume with a reading of Robbe-Grillet but also provides a useful redefinition of the category of author; Barthes has a piece on *Drame*, Sollers' novel of 1965; while Derrida explains *différance*. The unsigned introduction makes it clear that the group's general theory will resist being reduced either to formalism or structuralism.

The systematic trope of *Tel Quel* was the forceful yoking of writers noted for their formal experiments or unorthodox and innovative writing (among them Dante, Pound, Woolf, Céline, Joyce, Beckett, Artaud) with the names of Marx, Freud, then Lenin and Mao. Theory hesitated between a radical philosophical questioning of literary concepts and the more etymological sense of a "list" of authorities, or the ritual "procession" of tutelary figures invoked and yoked together. Patrick Ffrench's book on *Tel Quel* opened with this double meaning contained in "Theory": philosophical contemplation and collective witnessing, individual speculative thought and group procession of some chosen citizens. In its version of the dynamic union between Marxism and Freudianism, high theory was an updating of the old Freudo-Marxism of the 1930s in which, more often than not, rhapsodic references to Althusser and Lacan functioned as shorthand for "the real thought" of Marx and Freud. "Science" under these revolving strobe lights meant above all "Marx" after the epistemological break with Hegel's idealism and "Freud" without the biological naturalism of "instincts," but fully endowed with Lacan's formula of "the Unconscious is structured like a language." The quotation marks around these names indicate that these are not the historical thinkers themselves but their author-functions that are envisioned, according to Foucault's revision of the concept of the "author" as an "inventor of discursivity."

What mattered for the Tel Quelians was not to refine systems of literary *explications de textes* but to unveil the workings of textuality – a revolutionary process that subverts dominant ideologies, destroys the doxa that orders our perceptions of the self, the world, and God. The combination of Saussure read by Derrida, of Marx read by Althusser and of Freud read by Lacan, provided a trilogy which mapped out a new scientific and critical knowledge. Despite obvious shortcomings, much of what we call theory today found a synthesis in *Tel Quel*'s energies, an unstable amalgam that lasted less than a decade. Then it looked as if one could marshal together the concepts of Foucault, Althusser, Bataille, Derrida, Barthes, Lacan, and Kristeva. Literature was spoken of as a signifying practice whose subversive power was condensed in an "unreadability" (*l'illisible*) that nevertheless interacted with the social context. Avant-garde strategies deduced from close readings of Sade, Artaud, Roussel, Lautréamont or Joyce were applied to more conventional writers like Dante, Donne, or Hugo. Theory appeared as less assured than it claimed, since it was constantly hesitating between terrorism and theology, its recurrent hysteria significantly caught up between verbal dogmatism and endless dissidence. This is also what triggered a series of exclusions and fights – the main one was the departure of Jean-Pierre Faye, Mitsou Ronat, and their friends who founded *Change* in 1968, a review for which Joyce was also very important.

For the engagement with Joyce, the peak was perhaps in 1972, when Stephen Heath, who had worked with and on Roland Barthes, published "Ambiviolences" in two consecutive issues (50 and 51). Like most essays published in *Tel Quel*, it focuses on *Finnegans Wake*, but surveys the entire oeuvre and shows a real Joycean knowledge. Heath quotes elegantly Pound, Eliot, Vico, Jung, Jousse, Broch, and Svevo, and provides the usual theoretical guidelines: one finds the names of Barthes, Kristeva, Sollers, and Derrida, whose *différence* he reinscribes in Joycean terms as "hesitancy" or hesitation – in short, the signature of HCE. Heath was soon caught up in the rift between Derrida and Lacan, a rift which started in 1971, when Derrida answered to questions posed by the Tel Quelians in *Positions*. It culminated when Derrida chose the review *Poétique*, founded by Genette, Cixous, and Todorov, to publish the "Facteur de la Vérité," a wholesale attack on Lacan in 1975. Sollers and his friends decided to remain faithful to Lacan, and the break-up with Derrida was total.

1976 brought about a last reversal in alliances when the review opened its pages to the "new philosophers" who had launched a wholesale attack not just on Stalinism but on Marx, up to then sacrosanct. Resistance to communism became fashionable. Predictably, Sollers allowed himself to be seduced by the rediscovery of religion by the "new philosophers," either as the Jewish foundation embraced by Levy or as a more baroque Catholicism that might have been there all the time in Lacan's background. This is what marked the last round of essays on Joyce, often co-written by Sollers and Jean-Louis Houdebine. The concepts of "obscenity," transgression, blasphemy, and the like were then dominant. In the 81st issue (fall 1979), Jean-Louis Houdebine published "Joyce's signature" and then "Jung and Joyce." In the spring of 1980, number 83 was a special Joyce issue with a whole dossier on "James Joyce: obscentiy and theology," edited by Houdebine, some letters by Joyce, and "Joyce's Trinity," a discussion between Houdebine and Sollers. It contains an entertaining and interesting discussion of the trinitarian heresies in *Ulysses*. Finally, in number 92 (summer 1982), Beryl Schlossman, who had completed a French thesis on "the sacred and the comic in Joyce" directed by Julia Kristeva, published "Joyce and the gift of languages" (later a chapter of her first book, *Joyce's Catholic Comedy of Language*). Like Stephen Heath in 1972, and just ten years after, Schlossman is immersed in Joyce scholarship. She stresses the fascination for Jewish rituals and letters in *Ulysses* and the *Wake*, and gives a thorough analysis of the myth of Pentecost. She has also fully integrated the teachings of Julia Kristeva and those of Lacan.

Lacan remained the key influence on *Tel Quel*. After he had been excluded from the Ecole normale supérieure, where Derrida and Althusser still taught in 1969, he appeared like the most glorious heretic of theory. It was in this context that Lacan suddenly decided to turn to Joyce. We can note that he did this with reference to Sollers. In January 1973, Lacan put Joyce on a par with Sollers and himself:

> You must sit down and read a little the work by writers, not of your era – I won't tell you to read Philippe Sollers, who is unreadable, like me as a matter of fact – but you could read Joyce, for example. You will see therein how language is perfected when it knows how to play with writing (Lacan 1998: 36).

Lacan then added:

> I agree that Joyce's work is not readable – it is certainly not translatable into Chinese. What happens in Joyce's work? The signifier stuffs the signified. It is because the signifiers fit together; combine and concertina – read *Finnegans Wake* – that something is produced that, as a signified, may seem enigmatic, but is clearly what is closest to what we analysts, thanks to analytic discourse, have to read: slips of the tongue (Lacan 1998: 37, translation slightly modified).

One might object that *Finnegans Wake* has been translated into Chinese or argue that the difficulties of the text are not so insurpassable for some readers at least. Joyce appears here as the first writer able to teach psychoanalysts how to read, and he owes this to a unique use of language in which the signifiers float and mean halfway, move always elsewhere. All this was paving the way for the invitation extended by Jacques Aubert, who asked Lacan to give the major address at the 1975 International Joyce Symposium in Paris.

Lacan was entering into a domain that would durably inflect his later theories. He gave his talk on June 16, 1975, recalling as a promising coincidence his encounter with James Joyce at a reading of *Ulysses* at Adrienne Monnier's bookstore when he was only 20 (Aubert 1987: 22). Lacan was 74 by the time he returned to tackle the works of Joyce. This made him reminisce and re-create an image of himself as a "young man" meeting a slightly older Irish writer, already quite a celebrity, in Paris. In the seminar, he repeatedly played on the equivalence in French of *je nomme* and *jeune homme*: it is as if the detour that made him retrace the steps of Stephen Dedalus presented first "as a young man" and only later as an "artist" was the condition for his own rejuvenation. His encounter with Joyce was a fateful "coincidence" reawakened 50 years later by Jacques Aubert. All the new elements introduced into his theory in the early 1970s – the Borromean knot of the Real, the Symbolic, the Imaginary, the emergence of the Symptom in the real, the new importance given to *jouissance* in its connection with writing, the idea of writing as making a hole in reality, the theory of the lack of sexual rapport, the new figure of the Father as a perverse father – forcibly recur in the Joyce seminar, a seminar in which they find an elegant and final re-plotting: a re-knotting, in fact.

Lacan's speech at the Sorbonne mixed up brilliant insights with trite biographical readings (Aubert 1987). He could not digest at once the enormous Joyce scholarship, a whole library from which Jacques Aubert was lending him new volumes weekly. Lacan thus played the role of the uninitiated reader, distinguishing his approach from that of the specialists who thrive on Joyce. Lacan's starting point was simple, monolithic even: Joyce *embodies* the "symptom" as such, a symptom that has to be written "*sinthome*" to call up an older form of the word, used by Rabelais – seen as Joyce's predecessor in verbal experimentation. The two words (*symptôme/sinthome*) can be pronounced almost in the same way, since in certain French pronunciations, one skips the "p" in the first word. Thus it is that the archaic spelling subtly changes a common term and this gives a first hint of the crucial dimension of writing in naming here.

Having received this new name, the *Sinthome*, the Irish writer becomes a Saint through the rigorous homophony in French of "*sinthome*" and "*saint homme*," a depiction of him that accords quite well with the way Joyce wanted to present himself to his contemporaries and to posterity. The term also unleashes all sorts of punning associations, allusions to Aquinas, to "sin," and to literature ("tomes"). Joyce turns into the "saint and martyr" of Literature – the symptom of literature embodied by one man who has knowingly allowed himself to be devoured by letters, so as to be one with Literature.

Lacan's reservations about Joyce were nevertheless numerous and forceful: when Joyce plays with so many languages, the dimension of truth risks being lost. *Finnegans Wake* remains fundamentally a very masculine symptom overdetermined by the "Name-of-the-Father"; Joyce is seen as frantically erecting a literary monument in place of his father's real-life shortcomings; his writing compensates for failings that he excuses, negates, and sublimates at the same time. Although Joyce becomes the Symptom, he produces a text that can in no way deeply captivate its readers, since there is no clear reason why anyone should get interested in Joyce's own symptom. Joyce appears "unstuck," out of touch with the real unconscious process that he nevertheless tries to copy or imitate. Lacan detects a streak of megalomania: *Finnegans Wake* was a "stool" thanks to which Joyce hoped to reach immortality, but in fact he would owe it to the innumerable scholars laboring under the delusion that they would crack the code. Thus the *jouissance* that Joyce offers to his readers aims at the glorification of his name, a name that becomes a common noun when it translates that of Freud (in German, Freud is close to *Freude*, meaning happiness or enjoyment) into English ("joy" contained in "Joyce") and also into French, as *jouissance*.

This baffling, frustrating, and fascinating talk not only sketched what would become the theme of Lacan's seminar in the following year (1975–6), a seminar accordingly entitled "The *Sinthome*," but also maps out the theoretical task of his last productive years: the forceful confrontation with Joyce which obliges him to go beyond the three interlocking circles of the Real, the Imaginary, and the Symbolic (three concepts that had been the mainstays of his theoretical elaboration for 20 years) to show that their knotting depends upon the function of a fourth circle, often called Sigma for Symptom or *sinthome*.

Writing achieves a sewing together, a splicing of these partially loose circles of the Real, the Symbolic, and the Imaginary. Joyce was caught up in his father's symptoms: both father and son were spendthrifts, heavy drinkers unable to keep their families sheltered from disaster. While John Joyce could indeed imagine that he had "killed" his exhausted wife when she died of cancer, James Joyce's cross was Lucia, who started showing signs of derangement in the late 1920s and behaved more and more erratically until she was institutionalized in 1934. Lucia's fate appeared as a confirmation of Joyce's dangerous flirtation with psychosis. Lacan's reading is not far from Jung's; like Jung, Lacan stresses Joyce's wish to defend Lucia against psychoanalysis so as to ward off any suggestion that his own writing could be seen as "schizophrenic" or "psychotic," and like Jung he admits that Lucia drowns in the unconscious where a more experienced swimmer manages to reach back to the surface (*JJ* 679–80). However, Lacan also denounces Joyce's tendency to fall into the trap of Jungism when he writes about universal history in the *Wake*. The main consequence of these remarks was that Joyce's latest works seemed to offer the key to Lacan's latest conceptualization of psychosis.

Lacan was aware of the impact of his theories on contemporary avant-garde writers, especially Philippe Sollers and his friends from *Tel Quel*. But his reading was directly impacted by their theories of textual production, of an intransitive writing that functions outside meaning, and so on. The paradoxical consequence of this conflation was that all Lacanian psychoanalysts had to become Joyceans if they wanted to understand the right type of cure for psychosis or neurosis. The point of good psychoanalysis was henceforth to understand the function of the *sinthome* for each and every human subject. When the famous logician Quine asked Lacan during a tour of North American universities if the aim of psychoanalysis was to untie the knot made by the symptom, he answered in the negative: "No, it holds fast. One could state that if Freud demonstrates something, it is that sexuality makes a hole, but human beings have no idea of what it is. A woman is made present for a man by a symptom; a woman is man's symptom" (Aubert 1987: 60). Such an insight would play a crucial role in the later developments of Lacanian theory, especially for theoreticians like Žižek, and it is entirely founded upon a reading of Joyce.

Lacan's thesis on *Ulysses* revolves around the issue of paternity. The more Joyce denied his father, like Peter with Christ, the more he got entangled in the strings of the fourfold knot. Thus Lacan does not believe that Bloom is a likely father for Stephen nor that Stephen can figure a believable Telemachus (Aubert 1987: 27). He decided to stress the function of paternity while disentangling it from the Homeric structure: it is precisely the absence of real or symbolic fathers in the novel that shows how paternity is reduced to a name. A full discussion of this issue would entail a systematic examination of the theological substratum of the links between Shakespeare, God, and the Artist, which is precisely what the last issues of *Tel Quel* set out to do, following Lacan's hints, but only after Sollers and his friends had all reconverted to Catholicism.

In the last Joyce seminar, Joyce's Ego is promoted to the position of the fourth circle, where Lacan had previously put the Sigma of the Symptom before. Joyce's Ego is an effect of his writing and can be identified with his Symptom. There had been a mistake in the knotting of the three circles of the Real, the Imaginary, and the Symbolic, and to compensate the error, the Ego plays the role of a clamp keeping the circles together. "Why is Joyce so unreadable? Perhaps because he triggers no sympathy in us. What I am suggesting is that with Joyce, the ego comes to correct the missing relation. By such an artifice of writing, the Borromean knot is reconstituted" (*Ornicar?* 11, 1977: 8). Joyce's Ego is the symptom as it exploits the ruses of a literary enigma. It is a creative artifice, a "supplement" by which the spoken riddle turns into writing while reattaching all its components.

Lacan uses the signifier *ego* (conforming to the English use) and not *moi* to translate Freud's *Ich* (*Ornicar?* 9, 1976: 34). This suggests a renewed confrontation with British ego-psychology. The idea of the lability and supplementarity of the Joycean ego is confirmed by a passage taken from *A Portrait of the Artist as a Young Man*, when Stephen remembers how a number of schoolboys had tormented him because he would stubbornly claim Byron to be the greatest poet. After the schoolboys viciously lash at him, he is overcome by anger, and sobbing and clenching his fists, madly runs after them. Suddenly, he feels this anger falling from him, in a paradoxical moment of dispossession. Lacan remarks that this transformation of anger into disgust is suspect for a psychoanalyst. He sees in this emblematic scene the model of what might be called the Joycean body: a body that can fall from one's self, which is a mere envelope that by itself cannot really hold the subject.

Joyce's ego is a peel, a rim loosely captured by the Imaginary. It is labile, porous and artificial, and can be dropped just like that. For Joyce, then, as a consequence, the Real is not knotted to the Unconscious: it appears in symptoms that are linked with a place like Dublin. The concept of the ego that is proposed is not natural, it is artificial but cannot be reduced to the register of the Imaginary. The new Lacanian *ego* is indeed, as Ezra Pound wrote in his *Cantos*, an *Ego Scriptor* (Pound 1986: 472).

Like Heath in 1972 with his concept of hesitation, Lacan stressed the process of equivocation in Joyce's writing, while claiming that he had anticipated Derrida in this key insight:

> There is indeed another writing, which results from what one might call a precipitation of the signifier. Jacques Derrida insisted on this, after I showed him the way, by simply pointing to the signifier by writing it as S. It remains that the signifier, or what is modulated in the voice, has nothing to do with writing, which is perfectly demonstrated by my *Noeud-bo* (*Ornicar?* 11, 1977: 3).

Even though Lacan remained deaf to Derrida's suggestion that writing can be shown to inhabit the most intimate phenomenological link between our thinking and the inner language, both look to the central place of writing in Joyce's subjective constitution.

What Lacan added was that the linguistic equivocation deployed *ad libitum* by *Finnegans Wake* has practical uses for therapy:

> What in Joyce makes the symptom, the pure symptom of what is our relation to language, when it is reduced to symptoms – i.e. to what effect it has when this effect is not analyzed – I would even add when one forbids oneself to play with any equivocation that might move the unconscious of anybody (Aubert 1987: 27).

Such writing plays at the hinge between sound effects and written effects. Lacan analyzes the example of "Who ails tongue coddeau?," in which one hears "*Où est ton cadeau?*," to prove that Joyce always writes something that is meant to sound as something else, or in a different language. But this writing is essential to his ego. This is why the question of Lucia Joyce's madness and of her father's sanity acquires a crucial role. Lacan asked in February 1976:

> Was Joyce mad? The fact that I will not solve the question today will not prevent me from working with my distinction between Truth and the Real. . . . I began by writing *Inspired Writings*, this is why I should not be astonished to find myself confronting Joyce, and this is why I dare pose the question: Was he mad? By what were his writings inspired to him? (*Ornicar?* 8, 1976: 6).

This reference to his 1931 publication "Ecrits inspirés," one of Lacan's earliest medical papers, sends us back to the moment when he was trying to understand the logic of psychotic discourse.

In "Inspired Writings," Lacan refused any medical approach to the language of psychotics and preferred the experiments of the Surrealists:

> These texts . . . evince an actively ludic aspect whose intentional part, as its automatic part, ought not to be missed. The experiences made by certain writers on a mode of writing they have called Surrealist and whose method they have described very scientifically show the extraordinary degree of autonomy that graphic automatisms can reach, outside any hypnosis (Lacan 1975: 379–80).

Lacan refused to distinguish the artful simulation of psychotic delirium, such as one finds in *The Immaculate Conception* by Breton and Eluard, from "authentic" verbal productions of institutionalized patients: all these texts evince similar structures, are determined by preinscribed rhythmic formulas then subverted and filled with other meanings. Puns and homophonic patterns allow both poets and "mad" patients to use language as a chain of signifiers, letting desire move along with the chain, while metaphors manage to break through and pass through the Saussurean bar, to use Lacan's later terminology.

In a curious loop, we can note that Joyce's friends at *transition* were busy collecting and publishing such "inspired writings." For instance, in *transition* in 1929, Roger

Vitrac writes on "Le Langage à part," and extensively quotes a medical treatise by Dr. Seglas devoted to language trouble in alienated subjects before alluding to poetic texts by Prevert and Desnos as illustrations of the same linguistic process (*transition*, *18*, 1929: 176–90). All this, of course, is given in the context of the linguistic experiments of the "revolution of the word" launched by Joyce. Similarly, in a later issue of *transition*, Stuart Gilbert publishes an essay on "The subliminal tongue" in which he starts with Joyce and then examines a few cases of psychotic language, which include the psychical research on dissociation of personality by Morton Prince, who is also quoted in *Finnegans Wake*. At one point, Gilbert quotes Gide's *Paludes* with the allusion to "that part of unconscious that I would like to call God's part" (*transition*, *26*, 1937: 151).

The question of Joyce's potentially psychotic structure remained a haunting one for Lacan, and he never provided a definitive answer. Lucia Joyce figured as the remainder of her father's symptomatic formation. It is quite revealing to compare Lacan's own biographical trajectory with that of Joyce. Joyce's last years were darkened by his daughter's schizophrenia and the awareness that the irruption of political crises leading to a worldwide conflagration would prevent people from taking in the linguistic experiments of *Finnegans Wake*. Lacan had lost a daughter he adored, and, if his last years were more fulfilled and rewarding, they were darkened by political strife among disciples fighting for control of the school and the edition of his seminars. Like Joyce, he never stopped experimenting with new mathemes, knots, braids, bits of spliced strings, puns, and formulas.

It was, finally, Jacques Derrida who set an end to the moment of high theory identified as "poststructuralism" and he also did this with respect to Joyce. In 1985, in a major address given at the Frankfurt Joyce Symposium, Derrida took to task the very concept of a James Joyce Foundation. This deconstructive gesture was based upon previous readings of Joyce by him. Since the 1960s, in his discussions of Husserl's phenomenology, Derrida had defined *Ulysses* and *Finnegans Wake* as totalizing masterpieces, as "hypermnesic" machines that somehow managed to condense or quote a whole culture; by doing this these books play dangerously with an unmoored historicism while also modifying our reading habits. Reading these texts we discover that we are being read by them, we have been read in advance by the author, traversed by Joyce's encyclopedic culture. Stephen Dedalus spoke of Shakespeare as the father of his grandfather and his own grandson, presenting him as the paradigm of the self-generating artist. Hence the fascination of Joyce scholars for manuscripts, drafts, first editions, autographs, holographs, letters, and notebooks – such as are culled in the volumes of the *James Joyce Archive* – with the addition of recently discovered proofs and unpublished manuscripts sold for a fortune at auctions.

Facing such a formidably programmed archive, Derrida wielded a deconstructive scalpel, confronting the "Joyce scholars," who are perceived as an intimidating body and also an institution in need of a more secure foundation. The International James Joyce Foundation is a concrete example of a tradition that had invested cultural capital aiming at universality in a writer's name. It also needs someone who comes from the outside like Plato's Stranger, to authorize the foundation from a position of marginality. Even when Joyce scholars have at their disposal the "totality of competence in the encyclopedic field of the *universitas*" (Derrida 1992: 281), they crave the non-expertise of a foreigner who will question their "foundation" so as to reassure them. This foreigner will end up accusing them, "you do not exist, you are not founded to exist as a foundation" (284). Derrida poses a haunting question: under what conditions can "James Joyce studies" become a rigorous field, a recognizable discipline? Is there a type of Joycean competence that can be measured and posited as a prerequisite? Is it enough to have read the works and some critics, or should one commit oneself more actively and join Joycean reading groups or websites? Is Joycean knowledge inseparable from the rituals that accompany it, the International James Joyce symposia, Bloomsday celebrations in most important cities, the meetings of *Finnegans Wake* or *Ulysses* reading groups in universities or capitals throughout the world?

As we have seen, French theory is caught up both in the ritualizing performances that add up and constitute the competence of the expert, and in the decisive opening of the field to its "others." Then it plays a different game, less that of the expert than that of the avant-gardist and experimenter. This has left durable traces on the Joyce institution. Trevor Williams identified the 1975 Paris International James Joyce Symposium as a watershed in the internationalization of the institutions of Joyce criticism and as the moment when the apolitical view of Joyce was shattered (Williams 1997: 28). An exemplary panel, in which there was a dialogue going on about the "political perspectives on Joyce's work," gathered Bernard Benstock, Seamus Deane, Paul Delany, Leslie Fiedler, Suzette Henke, Maria Jolas, and Philippe Sollers. Sollers' provocations made the audience sense that a real discussion was taking place. He asserted that English had turned into a "dead language" after the publication of *Finnegans Wake* and dramatically showed the book (pointing to the adequately red hardback cover of the jacketless Faber edition of *Finnegans Wake*) with the declaration "I show you one revolution" (Aubert and Jolas, 1979: 107). Joyce's works had been banned just as Freud's books had been burned by the Nazis. Fiedler expressed an awareness of experimental language which tallied with Sollers', while Deane stressed the Irish point of view on Joyce as a colonial writer, caught up in a defeatist time warp. Henke reflected upon the then emergent feminist discourse on Joyce and Maria Jolas intervened to assert that Joyce had been political all along while an auditor quoted Frantz Fanon and concluded that Joyce was essential to debunk colonialist prejudice. Nearby, serious work on the generative linguistics of the *Wake* was being presented by *Change*.

What was rendered manifest was that the discourse of Jolas and his friends on the "Revolution of the Word" had joined with the language of high theory revised by the Parisian avant-garde. The experimentalism of the 1930s had returned to haunt the avant-gardism of the 1970s under the leadership of the *Tel Quel* group. Their pronouncements antagonized a more academic group influenced by New Criticism, whose dominant reading practice relied on close readings, source-hunting and communal discussions of textual riddles. A critical language inspired by Marxism, psychoanalysis, feminism, linguistics, poststructuralism, and deconstruction was brought massively to bear on Joyce for the first time. How could one stress the political element in Joyce given the biographical evidence testifying to his aloofness in Irish matters, his projection into a pure aesthete who leaves behind him Ireland's burden of tangled responsibilities, and his refusal to get involved in nationalist or internationalist causes after *Ulysses*?

The answer was the idea of a "revolutionary language," which for the Tel Quelians automatically placed Joyce in the avant-garde, on a pedestal including Lenin, Mao, and Artaud, whereas more conservative American Joyce specialists would stick to aesthetics or to biography. Sollers adapted Mallarmé's famous statement that "the Book was the bomb!", while other Joyceans only saw in the "artist's" politics non-involvement, detachment and indifference. It took another decade to allow the Joyce industry to digest the impact of 1975 – this is nowhere more visible than in the enormous compendium called *A Companion to Joyce Studies* edited in 1984 by Zack Bowen and James F. Carens. In more than eight hundred pages, the main aspects of Joyce scholarship are surveyed, with detailed analyses of all the individual works and important synthetic chapters like Scholes' and Corcoran's on the "Aesthetic theory and the critical writings." Yet Colin MacCabe's groundbreaking 1978 *James Joyce and the Revolution of the Word*, in which a neo-Marxist approach is coupled with Lacanian theory, is not even mentioned by Bowen and Carens, nor are the names of Eco, Lacan, or Derrida. Nothing is said of gender issues or of textual problems like the genetic versions provided by various manuscripts and editions. It is revealing to compare this thick book with the slim "introduction" by Alan Roughley, *James Joyce and Critical Theory* (1991), published seven years later. Roughley's chapters bear on Joyce as approached by various schools from structuralism, poststructuralism, semiotics, feminism, and psychoanalytic theory to Marxism. As Seamus Deane wrote in 1985, the prevalent critical assumption up to then had been that Joyce was apolitical and limited his genius to formal and stylistic innovation:

> Repudiating British and Roman imperialism and rejecting Irish nationalism and Irish literature which seemed to be in the service of that cause, he turned away from his early commitment to socialism and devoted himself instead to a highly apolitical and wonderfully arcane practice of writing. Such, in brief, is the received wisdom about Joyce and his relationship to the major political issues of his times (Deane 1985: 92).

The revision of this view would probably never have happened without the productive effort of French high theory facing Joyce.

NOTE

1 My first published piece on Joyce, "La Missa Parodia de *Finnegans Wake*" (1974) was partly devoted to genetic issues, raised by David Hayman's groundbreaking *First Draft Version of "Finnegans Wake."* In those years Hayman and Sollers also started meeting, leading to a later collaboration in *Tel Quel*.

BIBLIOGRAPHY

Attridge, Derek (ed.) (2004 [1990]) *The Cambridge Companion to James Joyce.* Cambridge: Cambridge University Press.

Attridge, Derek and Daniel Ferrer (eds.) (1985) *Post-Structuralist Joyce: Essays from the French.* Cambridge: Cambridge University Press.

Aubert, Jacques (ed.) (1987) *Joyce avec Lacan.* Paris: Navarin.

Aubert, Jacques and Maria Jolas (eds.) (1979) *Joyce & Paris, 1902 . . . 1920–1940 . . . 1975*, 2 vols. Lille and Paris: Publications de Lille-III and CNRS.

Beckett, Samuel et al. (1972 [1929]) *Our Exagmination Round His Factification for Incamination of Work in Progress.* London: Faber and Faber.

Bowen, Zack, and James F. Carens (eds.) (1984) *A Companion to Joyce Studies.* Westport, CT: Greenwood.

Deane, Seamus (1985) *Celtic Revivals: Essays in Modern Irish Literature 1885–1980.* London: Faber and Faber.

Derrida, Jacques (1968a) "La Pharmacie de Platon 1," *Tel Quel* 32: 3–48.

Derrida Jacques (1968b) "La Pharmacie de Platon 2," *Tel Quel* 33: 18–59.

Derrida, Jacques (1972) *Positions.* Paris: Minuit.

Derrida, Jacques (1992) "*Ulysses* gramophone," trans. T. Kendall and S. Benstock. In Derek Attridge (ed.) *Acts of Literature*, pp. 253–309. London: Routledge.

Ffrench, Patrick (ed.) (1998) *From Tel Quel to L'Infini: The Avant-garde and After.* London: Parallax.

Ffrench, Patrick and Roland-François Lack (eds. and trans.) (1998) *The Tel Quel Reader.* London: Routledge.

Forest, Philippe (1995) *Histoire de Tel Quel.* Paris: Seuil.

Gilbert, Stuart (1937) "The subliminal tongue." *transition* 26: 148–55.

Hayman, David (1963) *A First-Draft Version of Finnegans Wake.* Austin: University of Texas Press.

Hayman, David (1974) "Sollers interview." *Iowa Review* 5 (4): 10–15.

Heath, Stephen (1972a) "Ambiviolences: Notes pour la lecture de Joyce," *Tel Quel* 50: 22–43.

Heath, Stephen (1972b) "Ambiviolences – 2," *Tel Quel* 51: 64–76.

Houdebine, Jean-Louis (1982) "Joyce tel quel," *Tel Quel* 94: 35–44.

Jolas, Eugene (1929) "Super-Occident," *transition* 18: 176–90.

Kauppi, Niilo (1994) *The Making of an Avant-Garde: Tel Quel.* Berlin: Mouton de Gruyter.

Lacan, Jacques (1975) "Ecrits inspirés." In his *De la Psychose paranoïaque dans ses rapports avec la personnalité, suivi de Premiers écrits sur la paranoia.* Paris: Seuil.

Lacan, Jacques (1976, 1977) "*Le Sinthome*," *Ornicar?* 8, 9, 11.

Lacan, Jacques (1998) *Encore: The Seminar of Jacques Lacan, Book XX, On Feminine Sexuality, The Limits of Love and Knowledge, 1972–1973*, ed. Jacques-Alain Miller and trans. Bruce Fink. New York: Norton.

Lernout, Geert (1990) *The French Joyce.* Ann Arbor: University of Michigan Press.

Lernout, Geert and Wim van Mierlo (2004) *The Reception of Joyce in Europe.* London: Continuum.

Ogden, C. K. and I. A. Richards (1968 [1923]) *The Meaning of Meaning.* New York: Harcourt and Brace.

Paris, Jean (1967) "Finnegan, Wake!" *Tel Quel* 30: 223–35.

Pound, Ezra (1986) *The Cantos.* London: Faber and Faber.

Rabaté, Jean-Michel (1974) "La Missa Parodia de *Finnegans Wake*," *Poétique* 17: 75–95.

Rabaté, Jean-Michel (2001) *Jacques Lacan: Psychoanalysis and the Subject of Literature.* Houndmills: Palgrave.

Rabaté, Jean-Michel (ed.) (2004) *Palgrave Advances to James Joyce Studies.* Houndmills: Palgrave.

Roughley, Alan (1991) *James Joyce and Critical Theory: An Introduction.* Hemel Hempstead: Harvester, Wheatsheaf.

Sollers, Philippe (1981) *Vision à New York: Entretiens avec David Hayman.* Paris: Grasset.

Tel Quel: Théorie d'Ensemble (1968) Paris: Seuil.

Williams, Trevor L. (1997) *Reading Joyce Politically.* Gainesville: University Press of Florida.

17

Joyce, Music, and Popular Culture

R. Brandon Kershner

Literary Theory and Popular Culture

Joyce's work, especially the later books, *Ulysses* and *Finnegans Wake*, teems with references to popular culture. As his writing grew increasingly encyclopedic, it came to reflect directly and indirectly all the levels of cultural production of the periods that concerned Joyce – 1904 for *Ulysses* and the twentieth century before the Second World War in the *Wake* – and this emphatically included what is generally termed "popular culture" or, more pejoratively, "mass culture." In fact, since many of his characters were middle-aged in 1904 and were typically singing songs, reading books, or watching theatrical performances that had already been hallowed by tradition, much of the popular culture portrayed in *Ulysses* is actually mid- or late Victorian in origin. *Ulysses* mentions or features songs, from nursery rhymes to operatic arias; the bestselling magazines of the time; adventure novels and children's stories; works of pornography and women's romances; a large selection of newspapers; music hall performances; and unclassifiable snippets of gossip reflecting quotidian topics of 1904. Many Dubliners still insist that Joyce is not really an important writer because the whole of *Ulysses* is just a record of Dublin bar talk.

Given the pervasiveness of popular culture in his work, it would seem strange that, with the important exception of song, little serious attention was paid to popular culture by scholars of Joyce's work until the mid-1980s. But this situation simply reflected the political and ideological stance of literary academics in general between the wars and during the immediate postwar period. In a time when the study of modern literature was still struggling to assert its own legitimacy as an academic subject, it could not afford to concern itself with cultural material that was generally regarded as trivial and ephemeral. During the 1930s in England, F. R. Leavis' insistence on the bracing moral seriousness of both literature and literary criticism helped establish "Cambridge English" as a mature academic field. His extreme selectivity in setting a literary canon of the novel ranging from Jane Austen to George Eliot, Henry

James, and Joseph Conrad lent an air of authority to his sweeping judgments even as it helpfully restricted the amount of material students would be expected to master.

Extending their interpretations of the cultural criticism of T. S. Eliot and Ortega y Gassett, Leavis and his wife also portrayed popular culture as a degenerate, deadening form of the same cultural expression that at its highest – in the work of D. H. Lawrence, for example – has the potential to remake society and the individual conscience. Genuine literature, Q. D. Leavis asserted in *Fiction and the Reading Public* (1932), allows the reader "to live at the expense of an unusually intelligent and sensitive mind, by giving him access to a finer code than his own," whereas popular novels "substitute an emotional code which . . . is actually inferior to the traditional code of the illiterate." Thus popular fictions "actually get in the way of genuine feeling and responsible thinking by creating cheap mechanical responses and throwing their weight on the side of social, national, and herd prejudices" (Leavis 1932: 74). Articulating a metaphor which was to become increasingly common during the century, Leavis refers to the taste for popular novels as "a drug addiction to fiction" (Leavis 1932: 152). Meanwhile, the literary object was increasingly decontextualized by critics, in part through the process of "close reading" that proved so successful in disclosing the depths and complexities of Joyce's writing. As Terry Eagleton observes (1983: 44), "It was the beginnings of a 'reification' of the literary work, the treatment of it as an object in itself, which was to be triumphantly consummated in the American New Criticism." Reification removed the historical and cultural origins and connections from the work of art, and thus further disassociated it from examples of popular art arising from the same historical moment. The literary work was made timeless, in effect, by suppressing its temporality, its historical situation.

In America, the professoriate was similarly at pains to establish literary criticism as a professional discipline, and the variety of socially conservative formalism known as the New Criticism, with its emphasis on "organic" values and the timeless truths of myths, was well suited to the political quietism following the Second World War in the United States. Here, too, exclusivity was key to the literary-critical assertion of a subject matter and discipline. In offering the new, difficult work of the literary modernists for study and emulation, the New Critics found it all the more important to reject merely popular writing with the same broad gesture. Indeed, as Ezra Pound argued, if written work *did* find a large audience, that alone was probably enough to indicate that it was insufficiently challenging or serious.

Certainly the increasing dominance of T. S. Eliot as a cultural essayist during the postwar period, when literary modernism was establishing its hegemony, tended to give a conservative and antipopular coloration to criticism. His influential essay "*Ulysses*, Order, and Myth" suggested that in echoing the *Odyssey* Joyce provides a structuring principle upon whose scaffolding he can mount the otherwise unredeemed chaos of modern life. This "mythic method," he believes, is "a step toward making the modern world possible for art" (Eliot 1932: 681). Indeed, Eliot's assertion of a literary tradition that had many similarities to Leavis' *Great Tradition* (1948) implicitly upheld an exclusive, "timeless" canon whose selectivity was the key to its unassailable strength.

The branch of the American academy most invested in boosting modernist art – and this generally included its most imaginative, open-minded, and innovative members – found it effective to stress how the wealth of allusions to classical and canonical literature in Eliot, Joyce, Pound, Woolf, and the others demonstrated modernism's close relationship with the classics, including the acknowledged masterpieces of the modern European languages. Indeed, more than the writers themselves, it was modernist critics who canonized modernist works by stressing their continuity with great writing of the past (which on the surface they certainly did not resemble) and their complete disconnection with and rejection of the popular cultural forms with which they were contemporary. As Andreas Huyssen attempts to show, modernist criticism usually codes the popular as female, as a defining distinction from the male masterworks of the twentieth century. The very elements that gave popularity to bestselling work, such as melodrama, sentimentality, vigorous action, and easy reader identification, became regarded as the abjected hallmarks of bad art.

Among cultural commentators in Europe, the most influential were probably the intellectuals associated with the Frankfurt Institute for Social Research, including Theodor Adorno, Max Horkheimer, Erich Fromm, Leo Lowenthal, Herbert Marcuse, and Walter Benjamin. Although these thinkers differed in many ways in their approach to contemporary culture, there was a broad consensus among them (with the possible partial exception of Benjamin) that the effect of what Adorno called the "culture industry" was stultifying and helped prevent "the masses" from coming to full revolutionary consciousness:

> The total effect of the culture industry is one of anti-enlightenment, in which [. . .] enlightenment, that is the progressive technical domination of nature, becomes mass deception and is turned into a means for fettering consciousness. It impedes the development of autonomous, independent individuals who judge and decide consciously for themselves. [. . .] If the masses have been unjustly reviled from above as masses, the culture industry is not among the least responsible for making them into masses and then despising them, while obstructing the emancipation for which human beings are as ripe as the productive forces of the epoch permit (Adorno 1975: 18–19).

Aside from its Marxist inflection, there was nothing new about this attitude. As Patrick Brantlinger documents, characterizing mass culture as a means of distracting the people from consciousness of their true condition of exploitation – a kind of *panem et circenses* – is a theme among social commentators that exists in both "right" and "left" versions and has done so since classical times. For the Frankfurt School theorists, the division between authentic art and its spurious imitation was clear: real art was a form of critique, and could not be reduced to ideology, whereas mass art was simply a form of ideology and participated in its function of distraction and concealment. A number of American commentators, such as the leftist intellectuals associated with the *Partisan Review* and *Dissent* during the postwar period, shared this cultural orientation. Not all American intellectuals dismissed popular culture in favor of "serious" art, though, and during the 1920s there was a flurry of interest in what Gilbert Seldes termed the "lively arts." For Seldes, the best popular art – such as the films of Chaplin, jazz music, and experimental comic strips – were in fact engaged in the same work of cultural subversion of middle-class values in which modernists such as Joyce and Stein were embroiled. But Seldes was a public intellectual, and his views had little impact on the literary academy.

The formulation and codification of an alternative view of popular culture dates from the 1960s both in the United States and in Great Britain, and in both cases was tenuously but complexly connected with the emergence of a counterculture. In England the founding of the Centre for Contemporary Cultural Studies at Birmingham in 1964 helped consolidate the pioneering work of Raymond Williams in *Culture and Society, 1780–1950* (1958) and *The Long Revolution* (1961) as well as that of Richard Hoggart in *The Uses of Literacy: Changing Patterns in English Mass Culture* (1957). The writers associated with the Birmingham Centre took popular culture just as seriously as did the Leavises or the Frankfurt School, but unlike them believed that it might very well be a politically progressive force; in any case, the assumption was that each instance of popular culture, from Mills and Boon novelettes to workingmen's songs to punk subcultures, needed to be carefully investigated and analyzed. Above all, the implicit class-based condescension of the Leavises was abandoned even as their analytic methods were preserved and expanded, in part because many of the new intellectuals were themselves of working-class origin. Most were prepared to value and evaluate popular culture on its own terms – whatever that might mean – rather than as a pallid and debased reflection of "true" culture. As Paddy Whannel and Stuart Hall wrote in *The Popular Arts* (1964: 38), "It is not useful to say that the music of Cole Porter is inferior to that of Beethoven. The music of Porter and Beethoven is not of equal value, but Porter was not making an unsuccessful attempt to create music comparable to Beethoven's."

In the United States the two most significant figures are probably the Canadian Marshall McLuhan, with his hugely influential *Understanding Media: The Extensions of Man* (1964), and the maverick intellectual Leslie Fiedler, who staked out his position with a 1957 essay entitled "The Middle against Both Ends," in which he began an enthusiastic and nuanced celebration of popular cultural forms, specifically associating them with the rise of a consciously antibourgeois (and anti-intellectual) counterculture. As Andrew Ross (1989: 17) observes, "it is probably fair to say that popular culture has been socially and institutionally central in America for longer and in a more significant way than in Europe," so that it should not be surprising if most American critics have finally "abandoned the prestigious but undemocratic, Europeanized contempt for 'mass culture.'" No doubt this also is one of the reasons why American academics have generally been the leaders in studying the role of popular culture in Joyce. Starting in the 1960s American universities began to offer courses in science fiction and fantasy writing and films, in rock, blues, and folk music, and, eventually, in comic-book art. A great deal of activity centered on the Popular Culture Association, although most of this work would later be regarded as undertheorized by the proponents of what came to be called "cultural studies." By the mid-1980s there was something of a consensus among critics that the particular psychological and political effects of any particular example of popular culture could not automatically be assumed to be pernicious and needed individual investigation. As Jim Collins (1989: 16) put it, there was a shared "recognition that all cultural production must be seen as a set of power relations that produce particular forms of subjectivity, but that the nature, function, and uses of mass culture can no longer be conceived in a monolithic manner."

Joyce Studies and Popular Culture

Simply because Joyce's texts are so densely allusive — and because critics soon learned of his expressed desire to provide puzzles and riddles enough to keep professors busy for years, and promptly played along — occasional articles have explored the role of popular cultural figures and texts almost from the beginning of serious Joycean criticism. For example, Gerhard Friedrich in a 1954 article looks at correspondences between a Bret Harte novel and "The Dead," while a 1972 article by Marvin Magalaner explores the appearance of the popular novelist Marie Corelli and her work, especially *The Sorrows of Satan*, in *Ulysses*. The apparent rationale of critics doing this sort of work was that virtually anything mentioned in Joyce's work deserved investigation or at least identification. Neither Harte nor Corelli here was "taken seriously," insofar as neither critic looked for a significant dialogue between Joyce and the popular writer (in the relationship the critic M. M. Bakhtin termed "dialogism"). Neither critic looked to either Corelli or Harte to provide important insights into their culture and time. Rather, they were seen as the equivalent of the "street furniture" that Joyce often invoked to lend substantial detail to his novels. An exception to this rule in some ways, however, was the critical treatment of song and popular music, which will be discussed separately below.

Meanwhile, during the 1970s the gradual shift from mythical and New Critical paradigms toward the new European approaches, in particular structuralism, opened up the field of operations for American and British critics. Roland Barthes in *Mythologies* (1972) and Umberto Eco in *The Role of the Reader* (1979) demonstrated that the objects and events of popular culture, such as professional wrestling, the novels of Ian Fleming, or the figure of Superman, were susceptible to remarkably sophisticated analysis, even as structuralism's demystifying shift of emphasis from the individual genius behind the literary masterpiece to the system of language as a whole vastly broadened the field upon which analysis could act. The success of structuralism in the American academy was no doubt due in part to the fact that it could easily be seen as another kind of formalism that was putatively even more rigorous. In retrospect, it is clear that the gradual shift toward cultural studies had begun, although the turn toward history had not yet started to change the character of literary criticism. During this period those of us who were later to concentrate on the issue of popular culture in relation to Joyce were exploring and experimenting with a variety of approaches. I had dealt with that issue in a very introductory way in my 1971 dissertation on the novels of Raymond Queneau and James Joyce, primarily because when I looked at Joyce next to his French disciple it became clear that both were in some way seriously involved with popular culture in their writings – Queneau more obviously than Joyce, though perhaps actually triggered by something in Joyce's work that Anglophone readers had overlooked.

In 1975 at a meeting of the Southern Popular Culture Association in Tampa, Florida, I was able to discuss the issue with Leslie Fiedler. Fiedler, who had thought out the issue and its implications far more thoroughly than I, was very encouraging about my work, and I recall our agreeing that where Joyce was contemptuous of popular culture in *A Portrait* and had mixed emotions about it in *Ulysses*, by the time of the *Wake* he was outright celebratory. Only a few years before this, in a Joyce Symposium address that was published in the inaugural issue of the *Journal of Modern Literature*, Fiedler took the position that "the literary movement we have agreed to call "Modernism," and at the center of which Joyce stands, is . . . now dead" (Fiedler: 1970: 21). In part he was acclaiming the new movement we now term "postmodernism," in one of its early avatars, but he was also asserting that in his newfound enthusiasm for popular culture and his rejection of the mandarin values of modernism, he found himself rejecting Stephen and his values only to surprise himself by embracing Bloom and his. He asserts, "Like many of you here before me, like Joyce himself, I began by thinking that I was Stephen . . . began by thinking that I was the high flying boy doomed to fall in glory. . . . But I ended, as you will end, as Joyce ended, by knowing that I was Bloom, a comic, earthbound father who is also an apostle to the Gentiles" (Fiedler 1970: 29).

Fiedler's other major statement on Joyce is collected in a series of essays inspired by the 1982 Joyce centennial conference at Rutgers-Newark, and the editor, Heyward Ehrlich, has grouped it together with an essay by Zack Bowen centering on music in a section on "Popular Culture"; other categories include "Experimental Literature," "The New Sexuality," "Avant-Garde Music," and "Contemporary Philosophy" (including an excerpt from Margot Norris' *The Decentered Universe of* Finnegans Wake). The trace of the countercultural ferment of the 1960s and 70s is clear in the volume as a whole. Fiedler's essay, "To Whom Does Joyce Belong? *Ulysses* as Pop and Porn," tries to distinguish *Ulysses* from the classical type of modernist fiction, pointing out that both Joyce and the book itself have a status within popular culture, if only because there are pornographic aspects to *Ulysses* – "both Bloom and his author are readers of porn at a second remove: meta-porn savored over the shoulder, as it were, of a female reader" (Fiedler 1970: 30). Fiedler goes on to develop the idea that *Ulysses* is transgressive in that it gives a voice to a kind of female who has not previously been represented in literature, and he associates this with Joyce's knowledge of popular female novelists like Susan Warner, Mrs. E.D.E.N., Southworth, and Maria Cummins: "fully to understand [Joyce's] novel, one needs to have some sense of what *St. Elmo* is really about (or *The Wide, Wide World* or *The Lamplighter*)" (Fiedler 1970: 34). Clearly Fiedler here anticipates Huyssen's argument regarding the coding of popular fiction as female, and near the end of his essay he also suggests that it is essentially American.

As a leading intellectual, Fiedler was very much in a minority in the positions he took during this period, though I recall a man who in the 1950s had been a friend and colleague of his during the 1970s referring to him as a "clown." This kind of strong feeling arose because in the discussion of popular culture a great deal more was at stake than was immediately apparent: the recent "culture wars" descend directly from these early debates. For one thing, the traditionalists of literary criticism felt that if popular literature was seen as having cultural value (and if it was admitted that its interpretation by critics like Barthes and Eco yielded significant insights into culture), then that would threaten the profession's presumption that literary hermeneutics demanded special training only available within the profession because literary language was unlike other language uses. If, as Fiedler argued, some of the value assigned to classic texts reflected little more than class-based prejudice, then what would become of the whole idea of a canon? If the modernist proscriptions of sentimentality and melodrama are removed, then Fiedler's assertion that *Uncle Tom's Cabin* is an important text begins to seem not only reasonable but obvious. But if we professors of literature are not perpetuating a tradition with its attendant values, then what, it might be asked, are we professing?

Questions like these became increasingly pressing during the 1980s, as the new cultural movement Fiedler had hailed began to be celebrated (and reviled) under the name "postmodernism." Postmodernism was theorized in a variety of ways, changing as quickly as literary and artistic fashion changed, but in general was held to have a positive attitude toward popular cultural forms, in contrast to high modernism's presumed revulsion from the popular. Many postmodern texts, for example, themselves played on (or with) the conventions of mysteries or science fiction or pornography. While continuing and even exaggerating some features of modernism, postmodernism was imagined to be somehow populist in contrast to modernism's presumed elitism. But the discussion was further complicated by the revolution in critical approach that the academy was undergoing during the same period. The New Critical consensus began to give way to a group of newly arrived European critical approaches which became known collectively as "theory." First structuralism and semiotics, then a variety of poststructuralist approaches variously and sometimes jointly inspired by Derrida, Foucault, Lacan, and Bakhtin, as well as the delayed inheritance of the Frankfurt School and theoretically sophisticated neo-Marxists such as Louis Althusser, became increasingly influential through the end of the millennium. None of these approaches respected the old designation of the "literary" as a privileged category, and none particularly respected the set of values designated by the term "humanism." The newer critics worked on "texts," and began with the assumption that the author was in some sense dead: no text was any longer marked by the "aura" and the authority of the literary genius. Instead, all texts were in some way produced by the culture as a whole, and participated in a myriad shifting "discourses" none of which could be tracked back to an originating and authenticating voice or selfhood.

The first major work on Joyce and popular culture to reflect some of these assumptions was Cheryl Herr's groundbreaking study *Joyce's Anatomy of Culture* (1986). Herr's study demanded attention from Joyceans of all critical persuasions in the first place simply because of the mass of original archival research behind her writing. Still, there was considerable resistance to the book among more traditional critics because of her theoretical approach, which paid little attention to Joyce as an individual and far more to the participation of his writing in a wealth of public discourses. As Herr announces (1986: 11), "what has often led to discussion of individuality and selfhood may lead instead to consideration of the institutions and discursive forms constituting cultural experience." Thus Herr's work formed part of the new wave of Joyce studies initiated by critics such as Margot Norris, Karen Lawrence, and Colin MacCabe, although it differed from them – and led more immediately toward our current critical preoccupations – in directing attention away from the pure play of language and toward the historical and cultural surroundings of Joyce.

Herr's tactic was to investigate three major institutions of popular culture in Ireland: the press, the theater (especially the "panto" or pantomime and the music hall that were beloved by the working class, not to mention T. S. Eliot), and the clergy. Indeed, her book alternates between general discussions of each of these institutions and analyses of specific passages in Joyce's writings that allude to them. Herr's critical orientation is Marxist-semiotic, taking inspiration from the Tartu – Moscow group of semioticians that included Juri Lotman and Boris Uspenski, as well as from Umberto Eco, Terry Eagleton, and Fredric Jameson. The stage, the pulpit, and the press are only three areas of ideological play, but they help to determine the *Weltanschauung* of all Joyce's characters, even as they allow us entrance into the popular cultural matrix of Dublin around the turn of the century. One of Herr's presuppositions (1986: 4) is that "the daily newspaper, the popular play, and the sermon are [. . .] signs for the institutions whose ideological practices they embody and articulate." As she demonstrates, Joyce's frequent allusions to them in his work are far more than documentary local color or the product of an encyclopedic mind neurotically driven to reproduce all the particulars of his hometown, Dublin. Instead, they point to the cultural dynamics by which dominant institutions competed for discursive power over the demotic mind.

There is a major theme to the discussion in each section of *Joyce's Anatomy of Culture*: for the press it is censorship, for the stage dramatic transvestitism or "cross-dressing," and for the sermon it is the conflict between economic realities and the church's portrayal of the social order. Probably the most intriguing and influential section of the book is that dealing with the theater. Herr points to the apparent paradox that during a historical period when sexual ambiguity or impersonation was least tolerated in Anglo-Irish society as a whole, as the Wilde trial demonstrated, dramatic transvestitism flourished on the stage. Especially in the pantomime and music hall, beloved male performers appeared as female transvestites, just as well-known actresses impersonated males. Herr argues that the underlying function of the popular stage was to parade cultural anxieties about the essential nature of sexual difference, a difference that formed part of a series of class oppositions whose effect was to validate or legitimate oppression. Herr argues convincingly that the phantasmagoria of the "Circe" section of *Ulysses*, with its endless transformations and sexual impersonations, is one extended formal allusion to the pantomime. "Circe" destabilizes any essentialist notions of gender, she claims, not merely in Bloom's case but for all the characters. In fact, Herr sees Joyce's work as an assault upon the traditional notion of character, and an assertion that selves are cultural scripts, constantly written and rewritten in a complex palimpsest. And ironically, the implication is clear that the pantomime and music hall do much the same cultural work.

Herr followed up her interest in the popular stage with a significant anthology and critical study of turn-of-the-century Irish melodrama entitled *For the Land They Loved* (1991). The richness of Herr's historical investigations into the situation of the stage during this critical period has helped establish the cultural milieu within which Joyce was working. In a book that appeared in the same year, *Joyce, O'Casey, and the Irish Popular Theatre* (1991), Stephen Watt draws out further implications for our reading of Joyce from popular drama. Like most of the critics I discuss here, Watt endorses Jameson's call to reconceive the high culture/mass culture opposition "in such a way that the emphasis on evaluation to which it has traditionally given rise [. . .] is replaced by a genuinely historical and dialectical approach to these phenomena. Such an approach demands that we regard high and mass culture as objectively related and dialectically interdependent phenomena" (Jameson 1979: 133). Watt concentrates on the "New Woman" drama and its significance for Joyce, and in that respect he overlaps Richard Brown's important work in *James Joyce and Sexuality* (1985).

My own contribution to popular-culture studies, *Joyce, Bakhtin, and Popular Literature* (1989), complemented Herr's work in several ways. For one thing, my book focused on *Dubliners*, *A Portrait*, and the play *Exiles*, while much (though certainly not all) of Herr's book concentrated on *Ulysses* and *Finnegans Wake*. For another, my interest was primarily in popular literature, including familiar classics such as *The Count of Monte Cristo*, works of pornography such as *Eveline*, once-popular but now unknown novels such as Tom Greer's *A Modern Daedalus*, and even children's textbooks such as the Peter Parley series. Although in practice both Herr and I would at times perform similar ideological analyses on the popular works at hand, her overall approach was Marxist-semiotic, while mine was an attempt to adapt Bakhtin's criticism to Joyce. Thus my stress was upon ways in which Joyce's narratives entered into dialogical relationships with the popular literature of his time. I looked particularly carefully at books we know to have been in his library or which he discussed. At least some of my effort here was to recontextualize Joyce's writings, and a good deal of the new context toward which I pointed belonged to the nineteenth century. For instance, *A Portrait*, I felt, becomes a different book when it is seen among a group of well-known stories of public-school life, of which the most famous is *Tom Brown's Schooldays*. The dialogical relationship between the two is less obvious than at first might appear: whereas Joyce's book often plays ironically on the earlier work by reversing its apparent values, there are other occasions when the two books apparently endorse the same ideological position. Still, I was struck by the large number of occasions on which the popular works I examined seemed to be doing parallel cultural work to that of Joyce's literary productions.

The year before *Joyce, Bakhtin, and Popular Literature* appeared, a book was published only one of whose chapters deals with Joyce, but which has had a serious and growing influence on Joyce studies (as well as upon modernist studies in general). This was Jennifer Wicke's *Advertising Fictions: Literature, Advertisement, and Social Reading* (1988). Wicke argues that advertisement becomes fully constituted as a discourse (in Foucault's sense of the word) around the mid-nineteenth century, arising concurrently with the novel. The "dialectic between advertising and the novel reveals both how advertising was able to take on the status of a mass literature, enforcing its own codes of social reading, and how the novel relies on the conditions of advertising to permit it to become the major literary form" (Wicke 1988: 1). Wicke's book has separate chapters treating Dickens, James, and Joyce, as well as a chapter concentrating on P. T. Barnum that explores the role of advertising in nineteenth-century America. The chapter on *Ulysses* not only reviews the ubiquity of references to advertising in the book, but launches a radical argument that the situation of advertising, like Joyce's novel, has characteristics we often term "postmodern." Wicke (1988: 121) approaches advertising

> as typifying the modern condition of writing: it presages the "death of the human subject" of contemporary theory, produces the first intersubjectivity of reading and the formation of the subject in a uniquely historical and imagistic way, and offers a glimpse, however fallen, of the utopian powers of collective consciousness in a mass age.

Clearly, Joyce studies in the late 1980s participated in the general movement of critical attention toward cultural studies. Once advertising was seen as a fertile field of inquiry, Joyceans soon realized that it had always been a major subject of *Ulysses*. Jennifer Wicke and Garry Leonard co-edited a special issue of the *James Joyce Quarterly* (1993) on "Joyce and Advertising" that also included work by Michael Tratner, Mark Osteen, Ellen Carol Jones, Stephen Watt, Kevin Dettmar, Mary Lowe-Evans, and myself, displaying a remarkable variety of interests and approaches within the same general rubric. Lowe-Evans' *Crimes against Fecundity: Joyce and Population Control*, a study of the popular, scientific, and medical discourses surrounding that issue, had already dealt glancingly with popular culture. Watt and Dettmar's interest soon led to their editing a collection of essays on literary modernism that took a somewhat demystifying cultural-materialist approach. Garry Leonard, whose first book was a Lacanian reading of *Dubliners*, established himself as a leading exponent of popular culture study with his excellent *Advertising and Commodity Culture in Joyce* (1998). Tratner's book *Modernism and Mass Politics: Joyce, Woolf, Eliot, Yeats* (1995) touched only tangentially on popular culture, but in its treatment of mass politics and literature brought up most of the same issues. My own essay in this volume concentrated on the bodybuilder Eugen Sandow, and like most of my work since *Joyce, Bakhtin and Popular Literature* examined the culture portrayed in *Ulysses* rather than simply works of popular literature. In the light of work done since then, the Joyce and advertising issue demonstrated vividly how many different critical approaches and literary interests converged on the subject.

One area of popular-culture studies developed more or less independent of – or in parallel with – the movement I have been discussing, and that was the branch inspired by feminism. Because Joyce certainly recognized that the popular was generally coded as feminine we come upon his female characters surrounded by fashions, advertisements, books, and magazines explicitly addressed to them – and indeed in cases like Gerty MacDowell we find it difficult to disentangle the elements of her own consciousness from the restless brooding of the commercial culture of Irish womanhood. As early as 1978 Suzette Henke's study of Gerty dealt substantially with Maria Cummins' *The Lamplighter* and the other examples of commercial fiction that seem so important in shaping her views of the world. Since then there has been a steady stream of articles interrogating the implications for women of both the culture reflected in Joyce's work and Joyce's relationship with that culture. Even the articles specifically addressing the implications for feminism of the "Nausicaa" chapter would fill out a substantial anthology, with considerable dialogue among the participants, and of course Richard Pearce has in fact edited such an anthology of articles on "Penelope" (1994). Among many others, Margot Norris, Ellen Carol Jones, Shari Benstock, Kimberly Devlin, Bonnie Kime Scott, and Carol Loeb Shloss continued the pioneering work of Hélène Cixous, Marilyn French, and Florence Walzl. Of course, the concerns of feminist criticism are so broad that it inevitably overlaps related critical issues. For example, Carol Shloss and I edited a special issue of the *James Joyce Quarterly* entitled "ReOrienting Joyce," many of whose articles dealt with popular culture with a feminist slant, such as Shloss' essay on Western representations of the harem. This is hardly surprising, given the critical consensus that a fundamental feature of "orientalism" is the feminizing of the oriental Other. An excellent recent book that incorporates a great deal of archival research into popular culture with special relevance to the image of women is Katherine Mullin's *James Joyce, Sexuality and Social Purity* (2003). Some of Mullin's discoveries among popular magazines and newspapers demonstrate vividly how much we still have to learn from these sources that can seriously affect our reading of Joyce.

Meanwhile, during and after the late 1970s a great deal of work was being done investigating and establishing the details of Joyce's use of popular culture from a pragmatic rather than a theoretical viewpoint. Among the leading scholars in this regard is Mary Power, who is probably best known for her discovery of the "circus novel" by Amy Reade that Joyce called *Ruby, the Pride of the Ring* (1981). Other scholars who have made occasional but significant contributions include Joseph Heininger, Joseph Voelker, Daniel Schiff, Joseph Valente, Mark Osteen, and Coilín Owens. A treasury of popular culture is John Wyse Jackson and Bernard McGinley's *Dubliners: An Annotated Edition* (1995), which is full of period newspaper stories, advertisements, bits of street furniture, and period illustrations. Another good collection of images, far less scholarly but especially rich in photographs from the National Library, is Cyril Pearl's *Dublin in Bloomtime* (1969).

Aside from the publication of critical articles and books, one enterprise has been remarkably interesting and useful for Joyce scholars as a whole, and this is the "Documentary In-Sights" project begun around 1980 by Kathleen Rabl, under the supervision of Fritz Senn at the Zurich Joyce Foundation. Following a suggestion of

Hans Walter Gabler, Rabl began collecting items of material culture from Joyce's time that might bear interestingly on Joyce's work, items usually originating in Dublin, though more recently some coming from Trieste as well. The collection includes both period and modern photographs, slides, and CDs, pictures, postcards, books, pamphlets, journals, advertisements, programs, objects (such as a ceramic container for Plumtree's Potted Meat), articles of clothing, films, musical and spoken tapes and CDs, and more. The Documentary In-Sights Group has organized exhibitions at various locations. Among the most successful was "Le Donne di Giacomo," a Triestine exhibition organized by Erik Schneider and Simonette Chiabrando with the support of John McCourt and Kathleen Rabl. In addition to foundation staff, many Joyceans have contributed to the Documentary In-Sights project, including Schneider, Mary Power, Terrence Killeen, Peter de Voogd, Onno Kosters, and Marlene Corcoran. The material at the foundation is freely available for study by scholars, and will no doubt spark popular-culture studies for years to come.

Joyce and Music

Music can be an aspect of popular culture, but of course it need not be; it runs the cultural gamut from low to high, and one century's middlebrow music (much of opera in the nineteenth century) may well become the following century's highbrow entertainment. Joyce's rather traditional musical tastes disturbed many of the same people who were appalled to find this ultimate literary rebel living the life of the *haute bourgeoisie* in Paris. Be that as it may, Joyce is an author generally beloved of musical readers. He interlards his fiction with references to popular and music-hall songs, poems set to music, liturgical music, art songs, madrigals, cantatas, arias, and *lieder*, as well as folksongs, nursery rhymes, obscene ditties, and advertising jingles – virtually anything that could be sung; he was, after all, a concert-quality tenor capable of accompanying himself on piano or guitar, and his affection for music is obvious in his writings. A song in his work may be as obviously important thematically as "The Lass of Aughrim," which Gretta hears sung in "The Dead" and which sets her thinking of Michael Furey, or it may be as incidental as the vulgar rhyme Buck Mulligan belts out to amuse or offend his friends in "Telemachus."

But whatever their importance, songs are certainly ubiquitous: according to Zack Bowen, in *Ulysses* alone there are some 731 musical allusions (Bowen 1995: 24). Joyce is known for often writing "musical prose," whatever that may mean, and in the "Aeolus" chapter of *Ulysses* he announced his intention of creating the equivalent in prose to a musical composition – specifically a *fuga per canonem*, if we are to believe the "schema" he gave Stuart Gilbert – and this has finally brought him a small entry in the *Grove Dictionary of Music and Musicians*. Since Bloom's wife is a singer and middle-class Dublin a musical community, music arises as an explicit subject frequently in *Ulysses*, and almost constantly in the "Sirens" chapter. So there is no lack of subject matter here. The problem is that as soon as we set two distinct artistic modes against one another, we can only compare them or discuss their interaction in metaphoric and often vague terms. And this leads to considerable disagreement among critics about major matters. For example, while Stuart Gilbert insisted that "Sirens" was indeed a technical fugue with invariant, congruent repetitions of theme, Zack Bowen argues very persuasively that this simply does not describe Joyce's technique, no matter what we take to be his "theme" (Bowen 1995: 25–6).

As is the case with popular culture, much pioneering work in the identification of allusions was done by Adaline Glasheen in her multiple censuses of *Finnegans Wake* (1977) and Weldon Thornton in his *Allusions in "Ulysses"* (1968). But while song in Joyce's writing was the object of critical study almost from the beginning, the first substantial work on the subject was Matthew Hodgart and Mabel Worthington's groundbreaking volume *Song in the Works of James Joyce* (1959). Hodgart and Worthington pay special attention to the *Wake*, which is of course a treasure-trove of musical allusion, and were clearly well in advance of their time critically in asserting that "one of the most useful aids to reading *Finnegans Wake* is a grasp of modern popular culture, such as the press, advertisements, radio, low jokes, and most of all songs" (Hodgart and Worthington 1959: 40). The majority of the book is a simple identificatory listing of music references in Joyce's works from *Dubliners* and *Stephen Hero* through the *Wake*, with the great majority of the listings from *Ulysses* or the *Wake*. Hodgart and Worthington give page and line numbers for the songs, which are identified more completely in a listing near the end of the book. One introductory chapter deals with Joyce's sources. A second treats what are from a musical standpoint some of the more interesting passages from the *Wake*, and here the authors show how a knowledge of the songs allows for interpretation of passages that would otherwise be obscure.

It was a stroke of good fortune for Joyceans everywhere that among the graduate students working with Mabel Worthington while she was preparing this book was Zack Bowen. Bowen's mother had been a professional singer and had trained him with piano, organ, voice, and composition lessons. Although he had a fine tenor voice and performed professionally, Bowen was more attracted to academics. Under the influence of Worthington he discovered that he already possessed a great deal of musical lore that he could tap in the service of Joyce studies. As he continued to work in this vein he discovered that some of the thousands of allusions Hodgart and Worthington claimed were dubious, while there were still hundreds of others that had not been identified. Bowen and Worthington decided to divide their interests; Bowen's first major work was *Musical Allusions in the Works of James Joyce: Early Poetry through "Ulysses"* (1974), while Worthington did not live to complete her work on *Finnegans Wake*. Meanwhile, starting while he was still in graduate school, Bowen supervised the production of a series of record albums. These featured dramatic readings and musical performances of chapters from *Ulysses: Lestrygonians* (1961), *Calypso* (1963), *Lotus Eaters* (1964), *Hades* (1964), and *Sirens* (1966) were recorded by Folkways Records, now handled by the Smithsonian Institution.

Bowen's *Musical Allusions* was by a good margin the most sophisticated sustained treatment of music in Joyce to appear in its time. Although the book was in some respects a continuation of Hodgart and Worthington, Bowen pointed out (1974: 3) that where "they merely identified musical titles, I will attempt to fit the musical works to the text, to make them understandable as working, integrated elements in the works considered." Bowen does not simply look at the lyrics of a song for correspondences to Joyce's subject matter at that point in the book; he considers the implications of the particular version of the song, the style of its performance and accompaniment, and the emotional effect of the melody, its mood, dynamics, and pacing – what we might call the musical *gestalt*. Of course, Bowen is necessarily selective in the musical instances to which he devotes substantial attention. Indeed, since the publication of that book he has written a great deal more in the same area, much of which is collected in *Bloom's Old Sweet Song: Essays on Joyce and Music* (1995). At times, he has revisited passages he treated earlier and discovered an entire overlay of new meaning. In analyzing Joyce's use of music in *Ulysses*, Bowen distinguishes (1995: 10–11) five functions: (1) as a vehicle of association in a character's stream of consciousness; (2) to represent thematically dramatic situations, such as the Molly – Blazes liaison, sometimes working as a Wagnerian *leitmotif* emphasizing or pointing to themes; (3) to underscore points in the narrative and lend them weight; (4) to help characterize or embroider upon the scenes and characters Bloom encounters; and (5) itself becoming a part of the plot.

An important book for students of Joyce's relation to music is Timothy Martin's *Joyce and Wagner* (1991). Less musically focused than Bowen's books, Martin treats not only Joyce's relation to Wagner as musician but to Wagner as thinker, and indeed to literary Wagnerism as a whole. Most of his book proceeds thematically, via *topoi* such as "the artist-hero," "the Wandering Jew," and "redemption"; the later chapters are more formal, covering "the comic rhythm" and "the art of arts" (dealing with music as subject). A 35-page appendix lists allusions to Wagner and his work in Joyce's writings. Other well-known musical Joyceans include Michael Gillespie, Kathleen McGrory, Ulrich Schneider, Henriette Power, Myra Russel, Margaret Rogers, Sebastian Knowles, and Ruth Bauerle, whose *James Joyce Songbook* (1982) is both a delight to amateur Joyceans and a scholarly achievement. Bauerle's collection *Picking Up Airs* (1993) includes essays by several of these figures, while Sebastian Knowles' edited collection *Bronze by Gold: The Music of Joyce* (1999) features a large group of lesser-known scholars. A recent book dealing with Joyce and music more on the level of ideas than as an allusion study is Jack Weaver's *Joyce's Music and Noise: Theme and Variation in His Writings* (1998). Weaver takes seriously Joyce's relation to modernist musicians such as Schoenberg and Stravinsky. He finds the structure of a five-part rondo in *Portrait* and argues that *Ulysses* has the form of a sonata. Weaver also develops a radical theory that Joyce at times meant to refer to key signatures (and thus particular emotional associations) through lone capital letters. Weaver's study emphasizes the fact that while Joyce's works themselves may allude preponderantly to traditional works of music, his writing as an example of formal innovation has far stronger connections to the avant-garde music of the twentieth century. This represents another aspect of scholarship on Joyce and music, one to which a variety of scholars have contributed for decades.

Glancing through a list of articles, books, and dissertations from the past five years on the subjects "Joyce" and "music," I am overwhelmed by the wealth of inquiry represented. Clearly the subject is not near exhaustion, and at least as many of the authors are just beginning their careers as are established scholars in the field. As Zack Bowen has pointed out, there is no doubt that many allusions remain to be identified, considering how many basic identifications have been the result of chance; like popular culture as a whole, popular music was not carefully documented. What was assumed at the time to be ephemeral was given little consideration by the official guardians of culture, but it was cherished by Joyce, perhaps just because it was so fleeting. And every time a scholarly convention of Joyceans closes with the group singing "Just a Song at Twilight," it seems clear that he was right.

BIBLIOGRAPHY

Adorno, Theodor (1975) "The culture industry reconsidered," *New German Critique*, 6 (Fall): 12–19. Cited here as in Patrick Brantlinger (1983) *Bread and Circuses: Theories of Mass Culture as Social Decay*. Ithaca, NY: Cornell University Press, 235.

Barthes, Roland (1972) *Mythologies*, trans. Annette Lavers. New York: Hill and Wang.

Bauerle, Ruth (1982) *The James Joyce Songbook*. New York: Garland Press.

Bauerle, Ruth (ed.) (1993) *Picking up Airs: Hearing the Music in Joyce's Text*. Urbana: University of Illinois Press.

Bowen, Zack (1974) *Musical Allusions in the Works of James Joyce: Early Poetry through "Ulysses."* Albany: State University of New York Press.

Bowen, Zack (1995) *Bloom's Old Sweet Song: Essays on Joyce and Music*. Gainesville: University Press of Florida.

Brantlinger, Patrick (1983) *Bread and Circuses: Theories of Mass Culture as Social Decay*. Ithaca, NY: Cornell University Press.

Brown, Richard (1985) *James Joyce and Sexuality*. Cambridge: Cambridge University Press.

Collins, Jim (1989) *Uncommon Cultures: Popular Culture and Post-Modernism*. New York: Routledge.

Eagleton, Terry (1983) *Literary Theory: An Introduction*. Minneapolis: University of Minnesota Press.

Eco, Umberto (1979) *The Role of the Reader: Explorations in the Semiotics of Texts*. Bloomington: University of Indiana Press.

Eliot, T. S. (1923) "*Ulysses*, order, and myth," *Dial* 75: 480–3; reprinted in Richard Ellmann and Charles Feidelson Jr. (eds.) (1965) *The Modern Tradition*, pp. 679–81. New York: Oxford University Press.

Ellmann, Richard and Charles Feidelson Jr. (eds.) (1965) *The Modern Tradition*. New York: Oxford University Press.

Fiedler, Leslie (1957) "The middle against both ends." In Bernard Rosenberg and David M. White (eds.) *Mass Culture: The Popular Arts in America*, pp. 537–47. Glencoe, IL: Free Press.

Fiedler, Leslie (1970) "Bloom on Joyce; or, Jokey for Jacob," *Journal of Modern Literature* 1: 19–29.

Fiedler, Leslie (1984) "To whom does Joyce belong? *Ulysses* as parody, pop and porn." In Heyward Ehrlich (ed.) *Light Rays: James Joyce and Modernism*, pp. 26–30. New York: New Horizon Press.

Friedrich, Gerhard (1954) "Bret Harte as a source for James Joyce's 'The Dead,'" *Philological Quarterly* 33: 442–4.

Glasheen, Adaline (1977) *Third Census of "Finnegans Wake": An Index of the Characters and Their Roles*. Berkeley: University of California Press.

Henke, Suzette (1978) "'Nausicaa': romantic fantasy/'Oxen of the Sun': procreative reality." In her *Joyce's Moraculous Sindbook: A Study of "Ulysses*," pp. 153–69. Columbus: Ohio State University Press..

Herr, Cheryl (1986) *Joyce's Anatomy of Culture*. Urbana: University of Illinois Press.

Herr, Cheryl (ed.) (1991) *For the Land They Loved:*

Irish Political Melodramas, 1890–1925. Syracuse, NY: Syracuse University Press.

Hodgart, Matthew J. C. and Mabel P. Worthington (1959) *Song in the Works of James Joyce*. New York: Columbia University Press.

Hoggart, Richard (1957) *The Uses of Literacy: Changing Patterns in English Mass Culture*. London: Chatto and Windus.

Huyssen, Andreas (1986) *After the Great Divide: Modernism, Mass Culture, Postmodernism*. Bloomington: Indiana University Press.

Jackson, John Wyse and Bernard McGinley (1995) *James Joyce's Dubliners: An Annotated Edition*. London: Sinclair-Stevenson.

Jameson, Fredric (1979) "Reification and utopia in mass culture," *Social Text* 1 (Winter): 130–48.

Kershner, R. Brandon (1971) "Novels of James Joyce and Raymond Queneau" dissertation, Stanford University.

Kershner, R. Brandon (1989) *Joyce, Bakhtin, and Popular Literature: Chronicles of Disorder*. Chapel Hill: University of North Carolina.

Knowles, Sebastian (ed.) (1999) *Bronze by Gold: The Music of Joyce*. New York: Garland Press.

Lawrence, Karen (1981) *The Odyssey of Style in* Ulysses. Princeton, NJ: Princeton University Press.

Leavis, F. R. (1948) *The Great Tradition: George Eliot, Henry James, Joseph Conrad*. London: Chatto and Windus.

Leavis, Q. D. (1932) *Fiction and the Reading Public*. London: Chatto and Windus.

Leonard, Garry (1998) *Advertising and Commodity Culture in Joyce*. Gainesville: University Press of Florida.

Leonard, Garry and Jennifer Wicke (eds.) (1993) Special issue, "Joyce and Advertising,"*James Joyce Quarterly* 30 (4)/31 (1).

Lowe-Evans, Mary (1989) *Crimes against Fecundity: Joyce and Population Control*. Syracuse, NY: Syracuse University Press.

MacCabe, Colin (1978) *James Joyce and the Revolution of the Word*. London: Macmillan.

McLuhan, Marshall (1964) *Understanding Media: The Extensions of Man*. New York: McGraw-Hill.

Magalaner, Marvin (1972) "James Joyce and Marie Corelli." In Raymond J. Porter and James D. Brophy (eds.) *Modern Irish Literature: Essays in Honor of William York Tindall*, pp. 185–93. New York: Iona College Press and Twayne.

Martin, Timothy (1991) *Joyce and Wagner: A Study of Influence*. Cambridge: Cambridge University Press.

Norris, Margot (1976) *The Decentered Universe of Finnegans Wake: A Structuralist Analysis*. Baltimore, MD: Johns Hopkins University Press.

Pearce, Richard (ed.) (1994) *Molly Blooms: A Polylogue on "Penelope" and Cultural Studies*. Madison: University of Wisconsin Press.

Pearl, Cyril (1969) *Dublin in Bloomtime: The City James Joyce Knew*. London: Angus and Robertson.

Power, Mary (1981) "The discovery of Ruby," *James Joyce Quarterly* 18 (2, Winter): 115–21.

Ross, Andrew (1989) *No Respect: Intellectuals and Popular Culture*. New York: Routledge.

Seldes, Gilbert (1962 [1924]) *The Seven Lively Arts*. New York: A. S. Barnes.

Thornton, Weldon (1968) *Allusions in "Ulysses": An Annotated List*. Chapel Hill: University of North Carolina Press.

Tratner, Michael (1995) *Modernism and Mass Politics: Joyce, Woolf, Eliot, Yeats*. Stanford, CA: Stanford University Press.

Watt, Stephen (1991) *Joyce, O'Casey, and the Irish Popular Theatre*. Syracuse, NY: Syracuse University Press.

Weaver, Jack (1998) *Joyce's Music and Noise: Theme and Variation in His Writings*. Gainesville: University Press of Florida.

Whannel, Paddy and Stuart Hall (1964) *The Popular Arts*. London: Hutchinson.

Wicke, Jennifer (1988) *Advertising Fictions: Literature, Advertisement, and Social Reading*. New York: Columbia University Press.

Williams, Raymond (1958) *Culture and Society, 1780–1950*. New York: Harper and Row.

Williams, Raymond (1961) *The Long Revolution*. New York: Columbia University Press.

18

The Joyce of Manuscripts

Daniel Ferrer

Since the beginning of the twenty-first century, the Joycean world has been in a state of excitement: a number of unknown original documents have surfaced unexpectedly one after the other. In less than six years, close to a thousand pages of mostly very important manuscripts have come on the market. What, we might ask, is the excitement all about? What difference does this make when we already have at our disposal all the documents reproduced in the two beautiful volumes of color facsimile of the Rosenbach *Ulysses* manuscript and the 63 large volumes of facsimiles of the *James Joyce Archive* (11 volumes for the early works, 16 volumes for *Ulysses*, 36 volumes for *Finnegans Wake*, including the 16 volumes representing the 14,000 pages of the Buffalo notebooks)?

Confronted with this overwhelming bulk, we might even be tempted to ask a more basic question. Why should we waste our time studying Joyce's manuscripts? We sometimes feel that his books are already more than we can handle. Why should we burden ourselves with the additional tasks of deciphering his often almost unreadable handwriting, charting the maze of his proliferating archive and making sense of the maelstrom of his drafts?

One obvious answer is that if we were afraid of difficulty, if we were not somehow attracted by difficulty, we would not be reading Joyce at all. I once wrote that the point of studying the drafts of *Finnegans Wake* was not that they would solve the obscurities of the book, but on the contrary that they provided us with an inexhaustible store of supplementary obscurity. This was probably going too far: we have to acknowledge that manuscripts do help us to answer many questions, but at the same time they open up many more enigmas, revealing hidden dimensions of Joyce's works, and more generally of his *work*.

Books or Manuscripts?

First of all it should be noted that some of the books currently accepted in the Joyce canon are actually manuscripts, rather than works. Readers of the trade editions should remember that *Epiphanies*, *Stephen Hero*, and *Giacomo Joyce* were never published by Joyce: as far as he was concerned, they never went beyond the stage of manuscripts. Competent editors have made books out of these manuscripts, and we can read them, to a certain extent, as if they were self-contained literary works, but there is something artificial in the exercise. *Stephen Hero* in particular is so conspicuously unfinished, it is so clearly related to the genesis of *A Portrait of the Artist as a Young Man*, that it is difficult to consider that it has an autonomous existence. We spontaneously tend to read it genetically, both as an abortive version of the later novel and as a source of biographic data that help us understand the mind that created the subsequent masterpieces. At the same time we feel that this way of reading does not do justice to an interesting original writing project, but we cannot help the fact that this project was never brought to completion and was superseded by a new project that eventually produced *A Portrait*.

A few years ago, one of the best experts on Joyce's manuscripts, Danis Rose, expressed his intention to publish a new book, called *Finn's Hotel*, made of the sketches that Joyce wrote in 1923 ("Roderick O'Connor," "St. Kevin," "St. Patrick," "Tristan and Isolde," "Mamalujo," and so on) and later incorporated into *Finnegans Wake*. Rose was never allowed to proceed with what would have been a stimulating if scientifically questionable experiment. Joyce's writing projects at the time, as far as we can know them, seem to have been quite vague and it is dubious that Joyce ever intended to publish these sketches in a collection, as a kind of late counterpart to *Dubliners*. If he had chosen to publish them, it is probable that he would have added to their number and it is certain that he would have elaborated them beyond the state represented by the 1923 manuscripts. Such a book could only be an editorial artifact, constructed on a very shaky basis, but it would act as a useful reminder that the *Wake* was not all ready in Joyce's head when he started writing, that it only gradually took shape along the 16 years of strenuous work. On the other hand it could be misleading to hypostatize in the form of a book what must have been at most a very transitory intention in the course of the long evolution of the project that came to be known as "Work in Progress" and later resulted in the publication of *Finnegans Wake*.

Repairing the Text?

Publishing a manuscript as an autonomous work (as opposed to simply editing it as a manuscript) is the dream of many editors, as it is a rewarding experience in many respects, but it is not something that can (or should) often be done. Until the moment of final publication, a manuscript is not a work of art, but an instrument towards the elaboration of a projected work, not a literary text but a protocol for the fabrication of a text. Therefore, its most important feature is not its textual content but the direction(s) it indicates. Of course, if the final text is absent, or incomplete, we are glad to retrieve textual matter from the manuscript and to read it *as if* it was a text. On a similar basis, using manuscripts to improve the text of published works is a very common practice, sanctioned by a secular tradition. A whole branch of philology, known as "textual criticism," is devoted to establishing the best possible texts, usually by means of emendation of defective versions. In the case of works that antedate the modern period (biblical, classical or medieval), this can only be done by conjecture or by comparing different scribal copies. But when authorial manuscripts are available, they are considered the best expression of the author's intention and as such the ultimate recourse. Let us take a few examples from *Ulysses*.

In the first edition and in subsequent editions until 1984, the following sentence was to be found in the "Sirens" episode: "Miss Douce huffed and snorted down her nostrils that quivered imperthnthn like a shout in quest." The ending of this sentence is certainly puzzling, but we are used to being puzzled by the stylistic audacities of this episode. Readers certainly wondered what a "shout in quest" might be, but they took comfort from the fact that on the next line but one, Miss Douce is indeed "shouting." Or rather this is what they did before Hans Walter Gabler's edition showed that the last words should read: "imperthnthn like a snout in quest" (*U* 11 144–6). Looking at the typescript confirms that this is indeed what Joyce had written, but the compositor of the first galley proofs had misread an "n" for an "h" (the typed letters are not very well defined and his eyes may have been attracted by the "shouting" below). The new reading makes very good sense as it confirms that the sentence contains an echo of another passage, earlier in the episode: "Imperthnthn thnthnthn, bootssnout sniffed rudely" (*U* 11 100).[1] We might wonder whether the manuscript was really necessary in this case. The "snout/shout" substitution could have been conjectured by a good editor on the grounds that "shout in quest" is plainly absurd and that snout is called for by the echo of the earlier passage. But it is very dangerous to mend a text like this one on the basis of conjecture. This is what the proofreader of the 1926 edition tried to do in our next example, also from "Sirens." The first edition (1922) had this passage:

> — . . . . *ray of hope* . . . .
> Beaming. Lydia for Lidwell squeak scarcely hear so ladylike the muse unsqueaked a
> ray of hopk.

The 1926 edition, followed by all the subsequent ones until 1984, normalized the last word to "hope," on the assumption that "hopk" was a glaring typo. A look at the archive definitely confirms that it was "hopk" that Joyce wrote here and that the correction was indeed a corruption, but in order to understand what happened, we have to follow the development and radicalization of this segment.

The Dynamics of Invention

It all begins with two sentences inscribed in the margin of the second draft of the episode: "A ray of hope is beaming. Lydia for Lidwell unsqueaked a cork."[2] We can see that the first portmanteau in the sentence, "unsqueaked," expressive of the noise produced by the unscrewing of the cork, had already been coined at this early stage. On the fair copy,[3] Joyce changed this to

— . . . . ray of hope . . . .
Beaming. Lydia for Lidwell squeak scarcely hear so ladylike the muse unsqueaked a cork.

In this new context, "unsqueak" acquires a different meaning (a suppression or attenuation of the squeaking) and the pseudo-genteel affectation ("so ladylike the muse") actually draws our attention to the sexual connotations of the unscrewing noise. (*U* 15 1975; "Man and woman, love, what is it? A cork and bottle.") This version also emphasizes the interference between the song in the background and the narrative with the suppression of the word "beaming" from the italicized quotation and its integration in the authorial narration.

It was only on page proofs that Joyce all but replaced the material cork with an echo from the song in the preceding line, creating at the same time an onomatopoeic effect, imitative of the sound of the popping cork ("unsqueaked a ray of hopk"). This new portmanteau is much more disturbing than the first (hence the proofreader's feeling that it had to be a mistake), not a well-formed hybrid but a linguistic chimera. The final result is an amazingly rich sentence, counterpointing noises and music; spoken, sung or imagined voices; pretentious clichés and salacious innuendos. Thanks to the manuscripts we are able to follow the entry of the voices and the gradual densification of the polyphony.

Our next two examples, from "Circe," will confirm that the traditional project of textual criticism of using the manuscripts in order to *establish* the text is often an impossible task. On the contrary, a genetic investigation of the archives of writing tends to have a destabilizing effect on the text. In every edition until 1984, this was the beginning of the "Circe" episode:

(The Mabbot street entrance of nighttown, [. . .] Rows of flimsy houses with gaping doors. [. . .] Round Rabaiotti's halted ice gondola stunted men and women squabble. They grab wafers between which are wedged lumps of coal and copper snow [. . .].)

Gabler remarked that Joyce had actually written "grimy houses" instead of "flimsy houses" and "coral and copper snow" instead of "coal and copper snow": the typist had misread the very difficult handwriting of the fair copy and the corrupted words persisted in later versions. The 1984 edition (and all subsequent critically established editions) correct the mistakes and restore Joyce's original intention. They are probably right to do so – and yet some of us cannot help regretting the version of earlier editions. The flimsiness of the houses seemed particularly appropriate to the unreal atmosphere of the episode, suggesting the painted canvas of a stage setting. The grime is of course important too, but some of its associations are picked up and even reinforced by the coal color of the snow eaten by the dwarves in the same version. So the corrupted text could be considered to be, in some respects, superior to the version of the fair copy.[4] We cannot reject such considerations as purely subjective, as they may condition the way we interpret what happened after the fair-copy stage. We could wonder why Joyce never caught these mistakes on the typescript, the galley proofs, or any of the page proofs. There can be no question of flagging attention as this is the first paragraph of the episode. Joyce did look carefully, as he added a word and changed some punctuation. Could he have endorsed the changes, consciously or unconsciously? We can never answer such a question with any certainty. Eugene Jolas, who often worked with Joyce on the proofs of *Finnegans Wake*, confirms that it was not unusual for him to do so.[5] (The French translation cannot help us in this case: the translators did not find anything the matter with this version so they had no cause to ask Joyce.) An editor, however, has to make a decision. There is on the one hand the certainty that, up to the fair copy, Joyce intended to have "grimy" and "coral," and on the other the possibility that Joyce changed his mind, inspired by the mistake, and the fact that all the (numerous) subsequent changes in the episode were made in the context of a first paragraph that included the words "flimsy" and "coal."

Changes of intention are an editor's nightmare, as they often result in contradictions and dilemmas. On the contrary, they are the very substance of genetic criticism. The difference of perspective is particularly clear in the case of an addition to the proofs of "Circe" that did not make it into the published text and yet sounds strangely familiar to the reader of *Ulysses*. Towards the end of the messianic scene (*U* 15 1913), Joyce had intended to insert the following:

> Don Emile Patrizio Franz Rupert Pope Hennessy (in medieval hauberk, two wild geese volant on his helm, appears and, with noble indignation, disowns Bloom) Put down your eyes to footboden, big grand pig of Jude all covered with gravy! (Buffalo V.C.5b, *JJA* 26 175)

This genetically fascinating passage represents a culmination of Joyce's expansive creative energies. It has often been said that Joyce's mode of writing is mostly accretive: he adds much more than he deletes. After all, *Ulysses* was first conceived as a short story and progressively became the huge novel that we know. The expansive process was at its height in 1921 and it is particularly in evidence in the messianic scene of "Circe." By way of additions on manuscript and typescript, and several pullings of galley and page proofs, Joyce transformed two lines of dialogue into a 20-page scene. There is no way of knowing if this would ever have stopped or how much bigger *Ulysses* could have grown if Joyce had not set himself a final deadline: he wanted his novel to be published for his 40th birthday on February 2, 1922. By mid-December 1921 there was still half of "Circe" and most of the three last chapters to finalize, so it was necessary to make an end to this passage: Joyce sent Darantière, his French printer, the signed *bon à tirer*, the passed-for-press form authorizing its final printing. A week later, however, he sent him a duplicate of the last set of proofs with new additions (including the Don Patrizio passage) and, on top of the first page, the mention "Corrections supplémentaires si encore possibles James Joyce" ("Supplementary corrections if still possible James Joyce"). This sentence is important in several respects. It illustrates Joyce's creative energy, the intensity of his will to write, of his desire to improve his work, to go on *supplementing* until the last moment (actually beyond the last moment),[6] to keep open the *possibilities* of writing and to postpone the closure inherent to the written text as a finished product. It is almost as if he had signed the death sentence of his own work as a living creation and was now begging for a reprieve. But the indication is also fascinating because of its conditionality. It shows that a writer's purpose is not an absolute, but a fluctuating, time-bound transaction between a series of writing events and a series of external constraints: the text of a work cannot be defined with any certainty by the fiction of a unified authorial intention.

The further adventures of this passage prove it even better. As was to be expected, the supplementary proofs arrived too late and were never used by Darantière. Joyce was understandably reluctant to waste the amusing apparition of this composite figure of the Irish exiles. He therefore incorporated it, with a few variations, in the set of proofs for the end of the same chapter that he had at hand at the moment (*JJA* 26 316). The editorial problem raised by this writing event has no really satisfactory solution. The 1984 edition, answering Joyce's fervent prayer, incorporated the addition where he had wanted it to go, in the messianic scene (*U* 15 1914–17). But this reinsertion created an interesting but unintended echo with the very similar passage at the end of the chapter (*U* 15 4506–9). The 1986 edition (and all subsequent editions) wisely considered that the mid-January 1922 insertion canceled the indication on the mid-December 1921 proofs so that only the second passage was kept (*U* 15 4506–9). Another, drastic, solution would have been to reinstate the passage in the "Messianic Scene" and to excise the other one, on the grounds that it was only inserted at the end of the chapter as a second-best choice. This would not be a worse compromise than the other solutions, except that we would loose the changes introduced in the second incarnation of the piece.

This is how it was finally incorporated:

DON EMILE PATRIZIO FRANZ RUPERT POPE HENNESSY (*in medieval hauberk, two wild geese volant on his helm, with noble indignation points a mailed hand against the privates*) Werf those eykes to footboden, big grand porcos of johnyellows todos covered of gravy!

Some of the changes ("points a mailed hand against the privates" instead of "disowns Bloom," "johnyellows" instead of "Jude") are directly related to the new location: this archetypal incarnation of the Irish wild geese, who was adding his own very idiosyncratic voice to the general reprobation of Bloom at the end of the messianic scene, is now involved in the confrontation between Stephen and the British soldiers. The anti-Semitic outburst is thus converted, with the necessary adjustments, into anti-British insults. It is a process of interaction or transaction, for the contextual influence is reciprocal. The new environment is modified by the insertion of the element from the earlier background: the rather depressive end of the chapter acquires, through this insertion, something of the sheer exuberance characteristic of the messianic scene.

Retracing the genesis of a passage like this does not provide us with easy editorial solutions, but it is productive in different ways. It can affect our reading of the published text by strengthening some of our interpretations or helping us to develop new ones. For instance the fact that the Don Patrizio passage could be made to fit in two different contexts suggests an equivalence between those contexts, a similarity, also supported by the "Cyclops" episode, between Irish anti-British xenophobia and anti-Semitism. It draws a parallel between the ordeals of Bloom, excluded as a foreign element even by the arch-cosmopolitan Don Emile Patrizio Franz Rupert Pope Hennessy, and of Stephen, integrated by force in a community of hatred from which he cannot escape.

Apart from its value as an auxiliary for the interpretation of the text, the archive of writing reveals the dynamics of invention. The very fact that the insertion was suspended for a couple of weeks has induced an evolution. The passage is rewritten in accordance with a new temporal context (as opposed to the change of spatial context we have just described), reflecting at least a slight change of intention and perhaps even a stylistic evolution. The language of the cosmopolitan exile becomes even more international ("Werf those eykes to footboden," "big grand porcos") and seems to have moved one step forward towards *Finnegans Wake*.

Multiple Contextuality

By studying the traces of writing we are able to identify micro-contexts such as those defined by the one-week interval between the signing of the passed-for-press form and the change of mind that prompted new additions, or the four-week interval between the two versions of the insertion (or even the few moments that separate the writing of a word and its crossing out). We can then observe interferences between those micro-contexts and relate them to the macro-context of the general evolution of Joyce's work ("a book that in some aspects began as a sequel to *A Portrait of the Artist as a Young Man* ended as a prelude to *Finnegans Wake*"; Groden 1977: 13) as well as to the circumstances of Joyce's biography and the general political events of the time. There is, however, a very important intermediary contextual level represented by the sharply distinct phases of writing characteristic of *Ulysses*.

Any work of art bears the scars of the process of its making, but these scars are usually almost invisible on the smooth surface of the finished product. In the case of *Ulysses*, they are quite plain: anyone can see that there is very little in common between, for instance, the "Telemachus" and "Calypso" episodes and "Cyclops" or "Ithaca." The difference is so great that it can only be explained by radical changes in the writing project and any interpretation of the book that does not take into account the temporal dimension of its production is bound to run up against insurmountable difficulties. Michael Groden has shown decisively that *Ulysses* as we know it is the result of the layering (layering, not juxtaposition) of three large temporal contexts, corresponding to what he calls the early, middle and last stages (Groden 1977: 13). The early phase corresponds to what Joyce himself called the "initial style," a mixture, in various proportions, of monologues and third-person narration. The recent manuscript discoveries suggest that this phase was itself probably more complex than we imagined and that the "initial style" was actually the result of an evolution that took place around the year 1917. The middle stage represents a shift away from realism and an emphasis on parodies and stylistic pyrotechnics. The late stage exacerbates some of the earlier tendencies towards symbolism and schematism and the book seems to fold upon itself and to feed upon its own substance.

Although the three styles correspond primarily to the early, middle, and last chapters of the book, they are not merely juxtaposed in a linear sequence. Not only were the later chapters composed in continuity with the early ones – the inertia of what is already written is a condition of any writing – but one of the major aspects of the late style of *Ulysses* is precisely the rewriting of previous episodes: this is something that any reader of "Circe" will notice and that can also be detected in "Ithaca" and even in "Penelope." Studying the history of composition allows us to specify this process and to understand it as bidirectional. Because of the publication deadline, the printing schedule had been arranged in such a way that Joyce was writing the last episodes at the same time as he was correcting the proofs of the earlier ones. As a consequence, the (extensive) correction of the proofs for "Telemachus," "Nestor," "Proteus," "Calypso," and "Lotus Eaters" belong to the chronological context of the writing of "Ithaca" and "Penelope." This means that the early episodes, some of which had been drafted many years before, were actively present on Joyce's writing table as the end of the book was being written, but also that the revisions of the first part were introduced from the perspective of the late style. We can see also that during a single week of October 1921 Joyce marked proof for "Lotus Eaters," "Hades," "Aeolus," "Lestrygonians," "Scylla and Charybdis," "Wandering Rocks" and "Sirens": all the modifications entered at this moment in this wide array of episodes should be studied in the context of each other.

The counterpart of this temporal contextualization of spatially dispersed passages is the superimposition of temporal layers in a single location. We have seen an illustration of this with the "ray of hopk" passage of "Sirens," with its alterations reflecting a progressively radicalized treatment of language: the layers of revision coexist, as it were, in a single compound word (another anticipation of *Finnegans Wake*). On a larger scale, the "Aeolus" episode, originally perfectly representative of the initial style, bears the visible traces of its revision in the context of the late style: Joyce did not alter deeply the texture of the episode, but completely changed its external form by injecting the startling newspaper headlines in accordance with the radical modernist aesthetics of the later chapters.

Along the 16 years of the writing of *Finnegans Wake*, major inflections modified the original project, but the more drastic changes were structural reorganizations and the stylistic alterations were much more gradual, so that we cannot assign major "styles" as convincingly as we do in *Ulysses*, and given the nature of the published book it is not so easy to detect in it the traces of the process of evolution. However, if we take a bird's-eye view of the genesis of two of the more accessible passages in the book, the "Anna Livia Plurabelle" chapter (I.8) and the soliloquy of Anna Livia at the end of the book, we can make a few useful general remarks. "Anna Livia Plurabelle" was first drafted in 1924 and was revised at least 17 times during 14 years.[7] The main characteristics of the very first draft are still visible in the final text: the oral quality of the exchange between the two washerwomen, the fluidity of the rhythm, the humor. But many other features were added by the successive revisions, reflecting different visions of the work as it took shape between 1924 and 1928. The multi-lingual aspect, absent in the first layer, was introduced at different stages, beginning with an introduction of Scandinavian elements and northern dialects. The number of colloquialisms was then increased and the sound patterns were made more complex. But the most conspicuous feature is the addition of river names: for instance "Go on, go on," is replaced by "Garonne, Garonne" (*FW* 205 25). This began with a few scattered allusions, but became a major preoccupation of Joyce, who, for years, harvested hundreds of river names in his notebooks in order to weave them into his sentences. Most of these names are unknown to the majority of readers, so that the allusions cannot be detected without the help of a comprehensive encyclopedia or, even better, of Joyce's notebooks. It has often been pointed out that these elusive allusions obscure the original meaning of the sentences. Obviously, direct accessibility had ceased to be a concern. On the other hand, the final soliloquy (*FW* 619–28) was drafted, copied, typed five times and further revised on galley proofs within a few months at the end of 1938. In the process, the passage was considerably expanded – the two last short sentences ("I only hope the heavens sees us. Abit beside the bush and then a walk along the") were expanded to 87 lines in the printed book (*FW* 625 36–628 16) – but no spectacular change of direction is taken in this last and concentrated bout of writing, only a development and a progressive intensification. By this time, the stylistic evolution of *Finnegans Wake* had run its full course. We can even detect a certain *regression* towards a greater transparency, due perhaps to the fact that the final monologue of Anna Livia was a paradigmatic equivalent of Molly Bloom's soliloquy, so that the finishing of one book brought memories of the completion of another and the end of *Ulysses* formed a context for the ending of the *Wake*.

Over-Determination: A Genetic Aporia

The layering of successive levels of intentionality can be observed in any work that is produced in time (that is to say, everywhere except perhaps in very short extemporizations), but it is particularly accessible to a genetic approach within the framework of Joyce's aesthetics of saturation (as opposed, for instance, to an aesthetic model based on deprivation, like Beckett's). In Joyce, meanings pile up without canceling one another on the model of the portmanteau word (the "ray of hope" does not obliterate the underlying "cork," "go on" is still narratively and rhythmically perceptible beneath the surface of "Garonne"). Using the manuscripts to follow successive stages of writing produces an effect of ex-plication, a gradual unfolding of the packed riches. And yet it poses specific difficulties, linked with the paradoxes of the notion of over-determination. The multiplication of levels in a work like *Ulysses* implies that each element is heavily overdetermined: it is determined by its narrative import, by its various meanings, literal and symbolic, by its intertextual references, and by the tight web of symmetries and echoes that binds it to other parts of the book. It is impossible, however, logically and empirically, that these multiple levels should have been conceived at the same time. We hardly need the confirmation of the manuscripts to know that the infinitely complex structures of *Ulysses* and *Finnegans Wake* cannot have sprung fully armed from Joyce's brains (although Joyce managed to persuade some of his admirers that this had been the case). This implies that the majority of the determinations were discovered retrospectively rather than projected, so that they paradoxically reflect a basic indeterminacy. An open attitude towards the potentialities of writing is required on the part of the critic (reflecting Joyce's own disposition) to interpret genetically the mechanics of meaning.

Our first example, admittedly an exceptional one, takes us back to the late "Circe" proofs. In the Black Mass scene, just before the intervention of Adonai calling "Gooooooooooood!", Joyce made the following insertion:

The voice of all the blessed
Alleluia, for the Lord God Omnipotent reigneth!

(JJA 26 305)

What happened afterwards demonstrates in the most graphic way the inertia of the signifier and the dynamics of writing. Because of the poor quality of the paper on which the proofs were printed, Joyce's corrections, marked in ink, seeped through the page, so that they are clearly readable, in inverted mirror form, on the verso (*JJA* 26 306). This material accident, in the immediate context of the Black Mass (traditionally supposed to be celebrated as a literal inversion of the Holy Mass) suggested the inversion of the letters of the Alleluia and triggered the following expansion of the scene on the next proofs:

THE VOICE OF ALL THE DAMNED
Htengier Tnetopinmo Dog Drol eht rof, Aiulella!

(From on high the voice of Adonai calls)

ADONAI
Dooooooooooog!

(JJA 26 322–33)

The published version of the scene looks so integrated that it seems difficult to believe that its elements belong to different strata of writing and that its present form is the result of a material accident. Is it possible, for instance, that Adonai's "Goooooooooood" was not meant from the start to be an inverted echo of "Dooooooooooog"? Manuscripts show that the prolonged call was inscribed months before the writing accident.[8] This proves beyond any doubt that the canine echo, which is probably the most conspicuous element in the scene, is an afterthought, but this does not weaken the relationship established a posteriori between the two elements. Other retrospective links are automatically established with the Protean dog roaming the episode, with Bloom's "Dog of a Christian" addressed to the Man in the Macintosh during the messianic scene, with the mysterious answer (echo or dog whistle?) to Mulligan's call in the course of his initial blasphemous Mass, and so on.

The productivity of the accident does not stop there. A few days later, on another batch of proofs, Joyce added the words "from right to left" to the description of the apparition of Bloom's son Rudy reading a book. This links the inversion of letters to Hebrew script and connects the Black Mass to a network of pre-existent motifs such as the Kabbalah.

The potential for the diffusion of effects is even greater in *Finnegans Wake* as the next example demonstrates. It begins with a series of notes taken by Joyce in 1924 in notebook VI.B.14 about a particular feature of Celtic historical linguistics, the *p*/*k* (or *p*/*q*) split. It divides Celtic languages in two groups: Brythonic languages (such as Breton) admit the sound *p* where Goidelic languages (such as Irish) have the sound *k*. A consequence of this is pointed out in a note on page 218 of this notebook ("pascha I. casca/purpura Kurkura"), perplexing but clear enough when confronted with its source in a book by Stefan Czarnowski:[9]

> Dans les premiers temps les Irlandais remplaçaient le son *p* par *k* (écrit *c*) dans les mots empruntés, par exemple *purpura* devint *corcur*, *pascha – casc* [At first the Irish replaced the sound *p* by *k* (written as *c*) in words they had borrowed, for example *purpura* became *corcur*, *pascha – casc*] (Czarnowski 1919: 32 n. 2).

This national mispronunciation is a pattern of linguistic deformation that Joyce would exploit more than once in *Finnegans Wake*. But its meaning was enriched in the following year by another discovery. As Joyce was reading Freud's *Collected Papers*, he took note of an infantile phrase used by one of the young patients "do no 1" (from "Hans: 'Oh, I'll come up again in the morning to have breakfast and do number one,'" in "Analysis of a phobia in a five-year-old," Freud 1925: 160). Number one and number two are of course nursery euphemisms for urinating and defecating. This is taken up again further in the same notebook: "no 1 or no 2." Then, on top of the next page, we find the letters "pp or kk" followed by "keykey ahah." Passing from an English to a French version of the excremental functions (in French *pipi et caca* are precisely "number one and number two," with roughly similar childish connotations), Joyce starts playing with the sounds, relishing perhaps this coincidental historico-scatological homophony.

The game is continued on a page of a draft (47482a-23v, *JJA* 60 44) that is exactly contemporary with this notebook. Apparently, Joyce had written first:

> ~~earned~~ ^+forecast+^ by Cain, outflanked by Ham, reordered by Patrick, ~~delivered~~ ^+evaded+^ by Tristan, by Patrick's dear.[10]

He then takes up the Irish "kurkura" of notebook VI.B.14 to coin the amusing "kurkle katches," which gave him the key for a transformation of the passage, prompting a series of additions, substitutions, and overwritings:

^+kurkle katches+^ ~~forecast~~ by /C → K/ain, ~~outflanked~~ by /H → K/am, ~~reordered~~
^+inklored+^ by ~~Patrick~~ ^+Paw Kawdreg+^, ~~evaded~~ ysold by /T → K/ris/t → k/an
^+Kriskan+^, by ~~Patrick's dear~~, by Karnell ~~overagain~~.

The *p/k* substitution is at work on the name of Irish heroes (Partrick is transformed
into Kawdreg and, more surprisingly, Parnell into Karnell, with a hint of the carnal-
ity that caused his downfall), spreads to other words ("inklored," suggesting traditions
penned in ink), and seems to be getting out of hand, perhaps due to its newly discovered excremental connotation, with a surplus, an overflow of *k* (of *caca*), encroaching
over other letters (Kam and Kriskan!?).

Although this passage was never incorporated in *Finnegans Wake*, we find two occur-
rences of "kurkle" (*FW* 95 22 and 296 13). In the first appearance in particular ("Fine
feelplay we had of it mid the kissabetts frisking in the kool kurkle dusk of the lushi-
ness") the excremental connotation is clearly present (pissabed). But we should consider
that it is also present in each of the several instances of *p/k* inversion in *Finnegans Wake*.
Taking this a step further, we become aware that no *p* or *k* in the book remains unaffected: each *k* could be a *p* and a *k* may be hiding behind each *p* and in the shadow
of each of these letters lurks a marginal allusion to Celtic philology and to infantile
scatology.

Of course Joyce did not write every *p* and every *k* with this association in mind, but
this is not the point. Joyce knew that the signifying engine he had made up worked
autonomously like the printing press gone wild fantasized by Bloom in "Aeolus"
(*U* 7 102–4). It is interesting to compare a remark by Frank Budgen describing Joyce
in the early days of writing *Ulysses* ("Joyce . . . was a great believer in his luck. What
he needed would come to him. That which he collected would prove useful in its time
and place"; Budgen 1972: 173–4) and a note inscribed in 1924 in notebook VI.B.14
(p. 32): "JJ no gambler because/his style gambles/infinitely probable." By this time
Joyce knows that he does not need to gamble because his style does it for him, and it
cannot lose because its bets saturate the gambling table. Each word, each letter, opens
up an indeterminate number of meanings, or, to put it differently, produces retrospectively a multitude of determinations.

Discovering this has a sobering and a liberating effect on the reader. On the one hand,
manuscripts reveal a number of meanings and references that are almost undetectable in
the published text but that determined its present state. Knowing these opens up new
depths of understanding, adds new dimensions to the text. However, the recent discovery of long-lost manuscripts proves that the documents we have are far from complete,
and even if we had everything that Joyce ever wrote, it would only give us an incomplete
picture of the writing process: we cannot hope to ever recover everything that Joyce
intended. On the other hand, manuscripts also reveal that the productivity of the text
surpasses Joyce's intentions at any particular moment. Authorial intention cannot be
the last word on the text: it is something that we should not neglect, something that
we should pursue through its fluctuations and nuances by a rigorous interpretation of
the extant documents, but it cannot be a limitation of our powers of interpretation.

NOTES

1　This echo, by the way, was probably spotted by the translators of the 1929 French version, who produced a translation ("comme un groin qui furète") which is in this case more authoritative than the original first edition: translators are by nature close readers and these were lucky enough to have Joyce nearby, so that they had the possibility of asking him what he had really meant to say (Joyce 1929).

2　NLI MS 36,639/9, p. [10r].

3　The fair copy of this episode has been lost, but it can be reconstructed with the help of the typescript and the Rosenbach manuscript.

4　This passage has been discussed more than once. Some Joyceans think on the contrary that the "corrected" reading is superior to the previous version. Vicki Mahaffey, in her pioneering essay on intentional error, considers that "coal and copper snow" is a mere corruption that is detrimental to our understanding of the passage and its relation to other parts of the book.

5　"Joyce would improvise whenever something particularly interesting occurred to him during the reading, and occasionally even allow a coquille – a typographical error – to stand, if it seemed to satisfy his encyclopedic mind, or appeal to his sense of the grotesque hazard" (Jolas 1998: 11).

6　Again, Jolas shows us that Joyce's attitude had not changed ten years later, although he was working under very different affective and intellectual circumstances: "Once, I remember, I had just finished reading the last page of final proof and had given orders to go ahead with the printing. . . . As we settled back comfortably, the telephone rang. An excited voice announced that a heavy special-delivery letter from Paris had just arrived for us at the printshop. Joyce wanted to make further additions, one of them probably the longest he had yet invented: an onomatopoeia of over fifty letters expressing collective coughing in a church during a sermon. It was included" (Jolas 1998: 11).

7　This proliferation of version attracted early attention. Even before the manuscripts became available, critics such as Leon Edel and Edmund Wilson discussed the evolution of the chapter based on published versions. It was later studied by Fred H. Higginson, A. Walton Litz (1961), and Claude Jacquet (1985), among others.

8　See Rosenbach manuscript p. 79a.

9　The source was discovered by Geert Lernout. See notebook VI.B.14 (Deane, Ferrer, and Lernout 2002).

10　A simplified transcription system is used here: ~~deletion~~, ^+addition+^, /A → B/ (B written over A).

BIBLIOGRAPHY

Budgen, F. (1972) *James Joyce and the Making of "Ulysses."* London: Oxford University Press.

Crispi, L. and S. Slote (eds.) (2007) *How Joyce Wrote Finnegans Wake. A Chapter-by-Chapter Genetic Guide.* Madison: University of Wisconsin Press.

Czarnowski, Stefan Zygmunt (1919) *Le Culte des héros et ses conditions sociales: Saint Patrick, héros national de l'Irlande.* Paris: Félix Alcan.

Deane, V., D. Ferrer, and G. Lernout (eds.) (2001–4) James Joyce, *The Finnegans Wake Notebooks at Buffalo,* vols 1, 3, 5, 6, 10, 14, 16, 25, 29, 32, 33, and 47. Turnhout, Belgium: Brepols.

Deppman, J., D. Ferrer, and M. Groden (eds.) (2004) *Genetic Criticism: Texts and Avant-Textes.* Philadelphia: Pennsylvania University Press.

Ferrer, D. and C. Jacquet (eds.) (1998) *Writing Its Own Wrunes for Ever, Essais de génétique joycenne/ Essays in Joycean Genetics.* Tusson: Éditions du Lérot.

Freud, Sigmund (1925) *Collected Papers,* Vol. 3. London: The Hogarth Press.

Gabler, H.-W. (1988) "Joyce's text in progress." In *Texte* 7, "Ecriture – Réécriture – La Genèse du Texte," pp. 227–47; also in D. Attridge (ed.) *The Cambridge Companion to James Joyce,* 1st edn., pp. 213–36. Cambridge: Cambridge University Press.

Gabler, H.-W. (2005) "The rocky road to *Ulysses,*" *Joyce Studies 2004,* 15, Dublin: National Library of Ireland.

Groden, M. (1977) *Ulysses in Progress*. Princeton: Princeton University Press.

Groden, M. (1980) *James Joyce's Manuscripts: An Index*. New York and London: Garland.

Groden, M. (2007) "Joyce at work on Cyclops': toward a biography of *Ulysses*." *James Joyce Quarterly* 44 (2).

Herring, P. F. (ed.) (1972) *Joyce's "Ulysses" Notesheets in the British Museum*. Charlottesville: University Press of Virginia.

Herring, P. F. (ed.) (1977) *Joyce's Notes and Early Drafts for "Ulysses."* Charlottesville: University Press of Virginia.

Jacquet, C. (ed.) (1985) *Genèses de Babel: James Joyce et la création de Finnegans Wake*. Paris: Editions du CNRS.

Jolas, E. (1998) "Remembering James Joyce," *Modernism/Modernity* 5 (2): 2–29.

Joyce, J. (1929) *Ulysse*, traduit de l'anglais par M. Auguste Morel, assisté par M. Stuart Gilbert. Traduction entièrement revue par M. Valery Larbaud, avec la collaboration de l'auteur. Paris: La Maison des amis du livre.

Joyce, J. (1975) *Ulysses by James Joyce: A Facsimile of the Manuscript*, ed. C. Driver. New York: Octa-gon Books, and Philadelphia: Philip H. and A. S. W. Rosenbach Foundation.

Joyce, J. (1984) *Ulysses: A Critical and Synoptic Edition*, ed. H. W. Gabler with W. Steppe and C. Melchior. New York: Garland.

Litz, A. W. (1961) *The Art of James Joyce*. New York: Oxford University Press.

Hayman, D. (1963) *A First-Draft Version of "Finnegans Wake."* Austin: University of Texas Press.

Hayman, D. (1990) *The "Wake" in Transit*. Ithaca, NY: Cornell University Press.

Hayman, D. and S. Slote (eds.) (1995) *Probes: Genetic Studies in Joyce*. Amsterdam: Rodopi.

Mahaffey, V. (1991) "Intentional error: the paradox of editing Joyce's *Ulysses*." In G. Bornstein (ed.) *Representing Modernist Texts: Editing as Interpretation*, pp. 171–91. Ann Arbor: Michigan.

Rose, D. (1995) *The Textual Diaries of James Joyce*. Dublin: Lilliput Press.

Rose, D. and J. O'Hanlon (1989) *The Lost Notebook*. Edinburgh: Split Pea Press.

Scholes R. and R. M. Kain (1965) *The Workshop of Daedalus*. Evanston, IL: Northwestern University Press.

19

Joyce's Bridge to Late Twentieth-Century British Theater: Harold Pinter's Dialogue with *Exiles*

Mark Taylor-Batty

James Joyce's only play, *Exiles*, has never attained a production history of any substance. Written in 1915, it was first performed in Munich in 1918, was rejected by Yeats for the Abbey Theatre in Dublin, and eventually received its first London production, by the Stage Society at the Regent Theatre, in 1926. It subsequently received no significant airing in the British Isles until Harold Pinter's production at the Mermaid Theatre, London, in the winter of 1970–1, revived a year later for the RSC at the Aldwych Theatre. Productions of the play are still very rare. John MacNicholas points out that the reasons for this lack of interest in the dramatic work of one of the last century's most important literary figures are that "[i]t is generally agreed, perhaps especially among Joyceans, that *Exiles* is a bad play, opaque to both reader and viewer" (MacNicholas, 1981–2: 9) and that "the widest-held assumption [is] that *Exiles* is the aberration of a novelist, not the work of a playwright" (MacNicholas 1973: 33). The play is still generally disregarded in Joyce scholarship. Steven Connor, for example, in his survey of Joyce's literary achievement for a general readership, mentions *Exiles* only once as "additional" to Joyce's recognized works, and classes the play alongside Joyce's lyrics, critical essays, and juvenilia (Connor 1996).

Harold Pinter disagrees fundamentally with this appraisal of *Exiles*. In a recent interview he discussed the pleasure he extracts from communing with other artists in directing and adapting their work, and recalled his production of Joyce's play, which he considers to be one of the most satisfying directing experiences of his career:

> I certainly had a wonderful relationship with James Joyce. Unfortunately it was never embodied, for obvious reasons. But I always thought that I would love to have had a drink with him. I would have loved him to have seen my production of *Exiles*. Because remember, Ezra Pound said it was unstageable and I have to say that I proved quite cat-

egorically that it was not unstageable and I would have like Pound to have seen it also (Batty 2005: 83).

For Pinter, "Joyce has always been my boy, from the word go" (Gross 1980) and his "relationship" with the writer can be traced back to his youth, and his early attachment to *Ulysses*, a book his father refused to have on a shelf in a room where dinner was served. At the Hackney Downs Grammar School, at the age of 16, Pinter produced an essay on Joyce that was published in the school magazine, and which demonstrated not only that he had read *Ulysses* and *A Portrait of the Artist as a Young Man*, but that he was also familiar with *Finnegans Wake*. It is highly likely that the young Pinter, who left school to train as an actor and work in rep, would have read *Exiles* as a young man and, given his passion for Joyce, would have developed a desire to see the play performed. It is no surprise, then, once the appropriate vehicle was available to him in the form of the West End production company Shield, which he formed with friends in 1970, that he should have taken matters into his own hands and immediately committed to directing the work.

Some of the reasons for the play's early rejection were its challenge to contemporary moral values and an uneasiness produced by certain "unmentionable passages" (*JJ* 443 n.) that would meet with the censor's blue pencil. Such charges, of course, were commonly made against Joyce's literary output, but virtually guaranteed rejection by contemporary theater managements whose commercial concerns were dictated by the staid moral outlooks of the middle-class public who patronized their establishments. The plot of the play revolves around betrayal and infidelity. Bertha, common-law wife to author Richard Rowan, has lived in self-imposed exile in Italy with him and their child, Archie. The family has recently returned to Dublin, and faces a dilemma in the form of Robert Hand, a journalist and friend of Richard's, who propositions Bertha in the first act and invites her that evening to his private cottage. Richard, who advocates Bertha's freedom to respond as she sees fit, must nevertheless negotiate his own suspicions and jealousies, and turns up in the second act at Robert's hideaway before Bertha does to confront his friend and perhaps catch them in flagrante delicto. Meeting Bertha there too, he again suggests she does as she will and leaves the two together. The third act sees the resolution of this situation, with Richard tormented by the uncertainty of what has happened between his wife and his friend. In the final confrontations with Bertha and Robert, Richard wearily expresses his ingestion of the doubt that is to be his creative spur. Robert retreats into exile in England, and Bertha is hopeful of having regained her husband.

In Joycean terms, the play is short and verbally simple, and took the form of the kinds of modern social dramas that Joyce admired from the pens of Ibsen and Hauptmann, and that were being championed most notably by George Bernard Shaw. To this common perception of the piece, Kirsten Sheperd-Barr considers it against Oscar Wilde's work and, more interestingly, in terms of the symbolist stage of late nineteenth-century Paris which appealed to Joyce (Sheperd-Barr 2003).

Harold Pinter's writing up to 1970 had been suffused with attempts to mediate varied human responses to restrictive social, emotional, and interpersonal frameworks and Joyce's *Exiles* strove in some manner, as indeed does most of Joyce's writing, to approach similar concerns and provide concrete responses in artistic invention, as Raymond Williams (1982: 108) recognized:

> Those who are surprised by Joyce's close attention to Ibsen, through so much of his writing life, have been misled by the formulations and practice of the naturalist habit and have failed to see, beyond it, the directly connecting preoccupation with levels of being and communication and with the problems of writing them. Moreover, in Joyce as in Ibsen, there is a conscious relation between these general problems and a pervading sense of a network of illusions, self-deceptions, deceptions of others, and lies.

An appreciation of *Exiles* must begin from the same premises, and disregard the naturalistic form, already becoming old-fashioned in 1915, to consider the manner in which Joyce harnesses Ibsen's structure, and undermines the traditional communicative function of stage dialogue to demonstrate how individuals might exile themselves from those who might best bring them comfort. The theatricality that the text presupposes is a matrix of confrontations underscored by unspoken needs and overarticulated desires, and the rehearsal room, therefore, is the best environment for a complete study of the play through the trials of body language, shifts of eye contact, physical expression of distance, and hesitation in verbal enunciation that actors might supply. That Pinter, as a director, instinctively knew he had to erect these scaffolds of dialogic confrontations within spatial frames is evinced by some of the paring of the text that he engaged in prior to first rehearsals. The only significant cuts that he made to the play, with the permission of the Joyce estate and the Society of Authors, were to the part of the maid Brigid. Her first scene was cut altogether (the performance began with Beatrice alone on stage and Richard's entrance) and much of her part at the beginning of Act 3 was reduced. The result was to reduce some of the peripheral domesticity of the text and to concentrate on the substantial meetings between the four protagonists. The play, as a result, became a montage of significant dialogues, a concentrated dramatic series of confrontations and interrogations that expose the motives of the protagonists as they negotiate their interdependencies and desires. One reviewer, a Joyce specialist, considered these cuts to be "a permissible move, because these exchanges are indeed the meat of the play," and approved of the way in which this "made the play more claustrophobic" (Mason 1982: 5).[1]

Pinter discussed his proposed cuts to *Exiles* prior to rehearsals in correspondence with Samuel Beckett. "Your changes in the text are very understandable," Beckett assents, "But I wonder if there is not a purely acting way out of the difficulty whereby they could be dispensed with."[2] The response is typical of Beckett as director of his own work, for which he had a talent of seeking solutions in movement and space, and also of his well-known respect for the integrity of a writer's text. Pinter and Beckett had been correspondents since they had met in 1961 at the French premiere of *The Caretaker*, which starred Roger Blin as the tramp Davies and was directed by Jean Martin: Beckett's first Pozzo and Lucky actors.[3] The two authors exchanged manuscripts frequently and Pinter was happy to accept comments and advice on his work from his colleague. In the case of his project to resurrect *Exiles*, he found himself entering into a dialogue with someone who had been acquainted with Joyce socially, as an artist, and as an intellectual. Their brief dialogue concerns itself solely with the theatricality of the play, not its textual qualities, and is demonstrative of how both men had intuitive responses to the kinetic and gestural possibilities dormant in dramatic text, and how it might appeal to its audience. Speaking of *Exiles*, Beckett admitted that he had "often wondered how it could be done, that speech overcome and the deep wounding played"[4] and, in a letter which Pinter received the month before rehearsals were to begin, he mused on the "thinner ice" of the emotional terrain of Joyce's dramatic world:[5]

Dear Harold

Please forgive delay in writing to you about *Exiles* [. . .]

I feel the clue to the production is <u>apartness</u>. As much stage as possible as often as possible between the actors. When they have to come close it is reluctantly and to scatter again as soon as the situation permits. All exiled in one another from one another. Same principle to be applied vocally. Voices abnormally low from a distance. All speaking and listening more to themselves than to the others. Similarly for set. Elements isolated apart from one another.

No doubt this would create difficulties on other levels and I don't suggest it should be applied systematically throughout the three acts. I propose it simply as a predominant mood and a means of negotiating the thinner ice. [. . .]

Affectionately to you all

Sam [6]

Beckett's responses to Joyce's only play demonstrate the distinctive traits of his own approach to directing, and provide some small insight into his own approach to writing texts that have inscribed within their structure the modes of their own representation.

The structures of rhythm, pace, and space that define Beckett's theatricality were also recognizable in Pinter's oeuvre, which, in the 1960s, was renowned for being populated by characters who manoeuvre for psychological or spatial advantage. This preoccupation was first manifest in the non-dramatic Kullus texts,[7] and was easily translated into key staged moments of perceived or actual threat to occupancy and authority in *The Room* (1957), *The Birthday Party* (1958), *The Caretaker* (1960), *The Homecoming* (1965), and *The Basement* (1967). The need for "apartness" that Beckett suggests in acting relationships in *Exiles*, and the impulses to "scatter" upon the threat of connection or intimacy, was already very much a part of Pinter's own dramatic armory. The suggestion that the actors might speak "abnormally low" is also clearly Beckettian in the contract it demands of the audience's engagement with the onstage action. Whilst Pinter's actors were audible (and, of course, Beckett's suggestion was one more likely intended to be taken in the spirit rather than the letter), the audience/actor contract he demanded in performance certainly offered some of the tension that Beckett might have envisaged. His production was "riveting to the point of pain" (Mairowitz 1971) and, from the numerous reviews both his productions received, it was clear that he had prioritized a mode of performance that had been reached through a concentration on the delivery of dialogue that must have achieved something of Beckett's notion that characters might come across as "exiled in one another from one another." The performance was recognized as being a difficult but fulfilling experience, and Pinter's approach was widely endorsed. Speaking of the RSC revival in 1971, Zane Mairowitz (1971) approved of the steady-paced drama that the director had achieved:

> Pinter might then have decided to "jazz it up," to cut it mercilessly, play it fast. Instead, the production is slow and deliberate, uncut, acted for every moment, every twist, without an idea "thrown away" in the cause of "pace." [. . .] The fact is that it [. . .] is mere common sense, a hymn to everyone's intelligence.

The general critical response to the production was overwhelmingly positive. Many reviewers considered the success of the production as a validation of Joyce's play as a powerful and affective piece of theater: "He has lifted the lid of the coffin of one of the greatest plays of our time, revived an interest in the community supper of the Idea, and I, for one, feel ashamed and trivialized, but also replenished" (Mairowitz 1971). Irving Wardle (1970) considered that Pinter's contribution through rehearsal and execution of the play was to have offered

> the kind of insight which only one creative artist can perform in the service of another. *Exiles* is customarily dismissed as an unsatisfactory exercise in the Ibsen manner. That view is demolished by the Mermaid production which banishes the shade of Ibsen and reveals an extraordinary affinity between Joyce and Pinter.

This "extraordinary affinity" is worth exploring. Many critics certainly approached their appraisal of the production by filtering their responses to the show through their experiences of Pinter's plays, measuring one artist against the other. Given that both the play *Exiles*, with its spare production history, and Harold Pinter as a director were both relatively unknown entities, such a mode of approach was perhaps to be expected. Parallels between the work of the two men in such critical responses, however, seemed often only to provide a critical shorthand for assumed characteristics. Martin Esslin (1971) meaninglessly noted how one scene was "directed in a Pinter style by Pinter," demonstrating how the "Pinteresque" was, by now, a taken quality. "The success of Pinter's production is that it generates the cold tension of a play by himself,"noted another critic (Barber), echoed by yet another, who stated that "Harold Pinter's production at the Mermaid creates much the same illusion as the best of his plays" (Nightingale 1970). The banal comparison these comments imply was even turned into an accusation of appropriation in one review, in which it was claimed that Pinter had "not so much resuscitated as annexed James Joyce's *Exiles*," going on to clarify: "There are even characteristic Pinter ambiguities, like the two men comparing their hands, or the writer's brutal reading of a laudatory newspaper article about himself" (Marcus 1970). David G. Wright suggested that Pinter's own oeuvre already owed a debt to his interest in Joyce, and *Exiles* in particular:

Exiles (published in 1918) strikingly anticipates Pinter in its subtle use of ominous pauses; dramatizations of threat and hostility; patterns of territorial conflict, psychological and social displacement, and invasion; preoccupation with the power of the past; and exploration of nonverbal forms of communication (structurally and thematically) in the interactions of the characters (Wright 1988: 517–18).

Irving Wardle (1970) acknowledged such parallels, but did not attribute them to a presumed Pinter style directly:

> Some of the pre-echoes of Pinter are uncanny: such as the second act's forecast of *The Lover*, and the characters' habit of producing conflicting evidence of past experiences they both shared. But it is from the continuous style of the production that the play is really made to speak. It is played *sotto voce* with every phrase and every pause microscopically gauged. Joyce called it "three cat and mouse acts," and Pinter presents exactly that. The characters have practically no room for manoeuvre; they weigh every word they speak, and make not one superfluous gesture. Very little happens, but the effect is one of intense passion, fear and danger.

When considering what attracted Pinter to the notion of resurrecting *Exiles* for the stage, in the first instance there must have been a very simple allure in tackling this master's only stage play, consolidated, certainly, by a recognized affinity of thematic interests. One might conclude that it was by engaging in these shared artistic concerns through the act of directing – a form of surrogate authorship in the theater – that Pinter sought to engage his own creativity.

Interestingly, locating the production of *Exiles* within the biography of Pinter, it is placed at the end a period of creative stagnation (in terms of his own writing) that he himself recognized after the success of *The Homecoming*. In 1968 he described how his work had become "constipated" (Bosworth 1968) and bemoaned how writing "becomes more difficult the older you get, at least it does for me" (Billington 1996: 195). Over the summer before starting the rehearsals for *Exiles*, in his acceptance speech for the German Shakespeare Prize, he publicly admitted that "at the moment I am writing nothing and can write nothing. I don't know why. It's a very bad feeling, I know that, but I must say I want more than anything else to fill up a blank page again" (Pinter 2005: 43). Marking the end of that period, it is tempting to consider precisely how involvement with Joyce's work was a regenerating pursuit of some form for Pinter. The preparatory intellectual groundwork on *Exiles* had begun at least as early as spring 1969 – attested by Pinter's correspondence with Samuel Beckett on the subject – and this is almost two years before the production. It is unlikely, in the world of professional theater, for preparation for a production of this size to begin very much more than three months before opening. Ronald Knowles suggests that Pinter was closely contemplating *Exiles* even earlier, and isolates an association between Pinter's reading and his writing in his short play *Landscape* (1968), where Beth's words "if they touched the back of my neck, or my hand, it was done so lightly. Without exception. With one exception" (Pinter 1997: 170) mirror Robert's words in *Exiles*: "All then – without exception? Or with one exception?" (*E* 38) (Knowles 1998: 186). This period of contemplation and involvement with

Joyce's play, then, was bookended for Pinter by the writing of *Landscape*, before it, and *Old Times*, after it. The latter full-length play was written directly after the final, particularly intense, period of involvement with the text and during the run of the first performances of the play in the Winter of 1970–1: *Exiles* had opened at the Mermaid Theatre on November 12, 1970, and Pinter, when talking to Mel Gussow in December 1971, located the writing of *Old Times* as "last winter. About a year ago" (Gussow 1994: 26) The production of *Exiles*, and Pinter's pride in it, must certainly have left a lasting residue in his mind, for when he told Mel Gussow in December 1971 that he considered that "the past is not past, that it never was past. It's present" (Gussow 1994: 38) he was unconsciously echoing Robert's words from *Exiles*: "the past is not past. It is present here now" (*E* 108). Given such evidence of his passion for Joyce and his dedicated attachment to *Exiles*, and, as Billington reminds us, that he "sat down to write *Old Times* in the winter of 1970 while saturated in Joyce's play" (211), would it be too fanciful to wonder whether, in trying to find an appropriate title for this latest work, he, consciously or not, returned to a punctuating phrase that he had so recently been hearing daily in the rehearsal room?

> ROBERT [. . .] Lord, when I think of our wild nights long ago – talks by the hour, plans, carouses, revelry . . .
> RICHARD In our house.
> ROBERT It is mine now. I have kept it ever since though I don't go there often. Whenever you like to come let me know. You must come some night. It will be old times again. (*He lifts his glass, and drinks.*) *Prosit!*
>
> (*E* 48)

Arguably, the production of *Exiles* represents something of a synapse between Pinter's and Joyce's artistic agendas, and whilst the success of the production is of interest to Joyce scholars, the tangible evidence of "influence" it represents is of interest to Pinter scholars. It also provides meat for the consideration of what exactly is meant by "influence" in these circumstances. As the etymology of the word suggests, the impact is more one of osmotic absorption, dilution, and refinement within the receiving artist. It is not the parasitic lifting and appropriation of ideas or structures, nor is it the homage-paying urge to repeat and replicate. Instead, it is the excitement in discovering the statement or format of ideas in the work of one artist in manners that are attuned to the intuitive approach or conscious agendas of a second artist. Such a "meeting" might serve to ignite the creative processes of the second artist, or set in motion latent impulses to excavate responses to life-events and mediate human experience within art. Pinter's own artistic fraternity comprised numerous artists with whom he worked, or with whom he communed via artistic endeavor (in screenplay-writing, directing, and acting). These have included Margaret Atwood, Samuel Beckett, Joseph Conrad, Noel Coward, Henry James, Franz Kafka, Vladimir Nabokov, Marcel Proust, and William Shakespeare. In seeking to consider, through the prism of Pinter's interests in them, the common pursuits of the artists he has communed with artistically one might seek to define Pinter's sense of artistic self-definition as he positioned himself against or alongside them. In 1993, for example, he told Mel Gussow (1994: 118) that "I certainly believe I'm part of a tradition which undoubtedly includes Joyce and Eliot." Pinter's work on Joyce's play might well have permitted a satisfying concentration on another artist's expression of some of the concerns he shared, and if "influence" is to be considered it might be sought in subtle "gravitational shifts" to themes and concerns that were already characteristic of Pinter's writing.

Critics have sought the defining influence of Joyce in Pinter within *Old Times*. Michael Billington (1996: 211) hints at some of the similarities between *Exiles* and *Old Times*, pointing out, for example, that "both deal with the contest between two figures for the soul and body of a third, and with the ultimate unpossessability of the triumphant heroine." Katherine Worth details further comparisons, starts by noting the basic structural premise ("There again was the silent woman, the probing husband, the jealousy of the past and the nostalgia for it"; Worth 1973: 48) and provides a basic comparative study of the two plays, concentrating on similar exchanges between characters, such as the interrogation of Deeley and Kate and Richard and Bertha. She also perceives links with other, earlier Pinter plays as has been catalogued above. Rather than suggest incidences of "influence" of Joyce upon Pinter, Worth simply catalogues details and parallels that indicate his attraction to Joyce as a writer and *Exiles* as a play. David G. Wright, in his "Joyce's Debt to Pinter," goes further and charts comparisons of structure and pursuit of thematic goals in *Exiles* and *Old Times*, paralleling, for example, the plights and maneuvers of the characters of Richard and Deeley, to argue that "the associations between *Old Times* and *Exiles* are sufficiently close and sufficiently numerous that some degree of effect by Joyce on Pinter in this instance seems beyond dispute" (Wright 1988: 525). Wright's tight interweaving of the two plays to substantiate this claim of influence leads to some weakening generalizations. To identify Robert and Beatrice as intruders into Richard and Bertha's home, for example, and then make the association with the intrusive guest Anna in *Old Times*, or indeed with any Pinter invader, is a diluted observation; there are few plays by any author which do not contain some form of disruptive presence that engineers narrative or thematic development. His conclusion that "the quest for power in both plays comes to supplant the quest for love" (Wright 1988: 523) is more true of *Old Times* than it is of *Exiles*, where such an operation puts harmony at risk, but does not end in the kind of devastation that the curtain falls upon in *Old Times*.

One key affinity between the artists that Worth notes (1973: 51) is in how "[k]nowing and wanting to know lead into 'not knowing' in *Exiles*, as in all Pinter's plays." A condition of uncertainty in a character's status, security, and even identity had always featured highly in Pinter's drama. Originally it manifested itself as part of the patchwork of uncertainties that characters manipulated to out-maneuver one another, to gain advantage and control of a situation or of others. Ambiguities fueled power struggles and caused distrust and separation between individuals in such early plays as *The Birthday Party* and *The Caretaker*. In the early 1960s, Pinter introduced the technique to scenarios of interpersonal relationships in pieces such as *The Collection*, *The Lover*, and *Tea Party*. What Pinter developed in these short television dramas was the notion of the unpossessability of the other. His dramas demonstrated how, in order to achieve an intimacy of sorts, characters are compelled to construct narratives of their partners that accommodate their own emotional needs. In impressing these narratives, they force themselves into a position of unredeemable doubt, which either oils the wheels of further interaction in dissatisfying compromise or infects and engenders further, destructive, narratives. From *The Collection* (1961):

> James: You didn't do anything, did you? (*Pause*) He wasn't in your room. You just talked about it in the lounge. (*Pause*) That's the truth, isn't it? (*Pause*) You just sat and talked about what you would do if you went to your room. That's what you did. (*Pause*) Didn't you? (*Pause*) That's the truth . . . isn't it?
> Stella *looks at him, neither confirming nor denying.*
>
> (Pinter 1996: 145)

Exiles is constructed around the very same premises, and Richard Rowan's partially self-inflicted "deep wound of doubt" (*E* 147) compromises his future relationship with Bertha. Referring to her willingness to discuss her nocturnal liaison with his friend Robert Hand, telling her that "you will tell me. But I will never know" (*E* 133), he explains his anxiety at the elusiveness of truth. For Pinter, the key to the dramatic momentum is precisely that ambiguity which torments characters:

> Mel Gussow: From your point of view, the literal fact of a meeting or of a sexual relationship doesn't really matter.
> Harold Pinter: No, it doesn't. The fact is it's terribly difficult to define what happened at any time. I think it's terribly difficult to define what happened yesterday. You know that old Catholic thing, the sin in the head? So much is imagined and that imagining is as true as real.
>
> (Gussow 1994: 17)

Exiles offered nothing new to Pinter in this respect – he was speaking here of *The Homecoming* from 1965 (and the excerpt from *The Collection* dates from 1961) – but the intense emotional consequences between life partners of the seeds of doubt sown by previous or concurrent sexual relationships had yet to form a central motif in his work. In the earlier plays, the emotional consequences of relationships were treated as secondary to the need to conquer and control. In *The Collection*, for example, the threat to emotional security is dispatched with business-like coolness by Harry, and the role of Stella remains peripheral and enigmatic – a narrative device rather than a full-bodied role. Likewise, in *The Homecoming* the focus is significantly elsewhere, in the maneuvers to control and dominate a family unit. The "wound of doubt," though, proved its dramatic worth in *Exiles*, and Pinter is seen to adopt and adapt the potential in *Old Times*, *Betrayal* (1978), and, much later, *Ashes to Ashes* (1996). The fluidity and malleability of the concept of truth was a significant factor at work in these and other, later, works. Indeed, the enigma of *Old Times* is constructed around this fact, as indicated by the character of Anna: "There are some things one remembers even though they may never have happened. There are things I remember which may never have happened but as I recall them so they take place" (Pinter 1997: 269–70). In so depositing doubt as a tool, she applies it in her claim to possession of Kate through her discussion of their shared past, causing the eventual devastation of the wounded Deeley. This is another significant distinction between the two authors' use of doubt in interpersonal relationships: Joyce recognized the elusiveness of factual certainty occasioned by evoking past events, and demonstrates the effect upon the individual's emotional security; Pinter makes a currency of that elusiveness and the past becomes a battlefield of clashing memories, wielded in attempts to appropriate advantage in the present. Memory and the past had always operated as forces in his dramas, but first truly served this combative function in the period following *The Homecoming*. *Landscape* involves a married couple offering differing memories which, combined, chart or indicate the disintegration of their relationship to its present dysfunctional state, where she sits enwrapped in her world of remembered romantic liaisons and he strives to engage her in conversation with coarse and brutal imagery. This was explored further in *Night*, a sketch in which another married couple reminisce about the first days of their relationship, but now fail to agree on the details that should bind them. From the separation where the prioritization of completely different memories speaks of the impossibility of renewed intimacy in *Landscape*, to the evocation of the emptiness of a relationship in the incoherence of remembered fragments of its genesis in *Night*, Pinter arrives, via *Exiles*, at the manipulation of such fragments within acts of appropriation in *Old Times*.

> Kate: You were so unlike the others. We knew men who were brutish, crass. [. . .]
> Deeley: But I was crass, wasn't I, looking up her skirt?
> Kate: That's not crass.
> Deeley: If it was her skirt. If it was her.
> Anna (Coldly): Oh, it was my skirt. It was me. I remember your look . . . very well. I remember you well.
> Kate (to Anna): But I remember you dead. *Pause*. I remember you lying dead. You didn't know I was watching you.
>
> (Pinter 1997: 309)

The convergence of an increasing artistic interest in the potency of an unverifiable past with an older concern in the impossibility of defining truth in Pinter's work in the late 1960s runs in tandem with his shift towards greater attention to domestic sexual relationships. As shown, the fascination with the anatomy of truth forms a fundamental part of the manner in which these relationships are interrogated and examined dramatically. Whereas his plays had always examined the strategies that people employ in their social and domestic interactions, the specific focus from *Landscape* into the 1970s was upon closeness and intimacy, the question of how we attempt to negotiate our needs for such things, and the consequent failures and betrayals that can occur. Pinter's characters post-*Exiles* become more subjective in their expression of experience, and the emphasis on memory necessarily magnifies more personal perspectives. The substance of *Exiles*, built neatly around the emotional needs of four individuals and one established relationship, and presented through a series of confessional or confrontational dialogues, offered a model in which the ambiguity and doubt of motivation and purpose – which, as demonstrated, had always been a Pinter currency – casts a fog over the ability of individuals to communicate or resolve their interpersonal needs. The play's most potent scenes are those in which the characters attempt to expose or define their inner emotional processes through analyses and appraisals of past desires and ambitions, and their impact on the present situation, but do so without successful communication or communion.

Within the closer creative attention Pinter paid to sexual relationships, there was a gradual development in his attention to and crafting of female characters. Elizabeth Sakellaridou charts his progress from a writer who wrote female characters around male expectancies (effectively exposing such expectancies and the vocabularies that constructed and sustained them) to one who conveyed the reality of broader aspects of feminine experience. She locates a balanced representation of characters of both sexes within the more subjective forms of expression that Pinter used in the plays which examined sexual relationships, and states that it is not surprising that his "development into an androgynous writer coincides with his direct involvement . . . with the work of James Joyce and Marcel Proust, who are both associated with the idea of androgyny" (Sakellaridou 1988: 140). This is seen most clearly in *Old Times*, where nuances of homo- and heterosexuality level out evenly in Anna and Deeley's assertions of "ownership" of Kate, who subsequently rejects both their attempts to define and thereby possess her. It is possible that Pinter, in his portrait of Kate and Anna's relationship, expanded upon the "faint glimmer of lesbianism" (*E* 156) that he would have been aware Joyce had asserted should accompany the playing of Bertha and Beatrice. There is certainly something of their Act 3 solidarity, and the manner in which it further isolates Richard, in Anna and Kate's effective exclusion of Deeley. It is not impossible that Joyce's subtle writing of the dialogue between Bertha and Beatrice, and the sophisticated twist this added to the drama, offered Pinter the inspiration to further examine this similar female relationship in *Old Times*, which is notable in all his writing, being one of only two plays of his in which female characters outnumber the male.

In writing only one male role, thereby effectively eliminating the possibility of scrutinizing any male bond, Pinter is nevertheless seen to be moving tangentially away from *Exiles* with *Old Times*. Kate and Anna's "faint glimmer of lesbianism," if indeed it is present, is simply part of the play for advantage in Pinter's play, whereas in Joyce's it forms part of Bertha and Beatrice's pronounced escape from patriarchal coding. In direct contrast to this, a predominant theme through much of Pinter's writing, from his 1950s novel *The Dwarfs* through to *Celebration* in 2000, is the bond between male friends and associated homosocial behavior. It is perhaps in this respect that *Exiles* was particularly attractive to him and that his protracted work on its production served most to inspire him. Although the narrative development of the play focuses on Richard and Bertha's relationship and how it is affected by Bertha's meetings with Robert, it is certainly clear that the fundamental focus of the drama is the relationship between the old friends Richard and Robert. Suzette A. Henke argues (1990: 92) that "Richard is, for Bertha, Robert, and Beatrice, an elusive object of Lacanian desire who refuses to authorize erotic consummation" and that, specifically, Robert "seeks Bertha as a surrogate for homoerotic attachment." This is not out of keeping with Joyce's thoughts when compiling the play. In his preparatory notes, he queried the degree to which the two men share a physical attraction to one another which they defer and project through Bertha; Robert by attempting to seduce her, Richard by permitting and effectively staging this seduction: "The bodily possession of Bertha by Robert, repeated often, would certainly bring into almost carnal contact the two men" (*E* 156–7). On a primary, verbal level, he wove this suggestion into the play in expressions of affection or admiration between the men that involve the intermediary of Bertha. "You are so strong that you attract me even through her," Robert states to Richard, for example (*E* 78). Richard later claims to Bertha that her sexual intimacy with Robert only strengthens his bond with his friend:

> RICHARD [. . .] That I came first in your life or before him then – that may be nothing to you. You may be his more than mine.
> BERTHA I am not. Only I feel for him, too.
> RICHARD And I do too. You may be his and mine. I will trust you, Bertha, and him too. I must. I cannot hate him since his arms have been around you. You have drawn us near together.
>
> (*E* 95–6)

During their confrontation in Act Two, Richard insists on the opportunity to confess his purpose in licensing Bertha's pursuit of her interests in Robert. He begins with an appeal to their friendship, underscored with a physical hint of closeness:

> ROBERT Look here, Richard. We have said all there is to be said. Let the past be past.
> RICHARD (*Quickly and harshly.*) Wait. One thing more. For you, too, must know me as I am – now.
> ROBERT More? Is there more?
> RICHARD I told you that when I saw your eyes this afternoon I felt sad. Your humility and confusion, I felt, united you to me in brotherhood. (*He turns half round towards him.*) At that moment I felt our whole life together in the past, and I longed to put my arm around your neck.
>
> (*E* 87)

He continues to reveal how he has sought to engineer a situation where he would be betrayed and "dishonoured for ever in love and in lust" (*E* 88) and begins to intimate his various motives.

According to Joyce, Richard craves "to feel the thrill of adultery vicariously and to possess a bound woman Bertha through the organ of his friend" (*E* 158). It is this attempt at masculine union via a feminine intermediary and the precarious application of psychosexual impulses in resolving insurmountable desire that may have captured Pinter's attention. He himself had previously examined similar processes of male communion involving a catalytic female character, most notably in the novel of *The Dwarfs*, the writing of which pre-dates his dramas. Billington (1996: 138) points out that the characters of Pete and Mark in the novel "share an intellectual and social intimacy which is later reinforced by the fact that they both sleep with Virginia." The theme was further extrapolated in the screenplay of *The Servant*, *The Collection*, *The Basement*, and, of course, *The Homecoming*. But whereas Pinter, in these writings, had presented male bonds fragmented or challenged by a female presence (or, in the case of *The Homecoming*, a union achieved but with compromising consequences for the male unit), Joyce presented a scenario in which the victimization of the women – both Bertha and Beatrice – is evident, and resolution of their conflict is as important to the equation the play describes as that of the men. That is not to say that the tragic situations of Virginia (*The Dwarfs*), Stella (*The Collection*), or Jane (*The Basement*) are not apparent, but their abuse by the male characters forms part of the detritus of the failure ultimately to connect that characterizes their encounters. Ruth, in *The Homecoming*, takes an admirably active role in challenging masculine dogma, but her success is due to her unsympathetic skills as a schemer and our response to her is, at best, ambivalent (and this is further problematized by the variety of approaches adopted over the years by actresses and directors, further affecting our readings of her). Mark Silverstein applies Irigaray's concept of mimicry to Ruth, and to other Pinter women's behavior, to argue for a Foucauldian reading that a subject does not take control of power but simply articulates the power that constructs them. By subscribing to the syntax of control by submission to patriarchal projection of the female role, Ruth perhaps subjects herself to the emotional compromises that result from such dysfunctional strategies of achieving intimacy through dominance.

If the necessary inclusion of a female catalyst or foil within processes of male interaction is a determinable theme in some of Pinter's early writing, it was in many ways resolved and redefined with *The Homecoming*. During the transitionary period in his writing of the late 1960s, notions of fraternity are temporarily left aside and sorrow is instead expressed at an inability of the two sexes to commune successfully in and through the needs and desires they manifest for one another within established or fledgling relationships. *Landscape*, *Silence*, *Night*, and *Old Times* each document this form of paralysis in different ways. *Old Times*, written on the threshold of the *Exiles* experience, brings the movement to a close and, with the metaphoric "burial" of Deeley following his failed attempts at definition and thereby assured possession of his wife Kate, concludes the domination games of Pinter's earlier dramas. When, post-*Exiles*, Pinter was to return to his earlier interest in homosocial behavior and male interaction through the intermediary of a woman, it was to chart the dysfunction of that behavior, and the betrayals to self and to other that it occasioned. This is first manifested in his next directing experience, working on Simon Gray's *Butley* in the summer of 1971 (in between his two productions of *Exiles*). Gray's play, which charts the disintegration of the eponymous academic, provided a further focus on the homosocial aspects of Joyce's play that attracted Pinter:

> It seemed to me that Butley was a man living in a kind of no man's land – between women and between men. I understood from the play that his sexual experience was with women but that he probably liked men better. In other words, I didn't see him as

a homosexual [. . .] I think quite a number of men are in this position and it makes life very difficult for them (Pinter 1974).

Monologue (1972) was Pinter's first piece of writing after *Old Times* and with it he was clearly attempting to begin his own direct articulation of some of the concerns he had contemplated directly in the rehearsal rooms of *Exiles* and *Butley*. The play recalls the situation of the end of Pinter's novel *The Dwarfs*, and the dissolution of the friendship of two men following their sexual liaisons with the same woman. What is described is highly reminiscent of Bertha's cerebral attraction to Richard and sensual attraction to Robert:

> Now you're going to say you loved her soul and I loved her body. You're going to trot that one out. I know you were much more beautiful than me, much more *aquiline*, I know *that*, that I'll give you, more *ethereal*, more thoughtful, slyer, while I had both feet firmly planted on the deck. But I'll tell you one thing you don't know. She loved my soul. It was my soul she loved. [. . .] I loved her body. Not that, between ourselves, it's one way or another of any importance. My spasms could have been your spasms (Pinter 1998: 123).

This sexual binary is paralleled in the jocular recollection of how his friend should have been black, like the girl, in order to give an aesthetic purity to the image of him in his motorcycle leathers and helmet. In bringing into operation these body/soul, black/white polarities in his memories, the unnamed character of Man reveals his need for the implied potential for amalgamation that they carry – that is, his own full integration into the lives of both the girl and his friend. He embodies this integration in the fantasy of the mixed-color children that he would have loved, the fruits of the carnal/spiritual resolution he craves but so visibly lacks (the monologue is directed at an empty chair).

The results of failed or compromised attempts to achieve emotional independence or union through intimacy that Joyce presented in *Exiles* are defined powerfully by Pinter in *Monologue* as sterility and isolation. These he explored more fully in the all-male play *No Man's Land* (1975), which portrayed the results of choosing unproductiveness and distance over creative progression and intimacy within the character of Hirst. Ann Hall (1993: 76) notes how "Spooner is apparently offering Hirst an alternative to his current homosocial relations but using those relations to move Hirst beyond them." Again the warning the play offers is implicit, in that the dangers of a compromised existence lie within a personal risk of loss of genuine human bonds. With *Betrayal* (1978), though, Pinter was finally to close his personal examination of the anatomy of the fraternal bond, and with it his dialogue with *Exiles*, in an arrangement that most closely resembled some parallel universe to Joyce's play: the affair between Emma, wife of the publisher Robert, and his best friend, the literary agent Jerry. In the play's final scene, which in its reverse chronology is the first event, Robert's acceptance of his friend's behavior – flattering his wife at a party in the marital bedroom – might be read as an act of condoning the liaison and potential affair, in the

same way Richard promoted Robert Hand's pursuit of Bertha. Jerry's misplaced accusation of betrayal – that of his friend for not having admitted he knew of his affair
– mirrors Bertha's concern that Robert feels betrayed for her not having explained she
had revealed all to her husband. There is also the admission, albeit skewed, of mutual
admiration that Joyce activates, in Robert's statement to Emma: "I've always liked
Jerry. To be honest, I've always liked him rather more than I've liked you. Maybe I
should have had an affair with him myself" (Pinter 1998: 72). But, taking from the
germ of a failure to maintain a bond and profit on admiration and friendship, as first
demonstrated in *Monologue*, the mutual desire for a single woman in *Betrayal* is no
longer the psychological location of a struggle for dominance, as it was in pre-*Exiles*
Pinter. The reverse chronology of the play works in some way towards ensuring this,
as it denies an audience any appreciation of a causal chain in a way that might promote
a moralizing response. Instead, a sexual bond between men through the intermediary of a shared woman is accentuated as characteristic of an emotional immaturity, and
there is a compensatory emphasis on the will and need of the woman in the equation.
This places in strong relief the inefficiencies of the male manifestation and articulation
of need. Whilst Emma in *Betrayal* moves away from emotional paralysis to competent
independence, effectively moving towards creativity (from publisher, to literary agent,
to writer, to managing her own art gallery), the men, betraying their literary ideals to
market forces, move backwards and away from one another and her. *Exiles* presents the
plight of a woman abused by and isolated from the man she loves and to whom she has
dedicated herself, making personal sacrifices along the way. Encouraged to pursue the
advances of Richard's friend, Robert, she is torn between attempting to please Richard
and to please herself, given his seeming rejection of her. Ironically, he only reinforces
his isolation from her, despite his evident love for her, and it is by causing an audience
to respond to Richard's folly that Joyce foregrounds but problematizes a key Ibsenite concern – that one must pursue a duty to oneself. Henke (1990: 90) argues that
Richard

> feels convinced that like Christ and Charles Stewart Parnell, he will be betrayed by friends
> and disciples and, eventually, by the woman he loves. Like Kierkegaard, he defines ulti-
> mate spiritual possession as an act of sacrificial generosity: voluntary renunciation frees
> the individual from the ponderous burdens of jealousy and desire.

The fact that Richard resolves to hold Bertha, not in the security of assurance, but in
the bonds of a restless living wounding doubt, bears witness to a new inwardness and
a new passivity on his part. Joyce perhaps sought to examine the progression made
through the conflicts set in motion between his characters (possible spectres from
his own autobiography); the fact that Richard chooses to embrace and rekindle his
love for Bertha, albeit shackled by an inerasable wounding doubt, bears witness to an
emotional development or "closure" on his part. In contrast to this, Pinter, perhaps
also affected by spectres from his own autobiography, chooses to represent, and warn
against, failure and paralysis. In this way, perhaps, Pinter fulfills the Ibsenite doctrine
of duty to oneself by pointing to both Emma's success and Jerry and Robert's failure

and self-betrayal, and does so straightforwardly in a way that Joyce purposefully problematized in his so-called Ibsenite drama.

If, as argued above, Pinter's meeting with Joyce via a "dialogue" with *Exiles* can be detected in the ways in which his own writing moved tangentially away from established modes and themes to move in sympathy in directions recognizable within Joyce's play, then his production of *Exiles* represents a significant reintroduction of that play to the post-1956 British theater. In doing so, Pinter was considered to have redeemed the play. Frank Marcus (1970) of the *Sunday Telegraph* challenged the given wisdom on the play and stated that "what looks wordy and unwieldy on the page becomes miraculously spare, calculated, and fraught with passion." He went on to consider the achievement to be an act of literary resurrection, stating that "Pinter has given life to a forgotten literary curiosity, and this is the most profound kind of homage."

Perhaps much of the difficulty that Joyce scholars have had with the play is the dead end that is reached by reading the play as a textual artifact, as one would any other of Joyce's works. It simply does not match the satisfaction offered by the reading and rereading of Joyce's great prose. In facing this "weak" piece of "literature," a narrative has been developed within Joyce scholarship that maintains that the text must consequently be a weak piece of theater. MacNicholas concludes that as only Pinter's production (of all stagings of the play) was an unqualified success, "It therefore seems fair to say that the play itself is unusually dependent upon acting and directing skills to be effective" (MacNicholas 1981–2: 22). This is an astonishing piece of non-criticism, for the same can be said not only of any poor piece of dramatic writing but also of any sophisticated theatrical masterpiece. Like any complex work, *Exiles* requires an input of insight that sees past the demands of the naturalistic form and appreciates the intended thrust of the play's content, and can unravel and unpack with a group of actors the psychological cat-and-mouse game that Joyce inscribed. The narrative of *Exiles'* unplayability conspires against its being played, and therefore against the opportunity for it to be seen in the only context in which it might properly be judged (onstage as opposed to on page). Writing off Pinter's success as due simply to his exceptional skill serves to reinforce that constructed narrative.

MacNicholas (1981–2: 22) considers that "Joyce was struggling towards a new kind of theater" – which is certainly true – but argues that the experiment failed, and was therefore dropped. The failure may have simply been one of a mismatch with the cultural climate into which the work was born. His play was not commercially suited – on the grounds of moral temperament – to the kinds of theaters and audiences he sought to confront. Certainly, Joyce's significant contribution to European and world literature is unquestionably his experimentation in prose and the novel, but his experimentation in drama is worthy of further consideration, especially given the manner in which his mode of structuring a drama around subtle subtextual material and a failure of the apparatus of social and intimate communication has been wholly validated by a whole generation of writers, Pinter included, that followed the 1956 new wave of British theater writing. Joseph Voelker (1988: 500) noted how "In *Exiles*, Joyce carried realist dialogue to a point at which characters use language more to disturb than to communicate," and Worth recognized Joyce's attempt to introduce a new technique into the manner in which character relationships might be portrayed:

> a technique which no one had used in quite that way before in the English theatre for keeping the banal material taut and turning it towards a searching reading of character; a version of Ibsen's "investigation" technique with silence, pauses, visual movement used in something more like the Chekhovian way (Worth 1973: 53).

Worth might add August Strindberg to her chain of references, as an artist who sought to examine the processes of manipulation and inauthentic communication inherent within human interaction. Strindberg, of course, was not accepted into the "modern" world theater repertoire until the 1960s, when his distinctive approach to character and dialogue were more commonly pursued and admired. The postwar European theater (taking energy from the experimentations of the Left Bank pocket theaters in Paris and the successes of the English Stage Theatre in Britain) had begun to produce models that moved away from the narrative-driven "realism" of an essentially classical temperament, towards modes of representation that were rooted in both the socially aware impulses of early naturalism and the formalistic experiments of the symbolists, expressionists, and surrealists of the early twentieth century. This was the terrain in which *Exiles* might more firmly take root, given the manners in which it pre-empted the writing styles and agendas of those, such as Pinter, who rejected character-driven narratives and problem plays. Martin Esslin (1971) saw this most clearly:

> What was it that drew Pinter to a play which, outwardly at least, is in the style and spirit of Ibsen? In fact, of course, Joyce was the most modern of writers, his work contains all the preoccupations of the avant-garde. Behind the problem of the marital morals in *Exiles*, there lie unplumbed depths of psychological insight. The scene in which, having allowed herself to be kissed by her "seducer," Bertha then meticulously reports all that happened to her husband is of astonishing boldness: there is much here of Albee, much also of Ruth's nonchalance about sex in Pinter's own *The Homecoming*. On one level this is uncompromisingly honest Edwardian free thinking, on another it is sexual fantasy right out of Pinter's *The Lover*.

NOTES

1. Mason was, in fact, commenting on the radio broadcast of the Mermaid performance.
2. Samuel Beckett to Harold Pinter, letter dated September 17, 1970. Pinter's personal archive.
3. *Le Gardien*, Théâtre de Lutèce, Paris, January 1961. Roger Blin had directed the world premiere of *En attendant Godot* (*Waiting for Godot*) in 1953 as well as having taken the role of Pozzo. He had striven for four years to find a theater that would accept the play. Beckett dedicated *Fin de partie* (*Endgame*) to him.
4. Beckett to Pinter, letter dated April 4, 1969.
5. Regrettably, Pinter's letter to Beckett is no longer extant.
6. Beckett to Pinter, September 17, 1970; original emphasis.
7. *Kullus* (1949), *The Task* (1954), and *The Examination* (1955), all in *Various Voices* (2005).

Bibliography

Barber, John (1970) "Pinter's cold tension in Joyce's only play," *Daily Telegraph*, November 13: 14.

Batty, Mark (2005) *About Pinter*. London: Faber and Faber.

Billington, Michael (1996) *The Life and Work of Harold Pinter*. London: Faber and Faber.

Bosworth, Patricia (1968) "Why doesn't he write more?," *New York Times*, October 27, Sec. D: 3.

Connor, Steven (1996) *Writers and Their Works: James Joyce*. Plymouth: Northcote House.

Esslin, Martin (1971) "Exiles," *Plays and Players*, January: 38.

Gross, Miriam (1980) "Pinter on Pinter," *The Observer*, October 5: 25.

Gussow, Mel (1994) *Conversations with Harold Pinter*. London: Nick Hern Books.

Hall, Ann C. (1993) *"A Kind of Alaska": Women in the Plays of O'Neill, Pinter and Shepard*. Carbondale and Edwardsville: Southern Illinois University Press.

Henke, Suzette A. (1990) *James Joyce and the Politics of Desire*. London: Routledge.

Knowles, Ronald (1998) "Joyce and Pinter: *Exiles* and *Betrayal*," *Barcelona English Language and Literature Studies* 9: 183–91.

MacNicholas, John (1973) "Joyce's *Exiles*: the argument for doubt," *James Joyce Quarterly* 11: 33–40.

MacNicholas, John (1981–2) "The stage history of *Exiles*," *James Joyce Quarterly* 19: 9–26.

Mairowitz, Zane (1971) "Pinter does Joyce inch by inch," *Village Voice*, November 18.

Marcus, Frank (1970) *Sunday Telegraph*, November 15.

Mason, Michael (1982) "Exiles," *James Joyce Broadsheet* 8 (June): 5.

Nightingale, Benedict (1970) *New Statesman*, November 20.

Pinter, Harold (1974) "Butley," *The American Film Theatre/Cinebill*, January: 32–4.

Pinter, Harold (1991a) *Plays One*. London: Faber and Faber.

Pinter, Harold (1991b) *Plays Two*. London: Faber and Faber.

Pinter, Harold (1997) *Plays Three*. London: Faber and Faber.

Pinter, Harold (1998) *Plays Four*. London: Faber and Faber.

Pinter, Harold (2005) *Various Voices: Poetry, Prose and Politics 1948–2005*. London: Faber and Faber.

Sakellaridou, Elizabeth (1988) *Pinter's Female Portraits*. London: Macmillan.

Sheperd-Barr, Kirsten (2003) "Reconsidering Joyce's *Exiles* in its theatrical context," *Theatre Research International* 28 (2): 169–80.

Silverstein, Mark (1993) *Harold Pinter and the Language of Cultural Power*. London and Toronto: Associated University Presses.

Voelker, Joseph (1988) "The beastly incertitudes: doubt, difficulty, and discomfiture in James Joyce's *Exiles*," *Journal of Modern English Literature* 14 (4): 499–516.

Wardle, Irving (1970) *The Times*, November 13.

Williams, Raymond (1982) "Exiles." In Colin MacCabe (ed.) *James Joyce: New Perspectives*, pp. 105–10. Brighton: Harvester Press.

Worth, Katherine (1973) "Joyce via Pinter." In her *Revolutions in Modern English Drama*, pp. 46–54. London: G. Bell and Sons.

Wright, David G. (1988) "Joyce's debt to Pinter," *Journal of Modern Literature* 14 (4, Spring): 517–26.

20

The Joyce Effect:
Joyce in Visual Art

Christa-Maria Lerm Hayes

In the children's television and book series *Bob the Builder*, all supplies for Bob and the team come from JJ's building supplies yard. JJ's daughter is called Molly. She is an art student, who "works at the yard in her spare time, hiring out the skips" (Apsley and Clempner 2003). JJ stocks bricks, glass, and other materials suitable for erecting three-dimensional structures. JJ and Molly are seemingly of non-Western origin (Indian perhaps), while the colour scheme of Molly's clothes, as well as her name, point in another direction. A green-and-white jumper is combined with orange dungarees to generate a distinctly Irish flavor.

JJ's yard can serve as a fitting analogy for James Joyce's work and the ways in which visual artists are important heirs to Joyce. Taking artists seriously as Joyce's interpreters and scholars may yield new perspectives not only to the history of art, but also to Joyce studies. Fritz Senn has suggested that artistic interpretations have "a wider and more lasting effect than the sum total of our critical, scholarly comments" (Senn in Lerm Hayes 2004: 3). In JJ's yard, everything for the creation of two- and three-dimensional (art)work can be found. Art students need to spend a considerable time at JJ's yard – as Molly apparently does. They may become dismissive of traditions and have a skip ready to hand, challenging orthodoxies, but can also use the contents of that skip and the leftovers from chance accidents for their own creative ends. Molly's story also elucidates the fact that artists who have been attracted by Joyce are often those whose identity has become an issue and those who are students or are interested in subjectivity and identity formation.

James Joyce does not provide ready-made artworks or prescriptive aesthetic theories for the visual artist. What he stocks are tools and materials. He gives what he himself received from the skips that he raided: scaffolding. Joyce's work can – and in the best of cases does – function as a kind of builder's yard, a shared space where different backgrounds, knowledge, and creative skills are brought together for constructive ends.

Nevertheless, artists are only rarely consulted as interpreters of Joyce, and the writer's visual legacy is a field of scholarship that is only just emerging. I will here briefly outline this nascent field and some of the terms in which this interdisciplinary relationship can be discussed and include an account of some exhibitions related to Joyce. That gives me occasion for critical reflection on *Joyce in Art*, the book and exhibition project that I prepared for the Bloomsday centenary celebrations in Dublin in 2004. I will focus in particular on some irreverent artworks, seen as dialogical in the Bakhtinian sense, and add a few thoughts on Joyce in contemporary participative practice and the phenomenon of Joyce reading groups. This chapter will close with a consideration of one of several possible directions that the under-researched field of Joyce's visual legacy can take: Joyce's effect on the history of art.

In his review of my book *Joyce in Art: Visual Art Inspired by James Joyce*, Ruben Borg generously stated: "*Joyce in Art* is an ambitious work. It is no exaggeration to say that it inaugurates its own field of research and proceeds to codify that field, giving it a formal concreteness and a scarcely hoped-for accessibility" (Borg 2006: 189). While I was fortunate in having been the first to assemble so much fascinating material – beginning with Wyndham Lewis in 1914, as well as Joyce as a visual artist in 1929, and ending with artwork from 2004 – there are several excellent studies that have dealt with various aspects of this topic. These include my predecessor Archie Loss (1984), whose study ends in 1922, approximately where mine begins; Jo-Anna Isaac (1981); Robert Scholes (1992); and, dealing especially with postwar art, Evan R. Firestone (1982), Jean Fisher (2003), and Sarat Maharaj (1996). In art-historical literature, exhibition catalogues and interviews, one can often find an artist commenting on Joyce, though critics usually fail to follow up the invitation for further discussion. Tony Smith, Robert Motherwell, Richard Hamilton, Joseph Beuys, Martha Rosler, Lawrence Weiner, Brian O'Doherty (Patrick Ireland), and William Anastasi are among the artists whose knowledge and close reading of Joyce may often equal that of Joyce scholars. Most of their work remains to be considered in terms of the interpretations of Joyce's work they offer. Individual artworks that have an obvious relationship with Joyce are sometimes discussed in exhibition catalogues and sometimes literary scholars are asked to jump into the breach, such as with Declan Kiberd on Richard Hamilton's *Ulysses* illustrations (Hamilton 1988). Only occasionally does one find an art-historical text that analyzes an artist's work in its relation to Joyce's writing in a sustained way, though exceptions might include work by Marcelin Pleynet (1991), Vicki Mahaffey (1991), Suzanna Chan (2003), and Morris and Büchler (2001). Even rarer are texts that then focus on an artist's entire oeuvre (Lerm Hayes 2001). Evan R. Firestone was the only author to have focused on Joyce's legacy within a whole postwar art movement before I attempted my collection of material and issues.

Texts written from the Joycean perspective concern themselves with Joyce's aesthetics, Joyce's "art" in a more figurative use of the term, as well as with movements in visual art that may have influenced the writer's work such as Symbolism, Impressionism, Cubism, Expressionism, Futurism, and Dada. Such approaches are often exciting when they focus on Joyce as a participant in his era's culture (Kershner 1998), but they can remain troubled by general remarks about "Zeitgeist" and may leave themselves all too open to the inevitable reminder that Joyce was a "non-visual" writer (whatever that may mean), as well as one who suffered from eye problems.

Indeed, the current topic is one that its interdisciplinarity renders counterintuitive in many ways. Even when it is obvious that artists can both see and read Joyce, it might be asked how much use to them a writer can be who proposed the term "diaphane" (transparency) as an ideal for art, just at the time when art-historical modernism was at pains to emphasize the opacity of the visual artwork? How can Joyce's early concept of epiphany be reconciled with postmodernist tendencies that have sought to overcome the instantaneity with which the modernist work was supposed to be grasped? Though not treating Joyce himself, Grant Kester (2005) has placed "epiphany" and socially engaged art at opposite ends of the spectrum in current art practice. And how does one explain the fact that, at a time when minimalization, reduction, and simplicity were most prominent in the visual arts, a writer, whose strategy was the accumulative and the complex should become such a central point of reference?

Inspiration, Influence, Legacy, Effect, and Reverence

At this point, I should introduce some of the many terms that might be invoked to describe the relationship between Joyce and visual artists. When I used the term "inspiration" in the subtitle to *Joyce in Art*, I was motivated by Derrida's thoughts on spirit and echoed Joyce's penchant for secularized terminology (like epiphany). Here, however, I shall attempt to create some distance from the Romantic connotations of that term and thus also require the term "legacy," thereby only entering the "mysteriously romantic" idea of "afterlife" through the back door, since nothing "could be more overdetermined, unpredictable, nonlinear, and even mysterious than the notion of a writer's 'legacy'" (Cohen, Miller and Cohen 2001: xvi).

Joyce's own approaches towards traditions, most notably in his use of Homer as a scaffolding and as a quarry to be pillaged, may provide us with the appropriate background for approaching the strong legacy of visual artists working on him. It is true of artists' work in relation to Joyce that it

> cannot be fully justified in the straight line of a verifiable cognitive, hermeneutic interpretation. What Derrida in *Specters of Marx* says of his relation to the Marxian heritage might be said of the strongest [legacies.] Each is a "performative interpretation, . . . an interpretation that transforms the very thing it interprets." Only such faithful–unfaithful appropriation can be a responsible reception of such a legacy (Cohen, Miller and Cohen 2001: xvi).

It is difficult to speak of influence. No artwork is ever to be interpreted with just one reference; no relationship is just a one-way street. The title of Harold Bloom's study *The Anxiety of Influence* also does not quite apply to visual artists, who can reference their literary model directly without being called epigones. Joseph Beuys, for example, formulated a "confession of faith" in a work on Joyce (*Joyce with Sled*, 1985) that could not have been addressed to a visual artist. The influence of Joyce may, conversely, have been a motive behind the choice of some artists to work in the visual field rather than in that of literature. Martha Rosler, for example, began her career with a published essay on Joyce.

That said, however, I do concur with Harold Bloom's view that stronger works display a more independent, distanced relationship between the predecessor and the visual interpretation, which is also necessarily a misinterpretation (albeit a revealing one), and this may be heightened by the movement across disciplinary boundaries. Three of the six of Harold Bloom's revisionary ratios, which focus on such distance, thus describe the state of affairs most appropriately. *Clinamen, tessera,* and *kenosis* are, respectively: a swerve away from the model, its completion and antithesis, and a humbling movement towards discontinuity (Bloom 1997: 14). It should be possible both to use these categories in the following and to show them to be somewhat limited in their application to the interdisciplinary field, as well as in need of adjustment in relation to an art world that is sometimes characterized by the phenomenon of "postproduction." Joyce can be read between the lines of Nicolas Bourriaud's book, which established this term, as the precursor of a pillaging eclecticism that vitally includes ethical considerations of responsibilities and relationships beyond a merely consuming attitude.

I would develop this path further in order to argue that Joyce, the supposedly "apolitical" writer, has prompted a legacy in the visual arts that is clearly critical and often socially and politically committed. This might be explained with reference to the fact that for visual artists, following Walter Benjamin, it is common to see the book as distributed widely and relatively cheaply, already implying that it has a political significance. Such a reception among artists is now not as much at odds with positions taken by literary scholarship as it once might have been.

In those aspects of Bloom's argument which point towards a criticism, where influence becomes "antithetical" and "a series of swerves after unique acts of creative misunderstanding" (Bloom 1997: 93), we are not too far away from the concepts of the subversive and the dialogical that are so important to Bakhtin, and which I will invoke in the following in order to counterbalance the idea of reverence which is already always implicit in discussing artistic "legacy." I shall also employ a term that complements these ideas of influence and legacy: effect. And I shall introduce a short case study of the artist Richard Prince to show that eulogy and direct reverence do have their place in artists' works on Joyce – without crossing over into the realm of the unreflective.

David Hopkins' recent essay "Re-thinking the 'Duchamp-Effect'" begins by quoting Joseph Kosuth's statement from 1969: "All art after Duchamp is conceptual (in nature)." Hopkins rightly argues that "the lineage set up by Kosuth [i]s far too narrow [and must be] understood as a broad-based reaction originating in the later 1950s and 1960s to the formalist emphasis on visuality in the criticism of Clement Greenberg and Michael Fried" (Hopkins 2006: 145). Joyce's and Duchamp's approaches, biographies, and works show many uncanny parallels. In *Joyce in Art*, I escaped the shortsighted conclusion from this observation ("They must have met!") by arguing that Duchamp's rediscovery in the 1960s in both the US and Europe was led by visual artists (Kosuth himself and Richard Hamilton in the main) whose minds had been trained through the reading of Joyce, especially *Finnegans Wake*. They subsequently recognized Duchamp's notes as the conceptual foundation stones that they have ever since been seen as. I concluded that argument with the deliberately provocative assertion that the conceptual mindset in visual art may be as much a Joycean one as one owing to Duchamp (Lerm Hayes 2004: 143–8). Joyce epitomizes the paradigm shift to which Hopkins refers. Of course, there was a broader cultural shift under way and the call for breadth should not be answered with reference to just one additional figure. To introduce Joyce into the equation also means pre-dating the shift somewhat, to include the eager reading of Joyce among artists such as the New York School artists Tony Smith and David Smith, who had already set out to decompose high modernism's orthodoxies. In the retrospective reading of those who have felt their combined effect, Joyce and Duchamp colour each other's work, and they do share a view as fellow occupants of a position that is "never fully 'retinal' [read: formal] or 'conceptual' in approach, but something in between" (Hopkins 2006: 159). Hopkins finally asks,

> So how does the historian escape Duchamp's seduction? [. . .] One strategy would be to drop the "influence model" completely – however much Duchamp, perversely, obliges us to adopt it – and to think of "the Duchamp Effect" as more fundamentally generic and related to larger shifts in industrial production and mass media (Hopkins 2006: 145).

Effect is, indeed, an appropriate term for something with which most creative people have formed a relationship, conscious or otherwise, and which has also entered popular culture pervasively. It is in this sense that I will speak here of the Joyce effect or, accounting for their diversity, of Joyce effects.

Richard Prince is an American artist, whose photographs of the Marlborough Man are iconic, and whose images of the topless girlfriends of bikers at their group outings may even suggest an identification with or comment on Leopold Bloom, who sold advertising and bought erotic novels for his wife. Prince also has more "high" art interests, and he resolutely juxtaposes styles and registers. His sculptures include not only the hoods of modified cars and paintings covered with jokes, but also white pedestals, incorporating canonical novels, usually in two editions which are presented for comparison as well as for their "objecthood" (Figure 20.1).

In keeping with the many aspects of his work that are seemingly at variance with each other, Prince presents himself as a book collector, a connoisseur of the highest order, fantasizing about the most coveted of books:

> I want the best copy. The only copy. The most expensive copy. I want James Joyce's *Chamber Music*. I want the 1907 version, the variant, the first variant, the only with the lighter green binding, the taller, thin size, laid endpapers as opposed to wove [. . .] I want mine to be one of the advance review copies [. . .]. I want the tipped in letter to be dated May 3, 1907. I want this date because I know that the British Museum's copy (destroyed in World War II) was received on May 8 [. . .]. I want the earliest copy on record. I want the copy that is rarer than anyone had previously dreamed of. I want the copy of dreams (Prince 1992: 138–9).

He comments, "I've read *Chamber Music*. I've tried to read *Ulysses* about hundred times. It's hard. It's the kind of book written for a desert island" (letter to the author, January

Figure 20.1 Richard Prince, *Spoken English: Lolita* (2005)

5, 2007). The research he has undertaken into *Chamber Music* already seems to have taken up "desert island" time. When executing a work in 1987 that refers to Joyce even more clearly, he created a pseudonym to suit: John Dogg. The work is a steel loop (a "dog collar" shape?) with a rubber circle inside. It clearly shows a post-Duchampian aesthetic. On the rubber, one can enigmatically read "GGOD," while the title adds "*(Ulysses)*" (Figure 20.2).

Figure 20.2 John Dogg (Richard Prince), *GGOD (Ulysses)* (1987)

Here, the completion of Joyce (Bloom's *tessera*) would appear to most closely describe the relationship. Joyce's favorite wordplay on God and dog, in evidence when Stephen walks on Sandymount Strand in *Ulysses*, is combined with *Finnegans Wake*'s divine stutter. Prince seems to affirm and acknowledge Joyce in a very positive way as being engaged with both "high" and "low" – though not without a slight layer of irony. This shows the distance (at least in temporal terms) between Joyce and Prince. The writer, active in the times of connoisseurship, is met on his own terms, but as part of an oeuvre that deflates and banalizes. Joyce enables multi-stylistic work in all registers.

Exhibitions

From this example alone, it is evident that some visual artists' engagement with Joyce can go deep and has arisen out of lengthy research. One function that Joycean art exhibitions could have is to present and match such research, but they have often stopped well short of such ambition. Exhibiting Joyce is a topic that requires longer treatment than the current chapter can accommodate, but the practice is gaining in importance, as visual means are increasingly required to convey canonical authors to new readers. It has ranged from efforts at visualizing Joyce's Dublin through 3D animation computer technology (Gunn and Wright 2006), to publishing Joyce (Bishop 1994), to collecting and displaying first editions, as well as to illustrative artworks, and exhibiting Joyce's effects on visual artists.

The *James Joyce Broadsheet* has presented visual material related to Joyce in a sustained manner since 1980, with Pieter Bekker developing an early interest in this material. Many library and other literary exhibitions have shown first editions, memorabilia, and art since the important inaugural event of the 1949–50 Joyce exhibition in Paris and at the ICA in London, for which Richard Hamilton designed a broadsheet-like poster-catalogue. The 2004 National Library Joyce exhibition in Dublin was rightly praised for its excellent use of computer technology. It is that first exhibition's nearest neighbor. This juxtaposition of literary memorabilia and art is in evidence in all of the above and so widespread that it is hardly noticed. The Joyce Tower, the Dublin Writer's Museum, the James Joyce Cultural Centre and many library displays are characterized by this mixture that takes place when the visual culture of a writer's time is elucidated. The addition of more recent portraits and illustrations, or more loosely connected artwork, however, is likely to make it difficult for the viewer to decipher which interpretive attitude one ought to take – unless the equalizing and commodifying stance of the common high monetary value is allowed (Boscagli and Duffy 1996).

The Zurich James Joyce Foundation has organized two exhibitions on Joyce. Its holdings, like those of the Rosenbach Museum and Library in Philadelphia and the Harry Ransom Center at the University of Texas, in Austin, consist of both artworks and literary collectors' items of Joycean interest. In the exhibition "Thought through my Eyes" at the Strauhof Museum (adjacent to the Joyce Foundation) in 2000, strikingly simple but effective "reading aides" were presented in the effort to visualize

Joyce's work. Other items, like a giant copy of *Ulysses* that visitors could enter, gave a clear representation of the reader's becoming a part of this work. The artist Hannes Vogel co-curated the exhibition, helped with the "reading aides," contributed some of his own, and showed his larger, more independent work in a dedicated space. A major interest of this exhibition was that it reflected on that mixture in its comprehensive catalogue book (Zeller, Frehner, and Vogel 2000). Like Joyce's texts and artworks, such exhibitions require scholarly accompaniment, which was provided through wall texts by Heyward Ehrlich on a different occasion in 1982.

There have been countless art exhibitions held on the occasion of Bloomsdays and Joyce Symposia. In Szombathely, a festival featuring a mail art project takes place every Bloomsday. Marian Eide at the Rosenbach Museum and Library in 1995, and Jean-Michel Rabaté together with Aaron Levy at the Slought Foundation (both in Philadelphia), have curated small but thought-provoking Joyce exhibitions (Levy and Rabaté 2005). *Joycesight* in Rome focused on portraiture (Noon 1998) and Sheehan (2002) curated three witty, successive Bloomsday exhibitions of young, mostly Irish, artists' works. Bernd Klüser's Munich Gallery, as well as private collectors in Zurich and Cardiff, have commissioned and exhibited according to their particular interests in Joyce. *Joyce in Art* at the Royal Hibernian Academy, Dublin (June–August 2004), presented a larger and international version of such exhibitions. Before I take up the opportunity to reflect on this endeavor, I will turn to two shows that also coincided with the Bloomsday centenary.

One took place at the Atelier Augarten in Vienna and one at the Irish Museum of Modern Art, Dublin (IMMA) (Trummer 2004; Marshall 2004). They both began with first editions of *Ulysses* in glass cases. These were not copies owned by artists and the exhibition catalogues rightly did not claim the first editions to be visual artworks by the writer, though he had carefully picked the colour of the cover. While an artwork in a historical or literary exhibition can have the function of a piece of historical evidence, the reverse scenario can be more complicated, since a common denominator for all the exhibited material to be a part of canonical visual culture often seems to be sought. Works of contemporary art thus exhibited immediately vie for canonical acclaim and monetary value with the first edition. Its indexicality, however, appears to devalue their later and necessarily more "indirect" work.

In Vienna, the copy of *Ulysses* set the scene and it transformed the public for visual art into a group that sought to find out about *Ulysses*, not only through the art, through their previous knowledge, or through readily available sources, but through the exhibition catalogue. This included introductions to all the episodes of *Ulysses*, written mainly by the curator, as well as some reprinted essays on sensual perception in *Ulysses* and the like but not essays on the artworks presented, which were covered by two or three short pages each, without an attempt to generate an interpretation of what Joyce's effects on their art might have been or vice versa.

The exhibition at the Irish Museum of Modern Art had even larger problems to contend with. Apart from the first edition of *Ulysses* (which was borrowed) only works from the museum's own collection could be shown. This yielded about a dozen artists' works – mainly, but not exclusively, portraits and illustrations. In the wall texts (reprinted in the small catalogue), the curator distances both herself and the institution from their own exhibition. It is then especially interesting to note what the assumptions about Dublin's most famous son were in the premier government-funded contemporary art space in his native city, which had only two years previously exhibited Richard Hamilton's *Ulysses* illustrations. According to the catalogue, IMMA has "since its inception, dedicated itself to inclusive rather than exclusive art practices and programs, collecting quality artworks [rather] than famous named artists." It goes on:

> To cite Joyce in relation to one's own work could be read as an open sesame to the club of innovative and gifted people that Joyce himself epitomised but that is hardly a critique that could be levelled at any of the artists represented in this exhibition although it would certainly be true that some of them were as inspired by Joyce's legendary struggle to get his work published as others were excited by his texts (Marshall 2004).

Joyce's defining characteristic is apparently taken to lie in his canonicity, yet it remains slightly unclear what is meant here by notions of the "inclusive" and of "quality" which necessarily have a dependence on the canon. If Joyce is identified with the canon, does that mean that the exhibited artists do not belong to it, or that no relationship can be established between them and the writer? Neither reading would be borne out by the works. Perhaps the point is that these artists empathize with the as-yet non-canonical early Joyce, a view possibly supported by the exhibition's title, "high falutin stuff" and the explanation that was placed alongside it: "James Joyce took a very iconoclastic view of highbrow culture as his jocose reference to it in *Ulysses* . . . suggests: High falutin stuff" (Marshall 2004: 11). Misunderstandings multiply as Joyce is apparently no longer the canonical figure he is simultaneously accused of being, but rather an iconoclast. Much suggests that this text was written hurriedly and that the exhibition was the most unloved of any that the museum has so far presented. At the IMMA "Curating Now" symposium, held six months later, Enrique Juncosa, IMMA's director, stated in response to a question about political pressure that "without the Minister's say-so, we wouldn't have done that Joyce exhibition" – apparently a sad reflection on the missed opportunities for freedom and relevance that could have been recognized in the topic.

The Joyce in Art research project, completed in 2004, comprised a book and an exhibition, held at the Royal Hibernian Academy, in Dublin's city center, and curated in association with its director, Patrick T. Murphy. We showed approximately one hundred works from the last ninety years by over seventy international visual artists. The exhibition was launched in advance of the centenary of Bloomsday by the Minister of Art, as the Irish government had funded it generously.[1] Although the book and exhibition were intended to be encyclopedic, in response to Joyce's accumulative strategies, some of the central hypotheses of this project were that illustration and portraiture – the most common reactions by visual artists to literature – do not suit Joyce's works well. This is partly the case because both genres, as executed in traditional nineteenth-century fashion, are anachronistic in relation to Joyce's work and do not acknowledge that he broke radically with the conventions of pre-modernist times.

Artists more profitably reflect upon and interpret, and even extend, correct, and avoid, his work, demonstrating Bloomian *clinamen* and *tessera* to a particular degree. In such ways, Joyce's writings, thinking, and example have played a decisive if not central role at certain junctures of art history over the last ninety and especially the last fifty years. The role of Joyce's works for art may be compared to their influential function vis-à-vis critical theory during the same period. He was central both to the conceptualization of their works and to the identity-building of some of the leading artists in most postwar movements. Some (such as Martha Rosler) have found their Jewish identities and others (such as Jess, Tony Smith, David Smith, Patrick Ireland) their Irish or Irish-American identities to be particular incentives for studying Joyce. Artists attracted to Joyce since the 1960s have found in him a precedent for artistic emphasis on both form and content and for them he has also been an artist who could provide a legacy of committed art practices, those highlighting complex, typically postcolonial identities, "dislocutions" of all kinds and the fleeting nature of hierarchical power structures (Lerm Hayes 2004: 131–4).

What I wish to explore further arises from this last aspect of Joyce's effect. It is the observation that the artists who have most profitably responded to the challenge that is Joyce have done so obliquely and often irreverently or subversively: an observation powerfully confirmed when seeing the works come together in the exhibition. Many of the now-canonical artists shown might not always strike us today as struggling to forge their identities or fighting for recognition against all the odds. But they once were and Joyce for many of them has correspondingly remained a rebel, somewhat romantically eschewing canonization as well as commodification. This is true except, perhaps, for his faithful illustrators and portraitists. While Robert Motherwell and Richard Hamilton are testimony that the two camps cannot neatly be kept apart from each other, both have invented their Joyce and the question is to judge which responses are particularly valid today as interpretations of the writer's works and as examples of the Joyce effect.

Irreverent Appropriations

In order to pursue these appropriately irreverent appropriations of Joyce and their implications for who "owns" Joyce and which artists will own him in years to come, I will concentrate on a handful of artists and individual works, most but not all of them exhibited in "Joyce in Art."

It can be taken as a given that Joyce's works (especially *Ulysses* and *Finnegans Wake*) offer particularly good examples of the Bakhtinian forms of heteroglossia, dialogism, unfinalizability, the carnivalesque, folklore, the foregrounding of the body, and the view that form and content discourse are one (Kershner 1989). In keeping with the theme of faithful–unfaithful appropriations, it is partly the aim of this section to explore the extent to which these subversive and irreverent elements of Bakhtin's theories feed into these artworks in their responses to Joyce.

I find Miroslaw Balka a good example with which to begin. His figurative sculpture of a boy standing beside an table or altar, entitled *Remembrance of the First Holy Communion*, 1985, lays open moments of identification, in terms of their shared Catholic upbringing, between this young Polish artist and the young Joyce, and especially his alter ego in *A Portrait of the Artist as a Young Man*, Stephen Dedalus. Whilst there may be no exact precedent for the reduced color range of the body of Balka's boy or for the red heart and wound on the knee that are visible as its most strongly colored elements, this work illustrates *A Portrait* relatively faithfully. It represents Balka's own youth and is a moving work which captures the late nineteenth-century culture that is still well preserved in some parts of rural Poland. The artist has subsequently turned to producing works that focus on Stephen Dedalus' sensual experiences, such as wetting the bed, by his introduction of fountains, heated cushions and other unusual sculptural materials. Here, *A Portrait* is not illustrated so much as mediated via Joyce's thinking and material use of language in his later works. The whiskey fountain *250 x 280 x 120 (Sweets of Sin)* (2004), which Balka created for "Joyce in Art", merges many elements: biography (Joyce's fondness of alcohol); his literary use of synesthesia (the sculpture reeked and foamed for the duration of the show); the snow in "The Dead"; Balka's previous "bed" works on Joyce; Molly Bloom with her chamber pot; Bloom's and Stephen's urination at the end of *Ulysses*; and other bodily and sexually explicit, even abject, passages of the book. *Sweets of Sin* is a mildly pornographic novel that Leopold Bloom reads in the "Wandering Rocks" episode of *Ulysses*. Whiskey (in Irish *uisce beatha* or water of life) is literalized in *Finnegans Wake* into the water of life that resurrects Tim Finnegan. It thus provides yet another instance of or evidence for the cyclical nature of life and history on which that book is based. Balka's whiskey pump (Figures 20.3a and b) responds to Joyce's flowing cycles.

The result is a flowing sculpture in response to the bodily excretions featured in *Ulysses* and the flowing narrative of *Finnegans Wake*. The work comments on and inter-

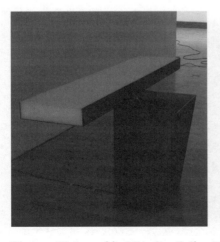 

Figures 20.3a and b Miroslaw Balka, *250 x 280 x 120 (Sweets of Sin)* (2004)

prets Joyce's oeuvre as a whole and in a semi-abstract way. It is a richer, more subversively humorous work than the *Holy Communion*, and it takes time and effort to decipher and interpret – akin to the process of reading the language of *Finnegans Wake*. The *Wake*, as the culmination of Joyce's oeuvre, merges previous motifs and Balka's procedures as well as his motifs may be said to appropriate this merging: faithfully but not too much so, having chosen to work on Joyce's legacy, but creating a sculpture that is clearly part of current artistic practice and of Balka's universe. It is this before it is anything that illuminates Joyce or – still less – echoes the writer's own taste in visual art. While Christian Orthodox faith was upheld in Bakhtin's work, the "answerable other" here, as in the following works, is made up both of Joyce and of contemporary viewers. In Balka's oeuvre, it even appears that a turning away from religious faith enabled a more pronounced dialogical trust in the recipients' capabilities to respond, to laugh, and possibly to interpret, and this is something that could be said about Joyce before him.

Joseph Beuys also proceeded in this Joycean–Bakhtinian fashion, letting one work emerge out of another, and his work provided another point of departure and another "dialogue partner" for Balka's. The nucleus of his sculptural and performance work is the practice of drawing, seen particularly his *Ulysses-Extension* from 1957–61. Ten double pages of these drawings were displayed in "Joyce in Art". The six exercise books where they originated are also the place where Beuys outlined his theory of social sculpture, his use of materials, as well as their social and ethical import all in a Joycean context. At first glance, these appear as monologues, interior ones. Featuring many inside views of the human body, they use the pencil and other substances to "think with the knee," as Beuys put it later in a postcard multiple. This is a dialogical way of thinking, creating a special kind of freely interpreted Joycean legacy, where not Bloom or Odysseus is the main protagonist, but a Penninus. This work is at once an extension and a "correction" of Joyce, a *clinamen*, and one that has itself had many effects and stood Beuys in good stead throughout his career (Lerm Hayes 2004: 175–6; 2001: 302–5).

Although *Ulysses* is mentioned in the title, I have shown elsewhere that the *Ulysses-Extension* as well as many sculptural formulations that emanated from this for the next thirty years are more closely related to the thinking of the later Joyce (Lerm Hayes 2004: 237–48). The fact that Beuys annotated almost every page of the *Wake* and issued a late, confession-of-faith-like text (*Joyce with Sled*, 1985), points to the immense importance Joyce had for the artist, whose work can, more than that of most artists of his generation, be called dialogical, especially in his dictum that the terms of his social sculpture will be dead and buried if not used and reinvented continuously (Hirschkop and Shepherd 1989: 41). Joyce served for Beuys as the "answerable other."

While most literary critics in the 1960s and 70s slighted Joyce for his supposedly apolitical stance, Beuys read Richard Ellmann's biography in 1972 (having already bought Jean Paris' earlier one) and annotated it selectively to highlight a certain partisan-like, anarchic image of the writer. His own work followed similar paths. Although Beuys did not always shy away from dogmatic statements, his overall intentions and especially his early work show a distinct link between the Joycean effect and his belief in answerability and social activism. The artist's interest in Ireland brought these elements together in the then rather unpopular recommendation to solve the "Troubles" in Northern Ireland through dialogue.

Patrick Ireland, who emigrated from Dublin to Manhattan in 1957, is another artist whose sociopolitical commitment is apparent and is even inscribed in his name, adopted by Brian O'Doherty for his visual art practice in response to the British presence in Northern Ireland and following Bloody Sunday in 1972. Patrick Ireland has returned to Joyce's texts, as many Irish emigrants and second, and subsequent, generation Irish-American artists have, finding in them a surrogate home (Lerm Hayes 2001: 121–5). He is also the artist who has most strongly expressed not only his admiration for but also his annoyance with Joyce that would apparently go well beyond even the more reactive categories of Bloomian influence. In 1963–4 he devised a game called *In the Wake (of)* where dice inscribed with words from *Finnegans Wake* could be rearranged. He explains that it

> is appropriately complex conceptually and had he [Joyce] seen it, it might have puzzled and bothered the wee bugger (not a very pleasant man I gather) by turning his own strategies against him. I think if you play with the great man, you have a chance of winning. Since I'm not in the tribute business, this is much more fun (Lerm Hayes 2004: 146–7).

This kind of playfulness approaches the subversiveness of the carnivalesque in Bakhtin.

Rebecca Horn's *Knuckle Dome for James Joyce* (2004) is another expression of an artist's love–hate relationship with Joyce (Figure 20.4). While her Kafka-inspired sculptures are sensitive, even nostalgic, Horn has created a simultaneously violent and humorous anti-Joyce piece that consists of ten knives with the letters "LOVE HATE" inscribed on their blades in red and black, like the knuckle tattoos of urban rebels. This

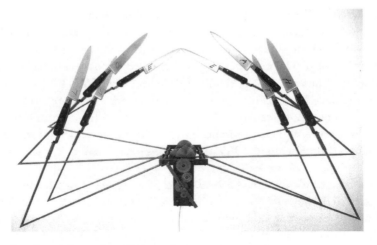

Figure 20.4 Rebecca Horn, *Knuckle Dome for James Joyce* (2004)

comments on the contemporary, impoverished urban lower class out of which Joyce had come a century earlier. Knives, being everyday items, also point to the kinds of domestic objects whose odyssey is a feature of *Ulysses*. That book overtly focuses far more on love and the dejection Bloom feels concerning his wife's unfaithfulness, but love and its "opposite" are juxtaposed when Bloom becomes the victim of nationalist anti-Semitism. Furthermore, the dome or delta-shape created by the converging knives is the sign or siglum for Anna Livia, the female protagonist in *Finnegans Wake*. It is a shape that simultaneously connotes the male (a mountain) and the female (the river delta), giving scope for a battle of the sexes that Joyce does not perform overtly. This is another "extension" of the writer or *tessera*, and is further in dialogue since the delta or Penninus motif was a leitmotif in Beuys' engagement with both *Ulysses* and the *Wake*. The dancing knives move like spiders' legs, adding a humorous suggestion to anyone who knows that Joyce was remembered by his friends for the spider dance he performed. Several criteria for dialogism and the carnivalesque are fulfilled.

James Coleman's overt occupation with Joyce originated in 1982, the Joyce centenary year. He used xeranthemum leaves, translated as "cheerfulness under adversity" in the appropriate language of flowers, for a garland on the bricked-up door of 7 Eccles Street, the fictional home of the Blooms, which was demolished in that year of Joyce celebrations (Figure 20.5).

A silver cast of this garland was on show at a Dublin art exhibition in the same year. In "Joyce in Art", this silver cast acted as the starting point for a new installation. Coleman mounted it on tinted Perspex, blocking the entrance to the second-largest room at the Academy, the one allotted to the artist, which he left empty. This void comments on the openness of Joyce's works – just like the near-white paintings in the central space of the main gallery, accompanied by a wall text that explains Umberto Eco's 1962 book *Opera Aperta* (*The Open Work*), whose main exemplar was Joyce, which was immediately influential among European artists and which informs such current concepts as the "Writerly Artist" (Mavor 2006). The open work is already a political manifestation, a statement of the active role and the recipients' freedom, which it theorizes. Additionally, Coleman's 1982 *Ulysses Project* was, despite its poetic manifestations, a scathing criticism of how Dublin and Ireland have treated their "exiled" son in the past. The artist's own "exile" in Italy, like Joyce's, adds another dimension or personal correspondence.

The function of Coleman's new installation was to serve as a reminder of the absences and voids that the writer found in his home country and turned into a feature in his work – this time activating the readers' responses and empowering them. The large empty space within an exhibition that featured many works that reflect on Joyce's accumulations is also an affront. It is the antithesis to illustration, one could say, and a reminder that Joyce's work retains its subversive potential.

The selection and layout of "Joyce in Art" played its part in the attempt to present a narrative that was critical and dialogically subversive (Figure 20.6), since it is not sufficient to give subversive works a platform which might possibly neutralize them. Many if not most of the viewers' expectations were for illustrations, possibly for such

Figure 20.5 James Coleman, *Ulysses Project* (1982)

Figure 20.6 "Joyce in Art" (2004). Installation shot showing (left to right) works by Man Ray, E. L. Kirchner, Gereon Inger, Raymond Pettibon, Tony Smith, Jürgen Parthenheimer, Joseph Beuys, and Joseph Kosuth (ceiling)

traditional features of the literary exhibition as a first edition here or a portrait there. A chronological arrangement might have been the norm. Initially, this seemed to be what was delivered, since the viewers were at the outset confronted with two nineteenth-century vitrines displaying the earliest exhibits (Wyndham Lewis, Matisse, and art by Joyce himself). But there was no first edition and viewers were then free to choose their own route through loosely thematic clusters. The "white paintings" in the central space of the main gallery gave openness and put the viewers themselves centre stage. Slightly off-centre stood a sculpture by Tony Smith, *The Keys to. Given*, with its angles pointing in all directions. There was not one key, instead a reference to the shape-shifting multiplicity of identities that Joyce pioneered with his sigla (Lerm Hayes 2004: 109–13, 128–9). Moreover, the synesthesia of Balka's whiskey fountain and many sound works sought to involve the viewers' physical bodies through their senses beyond the visual. This was particularly the case when they were actively involved such as in cycling on the bicycle in Jeffrey Shaw's *Legible City* installation, which took them through an interactive cityscape made up of writing. Here, they directly experienced a nonlinear way of reading, akin to that which Joyce had encouraged in the *Wake*. John Latham's roller blind with text from *Finnegans Wake* and entitled *The* after the cyclically "last" word, "the," also focused on nonlinearity (Latham had taught Shaw). *The* was one of the last pieces in the show, downstairs, before it was possible and encouraged by free entrance for visitors to complete the "commodius vicus of recirculation"

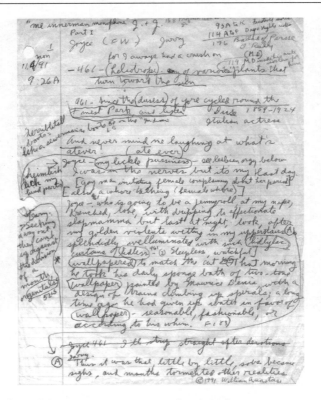

Figure 20.7 William Anastasi, *me innerman monophone* (2004)

(*FW* 3 2) and begin once more, echoing Joyce's last book's structure. The viewer could experience at first hand the absence of a "last word" that was important for both Joyce and Bakhtin (Hirschkop and Shepherd 1989: 113).

The presentation of thematic clusters and the freedom to choose one's own route are already standard practice within contemporary art display. As here, it carries the hope that visitors will create their own meanings. In "Joyce in Art" it was also a move that echoed the ways in which artists have responded to Joyce and to the dialogues that the writer himself had introduced via his sources and cultures. The fact that many virtually unknown artists were presented alongside the canonical ones was also an attempt to subvert the tendency towards the easily consumable spectacle that is inherent in large-scale exhibitions.

William Anastasi's *me innerman monophone* can serve to represent the time-consuming, work-intensive artworks in "Joyce in Art" that elude easy consumption (Figure 20.7). In researching and presenting the related, dialogical worlds of Jarry, Duchamp, and Joyce, it also aimed at the "coexistence of distinct languages which seems to define heteroglossia" (Hirschkop and Shepherd 1989: 18).

Works such as Martha Rosler's *Car Boot Sale* at the Project Gallery, Dublin (an exhibition with close ties to "Joyce in Art"), Rebecca Horn's knife sculpture, and James

Coleman's installation prompt the observation that the Bloomsday centenary inspired artists to focus in their own work on deviations from the uncritically celebratory and create works that anticipate how Joyce himself may have reacted to such festivities.

Artists often used banal, everyday items, like knives and all the bric-a-brac sold at Martha Rosler's *Car Boot Sale*. A critical and simultaneously caring message was conveyed, one that we might also call "cynical" since, as Wolfgang Wicht has explained,

> According to Žižek's definition, cynicism "represents the popular, plebeian rejection of official culture by means of irony and sarcasm [. . .] confront[s] the pathetic phrases of the ruling official ideology [. . .] with everyday banality and so hold[s] them up to ridicule[.]" Joyce's popular, pragmatic rejection of utopian thought corresponds to this classical method of criticising ruling ideology (Wicht 2000: 236).

"Joyce in Art" saw it as its task to facilitate such dialogical subversion. Although in its need for funding, and ensuing complicity in the attempt at spectacle, the exhibition clearly had its limitations, it was, I believe, necessary and possible to present such a survey-type display. I do not feel the wish to disown the project. It has given and still gives rise to many dialogues with artistic positions of exemplary thoughtfulness and it enabled me to write an "encyclopedic" book that is also organized chronologically then thematically in turn. It also introduces reminiscences of Joyce's complexity and what one can call *Finnegans Wake*'s "nonlinearity" or "hypertextuality" in its three modes of internal references, a feature that Ecke Bonk devised as an artistic response to Joyce and the text itself.

I did not make explicit the dialogistic implications of this and it has since also occurred to me what else was missing. The last work in "Joyce in Art" was John Cage's diachronic and anarchically dialogic *James Joyce, Marcel Duchamp, Eric Satie, an Alphabet*, 1990. In it, Joseph Beuys appears among many other characters from all ages and many countries. Cage much enjoyed playing or reading the part of Joyce himself. "Joyce in Art" has brought me to realize that Noel Sheridan's intended reading of (or performative departure from) passages of *Finnegans Wake* at the exhibition's opening, which could not take place for copyright reasons, would have been an important pointer towards the work that needs to be continued in order to encompass the dialogical more clearly and in order to renew and review Joyce for the future.

Reading Groups

Locating elements of dialogism, of the carnivalesque, of the focus on the body, of political activism, of ironic citation, of appropriation, and of an increasing distance from narrowly "text-serving" approaches in artists' reactions to Joyce should lead us to evoke the power of the reading group as a response to Joyce's later work that conjures up the dialogical again. *Finnegans Wake* requires to be read aloud and so transgress the boundaries of the written word and it also needs the simultaneously offered expertise of a great variety of specialists in such diverse things as nursery rhymes, Greek mythology, English literature, Dublin lore, comics, dance, the history of the book, and many more: non-coincident consciousnesses, in Bakhtinian terminology (Elkins in Lerm Hayes 2004: 325–9).

Finnegans Wake reading groups have a long pedigree of being held at independent venues like the Zurich Joyce Foundation or the Paula Cooper Gallery in New York (a space that opened with an exhibition of activist art against the Vietnam War) and of involving artists like Tony Smith, Brian O'Doherty/Patrick Ireland, and Susan Weil. Although reading in a group does not in itself constitute an artwork, I would argue that it bears the hallmarks of much current "relational" activity in the arts. The performance of artistic reading of Joyce would moreover be a perfect continuation of what had in the past taken place in László Moholy-Nagy's class at the School of Design in Chicago (Moholy-Nagy 1947); at the Black Mountain College, where John Cage, Susan Weil, Robert Rauschenberg, and others congregated; and during Noel Sheridan's perform-ances in New York and Australia.

Artists have also explored Joycean reading spaces. Joseph Beuys connected the "folded" roof of an Expressionist house with his reading of *Finnegans Wake* and Davide Cascio has devised a similarly multi-angled polyhedron, promoting multi-directional thinking, while reading *Ulysses*, complete with flowers in the corners (Figure 20.8).

In 1996 Kenneth Goldsmith extended Joyce by publishing every one of his utter-ances during a week (Goldsmith 2001). His colleagues Simon Morris and Pavel Büchler have conversed about this work, thereby creating yet another text-based visual artwork entitled *Extreme Reading*: a reaction to Goldsmith's reaction to Derrida's reaction to

Figure 20.8 Davide Cascio, "Space for Reading *Ulysses*" (2004)

Ulysses, presented as monologues, a subversive non-conversation in two disjointed parts (Morris and Büchler 2001).

Reading groups build collective identities and build on a "dialogical aesthetics [that] suggests a very different image of the artist [and reader]; one defined in terms of openness, of listening and a willingness to accept dependence and intersubjective vulnerability" (Kester 2005: 81). These artists and readers or interpreters have brought and will bring with them their skepticism and thus best faithfully–unfaithfully serve, (mis)interpret, appropriate, and transform Joyce, as well as their own enquiries.

Future Directions

One of the intended implications of my final statement in "Joyce in Art", that Joyce was an artists' writer, is that he is not so far an art historians' writer. A major anthology of recent art-historical texts does not contain his name (Jones 2006). Such exceptions as so far confirm the rule include essays by Carola Giedion-Welcker and Sarat Maharaj. Giedion-Welcker was among a number of Joyce's friends who were eminently knowledgeable about art, including James Johnson Sweeney, Samuel Beckett, and Thomas MacGreevy. Giedion-Welcker was misrepresented by major English-speaking art-historical figures, namely Rosalind Krauss and Lucy Lippard, who did not (wish to) realize that the author of the first monograph on modernist sculpture shared many of their own interests. Joyce quotations and references in her work are frequent.

Sarat Maharaj, who has considered far-reaching issues of translation and "typotranslation," thoughtfully complicates the issues of untranslatability and hybridity. Apartheid had taken essential "untranslatability" as justification for keeping the two parts of South African society separate and worse. Hybridity as the happy-clappy opposite, Maharaj rightly asserts, needs to remain problematic and can never quite be achieved, but must be kept alive. In this context, he invokes *Finnegans Wake*, the quintessential untranslatable text. It does not keep us apart, but in reading together makes us realize that we understand each other and the text by each understanding equally little. That empowering moment brings with it suggestiveness and, as a reward, not the easy translatability of Joyce into the realm of art, but the further complicating of the question of his effects in art. Joyce remains central in these eminently topical and far-reaching discourses.

Who in art will "own" Joyce in years to come was James Elkins' suggestive question in his envoi to *Joyce in Art* (Lerm Hayes 2004: 325–9). It can only partially be answered with recourse to interpretations of a near-encyclopedic selection of practitioners and works such as the one that I attempted to present in that book. It is a question that depends as much on the perspectives that those art historians whose thoughts, identities and approaches have been formed in reading Joyce have brought to art and will bring to it in the future. Joyce's effects in art history are one obvious direction in which my research is currently taking me. Carola Giedion-Welcker and Sarat Maharaj are this project's bookends. In anticipation of its findings, I can here attempt a preliminary answer to Elkins' question as far as the past is concerned. Art historians who have formulated a Joycean legacy are not the traditionalists occupied with style and iconography, nor those coopted by auction houses and the tribute industry. They are among those who have challenged orthodoxies in the field, who have promoted interdisciplinarity and developed a corresponding aesthetics of the "both–and," of hybrid reading and relevance. They keep art history alive.

It is only through further artworks like the ones here discussed and further studies in this field that artists, art historians, Joyceans, and readers can influence what will form Joyce's lasting visual effects and thus also shape our view of the writer's achievements: the canonical image of a round pair of glasses or the thought-provoking, subversive, conceptual works that (mis)interpret Joyce productively.

JJ's builders' supplies yard continues to be a meeting place. Molly's many friends and JJ's guests will certainly still be seen congregating there in the future, and, having put the welding torch aside for a moment, may be spotted huddling around annotated copies of a never-ending book.

NOTE

1 Research for the book and exhibition was supported by a Government of Ireland Post-Doctoral Fellowship, with which I was based at University College Dublin. The project was also sponsored by the Irish Government's ReJoyce Dublin 2004 Committee, MBNA Ireland, the National University of Ireland and the *Irish Times*. I am indebted to the Joseph Beuys Foundation, Basel, as well as the University of Ulster for my current sabbatical.

BIBLIOGRAPHY

Apsley, Brenda and Jane Clempner (2003) *Bob the Builder: Annual 2004*. London: Egmont Books.

Bishop, Edward L. (1994) "Re-covering *Ulysses*." In Thomas F. Staley (ed.) *Joyce Studies Annual 5*, pp. 22–55.

Bloom, Harold (1997) *The Anxiety of Influence: A Theory of Poetry*. New York and Oxford: Oxford University Press.

Borg, Ruben (2006) "Entwining our arts: a review of Christa-Maria Lerm Hayes, *Joyce in Art: Visual Art Inspired by James Joyce*," *Journal of Modern Literature* 29 (4): 189–93.

Boscagli, Maurizia and Enda Duffy (1996) "Joyce's faces." In Kevin J. H. Dettmar and Stephen Watt (eds.) *Marketing Modernisms: Self-Promotion, Canonization, and Rereading*, pp. 133–59. Ann Arbor: University of Michigan Press.

Bourriaud, Nicolas (2002) *Postproduction*. New York: Lukas and Sternberg.

Budgen, Frank (1972) *James Joyce and the Making of Ulysses and Other Writings*, introduction by Clive Hart. Oxford: Oxford University Press.

Chan, Suzanna (2003) "Looking for Molly Bloom: Frances Hegarty and Andrew Stones' art work *For Dublin*," *Irish Studies Review* 11 (3): 321–35.

Cohen, Tom, J. Hillis Miller, and Barbara Cohen (2001) "A 'materiality without matter'?" In their and Andrzej Warminski's *Material Events: Paul de Man and the Afterlife of Theory*. Minneapolis: University of Minnesota Press.

Eco, Umberto (1989) [Italian edition published 1962] *The Open Work*. London: Hutchinson Radius.

Ehrlich, Heyward (ed.) (1982) *James Joyce and Modernism: An Exhibit*. Newark: Rutgers.

Feshbach, Sidney (1989) "Marcel Duchamp or being taken for a ride: Duchamp was a Cubist, a Mechanomorphist, a Dadaist, a Surrealist, a

Conceptualist, a Modernist, a Post-modernist – and none of the above," *James Joyce Quarterly* 26 (4): 541–60.

Firestone, Evan R. (1982) "James Joyce and the first-generation New York School," *Arts Magazine* 56 (10): 116–21. Reprinted in Ellen G. Landau (ed.) (2005) *Reading Abstract Expressionism: Context and Critique*. New Haven, CT and London: Yale University Press.

Fisher, Jean (2003) "The enigma of the hero in the work of James Coleman." In George Baker (ed.) *James Coleman*, pp. 36–55. Cambridge, MA and London: MIT Press.

Gaiger, Jason and Paul Wood (eds.) *Art of the Twentieth Century: A Reader*. New Haven and Milton Keynes: Yale University Press and the Open University.

Giedion-Welcker, Carola (1973) *Schriften 1926–1971*. Cologne: Dumont.

Goldsmith, Kenneth (2001) *Soliloquy*. New York: Granary Books.

Gunn, Ian and Mark Wright (2006) "Visualising Joyce," *Hypermedia Joyce Studies* 7 (1), available at http://hjs.ff.cuni.cz/archives/v7/main/essays.php?essay=gunn (accessed February 2007).

Hamilton, Richard (1988) *Work in Progress: On Illustrations for James Joyce's* Ulysses. Derry: Orchard Gallery.

Hirschkop, Ken and David Shepherd (eds.) (1989) *Bakhtin and Cultural Theory*. Manchester: Manchester University Press.

Hopkins, David (2006) "Re-thinking the 'Duchamp-Effect.'" In Amelia Jones (ed.) *A Companion to Contemporary Art since 1945*, pp. 145–63. Oxford: Blackwell.

Isaac, Jo-Anna (1981) "James Joyce and the Cubist esthetic," *Mosaic* 14: 61–90.

Jones, Amelia (2006) *A Companion to Contemporary Art since 1945*. Oxford: Blackwell.

Joyce, James (1929) "Fluviana," *transition* 16 (17): between 296 and 297.

Kershner, R. B. (1989) *Joyce, Bakhtin, and Popular Literature: Chronicles of Disorder*. Chapel Hill: University of North Carolina Press.

Kershner, R. B. (1998) "The culture of Ulysses." In Vincent J. Cheng, Kimberly J. Devlin, and Margot Norris (eds.) *Joycean Cultures/Culturing Joyces*, pp. 149–62. Newark, NJ: University of Delaware Press.

Kester, Grant (2005) "Conversation pieces: the role of dialogue in socially-engaged art." In Zoyka

Kocur and Somon Lueg (eds.) *Theory in Contemporary Art since 1985*, pp. 76–88. Oxford: Blackwell.

Lerm Hayes, Christa-Maria (1997) *Hannes Vogel: Wylermeer – The Hill on which Vogel, Beuys, Joyce, Cage, Bartning . . . Meet With Ten Thunderclaps* (English, German, French), eds. Dirk Krämer and Klaus Maas. Bottrop: Peter Pomp.

Lerm Hayes, Christa-Maria (2001) *James Joyce als Inspirationsquelle für Joseph Beuys*. Hildesheim: Olms.

Lerm Hayes, Christa-Maria (2004) *Joyce in Art: Visual Art Inspired by James Joyce* with Fritz Senn (Foreword), James Elkins (envoi), Ecke Bonk (design). Dublin: Lilliput.

Levy, Aaron and Jean-Michel Rabaté (eds.) (2005) *William Anastasi's Pataphysical Society: Jarry, Joyce, Duchamp and Cage*. Philadelphia, PA: Slought Books.

Loss, Archie K. (1984) *Joyce's Visible Art: The Work of Joyce and the Visual Arts, 1904–1922*. Ann Arbor: University of Michigan Press.

Mahaffey, Vicki (1991) "The case against art: Wunderlich on Joyce," *Critical Enquiry* 17 (4): 667–92.

Maharaj, Sarat (1996) "'Transubstantiation': typo-translating the *Green Box*." In Martha Buskirk and Mignon Nixon (eds.) *The Duchamp Effect: Essays, Interviews, Round Table*, pp. 60–92. Cambridge, MA: MIT Press.

Maharaj, Sarat (2003 [1994]) "Perfidious fidelity: the untranslatability of the other." In Jason Gaiger and Paul Wood (eds.) *Art of the Twentieth Century: A Reader*, pp. 297–303. New Haven and London: Yale University Press/The Open University.

Marshall, Catherine (2004) "high falutin stuff." In Irish Museum of Modern Art. *high falutin stuff: IMMA Collection: Artists' Responses to James Joyce*, exhibition catalog, pp. 11–18. Dublin: IMMA.

Martyniuk, Irene A. (1998) "Illustrating *Ulysses*, illustrating Joyce." In Vincent J. Cheng, Kimberly J. Devlin, and Margot Norris (eds.) *Joycean Cultures/Culturing Joyces*, pp. 203–15. Newark, NJ: University of Delaware Press.

Mavor, Carol (2006) "The writerly artist: beautiful, boring, and blue." In Amelia Jones (ed.) *A Companion to Contemporary Art since 1945*, pp. 271–95. Oxford: Blackwell.

Moholy-Nagy, László (1947/1961) *Vision in Motion*. Chicago: Theobald.

Morris, Simon and Pavel Büchler (2001) *Extreme Reading*, available at http://intheconversation.blogs.com/art/2004/10/extreme_reading.html (accessed February 2007).

Nadel, Ira B. (1989) "Joyce and Expressionism," *Journal of Modern Literature* 16: 141–60.

Noone, Patricia (ed.) (1998) *Joycesight: Nove artisti irlandesi per James Joyce*. Exhibition catalog Trieste: Galeria d'Arte Moderna.

Pleynet, Marcelin (1991) "Art and literature: Robert Motherwell's *Riverrun*." In Stephen Bann and William Allen (eds.) *Interpreting Contemporary Art*, pp. 11–26. London: Reaktion Books.

Prince, Richard (1992) *Richard Prince*. Exhibition catalog New York: Whitney Museum of American Art.

Scholes, Robert (1992) "In the brothel of modernism: Picasso and Joyce." In his *In Search of James Joyce*, pp. 178–207. Urbana: University of Illinois Press.

Senn, Fritz (1993) "Transmedial stereotypes in the 'Aeolus' chapter of Joyce's *Ulysses*." In *Word & Image Interactions: A Selection of Papers Given at the Second International Conference on Word and Image*, pp. 61–8. Basel: Weise.

Sheehan, Declan (ed.) (2002) *Dedalus in Context: Bloomsday #1*. Derry: Context. (First in a series of three exhibitions: *B-Lomo Bloomsday #2*: 2003; *Molly*: 2004.)

Trummer, Thomas (ed.) (2004) *Ulysses: Die unausweichliche Modalität des Sichtbaren – Der Roman von James Joyce in der zeitgenössischen Kunst*. Exhibition catalog, Atelier Augarten, Vienna. Vienna: Christian Brandstätter.

Wicht, Wolfgang (2000) *Utopianism in James Joyce's* Ulysses. Heidelberg: C. Winter.

Zeller, Ursula, Ruth Frehner, and Hannes Vogel (eds.) (2000) *James Joyce "gedacht durch meine Augen"/"Thought through My Eyes."* Exhibition catalog, Strauhof, Zurich. Basel: Schwabe.

21

"In his secondmouth language": Joyce and Irish Poetry

Derval Tubridy

In his 1966 article "The Irish Writer" Thomas Kinsella (1928–) neatly encapsulates the dilemma of modern Irish literature, straining between the dual influences of W. B. Yeats and James Joyce:

> So, the Irish writer, if he cares who he is and where he comes from, finds that Joyce and Yeats are the two main objects in view; and I think he finds that Joyce is the true father. I will risk putting it diagrammatically, and say that Yeats stands for the Irish tradition as broken; Joyce stands for it as healed – or healing – from its mutilation (Kinsella 1967: 14).

What Joyce brings to an understanding of Irish literature is, in Kinsella's view, a recognition of the fractured and bilingual nature of the Irish tradition combined with an acceptance of modern social and political transformation. In short, Joyce embraces the "filthy modern tide" that so repelled Yeats.[1] It is Joyce's modernity, his ability to engage with the immediacy of Irish experience in all its aspects combined with his virtuoso transformations of language, that makes him a necessary exemplar for the Irish writer, and in particular the Irish poet.

Though Yeats and Joyce may be opposed in the minds of those who write in their wake,[2] Joyce's early writing was supported and encouraged by the elder poet who, in 1903, praised Joyce's writing, saying, "your technique in verse is very much better than the technique of any young Dublin man I have met during my time" (Yeats 1997: 13). In a letter to his family in December 1902 Joyce describes how Yeats introduced his work to the editors of periodicals such as the *Speaker* and the *Express*, and to others such as Arthur Symons and Maud Gonne who would be helpful in the future (*SL* 9). Joyce's first book, *Chamber Music*, was a collection of 36 poems that came out with Jonathan Cape of London (1907). However, even then, Joyce's attention was more clearly focused on his prose writing. On July 19, 1909, he wrote to a musician friend:

> There is no likelihood of my writing any more verse unless something unforeseen happens to my brain. I have written a book of stories called *Dubliners* and am in treaty with a

publisher about it. Besides that I am at work on a novel *A Portrait of the Artist as a Young Man* at which I have been engaged now for six years (*SL* 155).

Twenty years passed before the next collection, *Pomes Penyeach* (1927), was published in Paris by Shakespeare and Company. Written while Joyce was composing *Finnegans Wake*, the collection has been described as "a ploy to prove that Joyce, under fire for the lunacies of *Work in Progress*, could still be 'grammatically sane'" (Grennan 1999: 74). With the addition of "Ecce Puer," written to mark the death of his father and the birth of his grandson, both collections were gathered together in the *Collected Poems* published by the Black Sun Press of New York (1936). What is remarkable about the poetry here is the formal, almost staid quality of the language. Lines from "Ecce Puer":

> Of the dark past
> A child is born,
> With joy and grief
> My heart is torn

(PE 111)

are characterized by Seamus Heaney (1939–) as "well-tuned and well-turned" (Heaney 2002: 388). There is, he says, a "technical fastidiousness about them" (Heaney 2002: 388). "Ecce Puer," in his opinion, is "an unexpectedly unsophisticated performance for an artist who was at the same time splitting the linguistic atom in *Finnegans Wake*" (Heaney 2002: 389). Heaney's comments draw our attention to the marked difference in Joyce's use of language between the two modes of writing; the poetry looking back to an almost Victorian formalism, the prose looking forward to a modern experimentalism.

Two broadsides, "The Holy Office" (1904) and "Gas from a Burner" (1912), complete Joyce's verse. Even as he sought Yeats' approval and assistance, "The Holy Office" parodies Yeats' poem "To Ireland in the Coming Times." Joyce's broadsheet mocks key figures of the Irish Revival such as Yeats, Synge, and Gogarty, "But I must not accounted be / One of that mumming company–," placing the writer firmly on the side of the proletariat: "But all these men of whom I speak / Make me the sewer of their clique" (*PE* 104). Joyce refuses romanticism in favor of a modernity that Yeats had earlier disparaged in "The Statues": "We Irish, born into that ancient sect / But thrown upon this filthy modern tide" (Yeats 1983: 337), marking him as a writer who rejected the Revival's idealized Ireland in favor of the contingent and often brutal Ireland of the early twentieth century. Robert F. Garratt underlines how "the antiromanticism implicit in Joyce's treatment of Dublin's mean streets not only provides an antidote to Yeats' romantic Ireland but also shows to what extent ordinary experience might be used for art" (Garratt 1986: 83). The baton is passed, and a new cultural Ireland emerges. In "The Holy Office" Joyce makes clear where he stands: "That they may dream their dreamy dreams / I carry off their filthy streams" (*PE* 104). Though it was Joyce's verse that caught Yeats' attention, recent Irish poets such as Heaney look instead to the writer's prose for inspiration:

The great poetry of the opening chapter of *Ulysses*, for example, amplifies and rhapsodizes the world with an unlooked-for accuracy and transport. It gives the spirit freedom to range in an element that is as linguistic as it is airy and watery, and when the poems are compared with writing that feels so natural, spacious and unstoppably alive, they are seen to be what Yeats said the earliest of them were – the work of a man "who is practising his instrument, taking pleasure in the mere handling of the stops" (Heaney 2002: 389).

So it is to Joyce's prose – the measured clarity of *A Portrait of the Artist as a Young Man*, the ebullient music of *Ulysses*, and the extraordinary inventiveness of *Finnegans Wake* – that we look to find the kind of language that has invigorated and fortified Irish poetry. It is in Joyce also that we find a modern refiguration of themes central to Irish poetry today: language, place, and identity.

Loosely classified as Ireland's modernist poets, Thomas MacGreevy (1893–1967), Brian Coffey (1905–95), Samuel Beckett (1906–89), and Denis Devlin (1908–59) developed Joyce's continental and cosmpolitan aesthetic during the 1930s and 40s. Just as Joyce looks to the *Odyssey* in *Ulysses*, Coffey's poetic sequence *Death of Hektor* (1979) draws on Homer's *Iliad*:

A harp he   uses background for verses sung
He pared no fingernails not indifferent   not masked [. . .]
His ears open to spoken word and words down time like
                wind-blown sand
words of triumph unsleeping enmities wound-up spells malice
swirl of sound continual mixed in a perfect ear
surfacing coherent truer than history all and everything

(Coffey 1991: 156)

Here Coffey explicitly refers to the young Stephen of *A Portrait* when, in conversation with Lynch, he deifies the artist who "like the God of creation, remains within or behind or beyond or above his handiwork, invisible, refined out of existence, indifferent, paring his fingernails" (*P* 181).[3] However, for MacGreevy it was Joyce's Catholicism that was the point of connection. Writing in *Our Exagmination Round his Factification for Incamination of Work in Progress*, MacGreevy celebrates Joyce's Catholicism, emphasizing what he calls "the Catholic element" of Joyce's work with a reading of Stephen Dedalus' journey in *Ulysses* as a movement through "the inferno of modern subjectivity" (MacGreevey 1972: 117–27). Linking Joyce with T. S. Eliot, MacGreevy argues that Joyce's ability to encompass "the darker aspects of existence" is made possible by the "spiritual vocabulary of Catholicism" (Armstrong 1995: 50). In contrast, Joyce's ambivalent attitude towards Catholicism is shared by Austin Clarke (1896–1974), who identified closely with the novelist, describing how *A Portrait of the Artist as a Young Man* became confused with his own memories (Clarke 1962: 26). The repressive influence of the Catholic Church described by Joyce in the novel is explored by Clarke in poems such as "Ancient Lights" (1955). The fears that the Redemptorist sermon strikes in Stephen are echoed by Clarke's speaker: "But darkness / was roomed with fears. Sleep, stripped by woes / I had been taught, beat door, leaped landing / Lied down the banisters of naught"

(Clarke 1976: 27). Stephen's release at the close of *A Portrait* is figured in Clarke's work as a kind of baptism that echoes the "sweet rain" of Stephen's confessional experience, glorifying the natural elements in a celebration of the city:

> The sun came out, new smoke flew up,
> The gutters of the Black Church rang
> With services. Waste water mocked
> The ballcocks: down-pipes sparrowing,
> And all around the spires of Dublin
> Such swallowing in the air, such cowling
> To keep high offices pure: I heard
> From shore to shore, the iron gratings
> Take half our heavens with a roar.

(Clarke 1976: 28–9)

While Clarke's language may owe more to Gaelic prosody, such as *aicill*, *amus*, or *uaithne*,[4] than to a Joycean sense of linguistic experimentation, his investigation of the agonistic relationship between subjectivity and religious identity draws strongly on Joyce's example. By transmuting the religious rituals of Irish Roman Catholicism into his own aesthetics Joyce anticipated the new secular Ireland of the late twentieth century.

Joyce's writing provided an alternative vision of Ireland in a form which, by extending the possibilities of prose, opened new avenues for Irish poetry. Paul Muldoon (1951–) recognizes the vital presence of Joyce for all Irish writers, saying, "Joyce is marvellous, extraordinary; he has been an influence even on poets in Ireland as well as novelists in terms of his allowing for all the possibilities of language" (Muldoon 1988: 311). The wordplay that reached its apotheosis in Joyce's *Finnegans Wake* is exploited in Muldoon's poetry. Reviewing *Meeting the British*, John F. Deane describes Muldoon's writing as "rhythmically based, alert to the nuances of language and the sounds of words that chime and spark off each other" (Deane 1987). For example, the poet plays on variations on the consonantal pattern "rgn" with words like "organza," "arrogance," "oregano," "Arigna," "Aragon," and "Oregon" as a way of exploring the theme of origin in the collection.[5] Similarly, his play on the French word *quoi* in "Incantata" simultaneously recalls Lucky from Beckett's *Waiting for Godot*, whose own incantation "quaquaqua" brings us back to the sound of thunder in *Finnegans Wake*, a work that Beckett himself was only too familiar with: "Glass crash. The (klikkaklakkaklaskaklopatzklatschabattacreppycrotty graddaghsemmih sammihnouithappludдyappladdypkonpkot!)" (*FW* 44 19–21). Writing in praise of Joyce's "Work in Progress" Beckett underlines Joyce's attention to the sounds and rhythms of language in a manner that we expect from poetry far more than from prose. He argues that Joyce's writing "is not to be read – or rather it is not only to be read. It is to be looked at and listened to" (Beckett 1983: 27). Muldoon's "Incantata" may echo the sentiments of Yeats' elegy "In Memory of Major Robert Gregory," but the language owes much more to Joyce:

> I thought of you again tonight, thin as a rake, as you bent
> over the copper plate of 'Emblements',
> its tidal wave of army-worms into which you all but disappeared:

I wanted to catch something of its spirit
and yours, to body out your disembodied *vox
clamantis in deserto*, to let this all-too-cumbersome device
of a potato-mouth in a potato-face
speak out, unencumbered, from its long, low, mould-filled box.

(Muldoon 2001: 334)

For Eamon Grennan, these lines demonstrates how "plain phrasing and speech-syntax is fused" by Muldoon "to effective rhymes and half-rhymes, and rhetorically amplified by the way the sentence grows into the capacious breadth (and breath) of the stanza" (Grennan 1999: 347–8). A poem such as "Making the Move" uses language to destabilize the subject, taking us back, through Joyce, to the Homeric Ulysses and a meditation on love:

When Ulysses braved the wine-dark sea
He left his bow with Penelope,

Who would bend for no one but himself.
I edge along the bookshelf.

(Muldoon 2001: 334)

Cupid's bow becomes an emblem for the speaker's sexual ambivalence, pitting the two desires for love and learning within the context of a journey or *immram* that mirrors, in reverse, Bloom's marital fidelity: "Were I embarking on that wine-dark sea / I would bring my bow along with me" (Muldoon 2001: 91). The gender transformations and erotic exploits that Bloom enjoys in the "Circe" episode of *Ulysses* provide the speaker of "Yarrow" with an example as he wonders whether he is a bit player in a porn flick, "laid out on a da- / venport in this 'supremely Joycean object, a nautilus / of memory jammed next to memory'" within the eye of a "video / camera giving me a nod and a wink / from the blue corner" (Muldoon 2001: 380).

Muldoon is described as a poet who has "always adopted the Joycean strategies of exile and cunning" (Buchanan 1992: 313). These strategies are linguistic as well as biographical and provide a necessary example for poets writing in Irish as well as English. Seán Ó Ríordáin (1916–77), for example, found in Joyce a way out of the Irish Ireland that threatened to stifle the emerging poet. At the close of *A Portrait of the Artist as a Young Man* Stephen recounts John Alphonsus Mulrennan's return from the west of Ireland:

He told us he met an old man there in a mountain cabin. Old man had red eyes and short pipe. Old man spoke Irish. Mulrennan spoke Irish. Then old man and Mulrennan spoke English. Mulrennan spoke to him about universe and stars. Old man sat, listened, smoked, spat. Then said:
— Ah, there must be terrible queer creatures at the latter end of the world (*P* 212).

Here the old Gaelic Ireland meets with the new Anglophone Ireland in an exchange characterized by mutual incomprehension. Through Stephen, Joyce expresses the anxiety of the Irish writer who feels drawn toward the Irish language but knows he is most at home in English. Stephen voices this anxiety:

I fear him. I fear his redrimmed horny eyes. It is with him I must struggle all through this night till day come, till he or I lie dead, gripping him by the sinewy throat till . . . Till what? Till he yield to me? No. I mean him no harm (*P* 212).

Stephen flies the nets of language by leaving Ireland. Joyce too escapes the conflicting pull of two languages, Irish and English, by embracing a polylingual Europe with its interplay of languages and by developing a mode of writing characterized by the disruption of linguistic norms. The struggle between the modern Irish writer and the Gaelic language that Joyce circumvented rather than resolved became the central struggle for Ó Ríordáin. Influenced by Joyce, and choosing to write in Irish, Ó Ríordáin found himself caught between the modernist interplay of language and the new Ireland's need for linguistic purity. Born in the gaeltacht (Irish-speaking) area of Baile Bhuirne in West Cork, Ó Ríordáin published his first collection *Eireaball Spideoige* in 1952. He is described by Seamus Heaney as "a significant voice in modern Irish writing" (Heaney 1983: 115), and praised by Seán Ó Tuama as "a modern Gaelic poet who, more than any other, managed to combine the vision of European writers from Baudelaire to Beckett with the Irish language tradition – the result of which was poetry unequalled in the language for hundreds of years" (Ó Tuama 1973: 167).

His writing generated praise and controversy. Full of word-play, sprung rhythms and carefully constructed conceits, Ó Ríordáin's poetry has affinity with Eliot and Hopkins. But the strongest influence of all is Joyce. For Ó Ríordáin, Joyce was "as much part of myself / as the alphabet and gospels" ("Tá sé ina chuid díom chomh dearfa / Le soiscéal Chríost nó an aibítir").[6] In terms of linguistic and religious attitude, Joyce provided a way out of the inward-looking sensibilities characterized by *The Hidden Ireland* of Daniel Corkery who was Ó Ríordáin's early mentor:

> Corkery told me once not to write a single line that wasn't based on a line of the old poetry. But what can one do when things outside the tradition have gone into one – when the person is wider than the tradition?[7]

This is the very struggle that Joyce describes between Stephen and the red-rimmed horny-eyed old man. When Ó Ríordáin's first collection came out the poet was taken to task for his inventive use of the Irish language. The poet Máire Mhac an tSaoi greeted the new book with the exclamation "that Ó Ríordáin's language 'wasn't Gaelic at all' and that 'as long as his Irish is stuffed with English, he'll only have a kind of Esperanto!'"[8] The Gaelic purism that Corkery and Mhac an tSaoi espouse is undone by the impossibility of insulating Ireland from the influences of modernity. For Ó Ríordáin, Joyce provided the exit strategy. In his last collection, *Tar Éis Mo Bháis*, the poet invokes the older writer as exemplar and guide in his poem "Joyce":

> Tripping in his wake, I'm wracked;
> his Latin formalism so exact
> that when I think of him, I
> am not I – ego subsides.

Ag triopallacht a fhriotalú táim treascartha,
An fhoirmiúlacht laideanta,
Ní mé mé le linn dom machnamh air,
Ach é siúd – tá lagú ann.[9]

(Ó Ríordáin 1978: 21)

In his 1984 collection *Station Island*, Seamus Heaney also summons Joyce as guide and mentor. However, Heaney's relationship with Joyce is more ambiguous than Ó Ríordáin's, suggesting a relationship of influence that works both ways. In the twelfth verse of "Station Island" Heaney imagines Joyce as a source of strength and security:

Like a convalescent, I took the hand
stretched down from the jetty, sensed again
an alien comfort as I stepped on ground

(Heaney 1988: 266)

Once the younger poet has two feet planted on the ground the balance of power shifts, placing him in an uncertain position of responsibility as well as influence. He lands on the pier:

to find the helping hand still gripping mine,
fish-cold and bony, but whether to guide
or to be guided I could not be certain

(Heaney 1988: 267)

What Joyce's voice – "cunning, narcotic, mimic"– gives Heaney is the impetus to make language his own: "You've listened long enough. Now strike your note" (Heaney 1998: 268). The poet's need to absorb the linguistic and literary inheritance of home is problematic for Irish poets who, as Kinsella explains in "The Irish Writer," find themselves between Scylla and Charybdis. Drawing on the dual and interrelated traditions of Britain and Ireland, Irish writers needs to find their own linguistic space. Like Kinsella, who is concerned about the risks of writing in a language that is both foreign and one's own, Heaney explores his own linguistic pedigree in "Traditions," explaining how "Our guttural muse / was bulled long ago / by the alliterative tradition," "while custom, that 'most sovereign mistress', / beds us down into / the British isles." The inclusive "Our" raises the question of community. Heaney asks that question in Shakespeare's voice, quoting from *King Henry V*, "'What ish my nation?'" The answer is spoken by the gentle voice of Leopold Bloom:

And sensibly, though so much
later, the wandering Bloom
replied, "Ireland," said Bloom,
"I was born here. Ireland."

(Heaney 1972: 31–2)

Here Heaney draws on the 'Cyclops' episode of *Ulysses* where Bloom's idea of a nation is ridiculed:

— But do you know what a nation means? says John Wyse.

— Yes, says Bloom.

— What is it? says John Wyse.

— A nation? says Bloom. A nation is the same people living in the same place.

— By God, then, says Ned, laughing, if that's so I'm a nation for I'm living in the same place for the past five years.

So of course everyone had a laugh at Bloom and says he, trying to muck out of it:

— Or also living in different places.

— That covers my case, says Joe.

— What is your nation if I may ask? says the citizen.

— Ireland, says Bloom. I was born here. Ireland.

The Citizen said nothing only cleared the spit out of his gullet and, gob, he spat a Red bank oyster out of him right in the corner.

(*U* 12 1419–33)

The plurality of identities that Joyce promotes, pitting the monocultural Citizen against the cosmopolitan Bloom, is picked up also by Kinsella, who, in *Butcher's Dozen*, argues for an idea of community based on difference rather than identity:

We all are what we are, and that
Is mongrel pure. What nation's not[?]

(Kinsella 1996: 142)

Ownership of language, and the relationship between that language and the identity of a people, are key issues for modern Ireland. Founded with an aspiration of bilinguality the modern Irish state found itself drawn in two opposing directions: either towards a pure monolingual culture that emphasized the Gaelic past, or towards a bilingual (primarily Anglophone) culture that gave lip service to the Irish language while doing business in English. As a poet writing in Irish, Seán Ó Ríordáin found himself in the front line. After the sharp criticism his early writing received, Ó Ríordáin rejects his earlier attitude – "I wasn't thinking about Irish at all, I was thinking about poetry"[10] – in favor of a rejection of all taint of English. His 1964 collection *Brosna* argues for a linguistic purity that Seamus Heaney finds troubling, particularly in the poem "Fill Arís" ("Return Again") that Heaney translated for *Fortnight*:

. . . unshackle your mind
Of its civil English tackling,
Shelley, Keats and Shakespeare.

Get back to what is your own.
Wash your mind and wash your tongue
That was spancelled in a syntax
Putting you out of step with yourself.[11]

. . . bain ded mheabhair
Srathar shibhialtacht an Bhéarla,
Shelley, Keats is Shakespeare,
Fill arís ar do chuid,

Nigh d'intinn is nigh
Do theanga a chuaigh ceangailte i gcomhréiribh
'Bhí bun os cionn le d'éirim . . .

(Ó Ríordáin 1964: 41)

Ó Ríordáin's worry is refuted by Heaney, who sees in it a dangerous and impossible erasure of history, the very dilemma that Joyce addresses in the "Nestor" episode of *Ulysses*:

> — History, Stephen said, is a nightmare from which I am trying to awake.
> From the playfield the boys raised a shout. A whirring whistle: goal. What if that nightmare gave you a back kick? (*U* 2 377–9)

Joyce gives both Ó Ríordáin and Heaney a back kick, enabling both to come to terms with the tradition in which they find themselves and to move the game forward. It takes place on, as Heaney puts it, "the Feast of the Holy Tundish" when, in *A Portrait of the Artist as a Young Man*, Stephen realizes that the Dean of Studies' English is as much his as another's:

> That tundish has been on my mind for a long time. I looked it up and find it English and good old blunt English too. Damn the dean of studies and his funnel! What did he come here for to teach us his own language or to learn it from us? Damn him one way or the other! (*P* 212)

In "Station Island" XII Heaney's speaker hears Joyce's voice urging him to uncouple language from nation: "'Who cares,' / he jeered, 'any more? The English language / belongs to us'" (Heaney 1984: 268). It is this sense of appropriation and transformation that results in a sense of ownership, in being at home in a language, that Joyce gives to Irish poets, whether they write in Irish or in English. And this is why Heaney's Joycean figure urges the poet speaker to "Keep at a tangent" to the mainstream. Juxtaposing the poet with a larger unnamed community – "When they make the circle wide" – Joyce counsels the poet to find his own direction and his own voice: "swim / out on your own and fill the element / with signatures of your own frequency" (Heaney 1984: 268).

Medbh McGuckian's poetry is firmly established on its own distinctive frequency. Described as "daring and innovative," McGuckian's attitude to language echoes Joyce's own (O'Brien 1999: xxii): "English is this wonderful currency. I don't see it as an imperial language. It was originally, it was pushed into place, but I think now I see it as a hybrid, useful currency" (McGuckian 2003: 66).

Building on Stephen's postcolonial realization that the English language sits as easily on an Irish tongue as on an English one, McGuckian appropriates and reconfigures language. In "The Partner's Desk" the poet speaks of writing in an "un-English language." Her term describes language as *unheimlich*, a language in which one is both at home and from which one is exiled. Reading McGuckian we find our familiar language suddenly and inexplicably made strange. Compared with both Joyce and Gerard Manley Hopkins, the poet writes "a radically revised poetry, one . . . that flouts conventional syntax, proliferates ellipses, makes illogicality the only certainty" (O'Brien 1999: xxiii). McGuckian's language recognizes what Kinsella has termed the "broken tradition" of Irish writing, and it uses Joyce's example to extend the possibilities of poetry that it may more fully contain the "uncreated conscience" of twentieth-century Irish experience. Working from notebooks into which are written phrases and scraps drawn from a diverse range of materials, just as Joyce did in preparation for *Finnegans Wake*, McGuckian explains her approach: "I can't open a dictionary. I should, of course, but I like to find a word living in a context and then pull it out of its context" (McGuckian 2003: 67). McGuckian's is a resonant and complex poetry, written at a tangent to convention, as she explains in "Prie-Dieu":

> This oblique trance is my natural
> Way of speaking, I have jilted
> All the foursquare houses, and
> My courtyard has a Spanish air,
> Defiant as a tomboy;
>
> (McGuckian 1999: 97)

The Spanish air within which McGuckian writes recalls "Penelope" of *Ulysses* in which the Gibraltar-born Molly speaks of her experience as a woman on the most intimate level. The uninterrupted pattern of Joyce's prose, with its cadences and rhythms arising as much from phonetic counterpoint as from signification, has much in common with McGuckian's use of language. Describing her writing as a kind of river that necessarily allows for a polyphony of signification, McGuckian nevertheless argues for an exactitude within fluidity:

> So if you say *silver*, that word takes resonances as to what comes before it and after it, and maybe it rhymes with something here or there, that word is in an axis, once you put it in a poem it becomes very fluent, it becomes part of a river – there is nothing that is oppressive (McGuckian 2003: 67).

The tangent that Heaney's Joyce urges poets to travel can be understood in terms of a sense of place as well as a sense of language. The Joyce that stretches a steadying hand to Heaney is the same Joyce invoked by Thomas Kinsella. Heaney's Joyce "seemed blind, though he walked straight as a rush / upon his ash plant, his eyes fixed straight ahead." Kinsella's Joyce, in "Nightwalker," can also hardly see, though he is as perceptive as ever:

> Watcher in the tower,
> Be with me now. Turn your milky spectacles
> On the sea, unblinking.
>
> (Kinsella 1996: 80)

Gazing from the Martello tower of *Ulysses*, Kinsella's Joyce is an urban writer, attentive to the rhythms and cadences of the city. Writing in 1905 Joyce describes his surprise that Dublin had been so far overlooked by literature:

I do not think that any writer has yet presented Dublin to the world. It has been a capital of Europe for thousands of years, it is supposed to be the second city of the British Empire and it is nearly three times as big as Venice (*LII* 122).

This oversight is more than adequately remedied by *Dubliners*, *Ulysses*, and *Finnegans Wake*, works which do not simply give Dublin to the world, but reinscribe the city in terms of the emerging sense of identity instigated by Ireland's devolution from British control. In her study of *The Irish Ulysses*, Maria Tymoczko argues that

> Joyce retakes Dublin from the Irish Ascendancy, giving us a memorable Everyman's Dublin, an English-speaking Dublin upon which to build a free state. This attention to Dublin topography is an ironic expression of Joyce's nationalism, an expression not likely to be appreciated by the nativist nationalists who were interested in promoting and preserving a rural Irish Ireland (Tymoczko 1994: 159).

Here Tymoczko draws on a distinction, made by the historian F. S. L. Lyons in his *Culture and Anarchy in Ireland 1890–1939*, between the cosmopolitan and urban nationalist on the one hand, and the nativist and rural nationalist on the other hand. Emer Nolan eloquently criticizes Lyons' characterization of Joyce as a cosmopolitan, "refusing equally the calls of 'Anglo-Ireland' and 'Irish Ireland'," arguing instead for a more nuanced reading of Joyce's relationship with both representative communities (Nolan 1995: 48).

The interconnections between national identity and urban topography are evident also in the work of the contemporary Irish poet Thomas Kinsella. Like Joyce, Kinsella was born and brought up in Dublin, and that city forms the focus of, and provides the material for, his poetic development. With an overlap of 13 years between Kinsella's birth in 1928 and Joyce's death in 1941, Kinsella can be seen as a writer who inherits what Len Platt describes as Joyce's "very considerable investment in historical reconstruction, a motivation that was powerful, committed, even raw" (Platt 1998: 16). Kinsella's poetry exhibits a very strong commitment to the political and cultural development of the Republic of Ireland, and his voice occupies a unique position within a generation who felt that it was truly in their hands to shape and form the emerging nation. However, because of this commitment, Kinsella has occasionally adopted the stance of a scathing social critic. For example, the 1968 poem "Nightwalker" characterizes the politician Charles Haughey (who as Taoiseach had enormous influence on the development of the country throughout the latter half of the twentieth century but whose retirement was stained by evidence of corruption) as

> The Sonhusband
> Coming in his power, climbing the dark
> to his mansion in the sky, to take his place
> in the influential circle, mounting to glory
> On his big white harse!

(Kinsella 1996: 80)

The unmistakable insult contained within the portmanteau word "harse" – formed by joining "horse" with "arse" – takes issue with the implication of Haughey riding to hounds, his rise to power through marriage to a previous Taoiseach's daughter, and his establishment of a large personal demesne by means of an insidious perversion of political processes, known colloquially as GUBU politics. Kinsella's insult draws its power from Joyce's use of the word "harse" in *Finnegans Wake*:

> This is the Willingdone on his same white harse, the Cokenhape. This is the big Sraughter Willingdone, grand and magentic in his goldtin spurs and his ironed dux and his quarter-brass woodyshoes and his magnate's gharters and his bangkok's best and goliar's goloshes and his pulluponeasyan wartrews. This is his big wide harse. Tip (*FW* 8 16–21).

Kinsella's 1997 collection of poems, *The Pen Shop*, rewrites Bloom's odyssey in reverse as the poet-speaker journeys through the center of Dublin in the opposite direction to the protagonist of *Ulysses*. *The Pen Shop* explicitly references the "Hades" episode of *Ulysses* and "Grace" from *Dubliners*, using the poet-speaker's perambulations through a specifically delineated urban geography to explore the relationship between place and politics from the perspective of both the present and the past. And, as in Joyce's *Ulysses*, the act of walking in the urban space described by *The Pen Shop* allows for connections to be made between disparate times through an identity of place. Through *The Pen Shop* Kinsella maps Joyce's Dublin onto his own. In a reflexive movement of reiteration he folds Dublin in the first decade of the twentieth century onto that same city in the last decade of the same century. *The Pen Shop* enunciates a topography of Dublin through which the poet draws together the strands of personal and public history into the nodal point of writing. Divided into two sections – "To the Coffee Shop" and "To the Pen Shop" – with an prefatory poem at the beginning of the volume, *The Pen Shop* traces a journey from the General Post Office on O'Connell Street, over the Liffey, into Bewleys of Westmoreland Street, and on down to Nassau Street to the warm confines of a narrow establishment called "The Pen Shop." This journey also traces a movement from the mythical history of Ireland which so informed Kinsella's earlier volume *One*, through a meditation on pre-independence history alluded to in books such as *The Messenger* and *St. Catherine's Clock*, to an assessment of the poet's family history and his own mortality. Ghosting Kinsella's speaker's journey down O'Connell Street is Bloom's own journey in the opposite direction. Kinsella's solitary speaker walks, while Joyce's protagonist rides in a carriage with his companions Martin Cunningham, Jack Power, and Simon Dedalus, up O'Connell Street towards Glasnevin Cemetery.

Kinsella's poem opens in the General Post Office as the speaker posts a letter to the muse-mother figure whose "fierce forecasts" provoke this response: *"Rage, affliction and outcry!"* The GPO is a significant site in the history of modern Ireland in that it formed one of the key locations of the 1916 rising. The journey to the Pen Shop begins "under the cathedral ceiling" of the General Post Office. The customers that Kinsella's speaker sees in the General Post Office are envisaged as "souls" whose movements approximate Dantean circumambulation as they take their "places in line at the glass grills / or bowing at the shelves. / Following one another / out through the revolving doors" in a pilgrimage that mirrors Heaney's pilgrimage to Lough Derg in *Station Island*. These "souls" allude to the "silent shapes" glimpsed by James Joyce's

Leopold Bloom as he passes the yard of "Thos. H. Dennany, monumental builder and sculptor" – "Crowded on the spit of land silent shapes appeared, white, sorrowful, holding out calm hands, knelt in grief, pointing. Fragments of shapes, hewn. In white silence: appealing" (*U* 6 459–61) – and recall also the shades of the dead who gather around Odysseus in supplication when he arrives in Hades (Gifford 1988: 115).

At the center of the GPO stands a statue of Cúchulainn, the mythical figure vaunted in Joyce's "Cyclops" episode and Kinsella's earlier poem "At the Western Ocean's Edge," familiar too from the poet's translation of the epic mythological cycle the *Táin Bó Cuailnge*:

. . . Around the bronze hero
sagging half covered off his upright,
looking down over one shoulder at his feet.
The harpy perched on his neck.

(Kinsella 1997: [7])

This "bronze hero" depicts the dead Cúchulainn, the same figure that Yeats' Padraig Pearse "summoned to his side" in "The Statues." The vanquished Cúchulainn sought to cheat death by remaining upright, lashed to a pillar stone. It is only when the crow, symbol and manifestation of Mórrígan, goddess of war, lands on his shoulder that his enemies know that he is dead. The crow, or "harpy" as Kinsella puts it, is also a version of the cailleach figure who can be read as Hecate or the Jungian Terrible Mother. By focusing on the representation of Cúchulainn depicted by the statue in the GPO, Kinsella situates an aspect of the Irish mythology which is fundamental to his poetry in a specifically political context. Through subject and situation Kinsella questions the use of mythology for political purposes, evoking the rhetoric of Pádraig Pearse, key figure in the Easter Rising of 1916, for whom Cúchulainn was "the great prototype of the Irish patriot-martyr" (Shaw 1972: 593).

This rhetoric of blood-sacrifice embodied in the statue of the dead hero is subtly undercut in Kinsella's poem by the appearance of Joyce's pacifist "Mr Bloom." The introduction of Bloom adds a retrospective resonance to Kinsella's own description of himself in an earlier collection, *The Messenger*, as a "blackvelvet-eyed jew-child" who watches his father agitating against the fascist Blueshirts. On O'Connell Street Kinsella's speaker literally intersects with Leopold Bloom, who travels northward to the Prospect Cemetery in Glasnevin. In *The Pen Shop* Kinsella writes:

By Smith O'Brien. Dead thirty years, to the day,
when Mr Bloom unclasped his hands in soft
acknowledgement. And clasped them. About here.

(Kinsella 1997: [7])

Drawing on the "Hades" episode of Joyce's *Ulysses*, Kinsella joins the histories of mythological self-determination with those of a more recent political self-determination as he connects the statue of Cúchulainn with the statues of O'Connell Street, each of which commemorates a particular moment in Irish history. Here, Kinsella rewrites Joyce's passage from *Ulysses*:

Mr Bloom unclasped his hands in a gesture of soft politeness and clasped them. Smith O'Brien. Someone has laid a bunch of flowers there. Woman. Must be his deathday. For many happy returns. The carriage wheeling by Farrell's statue united noiselessly their unresisting knees (*U* 6 225–8).

The statue that Bloom notices as he passes is that of William Smith O'Brien (1803–64), Cambridge-educated MP for Limerick, who was involved in the insurrections of 1848 for which he was commemorated by a statue sculpted by Sir Thomas Farrell (1827–1900). On his way to Glasnevin to attend Dignam's funeral Bloom passes another statue by Thomas Farrell, that of Sir John Gray (1816–75): "Mr Power, collapsing in laughter, shaded his face from the window as the carriage passed Gray's statue" (*U* 6 257–8). John Gray is, of course, the owner and editor of the *Freeman's Journal* that Bloom carries around in his pocket. And significantly for Kinsella's *The Pen Shop*, it is in the offices of the *Freeman's Journal* that Stephen rejects the rhetoric of nationalist Irish culture.

Though Gray was commemorated for advocating disestablishment of the Church of Ireland, land reform, and free denominational education, he is now (as Kinsella writes) "unremembered on his pedestal" and denigrated, in Kinsella's poem, by the statement "None of the Grays was any good." Here Kinsella quotes directly from Joyce's story "Grace" in *Dubliners* in which Mr. Power – who, in *Ulysses*, shares the carriage with Bloom as they travel to the cemetery – pronounces that "None of the Grays was any good" (*D* 170). In their book on *John Stanislaus Joyce* John Wyse Jackson and Peter Costello note that this casual defamation is most probably borrowed from Joyce's father, who may have been "among the party at the June unveiling of a statue (by Farrell) of the late Sir John Gray MP" (Jackson and Costello 1997: 85). Terence Brown reads the insult as an "especially ungracious remark," considering the Gray family's "notable contributions to civic and national life," but suggests that "Mr Power is probably recalling the fact that in 1891 Edmund Gray's son deserted the Parnellite cause" (*D* 303–4 n. 70).

The next statue encountered in *The Pen Shop* is that of the socialist activist James Larkin (1876–1947). The orator is described in redemptive terms:

> Under Larkin with his iron arms on high,
> conducting everybody
> in all directions, up off our knees.
>
> (Kinsella 1997: [8])

In his earlier collection *The Messenger* Kinsella remembers the role that Larkin played in the development of his father's political consciousness: "He reaches for a hammer, / his jaw jutting as best it can / with Marx, Engels, Larkin." Larkin's struggle against capitalism rather than colonialism is seen, in these lines, to be inclusive and empowering. He stands outside the rhetoric of blood sacrifice promulgated by Pearse and provides a visual contrast, "arms on high," with the "sagging" figure of the dead Cúchulainn. Kinsella's Joycean connection underlines a certain antipathy to what Declan Kiberd has called "the Cúchulainn cult," which was "objectionable to Joyce because it helped to perpetuate the libel of the pugnacious Irish overseas, while gratifying the vanity of a minority of self-heroicizing nationalists at home" (Kiberd 1992: xii–xiii).

Just before crossing the River Liffey the speaker of *The Pen Shop* encounters the statue of Daniel O'Connell (1775–1847), aloft on his 28-foot pedestal. He is the "Hero as liberator" of Kinsella's earlier poem ("At the Western Ocean's Edge" in *Personal Places*), and also the "hugecloaked Liberator's form" by which Bloom's carriage passes in "Hades" (*U* 6 249). O'Connell, member of Parliament for County Clare and successful agitator for Catholic emancipation, described by Roy Foster as "the greatest leader of Catholic Ireland," stands "high in the salt wind" that blows in from the river Liffey (Foster 1988: 291 n. iii). The depth of O'Connell's commitment and his exceptional abilities as a politician are conveyed by his stance, "shirt thrown open and ready for nearly anything," and also his attitude, "with hand on heart and dealer's eye." Below O'Connell's statue gather personifications of the debates and issues of his time: "Church and Education in debate / around the hem of his garment; Honest Toil at his heel." By ghosting *The Pen Shop* with the Hades episode of *Ulysses* and "Grace" of *Dubliners*, Kinsella strengthens his inquiry into the role of memory and the place of the hero in the formation of history. The shades which Odysseus meets in Hades become both the "souls" in the GPO and the statues that Joyce's and Kinsella's travelers pass as they move through the center of Dublin.

The Dantean influence that joins Heaney's and Kinsella's evocations of Joyce is present also in David Wheatley's (1970–) *Misery Hill*. The title poem gives us a turn-of-the-century vision of Dublin's underbelly that is indebted to Joyce's example. Drawing much from Kinsella's own explorations of the psychic geography of Dublin, Wheatley's journey begins in the Dublin street Misery Hill and takes its tangent through history, politics, television culture and love to reimagine Joyce's Dublin for twenty-first-century minds. Wheatley also turns his gaze beyond Dublin to the 14-towered city on Ireland's western shore from where Joyce's wife, Nora Barnacle, hailed, and from where Joyce's own tribe comes. Wheatley prefaces his poem "Numerology" with an epitaph taken from Joyce's "The City of the Tribes":

> The cartographer lists and draws fourteen bastions, fourteen wall-towers, fourteen main thoroughfares, fourteen monasteries, fourteen castles, fourteen laneways (*OCPW* 198–9).

Wheatley's 14-line poem describes a visit to Galway with his lover. Through a subtle and humorous progression of numbers from 1 to 14, sex and the city unfold:

> Purity of heart is to will one thing.
> A pair of Trinity squares, down for the week:
> how could that salty longing not awake
> by Galway bay, our hearts gone for a song?
>
> Under the arch, over the Corrib, pent
> in a guesthouse, working it out again, the six-
> es and sevens of it, the algebra of sex,
> the octopus arms and legs out for the count

come 'breakfast at nine', at ten . . . Waking to
elevenses, a sleepy one on one,
we get up to the angelus' round of applause,

the tilly of a kiss in the street: the two
of us in the city of fourteen tribes, awash
with fourteen shades of light that colour us one.

(Wheatley 2001: n.p.)

The "tilly of a kiss" that unites the lovers is the addition that turns the angelus's 12
into 13. Wheatley's "tilly" evokes Joyce on two levels. It is the extra measure given by
the milkwoman in the "Telemachus" episode of *Ulysses*: "She poured again a measure-
ful and a tilly," recalling the sardonic eye that Joyce casts on the Gaelic romanticism
that colors Stephen's view of the workaday woman. It is also the extra poem in Joyce's
Pomes Penyeach which, costing a shilling, should by rights contain 12 poems. The thir-
teenth, called "Tilly," is extra, the unpaid for supplement traditional to local custom.

Though Joyce's verse is the minor "tilly" of his writing, his contribution to Irish
poetry remains central rather than supplemental. Joyce's virtuouso linguistic performances and his embrace of the "mongrel pure" of a modern Irish literary tradition was
central in the establishment of a modern Irish literary identity. Joyce's self-imposed
exile made it possible for future generations of writers to be, as Kinsella phrases it,
"out of Ireland" while still fully engaged with the issues and concerns of the place
itself. As Peter Fallon and Derek Mahon (1990: xxi) put it, "these writers *commute*."
To the extent that modern Irish poets have rendered obsolete the dichotomy Kinsella
outlined in 1966, it is in part testament to the rich potential of Joyce's example, and a
recognition of an Ireland "with fourteen shades of light that colour us one."

NOTES

1   See Yeats (1983: 336–7, 337). See also Elmer
    Andrew's introduction to *Contemporary Irish
    Poetry* (Andrews 1992: 9).
2   John Goodby takes issue with "the tendency
    to relate all subsequent Irish poetry to a pair
    of founding fathers," arguing that "the division
    of Irish poetry into what John Wilson Foster
    has called the 'Romantic' and the 'pluralist' is
    deeply unsatisfactory in many ways. It requires,
    for one thing, the conflation of (Protestant)
    Yeatsian Revivalism with 'myth' and (Cath-
    olic) Joyce with 'reality', effecting a progress
    from myth to realism which requires us to
    overlook Yeats' all-too-realist 1930s' interest
    in eugenics and fascism, as well as the myth-

saturated methods of *Ulysses* and *Finnegans
Wake*" (Goodby 2000: 4).
3   See Alex Davis' reading of *Death of Hektor* (1995:
    165).
4   For a discussion of Clarke's use of Gaelic prosody
    see Harmon (1989: 21–7).
5   Mick Imlah, review of *Meeting the British* in the
    Times Literary Supplement, quoted in Kendall
    (1996: 129).
6   Seán Ó Ríordáin, *Tar Éis Mo Bháis* (1978: 21).
    Translation by Frank Sewell in his *Modern Irish
    Poetry* (2000: 15–16).
7   Seán Ó Coileáin, *Seán Ó Ríordáin: Beatha agus
    Saothar* (1985: 210). Quoted in and translated
    by Frank Sewell (2000: 14).

8 Máire Mhac an tSaoi quoted by Seán Ó Coileáin, (1985: 241); translated and quoted by Frank Sewell (2000: 18).

9 Seán Ó Ríordáin (1978: 21–2). Translation by Frank Sewell (2000: 15–16).

10 "Seán Ó Ríordáin ag caint le Seán Ó Mórdha," in *Scríobh 3,* ed. Ó Mórdha, p. 174. Quoted by Frank Sewell (2000: 28).

11 Translation by Seamus Heaney (1983: 115).

BIBLIOGRAPHY

Andrews, Elmer (ed.) (1992) *Contemporary Irish Poetry.* Basingstoke: Macmillan.

Armstrong, Tim (1995) "Muting the Klaxon: Poetry, History and Irish Modernism." In Patricia Coughan and Alex Davis (eds.) *Modernism and Ireland: The Poetry of the 1930s,* pp. 43–74. Cork: Cork University Press.

Beckett, Samuel (1983) "Dante . . . Bruno. Vico . . Joyce." In Ruby Cohn (ed.) *Disjecta: Miscellaneous Writings and a Dramatic Fragment,* pp. 19–33. London: John Calder.

Beckett, Samuel et al. (1929) *Our Exagmination Round His Factification for Incamination of Work in Progress.* Paris: Shakespeare and Company.

Buchanan, Barbara (1992) "Paul Muldoon: "who's to know what's knowable."" In Elmer Andrews (ed.) *Contemporary Irish Poetry: A Collection of Critical Essays,* pp. 310–27. London: Macmillan.

Clarke, Austin (1962) *Twice Round the Black Church.* London: Routledge and Kegan Paul.

Clarke, Austin (1976) *Selected Poems,* ed. Thomas Kinsella. Dublin: Dolmen Press.

Coffey, Brian (1971) *Selected Poems.* Dublin: New Writers Press.

Coffey, Brian (1991) *Poems and Versions 1929–1990.* Dublin: Dedalus.

Corkery, Daniel (1925) *The Hidden Ireland.* Dublin: M. H. Gill and Son.

Coughlan, Patricia and Alex Davis (eds.) (1995) *Modernism and Ireland: The Poetry of the 1930s.* Cork: Cork University Press.

Davis, Alex (1995) "'Poetry is ontology': Brian Coffey's poetics." In Patricia Coughlan and Alex Davis (eds.) *Modernism and Ireland: The Poetry of the 1930s,* pp. 150–72. Cork: Cork University Press.

Deane, John F. (1987) "Review of *Meeting the British,*" *Sunday Independent,* July 12.

Deane, Seamus (ed.) (1991) *The Field Day Anthology of Irish Writing,* Vol. 3. Derry: Field Day.

Devlin, Denis. (1989) *Collected Poems of Denis Devlin.* ed. J. C. C. Mays. Dublin: Dedalus Press.

Fallon, Peter and Derek Mahon (eds.) (1990) *The Penguin Book of Contemporary Irish Poetry.* London: Penguin.

Foster, R. F. (1988) *Modern Ireland: 1600–1972.* London: Penguin.

Garratt, Robert (1986) *Modern Irish Poetry: Tradition and Continuity from Yeats to Heaney.* London: University of California Press.

Gifford, Don (1988) Ulysses *Annotated.* Berkeley: University of California Press.

Goodby, John (2000) *Irish Poetry since 1950.* Manchester: Manchester University Press.

Grennan, Eamon (1999) *Facing the Music: Irish Poetry in the Twentieth Century.* Omaha, NE: Creighton University Press.

Harmon, Maurice (1989) *Austin Clarke: A Critical Introduction.* Dublin: Wolfhound Press.

Heaney, Seamus (1972) *Wntering Out.* London: Faber and Faber.

Heaney, Seamus (1983) "Forked Tongues, Céilís and Incubators," *Fortnight* 197: 113–16.

Heaney, Seamus (1984) *Station Island.* London: Faber and Faber.

Heaney, Seamus (1998) *Opened Ground: Poems 1966–1996.* London: Faber and Faber.

Heaney, Seamus (2002) "Joyce's poetry." In his *Finders Keepers: Selected Prose 1971–2001,* pp. 388–90. London: Faber and Faber.

Jackson, John Wyse and Peter Costello (1997) *John Stanislaus Joyce: The Voluminous Life and Genius of James Joyce's Father.* London: Fourth Estate.

Kendall, Tim (1996) *Paul Muldoon.* Bridgend: Seren Poetry Wales Press.

Kiberd, Declan (1992) "Introduction." In James Joyce, *Ulysses.* London: Penguin.

Kinsella, Thomas (1967) "The Irish writer," *Éire-Ireland* 2 (2): 8–15.

Kinsella, Thomas (1996) *Thomas Kinsella: Collected Poems 1956–1994.* Oxford: Oxford University Press.

Kinsella, Thomas (1997) *The Pen Shop.* Dublin: Peppercanister Press.

Lyons, F. S. L. (1982) *Culture and Anarchy in Ireland*

1890–1939. Oxford and New York: Oxford University Press.

MacGreevy, Thomas (1972 [1929]) "The Catholic element in *Work in Progress*." In Samuel Beckett et al., *Our Exagmination Round His Factification for Incamination of Work in Progress*, pp. 117–27. London: Faber and Faber.

MacGreevy, Thomas (1991) *Collected Poems of Thomas MacGreevy*, ed. Susan Schreibman. Dublin: Anna Livia Press.

McGuckian, Medhb (2003) "'I am listening in black and white to what speaks to me in blue': Medbh McGuckian interviewed by Helen Blakeman," *Irish Studies Review* 11: 61–9.

McGuckian, Medhb (1997) *Selected Poems*. Meath: Gallery Press.

McGuckian, Medhb (1999) *Irish Women's Poetry: 1967–2000*, ed. Peggy O'Brien. Winston-Salem: Wake Forest.

Muldoon, Paul (1988) "Interview," *Contemporary Authors* 129: 311.

Muldoon, Paul (2001) *Poems 1968–1998*. London: Faber and Faber.

Nolan, Emer (1995 [1990]) *Joyce and Nationalism*. London: Routledge.

O'Brien, Peggy (ed.) (1999) *Irish Women's Poetry 1967–2000*. Winston-Salem: Wake Forest University Press.

Ó Coiléain, Seán (1985 [1982]) *Seán Ó Ríordáin: Beatha agus Saothar*. Dublin: An Clóchomhar Tta.

Ó Ríordáin, Seán (1952) *Eireaball Spideoige*. Dublin: Sáirséal agus Dill.

Ó Ríordáin, Seán (1964, rpt. 1987) *Brosna*. Dublin: Sáirséal agus Dill.

Ó Ríordáin, Seán (1978) *Tar Éis Mo Bháis*. Dublin: Sáirséal agus Dill.

Ó Tuama, Seán (1973) "Seán Ó Ríordáin agus an Nuafhilíocht," *Studia Hibernica* 13: 100–67.

Sewell, Frank (2000) *Modern Irish Poetry: A New Alhambra*. Oxford: Oxford University Press.

Shaw, Francis (1972) "The Canon of Irish History – A Challenge." Reprinted in Seamus Deane (ed.) *The Field Day Anthology of Irish Writing*, pp. 590–5. Derry: Field Day.

Platt, Len (1998) *Joyce and the Anglo-Irish: A Study of Joyce and the Literary Revival*. Amsterdam and Atlanta, GA: Rodopi.

Tymoczko, Maria (1994) *The Irish Ulysses*. Berkeley: University of California Press.

Wheatley, David (2000) *Misery Hill*. Meath: Gallery Press.

Wheatley, David (2001) "Numerology." http://english.chass.ncsu.edu/freeverse/Archives/winter_2001/poems/D_Wheatley.html.

Yeats, W. B. (1983) *The Poems of W. B. Yeats*, ed. Richard J. Finneran. New York: Macmillan.

Yeats, W. B. (1997) *Collected Letters of W. B. Yeats*, Vol. 2, eds. Warwick Gould, John Kelly, and Deirdre Toomey. Oxford: Clarendon Press.

22

"Ghostly Light": Spectres of Modernity in James Joyce's and John Huston's "The Dead"

Luke Gibbons

All spirits in fact are not, as far as psychic communications are concerned, spirits at all, are only memory.

George Yeats, writing to W. B. Yeats (Armstrong 2005: 127)

In an early essay on James Clarence Mangan, James Joyce wrote that "in those vast courses which enfold us and in that great memory which is greater and more gener-ous than our memory, no life, no moment of exaltation is ever lost" (*OCPW* 60). This observation dates from a period in which, despite all Joyce's skepticism towards the occult and spiritualism, he retained an interest in key theosophical concerns such as cyclical history and the pursuit of arcane, hermetic knowledge.[1] One particular aspect that held an enduring fascination was the possibility of world memory, an "akasic" medium, as described in *Ulysses*, that records "all that ever anywhere wherever was" (*U* 7 882–3). Such a medium is still memory, but it is not just psychological, isolated within individual skulls. In Ireland, this spectral memory was grounded in a collective past – the old Gaelic, pre-Famine order that lingered in the recesses of urban life, and of which, indeed, Mangan was the last literary representative in Joyce's eyes: "Those whom the flames of too fierce love have wasted on earth become after death pale phan-toms of desire" (*OCPW* 81).[2] It is difficult not to see in this a presentiment of "The Dead," for while the "shade" of Michael Furey is clearly lodged, at one level, in Gretta Conroy's unconscious, it also has a "trans-subjective" element, impinging on Gabriel's consciousness as if it had an (after)life of its own.[3] It is not that Joyce comes down deci-sively on one side or the other, designating ghosts as either psychic states or ethereal beings, but that certain traces of memory have a force independent of the minds that recall them. Their haunting is cultural, in the deepest sense, requiring a (re)connection with a world, exemplified by Gretta Conroy's and Michael Furey's upbringing in the west of Ireland, that colonial modernity consigned to oblivion. One of the achieve-ments of John Huston's adaptation of "The Dead," deriving perhaps from his residence in county Galway, is to bring out the latent cultural uncanny of Joyce's story, depicting the "ingenuous insularity" and "hospitality" (as Joyce described it) of an urbane, middle-class Dublin for whom life on the western seaboard is as strange as any paranormal phenomena (*JJ* 245). Instead of vanishing in the name of progress, many "anachronistic" features of peripheral cultures haunt the by-ways of modernity, hovering in the shadows of brightly lit cities or echoing the silences of empty streets.

"Pale Phantoms of Desire"

> The figure of the ghost is not just one figure among others. It is perhaps the hidden figure of all figures.
>
> Jacques Derrida (1994: 120)

In the closing sequence of "The Dead," Gabriel Conroy and his wife Gretta are shown to their room in the Gresham Hotel on O'Connell Street by a sleepy porter who has lit a candle for the purpose. There is a faint disturbance in the air as they begin their ascent for the porter has to halt "on the stairs to settle his guttering candle. They halted too on the steps below him" (Joyce 1995: 190). On entering the room, "the unstable candle" is placed on a toilet-table but its services are not required:

> The porter pointed to the tap of electric-light and began a muttered apology but Gabriel cut him short.
> — We don't want any light. We have light enough from the street. And I say, he added, pointing to the candle, you might remove that handsome article, like a good man.
> The porter took up his candle again, but slowly, for he was surprised by such a novel idea (Joyce 1995: 190–2).

The Gresham Hotel had proudly proclaimed its modernity to the Dublin public with advertisements announcing the installation of electric light and an electric elevator,[4] but there appears to have been a power shortage on the night of the epiphany. Fifty years earlier, it was unlikely the light from the street would have illuminated a room in the Gresham as a witness to an official inquiry claimed he could not even read his watch at the foot of the gas lamp outside the hotel (O'Brien 1982: 67). In the latter half of the nineteenth century, however, Dublin began to showcase its metropolitan status with the introduction of more extensive gas lighting in the city center in the 1870s, followed by electric light on a small scale in 1892, generated by a power station in Fleet Street. The major drive towards electrification did not take place until the completion of the massive Ringsend power station between 1899 and 1903, which facilitated the introduction of electric trams and the more widespread use of electric lighting. Crucially, the power was still not sufficient to produce a 24-hour supply (O'Brien 1982: 68), and it is this, perhaps, that accounts for the power cut when Gabriel and Gretta enter the Gresham. Gas lighting at the turn of the century had extended to several thousand lamps throughout the city but it is striking that, for all its modernity, it is barely able to keep the shades of the past at bay as events unfold on the night of the Misses Morkan's party. As the porter leaves the room and Gabriel turns the lock,

> A *ghostly light* from the street lamp lay in a long shaft from one window to the door. Gabriel threw his overcoat and hat on a couch and crossed the room towards the window. He looked down into the street in order that his emotion might calm a little. Then he turned and leaned against a chest of drawers with his back to the light (Joyce 1995: 192: my emphasis).

It is as if the movement of air that disturbed the candle (if not the electricity) on the stairs has made way for gaslight and, later, for an "air" of a different kind, that of the ballad "The Lass of Aughrim," associated with Michael Furey, who worked in the gasworks in Galway. In some editions of the story, "ghostly" is printed as "ghastly," a mistake to be sure, but one that in its own Joycean way catches the eerie connections between various manifestations of "air" and "light" in the story. In *Ulysses*, candlelight illuminates the apparition of Stephen's dead mother in a dream: "The ghostcandle to light her agony. Ghostly light on the tortured face" (*U* 1 274–5) and for Buck Mulligan the Holy Ghost is little more than a "gaseous invertebrate" (*U* 9 487);[5] if Michael Furey is the third person in another trinity, it is perhaps fitting that he assumes this airy form.

Earlier on the night, the associations between air and gaslight are established when Lily, the servant, opens the door and helps Gabriel off with his overcoat:

> A light fringe of snow lay like a cape on the shoulders of his overcoat and like toecaps on the toes of his goloshes; and, as the buttons of his overcoat slipped with a squeaking noise through the snow-stiffened frieze, a cold, fragrant air from out-of-doors escaped from crevices and folds.
> — Is it snowing again, Mr Conroy? asked Lily — (Joyce 1995: 159)

The release of air from the overcoat is picked up by three senses – sound, smell, and touch (if we include feeling the chill) – and no sooner has it made its presence felt than Gabriel's attention is drawn to Lily's voice and her appearance, illuminated by the light in the pantry:

> She had preceded him into the pantry to help him off with his overcoat. Gabriel smiled at the three syllables she had given his surname and glanced at her. She was a slim growing girl, pale in complexion and with hay-coloured hair. The gas in the pantry made her look still paler (Joyce 1995: 159).

This is the first mention of "gas" in the story, signaled by the escape of cold, wintry air, and the Gaelic inflections of Lily's pronunciation of Gabriel's name.[6] Later on, when the guests are leaving the party after the performance of "The Lass of Aughrim," Mr. Darcy walks out of the pantry and engages with Gabriel and others in some mild banter about his head cold, and the need "to be very careful of his throat in the night air" (Joyce 1995: 229). Michael Furey, we discover at the end, was not so careful of his

throat when he sang in the night air, and, as if with this in mind, the next lines turn to Gabriel, who now sees Gretta in the same kind of light that had illuminated Lily:

> Gabriel watched his wife, who did not join in the conversation. She was standing right under the dusty fanlight and the flame of the gas lit up the rich bronze of her hair, which he had seen her drying at the fire a few days before (Joyce 1995: 188).

Gretta seems lost in her thoughts, and then suddenly turns to Mr. D'Arcy:

> — Mr D'Arcy, she said, what is the name of that song you were singing? —
> — It's called *The Lass of Aughrim*, said Mr D'Arcy, but I couldn't remember it properly. Why? Do you know it? —
> — *The Lass of Aughrim*, she repeated. I couldn't think of the name —
> — It's a very nice air, said Mary Jane. I'm sorry you were not in voice tonight —
> (Joyce 1995: 188)

What begins as air in the physical sense – "cold fragrant air" – turns gradually into an acoustic, cultural medium, which is no less physical but which carries a component that cannot be reduced to sonic effects alone. This is, of course, no more than the resonances of music, language, and the human voice allow but in fact the mystery of how something can be heard, over and above what is *literally* present, mere sound waves, became an issue of central importance in modernist investigations of mind and matter, and of the indeterminate zones where outer and inner worlds collide.[7] Such investigations were greatly enhanced by the rise of new technologies, which carried energy – heat, magnetism, light, and sound waves – in a manner that was closer to magic in the popular imagination than to the dull laws of science, conventionally understood. The capacity of the wireless, for example, to send human communication on Hertz waves through an apparently invisible medium came to resemble thought transference itself, a new modernist mode of telepathy. As Helen Sword has commented, much was made of the numerous

> historical and thematic parallels between the rise of spiritualism in the late nineteenth century and the simultaneous development of new communications technologies [. . .] [A]s radios became an increasingly affordable household item, the notion that the dead can communicate via "etheric vibrations", using a special frequency undetectable by the living, became a commonplace (Sword 2002: 36).

Joyce was to make considerable use of such parallels with regard to photography and film in *Ulysses*, and, indeed, radio and television in *Finnegans Wake*, but in "The Dead" such "etheric vibrations" emanate from the more elementary technologies of city streets and domestic lighting.

Just as the streets were dark with something more than night, in Raymond Chandler's phrase,[8] so also the city resonated with something more than sound. That sound extends beyond its own physical – or sensory – boundaries is constantly suggested in "The Dead," as the ear picks up noises that are virtually inaudible, or would not be noticed by others. Gabriel's buttons slip through his frozen overcoat with a "squeaking

noise" (Joyce 1995: 159), which acts as a prelude for his detecting the three syllables with which Lily pronounces his name (but which, as readers, we do not "hear").
Ascending the stairs to the hotel room on returning from the party, the silence is such
that "Gabriel could hear the falling of molten wax into the tray and the thumping of
his own heart against his ribs" (Joyce 1995: 191). The latter is understandable, albeit a
sound from within; if the "falling" of the wax is audible, however, it is perhaps because
it is partly coming from within as well, in the manner of the "falling" snowflakes that
bring the story to an end. Following Gretta's sorrowful recollections of Michael Furey,
Gabriel is lost in reverie but is brought to his senses by a faint sound: "A few light
taps upon the pane made him turn to the window. It had begun to snow again. He
watched sleepily the flakes, silver and dark, falling obliquely against the lamplight"
(Joyce 1995: 198). It is as if sound imbues the natural world with agency, the action
of the snowflakes re-enacting Gabriel's earlier tapping on the window with his fingers
to compose himself before his speech. As the shading of sound into light indicates,
moreover, the word "tap" also alludes to "the tap of electric light" whose failure has
permitted the gaslight, or its ghostly shade, to infiltrate the room. "A vague terror"
seizes Gabriel when he discovers that Michael Furey had died out of love for Gretta "as
if, at that hour when he hoped to triumph, some impalpable and vindictive being was
coming against him, gathering forces against him in its vague world" (Joyce 1995:
195). While standing in the rain at the back of the house in Galway where Gretta was
staying, her young lover had thrown gravel up against the bedroom window to attract
her notice: "I can see his eyes as well as well!," Gretta says in a sobbing voice, "He was
standing at the end of the wall where there was a tree" (Joyce 1995: 196). The image
evoked by Gretta's words stays on in Gabriel's mind, and seems to slip its inner moorings to emerge in the dim light of the room: "The tears gathered more thickly in his
eyes and in the partial darkness he imagined he saw the form of a young man standing
under a dripping tree" (Joyce 1995: 197).

Air passes from sound into voice – the cold air of the night into the air of a song
– but then is transmuted into light. When the first notes of "The Lass of Aughrim"
reached him, Gabriel "stood still in the gloom of the hall, trying to catch the air that
the voice was singing and gazing up at his wife":

> The voice, made plaintive by distance and by the singer's hoarseness, *faintly illuminated*
> [emphasis mine] the cadence of the air with words expressing grief:
>
> > *O, the rain falls on my heavy locks*
> > *And the dew wets my skin,*
> > *My babe lies cold . . .*
> >
> > (Joyce 1995: 187)

If the air in this passage is physical, then perhaps it may be "illuminated"; but if it
belongs to the song, as "cadence" would suggest, then some indiscernible kind of
sensory transfer or synesthesia has taken place. In *Portrait*, Stephen and Cranly are
overtaken by the sound of a servant singing, which recalls "the *touch* of music" from

another female voice in a choir during Easter Week: "all hearts were *touched* and turned to her voice, *shining* like a young star, *shining* clearer as the voice intoned the proparoxyton and more faintly as the cadence died" (*P* 206; my emphasis). As Marina Warner has noted, the association of "air," as the principle of life and breath, with music took on particular currency during the Baroque era: "This synaesthetic equivalent between air and music gives the words 'aria' and 'air', which began in the same period to describe tunes and songs of especial, emotive potency" (Warner 2006: 79). In "The Dead," it is notable that it is not an "aria" of the kind discussed at length over the dinner table which inspires Gretta, but a homespun national "air," sung in the "old Irish tonality" (Joyce 1995: 187). Recalling the memory of Michael Furey, Gretta's own voice seem to hover between the visible and invisible:

> — I suppose you were in love with this Michael Furey, Gretta, he [Gabriel] said —
> — I was great with him at that time, she said —
> Her voice was *veiled* and sad.
>
>   (Joyce 1995: 195; my emphasis)

"Veiled" can be understood as a visual metaphor to mean something concealed through sound, but it is precisely the fact that it is more than a metaphor that adds to its precision in the context. As Nicolas Abraham and Maria Torok suggest, the melancholic inability to mourn involves acts of concealment in which the lost object is hidden away, preserved through "encryptment," though part of what is hidden is the pain of betrayal or abandonment that led to the loss. In this case, the suffering of the loved one is recast as devotion to the survivor, the subject who inflicted the pain in the first place:

> Freud is surprised that melancholics show no shame at all for the horrible things for which they blame themselves. Now we can understand it: the more suffering and degradation the [love] object undergoes (meaning the more he pines for the subject he has lost), the prouder the subject can be: "he endures all this because of me" . . . Melancholics embody their phantom object in everything that the phantom, frantic with grief, endured "for them" (Abraham and Torok 1994: 136–7).

"Phantom" is used here, Abraham and Torok's editor points out, "in the medical sense of 'phantom limb syndrome'," in which pain is still felt after its source is missing. Metaphor is not just a figure of speech but also a way of responding to what cannot be named, what is veiled from both sight and sound. In this sense, Gretta's voice is veiled throughout, inhabiting a zone of "extra" sensory perception in which the senses give way to one another under the pressure of events. Metaphors, as a rule, articulate experiences that exist "in the head" and do not literally correspond to reality, but central to Joyce's stylistic technique is a mode of "free indirect discourse" that confounds subjective and objective narration, leaving it unclear whether something belongs to inner experience or emanates from an indistinct, external world.

According to John Paul Riquelme, Joyce's use of language throughout "The Dead" carefully contrives situations in which "the narrator's [objective] perspective and the character's have been subtly mingled and merged . . . by a style that mediates between an internal and external view":

> The style signals the merger because it uses the third person, an ostensibly *external* view, to present not only what occurs *within* the character (in words that appear to mimic the character's language), but also . . . [the] act of hearing something that apparently lies *outside* . . . [This] is not just a matter of reading semantically. It involves also recognizing the ambiguous relations of literal to figurative, part to whole, internal to external, living to dead, and narrator to character that enable the sentence's words to carry implications they might not carry in other contexts (Riquelme 1994: 224; original emphasis).

As a telling example, Riquelme cites the merger between Gabriel's "swooning" and the "faintly" falling snow in the cadences of the final sentence: "His soul swooned slowly as he heard the snow falling faintly through the universe and faintly falling, like the descent of their last end, upon all the living and the dead" (Joyce 1995: 198). This blurring of inner and outer worlds, literal and figurative, goes back to the opening sentences of the story in which Lily's voice, ventriloquized through free indirect discourse, testifies to a world in which the literal is merged with the metaphorical: "Lily, the caretaker's daughter, was literally run off her feet" (Joyce 1995: 158). This is picked up in the next sentence in which the clanging of the "wheezy hall-door" has a materiality of its own, while yet hinting at the breathless condition of Lily, if not the fatal lung disease that befalls Michael Furey. What often goes unremarked is that such "free indirect discourse" is a stylistic signature of cinema itself, giving rise to its spectral powers as a narrative medium in which the camera can move effortlessly through walls and doors, position itself unobserved in rooms, merge past and present, or bend the material world to its own will. In Huston's film, the camera operates in an unobtrusive way to make room, as it were, for an uninvited guest at the Misses Morkan's party, to intimate a barely perceptible hinterland between word and image, the living and the dead.

Haunted Cinema: A "Second Spectre"

> Cinema "itself" become[s] not only a host for the spectres it images but itself a ghost, a second spectre.
>
> Alan Cholodenko (2004: 100)

The difficulty for cinema as a visual medium lies in the impossibility of "pure" subjective narration of the kind that is easily achieved in literature. No matter how "expressive" the shot, or subjectively marked the vision, there is always more in an image than is noticed, or could be accounted for in terms of point of view. This "gap" or visual "surplus" is ordinarily unproblematic, and is put down to the invisible presence of the camera in classic film – or, perhaps more accurately, Hollywood – narration.[9] In terms of film style, however, this space in endlessly exploited for narrative effect, as in the various unresolved enigmas raised by Orson Welles' *Citizen Kane*. In the famous opening scene of the film, the camera picks up Charles Foster Kane's utterance of his last fatal word, "Rosebud," but who hears the word? Is it the nurse who enters the room, the butler lurking outside, or the camera itself – the camera as the ghost of a sundered past breaking through the self-images of a life? When Kane first enters Susan Alexander's apartment on his way to the warehouse that stores his past, does he really see the snow-globe on a shelf beneath the mirror through the corner of his eye, thus making a subliminal connection between the loss of his mother and the hapless singer who becomes the object of his flawed fantasies? In Susan's own flashback sequence, she is shown unconscious on her bed with a half-filled glass in closeup in the foreground, a scene she clearly could not have apprehended herself even though she "recalls" it. Throughout the film, it is not just that the camera "sees" more than the various characters, but that in doing so it becomes a kind of shadowy character, offstage but central to the action. Parodying its role of omniscient or invisible narrator, the camera is subject in *Citizen Kane* to the same partial vision and blind spots as the other dramatis personae of the film: hence Borges' conclusion that for all the privileged access to the secrets of Kane's past, the film is still "a labyrinth without a centre" (Borges 1988). Innumerable "loose ends" are left unresolved, all the more to give the lie to the illusion that any one key can unlock the mysteries of a person's life.

In the case of the horror or haunted film, the gap between camera and "subject-position," between narrator and character, is prised open in a more manipulative way to unsettle not only characters in the movie but spectators in the audience. When the camera moves stealthily along the dimly lit privet hedges of suburbia in John Carpenter's *Halloween* (1978), coming to rest outside an illuminated ground-level window, the fear is that this is not just a film technique, a means of intensifying the atmosphere, but the point of view of the killer spying on his vulnerable teenage victims. The threat assumes an overt physical presence in the monster film, but it may be that "haunted cinema" is at its most effective when the source of terror is kept offscreen, as in classic films such as *The Uninvited* (Lewis Allen, 1944) or *The Innocents* (Jack Clayton, 1963). As Gary J. Svehla writes, "Unlike vampires, Frankenstein monsters, and creatures from black lagoons, the substance of ghost cinema resides well within the domain of the human psyche and solutions are never as easy as a wooden stake through the heart" (Svehla 1996: 202–3). Svehla is correct to emphasize the link with the "domain of the human psyche" but haunting cannot be reduced to this, or to the recesses of a particular character's mind. Such an approach rules out the possibility that the haunting may derive from another "character," emanating from an unrequited past that is not psychologically internalized, or contained within memory.[10] For Svehla, ghosts and hauntings "often become metaphors representing the external manifestations of a character's inner turmoil . . . and once these psychological demons have been exorcized, the external ghost also vanishes" (Svehla 1996: 202). But what if it is not so easy to distinguish between metaphor and external reality, or if metaphors have the force of presences – however offstage or liminal – in peoples' lives? This, it could be argued, is the state of affairs that pervades the Misses Morkan's party and its aftermath, the condition that is general all over the world of Joyce's and Huston's story.

In one of the earliest discussions to address spectral elements in "The Dead," Janet Egleson Dunleavy argued that it is

> a ghost story that features a veritable Who's Who of Irish dead who walk unseen through the substructure, perceived only in the subconscious of the Misses Morkan's living guests . . .. Perversely unwilling to reveal themselves that they may be given their due, these spirits nevertheless become malevolent when treated with disrespect (Dunleavy 1984: 308).

Dunleavy is at pains to establish that the "ectoplasmic" disturbances of the text cannot be attributed to narrative techniques alone, to Joyce's virtuosity in handling multiple perspectives in a story. Polyphony is not merely a literary technique but hints at presences that "cannot be ranked as multiple point-of-view narrators (because they are not given full responsibility for telling the tale) but who can be described as characters" over and above the more overt personages in the story (Dunleavy 1984: 309). Four such "personalities" are identified by virtue of their distinctive voices or narrative idioms, and while such an exercise in characterization ultimately fails to be persuasive, the suggestion that certain acoustic or visual effects extend beyond the psychologies of individual characters does point to the presence of "shades" or forces that have not yet passed into memory. As Riquelme and others have observed, it is vital for Joyce's story that the narrative voice in the final paragraph does not belong to Gabriel alone, since that would confine it to precisely the kind of enclosed, subjective world that is contested throughout the story. Yet it is this aspect of Huston's adaptation that drew some opprobrium in critical responses to the film, mainly on account of the introduction of a somnolent voice-over, enunciated by Gabriel, to accompany the final images. As Franz Stanzel remarked:

> The shift from third to first-person reduces the dimension of meaning from near-universal validity to Gabriel's subjectively limited personal view. Such a procedure, probably induced by the necessities of the camera art, throws light on the difficulty, if not the impossibility, of rendering in the medium of film the precarious equilibrium between figural and narrative voices achieved in the story through free indirect style (Stanzel 1992: 121).

Gabriel does indeed utter the words but it does not follow that everything on the screen emanates from his consciousness.[11] The images summoned up are both related to, and yet at one remove from, his mind as the camera travels not just across the snowbound countryside but through memorials of the Irish past before it reaches the graveyard where Michael Furey lies buried. The ruins that loom in silhouette on the screen – a castle, a round tower, an ancient abbey – are themselves "external manifestations" of memory in national iconography, and provide a crucial, *cultural* mediation for the "transcendental" impulse towards the "universal" that is often noted at the end of Joyce's story. In this, Huston is not departing from the spirit (if such is the appropriate word) of the text, for the ghosts that haunted Joyce belonged not to the séances of late Victorian spiritualism but to Irish folklore and popular superstition – a class apart from the tawdry metaphysics of ouija boards and table-turning in London (or Dublin) drawing rooms. In Huston's original screenplay, it was intended to break up Gabriel's reverie by a shot of:

A TREE IN THE COUNTRYSIDE
A young man, standing under a dripping tree.
DISSOLVE TO:
Other dark and mysterious shapes seen through a watery lens.

(Hart 1988: 34)

This literalization of Gabriel's twilight state of mind was wisely deleted, for the true mystery of Michael Furey is that he cannot be seen, even though he is apprehended with all the intensity of Gretta's memory. The film opens with a view from the street of the "shades" of dancers coming to life in an upstairs window, a viewpoint that could be that of an invisible shade, waiting for its moment to enter the Morkan household.

During the party-pieces earlier in the night, Mr. Grace (Sean McClory) – a character introduced by Tony Huston into Joyce's original story – recites a translation from a Gaelic poem, "Broken Vows," about the betrayal and death of a peasant girl by the lord of the Big House. The camera focuses at first on the speaker as his words, in the stage directions of the screenplay, cast "a spell" over his hearers (Hart 1988: 26). There follows an edit to a pensive Gabriel, but when the camera cuts to Gretta "a strange aura seems to surround her" as she passes into a rapt state: "It is almost as if she were in a trance. Though her gaze is inward, an enigmatic beauty pours from her like that of a fine unsentimental picture of the Annunciation" (Hart 1988: 27). At this point, the camera begins to move slowly of its own accord along the line of young women who are also transfixed by the plaintive words of the recitation, thus picking up an important suggestion in Joyce's original story that the response to "The Lass of Aughrim" is not confined to Gretta but part to a wider cultural receptivity to a vestigial past: "'O, Mr D'Arcy,' cried Mary Jane, 'it's downright mean of you to break off like that when we were all in raptures listening'" (Joyce 1995: 187).[12] When the focus switches back to Mr. Grace in Huston's film, he has, "despite being a corpulent middle-aged academic . . . somehow managed to transform himself utterly into the spirit of the young speaker," the forlorn peasant girl of the poem (Hart 1988: 27). The camera itself has become the "medium," the means by which the spirit of the "young speaker" enters the room, and when the rustle of Lily's clothes on the backstairs signals her appearance at the end of the scene, it is as if she has become a manifestation of the voice, the "back answer" of a silenced culture.

The challenge presented to any adaptation of "The Dead" is how to capture the tones, the verbal shading and premonitions in Joyce's story that prepare for the "apparition" of Michael Furey. Huston's stylistic achievement derives from the manner in which these ghostly echoes – constantly oscillating between voice and image, the inner and outer worlds of the characters – is conveyed by the choreography of the camera. When Miss Julia sings "Arrayed for the Bridal" in a faltering voice reminiscent of Maria in "Clay," the camera again appears to assume a dynamic of its own as it moves slowly up the same backstairs that Lily has ascended a short while earlier, except this time it is to explore the keepsakes and bric-a-brac of the Morkans' past – porcelain angels, faded photographs, old war medals, ornamental glass slippers, a needlework sampler, a crucifix with beads. These mementoes are redolent of imperial nostalgia, displaying the extent to which Catholic middle-class households in Joyce's Dublin had taken empire to heart – a theme relayed throughout the story in the account in Patrick Morkan's truncated ride to the Fifteen Acres to see a military review, the dance at the party (a quadrille called "Lancers"), Gabriel's writing for the Unionist *Daily Mail*, and, perhaps more obliquely, Aunt Kate's attachment to the "sweet English tenor voice" of Parkinson. When the action shifts again to another song heard on the stairs, "The Lass of Aughrim," it provides the setting for the re-emergence of a lost love, and the remnants of a discarded culture which may lie outside empire but which is no less part of modernity.

The Memory of the Dead

> The ghost is not simply a dead person, but a social figure, and investigating it can lead to that dense site where history and subjectivity make social life.
>
> Avery Gordon (1997: 8)

One of the criticisms directed at Huston's version of "The Dead" is that it is *too* Irish, implicating a story of deep personal grief in submerged narratives of political loss of the kind that Joyce (so this account goes) clearly rejected in his own life. Commenting on the insertion of Lady Gregory's translation of "Broken Vows" into the night's performances, Clive Hart writes, "Joyce would have hated the introduction into his story of a passage of Celtic Revival literature – especially, I believe, a passage from a writer for whom he had so little respect" (Hart 1988: 13). It is true that much of Joyce's animus against the Revival had to do with its Anglo-Irish leadership, and the "nativist" leanings of urban literati intent on re-creating the western seaboard in the image of Romantic Ireland. What is often overlooked, however, is that during the period of the composition of "The Dead," such hostilities to the Revival derived from modernizing *nationalist* sympathies on Joyce's part, as in his support for Sinn Fein protests against the Abbey's staging of Synge's *Playboy of the Western World*.[13] From this perspective, Miss Ivors' enthusiasm for an excursion to the Aran Islands can be seen as reclaiming the west of Ireland from romanticism for a modernizing project in keeping with the resurgent energies of Joyce's own generation. Galway is not just an outtake from modernity (though some Revivalists may have imagined it thus); Michael Furey, after all, was employed in the gasworks, and on visiting Galway himself, Joyce wrote of its new suburbs that one has to close one's "eyes to this unsettling modernity just for a moment" to see "the shadows of history" in the city (*OCPW* 196). Galway's connections to mainland Europe were clear from an encounter with Danish fishermen, whose presence prompts a turn towards the Irish past in Joyce's mind, if not in theirs:

They were out summer-fishing on the ocean, and stopped off at Aran. Silent and melancholic, they look as if they are thinking of the Danish hordes that burned the city of
Galway in the eighth century and of the Irish lands which, as legend has it, are included
in the dowries of Danish girls; they look as if they are dreaming of reconquering them
(*OCPW* 205).

So far from Miss Ivors being "a flat character," as the critic Allen Tate charged, she is
central to the imaginative spaces prepared in the text for the opening up of Gretta's
buried past, and the ghostly visitation of Michael Furey. As Tate himself concedes,

Miss Ivors stands for the rich and complex life of the Irish people out of which Gabriel's
wife has come, and we are thus given a subtle dramatic presentation of a spiritual limitation which focuses symbolically, at the end of the story, upon his relation to his wife
(Tate 1996: 391).

It is all the more inexplicable then to find Tate concluding, in one of the most cited
critical observations on the story, that "no preparation" is made for Michael Furey's
"sudden" appearance at the end, thus introducing a structural flaw in the continuity
of the narrative on Joyce's part (Tate 1996: 393). In fact, as we have seen, the semantic
charge attached to words such as "air," "snow," "cold," "gas," and "light"; the thematic
allusions linking Lily and Miss Ivors to Gretta's west of Ireland affiliations; the top-
ographical resonances of Aughrim and the political associations of the monuments
of "King Billy," Wellington, and Daniel O'Connell – all carry intimations from the
outset of the events that are going to unfold later in the night.[14]

It is not Huston, therefore, who introduces a nationalist undertow to Joyce's text;
rather he gives a "visual tonality" to nuances in the story that open up modernity
to its own excluded voices. In marked contrast with the nostalgia of the Revival,
there is no romantic regression, no attempt to escape from the world of gas, electricity, galoshes, light opera, connections to the continent or the wider world. As several
critics have noted, the story ends with an invocation of the universal as well as the
local as the journey westward towards Galway, like the snow that is general all over
Ireland, moves out into a wider, unbounded space. For Bruce Robbins, this recourse to
weather, whether figural or literal, is part of a linguistic shift beyond "place" and the
"national," as is signaled by the introduction of "universe" into the final reverie:

This is not just a moment of alternative nationalism. The snow that is general all over
Ireland cannot help but stand for patterns of weather and ecology which are notoriously
impossible to restrict within one's national borders, even those of an island – which
the Republic of Ireland notoriously both is and isn't. The phrase about the snow being
general that Gabriel repeats as he sinks into unconsciousness is a phrase from the newspapers, but he adds to it the words 'the universe', words which are not in the newspapers.
The impulse to detach and re-bond by forgetting can and does work on more than one
scale (Robbins 2003: 106–7).

The irony here is that for Joyce, even the weather can be marked with nationality: "The rain is falling on the islands and on the sea," as he wrote of Aran and Galway Bay, "It is raining as it can rain only in Ireland" (*OCPW* 205). This observation comes at the end of Joyce's essay on "The Mirage of the Fisherman of Aran" where he envisages a moving out into the wider world from Galway bound up with more worldly concerns, the regeneration of the city as the port of global importance it once was before colonial rule. Holding a map of proposed trade routes spreading out from the harbour, Joyce closes his essay in what could be read as a parody of the mystical journey outwards at the end of "The Dead":

> In the twilight, we cannot make out the names of the ports, but the lines that start from Galway, branching and extending outwards, recall the symbol placed next to the arms of his native city by the mystic, perhaps even prophetic Dean of the Chapters: *Quasi lilium germinans germinabit et quasi terebinthus extendens ramos suos* [It will flourish like a lily growing and like a terebinth tree spreading its branches] (*OCPW* 205).[15]

An apparition of sorts is introduced by Joyce earlier in the essay but it is the mirage of "Hy-Brasil," the legendary land beyond the sea in ancient Irish annals. Not only the weather but the otherworld is given a local habitation in the Irish imagination. Part of the undoubted appeal of theosophy and "world memory" was that it afforded the prospect of a unified cosmic consciousness beyond the ruin and fragmentation of modernity, but as W. B. Yeats wrly noted, even the otherworld may speak in a national accent: "If one questions the voices at séance they takes sides according to the medium's nationality":

> All spirits for some time after death, and the 'earth-bound' as they are called [. . .] those who cannot become disentangled from old habits and desires, for many years, it may be centuries, keep the shape of their earthly bodies and carry on their old activities [. . .]. [S]hould I climb to the top of that old house [. . .] where a medium is sitting among servant girls [. . .] the apparition will explain that, but for some family portrait, or for what it lit on rummaging in our memories, it had not remembered its customary clothes or features, or cough or limp or crutch (Yeats 1970: 324–5).

The cosmopolitan is haunted by both the local as well as the past, and if there is moving out into a wider world, it is that of a spectral modernity, emanating from the unrequited voices in the margins, the "servant girls," the lily flourishing and growing on the arms of Galway city.

NOTES

1 For Joyce's interest in theosophy, see Stanislaus Joyce (1958: 140–1; *JJ* 174).

2 In a later essay, Joyce wrote, "The ancient national spirit that spoke throughout the centuries through the mouths of fabulous seers, wandering minstrels, and Jacobite poets has vanished from the world with the death of James Clarence Mangan. With his death, the long tradition of the triple order of the ancient bards also died. Today other bards, inspired

by other ideals, have their turn" (*OCPW* 125). This picks up on a theosophical image given a nationalist inflection in the earlier essay on Mangan: "With Mangan a narrow and hysterical nationality receives a last justification, for when this feeble-bodied figure departs dusk begins to veil the train of the gods, and he who listens may hear their footsteps leaving the world" (*OCPW* 60).

3　For Joyce's abiding interest in "transpersonal" memory and its connection with theosophy and the work of psychologists such as William James, see the insightful discussion in Rickard (1999: 86–117). Rickard does not link these concerns, however, with the elements of Irish folklore and superstition that persisted within colonial modernity.

4　See the advertisement for the Gresham Hotel reproduced in John Wyse Jackson and Bernard McGinley's valuable illustrated and annotated edition of *Dubliners* (Joyce 1995: 193).

5　For the iconographical context of this remark and associations of the Holy Ghost with wings, air, spirits, and inspiration, see the section "Air," Part II, in Warner (2006: 77).

6　As John V. Kelleher remarks, Lily's "accent is Dublin lower-class; she intrudes a vowel into his name and calls him, not 'Mr. Conroy', but 'Mr. Connery'. Conroy derives from the Irish name Cu Roi; Connery from the quite different *Conaire*" (Kelleher 2002: 44).

7　This was central to the emergence of the philosophical school of phenomenology, associated with Edmund Husserl.

8　"The streets were dark with something more than night": Raymond Chandler, "The Simple Art of Murder" (1944), cited as epigraph to Naremore (1998).

9　For the problems posed by Joyce's distinctive modes of narration to cinema, see Gibbons (2004).

10　Such an approach is central to Abraham and

Torok's psychoanalytic concept of "the phantom" (Abraham and Torok 1994: 165–206).

11　As Jakob Lothe points out, responding to Stanzel's criticism, Gabriel's subjectively experienced thoughts are placed in a larger narrative frame through the use of images; if this is overlooked by Stanzel, "it is because (by concentrating on the voice) he places too little weight on the distancing effects of Huston's camera" (Lothe 2000: 155).

12　According to Kevin Barry, "this generalizing of affective response to the Gaelic west" is added by Huston's film and is not found in Joyce's original story: "In Joyce's story[,] it is Gretta alone who is susceptible to the memory trace of the West, the trace of her own distinctive past, [affections] that set her apart from everyone else" (Barry 2001: 61). In fact, Joyce, as well as Huston, extends memory beyond the personal to the collective.

13　See Joyce's letters to Stanislaus, February 1 and February 11, 1907, where he recounts details of the Abbey riots, relishing the affront to Yeats and Lady Gregory's self-importance, though his response to Synge is more favorable. Joyce mentions how it put him off working on "The Dead" (*LII* 207–9, 211–13).

14　For the relation between political allegory and the "deep history" of "The Dead," see Gibbons (1992: 358–75; 2002: 127–48).

15　As Kevin Barry observes in his notes on the essay, Joyce drew his arguments for the revitalization of Galway from a pamphlet, *Galway as a Transatlantic Port* (n. d. [1912]), which sought to exploit the prospect of an imminent world war to encourage England to open alternative transatlantic shipping routes to those of British ports (*OCPW* 342–3). In the "Cyclops" chapter of *Ulysses*, Galway's former glory as an Atlantic port is part of the nationalist case for the economic regeneration of Ireland.

BIBLIOGRAPHY

Abraham, Nicolas and Maria Torok (1994) "Mourning *or* melancholia: introjection versus incorporation." In their *The Shell and the Kernel: Renewals of Psychoanalysis*, ed.trans. N. T. Rand, pp. 125–

38. Chicago: University of Chicago Press.

Armstrong, Tim (2005) "The vibrating world: science, spiritualism, technology." In his *Modernism*, pp. 115–34. Cambridge: Polity Press.

Barry, Kevin (2001) *The Dead*. Cork: Cork University Press.

Borges, Jorge Luis (1988) "Citizen Kane." In Edward Cozarinsky (ed.) *Borges In/And/On Film*. New York: Lumen.

Burkdall, Thomas L. (2001) *Joycean Frames: Film and Fiction on James Joyce*. New York: Routledge.

Carver, Craig (1978) "James Joyce and the theory of magic," *James Joyce Quarterly* 15 (3): 201–15.

Cholodenko, Alan (2004) "The crypt, the haunted house, of cinema," *Cultural Studies Review* 10 (2 September): 99–113.

Derrida, Jacques (1994) *Specters of Marx: The State of the Debt, the Work of Mourning, and the New International*, trans. Peggy Kampf. New York: Routledge.

Dunleavy, Janet Egleson (1984) "The ectoplasmic truthtellers of 'The Dead,'" *James Joyce Quarterly* 21 (4 Summer): 307–20.

Gibbons, Luke (1992) "Identity without a centre: allegory, history and Irish nationalism," *Cultural Studies* 6 (3 October): 358–75.

Gibbons, Luke (2002) "'The cracked looking glass' of cinema: James Joyce, John Huston, and the memory of 'The Dead.'" In Dudley Andrew and Luke Gibbons (eds.) "The Theatre of Irish Cinema," special issue of the *Yale Journal of Criticism* 15 (1, Spring): 127–48.

Gibbons, Luke (2004) "Visualizing the voice: Joyce, cinema and the politics of vision." In Robert Stam and Allesandra Raengo (eds.) *A Companion to Literature and Film*, pp. 171–88. Oxford: Blackwell.

Gordon, Avery (1997) *Ghostly Matters: Hauntings and the Sociological Imagination*. Minneapolis: University of Minnesota Press.

Hart, Clive (1988) *Joyce, Huston and the Making of The Dead*. Gerrards Cross: Colin Smythe.

Joyce, James (1995) *"Dubliners": An Illustrated Edition*, ed. John Wyse Jackson and Bernard McGinley. London: Sinclair-Stevenson.

Joyce, Stanislaus (1958) *My Brother's Keeper*. London: Faber and Faber.

Kelleher, John V. (2002) "Irish history and mythology in James Joyce's 'The Dead.'" In *Selected Writings of John V. Kelleher on Ireland and America*, ed. Charles Fanning, pp. 40–56. Carbondale: Southern Illinois University Press.

Lothe, Jakob (2000) "The Dead." In his *Narrative in Fiction and Film: An Introduction*, pp. 127–56. Oxford: Oxford University Press.

Naremore, James (1998) *More than Night: Film Noir in Its Contexts*. Berkeley: University of California Press.

O'Brien, Joseph V. (1982) *"Dear Dirty Dublin": A City in Distress, 1899–1916*. Berkeley: University of California Press.

Rabaté, Jean-Michel (1996) *The Ghosts of Modernity*. Gainesville: University of Florida Press.

Rickard, John S. (1999) *Book of Memory: The Mnemotechnic of* Ulysses. Durham, NC: Duke University Press.

Riquelme, John Paul (1994) "For whom the snow taps: style and repetition in 'The Dead.'" In James Joyce, *The Dead*, ed. Daniel R. Schwarz, pp. 219–33. Boston, MA: Bedford Books.

Robbins, Bruce (2003) "'The newspapers were right': cosmopolitanism, forgetting, and 'The Dead,'" *Interventions* 5 (1): 101–12.

Stanzel, Franz K. (1992) "Consonant and dissonant closure in *Death in Venice* and *The Dead*." In Ann Fehn, Ingeborg Hoesterey, and Maria Tartar (eds.) *Neverending Stories*. Princeton, NJ: Princeton University Press.

Svehla, Gary J. (1996) "The uninvited." In Gary J. Svehla and Susan Svehla (eds.) *Cinematic Hauntings*, pp. 300–17. Baltimore, MD: Midnight Marquee Press.

Sword, Helen (2002) *Ghostwriting Modernism*. Ithaca, NY: Cornell University Press.

Tate, Allen (1996) "The Dead." In James Joyce, *Dubliners: Text and Criticism*, eds. Robert Scholes and A. Walton Litz, pp. 404–9. New York: Penguin.

Warner, Marina (2006) *Phantasmagoria: Spirit Visions, Metaphors, and Media into the Twenty First Century*. Oxford: Oxford University Press.

Yeats, W. B. (1970 [1914]) "Swedenborg, mediums, and the desolate places." In Lady Gregory (ed. [1920]), *Visions and Beliefs in the West of Ireland*, pp. 317–37. Gerrards Cross: Colin Smythe.

23

Joyce through the Little Magazines

Katherine Mullin

And once upon a week I improve on myself I'm so keen on that New Free Woman with novel inside.

(FW 145 28–32)

Chapter 6 of *Finnegans Wake* acknowledges Joyce's debt to the "little magazines" which brought his work before his public and kept it there. *The New Freewoman*, under its new title *The Egoist*, began to serialize *A Portrait of the Artist as a Young Man* on February 2, 1914. 1914 was, as Richard Ellmann observes, an "annus mirabilis" for Joyce, since *A Portrait*'s debut was followed by Grant Richards' belated decision to publish *Dubliners* (*JJ* 353). Within a year, one little magazine transported Joyce from expatriate obscurity to international acclaim. Little magazines were founded to print material appealing to a small group of intellectual readers. Their circulations were rarely more than a thousand: they disseminated work unattractive to commercially run periodicals, often because of its experimental nature, and sometimes because it risked prosecution under obscenity laws. Beset by censorship difficulties, wary publishers, and nervous printers throughout his career, Joyce would continue to resort to little magazines to find an audience for his risky experiments with the novel form.[1] *The Egoist* serialized *A Portrait* between February 1914 and September 1915, publishing the first book edition in 1917, and issued extracts from *Ulysses* during 1919. Meanwhile, *Ulysses* was appearing in the New York journal *The Little Review* from March 1918, despite skirmishes with the censor culminating in an obscenity prosecution in late 1920. During the 1920s and 1930s, little magazines offered Joyce a natural home for *Finnegans Wake*, then gestating as "Work in Progress," which appeared in the *Transatlantic Review*, *The Criterion*, *This Quarter*, and, above all, *transition*. Little magazines were crucial to Joyce's position at the heart of international literary modernism, and it is unsurprising that *Finnegans Wake* should pay them tribute.

Why do the circumstances of Joyce's publication matter? The minutiae of Joyce's progress through the little magazines of decades past might seem of small relevance to the interpretation of his work today. Jerome McGann has, however, suggested that the "price of a book, its place of publication, even its physical form and the institutional structures by which it is distributed and received, all bear upon the production of literary meaning" (McGann 1985: 4), and that argument has been strikingly advanced by Lawrence Rainey in relation to the 1922 first edition of *Ulysses*. Shakespeare and Company's strategy of issuing a limited, deluxe, subscription-only edition was, Rainey argues, financially astute, since a first edition rapidly became the object of investment and speculation:

> The scandal of *Ulysses*, or at least of the first edition, did not consist in the philistine hostility of mass culture, as opposed to the discerning judgement of elite readers. The real scandal lay elsewhere, in that intangible yet perceptible social space where aesthetic value became confused with speculation, collecting, investment, and dealing, a space in which modernism and commodity culture were not implacable enemies but fraternal rivals (Rainey 1998: 76).

Rainey's suspicion of those early "elite readers" who disdained commodity culture while conflating aesthetic and financial value might at first glance be plausibly mapped onto the subsidized, coterie-orientated little magazine. Yet Joyce's relationship with the little magazines is too complex and ambiguous to fit tidily into a similar paradigm. Instead, Joyce's recourse to little magazines reveals the ways in which his work nuances, or even disrupts, what is often assumed to be the cultural politics of "high modernism."[2] The little magazine has frequently been identified as an exemplary instance of a "high modernist" publishing space, yet the presence of Joyce's work within it repeatedly destabilizes any implied opposition between elite and mass cultures. My focus will be on the three magazines in which Joyce was a sustained presence, *The Egoist*, *The Little Review* and *transition*. In *The Egoist*, I will argue, *A Portrait* and *Ulysses* covertly unsettle Ezra Pound's proclaimed agenda to transform the journal from a "low" concern with sexuality, into an organ for "an aristocracy of the arts" ("The New Sculpture," *The Egoist*, February 16, 1914: 67). In *The Little Review*, *Ulysses* found a more plausible home, since its "obscene" presence there exacerbated an existing fault line troubling the cultural divide between the coterie and the popular. In *transition*, the mature Joyce, his reputation established, is as indubitably a contemporary celebrity as Charlie Chaplin, as "Work in Progress" becomes the exemplary art form through which to articulate its eccentrically democratic aesthetic vision.

The Egoist: Firing the Sex Problem?

In December 1913, Joyce, then stagnating unpublished in Trieste, received his first letter from Ezra Pound, who had heard of his travails with recalcitrant publishers. Explaining he was "informally connected" with *The New Freewoman*, "a new and impecunious paper," Pound invited Joyce to contribute "markedly modern stuff" (*JJ* 349–50). *The New Freewoman* was a resurrected version of *The Freewoman*, founded in 1911 by Dora Marsden and Mary Gawthorpe, two renegade suffragettes who wished to "break away from the monomania of the vote" (Lidderdale and Nicholson 1970: 47). More radical than mainstream feminism, it prided itself, as contributor Rebecca West put it, on "its unblushingness – *The Freewoman* mentioned sex loudly and clearly and repeatedly and in the worst possible taste" (*The Freewoman* September 19, 1912: 649). It debated "free love," birth control, "wages for motherhood," prostitution and "Uranianism," as homosexuality was then termed. Its daring preoccupations forced W. H. Smith to label the paper "unsuitable to be exposed on the bookstalls for general sale," and it duly folded in October 1912, only to be resurrected as *The New Freewoman* in June 1913, with Marsden as sole editor and Pound literary editor (*The Freewoman* September 5, 1912: 602). In writing to Joyce, Pound was pursuing an established agenda to transform a journal primarily concerned with sexual ethics into an experimental literary magazine. During the first six months of Pound's tenure, articles on "The Excitation of Sex Discussions," "Sex Oppression and the Way Out" or "The Problems of Celibacy" were accompanied by poems by HD, Amy Lowell, William Carlos Williams and Ford Madox Ford, yet for Pound and several of his contributors, the journal's crusading sexual radicalism distracted from its aesthetic innovations. His first step was to orchestrate an open letter to Marsden objecting to "the present title of the paper" and requesting "another title which will mark your paper out as an organ for individualists of both sexes" (*The New Freewoman* December 15, 1913: 244). Marsden acceded in the last issue of December 1913, announcing the journal's transformation into *The Egoist*, and early in the new year, when Marsden resigned as editor, Pound saw another opportunity. Amy Lowell was Pound's preferred editorial candidate, and he urged her to help him to "fire the sex problem" from *The Egoist*'s pages (Pound 1962: 71). Marsden, however, appointed her friend Harriet Shaw Weaver, who agreed that "the *Egoist* spark of intelligence is not to be extinguished under Miss Lowell's respectable bulk" (Lidderdale and Nicholson 1970: 87). *The New Freewoman*'s transformation has been widely read as a seismic moment of conflict between modernism and feminism (Ruthven 1987: 1300; DuPlessis 1990: 44–5). It might, however, be better understood as a more ambiguous contest between "respectable" literary innovation and "vulgar" sexual radicalism.

How might Joyce be located within this ideological struggle? His appearance in *The Egoist* in early 1914, alongside his status as protégé, might place him as a natural ally in Pound's crusade. But tracing Joyce's progress through the journal over the next five years allows a more complex picture to emerge. On January 15, 1914, Pound introduced "an author of known and notable talents" by printing Joyce's own "Curious History" of attempts to publish *Dubliners* through Grant Richards in London and Maunsel and Co. in Dublin (*The Egoist*, January 15, 1914: 27). Readers were primed to support Joyce as a victim of unjust censorship when the serialization of *A Portrait* began on February 2. The opening pages appear alongside Marsden's savage review of Christabel Pankhurst's polemic *Votes for Women and Chastity for Men*, a return to old *Freewoman* territory in contesting the sexual conservatism of suffrage ("Views and Comments: the Chastity of Women," *The Egoist*, February 2, 1914: 44). While *A Portrait* slowly progressed through consecutive numbers, further articles and letters debated "Passion v. the Suffragettes" and "Modern Writers on Chastity" (*The Egoist*, February 15, 1914: 77–8). By March, a protest from one suffragette appeared alongside letters on the perverse "Uses of Restraint," and an article on "Marriage" which attributed female frigidity to the upbringing of young men: "Parents teach them nothing, and prostitutes simulate only the characteristics of abnormal and perverted sexuality" (*The Egoist*, March 2, 1914: 98). The next issue debated the elusive female orgasm as "HSC" blamed his fellow men for "learning to play the flute or the shattering cornet" while remaining "pretty poor players on the female instrument, far too easily satisfied by the least squeak of harmony" (*The Egoist*, March 16, 1914: 120). Whether "the Catholic Church permits a woman to finish (by masturbation) what her husband has begun" (*The Egoist*, March 16, 1914: 119) preoccupied the letters pages until well into June. Against this competition, one might pity Pound, striving to attract his readers' attention with an article on "An Exhibition at the Goupil Gallery" or a contribution from Storm Jameson on "Modern Dramatists" (*The Egoist*, March 16, 1914: 98, 103).

These suggestive juxtapositions raise the obvious question of how far Joyce might be assimilated within Pound's campaign to displace "the sex problem" with literary experiment. In introducing Joyce through his account of how philistine publishers had for ten long years baulked at the sexual references in *Dubliners*, Pound had already muddied the waters, appealing to the common ground between readers primarily interested in sexual revolution and those more absorbed by modernism. Moreover, reading the first chapter of *A Portrait* within *The Egoist* emphasizes the extent to which the novel complemented the journal's twin preoccupations with aesthetics and sexuality. While correspondents debate chastity, sex education, masturbation, and the repressive role of the Catholic Church, *A Portrait* gives us the Christmas dinner conflict over priestly interference in the political repercussions of Charles Stewart Parnell's adultery, followed by the "smugging" episode, where a baffled Stephen attempts to discover the nature of his schoolmates' obscure transgression. When "HSC" wrote in to "thank and congratulate the Editor for having given so much space to a subject often hidden away" (*The Egoist*, March 16, 1914: 119), he was referring to his own contributions, but his words might as aptly have applied to *A Portrait*. This coincidence continued throughout June and July, when Stephen's sexual awakening, culminating in his encounter with the prostitute at the close of Chapter 2, ran alongside passionate debates over Pankhurst's condemnation of men who resorted to prostitutes. In August 1914, however, the outbreak of the First World War meant that both *The Egoist*'s serialization of *A Portrait* and its discussions of sexuality were abruptly suspended. The politics of war preoccupied correspondence columns and articles on ethical subjects, while Joyce was unable to send instalments from Trieste until December. When serialization resumed, the experience of reading *A Portrait* month by month in the journal had notably changed, in that the theme of sexuality was now almost entirely confined to the novel. The homoerotic undertones of Stephen's conversations with Cranly in the fifth chapter, for instance, were unaccompanied by debates elsewhere in the journal about "Uranianism" and sexology. Indeed, the balance between the literary and sexual content of the journal seemed at last to have tipped in Pound's favor. May saw the issue of the influential "Special Imagist Number"; typical articles included "Notes on Modern German Poetry" (*The Egoist*, June 1915: 96) and "The Poetry of D. H. Lawrence" (*The Egoist*, May 1915: 81).

While it might seem, therefore, that the "sex problem" had been successfully shelved, *A Portrait* is arguably not complicit with, but resistant to, that process. Indeed, after December 1914, Joyce's fiction can be seen as an important outlet of *The Egoist*'s former preoccupations, embodying the persistence of the journal's repressed. The extent to which Joyce's work came to reconcile *The Egoist*'s dual and conflicting commitments is increasingly apparent in the months following the completion of *A Portrait*'s serialization in September 1915, when Harriet Shaw Weaver proposed that *The Egoist* should become book publishers, since commercial publishers proved unwilling to take the risk.[3] The process of finding a printer willing to risk setting the unexpurgated type was frustrating, since British printers were jointly liable for the publication of "obscene" or "indecent" material, and, in the wake of the trial concerning D. H. Lawrence's *The Rainbow* in late 1915, all were conscious of the dangers. Negotiations dragged on throughout 1916, as Weaver used her editorial columns to report on her repeated failures to secure a printer, and to praise Joyce's ability "to penetrate with cool analysis and innocent of suggestiveness" (*The Egoist*, March 1916: 34) into sexual matters. She compared his frankness with bestselling writers who "worked up details saturated with the most heated sexual suggestiveness," invoking a telling cultural divide to think through the problem of "obscenity." "Suggestiveness" belongs to low culture; "cool analysis" is the provenance and indicator of high art; Joyce is heroic in "having won for the critical understanding intellect standing-room on a portion of the territory now held specially sacred to exhibitions of a vapid sentimentality tricked out with a furtive salaciousness" (*The Egoist*, March 1916: 35).[4] Here Joyce is invoked to draw together the journal's once competing strains: his work licenses sexuality as a proper concern for "the critical understanding intellect." When the New York publisher Ben Huebsch offered to step in as printer, finally enabling the novel to go to press, Pound himself acknowledged Joyce's ability to make "the sex problem" artistically respectable. "At last the novel appears," Pound announced in his editorial column of February 1917, adding, "I doubt if any manuscript has met with so much opposition, and no manuscript has been more worth supporting" (*The Egoist*, February 1917: 21).

This implied codependency between sexual censorship and literary merit could only escalate in 1918, when readers were promised a "new novel by Mr James Joyce, *Ulysses*" (*The Egoist*, January 1918: 15). Repeated delays were announced until the January 1919 number confessed that "printing difficulties" had "made it impossible to publish *Ulysses* in full in serial form" (*The Egoist*, January–February 1919: 11). During 1919, a series of extracts sporadically appeared: a draft of the "Nestor" episode in the January–February issue, "Proteus" in March–April, "Hades" spread over two issues from July to September, and "Wandering Rocks" in December. Finally, in December 1919, the journal announced its own demise: "*There will be no issue of The Egoist in journalistic form in 1920*" (*The Egoist* December 1919: 70; original emphasis). Weaver had decided to devote herself to the publication of *Ulysses* in book form, and used her final editorial column to protest that

> an intelligence abnormally acute and observant, an accomplished literary craftsman who sets down no phrase or line without its meaning for the creation as a whole, is faced with a situation in which the very possibility of existence for his work lies at the mercy and limitations of intelligence of – let us say – the printing work's foreman! (*The Egoist*, December 1919: 70)

For Weaver, matters of sexuality and censorship have become inextricably entwined with issues of cultural ownership. Pound's attempt to transform the journal from an excitable forum for the frank discussion of sexuality into a space to foster "an aristocracy of the arts" is curiously undercut by this final vision of "the printing work's foreman" as the arbiter of the fate of *Ulysses*.

Joyce's position amid the self-conscious culture wars at *The Egoist* is therefore notably ambiguous. On the one hand, championing Joyce as the arch high-modernist stylist increasingly dominated the journal, eventually becoming its raison d'être. Yet Joyce's subject matter was disconcertingly "low," as the juxtaposition of *A Portrait* with the controversies of the correspondence columns could only highlight. Prostitution, masturbation, the Catholic Church's role in the regulation of sexuality, sexual politics within and outside marriage are all questions of mutual interest both to a significant section of *The Egoist*'s readership and to Joyce's two novels. Indeed, one might speculate that this crossover had much to do with Joyce's success in *The Egoist*, alongside his more obvious role as experimental literary stylist. Certainly, one of the ways in which the journal reconciled its conflicting concerns was through deflecting those energies which had once been devoted to "the sex problem" onto the affiliated issue of the censorship of material deemed "indecent" or "obscene." Whereas *The Freewoman* had originally prided itself on debating sex "loudly and clearly and repeatedly and in the worst possible taste," *The Egoist* ended eight years later in vigorous defense of the similar "unblushingness" of Joyce's fiction. The apparent dichotomy between experimental modernism and sex radicalism was thus incrementally undermined by the adventure of publishing Joyce. As Weaver observed, the censorship of Joyce added another dimension to the sense of cultural politics which ostensibly animated her journal. In 1914, Pound could brashly declare, "Damn the man in the street, once and for all, damn the man in the street who is only in the street because he hasn't intelligence to be let in to anywhere else" (*The Egoist*, December 1919: 70). By 1919, Pound's "man in the street" had become Weaver's "printing works foreman," a far more formidable adversary. The foreman's supposed willingness to print bestselling "suggestiveness" while simultaneously prohibiting Joycean "frankness" inflected the journal's loudly theorized distinction between "the literary" and "the popular" through the troublingly "low" question of sexuality.

The Little Review:
Making no Compromise with the Public Taste?

I have so far argued that Joyce's central presence in *The Egoist* unsettled its contested attempts to transform itself from an organ of sexual radicalism into a forum for literary experiment. Joyce, so often understood as dominating the project of an "elitist" high modernism, is revealed within *The Egoist*'s pages as not so easy to locate on one side of a cultural divide between "high" and "low," "intellectual" and "mass," "artistic" and "vulgar." Turning now to the second of the journals to which Pound introduced Joyce allows further exploration of his ambiguous status within the volatile cultural politics of the little magazines. *The Little Review* was founded in Chicago by Margaret Anderson in March 1914, although it soon moved to New York, picking up a second editor, Anderson's lover Jane Heap, along the way. Initially subtitled "Literature Drama Music Art," the first issue self-consciously emphasized its commitment to youth, rebellion, and change, proclaiming a "profound unrest torments the modern man" since already "a cult of the new has sprung up" (*The Little Review*, March 1914: 14, 23). "Newness" meant modernism, and, between 1914 and its demise in 1929, *The Little Review* published work by T. S. Eliot, HD, Ford Madox Ford, Wyndham Lewis, Marianne Moore, Ezra Pound, Dorothy Richardson, May Sinclair, Gertrude Stein, William Carlos Williams, and W. B. Yeats, as well as Joyce himself. Encouraging opinionated debate about the nature and value of art, *The Little Review* frequently startled through its provocative, confrontational declarations of its own place at the pinnacle of high culture: "FOR VIRILE READERS ONLY," "MAKING NO COMPROMISE WITH THE PUBLIC TASTE," and "THE MAGAZINE WHICH IS READ BY THOSE WHO WRITE THE OTHERS" were three of its typically flamboyant strap-lines. The cheerful blatancy of such declarations might seem to epitomize modernism's frequently perceived hostility to mass culture, as one contributor protested:

> The mass – the lower class – are feared by anyone publishing a magazine such as yours. You protect yourself from mass action by throwing up an intellectual barrage. Not content to mingle with or become part of the mass you thereby make a choice to remain in power with the ruling class as long as possible and by whatever means (*The Little Review*, October 1919: 55).

Such earnest accusations of elitism, however, rather miss the point of *The Little Review*'s tone of exuberant self-parody. For the journal both flaunts and ridicules its own intellectual and aesthetic aspirations, undermining any tendencies towards high modernist seriousness in ways which made it the ideal location for the debut of *Ulysses*.

The ambiguity of *The Little Review*'s cultural politics is most strikingly displayed through its imaginative promotional strategies. One of the most flamboyant was the "blank issue" of September 1916, when Anderson and Heap resolved to publish "an issue of the magazine made up of sixty-four empty pages" as "a gesture of protest" (Anderson 1930: 124). Declaring *"The Little Review* hopes to become a magazine of

Art. The September issue is offered as a Want Ad" (1), the issue contained nothing except Heap's cartoons of Anderson at unexpected leisure. It promoted the magazine both by soliciting new work, and by parading, even parodying, its own aesthetic discrimination, thus exemplifying Anderson and Heap's flair for self-promotion, a talent which sits somewhat uneasily alongside articles boasting of its tiny circulation as a magazine making "no bid for popularity" and thus "not for sale on all the newsstands to casual readers" (*The Little Review*, December 1917: 42). Yet *The Little Review*'s discontent with its status as a coterie journal with fewer than five hundred subscribers can be inferred from its editors' eagerness to appropriate mass marketing techniques to broaden its circulation and increase its precarious revenues (Bishop 1996: 314). Always short of money, Anderson and Heap were voracious, indiscriminate solicitors of advertisements. In the June–July 1915 issue, for instance, blank pages were printed where advertisements might go, subscribers were offered a $5 bounty for each advertisement brought to them, and doubtful businesses were cajoled through advertorial:

> Mandel Brothers might have taken this page to feature their library furnishings, desk sets and accessories, for which they are supposed to have the most interesting assortment in town. I learned that on the authority of some one who referred to Mandel's as "the most original and artistic store in Chicago." If they should advertise these things in here I have no doubt that the 1000 Chicago subscribers to *The Little Review* would overflow their store (*The Little Review*, June–July 1915).[5]

Throughout its lifetime the journal ran "oddly eclectic" advertisements, placing articles on Emma Goldman alongside advertisements for Goodyear Tyres, or a promotion for *Diane of the Green Van*, "The Book Hit of the Year," a "Breezy Story," on the back cover of an issue promising "NO COMPROMISE WITH THE PUBLIC TASTE" (Bishop 1996: 304–6).

Such enthusiastic participation in the discourse of mass commercial culture may at first seem incongruous, but it is nonetheless in line with the curiously democratic flavor of the journal. For *The Little Review*'s elitist polemic was undermined by one of the its most important innovations, the "Reader Critic" column, where readers entered into dialogue with material printed in the magazine. Unlike the correspondence columns in *The Egoist*, which were free of editorial intervention and isolated from the rest of the magazine, the "Reader Critic" columns allowed a space for readers and editors to argue with one another. There, as Jayne Marek argues, Heap and Anderson radically altered the parameters of the editor's role, fanning controversy by skirmishing with readers and even with each other (Marek 1995: 63). While I would concur with Marek that this was new in a little magazine, it was, significantly, no novelty to the world of commercial journalism. Indeed, Anderson and Heap borrowed strategies of reader involvement pioneered some thirty years earlier in the popular press of the 1890s. As Kate Jackson has shown, *Tit-Bits* and its imitators, *Answers* and *The Million*, were ceaseless in their inventive efforts to include readers in the fabric of the text, inviting them to contribute through entering competitions, sending in questions and answers to correspondence columns, devising riddles and jokes, or submitting prize stories.

The readers of *The Little Review* were similarly invited to participate in their journal, through the "Reader Critic" column, through contributing articles, or even through brokering an advertisement for a $5 reward.

The Little Review's appropriation of promotional and editorial strategies more at home within a mass-market periodical like *Tit-Bits* makes it, in one sense, the ideal location for *Ulysses*, a novel which, as Joyce scholars such as R. B. Kershner and Jennifer Wicke have established, persistently subtends high and low culture, the commercial and the aesthetic. Most obviously, Leopold Bloom's job as an advertising canvasser keeps mass culture in the foreground, as he repeatedly muses on his profession, acknowledging successes like the *Freeman's Journal* logo of a "homerule sun rising up" (*U* 4 102), and keeping a shrewd eye out for failures: "Damn bad ad," he typically thinks in "Lotus-Eaters" as he surveys a poster of a "cyclist doubled up like a cod in a pot" (*U* 5 551–2). Tellingly, fascination in *Ulysses* with popular culture disconcerted Pound almost as much as the persistence of Joyce's focus on the body. As Paul Vanderham has noted, Pound was the book's first censor, writing to Joyce after reading a draft of the "Calypso" episode to object to the closing passage when Bloom, "seated calm above his own rising smell" (*U* 4 512–13) on the outside privy, read "Matcham's Masterstroke," Philip Beaufoy's *Tit-Bits* contribution, before he "tore away half the prize story sharply and wiped himself with it" (*U* 4 537; Vanderham 1998: 16–28). Pound's reservations are obviously impelled by the bodily frankness of this passage, but they are also, I would suggest, animated by the intrusion of his age's most successful popular magazine into the scene. Indeed, the resonance between bodily and cultural lowness was underscored by Pound in his advice to Joyce: "The chapter has excellent things in it, but you overdo the matter. Leave the stool to Geo. Robey. He has been doing 'down where the asparagus grows['] for some time" (Vanderham 1998: 19). Pound refers to the British music hall comedian George Robey, who was notorious for his lavatory humor: the allusion objects both to Bloom "at stool" (*U* 4 465) and to Bloom absorbed in mass culture. If *The Little Review* has more in common with *Tit-Bits* than might first appear, both through its immersion in promotional discourse and its dialogic relationship with its readership, then one might discern a submerged anxiety behind the force of Pound's objection. For the fascination in *Ulysses* with advertisements, popular journalism, and affiliated forms of mass culture could draw unwelcome attention to *The Little Review*'s tendency to disturb cultural hierarchies. The spectacle of Joyce's protagonist defecating while absorbed in an ephemeral, disposable piece of magazine fiction might well unsettle *The Little Review*'s defenders.

The subversive implications of the closing scene of "Calypso" is further illuminated by turning to the ways in which *Ulysses* itself increasingly became *The Little Review*'s most potent promotional tool. Joyce first appears in the journal in June 1917, when the "Reader Critic" column carried his message of good wishes and the promise "to send you something very soon – as soon as my health allows me to finish work" (*The Little Review*, June 1917: 34). The back cover of the issue carried a revealing advertisement for *The Egoist*'s edition of *A Portrait*:

Special Offer

James Joyce's *A Portrait of the Artist as a Young Man* and a year's subscription to *The Little Review* for $2.50.

We are glad to announce that through the courtesy of Mr Huebsch we are able to make the following unusual offer, available to anyone who sends in a subscription (or a renewal) to *The Little Review*:

    Mr James Joyce's *Portrait of the Artist as a Young Man*, the most important and beautiful piece of novel writing to be found in English today, retails for $1.50. The subscription price for *The Little Review* is $1.50. We will cut the latter to $1, and you may have the book and the subscription for £2.50. Or you may have Mr Joyce's *Dubliners* instead.

From the moment of Joyce's debut, he is positioned as an international celebrity, his good wishes acting as an endorsement of the journal. The advertisement confirms that impression, embedding Joyce within the surprising context of the "Special Offer," and it would not be long before Joyce would be placed at the center of *The Little Review*'s marketing drive. In February 1918, the back cover carried the announcement that the serialization of *Ulysses* would commence in the next issue, together with praise from Pound: "It is certainly worth running a magazine if one can get stuff like this to put in it." The frontispiece of the following issue for March 1918 reads simply "ULYSSES BY JAMES JOYCE," while the inside flyleaf was crowded with advertisements for *Dubliners*, *A Portrait*, and even a forthcoming edition of *Exiles*. Readers of the first episode were in no doubt about the dual value of Joyce's acquisition. "The April issue is first rate from a business standpoint also," wrote one reader critic: "May Sinclair and Joyce ought to be good business getters for any commercial magazine" (*The Little Review*, May 1918: 62).

    Indeed, such was Joyce's commercial potential that Anderson and Heap attempted to capitalize on it through the distinctly risky measure of sending out unsolicited sample issues. Subscribers were urged to write in with the names and addresses of "any friends who are not entrenched in mediocrity," who would be sent a copy and an invitation to subscribe (*The Little Review*, September 1917: rear flyleaf). This policy had infamous effects when Anderson mailed the July–August 1920 number to the teenaged daughter of a prominent New York lawyer. The issue contained the section of "Nausicaa" when Bloom masturbates before an entranced Gerty MacDowell on Sandymount Strand; the outraged father protested to John Sumner, chairman of the New York Society for the Suppression of Vice, who began the legal proceedings which would eventually lead to the banning of the novel throughout much of the Anglophone world (Vanderham 1998: 37–57). Ironically enough, this apparently catastrophic result of a misconceived marketing strategy had a far greater promotional value, for Anderson and Heap had long recognized that suppression on the grounds of obscenity could significantly increase their journal's profile. When in October 1917 the Post Office confiscated the number carrying Wyndham Lewis' "Cantleman's Spring Mate," describing the sexual conquests of a soldier about to depart for the Western Front, the editors made their delight plain, printing a "Notice to subscribers" on the back cover of the following issue: "We had no hope that such a good piece of prose would gain the interest of the Postoffice for a moment. OBSCENITY!!!" (*The Little Review*, November 1917, rear flyleaf). The trial of the "Nausicaa" episode brought unprecedented opportunities for such welcome publicity. During the trial, *The Little Review* reported excitably on "all the blatant ineptitudes of the court proceedings," and both editorials and the "Reader Critic" columns overran with discussions of the controversy (*The Little Review*, January–March 1921: 61). Meanwhile, it boasted, "REMEMBER: *The Little Review* was the first magazine to reassure Europe as to America, and the first to give America the tang of Europe" (*The Little Review*, December 1920: 3). After the journal lost its case, it turned the court's decision into a badge of avant-garde credibility, reminding readers the following year that "*Ulysses* ran serially in *The Little Review* for three years, issues were held up by the post office and destroyed, we were tried and fined for sections of the book – scarcely a peep from the now swooning critics except to mock it" (*The Little Review*, autumn 1922: 34). As in *The Egoist*, so in *The Little Review* the question of obscenity thus nuances and complicates Joyce's position within high modernism. On the one hand, Joyce was repeatedly invoked as a crucial guarantor of *The Little Review*'s lofty commitment to literary experiment. On the other, that invocation led to his increasing entanglement within a distinctly "low" promotional discourse. In its confirmed obscenity, *Ulysses* did more than any of the journal's colorful promotional gambits to bring *The Little Review* to international acclaim.

transition: A Revolution of the Word?

The publication of *Ulysses* in 1922 catapulted Joyce to an international notoriety stretching far beyond the coterie world of the little magazine. Yet he nonetheless continued to place his work within small, specialist literary journals, even though *Finnegans Wake*, gestating as "Work in Progress" throughout much of the 1920s and 30s, did not obviously lend itself to magazine serialization, as Joyce was forced to recognize. Between February 1924 and late 1925, three extracts from "Work in Progress" appeared in Ford Madox Ford's *Transatlantic Review*, T. S. Eliot's *Criterion*, and *This Quarter*, but none of these journals cared to repeat the experiment (McMillan 1975: 182). Two others, *The Dial* and Wyndham Lewis' new review *The Enemy*, solicited contributions from Joyce, only to turn down submitted extracts from the new project. Meanwhile, former supporters were expressing their doubts. "Nothing short of divine vision or a new cure for the clapp can possibly be worth all the circumambient peripherization," complained Pound, seconded by Weaver's more discreet dismay (*JJ* 584, 590). Bruised, Joyce turned for support to a new admirer, Eugene Jolas, an American journalist now living in Paris and in the minority among Joyce's circle to express unmitigated enthusiasm for "Work in Progress." As Joyce explained in a letter to Weaver, he wanted extracts from his new work "to appear slowly and regularly in a prominent place" (*LI* 245), and in Jolas's new journal *transition* he found his spiritual home. Founded in 1927 and running until 1938, *transition* situated itself firmly within an international avant-garde, championing Dada and Surrealism, publishing Gertrude Stein and the first English translation of Kafka's *Metamorphosis*, and printing illustrations by Man Ray, Marcel Duchamp, Wassilly Kandinksy, Piet Mondrian, and Henry Moore. Yet it devoted more space to "Work In Progress," its defense and its explication than to any other work of art. As Dougald McMillan notes, "the name Joyce became so synonymous with *transition* that attackers could not or would not tell them apart"; the journal became, as the French critic Marcel Brion put it, "la maison de Joyce" (McMillan 1975: 179). At the peak of his celebrity, Joyce had found his own fanzine.

From the moment of its debut in April 1927, *transition* passionately promoted its star contributor. Joyce's was the first name on the title page of the first issue, which began with a draft of the opening pages of *Finnegans Wake*. Until November 1929, *transition* published an extract from "Work in Progress" in each issue; when ill health forced Joyce to leave off work, the journal was also suspended until he could resume his contributions in March 1932. Not only did the journal offer a reliable home for "Work in Progress," it also permitted its explication, welcoming Joyce's scheme in late 1927 to publish a sequence of articles which would elucidate his experiment to a sympathetic audience. The series began with William Carlos Williams' vigorous defense of Joyce's new style, which both "leaves nothing out" and, in its "broken language . . . affords him relief from boneheaded tormentors" (*transition*, November 1927: 149). The next issues saw Elliot Paul's brave elucidation of "Mr Joyce's Treatment of Plot" (*transition*, December 1927: 196–9), followed by Eugene Jolas on "The Revolution of Language and James Joyce," which heralded "the disintegration of words and their subsequent reconstruction" as "some of the most important phenomena of our age," confounding those "timid minds" responsible for "an avalanche of jeers and indifference" (*transition*, February 1928: 109). Both Williams' and Jolas's essays attempt to understand Joyce's innovations through the context of past difficulties in finding an audience; Williams' "boneheaded tormentors" alludes to the censors who outlawed *Ulysses*, while Jolas's reference to "timid minds" indicts both an indifferent public and also, perhaps, former supporters like Pound and Weaver. This tone of critical explication to a small audience of enthusiasts continued through further essays by Samuel Beckett, Frank Budgen, Stuart Gilbert, John Rodker, and others, which were eventually published as *Our Exagmination Round His Factification For Incamination of Work in Progress*. Joyce himself was enthusiastic about *transition*'s value in promoting his work, supplying the editors with a list of around forty people who should be sent free sample copies and even paying them 400 francs a month to offset distribution costs (McMillan 1975: 184). What all this might suggest is Joyce's inevitable retreat in the latter years of his career into a coterie world still smaller and more select than that bound by *The Egoist* and *The Little Review* – a world from which even the editors of those journals were excluded. Yet, while not claiming for *transition* any popular appeal, I would, nonetheless, contest so apparently unproblematic an assimilation of Joyce into an impenetrable high culture. For *transition* shares Joyce's genuine intellectual fascination with the interrogation of cultural boundaries, an interrogation *Finnegans Wake* perversely achieves and celebrates.

Within a year of the journal's foundation, an article in *transition* proposed that it commit itself to "the breaking down of all snobbish barriers between the arts" (*transition*, February 1928: 177). Its writer, Syd Salt, was hardly speaking out of turn, since *transition*'s first issue declared its intention to assault such barriers, whether they were between nations or between cultural forms. Alongside its declaration that the journal would be "distinctly international" in flavor, facilitating "mutually helpful and inspiring" connections between Anglophone and other writers, and between America and Europe, the editors also proclaimed themselves to be unusually relaxed about the barbarians at the gate:

> We hear much talk, nowadays, about the encroachment of commercialism upon the field of art, of the dominance of the acquisitive spirit and the dwindling of the reflective or contemplative faculties. The threat does not seem grave to us (*transition*, April 1927: 135).

This insouciance about the supposed commodification of art was accompanied by a clear relish for the age's most obviously commercial aesthetic form, cinema. As Michael North has shown, *transition* was fascinated by the creative possibilities of cinema, devoting a special section in 1936 to directors as disparate as Eisenstein and Chaplin, which was illustrated with stills from Chaplin's *Modern Times* and Disney's first Mickey Mouse film, *Steamboat Willie* (*transition*, June 1936: 100–5). The "Cinema" section was a natural development from an absorption with the medium dating from the journal's inception, when it carried advertisements for the film journal *Close Up* and declared that "the importance of the cinema in modern art and literature is resulting in an ever increasing interest in this new technique" (*transition*, May 1927: 184). Indeed, as North argues, what Jolas termed "logocinema" was crucial to the journal's dedication to "the revolution of the word," through which writers were urged to throw off "the hegemony of the banal word, monotonous syntax, static psychology and descriptive naturalism" (*transition*, June 1929: 13) and turn to innovative modes of expression which borrowed from new technologies.

The ur-text here was naturally "Work in Progress," which, Jolas claimed, fulfilled the journal's twin ambitions of assailing national and cultural boundaries: "Whirling together the various languages, Mr Joyce, whose universal knowledge includes that of many foreign tongues, creates a verbal dreamland of abstraction that may well be the language of the future" (*transition*, February 1928: 115). That this "verbal dreamland of abstraction" might best be understood as quasi-cinematic was underlined in 1932:

> The mutation now going on, which is helped dynamically by the new technological means such as the cinema, the radio and other mechanical forces, is about to create a linguistic interpretation that will doubtless have its effects on the final morphological process of modern languages [. . .] The writer has new forms at his disposal, a fusion of forms in which all the senses come into their own (*transition*, March 1932: 104).

Throughout its run, *transition* thus advanced two mutually reinforcing arguments; firstly, that the art of the future would assail cultural boundaries by modeling its techniques in part on new mass technological forms, and, secondly, that "Work in Progress" offered a prototype for that new art form. These arguments, while not immediately convincing, were undoubtedly ingenious. In *transition*, "Work in Progress" appears not as the inaccessible, baffling, perplexing read as it first seems, available only to a readership of initiates, but as a paradoxically democratic text, which, through both its polyglottal language and its recourse to radio and cinema as models for its innovations, offers, as Joyce would put it, "funferall" (*FW* 111 15). In this context, the various essays published in *transition* and later collected as *Our Exagmination* seem touchingly sincere in their drive to "explain" Joyce's project to the confused. That drive is perhaps most striking in one of *transition*'s more curious projects, C. K. Ogden's attempt to translate the Anna Livia Plurabelle episode "into Basic English, the International Language of 850 words in which everything may be said" (*transition*, March 1932: 259). The purpose of this experiment, sanctioned by Joyce himself, was "to give the simple sense of the Gramophone Record made by Mr Joyce" (*transition*, March 1932: 259), and is surprisingly successful. Beginning "Well are you conscious, or haven't you knowledge, or haven't I said it, that every story has an ending and that's the he or the she of it" (*transition*, March 1932: 259), Ogden's translation does indeed preserve much of the sense and the flavor of the original through its relatively transparent prose.

Through invoking cinema, radio, and gramophone as both the contexts for and helpful routes into "Work in Progress," *transition* thus interrogates the cultural hierarchies it seems, at first glance, to preserve. In this, the last little magazine to publish Joyce, "Work in Progress" is deployed to unsettle the boundaries between "low" and "high" culture, between a mass and elite readership – boundaries which its notorious "difficulty" otherwise seems to impose. That paradox sustains a tension also integral to Joyce's earlier disruptive presence within little magazines. In *The Egoist*, both *A Portrait* and, eventually, *Ulysses* undermine that journal's self-conscious ideological conflict between a "low" concern with "the sex problem" and a more "respectable" dedication to "high modernism." In *The Little Review*, *Ulysses*, and the uses to which it is put, draws attention to the journal's disreputable borrowings of promotional strategies from the mass media, such as the interactive correspondence column, the advertorial, the celebrity endorsement, and the deftly orchestrated publicity stunt. In *transition*, "Work in Progress" appears not so much as the pinnacle of high-modernist experiment, as the text of a democratic future, international in audience and provenance, the product of new mass communications technologies. Reading Joyce through these little magazines, then, contributes to our understanding of how he can be located not only safely within "high modernism," but also at the center of what has recently been labeled "low modernism." For Joyce is equally at home on both sides of the cultural divide, as he reminds us when paying tribute to his beginnings in the world of the little magazine: "And once upon a week I improve on myself I'm so keen on that New Free Woman with novel inside" (*FW* 145 28–32).

In naming *The Egoist* under its former title, *The New Freewoman*, *Finnegans Wake* subtly reconfigures the cultural coordinates of the little magazine, for the speaker here is Issy, an adolescent girl elsewhere absorbed by a feminized popular culture of fashion and beauty tips, celebrity gossip and romantic fiction. Here, Joyce incongruously misrepresents "that New Free Woman with novel inside" as a popular women's magazine. His tribute to the journal which placed him so securely at the heart of literary modernism is thus typically astute and provocative in its playful flirtation with the problematic categories of "high" and "low."

NOTES

1 For an excellent and detailed account of Joyce's publishing travails, see Vanderham (1998).

2 For a stimulating yet contentious account of modernism's supposedly conservative and reactionary cultural politics, see Carey (1992).

3 Grant Richards was offered first refusal, but declined after six months' consideration. Martin Secker, Duckworth, John Lane and T. Werner Laurie were also unable to accept the manuscript without alterations and excisions of the sexual references. For a full account of these

travails, see Lidderdale and Nicholson (1970: 102–5).

4 As Richard Brown notes (1992: 243), *The Egoist* was thus instrumental in helping to secure Joyce's reputation as "the type of the avant-garde artist who stuck heroically to his vision despite the attempts of the narrow-minded and the hypocritical to silence him."

5 Bishop notes (1996: 304) that the real circulation figures of the journal in 1915 were less than half the thousand subscribers Anderson names.

BIBLIOGRAPHY

Anderson, M. (1930) *My Thirty Years' War: An Autobiography*. London: Knopf.

Barash, C. (1987) "Dora Marsden's feminism, the *Freewoman*, and the gender politics of early modernism," *Princeton University Library Chronicle* 49 (1): 31–56.

Beckett, S. et al. (1972 [1929]) *Our Exagmination Round His Factification for Incamination of a Work in Progress*. London: Faber and Faber.

Bishop, E. (1996) "Re:Covering modernism: format and function in the Little Magazines." In Ian Willison, Warwick Gould, and Warren Chernaik (eds.) *Modernist Writers and the Marketplace*, pp. 287–319. Basingstoke: Macmillan.

Brown, Richard (1992) "Joyce, postculture and censorship." In Paul Hyland and Neil Sammells (eds.) *Writing and Censorship in Britain*, pp. 243–58. London: Routledge.

Carey, J. (1992) *The Intellectuals and the Masses: Pride and Prejudice among the Literary Intelligentsia 1880–1939*. London: Faber and Faber.

Clarke, B. (1996) *Dora Marsden and Early Modernism: Gender, Individualism, Science*. Ann Arbor: University of Michigan Press.

Dettmar, K. and S. Watt (eds.) (1996) *Marketing Modernism: Self-Promotion, Canonization, Rereading*. Ann Arbor: University of Michigan Press.

DuPlessis, R. B. (1990) *The Pink Guitar: Writing as Feminist Practice*. London: Routledge.

Ferrall, C. (1992) "Suffragists, egoists, and the politics of early modernism," *English Studies in Canada* 18 (4): 433–46.

Garner, L. (1990) *A Brave and Beautiful Spirit: Dora Marsden 1882–1960*. Aldershot: Avebury.

Hanscombe, G. and Virginia L. Smyers (1987) *Writing for their Lives: The Modernist Women 1910–1940*. London: Women's Press.

Hoffmann, F., C. Allen, and C. Ulrich (1947) *The Little Magazine: A History and Bibliography*. Princeton, NJ: Princeton University Press.

Jackson, K. (2001) *George Newnes and the New Journalism in Britain*. Aldershot: Ashgate.

Kenner, H. (1971) *The Pound Era*. Berkeley: University of California Press.

Kershner, R. B. (ed.) (1996) *Joyce and Popular Culture*. Miami: University of Florida Press.

Knight, M. (1996) "Little magazines and the emergence of modernism in the *fin de siècle*," *American Periodicals* 6: 29–45.

Lewis, Wyndham (1927) "Editorial notes: art and 'radical' doctrines," *The Enemy* 2: xxiii–xxviii.

Lidderdale, J. and M. Nicholson (1970) *Dear Miss Weaver: Harriet Shaw Weaver 1876–1961*. New York: Viking.

McGann, J. (1985) *Historical Studies and Literary Criticism*. Madison: University of Wisconsin Press.

McMillan, D. (1975) transition: *The History of a Literary Era 1927–1938*. London: Calder and Boyars.

Marek, J. (1995) *Women Editing Modernism: "Little" Magazines and Literary History*. Lexington: University Press of Kentucky.

Morrisson, M. (1997) "Marketing British modernism: *The Egoist* and counter-public spheres," *Twentieth Century Literature* 43 (4): 439–69.

Morrisson, M. (2001) *The Public Face of Modernism: Little Magazines, Audiences and Reception, 1905–1920*. Madison: University of Wisconsin Press.

Mullin, K. (2003) *James Joyce, Sexuality and Social Purity*. Cambridge: Cambridge University Press.

North, M. (2002) "Words in motion: the movies, the readies and "the revolution of the word," *Modernism/Modernity* 9 (2): 205–23.

Pound, E. (1962) *The Letters of Ezra Pound 1907–1941*, ed. D. D. Paige. London: Faber and Faber.

Rainey, L. (1998) *Institutions of Modernism: Literary Elites and Public Culture*. London: Yale University Press.

Ruthven, K. K. (1987) "Ezra's appropriations," *Times Literary Supplement*, 20–26 November: 1300.

Sullivan, A. (ed.) (1986) *British Literary Magazines: The Modern Age, 1914–1984*. Westport, CT and London: Greenwood Press.

Thacker, A. (1993) "Dora Marsden and *The Egoist*: 'our war is with words,'" *English Literature in Transition, 1880–1920* 36 (2): 178–96.

Vanderham, P. (1998) *James Joyce and Censorship: The Trials of Ulysses*. Basingstoke: Macmillan.

Wicke, J. (1988) *Advertising Fictions: Literature, Advertisement and Social Reading*. New York: Columbia University Press.

24

Joyce and Radio

Jane Lewty

James Joyce considered abandoning "Work in Progress" after the death of John Stanis-laus Joyce, in December 1931. Grieving, he told Eugene Jolas that "I hear my father talking to me. I wonder where he is" (*JJ* 644). At times, Joyce confessed, the voice would seem to emanate from within his own body or throat, "especially when I sigh" (*LIII* 250). This was an insistent reminder of absence, coupled with the notion that attributes of John Stanislaus had remained within his son. In "Circe," Stephen's mother appears as a separate vision, "uttering a silent word" (*U* 15 4161) which Stephen cannot yet apprehend; his hallucination is at the borderline of fantasy but no one else can hear or see it. Adam Piette points to Stephen's bitter description of Hamlet's father, "the ghost from limbo patrum, returning from the world that has forgotten him," while Leopold Bloom performs a similar function, bridging a divide regardless of, and perhaps owing to, his alien status. Flitting from place to place, he is a transmutable figure, "like a ghost," as Piette argues, "invisible to most [. . .] people [and] absent in their eyes" (Piette 1992: 187–8). Stephen requires the ministry of Bloom in order that his mother may speak in "Circe" as a character in their auradrama, praying for him in her "other world," yet eerily present in Stephen's features; her face "green with gravemould" (*U* 15 4159) echoed by his fearful expression, "drawn and grey and old" (*U* 15 4222).

The collapse of disparate states into a coexistent plain is a central theme in Joyce's work, as shown by his early attraction to George Moore's lyric "O Ye Dead," where "shadows cold and wan" desire life once again. This is developed in "The Dead" where Michael Bodkin lingers wayward and flickering in Gretta's memory, ushered in by the "distant music" of an unidentified piano player (*D* 211). Richard Ellmann observes that Joyce's corpses rarely stay buried; they cause agitation by striving to maintain their existence (*JJ* 362). This is a process naturally accepted by Bloom, who not only muses over "[u]nderground communication," but knows that "warm fullblooded life" (*U* 4 1005) can be haunted by traces of the lost and forgotten. In "Hades," he considers the gramophone as a viable means of retrieval, which diminishes "poor old grandfather" to a "Kraahraark!" (*U* 4 965) but never fully experiences the intermediary state between two worlds until the second half of *Ulysses*, which, as John Gordon notes, "depends on effects deriving from . . . telepathy, psychically-engineered correspondence, telekinesis, ghost-visitations, the apparition of etheric doubles and (of course) metempsychosis" (Gordon 2003: 254). Gordon contends that Joyce actively pursued the possibility of "new instruments [which brought] the formerly occult into the realm of the experimentally observable," as exemplified by Bloom, whose inner components work in tandem with outer forces to create a hallucinatory, and codetermined, space of activity. Taking this to be a generative area of enquiry, it is fair to say that, in Joyce's final work, the subject's ability to stretch the boundaries of science, and pseudoscience, would be continued; that Bloom's sensitivity would evolve into an improved everyman figure, who uses channels of "phone, phunkel, or wire" (*FW* 502 32) in order to traverse the unknown . This essay will focus on conductors and conduits, namely the medium of radio and its capacities. It will suggest that radio, in itself, may be a portal through which to access the *Wake*, and a development of Joyce's concern with communication breakdown.

Radiospace

This term has, of late, been redefined as "transmissional space," an unquantifiable area that exists in the utter abstract, a representation given breadth and depth by a signal which bears some kind of sonic content, and is apprehended by a receiver. "Transmission" implies a proliferation of objects, free-flowing in an arena that is not acoustic. Sound is present at both ends of the exchange, but in between there is silence. Radiospace is an idea, something unstructured, generally considered to be a cacophony of every noise, and word, in existence. To complicate matters further, these bodies may be also resituated in terrestrial relations without compromising their singularity. In their groundbreaking book *Wireless Imagination*, Douglas Kahn and Geoffrey Whitehead describe transmission as the place where an object can exist in several forms. Devices of "inscription" and stasis (such as the gramophone, or phonograph) are combined with the "vibrancy" of a larger system – that is, the sonic characteristics of the universe, "everything from essence to cosmos, always ringing with voice and music" (Kahn and Whitehead 1992: 15). Fundamentally, "[f]igures of vibration [live] in the space of an imaginary world, whereas figures of inscription [destroy] the space of the world" (Kahn and Whitehead 1992: 20). Figures of transmission contain both traits.

The very fact of "wirelessness" denotes what Jeffrey Sconce describes as the "sublime paradox of distance" (Sconce 2000: 66), thus inspiring all the responses to early radio technology, "as queer as any transaction with a ghost in Shakespeare" (Kenner 1987: 36). Its global effect is juxtaposed by the location of the technology – that is, the whereabouts of the receiver itself, whether it be a fully functioning radio station, or a cat's whisker antenna. Kahn and Whitehead trace "initial ideas of unmediated communication," such as F. T. Marinetti's 1933 manifesto *La Radia* which looked forward to "the reception, amplification and transfiguration of vibrations" emitted by "living beings [. . .] or dead spirits," the "dramas of wordless noise states [. . .] the delimitation and geometric construction of silence" (Kahn and Whitehead 1992: 267–8). The mere suggestion of a boundless arena contracted into a single moment of consciousness was reflected in various artistic and literary endeavors, and "sent hurtling down onto individual means of expression, splintering them into fragments" (Kahn and Whitehead 1992: 22). Marinetti would acknowledge that wireless telegraphy caused the collapse of syntax and analogy, and that those born into electric utopia were vulnerable, as intervention by machines had exerted "a decisive influence on their psyches." Stephen Kern, in *The Culture of Time and Space*, observes at length the "broader cultural aspect" of simultaneity; how a growing sense of unity was matched by personal isolation (Kern 1983: 88). John Durham Peters similarly charts the dyadic element of communication, how large-scale message systems generate anxiety. The isolated soul in the crowd, he adds, resonates "through the art and social thought of the twentieth century" (Peters 1999: 15). Synapses are often faulty in modernist discourse; interpersonal connections are incomplete, often silent but ceaseless amid the ether. I have contended that the condition of modernist writing (that which, of course, fuses and amplifies its precursors) was deeply wrought by the ambiguity of radio, its potential and promise, its intimacy juxtaposed with a long-range remoteness. Adelaide Morris' edited collection *Sound States*, a vibrant, comprehensive investigation of "earplay" in twentieth-century experimental poetics, also makes a valid connection between the "tunings" of the wireless imagination and the modernist epic. Morris argues for a "newly reorganized sense [ratio] of secondary orality" (Morris 1997: 37) composed of the written and the spoken word, which "engages the newly energized ear of its audience" (Morris 1997: 34), an audience exposed to the dominance of radio, telephone, and loudspeakers, which are all methods of delivering information. Essentially, the "shifting, speeding, slurring, sliding, and slowing" (Morris 1997: 34) of these texts are "all about illogical connections," many of which are recognized as akin to technological effects: the crashing of a telephone exchange, the spinning of a record, the twiddling of a radio dial.

Wireless words are scattered into an abeyance; they are caught by any one of a multitude attuned to a particular wavelength. As early as 1900 it was realized that wireless had opened a vacuum where the one signal tracked may, or may not, be the one summoned. It was the "main prospector of the ether" (Dunlap 1937: 75), Guglielmo Marconi, who filed for a patent in 1900 which aligned both transmitter and receiver, following several experiments where unregulated "agents" distorted his Morse messages. Thereafter known as 7777, the patent revealed the blind spot of Marconi, as defined by his biographer Hugh Aitken, which was that of favoring the "dream of direct wireless rather [than] a world relay system," as preferred by his sponsors. Marconi's 7777 improvement was fueled by a concern that two senders could block each other out. His intent was to fix wavelengths in the radio frequency spectrum, to find the exact place on the dial, from where the "you," the absent voice, emanated. Despite Marconi's efforts, cross-fertilization is the nature of radiospace. Sound waves persistently collide with each other, regardless of technological stability or directives.

Another factor is the disruptive element of static – the official term being "generic radio interference" – which might construct an incorrect answer or meaning amid its sibilant white noise.

Radio Text

Thematically, any technology can be traced through the Joycean maze; being, as he was, a self-styled afficionado of popular culture. As Donald Theall notes, machines of communication operate on three levels, all of which are amalgamated into a "copresence" (Theall 1997: 139). Firstly, "traditional sign systems (hieroglyphics, alphabets, icons, drawings)"; secondly, "technologically mediated modes of reproduction (books, telephone, film)"; and lastly, "crafted modes of popular expression dependent either on the traditional or the technologically mediated (sermons, pantomimes, riddles, comics)" (Theall 1997: 151). It could be argued that radio encompasses all three, insofar as it affects the power of inscription, and provides a platform for every type of oral expression. Harry Levin's assertion that Joyce was replacing the archangel's trumpet with an electric amplifier has been since elaborated upon, along with his conviction that the "loudspeaker" of radio is indeed the "medium of *Finnegans Wake*" (Levin 1941: 67). Recent critical appreciations such as *Techne: James Joyce, Hypertext and Technology*, by Louis Armand (2003), have raised the necessity of mapping Joyce's work alongside communications technologies of the early twentieth century, as they not only affect the structural logic of his work, but, as Armand contends, reveal Joyce's own awareness of these developments. This is not universally seen as communicative in itself. Michael Begnal has added that, whilst radio may indeed be a "central symbol" in the *Wake*, the problem arises from lack of "recognition on the part of the reader" as to who is speaking (Begnal and Eckley 1975: 26). In an essay which partially addresses this issue, and thus provides a starting point for the topic in general, James A. Connor charts the ways in which Joyce reset the technologies of his environment into an "older form" (the novel) and, in doing so, reproduced the "audial" in his language experiments. This is asserted more forcibly by Theall, who places Joyce ahead of his contemporaries for his adaptation of "technoscientific phenomena" into "language, gesture, speech and print/writing" (Armand 2004: 29) rather than into the visual arts.

Connor deals with the experience of radio listening in the 1920s and 30s,"the "high-altitude skips [the] superheterodyne screeches" (Morris 1997: 18), and the "squeals and whistles, howls like banshees keening through the airwaves" (Morris 1997: 20), all caused by failure to perform the laborious tuning, and retuning, of the headset or speaker. He also highlights the issue of structure and content of radio, where a bandwidth is "broad enough to permit a multitude of conflicting ideas" (Morris 1997: 24). This correlates to Joyce's mixing of codes, and, as Eric McLuhan briefly remarks, the presenting of radio as "not only a mighty awakener of archaic memories, forces and animosities, but a decentralizing, pluralistic force" (McLuhan 1997: 307). Correspondingly, Laurent Milesi writes that Joyce's portmanteau idiom in the *Wake* is so pliable that it allows all languages to interact and coexist in a "cosmopolitics" (Milesi 2004). Joyce's ideal desire to let any fragment of the *Wake* speak to any citizen of the world is that of "the imaginative forces of poetry in bridging the post-babelian linguistic gap, if only in a dream" (Milesi 2004: 161). Global communication is not achieved through a common denominator, but by the cross-fertilization of single entities. When considering Joyce's trajectory from the particular to the universal, it is possible that the syntheticism of the *Wake* and its rejection of a single communicative framework is part of the author's notion of how the work might be accessed or received. Joyce's comment on the "simultaneous action" (Hoffmeister 1979: 132) of the *Wake* may comprise a response to the multiform structure of radio, which permitted the state of subversive encoding; yet also embodied the notion of an all-encompassing, instant mode of speech.

This might explain the prominence of radio advertising in the *Wake*, a sometime narrative which is cut and spliced with other genres. After all, in Book I Chapter 5,

> the ear of Fionn Earwicker aforetime was the trademark of a broadcaster with wicker local jargon for an ace's patent (Hear! Calls! Everywhair!) then as to this radiooscillating epiepistle to which, cotton, silk or samite, kohol, gall or brickdust, we must ceaselessly return (*FW* 108 21–5).

This is what Joyce himself would have heard in the 1930s, the nightly rabble from various European stations, including, significantly, commercials from the Ireland Broadcasting Corporation, most of which promoted cosmetics and patent medicines. Not only were some of these adverts censored for their tawdriness, but their more acceptable replacements were broadcast subliminally, often embedded within a scheduled radio talk or repeated *ad infinitum* as the station played on into the night, devoid of programs yet still present on the waveband. On one level, this might have consolidated Joyce's opinion of censorship; additionally, it displayed a controlled linguistic manipulation which cannot have gone unnoticed, or even uncopied. For instance, when did the message cease to be received "correctly," and when was it comparable to, or heard less effectively than, silence? Was it more successfully received in code, amid other lines? If language is a distorting medium, never revealing its processes to those who respond and interpret, then radio language (despite broadcasting to a multitude) must somehow surpass this distortion. It transmits a message intended to be the same for all. The *Wake* deliberately refutes this in Book II Chapter 3, which is retold several times in variants through the wireless. Conversely, the Mime of Mick, Nick, and the Maggies is "wordloosed over seven seas crowdblast in celtelleneteu-toslavendlatinsoundscript. In four tubloids" (*FW* 219 16–17). The second sentence infers that radio advertising must still subscribe to a specific type of language, readily identifiable in its lurid sensationalism and condensed meaning. In addition, Latin was once the lingua franca of the Western world; its syntax is conveyed through a system of affixes attached to a word stem. Here, Joyce is implying that, in radiospace, morphemes and even phonemes (the smallest linguistic unit) are randomly discharged and then recombined with intent. A more explicit reference to the public nature of radio is found in Book III Chapter 3, when the people sit over Yawn (Shaun) in judgment and the four old men who conduct the inquest are superseded by "the bright young chaps of the brandnew brainstrust" (*FW* 529 10). Here, the transformation from ancient and remote to energetic and modern is denoted by the use of a well-known broadcasting motif. *The Brains Trust* was a BBC discussion forum heard by 29 percent of the population in the 1930s, garnering 4500 letters a week from listeners who wanted their queries addressed by Dr. C. M. Joad and Julian Huxley. Its placing in the *Wake* is a comment on the idea of gaining attention, chiefly through early radio and its artful strategies. As shown, listeners could be lulled into submission by a popular refrain which secreted alternative information, or actively instructed by an all-knowing authority. Radio will always "let in" opposing frequencies, in a way that threatens the efficacy of the "planned" assault on the individual sensorium. If, as Connor suggests, Joyce deftly rendered this collision in his writing, then it points to a consistent, and practical, engagement with the medium itself.

Radio Set

As noted above, static was a continual presence in early radio. Long-range signals would bounce off the Heaviside layer (a covering of charged particles enveloping the Earth, which radio frequencies cannot penetrate and which subsequently reflect them back), thus swamping the short-wave frequency. The radio apparatus needed constant additions and readjustments to counter the static. "Blocks" were inserted to hold the frequency steady, and filters were applied to keep the hissing noise at a minimum. Magazines such as *Radio Craft* and *Popular Wireless* ran advice columns on how to identify mysterious problems such as sulphation of batteries, distortion from overloading the valves on a radio set; also how to upgrade by connecting transformers and amplifying equipment. A recurrent theme was how to achieve "oscillation," whereby the radio set would vibrate backwards and forwards, accepting one current and simultaneously giving out another. Other tempting offers included crystal-type variable condensers, ebonite strips, basket coils, and the weekly problem page devoted to solving "Trouble by heterodyning?" Such obsessive detailing was to avoid what one irate subscriber called "a cacophonous miscellany of bestial and obscene noises" (*Popular Wireless*, August 3, 1929: 654). In contrast to Marinetti's concern that radio might dissolve speech patterns, the overriding impulse was to celebrate the field of wireless technology as a vastly informative and codependent community, rather than isolated souls hunched over their untrustworthy models. One listener opined that "broadcasting has added about five hundred words to the average man's vocabulary, not including those he uses when the thing won't work" (*Popular Wireless*, March 17, 1928: 90). To temporarily deflect the opportunity of labeling the *Wake* as the epitome of this comment, it is useful to identify some direct allusions to radio technology, where there is "electrickery in attendance" (*FW* 579 6).

Amid the welter of Book III Chapter 3 – perhaps the least coherent chapter of the

Wake owing to its extensive activity prior to "Recorso" – the ghost-raising is overlapped by noises. Yawn/Shawn's first request, as a "temptive lissomer" (*FW* 477 18) is to ask for Issy's letter, which he believes to be part of their correspondence, but is in fact, as one of his accusers points out, in "a deutorous point audibly touching this" (*FW* 478 7) a challenge to his own "landeguage" (*FW* 479 10). The point is that, on one level, Yawn/Shawn is experiencing a breakdown in communication, and he cannot locate the desired, absent, voice beneath his own ventriloquial distortions. The projected selves of the four inquisitors also mutate into different patterns, like sliding frequencies, or "twinestreams twinestrains" (*FW* 528 17) as evoked in the Issy interlude. Her melody is ruptured by the Matthew figure, who interprets the sound of the fireplace as an errant radio signal: "Your cracking out of turn, my Moonster firefly, like always. And 2RN, and Longhorns Connacht, stay off my air!" (*FW* 528 27–9). Interestingly, this sequence focuses on the immediate "harrowd" (*FW* 527 3) situation and its jarring with Shawn/Yawn's suppressed memories, but suddenly there is a call to order: "All halt! Sponsor programme and close down. That's enough, genral, of finicking about Finnegan and fiddling with his faddles" (*FW* 531 27–9). After a regrouping, or clearing of static debris, the "priority call" (*FW* 501 15) is detected and decoded by people who have the "phoney habit" (*FW* 533 30). Shawn's "superstation" is "amp amp ampli[fied]" (*FW* 533 33) to the level of BBC airwaves, where "Calm has entered. Big big calm, announcer" (*FW* 534 4). This is not to say that radio dominates III.3; it is a séance, and its structure is based on reports from the Society of Psychical Research, which often detailed trivial encounters with spirits through the "oujia ouija wicket" (*FW* 533 18). However, its vocabulary may also reflect radio tropes, as the previous "fireless words" (*FW* 469 27) of Shaun the Boast in III.2 morph into a more emphatic description of radio tuning:

> Is the strays world moving mound or what static babel is this, tell us?
> — Whoishe whoishe whoishe whoishe linking in? Whoishe whoishe whoishe?
>
> (*FW* 499 33–4)

Whilst this is seen to represent a hookup with the spirit world, it may also be read as a momentary break in transmission, particularly with the repeated sound of "Zinzin. Zinzin" (*FW* 500 5) which imitates white noise. "SILENCE" falls after a truncated sentence, "What is the ti . .?" (*FW* 501 5–6) and the effort is resumed in order to obtain "somewhave from its specific" (*FW* 501 21). The action is resonant of a dial being manipulated: "Better that or this? [. . .] Follow the baby spot [. . .] Very good now [. . .] Moisten your lips for a lightning strike and begin again. Mind the flickers and dimmers! Better?" (*FW* 501 13–18).

The coexistence of acoustic technologies and spiritualism has been well documented (Sconce 2000), and invites the notion that Joyce was aware of, and capitalized upon, this parallel. In September 1925, the *New York Times* reported that a group of psychic researchers had convened in Paris to discuss "Wireless Talks With [the] Spirit World," chiefly aiming to "Eliminate Mediums." Joyce was in the vicinity, having returned from Arcachon after a bout of conjunctivitis, but there is little evidence to

prove that sections of the *Wake* are directly responsive to this event. A more reliable source of debate is Joyce's incorporation of radio stations and their whereabouts.
All stations had what was termed a "call-sign" (identification letters to be found on
the waveband). Switzerland, for example, was 2HB; Newfoundland was 2VO; the call
sign for Radio Eirann, or "Radio Athlone," as Joyce preferred to call it, was 2RN –
to which Matthew strongly objects – chosen in 1926 as a gesture from the British
Post Office. (It asked all expatriate listeners to "come back to Eirann," an obvious
pun.) Ireland played a variable role in the development of radio communications, as
shown by a piece in *Radio News* (March 1927) joking about the "primitive methods"
of the Wireless Society of Ireland, who had proudly detected signals through the kite-
flying method. This was something Marconi had achieved 20 years earlier. In actuality,
during the uprisings in 1916, the Republicans had carried a radio set from building to
building, in order to duck under the British News blackout, and in 1926 the first Irish
commercial station was aired on January 1 from Little Denmark Street in Dublin. By
1933, the transmitter was relocated two miles east of Athlone, operating on 60 kilo-
watts with a range stretching to middle Europe. It initially relied on relays from the
BBC, although the first director, Seamus Clandillon, introduced Irish-language programs. A typical evening agenda began with a stock exchange list, a news bulletin and
market reports, and closed with a weather forecast. Owing to financial restrictions, the
service functioned in a building without sound insulation; understandably, this caused
some improvisatory situations. One broadcaster recalled how a gramophone positioned
in the corridor provided the incidental music for programs by "opening and closing
the studio door" so that the sound would appear to be modulated (Gorham 1967:
101). For any listener in exile, once "home" was reached after sifting through the airwaves, the result may have been nothing more than confused knocking and snatches of
melody. It is likely that the third thunderword of *Finnegans Wake* replicates this frus-
tration, with its "Glass crash" (a special effect) (*FW* 44 19). Eric McLuhan writes on
the intervolving themes of technology and self-expression in Book I Chapter 2, with
all its attendant misfires. He notes that the "[a]rticulate speech is a form of stutter-
ing; consonants interrupt the songs of vowels" (McLuhan 1997: 81) and that HCE is
relying upon other forms such as watches and bells, or rather "outerings" of himself,
so that he may measure his defense. The allusion to Volapuk, an invented language,
in the words "villapleach, vollapluck" appearing in this chapter (*FW* 34 31–2) might
suggest Joyce's concurrence with McLuhan's idea that "technological utterance is also
an artificial language, and is therefore of grammatical interest" (McLuhan 1997: 82).
But the consonant-laden thunderword itself, with its "klikkaklakka" opening, may
also imply the earwig with its suppressed hearing, beset with sounds of eggs breaking, applause, alarms ringing, and a rapid stammering which is never consolidated.
If this can be associated with Joyce's radio listening, then it follows that, as a "grammatical" experiment, it ideally portrays the themes of reinvention and digression of
Book 1 Chapter 2, "resnored alco alcoho alcoherently" (*FW* 40 5), rendered through
the haze of a dream, a drunken stupor, or a blanket of sound. More generally, it enacts
the failure of words dispatched through technological means, and the knowledge that

a single utterance heard by any radio listener was a sound reproduced, altered, and mutated along the way.

Thinking, as he did, of Ireland "every day in every way" (*LI* 395), Joyce would have surely relied upon wireless as a link to his homeland. With failing eyesight, the solitariness of the act would be intensified, being "athlone in the lillabilling of killarnies," meaning that his native music/lullabies were often "disrecordant" (*FW* 450 25–6) through the radio. Of Joyce's listening, I imagine an incessant, restless switching of dials, calling for 2RN, which would invariably be barricaded by stronger frequencies. It is likely that Joyce had a three-valve, possibly five-valve, set with a radio-wave tuner (consisting of two coils and a variable condenser) as it was difficult to reach long-wave radio stations with a simple one-coil set. These developments were adapted into Dunham portable sets, Pye portables, and Lotus portables. If Joyce had no recourse to these more sophisticated models, he would spend considerable time adjusting a 1-valve set which demanded a regression to headphones. These mufflers exclusively fixed the wearer/listener on a sound edging its way down the ear canal, which then penetrated the tympanum. Noises from outer levels would impinge upon the operation, but this was largely an interiorized process, a suspension of other senses. In his discussion of the *Wake*'s hero as "the quintessential deaf-mute," John Bishop lists the "weltering proliferation of 'hardly heard' and mutely garbled forms" in the text (Bishop 1986: 269) insofar that the sleeper's mouth cannot emit a sound; but he nevertheless participates in an "unsounded talking-over," even "throwing his voice into the wooden space between his ears [and] playing ventriloquist to his own dummy" (Bishop 1986: 270–1). Bishop also succinctly adds that "a reader of the *Wake* would profit from a few lessons in 'How to Understand the Deaf'" (Bishop 1986: 269). Building upon this critique, one might consider the amateur "dummydeaf" (*FW* 329 27) radio listener, who cannot fully engage with the transmission. He cannot answer back, or even hear correctly, experiencing – in isolation – what may be termed the "Mute art for the Million" (*FW* 496 7). To obtain a connection on a typical one-valve set, the "reaction coil" must skim the "fixed coil," whereupon, if a clicking or breathing sound was heard through the headphones, oscillation would take place, and weaker signals could be snatched from the ether. Even then, a "sibspecious connexion" (*FW* 374 8) would occur – misinterpretation on the part of the listener. This is alluded to in the *Wake*: the sleeper who hears "his own bauchspeech in backwords" (*FW* 100 27–8), no doubt composing words out of torn vibrations. He is a "wrongstoryshortener" (*FW* 17 3–4) who is in sonic turmoil, despite being, as noted, a "radiooscillating epiepistle" (*FW* 108 24) with "dectroscophonious" (*FW* 123 12) abilities. As Issy deduces in regard to her secret message, "sure where's the use of my talking quicker when I know you'll hear me all astray?" (*FW* 472 12–13). The spiral of the sleeper's inner ear creates a "warping process" (*FW* 407 3) on top of the "uncontrollable nighttalkers" (*FW* 32 7–8), or "sharestutterers" (*FW* 28 27) who are already modulated by their passage from anode to cathode, and back again, much like the story of HCE.

During the 1930s, local Paris stations included Radio-Paris (known as "Radiola" or

PTT) and Radio Vitus. PTT was the official station owing to the fact that the Eiffel Tower, although equally well known, was the province of the French government, with its broadcasts dispatched by courtesy. Conceivably, Earwicker's "house of call" (*FW* 310 22) might represent the Eiffel Tower, with its "radio beamer" mast (*FW* 380 16–17) and multiplex conductors, as noted by McLuhan, who makes the connection between the "Arab muezzin tower motif in thunderword 1" (McLuhan 1997: 157) and the broadcast tower of radio "muzzinmessed for one watthour" (*FW* 310 25) which unites its listeners. Another impediment to Radio Athlone was a secret radio station, broadcasting within the Paris suburbs every day, from 9 a.m. to 6 p.m. every day. No one had the key to the elusive call sign (indeed, a genuine "subspecious connection"), but it was one of the many "noisances" (*FW* 14 6) alongside the 30 more powerful stations operating on wavelengths between 1000 and 4000 meters. Those closest to 2RN's wavelength were Rome, Langenburg, and Konigswusterhausen in Germany. There was supposed to be 10 kilocycles between broadcasting stations, but, during the daytime, this was impossible. Radio waves reaching beyond 900 miles were reflected back to earth from the Heaviside layer, this being known as the "skip" distance. After dark the skip distance was increased to over 10,000 meters (verifying Leopold Bloom's observation that black is a good conductor; *U* 4 79–80). Joyce would have heard Radio Athlone more clearly still, however, "picking up airs from th'other over th'ether" (*FW* 452 13) as there was nothing to lessen the intensity of sound, from any location. Notably, the best months of the year to receive long-wave radio transmissions were March and April, given that ionization of the atmosphere by the sun was likely to occur in summer, and this caused a delay in outgoing transmissions. The apparent date of the *Wake* is March 21 and 22; the wind is from the northeast, there is fog and mixed precipitation. The year is estimated as 1938, for the *Wake* is consistent with events of the time, such as the Irish Free State, actually invoked over the radio in "Recorso" (*FW* 604 23), as the final storm report "blow[s] a Gael warning . . . shearing aside the four wethers and passing over the dainty daily" (*FW* 604 24, 34–5). However, an article in *Popular Wireless* (April 11, 1936: 63–4), relates a thunderstorm of lightning and hail which moved across St. George's Channel in mid-March, "a night of considerable electro-magnetic disturbance in the either [whereupon] atmospherics were so bad that there was no pleasure in long- or short-distance listening." This would have been a freak manifestation for the usually conductive summer months. Amid a day of varying weather, the storm in *Finnegans Wake*, which begins as a "freakfog" (*FW* 48 2) and rises to a "hailcannon" onslaught (*FW* 174 22), may have been augmented by this genuine weather report and its effect on wireless function – most emphatically in Book II Chapter 3, which was drafted in 1936. This chapter is renowned for its "Enterruption[s]" (*FW* 332 36) and turbulence; it may be attributed to Joyce's experience of "pecking at thumbnail reveries, pricking up ears to my phono on the ground" (*FW* 452 12–13), and being harried by intrusive signals. A break in the action is marked by a "Check or slowback. Dvershen" (*FW* 332 36), probably the station at Prague-Kbely, Czechoslovakia, with its call-sign "OK," transmitting at 1600 meters and bringing news of German troops marching along the "danzing corridor" (*FW* 333 8). In itself, this line directly hints at Joyce's engagement with wireless; a frustrating though necessary pastime. It is also merely another component in the most radiogenic section of the *Wake*, which will now be analyzed accordingly.

Book II Chapter 3

A catalogue of debate exists on the "Tavernry," or "Norwegian Captain" sequence, where episodes in HCE's shameful life are recounted by patrons of his hostelry. For example, Campbell and Robinson trace nine interwoven yarns, all of which present the returning avenger who woos and wins the damsel, growing fat and base before angry deposition by his people. Persecuted, ghosted, and finally exiled, he retreats to the purgatorial river (Campbell and Robinson 1946: 100). The principal motif of II.3 is a radio, whose continual presence ensures that all dialogue is loud, rapid, and scattered; every item broadcast from the "earpicker" (*FW* 312 16) recasts the legend in another form. In essence, the majority of interpretation holds that the wireless is at a distance, exclusive of the sleeper and operating at the level of external noise, as, for example, the "Rolloraped" (*FW* 330 20), a rollerblind at the window which rips through the layers of unconsciousness and thus alters the subliminal arrangement of word-patterns. This would place the sleeper in sonic turmoil, compelled to filter sounds from his environment into the dream-flow. Derek Attridge ventures that, although Joyce was tolerant of those who used the strategy, "there is little evidence to suggest he associated his laborious project with [. . .] sleep or dreams" (Attridge 1989: 17–18). This would correlate to a comment made by Harriet Shaw Weaver, in 1954, which dismisses the *Wake*'s supposed dream form as a "convenient device," never intended to expand into the somnambulistic wanderings of HCE (Atherton 1954: 17). Indisputably, though, the sleeper is the auditory vigilance of the night, the "earwitness" (*FW* 5 14), someone "who will somewherise for the whole" (*FW* 602 7), an "Ear! Ear! Not ay! Eye! Eye" (*FW* 409 3). Bishop advances this notion brilliantly in his overview of pages 309–10, wherein Joyce compresses every element of wireless, and, in doing so, asserts its central place in the *Wake*:

> [A] high fidelity daildialler, as modern as tomorrow afternoon and in appearance up to the minute, (hearing that anybody in that ruad duchy of Wollinstown schemed to halve the wrong type of date) equipped with supershielded umbrella antennas for distance-getting and connected by the magnetic links of a Bellini-Tosti coupling system with a vitaltone speaker, capable of catching skybuddies, harbour craft emittances, key clickings, vaticum cleaners, due to women formed mobile or man made static and bawling the whowle hamshack and wobble down in an eliminium sounds pound so as to serve him up a melegoturny marygoraumd, eclectrically filtered for allirish earths and ohmes.
>
> (*FW* 309 14–310 1)

Here, radio science is described in fastidious detail (even the ohms, the unit of electrical resistance), probably gleaned from specialist weeklies. The "magazine battery" (called the Mimmim Bimbim patent number 1132) galvanizing the "harmonic condenser enginium" (*FW* 310 1–3) is a reference to cheap mail-order components, which, although very "modern," invariably needed to be "tuned up by twintriodic singulvalous pipelines (lackslipping along as if their liffing deepunded on it)" (*FW* 310 5–6). The patent itself is the Peterson coil for lightning protection; an instrument which will not be entirely dependable in II.3. As noted, the "marygoraumd" of radio signals, circling in the ether, must be "filtered" so that "liffing" (the Liffey) and all else Irish, can be detected by the "key-call." Centuries-old snippets of sound are included in this scanning of "Naul and Santry" (*FW* 310 13), as indicated by the reference to Piaris Feiritear (*FW* 310 11), an Irish-language poet (1600–63) still recalled in oral tradition. The consumerist nature of radio advertising is even present in the "vaticum cleaners," which double as the "vacuum," or "Etheria Deserta" (*FW* 309 9) of radiospace. Above all, the most startling feature of this device is the "howdrocephalous enlargement," which operates the "circumcentric megacycles" or "most leastways brung it about somehow" (*FW* 310 6–9). This "meatous conch" conducts all and sundry, a mulligatawny of concertos over the "hamshack" (slang for an amateur wireless station). Bishop writes at length on the "otological life" (*FW* 310 21) of the sleeper; how sound waves "pinnitrate" and revolve deep into the "lubberendth" of his ear (*FW* 310 9, 21) akin to other "sensing devices" such as radar or telegraphic posts. He proposes that "the real power source feeding this radio is our [. . .] hero himself"whose ears translate cryptic signs "for all within crystal range" (Bishop 1986: 276). Furthering this observation, I would accentuate the "Eustache Straight" (Eustachian tube) (*FW* 310 12) which connects the larynx to the ear (indeed, the "suckmouth ear" in III.3, *FW* 394 22). This points to a near-cyborgian portrait of a "man made static" (*FW* 309 22), as "highly charged with electrons as hophazards can effective it" (*FW* 615 17). Within this inventory of detail, there is a reminder of how any radio communication is complex and fallible. The listener enacts a circuitous, one-sided dialogue, regardless of, and alongside, the interactive experience.

It is worth recounting that Marconi, dubbed "the Gulliver of science" (Dunlap 1937: 179), had a "highly strung nervous system" which naturally incorporated a pair of ultra-sharpened ears. In addition to knowing the mechanics of "radiocasting from A to Z and back again," Dunlap emphasizes that Marconi literally "personifie[d]" wireless with his uncanny ability to dissect a multiplicity of sounds and pinpoint words from afar (Dunlap 1937: 179). For these purposes, not only do we remember that "the ear of Fionn Earwicker aforetime was the trademark of a broadcaster" (*FW* 108 21–2), but, as remarked upon by Roland McHugh, the sleeper "dialls" into the past (McHugh 1976: 77). He employs the radio for "Hystorical leavesdropping" (*FW* 564 31) and becomes "the cluekey to a world room beyond the roomwhorld" (*FW* 100 28). Whilst in accordance with Bishop's notion that "sounds from the real world are invariably impinging on Earwicker's ears with erratic constancy throughout the night" (Bishop 1986: 278), I would add that the "free association as a process of radioreception" (Bishop 1986: 278) which constitutes much of II.3 may be extended to include extraterrestrial noise, from an alternative plain of existence. After all, the sleeper is a "coaxing experimenter" (*FW* 582 3), perhaps even a "dweller in the downandoutermost where voice only of the dead may come" (*FW* 194 19–20), whose hearing cannot always be selective. The phrase "Listen, listen! I am doing it. Hear more to these voices! Always I am hearing them" (*FW* 571 24–5) is one which conveys the impression of disorder, a state where the sleeper is invaded by multiple dialogues. As a "Prospector projector" (*FW* 576 18), he receives, and amplifies, those ghostly whisperings otherwise dispersed (Lewty 2004: 1).

Therefore the reader may wish to reposition the wireless in II.3 as more than simply occupying a place in the tavern downstairs. It provides a linkage to the "Real Absence," or "Echoland" (*FW* 13 5) in addition to containing recognizable sonic components. For the sleeper, who frequently wonders "what are the sound waves saying" (*FW* 256 23–4), the radio, "the wickser in his ear" (*FW* 311 11), is regrettably a "harpsdischord" (*FW* 12 18). For any early radio listener attempting to listen to their favorite program, interference from nearby transmitters was of great concern insofar as carrier waves collided with the specific broadcast. If the radio dial alighted between stations, the result was a distorted combination of both signals, which restructed any attempt to differentiate between the two. As Shaun's persecutors point out in III.3, anyone with a wireless set "can pick up bostoons" (Boston) (*FW* 489 36) alongside short-wave items.

This is registered in II.3 by the conglomeration of sound, how the two primary broadcasts and a weather report, are interrupted and splintered by alternative noise, "crupping into our raw lenguage" (*FW* 323 5). The sermon emphasizes the Quinquagesima service, celebrated the previous month but aired at the present time; the weather forecast predicts a storm which will soon dismantle the window shutters upstairs. Initially, the sermon observes "the otherdogs churches," but after a "low frequency amplification" (*FW* 312 32–3) the speaker becomes a hellfire and damnation "agitator" (*FW* 333 4) causing confusion. Curses are delivered in tandem with the rising wind, wireless frequencies are assailed, and someone is held accountable for exposing the house to the elements, "for where the deiffel or when the finicking or why the funicking, who caused the scaffolding to be first removed[?]" (*FW* 313 36–314 2). The storm bursts into the sleeper's bedroom, in a thunderword of violent excitation:

> Upon this dry call of selenium cell (that horn of lunghalloon, Riland's in peril!) with its doomed crack of the old damn ukonnen power insound in it the lord of the saloom, as if for a flash salamgunnded himself, listed his tummelumpsk pack and hearinat presently returned him, ambilaterally alleyeoneyesed, from their uppletoned layir to his beforetime guests (*FW* 323 25–30).

O'Connell, the great liberator, and champion of the English language as a means of empowerment for the oppressed Catholic minority, is now an ineffective "doomed crack," heard through the "horn" of the wireless, whose superior battery power enables it to transcend Ireland's borders, as far away as Lough Allen/"lunghalloon." The sleeper must retune his hearing, in order to absorb all sounds (the "salmagundis" perhaps being a pun on the Joycean idea of "word-salad"?) "ambilaterally," meaning "from both sides," and consequently decide which waveband to settle upon. The demand to "change all that whole set" (*FW* 324 14) is a blatant response to this motion, an irritated cry to "Shut down and shet up. Our set, our set's allohn" (*FW* 324 15–16). The word "allohn," recalling the German *allein* (only), may imply that the sleeper's patrons are tiring of the interference, and clamor for a definitive "set" or station.

And they poured em behoiled on the fire. Scaald!
Rowdiose wodhalooing.

(*FW* 324 17–18)

"Wodhalooing" is possibly "Radio Atha-luin," sizzling above warnings of another "sodden retch of low pleasure" making its way "from the nordth" with "lucal drizzles" (*FW* 324 32–3, 25). An advert for tea ensues, only costing "one and eleven" (*FW* 325 5) and the announcement of a string quartet. The storm gathers momentum, and the roller-blind unravels over the window, becoming a "bombardment screen" (*FW* 349 8) for the Butt and Taff sequence. Evidently these "conjurations" (Gordon 1986: 205), project a sequence of moving images, and thus constitute a break in the sleeper's auricular experience. Nevertheless, they are "borne by their carnier walve" (*FW* 349 12), a carrier wave/valve which produces a "verbivocovisual" (*FW* 341 18) account of the horse race. This is evidence of HCE's "earsighted view" (*FW* 143 9–10). He interprets all events "phonoscopically" (*FW* 449 1), fixing on "stellar attractions" (*FW* 449 3) which are converted from sound amid the ether.

During the opening sequence of Book I, Chapter 1, we are advised to "lift we our ears, eyes of the darkness" (*FW* 14 29), and prepare for a multiform acoustic experience, which may inspire a "soundpicture" (*FW* 570 14), such as this point in II.3, where the wireless interjects with a barrage of visual tabloid gossip. Upper-class women at the race are no longer fashionable, after donning mackintoshes; America's moneyed "Yales boys" (*FW* 346 7) are ruining their reputations in New York; the final titbit is, bathetically, an advert for laxatives. Additionally, this passage underscores the profligacy of words, how nonsense and taletelling equates to the untrustworthiness of a wireless connection. Some order is resumed in the tale, with "fullexampling" (*FW* 356 14), but a reference to the sleeper's "static" body is once again invoked, as the patrons offer to "sock him up," [electrify him] like a "ham" [radio ham], "a ham pig" (*FW* 359 19–21), who listens in: the "eariewhigg" who deserts his post (*FW* 360 32). Ultimately, in the choppy climate of II.3, all elements are "rent, outraged [and] yewleaved" (*FW* 339 28), and mere "humble indivisibles in the grand continuum" (*FW* 479 21–2). As the section closes, the four avunculists, who recur in multiple form throughout the text, struggle to find their longitude and latitude: "Highohigh! Sinkasink! / Waves" (*FW* 373 7–8). As the chapter subsides, "[t]he auditor learns" (*FW* 374 6), perhaps that information should not be passed from "story to story" (*FW* 374 32), in the "wakes of his ears" (*FW* 382 25), where "flash becomes word and silents selfloud" (*FW* 267 16–17).

Radio Work

Of course, when reading the *Wake* through a specific idea, or conviction, the danger is simply to produce a catalogue of evidence. One way to sidestep this tendency is to withdraw from textual detail and view the *Wake* as a larger project, whose effect may also align to one's interpretation, but it nevertheless reduces the risk of overemphasis. To this end, when viewing the thunderwords as a collective construct, they seem to mimic the acoustic disturbance of static, whereupon white noise is visually rendered. They are not only fractions of noise, but also occur in linguistic variations of around a thousand letters. As readers, our eye notes cacophony that the ear silently translates into sound, and we can detect a perpetual, distant, noise, far more akin to the music of the spheres than a clunking verbal rendition. When perceiving Book II Chapter 2 in its entirety, the "Study Period – Triv and Quad" is a medley of crossings and intersections, "devoted to the appearance of . . . words on the page" (Hart 1962: 36), and comparable to Apollinaire's caligramme "Voyage," where the etching of a telegraph pole crossed by wires functions as a musical time signature for words printed below (Apollinaire 1980: 92–3). The order of II.2 may also suggest a playful experiment with how, and what, is received through a radio set. Situated in the center of the *Wake*, it implies a meticulous working method, whereby a list of sounds is compiled before being dismantled and turned back into static; in itself, an academic exercise. Before the chapter begins, an exclamation of "Uplouderamainagain!" (*FW* 258 19) indicates the manual operating of a radio, where "phonoised by that phenomenon, the unhappitents of the earth have terrumbled from fimament unto fundament and from tweedledeedumms down to twiddledeedees" (*FW* 258 22–4). Such "dial [. . .] doodling" (*FW* 306 8) creates an aural impression for the reader, where voices surge from the "unterdrugged" (*FW* 266 31) lower text. Radio is able to snatch voices by "ancient flash and crash habits" (*FW* 289 17), yet, the sub-harmonics on the same page imply that "live wire[s]" (*FW* 289 9) do not deliver consistent information, "they just spirits a body away" into the ether. Earlier, during the "daily dubbing" (*FW* 219 8) of the Mime, a message is "posted ere penned" (*FW* 232 17), due to "interfering intermitting interskips from them (pet!) on herzian waves" (*FW* 232 9–11), the "pip" and "pet" of telegraphic signals from, and to, Issy. As John Gordon notes, she is heralded by double "ii" notations – a reference to the "I" in Morse code – often speaking in a "chimney-borne" (Gordon 1986: 261) language, a "dewfolded song of the naughtingales" (*FW* 359 32), which may allude to the popularity of the nightingale's melody in early radio, due to the groundbreaking outdoor broadcast in 1924 when it became the first call from the natural world. Issy's "flispering" (*FW* 580 20) voice drops into HCE's room, and echoes in the fireplace where it is often distorted by the semiconscious speaker. The chimney flue is just one of the *Wake*'s conduits, as is the "contact bridge" of "two million two humbered and eighty thausig nine humbered and sixty radiolumin lines" (*FW* 285 17–19), mentioned in II.2. It has "kaksitoista volts yksitoista volts kymmenen volts, yhdeksan volts," and many more, implying a multi-lingual channel from, most importantly, the "poet's office" (*FW* 265 28); in other words, "where G.P.O is zentrum" (*FW* 256 29). This was the original site of Radio Eirann; three makeshift studios at the top of the General Post Office itself. Throughout the *Wake*, in "deafths of darkness" (*FW* 407 12), sounds are being transmitted and received like the 1902 experiment in transatlantic messaging, instigated by the success of patent 7777. Whether it be during a scene of fracture and disturbance, or a rare moment of concordance, the speakers relay their messages in a certain manner, conversing "across space like dream radios" (Connor 1997: 21), and almost "as softly as the loftly marcon-imasts from Clifden" which "sough open tireless secrets [. . .] to Nova Scotia's listing sisterwands" (*FW* 407 20–2) – a phrase which amounts to an unconcealed tribute to the pioneer of wireless.

Imagine a radio broadcast of the *Wake* which called attention to the possibilities of the medium itself. It would be as effective, surely, as Orson Welles' "panic broadcast" of 1938, where radio was used both as an art form and as electric amplifier for the Last Judgment. It is this purist notion of radio that Joyce investigates, as a vehicle for the cross-fertilization of words, mentioned earlier in this essay. Again, consider the various transformations of HCE, ALP, Shem, Shaun, and Issy, who oscillate and collide like opposing frequencies, becoming the fragments who speak to the world. The *Wake* may be our only ingress into radiospace, a void simultaneously vacant and populous, terrifyingly unquantifiable save for a writer who attempted to write the "science of sonorous silence" (*FW* 230 22–3). In 1941, the artist Edgard Varèse completed his draft for a radiophonic work which would "[split] up and superimpose" every language in the world, effected by "fantastic radios" (Kahn and Whitehead 1992: 23) carefully manipulated from select transmitting posts. Given that Joyce recognized the nature of a medium whose listeners are simultaneously passive and active, it is also possible to interpret the *Wake* as a vast radio project, where the reader's contractual obligation as a co-creator simulates oral/aural communication and its misfires. Such an idea would be motivated by the limitations of wireless in the 1930s. Its potential as a platform for artistic expression was rarely exploited by radio producers who grappled with how to blend literary adaptation with innovative sound pieces. Ideally, as Edward Sackville-West wrote – in a regrettable oversight – "an Ibsen of the ether" was required, "one who joins things together – words, music, all manner of sounds" (Sackville-West 1945: 8–9). A more recent observation by R. D. Smith, after several decades of broadcasting, contends that

> the ring as opposed to the straight ribbon describes many of the best works for radio. The sailor, explorer, or fugitive who comes back to his home port, the pilgrim who finds at the program's climax that 'in my end is my beginning' [are] typical figures in radio, as they are in a great deal of literature" (Smith in Lewis 1978: 222).

As the speakers of the *Wake* "recoup themselves: now and then, time and time again" (*FW* 577 20), it is tempting to agree with Clement Semmler's comment in *BBC Quarterly* (1949–50), that some "venturesome" program planner, or critic, might "put the seal" on Joyce's final novel.

BIBLIOGRAPHY

Apollinaire, Guillaume (1980) *Caligrammes: Poems of Peace and War 1913–1916*, trans. Anne Hyde Grant. Berkeley: University of California Press.

Armand, Louis (2003) *Techne: James Joyce, Hypertext and Technology*. Prague: Charles University.

Armand, Louis (ed.) (2004) *Joycemedia: James Joyce, Hypermedia and Textual Genetics*. Prague: Litteraria Pragensia.

Atherton, J. S. (1954) *The Books at the Wake: A Study of Literary Allusions in James Joyce's* Finnegans Wake. London: Oxford University Press.

Attridge, Derek (1989) "Finnegans awake: the dream of interpretations," *James Joyce Quarterly* 27 (1): 11–29.

Begnal, Michael H. and Grace Eckley (1975) *Narrator and Character in* Finnegans Wake. Lewisburg, PA: Bucknell University Press.

Bishop, John (1986 [1976]) *Joyce's Book of the Dark*. Madison: Wisconsin University Press.

Campbell, Joseph and Henry Morton Robinson (1946) *A Skeleton Key to* Finnegans Wake. London: Faber and Faber.

Connor, James A. (1997) "Radio-Free Joyce: Wake language and the experience of radio." In Adalaide Morris (ed.) *Sound States: Innovative Poetics and Acoustical Technologies*, pp. 17–31. Chapel Hill: University of North Carolina Press.

Dunlap, Orrin J. (1937) *Marconi: The Man and His Wireless*. New York: Macmillan.

Gordon, John (1986) Finnegans Wake: *A Plot Summary*. Dublin: Gill and Macmillan.

Gordon, John (2003) *Physiology and the Literary Imagination*. Gainesville: University Press of Florida.

Gorham, Maurice (1967) *Forty Years of Irish Broadcasting*. Dublin: Talbot Press.

Hart, Clive (1962) *Structure and Motif in* Finnegans Wake. London: Faber and Faber.

Hoffmeister, Adolph (1979) "Portrait of Joyce," trans. Norma Rudinsky. In Willard Potts (ed.) *Portraits of the Artist in Exile: Recollections of James Joyce by Europeans*, pp. 127–36. Seattle: University of Washington Press.

Kahn, Douglas and Geoffrey Whitehead (1992) *Wireless Imagination: Sound, Radio, and the Avant-Garde*. Cambridge, MA: MIT Press.

Kenner, Hugh (1987) *The Mechanic Muse*. Oxford: Oxford University Press.

Kern, Stephen (1983) *The Culture of Time and Space*. Cambridge, MA: Harvard University Press.

Levin, Harry (1941) *James Joyce: A Critical Introduction*. Norfolk, CT: New Directions.

Lewty, Jane (2004) "Losing control in Book II, iii," *Hypermedia Joyce Studies* 5: 1.

McHugh, Roland (1976) *The Sigla of Finnegans Wake*. London: Edward Arnold.

McLuhan, Eric (1997) *The Role of Thunder in Finnegans Wake*. Toronto: Toronto University Press.

Milesi, Laurent (2004) "Joyce: language and languages." In Jean-Michel Rabaté (ed.) *Palgrave Advances in James Joyce Studies*, pp. 144–61. New York: Palgrave Macmillan.

Morris, Adelaide (ed.) (1997) *Sound States: Acoustical Technologies and Modern and Postmodern Writing*. Chapel Hill: University of North Carolina Press.

Peters, John Durham (1999) *Speaking into the Air: A History of the Idea of Communication*. Chicago: University of Chicago Press.

Piette, Adam (1992) *Remembering and the Sound of Words: Mallarmé, Proust, Joyce and Beckett*. Oxford: Clarendon Press.

Sackville-West, Edward (1945) *The Rescue*. London: Hogarth Press.

Sconce, Jeffrey (2000) *Haunted Media: Electronic Presence from Telegraphy to Television*. Durham, NC: Duke University Press.

Semmler, Clement (1949–50) "Radio and James Joyce," *BBC Quarterly* 2: 92–6.

Smith, R. D. (1978) "One grain of truth." In Peter Lewis (ed.) *Proceedings of the Radio-Literature Conference*, pp. 219–29. Durham: University of Durham Press.

Theall, Donald F. (1997) *James Joyce's Techno-Poetics*. Toronto: University of Toronto Press.

25

Scotographia:
Joyce and Psychoanalysis

Luke Thurston

Introduction: Misnomering One's Own

"Psychoanalysis is out, under a therapeutic disguise, to do away entirely with the moral faculty in man." Although it was D. H. Lawrence who made this defiant statement in 1931, for once James Joyce might have agreed with him. In biographical terms, at least, Joyce's manifest hostility to Freud and all things "freudful" (*FW* 411 35) can hardly be disputed. Ellmann gives us a well-known list of Joyce's denigrating remarks about psychoanalysis, at one moment comparing its ideas unfavorably to Vico's, at another denouncing its practice as "neither more nor less than blackmail" (*JJ* 524). What certainly can be disputed, though – and has been at great length by critics – is the exact significance of Joyce's hostility; whether, that is, it testifies to an incisive, although largely unstated, critique of Freudian thought, or else (in a reversal implicitly sanctioned by "Freudian" interpretation) to a secret enchantment with it, and the consequent anxious disavowal of its influence.

On the surface, at any rate, Joyce was certainly not *mordu par l'analyse*, in Jacques Lacan's droll understatement, not "bitten" by psychoanalysis. And his disregard for the faddish ideas of the "new Viennese school" (*U* 9 780) can hardly have been lessened when, following the publication of *Ulysses*, one of the book's first reviewers warned readers that in *Ulysses* they would find Bloom's inner life "laid bare with Freudian nastiness" (Deming 1970: 199). It was as if, confronted with the perplexing task of having to describe Joyce to the reading public in 1922, all reviewers could think of was to say "Freud," and that name would be enough to conjure up a whole world of unmentionable (and of course very un-English) "nastiness."

But if the conjugation of Joyce and Freud had at first characterized some of the earliest and seemingly least-considered responses to Joyce, it did not (as Joyce may have hoped it would) simply disappear as Joycean criticism matured. On the contrary, as late as 1978 Philippe Sollers was to reinscribe that conjugation of names as a veritable signature for a criticism committed to the disruptive politics of cultural modernity: "Freud, Joyce: another era for manwomankind" (Sollers 1978: 120). But now "Freud" was no longer simply a way to explain Joyce in analogical terms: for Sollers, the names are equivalent, even somehow identical. There is a silent allusion here to the notion, which supposedly once struck Joyce as witty, that, as Ellmann puts it, "Joyce meant the same thing in English as Freud in German" (*JJ* 490). In Sollers' eyes, each name is a translation of something still better expressed in French: *jouissance*. "Freud, Joyce" therefore names a single epoch-making outbreak of sexual joy, something exhilarating but also outrageous, at odds with bourgeois propriety (so perhaps we have not traveled very far from the "Freudian nastiness" of the 1922 newspaper review).

But there is more: Sollers may not have been aware of it, but the translation of the two names had already occurred to Freud, and had featured in a text he published in 1905, a text which we know Joyce purchased in 1917: *The Psychopathology of Everyday Life*. There, as Jean Kimball notes, Freud analyzes his own misremembering of a name from a novel by Alphonse Daudet – he recalls a character as "Monsieur Jocelyn" when in fact the name is "Monsieur Joyeuse" – in terms of his unconscious repudiation of the "feminine" or passive situation he had been in as a young medical student in Paris (another uncanny pre-echo of Joyce). As Freud writes, "'Joyeux,' of which 'Joyeuse' is the feminine form, is the only possible way in which I could translate my own name, Freud, into French" (Freud [1901]: 149). In Kimball's view, it "thus seems entirely possible that Joyce himself originated the comment on the interchangeability of 'Joyce' and 'Freud', drawing on Freud's account" (Kimball 2003: 7). If to "originate" a comment by "drawing on" someone else's seems, at the very least, paradoxical, we might see in Kimball's blurred logic a symptom of the representational problem in question: that of the uncanny double, with its unsettling breach of signifying propriety. In the space of the uncanny, Freud discerns "a doubling, dividing and interchanging of the self" (Freud [1919]: 234); there, what or who is original is always in doubt.

From a certain perspective, then, the psychoanalyst appears as the double of the modernist artist (or vice versa); both Freudian and Joycean practices can be envisaged as a single, although "doubleviewed" (*FW* 296 1) – either distasteful or admirable – breach of established cultural protocols. Now, as we have seen, for Freud the double is *unheimlich*, uncanny; and we should pause over that term as we consider the precise sense of "modernity" implicit in this critical desire to link Joyce and Freud. The most useful definition of the uncanny is given (appropriately enough, perhaps) not by Freud speaking *in propria persona*, but when he quotes Schelling (and this act of quotation already raises questions about the *unheimlich* interrelation of psychoanalysis and idealist philosophy[1]): it is "the name for everything that ought to have remained . . . secret and hidden but has come to light" (Freud [1919]: 224). This sense of the uncanny – an improper enlightenment, an opening-up or making-appear of what should ("in all decency," we seem to hear) have been left in obscurity – might indeed be a way of naming, although with a sharply pejorative note, the different acts of "modernity" in Freud and Joyce. What would link the two names would therefore not be some supposed identity of purpose (something clearly contradicted by the biographical evidence), but the way that in each man's practice something unacceptable appears, an incriminating secret is broadcast. The notion that Joyce's name "meant the same thing" as Freud's is in this sense merely a lame footnote to a much more suggestive contention: that both psychoanalysis and Joycean writing are uncanny, self-conflicted participants in a "clearobscure" (*FW* 247 34) coincidence of modernity and traditional morality, of enlightenment and obscurity.

The ambiguity of *unheimlich* (caught up with its double/opposite *heimlich* in a semantic network which includes "homely," "secret" and "strange") may offer a good starting point for us to reflect on the varied relation between Joycean criticism and psychoanalysis. On one side, we have critics for whom psychoanalysis is thoroughly at home with the Joycean text, knows its most intimate secrets, and can shed light on its obscurest enigmas. The argument in support of this perspective may refer to Joyce's biography (in particular to the younger Joyce's sojourns in Trieste and Zurich, where psychoanalysis formed part of general intellectual currency as it certainly had not in Dublin) and especially to so-called "genetic" research into his reading and note-taking. From this point of view, it makes sense to use psychoanalysis in reading Joyce's texts primarily because Joyce himself used so much psychoanalysis in writing them. So Joyce's contemporary Mary Colum, regarding his development of the interior monologue, could contend that "he undoubtedly owes a great deal to Freud" (Colum 1937: 349); while for Lionel Trilling, Joyce "exploited Freud's ideas" more thoroughly than any other modern writer (40). These claims – these allegations, some might say – have, as we shall see, been revised and formulated more carefully in the light of more recent critical developments, especially those in genetic criticism.

In another sense, however, it may be argued that we do not need documentary evidence linking Joyce's writing to psychoanalysis in order to draw upon psychoanalytic concepts in reading his work. The concept of the unconscious would seem to complicate, to say the least, any reference to an author's conscious practice, as reconstructed by a critic from documentary records. Freudian theory remains eminently controversial, of course, but there can be little doubt that Freud's ideas – as well as Joyce's writings – have permanently altered our sense of the semantic consistency of an author's relation to the text. We are very unlikely today, for instance, to read Stephen's shouted *Non serviam!* in the "Circe" episode of *Ulysses* (*U* 15 4228) as a bold authorial declaration of independence, echoing the defiant "I will not serve" first voiced by the young Stephen in an earlier book (*P* 201) without also hearing in it an anguished, antagonistic plea, and if we still choose to picture Joyce's character as an authorial self-portrait, it will be as a subject irreducible to the conscious "I," if not yet the "dividual chaos" of *Finnegans Wake* (*FW* 186 4). If *Non serviam!* is to be read as the site of at least two kinds of meaning, only one of which is governed by the conscious ego, arguably it no longer matters whether or not Joyce *in propria persona* had heard or read about Freud's notion of a split psyche, or even whether or not he believed in it.

What quickly becomes apparent is that, like every prominent element in a Freudian dream, the question of Joyce-and-psychoanalysis is thoroughly overdetermined. As has been convincingly shown by, among others, Ellmann (1982), Ferrer (1985),

Van Mierlo (1997) and Kimball (2003), Joyce did read widely in psychoanalysis at various points in his writing. One should emphasize, however, that this is *not* a decisive argument for using psychoanalytic ideas to read his work; what it does show is that those ideas were of great interest to him in crucial periods of his development as a writer. But had no such evidence come to light, the case for using psychoanalytic ideas to understand his work would be essentially the same, since the argument is based not on contingent historical circumstances, but on general claims about the nature of the human subject.

It may be that it was the global ambition underlying these general Freudian claims that Joyce found at once repulsive (thus his critical utterances) and oddly seductive (thus his diligent reading and careful notes). Half a century ago, Frank Budgen gave us an illuminating picture of Joyce's intense response – and his marked gesture of non-response – to the psychoanalytic "world-view":

> If psychoanalysis cured sick people, well and good. Who could quarrel with that? But Joyce was always impatient or contemptuously silent when it was talked about as both all-sufficient *Weltanschauung* and a source and law for artistic production.
>
> "Why all this fuss and bother about the mystery of the unconscious?" he said to me one evening at the Pfauen restaurant. "What about the mystery of the conscious? What do they know about that?" (Budgen 1970: 356)

We should be extremely careful not to overinterpret this last remark, and in particular not to embrace it in our anti-Freudian gusto as a sign that Joyce had definitely seen through (or "deconstructed") the ontological mystification at the heart of psychoanalysis. The fact that "the mystery of the conscious" is central both to the radical phenomenological critique of Freud (see especially Henry 1993) and, in a completely different sense, to twenty-first-century brain science may indeed be a confirmation of Joyce's prophetic intuition, but it is perhaps risky to base such a lofty claim on the recollection of a single comment, a Joycean throwaway.

There is, however, a tradition in Joycean criticism that has wholeheartedly endorsed the negative tone of Joyce's anecdotal response to psychoanalysis. For this line of critics, the problematic of the uncanny double that seemingly links Joyce to Freud looks like an imaginary veil of "theory" cast over mere historical contingency – and an attempt to hide the mutual strangeness, the fundamental discrepancy, of Joycean and Freudian worlds. Maria Jolas, looking back in 1973 at her youthful involvement with Joyce, emphasized that discrepancy when she stated that "it was a remarkable sign of [Joyce's] intelligence that he didn't fall for psychoanalysis when it was so current. He started beyond it."[2] In Darcy O'Brien's view, likewise, Freudian theory is largely irrelevant to the task of interpreting Joyce; to use psychoanalytic ideas in reading "Circe," as O'Brien puts it (1976: 283), "is to look far beneath the episode, and why should we assume that the truer truth is that which lies beneath?" Psychoanalytic criticism, in O'Brien's eyes, is all too ready to draw up a convenient "diagnosis" to cut short our endless reading, and in its search for the deep and meaningful merely risks overlooking the polyvalent *surfaces* of Joycean writing.

Critics who adopt this anti-Freudian perspective can certainly point to a long history of reductive psychoanalytic "solutions" to aesthetic problems, beginning with Freud's infamous "Oedipal" reading of *Hamlet* (which Joyce, of course, knew from having read Ernest Jones' lengthy elaboration of it).[3] But they might also include in that same history of misreading another "freudful" struggle to solve the problem of Joyce, both in literature and outside it: that of Carl Gustav Jung.

Jungian and Joycean Triangles

For the C.G.'s not literary and his handymen are rogues.
For the C.G.'s about as literary as an Irish kish of brogues.[4]

The encounter of Joyce and Jung is often noted by critics as a double one, occurring both in history and in theory, in the domain of fact and that of speculation.[5] Our interest in Jung as a reader of Joyce is thus always supplemented and complicated by our knowledge of his role in Joyce's life: primarily, as a psychiatrist who briefly (and unsuccessfully) undertook the clinical treatment of Joyce's daughter Lucia. But we will argue that in this triangulation of reading – where our approach to the text finds itself looking sideways at the domain of the real – we find another version of a triangular structure that repeatedly links Joyce and Jung, in which their relationship is always mediated by a third term, the site of an exchange, of gift or debt.

On his first visit to Trieste, when Joyce was still quite young and curious (or still, in the celebrated Wakean phrase, "yung and easily freudened," *FW* 115 22–3), he had bought a pamphlet by Jung entitled *Die Bedeutung des Vaters für das Schicksal des Einzelnen* (The Significance of the Father in the Destiny of the Individual). Published in 1909, while Jung was still an orthodox psychoanalyst, this essay (which for Kimball is "aggressively Freudian"; 1997: 21) uses clinical material to argue for the predominant role of the father in the etiology of neuroses. Joyce never mentions the essay in his correspondence, and although it may seem highly plausible to link its argument to the insistent Joycean preoccupation with fatherhood – especially given the extraordinary picture provided by Stanislaus Joyce (1971) of the "crazy drunkard" who was the Joyces' own father – we will not do so here, for fear of wandering onto the speculative terrain of "what Joyce did or did not do" mocked in Darcy O'Brien's derisive title.

However, another text by Jung *does* find a place in one of Joyce's letters – precisely as an object of desire, something whose lack is insistently noted; and this brings us to the first of our triangles. In December 1919, Joyce wrote to Frank Budgen from Trieste, where he had recently arrived having spent most of the war in Zurich:

Since I came here I wrote a long letter to Mrs M, asking her very urgently to consider the "advisability of the revivability" of her aid. That distinguished lady never answered. W pretends he did not know my address here – another piece of fooling. He forgets only what he dislikes to remember, viz., that he promised me as a gift DOKTOR JUNG'S

(prolonged general universal applause) Wandlungen der LIBIDO (shouts *Hear! Hear!*
from a raughty tinker and an Irishman in the gallery). For God's sake give those louts the
go by (*SL* 244).

The paranoiac triangle is already fully at work here (although at this point, intrigu-
ingly, Jung is in the place of the object-gift). We need Ellmann's account to fill in
the details: "Mrs M" is Mrs. Edith Rockefeller McCormick, an American million-
airess who lived in Zurich; "her aid" was a monthly income of 1,000 Swiss francs
which she began to pay Joyce from March 1918 (*JJ* 422). A more ambiguous act of
generosity had been her subsequent offer to fund Joyce's psychoanalytic treatment by
Jung, an offer which Joyce had flatly rejected: "It was unthinkable," he told a friend
(*JJ* 466). Meanwhile, "W" is Ottocaro Weiss, a Zurich friend of Joyce's with whom he
had frequently dined and had discussed, among other things, psychoanalysis (Edoardo
Weiss, Ottocaro's brother, was an eminent psychoanalyst). But when Joyce discovered,
on calling at the bank in October 1919, that the regular gift from Mrs. M had been
stopped, "he quickly concluded that Weiss had persuaded her to cut off the subsidy"
(*JJ* 467). So Weiss now became, in Joyce's eyes, one of "those louts" who possess
something precious – money, psychoanalytic knowledge, or perhaps even "libidinal
transformations" (to translate the title of the non-delivered Jungian gift) – which they
appear to offer but then withhold in unjust, sadistic punishment. Frank Budgen was
slightly puzzled by the ferocity of this letter, noting Joyce's "big grouse about not
getting that book he was promised" (Budgen 1970: 200).

What characterizes the triangular antagonism at work here? It is tempting to
describe its structure as "Oedipal": Joyce imagines himself to be deprived of a gift –
marked as feminine or libidinal – by the intervention of another man. Thus, the desire
of a woman (Mrs. M) to give her precious object to Joyce is diverted by W; and in turn,
W's promised gift of "libidinal transformations" (to be relished by a "raughty" – perhaps
raunchy or naughty – Joycean tinker) is never delivered by W. It is clear, moreover, that
to Joyce's mind the gift, in the instance of both money and book, is not really a gift but
the *repayment of a debt*. We will see how this economy of paranoiac gift/debt returns in
the subsequent relations between Joyce and Jung, and how, more generally, it characterizes the "link" made by critics between Joyce and psychoanalysis (we have already seen it
at work in Mary Colum's assertion that Joyce "owes a great deal to Freud").

If Jung remained invisible in this first Joycean imbroglio of 1919 – although it has
been argued that in fact he probably played a decisive role in Edith McCormick's decision to terminate Joyce's allowance[6] – he was to reappear a decade later in another,
apparently altogether different, Joycean triangle. In 1930, Daniel Brody, who ran the
Swiss publishing house Rhein-Verlag, asked Jung to write an article about *Ulysses* for a
new literary review he was planning to launch. Jung agreed, but what he subsequently
wrote seemed too harsh and "clinical" to Brody, who nervously forwarded a copy to
Joyce. An account of what ensued is given by Jung's editors:

> [Brody] sent the article to Joyce, who cabled him, "Niedrigerhängen," meaning "Hang
> it lower" or, figuratively, "Show it up by printing it." (Joyce was quoting Frederick the

Great, who upon seeing a placard attacking him directed that it be hung lower for all to behold.) Friends of Joyce, including Stuart Gilbert, advised Brody not to publish the article, though Jung at first insisted on its publication. In the meantime, political tensions had developed in Germany, so that the Rhein-Verlag decided to abandon the projected literary review and Dr Brody therefore returned the article to Jung. Later, Jung revised the essay (modifying its severity) and published it in 1932 in the *Europäische Revue*. The original version has never come to light (Jung 1967: 132–3).

Another lost original! We can never know exactly what Joyce read and answered with the enigmatic telegram. But he wrote to Harriet Shaw Weaver on September 27, 1930, with a rather different story about Jung's article: "The Rheinverlag wrote to Jung for a preface to the German edition of Gilbert's book. He replied with a very long and hostile attack [. . .] which they are much upset about, but I want them to use it" (Jung 1967: 133). Now, Rhein-Verlag did indeed publish a translation of Stuart Gilbert's book in 1932, under the title *Das Rätsel Ulysses* (*JJ* 628), but it is unclear whether or not Jung's essay did serve as its preface, as Joyce thought it should (especially given Gilbert's opposition to the publication of the piece). At any rate, by 1932 Jung had rewritten the article "modifying its severity" and turning it into the text we now have: "Ulysses: A Monologue". And he sent it, the most ambiguous of gifts – one part-readerly appreciation, nine-parts ferocious critical assault – to Joyce with the following remarkable letter, which is worth quoting in full:

> Küsnacht-Zürich
> Seestrasse 228
> September 27th 1932
>
> James Joyce Esq.
>
> Hotel Elite
> Zurich
>
> Dear Sir,
>
> Your Ulysses has presented the world such an upsetting psychological problem that repeatedly I have been called in as a supposed authority on psychological matters.
>
> Ulysses proved to be an exceedingly hard nut and it has forced my mind not only to most unusual efforts, but also to rather extravagant peregrinations (speaking from the standpoint of a scientist). Your book as a whole has given me no end of trouble and I was brooding over it for about three years until I succeeded to put myself into it. But I must tell you that I'm profoundly grateful to yourself as well as to your gigantic opus, because I learned a great deal from it. I shall probably never be quite sure whether I did enjoy it, because it meant too much grinding of nerves and of grey matter. I also don't know whether you will enjoy what I have written about Ulysses because I couldn't help telling the world how much I was bored, how I grumbled, how I cursed and how I admired. The 40 pages of non stop run in the end is a string of veritable psychological peaches. I suppose the devil's grandmother knows so much about the real psychology of a woman, I didn't.
>
> Well, I just try to recommend my little essay to you, as an amusing attempt of a perfect stranger who went astray in the labyrinth of your Ulysses and happened to get out of

it again by sheer good luck. At all events you may gather from my article what *Ulysses* has done to a supposedly balanced psychologist.

   With the expression of my deepest appreciation, I remain, dear Sir,

Yours faithfully,
C. G. Jung
(Jung 1967: 133–4)

In Jung's letter, the exchange of gifts takes place within a triangular scenario strikingly similar to the one we saw in Joyce's letter of 1919: the object-gift is again marked as libidinal and feminine – just like a woman's libido, it is an "upsetting psychological problem," both a hard nut to crack and a forbidden fruit to relish – while the masculine rival is both munificent benefactor and sadistic assailant, both giver and withholder of precious knowledge. Ellmann notes a corresponding ambivalence in how Joyce responded to Jung's letter: at one moment declaring it "imbecile," at another proudly showing it off as a "tribute to his psychological penetration" (*JJ* 629). Note that each man can only give the other textual pleasure when it comes to the subject of woman: Jung hates the book but savours the peaches of Penelope; Joyce disdains the letter but is pleased with the official recognition of his power to penetrate the feminine.

   In the end, though, Jung was unsure as to whether he had actually enjoyed the whole experience of reading *Ulysses*, and Joyce felt that it was precisely *pleasure* that was missing from Jung's response to the book: "He seems to have read *Ulysses* from first to last without one smile" (*JJ* 628). Turning to the text of Jung's article, we can see how it makes the question of readerly pleasure a central element in its objection to Joyce's writing:

> Yes, I admit I feel I have been made a fool of. The book would not meet me half way, nothing in it made the least attempt to be agreeable, and that always gives the reader an irritating sense of inferiority. Obviously I have so much of the Philistine in my blood that I am naïve enough to suppose that a book wants to tell me something, to be understood – a sad case of mythological anthropomorphism projected onto the book! And what a book – no opinion possible – epitome of maddening defeat of intelligent reader, who after all is not such a – (if I may use Joyce's suggestive style). Surely a book has a content, represents something; but I suspect that Joyce did not wish to "represent" anything. Does it by any chance represent *him* – does that explain this solipsistic isolation, this drama without eyewitnesses, this infuriating disdain for the assiduous reader? Joyce has aroused my ill will (Jung 1967: 113).

(I'll say!) Our first response to this outburst may be complete puzzlement. What exactly is it Jung has been reading? Presumably he has begun with "Stately plump Buck Mulligan" and the opening scene in "Telemachus" – where is the "maddening defeat of intelligent reader" in this, at first glance a largely realist description of some young men shaving, talking, having breakfast? The opening of *Ulysses* shows that the book precisely *does* have a "content" and conform to the conventional narrative mimesis demanded by Jung – although of course as the text unfolds its status as representation will be variously disfigured, tested, and even jeopardized (but never simply denied).

And if the "suggestive style" in Jung's hapless parody is meant to correspond to Bloom's fragmentary interior monologue in the early parts of the book, it is again hard to see why Jung finds this so difficult to fathom, since this style, as critics often note, shows Joyce's writing at its *most* mimetic or verisimilar. Of course, there *are* enigmas in *Ulysses*, but amongst so many styles that are, precisely, "suggestive," that aim not to defeat the intelligent reader but to stimulate different kinds of readerly intelligence.

It is almost as if Jung were responding, with his anguished, writhing prose, not to *Ulysses* but to the work-in-progress Joyce had more recently been publishing in Eugene Jolas's *transition* and elsewhere. Indeed, to have described the text that would be *Finnegans Wake* as a "drama without eyewitnesses," a self-regarding artistic rejection of readerly values, would have had some plausibility, and it was precisely the kind of reaction that greeted the book's publication in 1939. But Jung is already using the same language of outrage to describe *Ulysses*; in his eyes, for all the radiance and apparent legibility of the book's opening, it remains a Wakean "*édition de ténèbres*" (*FW* 179 27), a book of the dark.

So what is it that darkens Jung's reading? There is no need for us to speculate as to whether he might have seen a copy of *transition* before he began expostulating on Joyce's "unendurable pages" (Jung 1967: 124); for when Jung approvingly quotes Ernst Curtius' perplexed comment that, in *Ulysses*, "The author has done everything to avoid making it easier for the reader to understand" (Jung 1967: 113), it becomes clear that his notion of Joyce being illegible is grounded not on textual evidence but on something beyond it. For, as we know, the truth is almost the opposite of what Curtius alleges: consider all of the schemas and introductory guides to *Ulysses* drawn up with Joyce's involvement. And when Jung speaks of the "infuriating disdain" shown by the book, it is the *clinical* resonance of the phrase – its implicit allusion to the clinical concept of "transference" – that is striking. Jung pursues this implied question of transference further as he struggles to find a way to understand the singular challenge of Joyce's work: the "tragi-comedy of the average man," he sighs wearily, is part of his daily grind, and this has hardened him to the various peculiarities of the human psyche:

> Nothing in all this shocks or moves me, for all too often I have to help people out of these lamentable states. I must combat them incessantly and I may only expend my sympathy on people who do not turn their backs on me. *Ulysses* turns its back on me. It is unco-operative, it wants to go on singing its endless tune into endless time – a tune I know to satiety – and to extend to infinity its ganglionic rope-ladder of visceral thinking (Jung 1967: 115–16).

How can a book, though, turn its back on someone? It is the previous line that makes sense of Jung's rhetoric: it is people, obviously, who can turn their backs, and the doctor can only help them deal with their psychological troubles if they – *unlike Joyce and his daughter* – refrain from doing so.

So we come to the third of our Jungian–Joycean triangles. In the first, of 1919, Joyce had turned his back on Mrs. M's gift of psychoanalysis with Jung; in the second, of 1930, *Ulysses* had turned *its* back on Jung, disdaining all his valiant efforts to read it; and last of all, Lucia Joyce was to take up the family dance of tergiversation. In September 1934, two years after Joyce had received Jung's hostile fan letter, he finally accepted that (as Maria Jolas urged long before), if anyone could help Lucia, perhaps Jung could. And the initial prognosis when treatment began at the end of September seemed to offer some hope, so that Joyce even agreed to meet up with Jung to discuss his daughter. It must have been at one of those meetings that Joyce wrote in Jung's copy of *Ulysses* words that transformed the book retroactively into a gift: "To Dr C. G. Jung, with grateful appreciation of his aid and counsel. James Joyce. Xmas 1934, Zurich" (Jung 1967: 134). Jung's editors deduce from marginal notes and marks in the text that this was in fact the same copy Jung had owned since 1922, rather than a new one presented by Joyce. Perhaps Joyce wanted to settle old debts, convert the old antagonistic triangle into an exchange of gifts (note that it took place at "Xmas") rather than another cycle of paranoiac recriminations. The "upsetting psychological problem" was now not Joyce's book but a much more serious one: his child's psyche. According to Ellmann, however, it was still impossible for the two men to agree about what amounted to a genuine gift.

When the psychologist pointed out schizoid elements in poems Lucia had written, Joyce, remembering Jung's comments on *Ulysses*, insisted they were anticipations of a new literature, and said his daughter was an innovator not yet understood. Jung granted that some of her portmanteau words and neologisms were remarkable, but said they were random; she and her father, he commented later, were like two people going to the bottom of a river, one falling and the other diving (*JJ* 679).

Lucia's artistic gift, the creative urge to innovate in language which she inherited from her father – as well as Joyce's more desperate attempts to imagine her as "clairvoyant," bathed in supernatural light – all of these treasured Joycean ideas were grimly negated by Jung's diagnosis. And if Lucia occupied the position of gift in the Jungian–Joycean triangle (formerly the place of Mrs. M's money, of Jung's text on "libidinal transformations," of Joyce's *Ulysses*), she herself would illustrate the ambiguity, the libidinal transformability, of that position by sealing her rejection of Jung's therapeutic advances with the famous quip: "To think that such a big fat materialistic Swiss man should try to get hold of my soul!" (*JJ* 679).

So the Joycean soul – equally manifested by the father, his book, and his daughter – was not for Jung, and refused to cooperate with him or give him transference-love. There was no point in attempting to intervene in the Joycean soul, Jung concluded: it was simply untreatable. Joyce did his best to put a positive gloss on this when he wrote in a letter that Jung "told me nobody could make any head of her but myself as she was a very exceptional case and certainly not one for psychoanalytic treatment which he said might provoke a catastrophe from which she would never recover" (*JJ* 681). This final anti-Freudian touch ("If I can't get hold of the soul *he* certainly can't!") was perhaps the only bit of Jung's "aid and counsel" that Joyce did appreciate gratefully.

What, then, have been the consequences of these interlocking textual–biographical triangles for the subsequent decades of criticism? Jungian critics, in all their variety, have tended to ignore Jung's Joycean episode; the *Cambridge Companion to Jung*, published as recently as 1997, contains not a single reference to Joyce, even though it includes an essay entitled "A Jungian analysis of Homer's Odysseus" which would seem to make the cross-reference inevitable.[7] On the Joycean side, there has been rather more interest in the Jungian connection: Elliott Coleman (1963) and William Walcott (1971) began by using Jung's ideas on telepathic or mystical connections between subjects and histories to read Joyce, in particular the "Circe" episode of *Ulysses*. Coleman notes the resonance of Jung's notion that a *participation mystique* united Joyce and his daughter, quoting the famous letter where Jung made this part of his diagnosis of Joyce's resistance to psychotherapy:

> If you know anything of my Anima theory, Joyce and his daughter are a classic example of it. She was definitely his 'femme inspiratrice', which explains his obstinate reluctance to have her certified. His own Anima, i.e., unconscious psyche, was so solidly identified with her, that to have her certified would have been as much as an admission that he himself had a latent psychosis. It is therefore understandable that he could not give in (*JJ* 679–80n.: cited Coleman 1963: 15).

For Walcott, likewise, Joyce intuitively grasped the idea that subjects could participate in a single psyche or psychical experience, and worked it into *Ulysses* as a mystical "synchronicity" between Bloom and Stephen, inscribed in "Ithaca" as the playful spoonerism "Stoom" and "Blephen" (*U* 17 549–52). More recently, Jean Kimball (1997) has taken up the theory of synchronicity to formulate an overall reading of Joyce as "a divided self working towards integration" – in short, a very Jungian self. Kimball traces what she considers to be parallel experiences of crisis and resolution in the lives of Joyce and Jung, before finding these experiences reflected in, on one side, Jung's theories of the self, and, on the other, the "Jungian patterns" supposedly legible in *Ulysses* (it is of course no surprise that Kimball's narrative does not cross the Rubicon into *Finnegans Wake*, where a self working towards integration is somewhat harder to discern).[8]

What is most intriguing in these Jungian accounts of Joyce is how the references to biography are simultaneously essential to the account and rendered problematic by it; that is, the notion of discrete selfhood underlying the narrative of Joyce's "integration" or development – both as artist and as human being – is difficult to square with the telepathic imbrications of subjectivity posited by Jungian theory and "cerebrated" (*FW* 421 18) in Joycean writing. Sheldon Brivic (1980) responds to this tension between an integral "I" required by biography and its dissolution into multiple textual simulacra by mapping that same tension onto Joyce's development as a writer, and this in turn, argues Brivic, broadly corresponds to the shift from a Freudian to a Jungian perspective:

> The grant of authority to the unconscious is a crucial distinction between Freud's thought and Jung's; and also between Joyce's early works, where the prime issue is whether people can control their own lives and the later ones in which they follow their destinies with growing dynamism (Brivic 1980: 11).

So if young Stephen's struggle for mastery over himself and others in *A Portrait of the Artist as a Young Man* constitutes a "Freudian" effort by the ego to wrest control from the unconscious (and how close we are once again to the language of the 1922 reviews Joyce loathed!), perhaps a biographical view of the text as a product of Joyce's self-analytic and self-integrating psyche makes sense, whereas the more "Jungian" subjectivity that for Brivic comes to characterize Joyce's later work would demand a different account, one that would displace authority from an authorial "I." But how does Brivic conceptualize this difference? Unlike Kimball, Brivic does not recoil before *Finnegans Wake*: indeed, he sees it as "Joyce's most Jungian book" (Brivic 1980: 203). How, though, can anybody be said to "follow their destinies with growing dynamism" in the *Wake*? The book certainly has characters confronting "the labyrinth of their samilikes and the alteregoases of their pseudoselves" (*FW* 576 32–3), perplexed by the duplicitous surfaces of identity, but it is hard to see how this pervasive unraveling of egos could form part of a positive, developmental project. Brivic's answer is to see the family of characters HCE, ALP, Shem, Shaun, and Issy as involved, in Chapter 9 of the *Wake* (*FW* II.1), in a complex game of desire and power with eminently psychoanalytic implications, where the purpose of the artist "is to expose to the world the genitals and primal sin of his parents" (Brivic 1980: 204). This infantile fantasy, while clearly not a destiny to be followed with too much dynamism, leads on to a scene of "castration" – the collapse of an illusory paternal phallic identity – in which Brivic (1980: 205) finds a sign of "maturity" in the artist's realization that "he too had a great big oh in the megafundum of his tomashunders" (*FW* 229 20–1). In other words, Shem's astounding discovery (which elicits "a great big oh") is that the masculinity he shares with his father is based not on some phallic corporeal totality but on a fundamentally deficient body, a sexuality perforated by desire, by the Other (also, conveniently enough, marked by "a great big oh"). For Brivic, the acts of identity dissemination in the *Wake* correspond to the transition from a youthful Joycean vacillation between totality and nothingness ("All or not at all," thinks Stephen trudging along the beach; *U* 3 452) to a "mature" sense of masculine subjectivity as compromised, hybrid, its phallic lack incessantly made up for, necessarily supplemented by, the Other's feminine letter ("her Lettyshape . . . had never cessed"; *FW* 229 21–2). If this transition finally takes place, according to Brivic, in Joyce's "most Jungian" book, it must correspond to the dynamic pursuit of destiny, the move beyond the limited perspective of the ego into some liberating engagement with the collective unconscious. We might, however, consider this a rather rose-tinted view of a text that repeatedly insists, "We are circumveiloped by obscuritads" (*FW* 244 15). For a less optimistic, and considerably more obscure, view of the Joycean assault on the "I," let us turn to the work of Jacques Lacan.

Lacanian and Joycean Knots

Haven't you pulled enough people's legs?

Mary Colum to Joyce (Colum 1958)

Everscepistic! He does not believe in our psychous of the Real Absence . . .

(*FW* 536 5–7)

We have seen, then, that Jung's importance for Joyce and for Joyceans derives above all from what we might call his real presence, from his actual encounter with the major crisis of Joyce's late period: Lucia's illness. It is perhaps surprising to discover that Lacan too ascribed great importance to his own youthful "encounter" with Joyce, although (as the scare quotes suggest) this was an event Joyce himself may not have been aware of. As we will see, Lacan's idiosyncratic engagement with matters Joycean in the mid-1970s forms part of a broad reorientation of his psychoanalytic practice and teaching that gave the real, in his singular understanding of that term, a new prominence.

In was in the real, then, that Lacan first came into contact with Joyce, and he looks back on his Joycean encounter as the mark, the fateful inscription, of that real. So what exactly happened? In the opening address Lacan gave at the 1975 James Joyce Symposium in Paris, he explains that as a young student he had often hung about at Adrienne Monnier's Left Bank bookshop, and it was there that he had twice bumped into Joyce (Aubert 1987: 23). As I have shown elsewhere (Thurston 2004: 17–20), only one of these encounters – the reading from *Ulysses* in 1921, which Lacan may well have attended, although he can hardly have been noticed by Joyce – is documented or certified by history; the other, which according to Lacan took place in either 1918 or 1919, is not (since Joyce did not actually move to Paris until 1920). In my view, the misremembering of the encounter is more than just a trivial biographical footnote; it can provide an insight into both Lacan's category of the real and his sense of how Joyce's writing can be seen as a unique manifestation of it.

The real, as it comes to be characterized in Lacan's late work, is precisely *not* reality, the latter understood as a discursive product whose primary function is to allow human subjects to escape from the real, to foreclose it from their world. When the real returns, it does so in "impossible," hallucinatory fragments that invade and invalidate reality, producing overwhelming moments of anxiety or ecstasy (both versions of *jouissance*). It was just such a return of the real that Lacan would identify as the primal scene, the "epiphany" or vocation, of Joyce's writing, its unspeakable fantasmatic "root language." Lacan's misremembered encounter, then, can be seen as his own Joycean "epiphany": something irreducible to history, both impossible and yet overwhelmingly significant.

After giving his talk at the Paris symposium, Lacan went on to spend a year of his bi-weekly public seminar discussing Joyce, in the twenty-third volume of the seminar (Lacan 2005). His title was *Le Sinthome*, an old French spelling of the modern "symptôme," which became a Lacanian "puncept" bringing *saint homme* ("holy man") together with "sin," "tome" and other senses (see Rabaté 2001: 160–2 for an illuminating

discussion of this wordplay). This title was offered as a new *name* for Joyce – a literary holy man, both a sinful saint and a hole-y man, a man with "a great big oh in
the megafundum" (*FW* 229 20–1). Just as Jung had done, Lacan linked Joyce's singular creative gift to a fundamental pathology, but in Lacan's view that pathology
could be precisely located: in a complete non-inscription, a radical foreclosure, of the
Joycean paternal signifier. Here Lacan referred back to his work much earlier, in the
mid-1950s, on the etiology of psychosis. In Seminar 3, he had proposed foreclosure –
an act of psychical negation far more effective than repression, the partial and uneven
negative mode governing neurotic experience – as the root of a psychotic structure like
that of President Schreber, and had argued, in particular, that what is foreclosed from
the psychotic's world is the name of the father, the normalizing guarantee of a successful escape from the Oedipal triangle.[9] The *sinthome* marked a point where foreclosure,
the dysfunction of the signifier, resulted in a practice of writing (and in this it recalled
both the Schreber case and Lacan's own doctoral research on psychotic "inspired writings"). But with Joyce, as Lacan saw it, the foreclosure was still more "radical" than in
Schreber's case: it bore not only on the paternal "metaphor" – disabling the instance of
signifying substitution that gave rise to the normal–neurotic functions of the unconscious – but also on the imaginary, dislodging the very root of the ego. This made
Joycean writing – not accidentally, but deliberately – *pas à lire*, not for reading.

Was Lacan, then, going a step farther than Jung in pathologizing Joyce's work, simply
declaring its author mad? For Jung, we recall, Joyce's psychosis remained "latent," but
he also spoke, more ambiguously, of "an insane person of an uncommon sort" whose
apparent abnormality may conceal "superlative powers of mind" (Jung 1967: 117). Once
again, here we find an unlikely confluence of Jungian and Lacanian ideas: for the *sinthome*
is precisely the name Lacan gives to a subject or formation irreducible to the diagnostic
category of psychosis, yet which shares many of its traits.

Lacan's work with topological figures in the 1970s – including the famous Borromean knot that showed as interlinked rings the registers of real, symbolic, and imaginary (see Figure 25.1)[10] – brought many of his former theoretical positions into

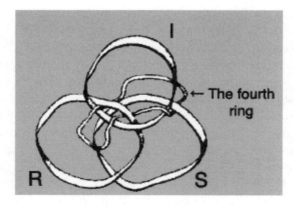

Figure 25.1 Lacan's Borromean Knot (1976)

question. The concept of foreclosure was a notable instance: whereas in Lacan's early teaching it specifically belongs to the theory of psychosis, in *Le Sinthome* it becomes a name for something confronting *all* human infants, not only those destined to become mad. In terms of Lacan's knot-topology, this could be expressed as follows: the three registers, initially distinct, are only interconnected by a fourth ring, whether an Oedipal symptom (as the name of the father is now termed) or another kind of forma-tion, perhaps a Joycean *sinthome*. The return of the real in Joyce's vocation or "epiph-any," as now read by Lacan, thus recalls a universal confrontation by each human infant with what is foreclosed, what cannot be spoken; but the Joycean response to that confrontation is singular, does not go by way of the repressive Oedipal metaphor that leads to the formation of the neurotic unconscious. The "Joycean knot" which Lacan amused himself with drawing on the blackboard thus points to the possibility of *non-repressive structures*: subjects "disinvested" from the unconscious (or the "Freud-ian unconscious," as Lacan began to dub it) that were not, or not explicitly, psych-otic. There was perhaps another echo here of Jung's diagnosis, for it was clear that the delightful singularity of the Lacanian–Joycean knot also comprised the vortex of Lucia Joyce, a subject whose "disinvestment" from normal–neurotic structure was undoubt-edly psychotic, and miserably so.

A central aspect of what Lacan attempted to do in his seminar, as each foray into Joyce's writing provoked a new topological sketch, concerned the status of meta-phor. The "Freudian unconscious," where the name of the father served as the fourth ring, brought real, symbolic, and imaginary together on the basis of signifying sub-stitution; it was governed, in other words, by a primal metaphor. What characterized the Lacanian–Joycean knot, by contrast, was a radical *failure* of metaphor — so that what bound the terms together was not a signifying operation, but a real *jouissance*, or rather a *jouis-sens*, as Lacan punned it: a singular, illegible coalescence of meaning and fantasmatic enjoyment. And for Lacan there is a rigorous continuity here between theory and what it theorizes: while the Freudian unconscious was properly mapped by a topography that remained only figurative, Lacan's knot is *no longer metaphorical*. This last assertion has been the hardest aspect of late Lacan for those outside the doctrinal fold to accept: surely, he was repeatedly asked after a seminar, this knot is just a model, isn't it? Lacan's "mad" response seemed almost to echo the scholastic theorizing of young Stephen: the knot itself, its *quidditas*, was simply beyond imagination.

This last idea — that both Joycean writing and Lacanian knot-topology surpass the imaginary, occupy a non-metaphorical real — has had curious, mixed effects. As Rabaté notes with some consternation, one consequence of the notion that Lacan's *sinthome* does not form part of the Freudian tradition of "applying" psychoanalytic theory to art has been the strange phenomenon of Lacanian analysts declaring Joyce an actual psychotic "case" to be considered in a clinical training, and recommending his texts to be read as good instances of the psychopathology of insanity. If this seems quite extraordinarily reductive, it is nevertheless consistent with some aspects of Lacan's own approach to Joyce; he has no time for what he sees as the nervous protocols of Joyce scholarship, and often says things that are simply ill-considered. (Is it only *false* naivety, we might wonder, that makes Lacan declare in one seminar that, at the opening of *Ulysses*, Joyce declares his wish to hellenize Ireland?)

What then, for all its "freudful mistakes," can Lacan's perspective on Joyce contribute to our readings of Joyce? We recall how Jung concluded that the Joycean soul was untreatable, and have seen something very similar in Lacan's notion that Joyce's writing is *pas à lire*, fundamentally unreadable; perhaps we should not expect, on such a basis, very much active engagement with Joyce's texts. Nevertheless, the Lacanian preoccupation with the various ways in which writing can encounter its own *limits*, the limits of its ability to make the world signify – in moments of unspeakable emotion or bodily abandonment, at points of mystical reflection or hellish violation – resonates powerfully with all of Joyce's work, from the first epiphanies to *Finnegans Wake*. The notion, however problematic, of the Joycean text as real in Lacan's sense, emphasizes its crucial relation to the objects foregrounded by psychoanalysis: above all the voice and the gaze. Critics have therefore been able to draw on Lacan's work in *Le Sinthome*, often elaborating what it only suggests or half-formulates, to develop some productive new explorations of such central themes as the ambiguous gift of proper names in Joyce, the problematic of sexual difference in *Exiles*, the question of Joyce's paternity, and his relation to literary tradition (Harari 2002: 217–20; Rabaté 2001: 166–7; Thurston 2004: 75–103). At its best, then, Lacan's knot remains an original, provocative – in sum, an eminently Joycean – work in progress.

Joyce's "x" Communicated

> You know people never value anything unless they have to steal it. Even an alley cat would rather snake an old bone out of the garbage than come up and eat a nicely prepared chop from your saucer.
>
> Joyce to Max Eastman[11]

"Modernist writers," writes Fritz Senn, "knew with Freud, though not necessarily from him, that mistakes have their own causation, are not to be dismissed as meaningless interferences. For writers, mistakes, errors are also economic devices, semantic loaves and fishes" (Senn 1995: 222–3). This idea of the fruitful, but not necessarily freudful, mistake is central to Joyce's literary practice, and its ambiguity may go some way toward accounting for his vexed relations with psychoanalysis. Criticism has largely abandoned the question, once considered so important by Mary Colum, of intellectual priority and debt, and sought rather to explore ways of interpreting the shared preoccupations, the rivalrous proximity, of Joyce and Freud (or Jung or Lacan). Thus, for Margot Norris (1976), the "intrepidation of our dreams" (*FW* 338 28–9) in *Finnegans Wake* points to a complex weave of parodic allusion to the foundational text of psychoanalytic theory, *The Interpretation of Dreams*, but Freud's text is viewed above all as a literary *resource* for Joyce, not as a source of his theoretical insight. Likewise, John Bishop (1986: 16) finds Freud's dream-book "everywhere implicit in Joyce's "nonday diary," but in a quite particular sense: namely as another way to add *obscurity* to the text, to deepen its epistemic gloom, its "eyewitless foggus" (*FW* 515 30). For both these critics, psychoanalytic theory is "scotographically arranged" (*FW* 412 3) by Joycean writing – reframed for its own peculiar ends, the decentering of the human subject, the writing of nocturnal obscurity (Greek *skotos*, "darkness"; *graphein*, "to write"). For John Rickard (1999), meanwhile, the best way to relate Joyce and Freud is to consider the latter's evolution as an interpreter, with an early "scientific" hermeneutic based on insight – the idea that knowledge itself could be curative, that grasping the truth could eradicate symptoms – giving way to a "narrative" hermeneutic, based not on a moment of insight but on an extended process of transferential working-through, of reinscription and reinterpretation. For Rickard, this transition from a confident herme-neutic to an ontologically undecidable perspective makes Freud's later work precisely more "Joycean," takes it closer to the "tenebrosity of memory" (Rickard 1999: 52) in Joycean writing, its disruption of ontology grounded in representation.

What becomes crucial here is the difference between psychoanalytic theory and its practice. Whatever one's reservations about mapping the shifting terrain of Freud-ian theory in order to explore modernist literature, if we consider the daily practice of the psychoanalyst – awaiting, with her ear open, the voice of the other in its irre-ducible peculiarity – we find something very close to Joyce's practice as a writer. The powerful otherness of the Freudian discovery resides not in its theoretical discourse but in the elusive *object* of that discourse, the object-voice that continually addresses and disorients psychoanalytic knowledge. And it is clear, as we shall see, that what sustained Joyce's writerly investment in psychoanalysis was not primarily its seductive and esoteric theorizing, but its clinical records: its case histories.

In an important article of 1985, Daniel Ferrer sought to intervene in the endless debate on Joyce and psychoanalysis by revealing "at last some irrefutable evidence of [Joyce's] direct (and close) contact with Freud's text in the English translation" (Ferrer 1985: 367). Ferrer had found, in one of the notebooks used in the composi-tion of *Finnegans Wake*, detailed notes made by Joyce on reading the third volume of Freud's *Collected Papers*, which comprised the five classic case histories, "The Wolf man," "The Rat man," "Dora," "Little Hans" and "President Schreber." Ferrer lists Joyce's associative and usually cryptic notes alongside the Freudian texts, interpolating his own suggestions for the "genetic" significance of the notes: how they inform and inhabit specific parts of *Finnegans Wake*. We should no longer base our interpretations, writes Ferrer (1985: 368), on vague analogies but on our knowledge of "precisely what caught Joyce's attention." Thus, the "Book of Shaun" (chapter 16) is shown to be densely interwoven with material from "The Wolf man," from the voyeuristic infan-tile sexuality in the case to the inverted Roman V which is revealed as one of its key signifiers, and which Joyce uses as Shaun's siglum (376–7).

What we learn from the work of Ferrer and subsequent genetic studies, then, is that Joyce responded actively, with the arcane methods he had developed to write *Finnegans Wake*, to the rich textuality of Freudian clinical practice, and perhaps above all to its powerful *interrogation* of human meaning, its refusal of the self-evident. The question

of determining "precisely what caught Joyce's attention," although offered by Ferrer as
an open, unfinished question, remains nonetheless problematic; for it risks returning
us to a pre-Freudian – that is, undivided, self-consistent – subject. As should be very
clear by now, Joyce's perspective on psychoanalysis was highly complex and inconsistent, so we should hesitate before attempting the difficult task of isolating it in a
specific set of reading–writing practices.

A good example of this difficulty comes in another useful contribution to genetic
Joyce studies, by Wim van Mierlo (1997). Van Mierlo supplements Ferrer's findings
by adducing documentary evidence of close intertextual links between *Finnegans Wake*
and the "President Schreber" case, but also seeks to emphasize what he considers many
accounts of Joyce and psychoanalysis to have neglected: namely, the eminently *parodic*
intention of these Joycean references. Van Mierlo seeks to construct, as precisely as possible, a history of how this parodic disfigurement of psychoanalysis grew with and
out of Joyce's reading. A passage often quoted in support of what Van Mierlo calls the
"rivalry theory" (of Joyce-and-Freud) can be located in this history thanks to the term
"cathexis":

> — You're a nice third degree witness, faith! But this is no laughing matter. [. . .] You
> have homosexual catheis of empathy between narcissism of the expert and steatopygic
> invertedness. Get yourself psychoanolised! (*FW* 522 27–32)

Since the technical-sounding term "cathexis" – Strachey's translation of Freud's *Besetz-
ung*, "investment" – does not enter English until 1922, Van Mierlo concludes that
Joyce must have come across it in a text by Freud or one of his disciples after that date.

The problem of Joyce's intention and attention here can be clearly seen if we pause a
little longer over "catheis." A traditional reading of the *Wake* would group this together
with all the other disfigured signifiers of psychoanalysis in the passage, perhaps linking
it to "cathering" (*FW* 382 15) and the ambiguous Greek root *kathairein* or *katheirein*,
to cleanse or to destroy, or to Freud's early work with the "cathartic" method. But one
of Van Mierlo's footnotes tells a different story: "Joyce corrected 'catheris' in the second
proofs for *transition* 15, but the printer probably mistook the 'x' above the 'r' for a deletion mark" (Van Mierlo 1997: 123 fn. 32). In other words, Joyce intended to write
"cathexis" – to use the *correct* term, that is, from Freud's text in English – but his "x"
was misread, first as "r," to produce "catheris" (see "cathering" above), and then as a
deletion mark. The letter that was supposed to mark the author's intended correction
ends up as the mark of his conscious, parodic misspelling: "You never made a more
freudful mistake."

NOTES

1 On this interrelation, see Henry (1993: esp. 289–90).

2 Kain (1974: 120). We should not forget that it was Maria Jolas who first suggested in 1932 that Joyce should consult Jung about Lucia's problems (*JJ* 679).

3 See Thurston (2004: 31–54).

4 These lines from Joyce's "amusing parody on Tipperary," as Frank Budgen describes it, are of course "really" about the Consul General in Zurich (Budgen 1972: 205). But what about the unconscious subtext?

5 See Thurston (2004: 130–48), and in a very different sense, Kimball (1997: 19–22).

6 See Stern (1976: 150); Roughley (1991: 175).

7 See Young-Eisendrath and Dawson (1997: 240–54).

8 For more detailed criticism of Kimball's book, see Thurston (2002).

9 See Lacan (1993: 143–57). For a detailed and incisive discussion of these points in Lacanian theory, see Grigg (1998).

10 See Grigg (1998: 65–9); Thurston (1998).

11 As recorded by Ellmann; *JJ* 495 n.

BIBLIOGRAPHY

Aubert, Jacques (ed.) (1987) *Joyce avec Lacan*. Paris: Navarin.

Beckett, Samuel (1972 [1929]) "Dante . . . Bruno. Vico . . Joyce," in Samuel Beckett et al., *Our Exagmination Round His Factification for Incamination of Work in Progress*. London: Faber and Faber.

Beja, Morris (1977) "Dividual chaoses: case histories of multiple personality and *Finnegans Wake*," *James Joyce Quarterly* 13 (3, Spring): 241–50.

Bishop, John (1986) *Joyce's Book of the Dark*. Madison: Wisconsin University Press.

Brivic, Sheldon (1980) *Joyce between Jung and Freud*. Port Washington, NY: Kennikat Press.

Budgen, Frank (1970) *Myselves When Young*. Oxford: Oxford University Press.

Budgen, Frank (1972 [1934]) *James Joyce and the Making of "Ulysses" and Other Writings*. Oxford: Oxford University Press.

Coleman, Elliott (1963) "A note on Joyce and Jung," *James Joyce Quarterly* 1 (1, Fall): 11–19.

Colum, Mary (1941 [1937]) *From These Roots*. New York: Cape.

Colum, Mary and Padraic Colum (1958) *Our Friend James Joyce*. London: Victor Gollancz.

Deming, Robert H. (1970) *James Joyce: The Critical Heritage*. London: Routledge.

Ferrer, Daniel (1985) "The freudful couchmare of Λd: Joyce's notes on Freud and the composition of Chapter XVI of *Finnegans Wake*," *James Joyce Quarterly* 22 (4, Summer): 367–82.

Freud, Sigmund (1960 [1901]) *The Psychopathology of Everyday Life*. In *The Standard Edition of the Complete Psychological Works of Sigmund Freud*. General Editor James Strachey. Vol. VI. London: Hogarth Press, 1953–74.

Freud, Sigmund (1955 [1919]) "The 'Uncanny.'" In *The Standard Edition of the Complete Psychological Works of Sigmund Freud*. General Editor James Strachey. Vol. XVII. London: Hogarth Press, 1953–74.

Grigg, Russell (1998) "From the mechanism of psychosis to the universal condition of the symptom: on foreclosure." In D. Nobus (ed.) *Key Concepts of Lacanian Psychoanalysis*, pp. 48–74. London: Rebus Press.

Harari, Roberto (2002) *How James Joyce Made His Name: A Reading of the Final Lacan*, trans. L. Thurston. New York: Other Press.

Henry, Michel (1993) *The Genealogy of Psychoanalysis*, trans. D. Brick. Stanford, CA: Stanford University Press.

Joyce, Stanislaus (1971) *The Complete Dublin Diary*, ed. George Healy. Ithaca, NY: Cornell University Press.

Jung, Carl Gustav (1967) "Ulysses: a monologue." In his *The Spirit in Man, Art and Literature*, pp. 109–34. London: Routledge.

Kain, Richard (ed.) (1974) "An interview with Carola Giedion-Welcker and Maria Jolas," *James Joyce Quarterly* 11 (Winter): 94–122.

Kimball, Jean (1997) *Odyssey of the Psyche: Jungian Patterns in Joyce's* Ulysses. Carbondale: Southern Illinois University Press.

Kimball, Jean (2003) *Joyce and the Early Freudians*. Gainesville: University Press of Florida.

Lacan, Jacques (1993) *The Seminar of Jacques Lacan. Vol. 3: The Psychoses, 1955–1956*, trans. R. Grigg. London: Routledge.

Lacan, Jacques (2005) *Le séminaire livre XXIII: Le sinthome*. Paris: Seuil.

Norris, Margot (1976) *The Decentered Universe of Finnegans Wake*. Baltimore, MD: Johns Hopkins University Press.

O'Brien, Darcy (1976) "A critique of psychoanalytic criticism, or what Joyce did and did not do," *James Joyce Quarterly* 13 (3, Spring).

Rabaté, Jean-Michel (2001) *Jacques Lacan*. London: Palgrave.

Rickard, John (1999) *Joyce's Book of Memory*. Durham, NC: Duke University Press.

Roughley, Alan (1991) *James Joyce and Critical Theory*. London: Harvester.

Senn, Fritz (1995) *Inductive Scrutinies: Focus on Joyce*. Baltimore, MD: Johns Hopkins University Press.

Sollers, Philippe (1978) "Joyce & Co." In his *In the Wake of the Wake*, trans. S. Heath and E. Anderson, pp. 107–21. Madison: Wisconsin University Press.

Stern, Paul (1976) *C. G. Jung: The Haunted Prophet*. New York: Braziller.

Thurston, Luke (1998) "Ineluctable nodalities: on the Borromean knot." In D. Nobus (ed.) *Key Concepts of Lacanian Psychoanalysis*, pp. 139–63. London: Rebus Press.

Thurston, Luke (2002) "Review of Kimball, *Odyssey of the Psyche: Jungian Patterns in Joyce's Ulysses*," *James Joyce Broadsheet* 62 (June): 3.

Thurston, Luke (2004) *James Joyce and the Problem of Psychoanalysis*. Cambridge: Cambridge University Press.

Van Mierlo, Wim (1997) "The freudful couchmare revisited: contextualizing Joyce and the new psychology," *Joyce Studies Annual* 8 (Summer): 115–53.

Walcott, William (1971) "Notes by a Jungian analyst on the dreams in *Ulysses*," *James Joyce Quarterly* 9 (1, Fall): 37–48.

Young-Eisendrath, Polly and Terence Dawson (eds.) (1997) *The Cambridge Companion to Jung*. Cambridge: Cambridge University Press.

Index